RICHARD SCHLATTER, GENERAL EDITOR

Humanistic Scholarship in America
◄§ THE PRINCETON STUDIES §►

THE COUNCIL OF THE HUMANITIES
WHITNEY J. OATES, CHAIRMAN
PRINCETON UNIVERSITY

ANTHROPOLOGY

Eric R. Wolf

ART AND ARCHAEOLOGY

James S. Ackerman   Rhys Carpenter

CHINESE PAINTING

Wen Fong

CLASSICS

Eric A. Havelock

ENGLISH LITERATURE

David Daiches

HISTORY

Felix Gilbert   John Higham
Leonard Krieger

LINGUISTICS

Eric P. Hamp   Karl D. Uitti
Rulon Wells

Their Authors

MODERN AMERICAN CRITICISM

Walter Sutton

MUSICOLOGY

Frank Ll. Harrison   Mantle Hood
Claude V. Palisca

THE ORIGINS OF AMERICAN
HUMANISTIC SCHOLARS

Robert H. Knapp

PHILOSOPHY

Roderick M. Chisholm   Herbert Feigl
William K. Frankena   John Passmore
Manley Thompson

RELIGION

Paul Ramsey, ed.
Philip H. Ashby   Robert M. Grant
James Gustafson   J. H. Nichols
Harry M. Orlinsky   John E. Smith
Claude Welch

RELIGION, A HUMANISTIC FIELD

Clyde A. Holbrook

The aim of these volumes is to present a critical account of American humanistic scholarship in recent decades. They have been commissioned by the Council of the Humanities, Whitney J. Oates, Chairman, of Princeton University and were made possible by a grant from the Ford Foundation.

—Richard Schlatter, General Editor.

PHILOSOPHY

୶ଟ ଟ୭

RODERICK M. CHISHOLM
HERBERT FEIGL
WILLIAM K. FRANKENA
JOHN PASSMORE
MANLEY THOMPSON

PRENTICE-HALL, INC.   ENGLEWOOD CLIFFS   NEW JERSEY

PRENTICE-HALL INTERNATIONAL, INC., LONDON
PRENTICE-HALL OF AUSTRALIA, PTY., LTD., SYDNEY
PRENTICE-HALL OF CANADA, LTD., TORONTO
PRENTICE-HALL FRANCE, S.A.R.L., PARIS
PRENTICE-HALL OF INDIA (PRIVATE) LTD., NEW DELHI
PRENTICE-HALL OF JAPAN, INC., TOKYO
PRENTICE-HALL DE MEXICO, S.A., MEXICO CITY

FOREWORD

What is the purpose of humanistic scholarship? What, in fact, does the humanist scholar do?

The job of the humanist scholar is to organize our huge inheritance of culture, to make the past available to the present, to make the whole of civilization available to men who necessarily live in one small corner for one little stretch of time, and finally to judge, as a critic, the actions of the present by the experience of the past.

The humanist's task is to clear away the obstacles to our understanding of the past, to make our whole cultural heritage—primitive, pre-Columbian, African, Asian, aboriginal, Near Eastern, classical, medieval, European, American, contemporary, and all the rest —accessible to us. He must sift the whole of man's culture again and again, reassessing, reinterpreting, rediscovering, translating into a modern idiom, making available the materials and the blueprints with which his contemporaries can build their own culture, bringing to the center of the stage that which a past generation has judged irrelevant but which is now again usable, sending into storage that which has become, for the moment, too familiar and too habitual to stir our imagination, preserving it for a posterity to which it will once more seem fresh.

The humanist does all this by the exercise of exact scholarship. He must have the erudition of the historian, the critical abilities of the philosopher, the objectivity of the scientist, and the imagination of all three. The scholar who studies the history of science, for example, must combine a knowledge of languages, history, and philosophy with the knowledge of a scientist. And so on with the scholars who study music, art, religion, literature, and all the rest.

The job is, obviously, impossible for any man; and the humanist scholar, knowing he can never attain his true goal, is always tempted to run after wooden idols whose cults are less exacting and which proffer an easy bliss.

Sometimes the humanist is tempted to bypass the rigorous training of the scholar and to wrap himself in the cloak of the sophist. Then he lapses into a painful wooliness and becomes the "literary" sort of humanist whose only accomplishment is a style which achieves the appearance of sublimity at the cost of an actual inanity. His opposite number is the hardheaded humanist who reacts against empty loftiness by becoming a pedant: he devotes himself to antiquarian detail no less trivial than the banalities of some social science or the mere collecting spirit which is sometimes found in the natural sciences. "Physical science can be at least as trivial as any other form of inquiry: but this is less obvious to the outsider because the triviality is concealed in the decent obscurity of a learned language."

Given the magnitude of his task and the impossibility of total perfection, the humanist scholar must, of course, specialize and his works will often be esoteric. But the belief persists that somehow specialization must be converted to generalization if the humanist scholar is to complete his job. Humanist scholars have not solved the problems of excessive specialization and must share the blame for that catastrophe of communication which besets modern learning.

Humanist scholars have been accused of being overly genteel, contemptuous of popular culture, snobbish and antidemocratic after the fashion of their aristocratic Renaissance progenitors, backward looking, hostile to the present, fearful of the future, ignorantly petulant about science, technology, and the Industrial Revolution—"natural Luddites." "It is a sad thought indeed that our civilization has not produced a *New Vision*," a modern technologist complains, "which could guide us into the new 'Golden Age' which has now become physically possible, but only physically. . . . Who is responsible for this tragi-comedy of Man frustrated by success? . . . Who has left Mankind without a vision? The predictable part of the future may be a job for electronic predictors but the part of it which is not predictable, which is largely a matter of free human choice, is not the business of the machines, nor of scientists . . . but it ought to be, as it was in the great epochs of the past, the prerogative of the inspired humanists." (Dennis Gabor, "Inventing the Future," *Encounter*, May 1960, p. 15.)

Scholars in the humanities may modestly reject the suggestion that they can ever be the inspired prophets of a new age. But their scholarship is essential to enable us to distinguish the inspired prophets from the fanatical Pied Pipers.

The Ford Humanities Project under the direction of the Council of the Humanities of Princeton University is looking at American humanistic scholarship of recent decades, describing it, and attempting to sift the imaginative, the original, and the admirable from the pedantic, the conventional, and the superficial.

We have commissioned about a dozen volumes by recognized scholars in each field. These volumes will give us an account of American humanistic scholarship enabling us to see just what that scholarship has contributed to the culture of America and the world.

The distinguished philosophical scholars who have written essays for this volume have, like good scholars and philosophers, given no final answers to the questions we have asked. But they have made searching analyses and they have continued the discourse which the Greeks began and which is still, perhaps, the principal task of humanistic scholarship.

In the beginning of the modern era, philosophy replaced theology in the university curriculum and in the honorific hierarchy of intellectual disciplines. In spite of the attacks of positivists in the nineteenth century, philosophy has never quite lost its exalted status. But it has, in recent decades, had its critics.

Already in the seventeenth century when philosophy had just come into its own as the Queen of the Sciences, Descartes and Bacon noted that it suffered in comparison with the mathematics and the natural sciences since it was neither progressive nor certain: it does not settle one set of problems once and for all and move on to a new set. Most of the essays here accept this charge with equanimity.

The usual answer to the charge is that philosophy, in common with the other humanistic disciplines, does not get better and better, or provide final solutions to problems, but that it is a daily discourse about truth and about the good life and that this discourse itself is the very marrow of culture, of the life of reason. Philosophy does, in this view of it, serve as a guide to life, but it does this without being dogmatic, without pontificating. "Nothing," the historian of thought tells us, "is more striking in the history of thought than the immediate transience, and the final permanence, of genial philosophical ideas. It is as if the human mind, stimulated and exercised in a genial period of prolific excellence, returns always to criticize what it has been given to feed upon, but that when, after a time of slumber, a new age begins, new minds seize once again upon one or more of the limited patterns of ideas in which men can express their comprehension of the universe. In this, thought differs from science, which is ever advancing to a fuller grasp." (David Knowles, *Evolution of Medieval Thought*, p. 16.)

But recent critics have complained that too much modern philosophizing is concerned merely with analyzing the meaning of statements and does not attempt to talk about good and evil, beauty and ugliness, truth and falsehood. Professors Frankena and Feigl accept this criticism, in part, and urge their colleagues to return to the traditional task of the philosopher. But Professor Thompson cautions us not to expect too much from the philosopher who does discourse about the basic truths and about the good life: "Philosophy in its maturity becomes infected with Socratic questioning even while it remains speculative, and it inevitably appears dangerous or useless to those who do not question."

The present essays demonstrate that in one field the Americans excel—we are good scholars and historians. Both in the history of philosophy and in the related field of intellectual history a number of American books are standard; and our scholarly monographs and editions are admirable, although some of them are too meticulous and too narrow in scope for the taste of Professor Passmore, whose roots are in the British tradition—he must lament the fact that the British universities are now coming to admire and imitate the American Ph.D. mill. Scholarship and history are our strong points. On the other hand, if we exclude the names of immigrant philosophers like Whitehead and Carnap, the present essays leave me with the impression that we have had in recent years no giants who are philosophers pure and simple rather than scholars and historians. Not many of the names mentioned in these pages are recognizable as those of great intellectual leaders and many are unknown even to an old academic hand like myself who has a fair speaking acquaintance with the various humanistic disciplines in America.

The generalization about philosophy lacking the progressive and problem-solving character of the sciences must be qualified in one instance—appropriately, in the case of the history of science. Professor Feigl's essay radiates an optimistic progressivism which is not shared by his colleagues.

Finally, the one difficult child in the house of modern philosophy has troubled us in these studies. Professor Hilary Putnam undertook the essay on logic. But the discipline appears to be so intractable, so specialized, so technical, in its present stage of development, that it could not be dealt with in our relaxed fashion and could not be so easily made intelligible to the nonphilosopher in the scope of one short essay. Hence, Professor Putnam's examination of modern American studies in logic will be published as a separate volume.

RICHARD SCHLATTER
General Editor

CONTENTS

CONTENTS

PHILOSOPHICAL SCHOLARSHIP IN THE UNITED STATES, 1930-1960

JOHN PASSMORE

PROFESSOR OF PHILOSOPHY
THE INSTITUTE OF ADVANCED STUDIES
AUSTRALIAN NATIONAL UNIVERSITY

My principal object in this essay has been to pick out and illustrate what I take to be the main tendencies in American philosophical scholarship. I hope I have not overlooked any work of the first order of importance, but no doubt I have failed to mention a good many studies which are quite as important as many of those to which I have referred; I have not attempted to compile a complete, or even a nearly complete, record of American scholarship since 1930. A further warning should be added: since this book does not contain essays on aesthetics or political philosophy, I have had very little to say about scholarship in those areas.

THE CONCEPT OF
PHILOSOPHICAL SCHOLARSHIP

In his *History of Philosophy,* Wilhelm Windelband distinguished three different types of philosophical scholarship: the logical, the historical, the biographical. The distinctions he was making can be illustrated from Kant scholarship. Kant attempted to solve certain philosophical problems—problems set for him, for example, by the difficulty of reconciling Hume's account of causality with what, so Kant thought, was the certainty of Newtonian mechanics. If the Kant scholar asks himself, simply, what those problems were, in what manner Kant tried to solve them, and with what success, he is taking the *logical* approach. At the same time, Kant was an eighteenth century German, influenced by and helping us to understand the Enlightenment. If the scholar considers Kant primarily as a figure in the history of European culture, he is adopting the *historical* approach. Then, Kant was a person, with a particular type of upbringing, in whose life the publication of a philosophical work was an episode, a special occasion. The scholar who considers Kant thus assumes a *biographical* approach.

Ideally, no doubt, the Kant scholar is all the time conscious of Kant as a philosopher, as a historical figure, and as a person. But few, if any, scholars live up to that ideal. At one extreme, Kant is discussed precisely as if he were a contemporary; a thesis is extracted from his work and critically examined as a possible solution of a philosophical problem (which may not at all be Kant's problem), just as if his writings were hot from the press. When an article on Galileo appears in a scientific journal, it will certainly be an attempt to understand Galileo, not to controvert him; but no philosopher is surprised to find in his *Philosophical Review* an article, say, on "Benevolence and Virtue" which begins from Hutcheson's *Inquiry Concerning the Original of Our Ideas of Beauty and Virtue* (1725) in order "to discuss, as if they were contemporary theories, two propositions which are easily detached from the context in which they occur, and which have a sufficient initial plausibility to render them attractive hypotheses even today" (W. C. Swabey, *Phil. Rev.,* 1943, p. 452). Or if he is surprised it will be by Swabey's unusually self-conscious apologia, not by the general character of his article. Many essays, or even books, which seem at first sight to be examples of philosophical scholarship—they begin from a passage in Hume, or Berkeley, or Plato—in fact lie quite outside our present concern: they are not contributions to what Windelband called "logical scholarship," they are contributions to philosophy, pure and simple.

At the other extreme, there is scholarship *about* philosophy, which is itself not at all philosophical—it may even be antiphilosophical—in intent or performance. A professor of Latin, or Greek, or Hebrew, or Arabic, sets out to establish a text; he is an expert philologist; he collates his texts with diligence, scrupulously annotating their more obscure allusions. Although the result is a work of potential usefulness to the philosophical scholar, the philologist himself may have little or no interest in philosophy. He may never have been present at a philosophical discussion; he may never have read a philosophical book except insofar as his philological studies compelled him to do so. He has edited an Arabic philosophical text rather than an Arabic mathematical text, not because he is more interested in philosophy than in mathematics, but solely because of the philological problems it presents.

A historian, similarly, may interest himself professionally in Plato, or in Locke, or in Hegel. He may be profoundly skeptical about philosophy as a form of inquiry, just as he may be bored by poetry; but he is professionally concerned with both philosophy and poetry insofar as they provide a clue to the peculiar mentality of a period. Many historians, indeed, have little feeling for general theory; they may pick up enough philosophy, "relativist" or "pragmatic" or "instrumentalist," to give some appearance of justification to their lack of interest in theory, but that is as far as their philosophical concern carries them. Yet because they are expert in a given period, certain types of scholarship about philosophers may fall, quite naturally, into their hands. Similarly, a biographer may be scarcely interested in the philosophical writings of his subject, except insofar as those writings reflect his subject's character or affect his reputation; in the eyes of such a biographer of Hume, for example, Hume's personal relations with Rousseau are of much greater importance than his—philosophically fundamental but impersonal —relations to Malebranche. A philosophical scholar would certainly reverse the emphasis.

Philosophical scholarship proper falls somewhere between the extreme of pure dialectic on the one hand and pure "scholarship *about* philosophy" on the other. The main objectives of the philosophical scholar are exposition and clarification rather than debate, but the exposition and the clarification are carried out in a critical philosophical spirit, not simply as a contribution to biography, philology, or history. The philologist who is attracted to Plato rather than to Homer, not because Plato's range of expression is more diversified than Homer's but because Plato is, and Homer is not, a philosopher; the historian who is genuinely interested in the structure of philosophical systems; the biographer who is interested in Hume as a person mainly because that person was a philosopher; the philosopher who is attracted to scholarship because his gifts lie in historical understanding and sympathetic elucidation rather than in debate—these, neither pure dialecticians nor scholars only accidentally concerned with philosophy, are the most typical figures. They converge in the figure of the philosopher-scholar, whose principal training may have been in philosophy, in philology, or in history, but who now concentrates his attention on the understanding of philosophical ideas.

Especially perhaps in America, as contrasted with Great Britain, can one pick out a distinct class of philosopher-scholars. There has been a considerable degree of specialization within American philosophy: a lively concern for contemporary philosophy and a scholarly interest in the past are only seldom conjoined in the same person. American scholarship, taken by and large, is not so dialectical as British scholarship, just because it is less often the work of philosophers with some interest in the past and more often the work of scholars with some interest in philosophy.

This latter fact largely accounts for what (from a British point of view) are the leading peculiarities of American philosophical scholarship. Most of the leading British philosophical scholars— Ross, Kemp Smith, Paton, Taylor, Webb, Findlay, Joachim—have written freely on general philosophical questions, and no one is surprised when philosophers like Russell, Ryle, Hampshire, Warnock, Ewing, Urmson, Kneale, Anscombe, and Geach come out with contributions to the history of philosophy. There are exceptions—especially in the field of Greek philosophy—but most British philosophers firmly believe that only a man who is deeply interested in philosophy can show that sort of understanding of philosophical problems which a philosophical scholar needs. In sharp contrast, very few of the important works of philosophical scholarship produced in America have been written by men who have made an independent mark, even the slightest mark, in any branch of pure philosophy. They are, most of them, written by philosophical scholars for philosophical scholars, not by more scholarly philosophers for less scholarly philosophers. Both their virtues and their defects flow from this fact.

My emphasis in this essay will be on the more philosophical sort of scholarship, but it is impossible wholly to ignore the contributions of men who are pure scholars, writing *about* philosophy; although they may not make direct contributions to the understanding and advancement of philosophy, the pure philologian, the pure biographer, the pure historian lay essential foundations for serious philosophical scholarship. I shall begin, therefore, with some account of those genres in which the pure scholar is most at home; but shall reserve for more detailed consideration those other genres—involving the direct exposition of, and a commentary on, philosophical ideas—which are naturally the main concern of the scholarly philosopher.

SCHOLARSHIP *ABOUT* PHILOSOPHY

1. Bibliographies. 2. Dictionaries and glossaries. 3. Biographies. 4. Editions and translations. 5. The history of ideas. 6. General histories. 7. Commentaries: general reflections.

1. Of all aids to scholarship, bibliographies are perhaps the most important, especially for the scholar who has not immediate access to the resources of a vast library. In this respect, philosophers have not, until recently, been well served. One of the earliest, and still respected, monuments of American scholarship—J. M. Baldwin's *Dictionary of Philosophy and Psychology* (1901)—contained, in its third volume, most extensive bibliographies; but unfortunately the supplementary bibliography for 1902-32, prepared by the American Philosophical Association, has never achieved publication. Nowadays, the most extensive current philosophical bibliographies originate on the continent of Europe; there is no American analogue to the *Répertoire bibliographique* of the Institut Supérieur of Louvain or the quarterly bibliography published by the International Institute of Philosophy. Nor is there a bibliography of American philosophy to compare with, say, the *Bibliografia filosofica italiana dal 1900 al 1950* (Rome, 1950). Indeed, there would be considerable practical difficulties—which also affect the present essay—in preparing such a bibliography: difficulties in determining who counts as an American, or in picking out from a wide variety of international journals the increasingly many American contributions. One might also add that in an age when philosophical activities are more and more confined within nationalistic boundaries, American philosophy is not in the least degree insular. A bibliography of purely American work, although it might properly be a source of national pride, would not serve even as an everyday working list for the American philosopher, as a similar national list would serve in a great many countries.

7

When it comes to special bibliographies, however, American assiduity and accuracy are deservedly famous. Almost every American scholarly work contains a bibliography which is at least adequate and reliable; most often, it will be the best bibliography in its field. The volumes of readings which have recently appeared from American presses normally contain bibliographies of exceptional usefulness; if I cite the selective bibliography in Herbert Feigl and May Brodbeck's *Readings in the Philosophy of Science* (1953) or the remarkably far-reaching bibliography prepared in America for A. J. Ayer's *Logical Positivism* (1959), this is only because they happen to be on my desk as I write—there are many other comparable examples. The bibliographies in the *Journal of Symbolic Logic,* too, have earned a reputation beyond the ranks of symbolic logicians; they are distinguished not only for their accuracy and exhaustiveness, but also for the quality of the critical commentary they incorporate.

Then there are bibliographies on particular persons and topics, such as M. H. Thomas's *Bibliography of John Dewey* (1939) or V. J. Bourke's *Thomistic Bibliography 1920-1940* (1945). In his "Plato, 1950-57"—published in *Lustrum* (1959-60)—H. F. Cherniss has set an unmatchable standard for all such specialist bibliographies; more exhaustive in a temporal sense than its title suggests, this bibliography in its completeness, its accuracy, its cross referencing, and the quality of its incidental summaries and critical commentaries, is a demonstration just how useful a well-constructed bibliography can be.

Bibliographical work of a still more specialized and professional kind is to be found in, for example, S. H. Thomson's *The Writings of Robert Grosseteste* (1940). This, however, is a striking example of "scholarship *about* philosophy" as distinct from "philosophical scholarship." Its author was, at the time of its publication, Professor of History at the University of Colorado; his book is an important contribution to medieval bibliography which, as we might express the matter, "happens to be" useful to philosophers. Much the same is true of George Sarton's *Introduction to the History of Science* (3 vols. in 5, 1927-48), which is certainly one of the most remarkable works of accumulative scholarship ever published.

"Accumulative scholarship," I said, and if American bibliographi-

8

cal works have a weakness, it is that they tend—with notable exceptions, to some of which I have already drawn attention—to be purely accumulative. In a prefatory note to the bibliography in *A Treatise on Probability* (1921) J. M. Keynes comments thus: "There are here enumerated many dead treatises and ghostly memoirs. The list is too long, and I have not always successfully resisted the impulse to add to it in the spirit of a collector. . . . At present, a bibliographer takes pride in numerous entries; but he would be a more useful fellow, and the labours of research would be lightened, if he could practice deletion and bring into existence an accredited *Index Expurgatorius*" (p. 432). As Keynes confessed, this is advice it is easier to give than to take; and the accumulative bibliographer might well justify himself on the ground that it is not for him to decide whether a treatise is dead, or a memoir ghostly. But certainly a bibliography which is a bare list, without estimates of importance, which makes no distinction between a worthy but labored and unoriginal doctoral dissertation and a notable contribution to scholarship, can be, as Keynes suggests, as much a hindrance as a help to a scholar. This is especially true if he is the sort of scholar to whom bibliographies are particularly useful, who is geographically so placed that he cannot rapidly scan a book in a large library but must take special steps to have access to it. Naturally, a bibliographer does not wish to proceed as if he were examining students, but he does need to help us determine which of the works he so painstakingly lists are likely to be of special usefulness; otherwise, if his bibliography is a mere uncritical collection, it may hinder rather than facilitate inquiry. But this is a disputed question: there can be no dispute, on the other hand, that American bibliographical scholarship is of a generally high level, and sometimes of quite exceptional quality. Here, at least, the graduate schools have done their work well.

2. The best-known "philosophical dictionaries" in the English speaking world would more accurately have been named "concise encyclopedias." As such, they have depended for their success upon the editor's capacity to attract the support, for a task more onerous, usually, than it is intellectually profitable, of the very best philosophers; nobody else knows enough to write a short article on a funda-

mental philosophical topic. The most substantial of such "dictionaries" is still J. M. Baldwin's *Dictionary of Philosophy and Psychology* (1901) which contains many articles of considerable importance, by men of the caliber of C. S. Peirce, Josiah Royce, and John
Dewey. On the scholarly side, however—leaving aside the third,
bibliographical, volume—it is much less satisfactory. The articles
on philosophical terms are usually adequate; those on individual
philosophers are meager in the extreme.

More recently, a shorter philosophical dictionary was edited by
D. D. Runes (1942). This ought to have been an important work:
the list of contributors was a notable one; the arrangement of topics
was reasonably well-conceived. In the outcome, however, a number
of the distinguished contributing editors were moved to protest, in
a letter to the *Philosophical Review* (1942), that they disowned all
responsibility for the general organization of the dictionary and even
for contributions signed with their own name.[1] There is still need,
then, of good philosophical reference books, both of substantial
works along the lines of the Italian *Enciclopedia filosofica* (1957)
and a scholar's handbook of the sort exemplified in the Oxford
"Companions." The first of these needs will, it is hoped, be met by
the projected *International Encyclopedia of Philosophy* to be published in America; the second, where the emphasis would be on
compact information about a multitude of terms and authors, still
remains a desideratum.

Word lists, concordances, and glossaries have been a special feature of French and German rather than of Anglo-Saxon philosophical scholarship. There are, however, some American examples; the

---

[1] This is as good a time as any to draw attention to the fact that there is a
disreputable fringe, associated with one or two publishers, to American philosophical scholarship: translations of a barbarous ineptitude, collections of old
essays masquerading as new works, mutilated and misprinted texts. I have not
commented on works of this sort, which are clearly not representative of the
achievement of the American scholar. This irresponsible fringe, which so far as
I know has no analogue elsewhere, sometimes brings American scholarship into
disrepute, especially on the continent of Europe, where readers do not always
know the ropes sufficiently well to discriminate between imprints. Continental
philosophers, too, have particularly suffered from iniquitous translations which,
in their ignorance of English, they can sometimes be persuaded to praise. The
only way of dealing with such unscrupulous publishing is to scourge it merci-
lessly; reviewers have not always been sufficiently outspoken.

most notable, perhaps, is the *Lexicon of St. Thomas Aquinas* (1948), prepared by R. J. Deferrari, M. I. Barry, and Ignatius McGuiness. This is a vast lexicon which takes as its province the vocabulary of the *Summa theologica* and "such other words from the remaining works as seem in the judgment of the authors to be of great importance." The preface claims that "this monumental work has brilliant significance"; however dubious the English, the sentiment is unimpeachable. T. W. Organ's *Index to Aristotle* (1949) is another example. This is rather more than a word list; it is an attempt, based on the Oxford translations, to list and group together the leading concepts in Aristotle's thought. The philosophical entries are somewhat submerged beneath the zoological and astronomical; and the work has been criticized (see, for example, D. A. Rees in the *Classical Review,* 1951) on the ground that it falls between the stools of being a complete word list such as Bonitz constructed and a genuine subject analysis. No single scholar, it has been suggested, could accomplish the task Organ had set himself. The very usefulness of such a work makes its errors and omissions particularly dangerous; the standards of accuracy and completeness in a reference book must be set extremely high. So far these standards have not been wholly satisfied in American philosophical reference works, nor, indeed, in any such publication which has appeared in the English language.

3. Philosophical biography is a troublesome genre. Even when the biographer is himself a philosopher, his responsibilities as a biographer are not easily reconcilable with any extensive investigation into the ideas, as distinct from the actions, of his philosopher-subject. In his preface to *The Life of David Hume* (1954) E. C. Mossner wrote as follows: "As I conceive his task, the biographer must present enough of the thinking of his subject to be able to interpret his actions without, at the same time, going so far as to overburden the narrative with *systematic* exposition, making it difficult of comprehension for a reader less interested in the ideas than in the man" (p. ix). In biography, as Mossner goes on to say, "the man predominates"; a biography is a narrative analysis of a character in action, and to intersperse it with lengthy exposition is to destroy its unity of style. So most philosophical scholars, if they engage in biography

at all, restrict it to a brief, often rather perfunctory, introduction to a commentary. The philosophical scholar may undoubtedly learn from a biographer something which will aid him in his task of philosophical comprehension, but it would be absurd of him, for example, to go to Mossner's biography of Hume for a substantial elucidation of Hume's ideas, however successful it may be in its full-length portrayal of Hume as a personality.

That personality was attractive in virtue of its humanity, rather than strikingly heroic or picturesque—not the natural stuff of which biographies are made. When it comes to more complex, fiery, scandalous characters like Nietzsche or Diderot or Kierkegaard or Voltaire—scarcely philosophers in a technical sense but rather, in Nietzsche's own phrase, "physicians of culture"—then the biographer is less likely to be himself a philosopher and more likely to subordinate the exposition of ideas to the analysis of a character in action or, alternatively, to an estimate of his historical importance. Thus, for example, Crane Brinton's *Nietzsche* (1948) "does not attempt," he writes, "to analyse his work from the point of view of a professional philosopher. . . . This study is rather an attempt to place Nietzsche's work in the more general currents of 'opinion' in our time" (p. ix). Indeed, Brinton exemplifies that historian's hostility to philosophy on which I previously remarked, as when he writes that "Nietzsche's reading and education . . . was that of a serious dabbler—or, if you prefer, a philosopher" (p. 81).

Reviewing in *Encounter* (January 1961) Sylvia Sprigge's *Berenson: A Biography* (1960), Meyer Schapiro comments thus: "Mrs. Sprigge's biography is not the work of a writer who shared her subject's philosophical interests and can deal critically with his aims and accomplishments. *What she says about his work and ideas is largely reporting*" (p. 57, my italics). The same comment could be made on a good many philosophical biographies; they report ideas rather than depict them as attempts to solve a problem. But there are exceptions, of which perhaps the most notable is R. B. Perry's *The Thought and Character of William James,* first published in what Perry calls "two ample volumes" in 1935, and in a reduced, less philosophical and more personal, one-volume form in 1948. The construction of Perry's book, especially in its original form, has come in for a certain amount of criticism; Perry included a considerable number of James's unpublished papers which certainly interrupt the biographical flow. But the fact remains that Perry, writing as a philosopher, brings out—as no pure scholar could, however learned, or no pure biographer, whatever his degree of psychological insight —just what problems were troubling James, and what he learned from his contemporaries in his attempt to solve them. No one seriously interested in James's philosophy ought to neglect Perry's biography; but there are very few biographies about which a comparable point can be made. For the most part, therefore, I shall simply ignore biographies as belonging to literature rather than philosophy, except when they take the form, essentially, of philosophical commentaries with biographical interludes.

4. Editions differ very greatly in character. Sometimes it is their object, simply, to make available for undergraduate use, in a form judged to be convenient for their pocket or suitable for their intellects, the text of a philosophical classic. In general, such enterprises are not only harmless but positively useful, although they are not of any scholarly interest.

When, however, they present the undergraduate with truncated selections (often from great and readily available works, from Locke, or Berkeley, or Hume, for example), their harmlessness is, to say the least, more dubious. For inevitably, such selections will reflect a particular, usually a fashionable, interpretation of the mutilated text: what is judged to be of "central importance" in it. Of course any teacher has to make a comparable judgment; he will direct an undergraduate's particular attention to certain sections of, for example, Locke's *Essay on the Human Understanding*—inevitably, considering the dimensions of that book. But if most undergraduates are only too happy to restrict their reading to what is thus explicitly demanded of them, the more inquiring undergraduate eye may stray elsewhere. That it cannot do, if only the "official" version of what is important lies in the text in front of him. Even when the original text is as unwieldy as J. S. Mill's *System of Logic,* and even when the selections are as judicious, and are accompanied by a commentary of such quality, as they are in Ernest Nagel's *Mill's Philosophy of Scientific Method* (1950), the scholar will have qualms and reservations; where the abbreviator is a philosopher of less insight the effect can be disastrous. Such works, if they have no positive, have at least a negative, importance for the scholar; they help to perpetuate legends and imperfect interpretations beyond their normal span.

Sometimes, of course, there is no option to selections. A case in point is the writings of C. S. Peirce. The *Collected Papers* edited, in the first six volumes, by Charles Hartshorne and Paul Weiss (1931-1935) and, in volume seven and eight, by A. W. Burks (1958) already, and inevitably, bear the mark of an editor's hand. The editors were obliged not merely to reprint but to bring into some order Peirce's scattered writings—a labor of love which made a considerable demand upon their philosophical insight. Both the bulk and the character of the *Collected Papers* justify the preparation of selections ordered on a different principle, such as Justus Buchler's *The Philosophy of Peirce* (1940) and P. P. Wiener's *Values in a Universe of Chance* (1958). Nor is it difficult to think of other cases in which the publication of selections is an important scholarly enterprise. Richard McKeon's *Selections from Medieval Philosophers* (1929-30) attracted attention to otherwise largely inaccessible material; this is even more obviously true of Philotheus Boehner's selections from William of Ockham (1957). Many of Leibniz' most important writings are, like Peirce's, fragmentary, justifying a volume of selections like P. P. Wiener's (1951); Newton's philosophical comments are scattered throughout his scientific works and H. S. Thayer's *Newton's Philosophy of Nature: Selections from his Writings* (1953) usefully brings them together; M. R. Cohen and I. E. Drabkin's *A Source Book in Greek Science* (1948) is a scholarly contribution of considerable importance. But allowing such exceptions—and there are many others—one must at the same time register a scholarly concern at the multiplication of volumes of selections and readings, insofar as they provide a way by which the lazy undergraduate, to say nothing of his seniors, can postpone indefinitely the task of making his own way through the literature.

Some editions of integral texts clearly fall into the area of scholarship *about* philosophy, rather than philosophical scholarship. Werner Jaeger's plain text of Aristotle's *Metaphysics* (1957), for example, offers no direct aid whatever to the philosopher-reader, and the same is true of a series of volumes prepared under the auspices of the Medieval Academy of America in order to present to a wider world Averroes' commentaries on Aristotle. The general plan of this edition was laid down by H. A. Wolfson in *Speculum* in 1931; a number of volumes have now been published. For the most part, these are scrupulous critical editions of the Latin and Hebrew texts, but in 1958 there appeared Samuel Kurland's translation with critical notes of *On Aristotle's De Generatione et Corruptione: Middle Commentary and Epitome,* the notes relating Averroes' texts to passages in Aristotle, to subsequent Aristotelian commentaries, and to the "super-commentators" on Averroes. The whole enterprise is a contribution to pure scholarship of the first order. The same is true of the *Scholia Platonica* (ed. W. C. Greene, 1938), in which American scholars notably participated (Philological Monographs, no. 8, published by the American Philological Association). Works such as these provide the materials on which the scholar-philosopher can comment; they are a starting point for philosophical scholarship, although only a starting point. They must be judged, however, by philological standards; no other standards are relevant to them.

At the opposite extreme are editions in which the text is supplemented by commentary and interpretation on such a scale that the work is a direct contribution to philosophical scholarship; such editions will be reserved for subsequent discussion as the occasion arises. In an intermediate position lie works like the translation by Y. R. Simon, J. J. Glanville, and G. D. Hollenhorst of *The Material Logic of John of St. Thomas* (1955). This is less scholarly from a purely philosophical point of view than the editions to which I have just referred or than many other American editions of medieval texts—it is based on an Italian edition which is itself not critical —but it contains, unlike the texts supplied by the pure medievalist, a brief preface by Y. R. Simon defending the conception of a "material" logic, and a considerable number of explanatory notes of a philosophical sort.

However, neither notes nor preface confront the final question: "What did John of St. Thomas actually contribute to philosophy, what did he help us to see which we might not have seen without his help?" Or even the preliminary questions: "What was puzzling John? What problems did he set out to solve? What traditions meet in him?" Furthermore the explanatory notes fail to fulfill their proper scholarly purpose—to help those who belong to a different tradition to see what is important in this tradition. To defend the possibility of a material logic with such remarks as: "Over and above the primary existence they enjoy in Nature, things enjoy, as objects of understanding, a new existence—objective, intellectual, intelligible—which brings forth in them a new system of properties" (p. 2) is not, at this stage in the history of philosophy, to advance understanding. The translators, by preparing this edition, have so far helped to bring John of St. Thomas back into intellectual circulation, but they have not taken the second step—the step of the philosophical scholar—of placing John in our general intellectual tradition. This defect is particularly likely to appear in editions prepared by neoscholastic philosophers, but it is not peculiar to them. Another example is Frederick de Wolfe Bolman's translation of Schelling's *The Ages of the World* (1942), the introduction to which was properly rebuked by E. L. Schaub in the *Philosophical Review* (1943) for falling back on Schelling's own expressions, without any real attempt to elucidate them. What has been said of some translations of Aristotle—"You can usually follow them if you know the Greek"—applies also to such introductions. Those who are already well acquainted with the author being introduced can usually understand the introduction.

In other cases, the introduction makes no pretence to be philosophical; it is of interest only to philologians or historians. An important example is D. D. McGarry's edition (1955) of the *Metalogicon* of John of Salisbury. There is much in the *Metalogicon* which is of considerable interest to the contemporary philosopher, e.g., John of Salisbury's thorough discussion of the distinction between falsity and "absurdity." But that fact McGarry does not bring out; his annotation is a medievalist's, not a philosopher's. Of course, on the other side, nothing dates more rapidly than an introduction which is merely fashionable in its philosophical approach; the important thing is to bring out the philosophical content in a vocabulary which is deliberately neutral. On the whole that objective has been achieved, although the author is not a philosopher, in Aram Vartanian's edition of La Mettrie's *L'Homme machine* (1960). This can be studied with profit by historians of ideas, historians of science, and historians of philosophy alike, because Vartanian has brought out the importance of La Mettrie's book in such a variety of respects. *L'Homme machine* is not a work of the first order, philosophically considered, but at least Vartanian sets its philosophical character in the clearest possible light; the principal objective of philosophical scholarship is thereby achieved.

One feature of the editions so far mentioned may have struck the reader, and that is the willingness, and indeed the tendency, of American scholars to devote themselves to figures who are of considerably less than major importance. If the present monograph were a *catalogue raisonné* rather than an attempt to detect tendencies, that impression would be reinforced; we could refer to recent editions of Pico della Mirandola, Philodemus, Herbert of Cherbury, Thomas of Bradwardine, and many another. For a modern edition of a minor writer, one naturally looks first to America. On the other hand, one does not turn to America for a classical edition of a major writer.

There are a few editions which concern themselves, at least, with the writings of major philosophers, even if not of their most important works, L. E. Loemker's edition, for example, of Leibniz's *Philosophical Papers and Letters* (1956) and L. W. Beck's translation and edition of Kant's *Critique of Practical Reason and Other Writings in Moral Philosophy* (1949). But in general the comment may stand: there is, to mention only recent British works, no American analogue to Ross's edition of Aristotle, or to the many editions and commentaries on Plato's dialogues prepared by Taylor, Cornford, Hackforth, Raven, Bluck, and others; or to the Jessop-Luce *Berkeley.* This is not because the work is now done, and need be done no more; to mention only a few cases, there is a real need for good modern editions of Locke, Mill, and (in translation) Hegel. Here, American scholarship has the opportunity, which it has not yet taken, to show its strength in ways which allow of direct comparison with the classical achievements of British and Continental philosophical scholarship. Few British philosophers have had the patience to devote themselves, with the American sort of scholarly assiduity, to the study of minor writers. For the American editions of such writers every scholar must be grateful. There certainly has been, in England, an undue tendency to concentrate attention upon a very few masters. But do American scholars, on the other side, lack the confidence to measure themselves against the truly great? Or does the solution lie elsewhere?

Boas, writing of A. O. Lovejoy as historian of philosophy (*JHI,* 1948), says of his works that "each of them indicates his profound sympathy with the less recognized genius, with those initiators of great traditions who at best find fame in a footnote" and connects that interest in minor writings with his moral sympathies: "is it not that same sympathy which has led him to participate in every movement which has had as its target the elimination of unfairness and the encouragement of justice" (p. 404). Are we to see in the American resuscitation of minor philosophers a demand for equal treatment? Or simply the influence of Lovejoy or of the Ph.D. requirement?

5. The history of ideas is very much an American preoccupation; German scholars are often suspicious of what they regard as its atomism—since it describes the history of unit-ideas rather than the development of *Geist*—and many British scholars have condemned it on the ground that it concentrates its attention on third-rate rather than first-rate thinkers. "The history of ideas," writes an English critic, "seems to consist of little more than those ideas and theories which philosophers and scientists have outgrown or rejected or which have never even achieved the status of serious candidates for criticism. The history of philosophy, on the other hand, is the story of those ideas and theories which have proved to offer a lasting intellectual stimulus. It is perhaps odd that this distinction should ever have come to be made, but even a casual acquaintance with what has been written in these fields makes the difference only too plain. One result of the cleavage has been that philosophers pay little attention to the history of ideas on the reasonable ground that they have more profitable ways of spending their time." [2] One is reminded of Hegel's definition of "erudition": "acquaintance with a number of useless things, that is to say, with that which has no intrinsic interest or value further than being known" (*Lectures on the History of Philosophy,* trans. E. S. Haldane, vol. I, p. 12). If this were a wholly correct definition of "the history of ideas," the philosopher might well leave it to the antiquarian. But, as Hegel suggests,

[2] Review by D. J. O'Connor of J. W. Yolton's *John Locke and the Way of Ideas* in *Philosophical Review* (1958), p. 269.

this sort of erudition is often confused with the history of philosophy; we need at least carefully to distinguish their respective fields. Furthermore, even if the history of ideas is quite distinct from the history of philosophy, the two may be intimately, and usefully, related.

Sometimes, of course, the history of ideas and the history of philosophy are simply identified; or rather, perhaps one should say, the history of philosophy is regarded as a particular species—along with the history of economic thought, the history of science, the history of social thought—of the history of ideas, understood as including any variety of historical study where the subject matter is intellectual, rather than political, legal, military, or diplomatic. Thus most of the essays included in the *Columbia Studies in the History of Ideas* (vol. 1, 1918; vol. 2, 1925; vol. 3, 1935) clearly fall within the history of philosophy. The title of these volumes, the preface somewhat oddly remarks, "represents a larger field of inquiry than the matter here included would indicate, a field in which others than philosophers are engaged and in which it appears that ideas have a history and that their history is influenced by contact with lines of experience not commonly called philosophical." Was there a last minute protest against the title? Certainly, *Studies in the History of Philosophy* would have been more appropriate, but the distinction did not, as late as 1918, seem to be of any great importance.

At the opposite extreme, there is work in the history of ideas which clearly has nothing to do with the history of philosophy—or has no more to do with it than have other varieties of history. The student of Hobbes certainly needs to know something about the political situation in seventeenth century England; the student of eighteenth century philosophy may well be grateful for such works as Marjorie Nicolson's *Newton Demands the Muse* (1946). The fact remains that this book, as much as studies of British constitutional history, lies outside the field of philosophical scholarship.

There is, however, a middle area, where the situation is more debatable; and it is works belonging to this area which have been particularly subject to criticism, as being merely the history of inferior philosophical ideas as distinct from the history of good philosophical ideas. Yet the development of the history of ideas as a discipline in the United States was very largely the responsibility of A. O. Lovejoy, a philosopher of very considerable ability, as he proved in his *The Revolt Against Dualism* (1930). He had already shown himself, in his essay on "The Thirteen Pragmatisms" (*Journal of Philosophy,* 1908), to be a quite exceptionally gifted disentangler of threads, able to detect and analyze the ingredients in a complex of ideas disguised as a single concept; these gifts he was to turn to good account in his work on the history of ideas.

Indeed *The Great Chain of Being* (1936) is the classical example of the more philosophical sort of history of ideas; it includes, too, by way of an introduction an important statement about the aims and objects of the history of ideas as compared with the traditional histories of philosophy. "In dealing with the history of philosophical discussions," Lovejoy writes, ". . . it cuts into the hard-and-fast individual systems and for its own purpose breaks them up into their component elements, into what may be called their 'unit-ideas.'" Now, of course, there were already plenty of books on the history of the idea of God, or the history of the idea of the soul; there were, too, histories of idealism, of materialism, of Christianity. But God, the soul, Christianity, materialism, idealism are not, Lovejoy argues, unit-ideas as he understands the phrase. People who call themselves Christian, for example, have "held under that name a very mixed collection of ideas the combination of which into a conglomerate bearing a single name and supposed to constitute a real unity was usually the result of historic processes of a highly complicated and curious sort" (p. 6). The task of the historian of ideas, looking at— to mention instances with which Lovejoy has particularly concerned himself—pragmatism, or primitivism, or romanticism, is to break up the conglomerate concept into the ideas which constitute it, ideas which have a history of their own, independent of, although affected by, their presence in that conglomerate.

What is meant by "idea"? According to Lovejoy, a very miscellaneous collection of entities: mental habits, like the habit of supposing that to any problem there must be a single solution; susceptibilities, like the susceptibility to the conception of immutability —what Lovejoy called "metaphysical pathos"; words or phrases like "rational conduct" which, by their very ambiguity, make it possible for men to move painlessly from one system of thought to another, while still supposing that they are governed by a single principle;

explicit beliefs. The concept of a unit-idea is, indeed, not itself a notably clear one—perhaps it has facilitated a painless transmission from one conception of the history of ideas to quite another—since the items in Lovejoy's list are not, in any ordinary sense of the words, either ideas or units.

George Boas, Lovejoy's colleague at Johns Hopkins and another of the more philosophical historians of ideas, defines "idea" much more narrowly as "something which might be asserted in a declarative statement, an assertion of belief, the solution of a problem, not necessarily one's own problem, but someone's in the last analysis" ("Some Problems of Intellectual History," p. 3, in Boas *et al., Studies in Intellectual History,* 1953). But Lovejoy's wider definition seems to conform more closely to the actual practice of the historian of ideas: intellectual habits are of as much importance to the historian of ideas as explicit principles.

On the face of it, the analysis of ideas is an admirable area of study: a particular way of investigating the history of philosophy, which seeks to uncover the tensions in a philosopher between the new ideas he is introducing and the habits of the tradition in which he is writing. Certainly a book like Lovejoy's *The Great Chain of Being* is of permanent interest to philosophical scholars. But this is largely because its central concern is with great figures in the history of philosophy—whether Lovejoy is right or wrong in his much debated interpretation of Aquinas, for example, nobody could doubt that his interpretation is philosophically relevant—and with ideas which, according to Lovejoy, originated in Plato. Indeed, Lovejoy has always maintained that "in the history of philosophy is to be found the common seed-plot, the *locus* of initial manifestation in writing, of the greater number of the more fundamental and pervasive ideas, and especially of the controlling preconceptions which manifest themselves in other regions of intellectual history" (*Essays in the History of Ideas,* 1948, p. 8). His concern, only, was to break down barriers between fields of inquiry, to persuade the philosophically trained scholar to follow up the history of the ideas which originate within philosophy as they pass into literature, science, and the general culture of society, not to move outside the field of philosophical scholarship altogether.

Had this in fact been the general procedure of historians of ideas, any investigation of American philosophical scholarship might have had to devote itself largely to their work. But in fact, the history of ideas has come to have less and less to do with philosophy, as can easily be seen from a perusal of the files of the *Journal of the History of Ideas* (1940-   ), and, as I have already suggested, it is now often regarded with positive suspicion by philosophical scholars. What do they dislike in it, and with what justification?

Sometimes they dislike the special sort of metaphysics with which the history of ideas has come to be associated. Thus, in the preface to his *Diderot and Descartes: A Study of Scientific Naturalism in the Enlightenment* (1953) Aram Vartanian writes that "the history of ideas deals primarily with ideas which have in the proper sense a history. . . . There are ideas whose successive development, or life-cycle, may be viewed as in itself constituting a form of organic existence in relation to which places, periods and persons, however significant, remain subordinate. This 'historical transcendence' of certain ideas must often be a tacit assumption on the part of their biographer." Vartanian does not make this remark as one who expects to be contradicted; but such a metaphysical-Darwinian approach to the history of ideas would certainly be regarded with suspicion by those scholars for whom the "unit" is a "person-holding-an-idea," not the idea itself. This connects, indeed, with a criticism which was raised at an early stage against the history of ideas, that it is too little historical; that it is concerned to pick out similar ideas in different forms at different times and places—as a classificatory geologist might recognize similar fossil forms in different strata—rather than to explain why the idea persisted or why it changed as it did, why it won new popularity at a certain time, and waned at another. Beginning from the premise that ideas are self-contained, the work of a historian of ideas easily degenerates into a mere collecting of instances and does not produce a truly historical study.

The association of the history of ideas with historical relativism has done nothing to advance its popularity with philosophers. "To Aristotle and to Plato," writes Harold Cherniss, "the very possibility of what we call a history of ideas would have seemed to be incompatible with philosophy, which to them implied an objective and eternal truth discernible by each individual human mind directly." ("The History of Ideas and Ancient Greek Philosophy," in *Studies in Intellectual History,* 1953, p. 45). If, of course, Plato or Aristotle denied that historical circumstances can affect what men believe, they would clearly have been wrong; but it does not follow, as it is sometimes taken to follow, that they were wrong in believing that there is such a thing as objective truth. A tired skepticism is the prevailing note in a good deal of the writing in the history of ideas, an arid egalitarianism for which the great thinker and the minor epigone each count as one, as hosts to the same philosophical virus, occupants of neighboring hospital beds. Indeed, the epigone is a more interesting demonstration-case than his master; his intellectual resistance is lower, he shows the effects of infection more clearly, in a form which the rawest of medical students can diagnose. Now we begin to understand why the history of ideas should so easily degenerate into mere parallel hunting, with third-rate writers as its territory of choice.

This is apparent even in the relatively early *Documentary History of Primitivism and Related Ideas,* the first volume of which, *Primitivism and Related Ideas in Antiquity,* prepared by Lovejoy and Boas, was published in 1935, the second volume, *Essays on Primitivism and Related Ideas in the Middle Ages,* by Boas, in 1948. These volumes, as the titles suggest, were largely designed as source-books, and it would be unfair to judge them as history. Nor are Lovejoy and Boas, insofar as they engaged in comment, wholly uncritical in their philosophical and historical attitude. But work of this sort, at lesser hands, degenerates into the mere accumulation of references, and even at the hands of Lovejoy and Boas, one wonders how much it has contributed to the growth of philosophical understanding.

It can easily encourage, too, the attitude summed up in the phrase "this has all been said before," a refusal to admit the possibility of novelty, which is no less absurd than the antithetical, antihistorical, identification of the latest with the most novel. The twin evils of relativism and what Peter Gay calls "the trap of spurious persistence" [3] are nowhere better exemplified than in what is, all the same, one of the most notable contributions of American intellectual history, Carl Becker's *The Heavenly City of the Eighteenth-Century Philosophers* (1932). On the one side Becker attacks logic as "something the mind has created to conceal its timidity and keep

[3] In *Carl Becker's Heavenly City Revisited,* ed. R. O. Rockwood (1958), p. 31.

23

up its courage, a hocus-pocus designed to give formal validity to conclusions we are willing to accept if everybody else in our set will, too" (p. 25); on the other side, he attempts to show that "the underlying preconceptions of eighteenth-century thought were still, allowance made for certain important alterations in the bias, essentially the same as those of the thirteenth century" (p. 31). And this latter thesis, as his critics have pointed out, is made plausible only by defects in Becker's powers of logical analysis; he fails to notice, beneath a similarity in verbal formulas, the operation of quite distinct concepts.

Undoubtedly, the history of ideas and the writings of "intellectual historians" like Becker have had a considerable effect upon philosophical scholarship in America. This effect has been a good one insofar as it encouraged scholars to think of philosophers as working in an intellectual and public setting, as distinct from being each a pure Cartesian Cogito; it has been a bad one insofar as it has encouraged merely accumulative scholarship. We shall see its effects, and examine some of its products in what follows; but the greater part of what is now regarded as "the history of ideas" lies wholly outside our province. For good or ill—as I believe, for ill—the history of ideas has passed out of the hands of philosophers, into the hands of departments of modern languages. "I like to think," writes Marjorie Nicolson, "that Lovejoy has found more cooperation among his literary students and followers than among philosophers" ("A. O. Lovejoy as Teacher," *JHI,* 1948, p. 432). What Nicolson likes to think is certainly true; and largely because the literary scholar is less suspicious of "mere erudition" than the philosopher—although even so there have been complaints that in literature, too, the application of Lovejoy's method has "helped to divert attention from literature of the first rank to works of the second and third or even lower rank."

6. A general history of any field of inquiry is difficult to write; and it becomes more and more difficult in a period like our own, which has witnessed a scholarship explosion scarcely less disconcerting than the population explosion and equally international in its incidence. No one can keep himself even reasonably in touch with the monograph and periodical literature—or even the books—

on the classical, medieval, and modern periods of Western philosophy, to say nothing of Eastern philosophy (which I shall be obliged wholly to ignore). This problem, no doubt, affects the political historian as much as it does the historian of philosophy. But there is a special problem in philosophy: to give any indication of the quality and importance of a philosopher one must be able to show how he argued, not merely what he concluded. This takes time and space; the need for restricting the length of a general history of philosophy to a manageable bulk does not allow the space to expound, nor does the labor of writing it allow the time to understand.

Of course the difference in this respect, too, between a history of philosophy and other histories can be exaggerated; a history book which is content to tell us that Hitler invaded Russia without explaining why he did so, what he hoped to gain by taking this particular step rather than some other, is not likely to advance our historical understanding. But still, it is an important fact that Hitler invaded Russia—a fact worth knowing, to be reckoned with in our understanding of past and present. In contrast, it is useless knowledge that Aquinas believed that there is an infinite God, James that there is a finite God, McTaggart that there is no God. Knowing that Hitler invaded Russia we see at once that, at least, he was an important figure in the history of Western civilization, whereas if all we know about Bradley is that he thought there was an absolute we have not the slightest conception why he was an important philosopher, in a sense in which the absolutist Ferrier—to say nothing of some enthusiastic theosophist—was not. "If the history of philosophy merely represented various opinions in array," wrote Hegel, "it would be a most superfluous and tiresome form of inquiry, no matter what advantage might be brought forward as derived from such thought-activity and learning. What could be more useless than to learn a string of bald opinions, and what more unimportant?" (*Lectures in the History of Philosophy*, trans. E. S. Haldane, p. 12). A history of philosophy which does not enable us to watch philosophical minds in action is, at best, a reference book with the entries arranged in chronological rather than alphabetical order—useful if we forget a date, or half-remember somebody's name or the title of a book, but not deserving to be called a history.

Unfortunately, the first histories of philosophy in the modern period were mostly of this form; the learned Joseph Brucker, for example, sets out for us in his immense *Historia critica philosophiae* (1742) the fifty-three logical opinions of Aristotle under numbered heads but displays no insight whatever (he was a scholar, not a philosopher) into Aristotle's problems or manner of thought. This pattern, deriving from Diogenes Laertius, set an unfortunate example for subsequent historians of philosophy. "There can be no real history of philosophy," as Harold Cherniss writes, "unless the historian philosophises, philosophises within the framework of his subject and at the same time keeps his critical faculty detached and vigilant over the philosophy which he is rethinking. That is why the ancient doxographers were not historians of ideas; it is why so much of the modern history of ancient philosophy is little better than doxography" (*Studies in Intellectual History,* p. 47).

But to philosophize over a wide variety of philosophers, diversified in interest, in method, in background, as the critical historian of philosophy is expected to do, involves an intellectual effort of a kind which Brucker, for example, did not have to make; yet it is at the same time expected of the general historian that he should satisfy the strictest standards of scholarship. Thus it is not surprising that there is no American equivalent of Windelband, or Bréhier, or Ueberweg; works of that magnitude and quality are sufficiently rare in any country. What one finds in America, rather, are undergraduate texts—largely, and naturally, doxographical in character and so subject to the strictures of Hegel and of Cherniss. They are scarcely to be taken seriously, as contributions to scholarship. One of the best known of them, B. A. G. Fuller's two-volume *History of Philosophy* (revised in 1945), is unusually candid in acknowledging its dependence on secondary sources; Fuller prefaces his discussion of medieval philosophy with the remark: "I have no first-hand knowledge of Patristic and Scholastic thought and texts. The following passages are founded for the most part upon the histories of medieval and scholastic philosophers by Gilson and de Wulf, and upon Ruggiero's *Filosofia del Cristianismo.*" Indeed such histories-for-undergraduates are almost all of them watered-down versions of more detailed histories; if, occasionally, they spring into unexpected life—as in Fuller's account of Plato and Plotinus, where he leaves himself enough space to discuss problems as distinct from merely summarizing doctrines—one can be sure one has discovered the genuinely scholarly concern of the author. For the most part, one hates to think of an undergraduate using such "histories" as anything but a rapid reference book. To attempt to learn philosophy or to understand its history by studying such a survey would be like trying to learn to swim by reading the list of Olympic record holders.

The problem of selection is perhaps easier when the subject is not the history of the whole range of philosophy but some branch of it, especially those branches which do not intimately involve the more intricate sort of philosophical argumentation. Thus in his *History of Political Theory* (1937), G. H. Sabine, by adopting a policy of rigid selection, succeeded in producing a work which is philosophical in tone, as historically descriptive as his field of inquiry demands, and sufficiently detailed to enable the intelligent reader to obtain a general understanding of the writers upon whom Sabine concentrates his attention, an understanding of their problems and their principles. This is certainly the most important general history of political theory yet produced, a work of which American scholarship can justly be proud.

Yet, as Sabine confesses, there is one great weakness in his book; the treatment of recent political theory—the last fifty years or more —is grossly defective; we are not led into recent controversies as a historian of thought can reasonably be expected to lead us. The same phenomenon is even more noticeable in K. E. Gilbert and Helmut Kuhn's *History of Esthetics* (1939; rev. ed., 1953). In the opening chapters there is a rare sense of spaciousness; some fifty pages on Plato's aesthetics leave room for explanation, discussion, illustration. By the time Gilbert and Kuhn reach the middle of the nineteenth century, however, their history has already degenerated into a chronicle, and their final chapter on "Twentieth-Century Directions" is quite pitifully inadequate. Throughout their work, too, the more difficult philosophical questions which arise within aesthetics are very largely neglected. The problems involved in writing a general history of philosophy on a small scale could scarcely be better illustrated than in this, still perhaps the best, history of aesthetics.

7. At the heart of philosophical scholarship lies the study of individual writers or of relatively brief periods of philosophical history; such studies permit a thoroughness precluded by general histories; the scholar has room enough, as it were, to show his powers. Yet the conclusion does not follow, that the scholar ought to specialize on a person or a period, if this involves becoming absorbed in that chosen period or person to a degree which prohibits any understanding of what lies beyond. General histories are often, no doubt, superficial doxographies; but specialised monographs may be quite as jejune, philosophically and historically, and even more misleading. For to understand a philosopher's problems and to estimate his success in meeting them, we need to know more than a little of the traditions which intersect in his work; the commentator who reads nothing, over long periods of years, except the writings of a single—often very minor—philosopher or school of philosophy is unlikely to produce a penetrating contribution to philosophical scholarship.

The more minor a writer is, the more important it is to see him against a wider intellectual background; otherwise one is almost certain greatly to overestimate his philosophical importance. This is a mistake to which the monographer is more liable than the general historian; and it is a recurrent defect in American scholarship.

A striking feature of the American scholarly scene, indeed, is the number of books written by "one-book" men. For their doctoral dissertation, it would seem, they have chosen to write about some minor philosopher, perhaps on the ground that no one has ever written about him before. It has been said that when five books have been written on a subject, it is easy to write a sixth; equally, one might retort, when nobody has written a book on a subject, it is easy to write the first. The doctoral student can be more confident that he will "make an original contribution to learning" if he sets out to comment on a previously neglected author or a previously unedited text than if he tries to throw fresh light on a great philosopher. He will learn more about philosophy by trying to understand Kant than by writing a thesis on Bolingbroke—but he is less likely to complete his dissertation, to satisfy his examiners, or to be able to "make a book" out of it.

Thus the scholar in search of a book about a minor writer soon develops the habit of looking first to America. Few English scholar-philosophers have been prepared to face the drudgery involved in the study of minor, or relatively minor, philosophers, whose genuine achievements are rare hummocks in a marsh of commonplaces. It is to the credit of American scholars that they are not in the least terrified by such arduous labors; and occasionally their patience is rewarded.

But to be able to see the significance of a minor figure is one of the last rewards of mature scholarship, not the first fruit of learning. The scholar can understand just what, for example, Joseph Glanvill stood for and just why and in what respect he was important, only when he has a considerable understanding of the period in which Glanvill worked and a sound knowledge of his great contemporaries. The one-book study of a minor figure may be conscientious—a useful source of bibliographical or biographical material—but it is scarcely likely to throw a discriminating light on its subject. Indeed, the reviewers of such books are forced monotonously to make the same comments: "thorough but pedestrian," "grossly overestimates the importance of X's philosophy, because he does not realize how largely it derives from Y," "quite misleading wherever it ventures a remark about other philosophers of the period." In the circumstances, nothing else is to be expected. A period of reflection, of reading outside the chosen field, before publication, might in some cases have worked wonders.

I cannot possibly comment in detail upon this regiment of well-drilled dissertations. Occasionally a particular dissertation will demand attention, or the prevalence of dissertations in a certain field will be particularly striking, but of the bulk of such works nothing will be said. Yet their multitudinousness and character must at least be noted. They constitute the major ingredient, numerically speaking, in American scholarly publication, explaining, to a certain degree, its ambiguous reputation in the world of learning. Within that flood of dissertations, we have somehow, and naturally imperfectly, to discern the course of the main, life-giving stream.

⋙ 3 ⋘

GREEK PHILOSOPHY

1. Pre-Socratic philosophy.   2. Platonic scholarship.   3. Aristotelian studies.   4. Post-Aristotelian philosophy.

"Classical students of Plato," writes W. C. Greene, "have too seldom been aware of the criticism of their author by modern philosophers, while even excellent modern philosophers are too rarely acquainted with the results of the philological study of Plato" ("Platonism and Its Critics," *Harvard Studies in Classical Philology,* ed. E. A. Havelock, 1953, p. 39). It is indeed a recurrent complaint by philologians that the most philosophical commentaries on Plato are philologically inadequate; sometimes the philologian can point, even, to schoolboy howlers. Especially, perhaps, in America. Generally speaking the British or Continental philosopher-scholar is more likely to have had a sound philological training than his American colleague; and those who have not had such a training are too intimidated by their classical colleagues to dare to publish their reflections on classical philosophy. On the other hand, philosophers can rightly retort that more scholarly commentaries often reveal a startling lack of philosophical sophistication. This is certainly true of Greene's own *Moira: Fate, Good and Evil in Greek Thought* (1944; see, for example, pp. 283-84) for all the notable virtues of that work.

The present commentary is entirely a philosopher's report. I cannot pretend to speak for the philologians, even in the most modest way. Were it possible, I should like to begin by drawing a sharp line between philological Greek scholarship and philosophical Greek scholarship, and to confine my attention thereafter to scholarship of the latter sort. But no such line can be drawn. Thus even if, as I suggested, Greene's *Moira* is in some ways philosophically innocent, it is of considerable assistance to the philosophical interpreter of, say, Plato; it is in part directly about Plato's work, and places it in an unusual, and revealing, context.

30

Indeed, some scholars would go further and insist that any book about Plato which is primarily philosophical must be bad; for Plato, they would say, was not in any modern or systematic sense a philosopher at all. He was a politician, whose philosophical "theories" are a hastily constructed earthwork designed as a defense for his political policies; he was a literary artist, a moralist, an educator, but not, except in the most incidental way, a logician or a metaphysician. Should we wish to understand Greek politics, they would say, or Greek ideas about education, or Greek art, or Greek religion, if we are in search of literary enjoyment, moral improvement, or political enlightenment, we should look to Plato, under the guidance of a classical scholar; but to look to him, under the guidance of a historian of philosophy, for systematic philosophical doctrines, is quite to misunderstand the character of his work. The rights of the philosopher-scholar, as distinct from those of the philologian, in the field of Platonic scholarship are by no means unquestioned—especially perhaps in America, although in some measure also in Germany. His role is one of the major points of controversy.

1. When it comes to the pre-Socratics, the position of the philosopher-scholar is even weaker. He is faced by philological problems so formidable that few philosophers now venture upon an interpretation of pre-Socratic philosophy, although the enigmatic aphorisms of Heraclitus, in particular, present a challenge to the philosophical imagination which is difficult to resist.

Nor is philological complexity the only obstacle the philosopher-scholar has to overcome if he turns his attention to the pre-Socratics. He has also to meet the objection that pre-Socratic thought belongs to the history of science, not to the history of philosophy—or, at the opposite extreme, that the pre-Socratics were myth makers rather than philosophers. At the very least, he must pay close attention not only to the philologians but also (as R. K. Hack has done in his brief essay on *God in Greek Philosophy, to the Time of Socrates,* 1931) to the historians of Greek religion and the historians of Greek science—not the less so, because philological interpreters have often been remiss in this respect.

To help him to cope with the history of science, the American scholar has at his disposal the fantastic erudition of George Sarton, as displayed in his reference work *Introduction to the History of Science* (1927-48) and in a more digestible form in *A History of Science: Ancient Science through the Golden Age of Greece* (1952), to say nothing of *Isis,* the journal he founded in 1913. Sarton had no great love for philologians, and he was no philosopher. But he did a great deal to foster interest in the history of science, even if in some respects his unmatchable learning has tended to clog the processes of inquiry; not all his successors have heeded his warning that "erudition without pedantry is as rare as wisdom itself."

Of other American histories of science, many have something to say about the pre-Socratics, but few are largely devoted to them. An exception is W. A. Heidel's *The Heroic Age of Science* (1933). Heidel—as later in his *Hippocratic Medicine: Its Spirit and Method* (1941)—sets out to show that Greek science was experimental in spirit, as opposed to the view that it is a priori. His work is not so much a history of science as a defense of the view that the Greeks were scientists, a defense which proceeds by discussing the use they made of what Heidel takes to be the main ingredients in scientific method. Such a task requires a combination of philological, scientific, and philosophical insight; Heidel's work was not meant to be more than preliminary, but even at that level it lacks the bite which we can reasonably expect from a quasi-theoretical study. Not surprisingly, recent historians of science—like Marshall Clagett in his *Greek Science in Antiquity* (1955)—have preferred to concentrate their attention on the Alexandrian period, where the problems of interpretation involve scientific rather than philosophical gifts; such works, however, are of no direct interest to the philosopher.

The most substantial American work on the pre-Socratics, considered as philosophers rather than as scientists, lies hidden within Harold Cherniss' *Aristotle's Criticism of Presocratic Philosophy* (1935). The phrase "lies hidden within" is used advisedly. Cherniss' theme is not pre-Socratic philosophy as such but rather the deficiencies of Aristotle as a source of information about it. This naturally forces Cherniss to compare the correct with the Aristotelian interpretation of the fragments, and so far involves him in a direct consideration of the ideas they present, but the product of that direct consideration can only with difficulty be extracted from the bulky complexities of Cherniss' work—especially since his indexing is of the most primitive kind. To find out what Cherniss thinks about the interpretation of a particular passage in, say, Empedocles involves looking through some hundreds of index references to "Empedocles," simply—references scattered throughout the entire length of the book—and with no guarantee that Cherniss will have discussed that passage at all. Yet, if he has discussed it, what he has said about it will almost certainly be important. Cherniss' essay on "The Characteristics and Effects of Pre-Socratic Philosophy" (*JHI*, 1951) stands at the opposite extreme; it is a masterly account of the whole course of pre-Socratic philosophy, but no more than a summary. The effect is that although the great merits of Cherniss' work have been widely recognized, it has not received, in detail, the attention it deserves.

Taken together with J. B. McDiarmid's essay on "Theophrastus on the Pre-Socratic Causes" (*Harvard Studies in Classical Philology,* ed. E. A. Havelock, 1953), Cherniss' work, however, made necessary a drastic revaluation of the accepted methods of interpretation of pre-Socratic philosophy. Theophrastus, according to McDiarmid, far from being an independent source of information about pre-Socratic philosophy, largely derives his analysis of the pre-Socratics from Aristotle; and Cherniss had already shown that Aristotle systematically distorts the doctrines of his predecessors for his own philosophical purposes. The effect has been to drive scholars back to the actual fragments, which now have to be carefully re-examined in a more independent way, less influenced by the presumption that Aristotle and Theophrastus can be relied upon as interpreters. That work of re-examination, however, has been undertaken in England rather than in America: for example, by G. S. Kirk and J. E. Raven in *The Presocratic Philosophers* (1957). They begin from the principle that "it is legitimate to feel complete confidence in our understanding of a Presocratic thinker only when the Aristotelian or Theophrastian interpretation, even if it can be accurately reconstructed, is confirmed by relevant and well-authenticated extracts from the philosopher himself" (p. 7). Similarly G. S. Kirk in his *Heraclitus: The Cosmic Fragments* (1954) presumes that "Cherniss has shown irrefutably in his *Aristotle's Criticism of Presocratic Philosophy* the extent and serious nature of Aristotle's historical perversions" (p. 30). Here then is a case in which American philosophical scholarship has had a striking effect upon the whole course of scholarship. There is a sense in which the study of pre-Socratic philosophy has had to be begun again. So far, however, American scholarship has not produced the modern equivalent of Burnet's *Early Greek Philosophy;* Cherniss' *History of Ideas* article is only a sketch-plan for such a book.

The only recent American work at all comparable with Kirk and Raven's—C. H. Kahn's *Anaximander and the Origins of Greek Cosmology* (1960)—is less critical in its attitude to Theophrastus, not surprisingly in view of the impossibility, in Anaximander's case, of basing an interpretation on the fragments. In general, indeed, Kahn recognizes that it is impossible now to determine quite what Anaximander did teach. "In a sense," he writes, "the name of Anaximander stands here as a symbol for the anonymous creative spirit of Ionian thought in the sixth century" (p. 8). Kahn is less concerned to establish what Anaximander himself thought than to describe the Ionian spirit; this he does admirably.

From the point of view of the philosopher-scholar, some of the most important work on the pre-Socratic philosophers has been produced by Gregory Vlastos. Unfortunately, this has not yet taken shape as a book; it is scattered over a wide variety of philosophical and philological journals. I have noticed articles in the *Philosophical Review* (1945-46 and 1950) on Democritus and on Anaxagoras; in *Classical Philology* (1947) on "Equality and Justice in Early Greek Cosmologies"; in the *American Journal of Philology* (1953 and 1955) on Alcmaeon and on Heraclitus; in the *Philosophical Quarterly* (1952) on "Theology and Philosophy in Early Greek Thought"; in *Transactions of the American Philological Association* (1946) on Parmenides. No doubt this is not a complete list, but it sufficiently illustrates the range of Vlastos' work. His essays are distinguished by their concern for philosophical implications; the richness of his annotation, if it is sometimes still a little indigestible by British standards, does not interfere with the freshness of his writing. The clogged, murky, abstract Teutonic literary style which mars so much American scholarship is in this instance—for once a cliché is justified—conspicuous by its absence.[1]

[1] I count Vlastos as an American, because he was largely trained in America

For the rest, American works on pre-Socratic philosophy are, for the most part, either marginal to philosophy or not of any great consequence. Felix Cleve—of European origin—makes large claims for his *The Philosophy of Anaxagoras* (1949); he pays scarcely any attention, however, to American scholarship, or indeed to any English language scholarship subsequent to Burnet, and his belief, expressed in a highly rhetorical way, that he has produced a new interpretation of Anaxagoras, is largely, although not quite wholly, based on ignorance of that literature.

Philip Wheelwright's *Heraclitus* (1959) is philosophically adventurous, as Kirk's meticulous commentary does not aspire to be, but it is scarcely notable for the exactness of its interpretations. What does Wheelwright mean, for example, when he writes that for Heraclitus "paradox lies inextricably at the very heart of reality" (p. 92), or that Heraclitus' attitude to community is "forcefully ambivalent" (p. 84)? There have been a great many articles on Heraclitus, including a number by the German-American scholar Hermann Fränkel, brought together in his *Dichtung und Philosophie des frühen Griechentums* (1951); and, of course, there have been articles of considerable quality about the other pre-Socratics, too—but little in the way of substantial books.

The Pythagoreans have been somewhat more exhaustively investigated. Kurt von Fritz's *Pythagorean Politics in Southern Italy* (1940) is an essay in source analysis, which, although published in America, belongs more properly, like Werner Jaeger's *Theology of the Early Greek Philosophers* (1947), to Continental than to American scholarship. At almost the same time Fritz was writing, E. L. Minar was preparing his monograph on *Early Pythagorean Politics in Practice and Theory* (1942). Minar makes some attempt, as Fritz did not, to relate Pythagorean politics to Pythagorean philosophy; he sees in the peculiarities of that philosophy the key to the success of Pythagoreanism considered as a social and political movement. "This doctrine helped to bring about a solidarity of the aristocrats in the face of new opposing forces" (p. 132). Here we notice for the first time the political emphasis which is characteristic of a great deal of recent American work in Greek philosophy.

and has taught there since 1948. But he was born and had his early education in Istanbul and taught in Canada for some seventeen years.

Other scholars have been interested in the religious aspect of Pythagoreanism, but much of their work has been in the form of doctoral dissertations; like most such dissertations, these would have been better had they been considerably reworked before being published. One of the better examples is Alister Cameron's *The Pythagorean Background of the Theory of Recollection* (1938).

A more important work is I. M. Linforth's *The Arts of Orpheus* (1941), a learned and iconoclastic study of the Orphic religious movement. Linforth's attack upon the whole notion of an Orphic religion has not, in its fullest extent, been widely accepted, but this sort of critical, debunking scholarship is highly important. A crude inductive conception of scholarship still survives in some quarters —scholarship is thought of as accumulation, pure and simple—but in fact a good deal of scholarship, like a good deal of science, consists in the criticism of myths. To this sort of enterprise American scholarship has made important contributions. Linforth's book, although its philosophical relevance is only indirect, is a striking example, which at worst forces a reconsideration of the often very shaky evidence. It is amazing how rapidly in the world of scholarship a dubious hypothesis can come to be regarded as an established fact, especially in fields like pre-Socratic scholarship where the evidence is in any case so scanty. Facts are so scarce that there is a great temptation to make them out of guesses.

2. The American record in Platonic scholarship is much more extensive. "Plato is philosophy, and philosophy Plato," Emerson wrote in his essay on "Plato or the Philosopher," and again, in a manner reminiscent of a familiar German attitude to Shakespeare, "Plato seems to a reader in New England an American genius." Emerson's successors have not been so tempted to think of Plato as an American, but there is no questioning that Plato has acted as a spur to the American imagination or, less often but still notably, as a thorn in the American side.

In Platonic scholarship, as is not the case in many areas of American scholarship, there is a great man to be reckoned with: irascible, sometimes hasty in his judgment, not always just in his references to his fellow scholars, but still a man of remarkable force and no less remarkable influence—Paul Shorey. *The Unity of Plato's*

Thought was published very early in the century (1903), but the point of view which Shorey there formulated he consistently maintained throughout his life; it has done a great deal to shape the course of American Platonic scholarship—and remarkably foreshadowed, even when it did not directly influence, the main tendencies of that scholarship. These tendencies can be set out thus: negatively, a relative indifference to textual criticism and to criticism of individual dialogues; positively, a critical attitude to the sources of Platonic biography, an emphasis upon the unity of Plato's thought, a concern for Plato the moralist and politician rather than for Plato the logician and metaphysician, an unusual degree of interest in Plato's *Laws*.

In the second volume of his Loeb edition and translation of Plato's *Republic*, Shorey remarks that "to put it drastically, for all practical purposes of the student of the Greek language, literature and philosophy, Hermann's text of the *Republic* is quite as good as the more scientific text of Burnet" (p. lxxii). One does not in fact look to America for critical editions of Platonic texts. Nor, although there are a few translations of Plato for school and university use, has there issued from America anything to compare with the translations and commentaries on individual dialogues recently prepared by Taylor, Cornford, Hackforth, Bluck, Dodds in England, and on the Continent by a considerable diversity of French, German, and Italian scholars. In general, the Platonic scholar will be working with a text and commentary prepared by a non-American scholar—Shorey's text of the *Republic* is perhaps the sole exception; what the scholar will find in America, rather, are general studies of Platonic thought, based on the presumption that Plato should be commented on as a whole rather than studied dialogue by dialogue. (Although Shorey's own *What Plato Said*, 1933, is in some measure an exception, insofar as it considers Plato's dialogues one at a time, the distinctive feature even of that work is the degree of cross reference from one dialogue to another.)

America has produced, however, editions and translations of Plato's *Epistles*, as distinct from his dialogues. The introductory chapter to *What Plato Said* contains a characteristic Shorey diatribe against "divinatory biography" and ends with a disavowal of confidence in the authenticity of the main biographical source—

37

Plato's *Epistles*. Shorey had previously expressed similar views in a number of articles and critical reviews. The main American editions of the *Epistles* are somewhat more conservative, reflecting an independent American interest in Plato as a political figure, rather than the special animus of Shorey against Platonic biographers. L. A. Post's edition of *Thirteen Epistles by Plato* (1925) rejects only the first, fifth, ninth, and twelfth letters; G. R. Morrow in his *Studies in the Platonic Epistles with a Translation and Notes* (1935) is considerably more skeptical, expressing some hesitation about, or rejecting, all but five of the epistles. But he still accepts the biographically vital seventh epistle. The Shorey tradition of complete skepticism about the epistles in particular and Platonic biography in general is, however, carried on by Harold Cherniss in *The Riddle of the Early Academy* (1945). Cherniss, discussing the view that Plato eventually abandoned the theory of ideas, makes the distinctly odd parenthetical remark that "for the sake of those who, like Professor Burnet, believe the *Epistles* to be genuine, they [the ideas] also appear in two *Epistles* which would have to be assigned to the latest years of Plato's life." This suggests that Burnet was idiosyncratic in believing that these late epistles—the sixth and seventh—were genuine, whereas, on the contrary, their genuineness is nowadays scarcely impugned except by the followers of Shorey. Such is the power of Shorey's name! It is invoked, too, by George Boas in his "Fact and Legend in the Biography of Plato" (*Phil. Rev.*, 1948). "Out of the mass of gossip and legend," he writes, "a life of Plato has been combed which is still repeated in histories of philosophy. It is in vain that scholars like Shorey and his pupils have pointed to the inanity of such biographical exercises" (p. 448). This skeptical tradition is, indeed, an important element in American Platonic scholarship.

Skepticism has been directed not only against Platonic biographies but also against the view that there was a secret Platonic doctrine, to be glimpsed in such dialogues as the *Philebus* and the *Timaeus*, but only expounded in detail in Plato's lectures at the Academy. In his 1884 dissertation, "De Platonis idearum doctrina," Shorey had doubted the existence of such an esoteric philosophy, and Cherniss' *The Riddle of the Early Academy* is a detailed critical examination of the whole conception of a secret teaching. This, like *The Unity of Plato's Thought*, is a short book; for once it is possible to pick out the main line of Cherniss' argument without being overwhelmed by detail. Cherniss may be wrong—certainly, he has won few converts—but he has compelled a re-examination of evidence in a field of scholarship which stood badly in need of iconoclastic criticism. In the end, it is by critical work such as this —which forces a radical rethinking—rather than by mere meticulousness that American scholarship will come to maturity. In that respect, as I have already suggested, the history of scholarship is more like the history of science than is commonly supposed: it is the bold step, based on firm scholarship, which counts, as distinct from the exercise either, on the one side, of an uninformed or uncritical imagination or, on the other hand, of pedestrian fact collecting, useful though that can be.

In the Shorey tradition, then, Cherniss argues that Plato's thinking was all of a piece, as opposed to the view that Plato worked out in later life a doctrine quite at odds with, say, the *Phaedo*. It is very strange that Raphael Demos, in the preface to his *The Philosophy of Plato* (1939), should write that "for the most part, writers on Plato have confined themselves to separate dialogues" or regard it as a peculiarity of his own work that it attempts to study the Platonic texts as "the exhibition of a single mind, now occupying itself with one problem, now with another, or with the same problem but with a different emphasis at different times" (p. ix)— strange, at least, if he is thinking of his fellow Americans, for his criticism could not be directed against Shorey's point of view. The contrast with the view of a British scholar like A. E. Taylor could scarcely be more striking: "If we try to isolate the topics, putting together under one head all Plato has to say [on a particular topic] we run the very serious risk of confusing what may be views learned very early in life, and very largely taken over receptively from a predecessor, with the very ripest fruits of a life of intense personal thought. . . . A work on Platonic philosophy composed on these principles may be an admirably digested 'cram-book'; it is certain to obliterate every trace of the development of Plato's thought" (*Plato: The Man and His Work*, 1926, p. 28). Scarcely an American scholar would agree with Taylor; for American scholars there is no "development" to obliterate.

39

Shorey wrote *The Unity of Plato's Thought* not long after Campbell and Lutoslawski had established, in general terms, the order of Plato's dialogues, and he is in part protesting against the view that their work is of any substantial help in understanding Plato. "The essential quality of Plato's thought remains for some Platonists a more interesting topic of discussion than the conjectural chronology of his writings" (p. 3). Perhaps this is why American scholars, with one important exception, have had very little to say about the chronology of the dialogues. When G. E. L. Owen of Oxford set out to show (*Classical Quarterly*, 1953) that the *Timaeus* was written at about the same time as the *Republic* and before the *Parmenides* and the *Sophist*, Cherniss protested in a number of articles, most notably in "The Relation of the *Timaeus* to Plato's Later Dialogues" (*American Journal of Philology*, 1954). The *Timaeus* is the greatest obstacle in the path of those who believe that Plato substantially changed his mind in the later dialogues; Cherniss sets out to show that the *Timaeus* is not only quite certainly later than the *Parmenides*, but also that the doctrines of the *Timaeus* in no way conflict with those expounded in Plato's earlier dialogues—or, for that matter, in the other late dialogues.

There is an interesting difference at this point in the approach of (most) British and the approach of (most) American Platonic scholars. The assumption in American scholarship is that Plato's status as a philosopher would be diminished if it were proved that he ever changed his mind on any important topic. In sharp opposition, J. L. Ackrill, an Oxford scholar, argues that "it would be odd if a lively and long-lived philosopher . . . never came to abandon views or arguments he had previously accepted" (*Phil. Rev.*, 1960, p. 133). Indeed, most British scholars would think the worse of Plato should it turn out that, in spite of living in the lively and rapidly changing intellectual and political atmosphere of Athens, he never seriously reconsidered his views on any important question. Of course, the final question is whether there is any *evidence* that Plato changed his mind; neither the possibility that he changed his mind nor the possibility that he did not can be ruled out a priori. Undoubtedly, however, the American scholar approaches the dialogues with the expectation that no change of doctrine will be found there; very often, indeed, he takes that for granted. This expectation is as conspicuous in the scholarly works of Shorey and Cherniss as in such free interpretations as Raphael Demos' *The Philosophy of Plato* or John Wild's *Plato's Theory of Man* (1946).

Demos' book is an exception to the general American tendency to emphasize Plato the moralist rather than Plato the metaphysician. But it is also exceptional in not even pretending to be a work of close scholarship; it refers scarcely at all to the interpretations of other scholars. At the beginning of Chapter XI Demos confesses that "our discussion will rely for the most part on insights which Plato himself has left undeveloped. We will try to elaborate and interpret hints rather than to summarise explicit doctrines; and our theory will not be capable of strict verification or disproof by reference to Plato's writings" (p. 197). Many of his critics have felt that some such warning ought to have prefaced the whole work, rather than a particular section of it; for all that it refers freely to the dialogues, this, as Cherniss has said, "is less a responsible, scholarly interpretation of Plato than a systematic variation *à la Whitehead*, on themes suggested by Platonic texts" ("Plato, 1950-57," *Lustrum*, 1959-60, p. 282).

For the rest, however, the "practical" interpretation of Plato has largely prevailed. Commenting on the analogy of the divided line in Plato's *Republic*, Shorey wrote: "It is permissible to develop these metaphysical implications in a systematic exposition of what we suppose to be Plato's 'philosophy.' But we should be as scrupulous as Plato himself is to distinguish the practical application of his principles in education, ethics, politics from *the metaphysics which he suggests but never affirms*. The main argument of the *Republic* is entirely independent of them, as Plato himself repeatedly indicates" (*What Plato Said*, p. 234, my italics). Indeed, a perusal of the dialogue-summaries, with cross references, which make up the (very useful) body of *What Plato Said*, leaves one with the impression that Plato's theory of ideas is a kind of overbelief, not to be taken seriously or literally as an ingredient in Platonism. The fifty pages Shorey devotes to Plato's *Laws* contrast strikingly with six pages on the *Parmenides* and thirteen on the *Sophist*. After discussing the *Sophist*, furthermore, Shorey remarks that "the old puzzle, how is illusion, error, false opinion, possible" seems to us a "foolish quibble," except insofar as there underlies it

41

a difficulty in giving "the full psychological explanation of error" (p. 297). We have only to read such a passage—or the discussion of the "method of hypotheses" in the *Phaedo* (pp. 179-80)—to see why Shorey places so little stress on Plato's logic and metaphysics; he simply does not see their importance. And, of course, since it is precisely in respect to Plato's attitude to "ideas" that most commentators have thought they could detect a fundamental change in his philosophical teaching, any scholar who denies that the theory of ideas is of the first importance or who will not admit that crucial consequences would follow even from relatively slight changes in its formulation, will naturally find it easier, if still by no means simple, to argue for "the unity of Plato's thought." Shorey's phrase and emphasis in fact go along with his belief that in a sense Plato has no thought—that he commits himself to no explicit ontological or metaphysical doctrines.

In the preface to his *In Defense of Plato* (1953) R. B. Levinson announces that for all his great indebtedness to Shorey he will "treat more seriously than . . . [Shorey] was wont to do the Platonic metaphysics"; that Levinson should make this comment in a book almost wholly devoted to Plato's morals and politics—naturally enough in view of its special purpose of defending Plato against Karl Popper and his fellow detractors—testifies to the very minor importance indeed which Shorey was accustomed to attach to Plato's metaphysics. It is the more startling, then, that Wild should preface his *Plato's Theory of Man* (1946) with the remark that "there is a widespread tendency at the present time to think of Plato as a soaring *metaphysician* or *abstract philosopher* having little to say of direct relevance to the concrete life of living men"— especially as his Plato is more, not less, metaphysical than Shorey's Plato. For the greater philosophical interest of Wild's book, however, one has to pay a heavy price. He says himself that "its aim is not so much to reveal the thought of Plato as to reveal the nature of human culture and its inversion, using Plato, the philosopher, as a guide" (p. 1). This aim however does not justify ascribing to Plato words he never uttered, nor does it justify ignoring the work of American scholars. Cherniss' name is nowhere mentioned, Shorey's only as a translator of the *Republic,* and Wild is free with such *obiter dicta* as "Epistles VI, VII, VIII are now universally accepted as genuine" (p. 13), or "no doubt this sense of contrast [between Plato and Aristotle] would be mitigated if one knew more about Plato's later esoteric teaching" (p. 16). American academics are the least insular of men, except where it is a matter of the intellectual islands within their own continent!

Wild, then, is not a follower of Shorey, but nevertheless still looks for a "practical" Plato. The same is true of R. E. Cushman; his *Therapeia: Plato's Conception of Philosophy* (1958), a good deal influenced by Wild, carries the conception of Plato as a moral-religious teacher, a precursor of Christianity, to what, one hopes, is its extreme point. For Plato, according to Cushman, "the index to truth about reality is the whole man, faithfully interrogated with reference to the entirety of his experience" (p. 273) and the central feature of Plato's teaching is "his preference for decisional, as distinguished from apodictic knowledge" (p. 271). It is, of course, very important to draw attention to the fact that for Plato moral and intellectual improvement are bound up with one another; it is quite another matter to read into him contemporary existentialist-theological conceptions of moral improvement and to identify *that* sort of moral improvement with intellectual improvement.

Not all Americans, however, have been happy about the moral and political implications of Plato's teaching; in certain important respects they constitute a challenge to the official Enlightenment philosophy of American democracy. J. J. Chapman, best known as a literary critic, in his *Lucian, Plato and Greek Morals* (1931) saw in Plato a frivolous dialectician; and Warner Fite in *The Platonic Legend* (1934) condemned Plato's politics and ethics—Fite's sole concern—on the grounds that his politics were totalitarian and his ethics showed no respect for the individual. (The range of Platonic interpretation is wide indeed: Fite attacks Plato for turning moral decisions into mathematical calculations; Cushman—who does not refer to Fite's book—praises him for turning mathematical calculations into moral decisions!) A. D. Winspear, classicist and Marxist, argues that Plato was an active antidemocratic politician, who hoped but failed to bring about a union between the landowning aristocrats and the rising commercial classes. Winspear's *The Genesis of Plato's Thought* (1940) ought not to be dismissed as simple-minded Marxist propaganda. No doubt, much of it is; but Winspear

43

at least tries to set Plato's political philosophy in a political context, and does so with some regard for evidence. Unlike Shorey, he sees Plato as responding to the ever changing conditions of Greek society, and as modifying his philosophical position accordingly; Winspear's argument depends, too, upon accepting as sound evidence much that Shorey and his followers rejected—especially the *Epistles.* Winspear, like Wild, does not mention Cherniss, and Shorey scarcely, except as translator of the *Republic.*

These home-bred attacks on Plato were largely ignored, but Karl Popper's *The Open Society and Its Enemies* (1945) really created a stir. (Popper knew nothing of the American critics of Plato when he wrote the first edition of *The Open Society,* but refers to them in the second edition, pp. 485-86.) The most detailed reply to Popper came from R. B. Levinson, whose *In Defense of Plato* can be read independently as a substantial contribution to our understanding of Plato's moral and political philosophy. Levinson's own attitude to Plato is by no means uncritical; he tries, however, to distinguish sharply between the political mechanisms Plato proposed, and the general philosophical spirit of the dialogues, in which he sees not a betrayal of Socrates, as Popper argues, but, substantially, a continuation and development of the Socratic tradition. This implies, as well, a rejection of the view that Socrates himself was a democratically minded free thinker. Levinson's Plato is more liberal than Popper's Plato, and his Socrates less radical. G. R. Morrow in his "Plato's Conception of Persuasion" (*Phil. Rev.,* 1953) argues, as he usually does, in a sober and independent way: there was, he thought, a certain tension in Plato's thought between his belief in critical inquiry and his strong moral feelings, a tension which he was never able wholly to resolve, and which led him in the end to place the claims of morality above the claims of reason. The admission that Plato, like other philosophers, might have been torn in different directions, is rare in American scholarship.

Not all replies to Popper were so considered and measured: Robert Jordan's "The Revolt against Philosophy: The Spell of Popper," for example, reverses Popper's charges against Plato, seeing in Popper the enemy of rationality. Jordan's essay appears in a volume edited by Wild—*The Return to Reason* (1953)—and is conceived very much in Wild's spirit. Wild himself took up the attack in *Plato's Modern Enemies and the Theory of Natural Law* (1953) arguing, as Jordan had done, that what Popper is condemning is not Platonism but philosophy. But Wild's attempt to ascribe a natural law theory to Plato rests upon a very sketchy and inadequate reference to natural law philosophers, which at times (pp. 35-36) runs very oddly together the conception of natural law and of a law of nature. This is the sort of "philosophical scholarship" which invites the criticism of philosopher and of scholar alike.

A characteristic feature of American Platonic scholarship, I said, is the extent of its interest in Plato's *Laws*. In *The Unity of Plato's Thought,* Shorey protested against "the notion that it [the *Laws*] may safely be neglected by the serious student" and went so far as to assert that it "may often be quoted for the true Platonic solution of problems which Socratic irony or dramatic art seems to leave unsolved in the earlier dialogues" (p. 85). Shorey himself devoted considerable attention to the *Laws* in his *What Plato Said* and wrote a number of notes on the text, as did L. A. Post ("Notes on Plato's Laws," *American Journal of Philology,* 1939); it has been much discussed, too, by the critics and the defenders of Plato's moral and political philosophy. But it has also served as the starting point for studies in Plato's relation to the political life of his time, in this case under Sabine's rather than Shorey's influence. The work of G. R. Morrow is in this respect particularly important. He diverges from Shorey, insofar as he sees in the *Laws* a rather different approach to politics, more sober and empirical, from that which prevails in the *Republic*. (A similar view is taken in David Grene's less technical essay on Plato in *Man in His Pride,* 1950.) In his *Plato's Law of Slavery in Its Relation to Greek Law* (Illinois Studies in Language and Literature, 1939) Morrow's main concern is to show, against the less discriminating defenders of Plato, that Plato's attitude to slavery was more strict, especially in widening the gulf between freedmen and free men, than the attitude incorporated in Athenian law. The interest of Morrow's book is only marginally philosophical; this is true, too, of *Plato's Cretan City: A Historical Interpretation of the Laws* (1960), which closely relates the *Laws* to Greek, and especially to Athenian, political and legal structures. We are now at that margin at which philosophic scholarship meets political theory and history—but certainly no student of the *Laws* can possibly ignore Morrow's substantial and illuminating study. Nor should he ignore Huntington Cairns's *Legal Philosophy from Plato to Hegel* (1949), a work written by a lawyer, indeed, but a lawyer with one eye for the philosophical connections of his subject.

In Friedrich Solmsen's *Plato's Theology* (1942) the *Laws* is again of central concern. Solmsen has made a careful study of American scholarship, but he does not accept the main conclusions of that scholarship; one can see clearly enough his Continental background. For him, Plato is an inquiring metaphysician, and a deeply puzzled one, trying out new ways of solving a problem with varying degrees of success. In reviewing *Aristotle's Criticism of Plato and the Academy,* Solmsen refers to "Cherniss' conviction that a closed and rather rigid system is a *conditio sine qua non* for a reputable philosopher" (*Phil. Rev.,* 1948, p. 287). That conviction Solmsen does not share; he is more ready than most American scholars to recognize that there are unresolved tensions in Plato's thinking.

The mention of Solmsen raises a difficulty; if we were to refer at this point to all the major works of scholars once, or now, resident in America, but not educated in America, the list would be a long and diversified one and any conclusions which followed from its character not very relevant to American scholarship as such.

Although the latest and considerably enlarged edition of Paul Friedländer's *Plato* (1st ed., 1928; American publication of the new vol. I, 1958) was published in America and owes a little to American scholarship, its intellectual background (with the mandatory references to Goethe and Schiller) and its general method of approach are unmistakably German, even if its emphasis on the "practical" character and on the unity of Plato's thought accord with leading tendencies in American scholarship. Similarly, although the second and third volumes of Werner Jaeger's *Paidea: The Ideals of Greek Culture* (1943-44) were first published in America, Jaeger's account of the *Republic* and *Laws* as treatises on education was worked out in Germany and has been little influenced by his sojourn in America, except in points of detail. These examples could easily be extended by reference to the essays on Plato included in Erich Frank's *Wissen, Wollen, Glauben* (1955) or to Richard Kroner's *Speculation in Pre-Christian Philosophy* (1956) or to Richard Robinson's *Plato's Earlier Dialectic* (1941), written while Robinson was teaching in America but representative of British scholarship in its emphasis on Plato's logical interests. It would not be appropriate for our present purposes to discuss such works in detail, but the presence of such scholars in America, even for short periods of time, will no doubt strengthen Platonic scholarship still further.

The general impression left by American Platonic scholarship is one of great richness and diversity. Yet I have by no means mentioned all the books which American scholars have devoted to Plato —such books as R. S. Brumbaugh's *Plato's Mathematical Imagination* (1954) or W. F. Lynch's *An Approach to the Metaphysics of Plato through the Parmenides* (1959) add to the impression of diversity—and I have said almost nothing about the multitude of articles and essays, sometimes of considerable importance, which have been written by American scholars since 1930. Many of them, of course, are examples of scholarship *about* philosophy rather than of philosophical scholarship, but it can by no means be presumed that because an article appears in the *American Journal of Philology* it is of no concern to philosophers.

One article, however, should be specially mentioned because it serves better than a thousand generalizations to make clear the special interests of philosophers as distinct from scholars: Gregory Vlastos' "The Third Man Argument in the *Parmenides*" (*Phil. Rev.*, 1954). This article has excited a quite exceptional degree of controversy, both inside and outside America; in it Vlastos attempts a philosophical reconstruction and a philosophical criticism of Plato's argument in the first part of the *Parmenides*. Of course, the approach is hardly a novelty, having been adopted earlier by Taylor, Cornford, Hardie, Ryle, and Ross, to mention only a few British writers. But when one looks at Vlastos' article again, after having inspected so many American books on Plato, one realizes how unusual it is in American classical scholarship—unusual in looking in detail at Plato's arguments, considering their validity, trying to uncover their hidden assumptions. It exhibits the sort of scholarly procedure which particularly interests the philosopher. Vlastos wants to know: "Was Plato right?" and he looks to scholarship, on the whole, to help him in answering the question. But American Platonic scholarship, has, for the most part, been directed toward making Plato less, rather than more, interesting to philosophers—or at least to those philosophers for whom logic, in however broad a sense, lies at the heart of philosophy.

American scholars have depicted Plato as a moralist, or a politician, or an educator, rather than as a logician or a metaphysician. Often enough, too, they have been concerned to show how Greek he was rather than what he contributed to a continuing philosophical dispute, a dispute in which he participates, as it were, with Hume and Russell and Quine. American scholars often describe themselves as reacting against what they like to call—for it is now the most favored term of abuse—a "nineteenth century" view of Plato, a view which they ascribe to Hegel and which, so they say, absurdly overemphasizes Plato's logic, metaphysics, and epistemology. If they are right, if Shorey is right, for example, in scarcely discussing "the much-talked-of ideas" in his summary of Plato's *Phaedo,* then certainly the position of Plato in Western thought is transformed; that they are right most American scholars seem not at all to doubt.

3.   Had this commentary been written even as late as 1950, it would have said very little indeed about Aristotelian studies. Aristotle had, until recently, a "bad press" in the world of American philosophy—at least outside neoscholastic circles. Dewey thought poorly of him; and Cherniss' *Aristotle's Criticism of Presocratic Philosophy* (1935) and *Aristotle's Criticism of Plato and the Academy* (vol. I, 1944) were mainly dedicated to the proposition that he was an unreliable guide to the doctrines of his predecessors. "When the question of consistency arises," Solmsen has commented, "Cherniss gives Plato always, Aristotle only sometimes, the benefit of the doubt." Certainly the general effect of Cherniss' work is not to advance Aristotle's philosophical reputation. (It incorporates, all the same, a considerable amount of detailed interpretation of Aristotle's philosophy.) Lane Cooper set out to popularize Aristotle's rhetorical writings by preparing modernized versions of them, as in his *The Rhetoric of Aristotle: An Expanded Translation with Supplementary Examples for Students of Composition*

48

and Public Speaking (1932), but he wrote as a literary critic rather than as a scholar. His *Aristotle, Galileo, and the Tower of Pisa* (1934) is, however, an interesting example of demythologizing scholarship, examining in a critical spirit the familiar tale about the manner in which Galileo disproved the doctrine that heavy bodies fall to earth more rapidly than light ones.

At Columbia in the 1920's, F. J. E. Woodbridge was sympathetically interpreting Aristotle to his graduate classes, which included Richard McKeon and J. H. Randall, both of them to write about Aristotle, as Woodbridge himself scarcely did. Such doctoral dissertations as H. D. Hantz's *The Biological Motivation in Aristotle* (1939) with its emphasis on the biological origins of Aristotle's metaphysics, reveal the direction of Woodbridge's teaching.

The Random House edition of *The Basic Works of Aristotle* (1941) helped to make the Oxford translations of Aristotle more readily available to a wider public. McKeon's introduction to the volume is scarcely a model of clear prose, but he does bring out the importance of concentrating attention upon Aristotle's method of inquiry—a method which he explores further, if not more lucidly, in his "Aristotle's Conception of the Development and the Nature of Scientific Method" (*JHI,* 1947). He has written, too, on "Aristotle's Conception of Moral and Political Philosophy" (*Ethics,* 1941) and on other Aristotelian topics, but has not published his major reflections.

A good deal of attention has been given to the relation of Platonism to Aristotelianism; some of the controversy has turned around the more special problem of the extent to which Aristotle's logic—his theory of the syllogism in particular—is derived from Plato, whether from the theory of division worked out in such dialogues as the *Sophist* and the *Statesman* or from a passage in the *Phaedo* (104-05). This latter origin had been suggested by Shorey, and his view was adopted in England by W. D. Ross; it is attacked, and an origin in the theory of division proposed, by Friedrich Solmsen in "Aristotle's Syllogism and Its Platonic Background" (*Phil. Rev.,* 1951). Other scholars, including McKeon in his introduction to *The Basic Works of Aristotle* and M. W. Heitzmann in the *Proceedings of the American Catholic Philosophical Association* (1954) have insisted on Aristotle's originality in this matter. The

49

battle between those who see in Aristotle, mainly, a somewhat pedantic systematizer of Plato and those who see in him "the master of those who know" is unlikely soon to abate.

Perhaps the most interesting suggestions about the origins of Aristotle's logic have been put forward by a German-educated scholar, Ernst Kapp. His *Greek Foundations of Traditional Logic* (1942) brings out the connection between Aristotelian logic and the practice of philosophical discussion, as that is illustrated in Plato's dialogues. Although it appeared at a time when men's minds were not entirely concentrated upon classical scholarship, this small book has been one of the most highly regarded and most widely quoted contributions to Aristotelian scholarship originating in America. It illustrates, once more, the virtues of brevity and a sharply defined theme in scholarly writing.

In the last decade—and at an increasing rate over the last two or three years—there has been a substantial increase in the volume of American publications on Aristotle, which have not as yet been digested by the world of scholarship. They are strikingly varied in character and quality. G. R. Morrow in his "Aristotle's Comments on Plato's *Laws*" (in *Aristotle and Plato in the Mid-Fourth Century*, ed. Ingemar Düring and G. E. L. Owen, 1960) is concerned to make the relatively minute but somewhat startling suggestion that Aristotle, when he criticized Plato's *Laws*, did not have before him the present text; a view which, if accepted, would somewhat improve Aristotle's reputation as a historian of philosophy—for his report of the *Laws*, if we work with the assumption that he is talking about the text we have, is perhaps the most striking and indisputable example of his unreliability. The book in which Morrow's essay appears is a record of a conference held at Oxford which was very largely concerned with Aristotle's *Protrepticus*. The authenticity of that work was challenged in the same year by W. G. Rabinowitz in his *Aristotle's Protrepticus and the Sources of Its Reconstruction* (University of California Publications in Classical Philology, 1957), a very detailed study by a pupil of Cherniss.

At the opposite extreme from this relatively minute work is J. H. Randall's *Aristotle* (1960), which attempts to set forth "what one man has found to be the significance for the present day" of Aristotle's philosophy. Randall tries to show that Dewey made a mistake in condemning Aristotle as a formalist and an antiscientific teleologist; he admits that Aristotle never quite broke loose from the Platonic modes of thinking which Dewey castigated, but what is original and distinctive in Aristotle, he argues, is a functionalism and contextualism akin to Dewey's own. So it turns out that "Aristotle aimed to understand Greece: he never forgot that aim" (p. 3). It also turns out that "his may well be the most passionate mind in history; it shows through every page, almost every line" (p. 1) and that "clearly Aristotle did not say everything; though without what he first said, all words would be meaningless, and when it is forgotten, they usually are" (p. 300). These, to put it mildly, are somewhat surprising views. But by pushing hard his "functionalist" interpretation of Aristotle, even although in a semipopular and unguarded way, Randall draws attention to an important, and not always sufficiently appreciated, tendency in Aristotle's thinking.

This is not the sort of work—to hazard a prediction—which will escape serious criticism in the world of international scholarship. It will, no doubt, be widely regarded as an attempt to Americanize Aristotle. But there is no objection to looking at Aristotle from the standpoint of American philosophical ideas; this, *mutatis mutandis,* is what the scholars of the past have done, if less openly. Ross's Aristotle is unmistakably an Englishman.

One may well regret, however, Randall's occasional wildness of judgment; one may regret, too, his jocular style. It seems to be very difficult for American philosophers to discover for themselves a style which is neither unduly colloquial and familiar in manner, nor so abstract and convoluted as to be scarcely intelligible. Surely "May I go?" need become neither "Can I push off?" nor "Is it permissible that I should egress from the subsistent environment pertaining to my location?"

This latter sort of style is certainly exemplified in J. P. Anton's *Aristotle's Theory of Contrariety* (1957), not only in such relatively technical passages as "the fundamental role of contrariety as the formal demand for determinateness and the grounds on the basis of which distinctions can be made for the cognisance of process" (p. 9), but even when Anton is doing no more than informally announce his intentions: "My predilections might have occasioned misinterpretations that I am not aware of, and for this reason

51

I am ready to assume the responsibility for any discrepancy in the consistency of the argument" (p. 9). To read this book is like trying to walk through a bog: clearly, it cannot after all be claimed for the classics that they train the student in the writing of a clear, precise, and sensitive English style. Anton, too, is a product of the Columbia graduate school, and he follows Randall in believing that Dewey's attack on Aristotle "exhibits the dimensions of a severe hyper-criticism" (p. 203), that "it were not difficult to exhibit Dewey as an Aristotelian more Aristotelian than Aristotle himself" (p. 206). I have drawn special attention to Anton's work because it is the sort of book which is often taken to be representative of American scholarship; such a judgment is grotesquely unfair, but there are enough books like Anton's to lend some appearance of justification to it.

A study of a very different kind in character and conclusions is G. S. Claghorn's *Aristotle's Criticism of Plato's Timaeus* (1954). Claghorn is a pupil of Morrow's and, like Morrow, wishes to defend Aristotle's reliability as a historian against Cherniss' attacks. But he goes further than that; he rejects the view that there is a sharp contrast between Aristotle's and Plato's physics. Just as Shorey had argued that there was a basic unity in the thought of Plato, so Claghorn wishes to maintain, he tells us, that where Plato and Aristotle "appear to differ this is often due to the method of investigation or exposition, rather than to an actual difference of conclusions" (p. 3). But there is no sign yet that this reconciliation of Plato and Aristotle will come to prevail, as Shorey's views did—quite the contrary, to judge from Randall and Anton. (Although Wild, too, suggested that Plato and Aristotle differ in emphasis rather than in doctrine.)

American scholarship has now produced, as it has not in the case of Plato, a substantial commentary on a single work of Aristotle in G. F. Else's *Aristotle's Poetics: The Argument* (1957). This monumental work—six hundred and seventy pages in all—is a line-by-line analysis of the *Poetics,* omitting only those sections which Else takes to be of technical, as distinct from theoretical, interest, but including a good many proposed amendments to the text. Some of his interpretations, and some of his amendments, have been seriously challenged; that is only to be expected. But Else's book, one hopes, will lead the way to other such patient and illuminating commentaries.

Another, quite different, variety of scholarship to be found is George Boas' lengthy study of "Some Assumptions of Aristotle" (*Transactions of the American Philosophical Society*, 1959). Boas applies one of Lovejoy's characteristic methods to Aristotle, insofar as he tries to bring out the assumptions on which Aristotle's argument rests—rejecting, incidentally, the view that "a principle of hierarchy is one of those assumptions." Unlike so much of the work inspired by Lovejoy—perhaps because Boas was a collaborator of Lovejoy, not a disciple—it is by no means overweighted with scholarship. "There comes a time in every man's life when he wishes to read a document for himself, as if no one had ever read it before," writes Boas, "and to draw his own conclusions." Indeed, he makes very little reference to Aristotelian scholarship, in part because, he says, he is approaching Aristotle from a novel point of view. If, indeed, there is a criticism to be made of the general structure of this particular essay, it is that it contains too much un-digested philosophy (Boas' own philosophy) rather than, as is the more common complaint, too obtrusive a scholarly apparatus. The balance in philosophical scholarship is, indeed, a delicate one; too much philosophy, as well as too little, can blur the image.

There have been other important studies of special aspects of Aristotle's thought. For example, Max Hamburger's *Morals and Law: The Growth of Aristotle's Legal Theory* (1951) is a scholarly study of the interplay between moral, political, and legal ideas in Aristotle. In E. A. Havelock's *The Liberal Temper in Greek Politics* (1957)—a vigorous attempt to rediscover what Havelock takes to have been the liberal tradition in Greek politics—Aristotle plays a large part. His *Ethics and Politics* (especially the eighth and the ninth books) are read by Havelock as an attempt to emasculate the liberal tradition by reconciling it with a traditional conservatism, by reinterpreting, for example, the traditional ideal of friendship in a way which seems, but only seems, to incorporate the liberal ideal of the love of mankind. Both Hamburger and Havelock are concerned to establish the "true present value" of Greek ideas; for Hamburger "there is a perfect harmony between Aristotle's ethical, legal and political ideas" and that harmony, as

53

distinct from a mere formal legal consistency, is the secret of any satisfactory legal system; for Havelock, on the contrary, Aristotle is in large degree the villain of the piece, the sophist Antiphon is more nearly the hero. "The twentieth-century note in his teaching is there. It sounds almost uncanny. Was he an apostle of the new education? Would he have approved a progressive school? Is it possible that in his Greek, we catch, across the centuries, the accent of Sigmund Freud?" (p. 294). Hamburger's meticulous essay is at the opposite pole of scholarship from Havelock's only too imaginative and belligerent reconstruction, but they both see in Aristotle ideas to be reckoned with, not simply occasions for erudition.

In a work of a very different character, *Aristotle's System of the Physical World: A Comparison with His Predecessors* (1960), Friedrich Solmsen looks backward from Aristotle rather than forward. He sets out to describe the major concepts in Aristotle's physics in their relation to pre-Socratic philosophy and the later dialogues of Plato, emphasizing particularly the way in which Aristotle uses Plato's conception of genesis and movement in order to reinstate physics—"reinstate" because its very possibility had been denied by Parmenides. Whatever criticism may in the end be directed either against Solmsen's general account of Aristotle's relationship to Plato and Parmenides or against the detail of his analysis of Aristotle, his book, certainly, is one that will have to be reckoned with as a contribution to Aristotelian scholarship. And by this time Solmsen may fairly be reckoned an American scholar.

In short, although America has not yet produced an Aristotelian scholar of the stature of W. D. Ross—and few countries have—the range of recent Aristotelian scholarship is quite remarkable. It is too new, as I said, to have established itself in the literature, but it certainly represents a notable revival of interest in Aristotelian studies. This extends in enterprising directions: a recent work by Lewis Hanke bears the title *Aristotle and the American Indians* (1958). The title is delightful; the contents I have deliberately, fearing disillusionment, left to the imagination.

4. Post-Aristotelian studies on the whole—neo-Platonism apart —have not been of great importance. There is one conspicuous exception: Benson Mates's *Stoic Logic* (University of California

Publications in Philosophy, 1953). Mates quite properly takes the work of Lukasiewicz as his point of departure; but he has gone in search of new evidence in support of Lukasiewicz' interpretations, has developed his ideas in a number of directions, and has added new translations of important fragments. Mates's work can truly be described, in an often employed but seldom justified phrase, as a model of philosophical scholarship. Firmly basing himself on the texts, alert to the scholarly literature, Mates at the same time displays a thoroughly philosophical appreciation of the points at issue in logical controversies. With his aid we come to understand the stoics, to place them in the history of logic, and at the same time to advance our philosophical, as distinct from our merely historical, understanding. Whether Mates is right or wrong in his interpretation of stoic logic only the experts can say—perhaps, as can easily happen, his interest in recent logic leads him to read too much of it into the stoics—but at least the critics will be able to find out what his interpretation amounts to, as is by no means the case in all works of scholarship. Indeed they often seem to take as their motto "obscurum per obscurius."

The comparison is interesting with P. H. DeLacy and E. A. De-Lacy's edition of *Philodemus: On Methods of Inference* (1941), to which Mates adversely refers. This edition, too, is an important contribution to scholarship—its authors have prepared and translated the text of Philodemus' essay, annotated it, written a biography of Philodemus, and added short essays on Epicurean and stoic philosophy. (They have written, as well, a number of articles, scattered through the classical journals, on skepticism, stoicism, and Epicureanism.) But they have quite failed to make clear what the logical issues were—exactly what, for example, Philodemus meant by his key concept, contraposition. Phrases like "the relation of necessary consequences, or contraposition" simply add to the confusion; it never becomes clear whether contraposition is the purely formal relation expressed in *"if p, q* implies *if not-q, not-p"* or whether, as the examples quoted by the DeLacys suggest, it consists in denying the consequent, or whether, a third possibility, the stoics would not have distinguished the formal relation from the inference. Yet this is just the sort of help we need in order to understand Philodemus' text.

There have been, of course, other works on the philosophy of this period. Ludwig Edelstein, for example, has written one of the rare essays on the stoic Posidonius (*American Journal of Philology*, 1936), whom, as Shorey puts it, "German ingenuity reconstructs." Farrand Sayre's *Diogenes of Sinope: A Study of Greek Cynicism* (1938) sets out, so it would seem, to quote every available piece of information about Diogenes or cynicism; it ends up, like so many doctoral dissertations, as a collection of paragraphs rather than a book, but no one can deny Sayre's thoroughness. He returned to the same subject in his *The Greek Cynics* (1948).

There have been, too, a number of editions and translations, some with valuable introductions and commentaries, for example, R. B. McKeon's introduction to the translation by H. N. Poteat of Cicero's philosophical writings (1950). Only Epicurus, however, seems to have been made the subject of a lengthy study, in a book which exhibits all the partisanship which Epicurus seems to call forth from his commentators. One may well agree with N. W. DeWitt in denouncing A. E. Taylor's *Epicurus* as a work quite unworthy of a great scholar, but that does not excuse DeWitt's own aberrations. His *Epicurus and His Philosophy* (1954) is so full of startling judgments—"Plato thought of abstract notions as having an independent existence just as geometrical figures exist, a false analogy" (p. 17)—that the reader can be sure of a shock on every page. He can, however, be sure of nothing else.

In general, then, with the striking exception of Mates's work, one does not turn to America for studies of stoicism, skepticism, or Epicureanism. This is not surprising; many philosophers would agree with Shorey when he wrote (and he said much the same of Epicurus) that "no genuine appreciator of Plato can take Stoicism quite seriously" (*Platonism*, 1938, p. 20), and described it as "an episode, a form of ethical culture for matter-of-fact and semicultural minds, something that does not really count when compared with Plato and Aristotle on the one side or even with Plotinus and the neo-Platonists on the other" (p. 23).

Note the phrase "*even* with Plotinus and the neo-Platonists"; Shorey is by no means enthusiastic about neo-Platonism and even less enthusiastic about its interpreters. The dialectic of the neo-Platonists, he says, belongs to the same general type as Hegelian dialectic—"the indeterminate and uncontrolled concatenation of equivocal and contiguous words in long chains of unverified and unverifiable ratiocinations" (p. 38). At most, Shorey is prepared to allow some degree of merit to Plotinus, but all neo-Platonists, in Shorey's eyes, made the fatal mistake of taking Plato's metaphysical suggestions seriously.

Many American scholars, however, have been attracted to neo-Platonism. Although their emphasis, like Shorey's own, has been on the predecessors of Plotinus rather than on his successors, there has in fact been an extraordinary degree of concentration on Philo. On Plotinus himself very little has been written, except a short sensible monograph by Joseph Katz on *Plotinus' Search for the Good* (1950) in which he sets out "to penetrate behind Plotinus' statements to the *problems* that faced his philosophy"; for the rest, there are only scattered essays. Not that other neo-Platonists have been wholly neglected. The vexed question how neo-Platonism derived from Platonism has been discussed by Philip Merlan—by origin a Continental scholar—in his *From Platonism to Neoplatonism* (1953). Merlan sets out to show that neo-Platonism has its roots in the Academy, in the manner in which Aristotle and his fellow Academicians—especially Speusippus—interpreted Plato. It is interesting to observe in this case, too, how a scholar's interpretation is influenced by what seems to him "reasonable." Approaching philosophy from the standpoint of an admirer of Schelling—compare Shorey on Schelling!—Merlan sees sense where English and Americans have seen nonsense, in, for example, the identification of the soul and the mathematicals (pp. 49-51). He is in consequence willing to ascribe to Plato himself, or at least to Aristotle, doctrines which most British and American Aristotelian and Platonic scholars have been most unwilling to admit they would have been so foolish as to hold.

The neo-Platonists, indeed, belong to that class of philosophers extensively studied only by those who admire them; even their severest critics enjoy reading Plato or Hume, but the neo-Platonists, on the whole, are either not read at all or worshipped. As L. J. Rosán points out in *The Philosophy of Proclus* (1949), estimates of Proclus' philosophy range "from an unusual antipathy to an unusual enthusiasm" (p. 225). He is described either as "one of the

greatest of philosophers" or as "not really a philosopher at all";
nobody speaks of him in tones of modified rapture. Rosán's own
book is an example of pure doxography. Rosán lists and briefly
describes the Proclus literature, translates Marinus' life, lists and
mentions the contents of Proclus' major works, summarizes his philosophy, sketches his influence (in a page or two), and quotes
evaluations of his work from historians and commentators. But he
makes no attempt to relate Proclus to the history of post-Platonic
philosophy, and in his own brief evaluation (pp. 227-29) he is
content to make such judgments as that Proclus was more systematic, more religious, and more emotional than Plato—judgments
not of any philosophical interest. In so obscure and difficult a field
as Proclus studies, even doxographical work is very welcome, but
the task of placing Proclus in the history of philosophy has still to
be undertaken.

In turning to studies of Philo, an initial difficulty is that much
of the recent work is only slightly concerned with Philo as a philosopher. Indeed E. R. Goodenough in his *Introduction to Philo
Judaeus* (1940) denies that Philo was an original philosopher at
all. Since he was trying, as Goodenough reads him, to show that
Greek philosophical ideas reached their highest expression in Hebrew religious teaching, he would not set out deliberately to invent
new philosophical ideas, any more than, as Goodenough says, a
modern reconciler of religion and science deliberately invents the
science he is reconciling into religion. Philo's ideas, then, "must be
assumed to be contemporary commonplaces," even though Philo's
work is sometimes the only clue we have to what were the commonplaces of the Hellenistic world.

Goodenough's very effective *Introduction to Philo Judaeus* includes a brief summary of Philo's philosophical ideas, but Goodenough's own main interest has been in Philo's mysticism (*By
Light, Light: The Mystic Gospel of Hellenistic Judaism*, 1935) and
in his political program, which Goodenough describes in *The Politics of Philo Judaeus* (1938), a work which contains a most
extensive and most scholarly bibliography of Philo's works (pp.
128-321) by Goodenough and H. L. Goodhart. Similarly, Samuel
Belkin in his *Philo and the Oral Law* ("Harvard Semitic Series," XI,
1940) sets out to show that Philo's knowledge of Jewish religious

teachings was considerably more thorough than has sometimes been supposed; Philo's strategic position in relation to Hellenistic Jewish and Christian thought naturally makes him a center of controversy.

No one can hope to study adequately Philo's place in the history of philosophy, so much is clear, unless he is more than superficially acquainted, on the one side, with Jewish and Greek thought in the Hellenistic period, and, on the other side, with medieval Christian and Jewish philosophy. One scholar of our time, and perhaps only one, has the learning needed to undertake the vast task of commenting on Philo as a Jew, as a Platonist, as a precursor of medieval thought: H. A. Wolfson. The figure of Philo has for him a quite special significance; he sees in him the source of all that is most characteristic in Western philosophy and theology until the time of Spinoza, during a period when philosophy was almost wholly preoccupied, as Wolfson interprets it, with problems arising out of Philo's Hellenistic Judaism and the impact of that Hellenistic Judaism—as represented, it is true, not only by Philo but also by Paul—upon Christian theology. Wolfson has embarked upon a vast enterprise: a detailed study of the structure and growth of philosophical systems "from Plato to Spinoza." He began the publication of the massive volumes that will make up that study, not at the beginning, with Plato, but with Philo, just because he sees in him the central figure in the whole story. His *Philo* (1947) was succeeded by *The Philosophy of the Church Fathers,* Volume 1, *Faith, Trinity, Incarnation* (1956), in which, again, Wolfson emphasizes Philo's influence, although he grants that the patristic doctrines of the trinity and the incarnation, in particular, arose outside the Philonic scheme.

Only a fragment of Wolfson's vast work, although a stupendous fragment, lies before us. Whether he will establish his main thesis, and so justify the central importance he attaches to Philo, has yet to be seen. He has come in for a good deal of criticism; he has been accused, for example, of greatly exaggerating Philo's originality by ignoring those "commonplace" Hellenistic philosophical sources which Goodenough emphasized; it has been suggested, too, that even Wolfson's vast learning is insufficient for the work upon which he has now embarked. But whatever the outcome—which will be, at least, to bring into greater prominence the Hebraic elements in Western philosophy and theology—Wolfson's work represents one of the few really ambitious tasks which American philosophical scholarship has undertaken to complete.

◄§ 4 §►

MEDIEVAL PHILOSOPHY

1. General histories. 2. Patristic studies. 3. Early medieval philosophy. 4. The thirteenth and fourteenth centuries.

1.   For a general history of medieval philosophy, one does not turn to America; there is no American equivalent of Gilson, Grabmann, de Wulf, or Copleston. In F. B. Artz's *The Mind of the Middle Ages* (1953), philosophy is only one, and not the main, ingredient; such books are contributions to intellectual history rather than to philosophical scholarship. Nor has Lynn Thorndike's gigantic *History of Magic and Experimental Science* (1923-41) any direct relevance to philosophy. Even George Boas' *Essays on Primitivism and Related Ideas in the Middle Ages* (1948) belongs rather to the history of ideas than to the history of philosophy proper, although no medievalist ought wholly to neglect this extraordinary anthology. In a sense, the only important American history of medieval philosophy is the series of introductions included in Richard McKeon's *Selections from Medieval Philosophers* (1929-30). Although not, of course, in any formal sense a history, this work has served as one for a great many philosophers.

2.   Those of the church fathers who were not actively hostile to philosophy made use of philosophical concepts in order to defend and expound Christian doctrine rather than in order to advance philosophy itself; except insofar as they can be read as chapters in the history of neo-Platonism, their writings, however important they may be to the church historian, are of only marginal interest to the philosopher-scholar. To the neo-Platonic reading of the fathers, Wolfson's *The Philosophy of the Church Fathers* is a notable, but almost isolated, American contribution; for the rest, leaving Augustine aside, one need only refer to Cherniss' monograph on *The Platonism of Gregory of Nyssa* (University of California Pub-

lications in Classical Philology, 1930), in which he sets out to show that Gregory had closely studied Plato himself, as distinct from his neo-Platonic interpreters.

Augustine, however, was an exceptional church father; to some degree, he had philosophical ideas of his own. In his case, too, American scholars have been interested in the character and extent of Platonic influences upon his thinking—as in M. P. Garvey's dissertation on *St. Augustine: Christian or Neo-Platonist?* (1939) and Bruno Switalski's *Neoplatonism and the Ethics of St. Augustine* (1946). Much has been done, as well, to make Augustine's philosophical writings more generally available; M. P. Garvey has prepared an annotated translation of *Against the Academicians* (1942); G. G. Leckie has translated *Concerning the Teacher and on the Immortality of the Soul* (1938); W. J. Oates's *The Basic Writings of Augustine* (1948) is a convenient compendium. As well, there have been commentaries, although they have tended to report Augustine's views in summary form rather than to analyze them philosophically. This is true both of V. J. Bourke's *Augustine's Quest of Wisdom* (1945)—in which the emphasis is popular rather than scholarly, biographical rather than philosophical—and of the chapters on Augustine's philosophy included in the collection edited by R. W. Battenhouse as *A Companion to the Study of St. Augustine* (1955). These titles by no means complete the list: American scholars have written monographs on special aspects of Augustine's philosophy, such as Emmanuel Chapman's *Saint Augustine's Philosophy of Beauty* (1939) and lengthy essays on his philosophico-theological outlook, of which the most important, perhaps, are A. C. Pégis' "The Mind of St. Augustine" (*Mediaeval Studies,* 1944) and "In Defense of St. Augustine" (*New Scholasticism,* 1944). Considerable as work on Augustine is in volume, it has not made any very substantial contribution to the exploration, as distinct from the exposition, of Augustine's more purely philosophical ideas about, say, knowledge and language. Augustine's theory of freedom, however—the point at which his theology and his philosophy meet —has been philosophically explored in M. T. Clark's *Augustine, Philosopher of Freedom* (1959), which effectively brings out the philosophical roots of Augustine's thinking.

3. Wolfson, again, is the giant of scholarship on early medieval philosophy. His *Crescas' Critique of Aristotle* (1929) is described by Georges Vajda in his *Introduction à la pensée juive du moyen âge* as "la meilleure monographie qui ait jamais été écrite sur un sujet d'histoire de la pensée juive médiévale" (p. 235), and it displays no less Arabic than Jewish learning. As well, Wolfson has written a considerable number of learned and controversial essays on Jewish, Arabic, and Christian thought in the medieval period, many of which are designed, no doubt, to be absorbed into his magnum opus on the Philonic tradition.

Leaving aside Wolfson's work, the record, except in Jewish studies, is a slight one. The *Aristoteles latinus* edited by Georges Lacombe (vol. 1, 1939) is an international rather than a purely American venture. H. R. Patch has written a scholarly essay—very much for medievalists—on the transitional figure of Boethius (*The Tradition of Boethius,* 1935); G. B. Burch has edited, translated, and annotated Bernard of Clairvaux' *The Steps of Humility* (1940) and, in *Early Medieval Philosophy* (1951), has rapidly sketched the philosophical and logical ideas of Erigena, Anselm, Abelard, Bernard, and Isaac of Stella. There is little more to add. Medieval Arabic philosophy—especially since the editions of Averroes prepared for the Medieval Academy of America have already been cited—could almost be let pass without a mention; occasional essays like B. H. Zedler's "Averroes on the Possible Intellect" (*Proceedings of the American Catholic Philosophical Association,* 1951), or Gerard Smith's "Avicenna and the Possibles" (*New Scholasticism,* 1943), or E. A. Moody's "Galileo and Avempace" (*JHI,* 1951), and slight monographs such as Rom Landau's *The Philosophy of Ibn 'Arabī* (1959) do not together amount to a considerable contribution to scholarship, although they do show that Arabic philosophy has not been entirely neglected.

Of scholarship on medieval Jewish philosophy a little more must be said. In an older generation, Isaac Husik led the way by looking at Jewish philosophy not as the theology of a sect but as part of the more general movement of philosophical ideas; his *A History of Mediaeval Jewish Philosophy* (1916) is still the standard introductory manual. Wolfson has displayed this same wealth of vision.

The fact remains that although a great deal has been written on Jewish medieval thought, little of it is of any great philosophical interest. *The Essays on Maimonides* (1941) edited by S. W. Baron are not, for the most part, directed at philosophers, and B. Z. Bokser's *The Legacy of Maimonides* (1950) does not penetrate far beneath the surface. I. I. Efros has produced a critical edition of Maimonides' *Treatise on Logic* (1938), but this prepares the way for, rather than exemplifies, philosophical scholarship. Saadia has been a good deal written about; he has been translated by Samuel Rosenblatt (1948), and made the subject of two commemorative volumes, one published by the American Academy for Jewish Research in 1943 and another, edited by Louis Finkelstein, in 1944; his philosophical ideas have been discussed in the *Jewish Quarterly Review* by such scholars as H. A. Wolfson (1946) and I. I. Efros (1942). But Saadia, like Maimonides, was a man of many parts, concerned to educate his people rather than to philosophize. The literature on Saadia is only to a very limited degree of philosophical interest.

Altogether, while American scholars are doing quite a little to bring out the connections between medieval Jewish thought and the main stream of Western culture, the general philosophical world has still to be persuaded that medieval Jewish philosophy is of interest to any but the specialist historian.

4. The traveler across a closely settled plain is, in a sense, unjust when he complains of its monotony. The scenery is not wholly devoid of interest: this farm has more fertile soil, that farm is more carefully tilled, their crops are not of equal quality, the layout of some of the farms displays a measure of personal taste. To the local inhabitant, indeed, the diversity is endless. Yet in another sense, of course, the tourist is right: the scenery is, as he might say, nothing to write home about.

American thirteenth century medieval scholarship is, in some degree, like that plain. The scene which confronts the commentator is not an empty barren waste; there are signs everywhere of careful and devoted work, varying, too, in quality, even if only within a certain range. But there is very little the foreign observer will report with excitement, or distinguish, as an eminence, from the general level of its surroundings.

This is the region, par excellence, of doctoral dissertations. They create scarcely a ripple; seldom reviewed in the major philosophical journals—especially over the last twenty years when the space available for reviews has been severely curtailed—they achieve a modest degree of recognition only in the most extensive bibliographies.

Even some apparently quite ambitious works on medieval philosophy, indeed, are obviously written by seminarians for seminarians, not as contributions to general scholarship. E. A. Sillem, himself a seminary teacher, speaks for many another reader of many another book—although more often of thirteenth than of fourteenth century studies—when he says of Stuart MacClintock's (all the same, important) *Perversity and Error: Studies on the "Averroist" John of Jandun* (1956): "It has not been written in a way that is calculated to make the meaning of mediaeval philosophical discussions comprehensible to those who are not familiar with the technical jargon current at the time. Instead of showing how John approached and considered the philosophical problems in which he was interested, and then explaining what we are to understand by the technical terms used, the author takes terms like 'intellectus agens,' 'sensus agens' . . . for granted as if they were still in currency today as they were in the Middle Ages." And, of course, they still are in currency—in the seminary.

Evan Roche is vulnerable to similar criticism. Introducing his text and translation of Scotus' *De primo principio* (1949), he tells us that his object is to satisfy the "crying need for a better acquaintance with the authentic writings of John Duns Scotus, especially among readers whose mother tongue is English"; nevertheless, the language he uses in his translation is not English, at least as that language is spoken outside the philosophy classes in seminaries. Consider the very first philosophical sentences: "There are many properties of 'being,' the consideration of which would be valid for the pursuit of our purpose. However, from the essential order as from a more fruitful means, I shall first proceed in the following manner" (p. 3). Would anybody be encouraged to study Duns Scotus by reading such a translation?

To take still another example, G. G. Leckie, in the introduction to his translation of Aquinas' *De ente et essentia* (1937), sets out to help us, he tells us, by "explaining and elucidating the principal concepts of the text" (p. xii)—a text which the beginner, he admits, may find "slightly obdurate" (p. xliii). This is the sort of help the unfortunate reader in fact receives: "Science has an *analytic remotion,* or formal distance, from individuated natures, seeing that science deals with the universal which is always true or at least true for the most part. From this it is to be understood that the terms which enter into propositions of science must be univocal signs of many, namely universals abstracted from all contingent increments, so that the abstracted quiddity or whatness of the thing is grasped by way of a mode of rational being expressive of the essential or necessary features of the thing of nature" (p. xix). No text could be more "obdurate" than this interpretation. One can see why R. E. Brennan in his editorial essay to *Essays in Thomism* (1942) should call upon Thomists to cultivate "a clearer and more sympathetic medium of expression, a more fluent and abounding style" (p. 22); reflection upon the subsequent essays in the same volume would sufficiently justify the sentiment, if not the expression, of this plea.

It would be wrong, however, to dismiss the shelves of gray paper-covered texts and commentaries—to say nothing of the multitudinous articles in the *Modern Schoolman* and the *New Scholasticism* —as wholly unworthy of serious attention. The Philosophical Studies of the Catholic University of America, for example, are generally concerned with some special aspect of the philosophy of Aquinas, sometimes his social teaching, sometimes a point in his metaphysics. Not seldom, they are the only essays on their particular themes in the English language; to that degree the volume of work on Aquinas in America is quite impressive, even if little of it is of the first, or even of the second, importance. An occasional monograph, indeed, has won for itself some degree of international recognition; as examples one may cite J. D. M. Goheen's *The Problem of Matter and Form in the "De Ente et Essentia" of Thomas Aquinas* (1940) or J. M. Marling's *The Order of Nature in the Philosophy of St. Thomas Aquinas* (1934). More substantial translations and commentaries on Aquinas, too, are beginning to appear in greater numbers. R. W. Mulligan's three-volume translation of Aquinas'

De veritate (1952) is the first translation into any language of a work which modern philosophers may well find more approachable than the *Summa;* Mulligan's translation runs as smoothly and idiomatically as can reasonably be expected and the annotation usefully relates the text to Aquinas' sources.

Mulligan has added a glossary, however, intended "for readers unfamiliar with the terminology of St. Thomas," which admirably illustrates the defects of so much medieval scholarship, and especially, perhaps, of Aquinas scholarship. If the nonscholastic philosopher looks up "being" in Mulligan's glossary, he will read: "that whose act is to be." The word "act" will certainly puzzle him. How, he will naturally ask, can "to be" be an act? If in search of further enlightenment he proceeds to look up "act," he will discover: "a perfection, as that of existence; an actuality." *Obscurum per obscurius,* with a vengeance. A glossary could be useful; this one, however, is likely to confirm the philosopher in his belief that Locke was right when he rejected medieval philosophy as mere word spinning. (Incidentally, the puzzled reader will do rather better if he turns to Bernard Wuellner's *Dictionary of Scholastic Philosophy,* 1956, an elementary dictionary which does to some degree recognize that to define the basic expressions of scholastic philosophy in scholastic terms is not likely to advance communication.)

Of course, there are many American works on Thomistic philosophy, and these generally include some sort of commentary on Aquinas. As examples, one may refer to J. F. Anderson's *The Cause of Being* (1952) and J. F. Peifer's *The Concept in Thomism* (1952). Neither work, however, does anything to clarify the teachings of Aquinas for those who are not already Thomists. Peifer's criticism of "modern philosophy" as represented by Locke, Berkeley, Hume, and Kant is hasty and superficial, and his exposition of Aquinas is intended, it would seem, only for those who are already Thomists; of Anderson's *The Cause of Being* much the same can be said. Neither work is in any serious sense a contribution to scholarship.

In contrast, although he describes his achievement in modest terms, R. J. Henle has performed a very useful scholarly task in bringing together the Platonic references in the writings of Aquinas (*St. Thomas and Platonism,* 1956), and has appended to his edition a lengthy study—influenced, one would guess, by Cherniss— of Aquinas' method of using Platonic doctrines. H. V. Jaffa's *Thomism and Aristotelianism* (1952) is not, as the title might suggest, a comparable study of the Aristotelian elements in Aquinas; it is in fact a detailed critical study of Aquinas' attempt, in his commentary on the *Nicomachean Ethics,* to reconcile Aristotelian and Christian ethics in order to construct an ethics for mankind. Such critical studies are badly needed; so far, few scholars except those who would subscribe themselves Thomists have been bothered to study Aquinas in detail—partly because, no doubt, so many of his problems in the *Summa* only arise for those who are committed to a Roman Catholic theology. Who else can be even mildly interested in such questions as whether a demon, having been resisted, has lost forever his demoniac powers? The effect, whatever the reason, is as if no one but a Platonist had ever written about Plato; philosophical scholarship about Aquinas would undoubtedly be more lively, more fruitful, and more illuminating if Aquinas were more often criticized in detail. (As it is, except for passing criticisms in reviews, I can think only of the Aquinas section in Lovejoy's *The Great Chain of Being*—a relatively brief discussion of a special topic—as an example of such a critical examination. It is significant that articles on Aquinas are almost wholly confined to neoscholastic periodicals.)

There is one piece of Aquinas literature, Walter Farrell's *A Companion to the Summa* (4 vols., 1938-42), which looks impressive on the shelves, but which is, to put it mildly, a strangely conceived work. It seems to be intended as a substitute for the *Summa* rather than as, in any ordinary sense, a "companion" to it. Farrell describes it, indeed, as "the *Summa* reduced to popular language"— an apt description, anyhow, of the language. ("Why should God have to grub about the corners of the world?" p. 79.) Farrell nowhere quotes, nowhere makes a direct reference to the text; much of his "companion," too, is an attack upon unnamed and unquoted "modern philosophers." It is inconceivable that anybody should write, or find a publisher for, a similarly constituted "companion" to any other philosopher; the very peculiar position of medieval studies, in their relation to seminary exercises, could scarcely be better brought out than by the mere existence of such a book as Farrell's *Companion*.

Perhaps the best known of American Aquinas scholars is A. C. Pégis, whose abilities have been very largely devoted to the preparation of anthologies, most notably *The Basic Writings of St. Thomas Aquinas* (1945) and the shorter *Introduction to St. Thomas Aquinas* (1948). In his introductions to these works, Pégis is particularly concerned to distinguish the writings of Aquinas from the teachings of Plato and the teachings of Aristotle—a theme he developed at greater length in his Aquinas lecture on *St. Thomas and the Greeks* (1939). Here, again, however, just at those crucial points where the philosopher looks for illumination, he does not get it; he is told, for example, that "because a thing is called a being from its act of to be, to ask what a being is is to be concerned with the sortness of its act of to be" (p. xxv). Perhaps it is impossible to express the teachings of Aquinas in the English language; if so, this point needs to be made clear and the reasons for it discussed. The pretend-English indulged in by most Thomists—Pégis is one of the clearest of all—does no good to anybody.

Pégis has also been a lively controversialist. In *Philosophy and Phenomenological Research* (1948) he engaged in a vigorous controversy with A. O. Lovejoy about that chapter in *The Great Chain of Being* in which Lovejoy pointed to an unresolved tension in Aquinas' ideas about God's creative powers. Pégis' "Some Recent Interpretations of Ockham" (*Speculum,* 1948) is an equally vigorous counterattack upon recent attempts to rehabilitate Ockham by showing that he is not, as de Wulf describes him, "a destroyer, an agnostic and fideist."

The defenders of Ockham have been particularly active in the United States; indeed, it is fair to say that the most important American contributions to medieval philosophical scholarship—I am, of course, excluding the Canadian Institute of Mediaeval Studies from my purview—have been written by men who set themselves deliberately in opposition to Thomism or, at least, to the interpretations of Thomistic historians.

In an important article on "Empiricism and Metaphysics in Mediaeval Philosophy" (*Phil. Rev.,* 1958), E. A. Moody proclaims the need for a radical rewriting of medieval philosophy. Thomistic historians like de Wulf, Moody suggests, leave completely mysterious the rise of empiricism in the fourteenth century; they are content to condemn it as a "decline," arising out of "an avid search for novelties," but they do not at all attempt to explain why the "novelties" were empiricist in character. The Thomistic historian presumes that the aim of philosophy is to provide a metaphysical justification for the Christian faith; Ockham's rejection of natural theology and, indeed, of an a priori metaphysics, is in their eyes an abandonment of philosophy. To make this assumption, Moody argues, is to read back a modern Thomistic doctrine into the medieval period. The medieval church thought of philosophy as an enemy; Ockham's fideism expresses the church's attitude to philosophy much more accurately than Aquinas' attempt to come to terms with metaphysics.

In any case, Ockham's criticisms, according to Moody, were strictly philosophical; and from the point of view of the historian of philosophy—as from the point of view of the historian of logic and of science—it is quite impossible to think of the fourteenth century as a period of decline. It was a period of criticism, no doubt, but criticism and decline are not the same thing.

Moody's *The Logic of William of Ockham* (1935) was the first major work to draw the attention of English speaking philosophers to Ockham's philosophy. Possibly they had previously noticed extracts from, and the essay on, Ockham in McKeon's *Selections from the Medieval Philosophers* (vol. II, 1930), but Moody's was the pioneering work, a summary of the main themes in Ockham's very difficult writings. Preceding the main wave of Ockham scholarship, it brought out very clearly, all the same, the need for a complete reconsideration of the traditional judgments about Ockham's philosophy. S. C. Tornay's *Ockham: Studies and Selections* (1938) is more conservative and less illuminating, but helped to underline the claims of Ockham to be taken very seriously as a philosopher.

Moody has also published an important study of *Truth and Consequence in Mediaeval Logic* (1953), especially notable because he looks at medieval logicians as contributing to the advance of philosophical inquiry, rather than as heads of a school which we have to decide whether to join. Moody reads medieval logic as a student of Carnap; he sets out to discover what the "rules" of a medieval logician would amount to if we were to think of them as the axioms of a formal system; in that manner, he helps us to understand the "rules," to see more clearly with what problems they were designed to deal, and to evaluate them historically. Medieval logicians, as he points out in his preface, "wrote in a word-language which, though perhaps quite precise for those who used it, is for us a foreign and only half-understood language." No doubt, there is a serious risk that the scholar who, like Moody, tries to translate this language will seriously misunderstand it. If, on the other hand, he is content to employ the medieval logicians' own words, his readers will not understand him at all—although they may imagine that they do so, just as a person can persuade himself that he understands a medieval Latin text because he can translate "Primum effectivum est actualissimum quia virtualiter continens omnem actualitatem possibilem" into "The first effectuality is the most actual because it virtually contains every possible actuality."

Moody has also worked on the boundaries of medieval logic and medieval science, by editing Buridan's *Quaestiones super libris quattuor de caelo et mundo* (1942), and by directing the attention of his students to such philosopher-scientists as William Heytesbury. One outcome is Curtis Wilson's *William Heytesbury: Medieval Logic and the Rise of Mathematical Physics* (1956), a scholarly interpretation of a difficult but important contribution to the rise of mathematical physics, bringing out its connection with "the new logic." (The sources of "the new logic" lie in Peter of Spain, the seventh tract of whose *Summulae logicales* was edited and translated by J. P. Mullally in 1945, under Moody's supervision.) Wilson's book was published by the University of Wisconsin Press; Wisconsin is now, indeed, thanks to the work of Marshall Clagett, an important center of medieval studies, especially studies of fourteenth century science. In conjunction with Moody, Clagett brought together in *The Medieval Science of Weights* (1952) the major medieval texts on statics; he has written a monograph on *Giovanni Marliani and Late Medieval Physics* (1941), and has produced a truly magnificent work—in this case, published in a manner to match—on *The Science of Mechanics in the Middle Ages* (1959). This book lies a little outside our field, but only a little; and it sets a standard of scholarship which the philosopher-scholar must regard with admiration.

The Franciscan Institute of New York is another important center of fourteenth century studies. The leading figure in the institute was a European scholar, Philotheus Boehner, who for fifteen years before his death in 1955 was so active in the world of American scholarship that it would be improper to ignore his work. His scholarship was highly diversified in character: textual, expository, dialectical. Specimens of each kind are included in his *Collected Articles on Ockham* (ed. E. M. Buytaert, 1958). Boehner's general object is to contribute to that "truer picture of Ockham" which was, he thought, "slowly beginning to emerge from a maze of prejudices and uncritically repeated opinions about his life, works and doctrines" (p. 23)—prejudices which Boehner delights to discover and demolish. Ockham is not an agnostic, according to Boehner, even though he limits the range of matters on which the truth of Christian doctrine can be demonstrated; he is, in metaphysics at least, a "realist conceptualist," not, as tradition has it, a nominalist; he is not a skeptic, since he accepts the Augustinian doctrine of "the infallibility of judgments regarding immediately given facts" (p. 27). Fairly obviously, Boehner is trying to make Ockham—from a theological point of view—more respectable, to depict him as a candidate for the post of official Roman Catholic philosopher. Not all medieval scholars are convinced that Ockham can be groomed for this position; Boehner has vigorously and lengthily disputed the counterinterpretations and criticism of de Wulf, Gilson, and, in particular, Pégis.

To establish his interpretation of Ockham, Boehner had first to show what Ockham wrote and what he did not write, and the texts of his works had to be accurately edited. So, for example, Boehner prepared a critical text of the *Tractatus de praedestinatione* (1945) which he supplemented by an explanation of the key expressions in Ockham's essay and a study of the degree to which he can properly be said to have developed a three-valued logic; Boehner's text of the *Tractatus de successivis* (1944)—attributed to Ockham and in fact, if Boehner is right, derived from his *Expositio super octo libros physicorum*—is supplemented by a life of Ockham and a bibliography of his works. Boehner's scholarly selections from Ockham—with Latin text and English translation, and a general introduction—partly overcome the difficulty in gaining access to Ockham's writings; his *Medieval Logic* (1952), although it is a slight work, designed "to foster an understanding between modern and neo-scholastic Logic," admirably fulfills that limited purpose, for all that scholars have quarreled with it on points of detail. Boehner was, indeed, the philosophical scholar par excellence, who conjoined substantial scholarship with philosophical insight. If his controversial zeal sometimes outran his scholarly discretion, it never interfered with the clarity of his exposition; his interpretations are formulated with force and philosophical accuracy, and the grounds for them are laid lucidly before us. Nor did he ever in the arduous toils of serious scholarship lose the precious gift of enthusiasm.

Other notable work on Ockham has originated in the Franciscan Institute. The institute's journal, *Franciscan Studies,* has printed a number of articles on aspects of Ockham's philosophy and editions of his shorter writings; the Publications of the Franciscan Institute include still other important monographs on Ockham as well as studies of such fourteenth century philosophers as Scotus and (philosophically less interesting) Bonaventura.

A. B. Wolter's *The Transcendentals and Their Function in the Metaphysics of Duns Scotus* (1946) is in the Boehner tradition. Wolter does not conceal himself behind a terminological wall— he quotes with approval a description of "the pseudo-science of ontology" as "little more than a non-alphabetic dictionary of scholastic terms." He tries to show how Scotus' theories arose out of the philosophical problems which confronted him; he helps us to understand Duns Scotus as a historical figure and as a philosopher, as distinct, merely, from helping us to become more learned about Scotus. Other important, if more purely expository, work on Duns Scotus has been produced by M. J. Grajewski as in, for example, his *The Formal Distinction of Duns Scotus* (1944).

Such lesser-known figures as Walter Burleigh, Thomas Bradwardine, and Nicolaus of Autrecourt have also attracted the attention of scholars, as part of the general revival of interest in fourteenth century philosophy and science. Boehner edited (1951) Burleigh's *De puritate artis logicae;* and at Wisconsin H. L. Crosby edited (1955) Bradwardine's *Tractatus de proportionibus.* Julius Wein-

berg's *Nicolaus of Autrecourt* (1948) is a philosophically penetrating exposition of Nicolaus' philosophical ideas; Nicolaus' criticism of medieval Aristotelianism, Weinberg argues, ought to have
made quite impossible the attempt in our own century to revive
Aristotelian metaphysics and ontology. This is one of the few contributions to medieval scholarship which every philosopher could
read with interest, if not always with agreement. For once, one gets
the feeling that the author is genuinely interested in philosophy,
and in the history of philosophy as a way of advancing philosophical understanding, without for a moment departing from the highest standards of scholarship. Finally, S. J. Day has made a careful
study of *Intuitive Cognition* (1947) considered as "a key to the
significance of the later scholastics." Day argues that the conception of intuitive cognition as it appears in the writings of Scotus
and Ockham—he rejects the common view that Ockham's attitude
to Scotus is one of simple opposition—overcomes problems which
are insuperable within the intellectual framework of Thomism,
the problem, in particular, of giving a satisfactory account of our
knowledge of particular entities. Pégis, in his *Speculum* article, has
vigorously criticized Day's reliance upon Rudolf Allers as a source
of Thomistic doctrine, but the philosophical issues which Day
sharply raises are certainly of the first importance.

It would be easy to add still further to this striking list of fourteenth century studies by venturing into political theory, so as to
refer, say, to such notable works as Alan Gewirth's commentary
(1951) and translation (1956) of Marsilius of Padua. But enough
has by now been said to demonstrate that fourteenth century studies are the high point of American medieval scholarship and, indeed, one of the most fruitful areas in American scholarship as a
whole. Even in a brief bibliography of fourteenth century philosophical scholarship, American contributions could not but be prominent. In contrast, a relatively extensive bibliography of Aquinas
studies might well refer to American scholarship only on an occasional special point. (See, for example, the bibliography in F. C.
Copleston's *A History of Philosophy,* vol. II, 1950.) Certainly, we
could add such thirteenth century studies as S. C. Easton's critical
biography *Roger Bacon and His Search for a Universal Science*
(1952), C. K. McKeon's careful and thorough *A Study of the*

Summa Philosophiae of the Pseudo-Grosseteste (1948), and a number of monographs on Duns Scotus, but, even then, the record would not compare with the achievements of scholars who have taken the fourteenth century for their province.

5

RENAISSANCE STUDIES

In one important respect, Renaissance scholarship bears a close resemblance to medieval scholarship; the source materials are hard to come by, so a good deal of the energy of scholars has had to be devoted to collecting, editing, and translating texts. A step forward in this direction was taken by the group of scholars who prepared in 1940 an annotated *Catalogue of Renaissance Philosophers (1350-1650)*; more recently, under the editorship of P. O. Kristeller, publication has commenced of a *Catalogus translationum et commentariorum: Mediaeval and Renaissance Latin Translations and Commentaries* (vol. 1, 1960). Editions of particular works include S. R. Jayne's text and translation (1944) of Ficino's *Commentary on Plato's Symposium;* there have also been modern editions of the Renaissance English translations of Lipsius' *Two Books of Constancy* (ed. Rudolf Kirk and C. M. Hall, 1939) and Guillaume du Vair's *The Moral Philosophy of the Stoics* (ed. Rudolf Kirk, 1951). But from the philosopher's point of view, the most important of such publications was the series of annotated translations brought together by Ernst Cassirer, P. O. Kristeller, and J. H. Randall as *The Renaissance Philosophy of Man* (1948)— another cooperative project involving the collaboration of a considerable group of young scholars. For most philosophers Valla, Pomponazzi, Vives, and even Ficino and della Mirandola had been little more than names; now it was possible, in some measure, to pass judgment upon them.

The Renaissance Philosophy of Man was published from Columbia, which has been the leader in Renaissance philosophical scholarship—especially since it offered a home to the German scholar Kristeller. Like Boehner at the Franciscan Institute, Kristeller has not only made important contributions to scholarship himself, but has inspired others to do likewise. His *The Philosophy of Marsilio Ficino* (1943)—based on research completed in Europe—is the standard book on Ficino, and his *Studies in Renaissance Thought and Letters* (1956) displays the range, variety, and depth of his scholarship. In his introduction to the *Studies* he makes two important points. The first is that although his own writings had emphasized the continuity between medieval and Renaissance thought, he does not wish to deny that the Renaissance was "in many ways also novel and original"; the second point is that "many writings of the humanists fall entirely outside the range of philosophy, even in the broadest possible sense of that term."

The question Kristeller here raises, whether the Renaissance is medieval or modern, has been one of the most hotly disputed scholarly controversies of our time. In his *Science and Thought in the Fifteenth Century* (1929), Thorndike wrote with scorn of the "so-called Renaissance"; so far as there was a Renaissance at all, he argues, it occurred in the twelfth century. His view of the matter has not won wide agreement. Sarton, in his *The Appreciation of Ancient and Medieval Science during the Renaissance* (1955), brought the full weight of his bibliographical learning to bear in detailing the publication of medieval and classical scientific works during the period 1450-1600 and expresses his conviction that the Renaissance, in important respects, worked a revolution in modes of thought, for all that Renaissance thinkers by no means abandoned their medieval heritage. Kristeller takes the same view, but at the same time draws attention to philosophical continuities which had previously been dismissed as unimportant. Thus, for example, he emphasized that "Renaissance Aristotelianism continued the mediaeval scholastic tradition without any visible break" (*Studies*, p. 578) and denied that it was no more than a sterile survival.

In general, American philosophical scholars have had a great deal to say about the medieval ingredients in Renaissance thought, and have helped to set the character of the Renaissance in a much clearer light. J. H. Randall, in a fundamental, much-referred-to article on "The Development of Scientific Method in the School of Padua" (*JHI*, 1940), brought out the importance of late Italian Aristotelianism in the development of ideas about the nature of scientific reasoning; a series of essays on *Jesuit Thinkers of the Renaissance* (ed. Gerard Smith, 1939) drew attention to an influential group of writers whose work has been too little considered by English speaking scholars; W. H. Hay's "Nicholaus Cusanus: The Structure of his Philosophy" (*Phil. Rev.,* 1952) pointed to the medieval elements in Nicholas of Cusa's thought. Partly under the influence of Kristeller's article on "Florentine Platonism and Its Relations with Humanism and Scholasticism" (*Church History,* 1939), a young scholar, Avery Dulles, emphasized in his *Princeps concordiae* (1941)—which bears the subtitle *Pico della Mirandola and the Scholastic Tradition*—the "Christian and scholastic background" from which, he tries to show, Pico's philosophy derived, in opposition to the view that scholasticism was an important ingredient only in Pico's early writings.

It is important to observe that most of the recent essays devoted to Renaissance philosophical scholarship have appeared in the *Journal of the History of Ideas* or in such journals as *Renaissance Studies,* not in the purely philosophical journals. For as Kristeller emphasized, studies in Renaissance thought are largely concerned with writers who are of little or no importance as philosophers. The Renaissance is of considerable interest to the historian; it is of considerably less interest to the historian of philosophy. Thus, for example, E. F. Rice, in his *The Renaissance Idea of Wisdom* (1958), writes as a historian, not as a philosopher, for all that he has carefully scrutinized the more philosophical, as well as the purely humanistic, texts. "Wisdom" is one of those ideas, like "the imagination," which philosophers sometimes refine for their own purposes, but the main history of which lies outside philosophy, in the writings of humanists, critics, and moralists.

Kristeller shows himself to be well aware of the pitfalls which confront the young scholar, pitfalls into which the American one-book scholar is particularly likely to fall, and to fall disastrously. Writing (with Randall) on "The Study of Renaissance Philosophers" (*JHI,* 1941) he points out that inexperienced students are often unable to determine what is original and significant in the writings of the thinker they have taken as their sole theme. That is why, he continues, "so many monographic studies of the last generation are so unsatisfactory and have made no important contribution to the understanding of the material which they have approached without sufficient preparation" (p. 488). A good example is J. L. Saunders' *Justus Lipsius: The Philosophy of Renaissance Stoicism* (1955). "It is to Lipsius," according to Saunders, "that one must turn to understand the place of Stoicism, its formulation and transmission, in the later Renaissance" (p. ix). To make good this claim, obviously, Saunders would need to describe in detail the character of Renaissance stoicism and Lipsius' place in its history. But in fact what Saunders provides us with is a detailed account of Lipsius' life and a close summary of his writings; for the rest, he is content with *obiter dicta* about Lipsius' influence. He tells us several times, for example, that Lipsius had a considerable influence on Montaigne, but he never considers the possibility that in fact the main influence was in the reverse direction. Saunders has made available to us a reasonably close summary of what Lipsius says, but he is not to be trusted whenever he ventures into the wider world of Renaissance thought. Yet Lipsius' revival of stoic ideas is of no philosophical interest in itself. He is a philosopher whose importance is historical, merely. But about his place in the history of thought we are no wiser, after reading Saunders' book, than we were before.

In his *Telesio: The First of the Moderns* (1935), Neil van Deusen set out to do belated justice to a thinker, highly regarded in his own time but speedily forgotten, whom some historians have described as the first modern empiricist. Van Deusen's book has the general characteristics of a justice-doing doctoral dissertation; its virtue is that it quotes copiously instead of merely summarizing. Bruno has come in for considerably more attention: Sidney Greenberg's *The Infinite in Giordano Bruno* (1950) does what it can for Bruno's philosophy and includes a translation of one of his major works, *Concerning the Cause, Principle and One; I. L. Horowitz in his *The Renaissance Philosophy of Giordano Bruno* (1952) detects in Bruno a dialectical method, which makes him a precursor of Hegel and Marx; and J. C. Nelson has published a study of Bruno's *Eroici furori* as *The Renaissance Theory of Love* (1958). One may be permitted to doubt, on the evidence of these volumes, whether Bruno deserves so concentrated an attention, but he is the sort of dramatic figure on whom a diversity of inquiries converge. For Horowitz, basically, he is a "martyr of science," for Nelson a "Renaissance personality," for Greenberg a philosopher.

The question "What happened to logic in the sixteenth century?" is, on the other hand, a philosophically important one. The rejec-

79

tion of formal logic by Descartes and Locke had serious consequences for logic and for philosophy alike, and it is foreshadowed by, and partly a response to, the sixteenth century emphasis on method at the expense of logic. The historic importance of Ramus in this connection has been emphasized by Perry Miller in *The New England Mind* (1939). Miller's work inspired W. J. Ong's *Ramus: Method and the Decay of Dialogue* (1958), which is accompanied by a *Ramus and Talon Inventory*—a short-title list not only of the published works of Ramus and of his leading followers, but also of the literature of the Ramist controversy. Ong's work—like W. S. Howell's *Logic and Rhetoric in England, 1500-1700* (1956)—is literary-historical rather than philosophical in its emphasis and concern. It displays considerably more insight than most works of this character, certainly more than Howell's, but Ong does not bring into sharp focus the facts which would particularly interest the historian of philosophy. His scholarship, however, is thorough and substantial; he has provided a mass of material, which now has to be worked into an adequate account—sadly lacking—of what happened to logic between Ockham and Locke.

N. W. Gilbert's *Review of Renaissance Concepts of Method* (1960) is another important contribution to the elucidation of the history of ideas about scientific and philosophical method. His point of departure is Randall's article on scientific method in the School of Padua, an article which has turned out to be of great seminal importance. Gilbert offers us a learned and meticulous study not only of Ramus but of a variety of minor Renaissance methodologists. What is now needed, once again, is a renewed investigation of the more major figures in the history of philosophy in the light of all this fresh information about their intellectual backgrounds; one comes away from such studies of minor figures with a greater, not a diminished, respect for the men who made the great breakthroughs.

6

MODERN EUROPEAN PHILOSOPHY

1. General histories.   2. The major European philosophers. 3. The secondary philosophers.   4. Secondary philosophers: the seventeenth century.   5. Secondary philosophers: the eighteenth century.   6. Secondary philosophers: the nineteenth century.   7. Philosophy of the recent past.

1.   America is unusually rich—if that is the right adjective—in outline histories of modern philosophy, designed to serve as textbooks for survey courses. Of these it is scarcely necessary to speak. They are not contributions to scholarship and do not pretend to be, but compared with the textbooks a British philosopher might write they sometimes display certain peculiarities which are not without relevance to our present theme.

Take, for example, a rather good representative of its type, W. K. Wright's *A History of Modern Philosophy* (1941). One peculiarity, from the point of view of a British observer, is that Wright freely refers, although he is writing for beginning students, to writers of whom the British-educated philosopher may barely have heard or whom he would not admit to be philosophers. Shameful as this will no doubt seem to my American readers, I doubt whether I had ever known that Ampère wrote books on philosophy until I read Wright's paragraph on his philosophical ideas; and I still have to be persuaded that Thomas Paine, admirable controversialist as he was, counts as a philosopher. If even relatively learned British philosophers were to be confronted by the quiz "Who were Ernest Dimnet, Alfred Espinas, Ethan Allan, Dorothea Veit, E. S. Beesly?" I suspect that few of them would get high grades. In this sense, the American student is certainly "better informed" than most senior British philosophers, a result of the fact that American teachers are very likely to have a conception of the history of philosophy which is quite different from—although not necessarily worse than—the British conception.

A second striking feature of Wright's book is that although he carries his story into the twentieth century, he says nothing whatever about any empirical philosopher subsequent to Mill. Thus the American student who makes use of Wright's book will have heard of Spencer, Royce, James, Dewey, and Alexander but all he will know of Russell or Moore is that they helped to establish the realist movement which gave rise to Alexander. Mach and Meinong have half a sentence apiece, there is not a word about Frege and Brentano. In short, the modern empiricist movements do not exist, and British philosophy after Mill consists of Spencer and Alexander. Bradley appears only as a name.

Recent philosophy is even more queerly envisaged in a very different introduction, written by a Thomist and "designed primarily for students who have some acquaintance with scholastic philosophy and who seek an introduction to the vast field of modern thought," James Collins' *A History of Modern European Philosophy* (1954). Although the nonscholastic may be puzzled by some passages in Collins' *History* and will most likely be unconvinced by others, it is in many ways a very good introduction to the history of philosophy. Collins discusses only a few philosophers, but deals with them very thoroughly, and in the bibliographical notes does something to fill in the historical gaps. But, once again, empirical philosophy ends with Mill; the student will be left with the impression that recent philosophy is entirely irrationalist in spirit, since the only writers of whom he will hear are Nietzsche and Bergson. Collins' history is almost useless as a preparation for participating in contemporary philosophical discussions; yet one would expect this to be at least one object of any historical survey of modern philosophy.

George Boas' *Dominant Themes of Modern Philosophy* (1957) is certainly not an introductory text. For a reader who already has a reasonable notion of the main issues in philosophy, it is extremely useful; for when Boas deals, as he does to a striking degree, with minor writers, it is not as mere names or views but in sufficient detail to let the reader see their importance. Some of his judgments are highly idiosyncratic, but the book as a whole is impressive in its constant concern with philosophical problems. Once again, however, the fact is conspicuous that although Whitehead, Jaspers, and

Sartre are all discussed, British philosophy stops at Mill and Spencer, and nineteenth century German empiricism is wholly neglected. Perhaps it might be set down to sheer chance that the three general histories which I have inspected all have the same emphasis—few works of this sort reach Australian libraries—but the same tendency is manifested, as we shall see, in monographs: post-Humean empiricism is scarcely studied at all. Perhaps no American is both interested in history and empiricist in his philosophical attitude, but it is very difficult to understand why this should be true, if it is true.

One book gives promise in its title of being both historical in character and particularly concerned with empiricopositivist philosophies: Hans Reichenbach's *The Rise of Scientific Philosophy* (1951). In fact, it turns out to be, for the most part, an account of Reichenbach's own philosophical views; his judgments on his predecessors reveal little or no historical insight. Even though, as I have been arguing, the historian of philosophy needs to possess philosophical insight, Reichenbach's book will serve to remind us that philosophical ability is no substitute for historical imagination.

What can happen, on the other hand, if the history of philosophy is left to "intellectual historians" is well illustrated in Jacob Bronowski and Bruce Mazlish's *The Western Intellectual Tradition from Leonardo to Hegel* (1960). Bronowski and Mazlish do not entirely neglect philosophers; they have quite a little to say about Hobbes, Locke, and Descartes, but do not so much as refer to Spinoza. This is no doubt as it should be from the point of view of an intellectual historian—which brings out the importance of developing the history of philosophy as an independent inquiry. If the history of philosophy is merged into general intellectual history, the purely philosophical perspective is certain to be distorted. Only by being "narrow," sharply distinguishing between philosophers on the one hand and publicists, sages, or reformers on the other, can one do justice to the philosophical tradition and its contribution to Western civilization. Every culture has its prophets and sages, but few societies have cultivated philosophy or science.

2.   Knowing something of the American educational curriculum and the small part that Latin and Greek play in it, one would

naturally expect the strength of American scholarship to be fully revealed only in the modern period. In fact, however, the American record in modern philosophical scholarship is more than a little disappointing. A bibliography which mentioned only the major commentaries on major European philosophers would scarcely have occasion to refer to a single American contribution to scholarship, nor is the record in regard to a great many of the more important minor philosophers very much better. Consider the following list of philosophers: Bacon, Hobbes, Descartes, Leibniz, Spinoza, Locke, Berkeley, Hume, Kant, Hegel, Mill—philosophers to whom no history of modern philosophy, however "outline," could fail to refer. On most of these philosophers, American scholars have written studies which deserve a mention, but only in the case of Spinoza and Kant, I shall be suggesting, have they made contributions to scholarship which it would be quite monstrous to ignore.

Bacon is an *uomo universale,* whose claims to be a great philosopher have been seriously disputed; but even that dispute has been neglected in the United States, where such substantial studies of Bacon as have been published are devoted to Bacon the writer as distinct from Bacon the philosopher or else, like C. W. Lemmi's *The Classic Deities in Bacon* (1933), are of only marginal relevance to philosophy. In search of a general commentary on Bacon, the scholar would do better to turn to France or to Italy or to Canada than to the United States.

In the case of Hobbes, Germany takes the lead, and one of the most notable of German Hobbes scholars, Leo Strauss, is now at Chicago. But Strauss completed *The Political Philosophy of Hobbes* (1936) before he left Germany. American political theorists have written quite a few essays on Hobbes, and Clarence De Witt Thorpe, writing as a "mere literary man," has made a detailed study of *The Aesthetic Theory of Thomas Hobbes* (1940) "with special reference to his contribution to the psychological approach in English literary criticism." The only work of any consequence on Hobbes's general philosophical position considerably predates 1930.

Cartesian studies are, at first sight, in a stronger position; one can point to two substantial works by A. G. A. Balz: *Cartesian Studies* (1951) and *Descartes and the Modern Mind* (1952). No one, however, in search of a general commentary on Descartes,

84

would go to either book. *Cartesian Studies* is a series of essays—originally published over a period of some twenty years and quite independent of one another—on "the diffusion of Cartesianism," and more especially on the diffusion of Descartes's ideas about mind and body. "If the student stray from the great highway of philosophy's history, to wander in its collateral byways," Balz writes, "he may be sure of adventures" (p. 218)—but the adventures Balz has in store for us are, on the whole, historical rather than philosophical. "It is to be hoped," he says of his essay on Louis de la Chambre, "that in the diagnostic sense this study of La Chambre possesses some value. His writings can scarcely deserve any other use" (p. 63). In short, we are now in the province of the history of ideas, not of the history of philosophy proper. Indeed, although it can be very usefully consulted as a set of exceptionally scholarly encyclopedia articles, Balz's book is too discontinuous to be read even as a history.

Descartes and the Modern Mind is in a rather different position, but is still not a commentary in any orthodox sense. Balz sets out to show that Descartes is "in spirit, in prophetic insight, and in generous ideality the father of the modern mind" rather than to concentrate upon "meticulous attention to detail," especially with respect to the "more ephemeral elements of doctrine" (p. viii). Without meticulous attention to detail, however, one cannot really understand what Descartes was doing; Balz substitutes for detail a curious variety of metaphysical interpretation—not assisted by a diffuse and abstract style—which blurs, rather than sharpens, our image of the Cartesian philosophy. Nor are we in compensation shown in detail just how Descartes has affected "the modern mind." Not uniquely in American scholarship, Balz's book is neither a close philosophical analysis nor a detailed historical study; a work of either sort would have its virtues, but Balz's compromise leaves the reader puzzled and dissatisfied.

Only one American work on a modern European philosopher, perhaps, could not possibly be excluded even from a brief, if serious, bibliography, and that is H. A. Wolfson's *Spinoza* (1934). Even so much is sometimes questioned. No doubt, it has been objected, Wolfson's *Spinoza* does a great deal to reveal the scholastic-Jewish sources of Spinoza's philosophy, but it does not help us to under-

85

stand Spinoza's philosophy for and in itself. The interpretation of Wolfson's book implicit in this objection is, I should say, mistaken. Wolfson does not set out, merely as some dry-as-dust scholar might, to list and analyze the Jewish sources which conceivably or actually influenced Spinoza. "The first step, the basic step, in the understanding of any philosopher," he writes, "is the determination by the method of historical criticism of what the philosopher meant by what he said, how he came to say what he said, and why he said it in the manner in which he happened to say it" (p. vii). The study of sources is, for Wolfson, only a means to the scholar's end: to help us look through the written word and the external form to the author's thought. In Spinoza's case, he argues, this is peculiarly necessary, just because the external form is so rigid and artificial, the mode of expression so technical and compact. How are we to tell whether Wolfson has "looked through" correctly? "The *Ethics*," Wolfson answers, "emerges as a logically constructed work throughout which there is order and sequence and continuity; propositions, apparently disconnected, group themselves into unified and coherent chapters; words, phrases, and passages, apparently meaningless or commonplace, assume meaning and significance; and the philosophy of Spinoza, as a systematic whole and in all its fulness of detail, appears in a new light and in a new setting and perspective" (p. viii).

To take over a contrast of Matthew Arnold, Wolfson helps us to see the soul of an explorer beneath the gown of the doctor. He writes, too, with dignity, lucidity, and point. Whether his interpretation is at all points correct is quite another matter; some of his critics have accused him of misunderstanding the Thomistic ingredients in Spinoza's thought and others of underplaying the influence of the new science. His interpretation of Spinoza's attributes, too, has come under criticism, as in F. S. Haserot's essay on "Spinoza's Definition of Attribute" (*Phil. Rev.*, 1953). Anyone who sets out to interpret a major thinker must expect, and will certainly in some measure deserve, to be criticized; no account of a great thinker is ever the whole story. The fact remains that it would be quite monstrous for a Spinoza scholar to ignore Wolfson's book; the same can be said, *mutatis mutandis,* for very few American commentaries on great modern European thinkers.

86

In a sense, however, David Bidney, in his *The Psychology and Ethics of Spinoza* (1940) does ignore Wolfson; his object, he says, is "to let Spinoza speak for himself," rather than to attempt to interpret him in the light of the teachings of his predecessors. Wolfson, Bidney suggests, began from the quite unwarranted assumption that Spinoza had a wholly coherent system, so that if we think we can detect inconsistencies in Spinoza we must be misunderstanding him. Bidney proposes, on the contrary, to point to inconsistencies whenever the "actual text" exhibits them. Bidney's interpretation of Wolfson is, I should say, mistaken: Wolfson is presuming, only, that Spinoza's inconsistencies are unlikely to be blatant and wholly inexplicable, that it is improbable that Spinoza's propositions have no connection whatever one with another, that what Spinoza is saying is unlikely to be transparent nonsense. This still leaves it possible that there are conflicting tendencies in Spinoza—conflicts between what Wolfson himself calls "Benedictus the first of the moderns" and "Baruch the last of the mediaevals"—and that as a result of the operation of these conflicting tendencies, there are inconsistencies in Spinoza of a more fundamental kind than those which immediately affront the eye.

After reading Wolfson, Bidney's book is bound at first to impress us as being somewhat ill-informed—a first impression that is in some respects also our last impression. It is, all the same, a close study of an unduly neglected aspect of Spinoza's philosophy, which usefully emphasizes the emergence of a modern point of view within Spinoza's psychology. Although L. S. Feuer's *Spinoza and the Rise of Liberalism* (1958) is not of the same philosophical interest, it sets Spinoza firmly in the context of Jewish-Dutch political thought and political experience.

No American work on Leibniz is of comparable importance. L. E. Loemker's edition of Leibniz' *Philosophical Papers and Letters* (1956) is a valuable collection—as is P. P. Wiener's *Leibniz* (1951)—and his introduction is competent and wide-ranging; both Loemker ("Leibniz' Doctrine of Ideas," *Phil. Rev.*, 1946) and Wiener ("Notes on Leibniz' Conception of Logic," *Phil. Rev.*, 1939) have written scholarly articles on Leibniz; a special number of the *Journal of the History of Ideas* (September 1946) contains a set of slighter essays on different aspects of Leibniz' thought. Lovejoy's chapter in *The Great Chain of Being* on "Plenitude and Sufficient Reason in Leibniz and Spinoza" brings out the conflicting strains in Leibniz' conception of the best of all possible worlds. There is, however, no substantial commentary on Leibniz. R. M. Yost's *Leibniz and Philosophical Analysis* (University of California Publications in Philosophy, 1954) is, however, an essay of a type seldom to be met with in America. Yost's interests are genuinely philosophical; if he does not move outside Leibniz' better-known writings, he makes us very conscious of the fact that Leibniz was a philosopher, a man whom we might have met and argued with as we might meet and argue with one of our contemporaries. Such comments as "Leibniz' attempts to analyze the concept of law were feeble and desultory" will strike some scholars as being irreverent; in fact, Yost is treating Leibniz with greater respect than most scholars do—as a live and vigorous thinker, not as a glassy-eyed exhibit in a museum of ideas. Not all books on great philosophers should be like Yost's, but more certainly should be, if the history of philosophy is not to collapse into an area of specialization within modern history or modern language departments. The fact remains that Yost's book neither is, nor aspires to be, a great commentary.

The weaknesses of the "modern language" approach to the history of philosophy are clearly exhibited in E. L. Tuveson's *The Imagination as a Means of Grace: Locke and the Aesthetics of Romanticism* (1960). Tuveson is by no means incompetent, yet his elementary misunderstandings of Locke (cf. pp. 23-24, pp. 28-29) are startling in the extreme. He includes no bibliography and to judge from his notes he has thought it proper to write about Locke without consulting any of the major commentators, although his own training, it would seem, was wholly literary. If the educated American is to derive his ideas about Locke from such books as Tuveson's, accurate knowledge about the philosophical past will simply disappear. J. W. Yolton's *John Locke and the Way of Ideas* (1956) is in contrast, even though its theme is historical, an essentially philosophical work; by studying the reception of Locke's *Essay,* the sorts of criticism that were directed against it, Yolton throws a certain amount of light on the *Essay* itself. A good example of thorough American scholarship (although it was actually written in England) Yolton's book is, all the same, only of modest importance and in a sense a little alarming insofar as it is a manifestation of a tendency to be more interested in the reputation of philosophers than in their achievement. For the rest, Benjamin Rand produced a much-criticized edition of an early version of Locke's essay (1931) and a number of doctoral candidates have taken some aspect of Locke's philosophy as their theme. Two dissertations, Albert Hofstadter's *Locke and Scepticism* (1936) and S. M. Thompson's *A Study of Locke's Theory of Ideas* (1934) stand out, written as they were by philosophers who were already revealing something of the quality of their subsequent work. But it would be absurd to expect important contributions to philosophical scholarship from young men; one sometimes feels that nobody ought to be permitted to publish scholarly work before, at least, the age of thirty. In a great many dissertations there are the seeds of really important work; early publication gives the author no chance of bringing the seeds into full growth by further reflection and reading, especially outside the area of his dissertation subject.

On Berkeley, there is an ambitious book to be reckoned with—John Wild's *George Berkeley: A Study of His Life and Philosophy* (1936)—but it has not advanced the reputation of American scholarship. Wild's thesis is that only in *Siris* does Berkeley "at last become a philosopher." T. E. Jessop's review in *Mind* (1937) sums the matter up: "In size and wealth of documentation it challenges comparison with Fraser's *Life and Letters of Berkeley*. But—I am sorry to have to say these things—its size is due to a quite remarkable prolixity and repetitiousness; its documentation, outside the biographical sections, will bear little inspection; and its expository sections expound not Berkeley but Wild" (p. 232). "All the usual principles of textual interpretation," Jessop continues, "seem to have been suspended" (p. 234). Even if Wild is in some measure right—opposing the Irish scholar Luce (see Wild's "The Unity of the Berkeleian Philosophy" in *Mind*, 1937)—in emphasizing the differences between the *Principles* and *Siris*, one must still regretfully concur with Jessop's judgment, regretfully because Wild is at least attempting to write a book which shall be at once scholarly and philosophical. Wild aside, one can point only to essays on Berkeley: especially perhaps to the series of essays included in the

George Berkeley issue of the University of California Publications in Philosophy (1957). These are understandably brief, but together they constitute a useful, if distinctly uneven, introduction to the whole range of Berkeley's thought, political and theological as well as philosophical. John Myhill's essay on "Berkeley's *De Motu*— An Anticipation of Mach" is a particularly illuminating study of a little considered work, even if one reserves the right to differ from Myhill's general judgment that "roughly speaking, one can say that Berkeley had, and Hume did not have, a respect for natural science" (p. 151). In a different genre, H. M. Bracken's *The Early Reception of Berkeley's Immaterialism, 1710-33* (1959) is yet another account of the growth of a reputation—Berkeley's reputation as a skeptic and a solipsist—assiduously worked out through a close study of his minor critics.

What of Hume? Biographical studies by E. C. Mossner, a careful scrutiny by A. B. Glathe of *Hume's Theory of the Passions and of Morals* (University of California Publications in Philosophy, 1950), a sober monograph by R. W. Church on *Hume's Theory of the Understanding* (1935). This latter, the most substantial work, was largely prepared before Church, American born but English trained, returned to the United States. Of course, there are very many articles: Church's "Malebranche and Hume" (*Revue internationale de philosophie,* 1938); Paul Marhenke on "Hume's View of Identity" (University of California Publications in Philosophy, 1937); R. H. Popkin's "David Hume and the Pyrrhonian Controversy" (*Review of Metaphysics,* 1952) will illustrate the range. Compared with French or Italian scholarship in the same period, to say nothing of English, the record is extraordinarily slight.

The situation in regard to Kant studies is rather better: especially in regard to Kant's ethics. Of P. A. Schilpp's *Kant's Pre-Critical Ethics* (1938; rev. ed., 1960), the English Kant scholar Paton remarks in its preface that "on its chosen topic Professor Schilpp's book is without a rival in the English language." As much might be said of a great many very bad American works of scholarship, but in Schilpp's case the topic is an important one. Kant's mature ethical writings are in many respects difficult to comprehend, and Schilpp's careful study of his earlier ethical opinions, as revealed in scattered writings, helps us to grasp the moral assumptions of the more mature works. L. W. Beck's edition (1949) of Kant's *Critique of Practical Reason* also contains a number of Kant's less accessible writings, and his *Commentary on Kant's Critique of Practical Reason* (1960) will establish itself, one can fairly confidently predict, as the standard commentary on a work of Kant's which has been somewhat neglected in the last few decades. Beck's *Commentary* is not a mere summary, but attempts to bring out the structure of Kant's thinking; sympathetic to Kant's intentions, it is often quite sharply critical on particular points, sometimes fundamental points, in Kant's argument. Nor is this one of those commentaries which is more obscure than the text itself; for the most part, Beck's interpretation is as sharp and clear as the subject matter permits.

W. T. Jones's Oxford dissertation on *Morality and Freedom in the Philosophy of Immanuel Kant* (1940) is a serious philosophical study of a crucial question in Kantian ethics. Jones is concerned to pick out from Kant's ethical writings what Jones regards as a truly critical account of the relation between morality and freedom, and to consider whether it can be sustained. This is scholarship in the (typically) English rather than in the (typically) American manner. A considerable number of articles by American scholars in American and European philosophical journals still further illustrate American interest in, and competence in discussing, Kant's ethical teachings. In closely related fields, T. M. Greene and H. H. Hudson have translated—with a considerable introduction by Greene on Kant's theology—*Religion Within the Limits of Reason Alone* (1934). Israel Knox's *The Aesthetic Theories of Kant, Hegel, and Schopenhauer* (1936) is one of the rare works in the English language on *The Critique of Judgment*, but like so many writings on aesthetics it is made an occasion for "fine writing" rather than for critical analysis.

No one could reasonably complain, then, that Kant's ethical, religious, and aesthetic writings have been neglected in America: there were gaps to be filled, and American scholarship has partly filled them. In a sense, no such gap is obvious in respect of Kant's logical and metaphysical writings. There are plenty of commentaries on Kant's *Critique of Pure Reason,* but in fact, for all the recent commentaries, Kant's philosophical ideas are by no means fully explored, if only because so many commentators have been concerned to defend Kant's metaphysics or epistemology rather than to bring out the very important pragmatic and positivist tendencies in his teaching. From American scholars one might reasonably expect a reading of Kant which would stress the positivist-pragmatic side of his philosophy, which has had so profound an influence on contemporary philosophy. Seeing that traditional metaphysics flourishes in the United States, one might also expect commentaries which would concentrate on the *Dialectic,* in contrast with the English tendency to lay all the stress on the *Analytic.* The actual situation is that, except for the short essays included in G. T. Whitney and D. F. Bowers' *The Heritage of Kant* (1939)—only a few of which are, in any case, concerned with logical and metaphysical questions —and a certain number of scattered essays such as George Schrader's articles on Kant's metaphysics in the *Review of Metaphysics* (1949 and 1951) one can point, as an example of American Kant scholarship, only to C. B. Garnett's *The Kantian Philosophy of Space* (1939). This is a study of Kant's doctrine of space in its relation on the one side to Newton and Leibniz and on the other to Alexander, Whitehead, and Broad. It is useful insofar as it gives an account of Kant's theory of space in his earlier writings, but to compare it with the great European commentaries on Kant would be absurd.

As for Hegel studies, it is difficult to find anything at all to report, so far as work on Hegel's metaphysics and his logic are concerned. Jacob Loewenberg's important articles on Hegel's *Phenomenology* (*Mind,* 1934 and 1935) did not, as one had hoped, serve as preliminary sketches for a major work. An occasional dissertation— for example, J. G. Gray's *Hegel's Hellenic Ideal* (1941)—has been devoted to some special aspect of Hegel's thought; Josef Maier's very brief monograph *On Hegel's Critique of Kant* (1939) begins with a quasi-Marxist flourish of trumpets about bourgeois philosophy but settles down into a useful, if inevitably sketchy, account of the various stages in Hegel's movement away from Kant. There is desperate need of new translations of Hegel. In a period which has seen translations of so many relatively unimportant works, nobody has turned to Hegel, except insofar as American scholarship can claim the credit for the publication by Chicago University Press of the Scottish philosopher T. M. Knox's translations of Hegel in *Early*

Theological Writings (1948). This volume also includes a few short translations and an introduction by Richard Kroner—not calculated to persuade the skeptic that Hegel is intelligible.

By far the most important work on Hegel to emanate from the United States is Herbert Marcuse's *Reason and Revolution: Hegel and the Rise of Social Theory* (1941). But Marcuse wrote that book as a German scholar, only recently arrived in America. Marcuse's interest, moreover, is in Hegel's influence on social theory rather than in his philosophy, although he does discuss that philosophy in the context of social theory—and one might well argue that this is the best way of coming to understand it. "German idealism," Marcuse writes in a revealing passage, "rescued philosophy from the attack of British empiricism, and the struggle between the two became not merely a clash of different philosophical schools, but a struggle for philosophy as such" (p. 16). A great many British and American philosophers would precisely reverse this interpretation of the situation: James and Russell and Moore, they would say, rescued philosophy from the attacks of German idealism. Both views seem to me to be mistaken; neither Hegel nor Hume ought to be dismissed as an "antiphilosopher."

One might expect that J. S. Mill would have been more freely discussed in America than Hegel, but that is scarcely the case. One or two dissertations have been published, including a quite useful one by O. A. Kubitz on *The Development of John Stuart Mill's System of Logic* (1932); Ernest Nagel's introduction to his *John Stuart Mill's Philosophy of Scientific Method* (1950) is an excellent conspectus; there is a surprisingly brief essay on "John Stuart Mill's System of Logic" in *Theories of Scientific Method* (ed. R. M. Blake, C. J. Ducasse, E. H. Madden, 1960); and every now and then a flurry of controversy arises in the journals about some point in Mill's ethical or political theory. What else? I. W. Mueller's lengthy study of *John Stuart Mill and French Thought* (1956) is a useful account of the French background to Mill's reflections on human society, but has very little indeed to say about Mill's logical or metaphysical ideas. Ney MacMinn, J. R. Hainds, J. M. McCrimmon have prepared an important *Bibliography of the Published Writings of John Stuart Mill* (1945)—important because so many of Mill's writings are scattered through periodicals. Very many

writers on scientific method, of course, have referred in more or
less detail to Mill's *System of Logic;* the fact remains that for a
really substantial study of Mill one looks in vain to the United
States.

3. Enough, more than enough, has now been said to substantiate
my general claim that American scholars have not contributed as
considerably as one might have expected to the major scholarly
literature on major philosophers. Now we shall turn our attention
to what, speaking relatively, are "secondary" European philosophers
—thinkers whose names are familiar to most present-day philosophers in English speaking countries, but whom philosophers (as
distinct from intellectual historians) seldom read, except perhaps
in a volume of miscellaneous selections. The list is a long one: it
would have to include the Cambridge Platonists, the Cartesians, the
French *philosophes,* the British moralists, the Scottish common-
sense philosophers, eighteenth century deists, British and German
idealist logicians, German romanticists, nineteenth century agnos-
tics, Helvétius, Vico, Whewell, Bolzano, Brentano, Meinong, Nietzsche, and Schopenhauer. These writers differ very greatly in quality
and in philosophical interest. Some of them, certainly, are major
figures in the history of Western culture, even if they are seldom
read or discussed by professional philosophers, at least in Anglo-
Saxon countries; with others, philosophers of the less learned sort
might profess to no previous acquaintance. For our present purpose,
however, the list will serve well enough as a starting point.

Many of the "secondary" philosophers have been entirely, or
almost entirely, ignored by American scholars. For example, I know
of no serious study of Herbart's philosophy and nothing of any
fundamental importance on the logical and metaphysical theories
of Brentano or Meinong. H. O. Eaton's *The Austrian Philosophy
of Values* (1930), however, painstakingly summarizes the ethical
theories of Brentano, Meinong, and von Ehrenfels; Eaton's book
was designed as a prolegomenon to critical discussion, but was, perhaps, too even in tone to act as a stimulant.

Very little has been published, either, on the British moralists—
Shaftesbury, Hutcheson, Balguy, Price—or on Hartley and Priestley,
or even the common-sense Scottish school. Gladys Bryson in *Man*

94

and Society: The Scottish Inquiry of the Eighteenth Century (1945)
has described the rise of social theory within eighteenth century
Scottish moral philosophy; and in the process has had a little to say
about the more elementary philosophical ideas of the Scottish moralists and metaphysicians, but she does not even profess to be em-
barking upon a serious investigation either of their ethical or of
their metaphysical teachings. This list of total or partial absentees
could be considerably enlarged: it is surprising how many intellectually respectable and historically influential philosophers have
scarcely been discussed by American scholars. That point having
been made, it is time to turn to a more positive description of what
has actually been achieved.

4. First, in seventeeth century studies. Only More, of the Cambridge Platonists, has been individually investigated; generally
speaking, the emphasis in writings on the Cambridge Platonists has
been on intellectual history rather than on critical commentary.
R. L. Colie's *Light and Enlightenment* (1957) is of fundamental
importance as a study of English-Dutch intellectual relationships
in the seventeenth century; unfortunately, she is quite unreliable as
soon as she moves outside the very minor writers who are her main
concern in order to say something about their influence on, say,
Cambridge Platonism. R. S. Westfall's *Science and Religion in Seventeenth-Century England* (1958) is in much the same position;
its emphasis is on the *virtuosi,* as distinct from the philosophers.
Westfall mentions the Cambridge Platonists only in passing; he has
a great deal to say about Locke but is interested in his "attitudes"
rather than in his arguments. In short, this too is, and only pre-
tends to be, intellectual history.

Henry More, however, has been more philosophically considered.
E. A. Burtt set the fashion in his *Metaphysical Foundations of Modern Physical Science* (1925), a brilliant and influential book which
persuaded a good many scholars that there was an intimate relation
between seventeenth century metaphysical speculation and seventeenth century scientific theorizing. Burtt's interpretation of the
historical situation was challenged by E. W. Strong in his difficult
and densely written *Procedures and Metaphysics* (1936). Strong
set out to show that mathematical procedures—especially as devel-

95

oped by the Italian mathematicians of the seventeenth century—
rather than metaphysical ideas were the real source of seventeenth
century mathematical physics. Burtt's influence, however, has persisted and his suggestions about More were followed up by J. T.
Baker in his *Historical and Critical Examination of English Space
and Time Theories* (1930) and "Henry More and Kant" (*Phil.
Rev.*, 1937). P. R. Anderson's *Science in Defense of Liberal Religion* (1933), which the subtitle describes as "a study of Henry
More's attempt to link seventeenth century religion with science,"
is a meticulously detailed account of a special theme in More's
thought. Marjorie Nicolson's edition of *The Conway Letters* (1930)
provides us with important biographical clues to the understanding
of More. Altogether, More cannot complain of neglect—if anything, there has been a tendency to exaggerate the historical importance of his theory of space—although attention has been mainly
concentrated on one or two aspects of his thought. A rounded study
of More is still needed.

Glanvill, too—as much a Cambridge Platonist as an Oxford
man could be—has attracted some attention, largely because he is
important as a publicist, as a clue to what was going on intellectually. R. F. Jones in his *Ancient and Moderns: A Study of the
Background of the Battle of the Books* (1936) talks about Glanvill
—as about Bacon—because his writings help us to understand the
intellectual background of seventeenth century literature; the merits
of Glanvill's philosophical writings are no part of Jones's concern.
The title of J. I. Cope's *Joseph Glanvill: Anglican Apologist*
(1956) speaks for itself, although Cope does in fact give a fairly
detailed account of such of Glanvill's philosophical ideas as closely
touch upon theology. In M. L. Wiley's *The Subtle Knot: Creative
Scepticism in Seventeenth-Century England* (1952) Glanvill appears as one of a group of poets, essayists, and churchmen, quite
out of philosophical company. R. H. Popkin's "Joseph Glanvill:
A Precursor of David Hume" (*JHI*, 1953) is more specifically
philosophical in its interest, insofar as it investigates Glanvill's
theory of causality; on the other hand his "The Development of the
Philosophical Reputation of Joseph Glanvill" (*JHI*, 1954) reverts,
in a now only too familiar manner, to the study of Glanvill's reputation as distinct from his actual achievement. (From a purely his-

torical point of view, of course, what a man is reputed to have said may be more important than what he actually said.)

Popkin's many studies in skepticism are now being brought together in book form; the first part of what is intended to be a general history of skepticism has appeared as *The History of Scepticism from Erasmus to Descartes* (1960). This incorporates a fairly considerable study of minor seventeenth century writers, as well as a more detailed account of Descartes's skepticism. Although Popkin's work suffers in respect of both freshness and continuity from the circumstances of its composition over a long and broken period of time, it is a work of quite exceptional thoroughness. If one still feels free to question whether Popkin has not exaggerated the Pyrrhonian influence on European philosophy, he has certainly made it impossible any longer to neglect what has been, at least, an important underground movement. The book is a striking example of American erudition, although, as so often, the clumsiness of the writing produces an effect of uncertainty and ambiguity. (Consider "All this does not answer the problem, but, like the solution of the Calvinists, is merely a reiteration of the idea that subjective certainty is true, and anyone who experiences it will believe this," p. 205.)

Herbert of Cherbury's *De religione laici* has been edited and translated by H. R. Hutcheson (1944). This is a work of less philosophical content than Herbert's *De veritate,* but Hutcheson's edition—published, it is interesting to note, for Yale Studies in English—contains a good deal of useful scholarly material. Other minor seventeenth century moralists and metaphysicians seem to have been almost entirely neglected. In contrast, quite a little has been written on Boyle and Newton, but most of it is biographical or theological in its emphasis—for example, M. S. Fisher's *Robert Boyle, Devout Naturalist* (1945). R. M. Blake's essay on "Sir Isaac Newton's Theory of Scientific Method" (*Phil. Rev.,* 1933) is characteristic of the more philosophical writings on Newton, not least in its dependence upon Burtt.

To turn now to the minor Cartesians, there are competent essays on Cordemoy, Clerselier, Rohault, de la Chambre, Clauberg, and de la Forge in Balz's *Cartesian Studies;* historians of ideas, as in Leonora Rosenfield's *From Beast Machine to Man Machine* (1941)

97

have been interested in tracing the emergence of eighteenth century materialism by way of the minor Cartesians out of Cartesian dualism. But, remembering that R. W. Church's fundamental *A Study in the Philosophy of Malebranche* (1931) was published in and from England, little or nothing has appeared on such more important Cartesians as Malebranche, Arnauld, and Geulincx. Gassendi has been equally neglected.

The somewhat enigmatic figure of Pierre Bayle has, in the last few years, come to the fore, now that commentators, especially on Hume, have drawn attention to the historical importance of seventeenth century skepticism. The best general study is still Howard Robinson's *Bayle the Sceptic* (1931). R. H. Popkin's essay on "Pierre Bayle's Place in Seventeenth-Century Scepticism" (in *Pierre Bayle,* ed. Paul Dibon, 1959) usefully compares and contrasts Bayle's skepticism with the skepticism of his contemporaries in such a way as to bring out its peculiarities. L. P. Courtines' *Bayle's Relations with England and the English* (1938) is, in a manner by now somewhat wearisomely familiar, historically thorough rather than philosophically illuminating, and R. E. Cowdrick's *The Early Reading of Pierre Bayle* (1939) illustrates the sort of scholarly study which is becoming increasingly common in America, as modern language departments and intellectual historians take over the history of ideas. Such investigations are by no means useless—far from it—but there is no point in knowing what Bayle read, or what his relations with England and the English were, except as a scholarly aid to understanding his ideas. More and more, we find ourselves confronted by innumerable "aids" which in fact aid us not at all in understanding.

Although an exploring party setting out to climb Everest will need to reconnoiter the foothills, it will not be for long content with the occasional glimpses of the peak obtainable from them. American scholarship about philosophy seems positively to prefer the foothills, and, indeed, those whose training has been in literature and history, solely or mainly, will do well to venture no further. Meanwhile, the zeal and industry, the careful organization, of the foothills party intimidates the philosopher who might otherwise have been disposed to make an assault upon the peak. So the philosophical commentary proper disappears, in a no man's land where the philosopher will not, and the scholar cannot, venture.

These critical reflections apply, in some measure, even to works for which scholars have every reason to be grateful: M. H. Fisch and T. G. Bergin's translations of Vico's *Autobiography* (1944) and *The New Science* (1948)—a translation of Vico must also be an interpretation—together with the introduction to Vico which appears by way of preface to the translation of the *Autobiography*. In this case, too, the gratitude is tinged with disappointment. *The New Science* is a peculiarly difficult work; its organization is, to say the least, so idiosyncratic that the ordinary reader stands in need of an experienced guide if he is to find his way profitably through its devious turnings. But of the hundred and four pages of Fisch and Bergson's introduction only fourteen are devoted to *The New Science* itself; those fourteen pages are a general summary—hard enough to construct, admittedly—rather than what the ordinary philosopher so badly needs, an elucidation of Vico's problems and of the structure of *The New Science*. Compare these fourteen pages with the forty-three devoted to "Vico's reputation and influence"!

Other works on Vico include R. A. Caponigri's *Time and Idea: The Theory of History in Giambattista Vico* (1953) and Thomas Berry's Catholic University of Washington dissertation on *The Historical Theory of Giambattista Vico* (1949), which is, at its level, a competent general interpretation of Vico's works, considered as "the product of a man of letters who was attempting to be a philosopher" (p. 28). Caponigri sets out to show that "Vico offers to modern man an alternative principle for the vindication of his own spirituality and subjectivity" (p. 3)—an alternative, that is, to a reversion to classical naturalism. As even this brief quotation may suggest, *Time and Idea* is a somewhat overwritten and by no means always clear account of Vico's thought, but it does at least make a direct attack upon the problem of interpreting Vico; in that sense it belongs to the Italian tradition of scholarship even though Caponigri is critical of the interpretation which men like Croce have offered of Vico. At the same time Caponigri supports his interpretation by close reference to the text of Vico's writings; *Time and Idea* is not, that is, a purely imaginative reconstruction.

5. Of eighteenth century British philosophers of the second order, only Butler has come in for any substantial consideration. Thomists have shown some slight interest in Reid and the common-sense school (see the articles in *Modern Schoolman,* 1956) and A. O. Aldridge has published a number of articles on Shaftesbury; the most interesting philosophically is "Shaftesbury and the Test of Truth," which appeared, significantly enough, in the *Publications of the Modern Language Association* for 1945. There have been odd articles, too, on Hutcheson and Mandeville, but no considerable study.

Butler, in contrast, has been well done by, with E. C. Mossner's *Bishop Butler and the Age of Reason* (1936), W. J. Norton's *Bishop Butler: Moralist and Divine* (1940), and W. G. Harris's doctoral dissertation on *Teleology in the Philosophy of Joseph Butler and Abraham Tucker* (1941). Mossner's book is rightly subtitled "a study in the history of thought." He devotes only twenty pages to Butler's ethical theory, pages from which the reader could scarcely guess that there has been more than a little controversy about the interpretation of Butler's ethics. In contrast, some seventy-five pages tell the story of the growth of Butler's reputation. The rest of the book is an outline—clear and lively, if somewhat sketchy —of the rise and fall of the deistic movement. Of Norton's book, in the sharpest possible contrast, no one could complain that it fails to concentrate upon Butler himself and upon his teachings; any complaint would lie precisely in the opposite direction. Norton says so little—almost nothing—about the intellectual atmosphere in which Butler was working that we are not helped to understand what problems were confronting Butler, or why it was that he wavered at crucial points in his thinking; this book belongs to the "summary" school of scholarship, as distinct from the "background and reputation" school. Still, Norton has made a very careful study of the whole corpus of Butler's writings; his object is to present Butler's ideas as a single system of metaphysics—a Protestant metaphysics. "How typically true it is of all Protestant creeds and sects *au fond,"* Norton writes in a sentence which will sufficiently illustrate those stylistic defects which so seriously detract from the value of his work, "is not for me to say; nevertheless it can respectfully take its place along with systems of other metaphysical expression"

(p. x). Of other eighteenth century moralists only Bentham has been seriously considered, and David Baumgardt's *Bentham and the Ethics of Today* (1952), well informed but ill formed, was prepared in Germany and England, although it makes some reference to contemporary American thought.

Bolingbroke, of the minor metaphysicians, if one can describe him in such complimentary terms, has come in for an extraordinarily detailed treatment in W. M. Merrill's *From Statesman to Philosopher* (1949); this is an excellent example of the sort of book which makes extravagant claims for its chosen hero through simple ignorance of his intellectual environment.

Eighteenth century German philosophy of the minor sort has never been of great interest to English speaking philosophers. It has, indeed, been wholly abandoned to modern language scholars; in consequence the emphasis has been on writers like Lessing rather than on philosophers like Wolff. J. C. O'Flaherty has published a revised version of his thesis on J. G. Hamann as *Unity and Language* (1952) in which he emphasizes the more philosophical aspects of a philosophically not very interesting thinker. Another modern-language scholar, R. T. Clark, has dealt at length, and thoroughly, with the life and ideas of Herder in his *Herder, His Life and Thought* (1955). Clark does not make exaggerated claims for Herder; as an epigraph, he quotes Nietzsche's judgment of Herder that "he did not sit at the banquet table of those who were truly creating; and his ambition did not permit him to take a modest seat among those who were truly enjoying." Clark's book is, indeed, a careful study of the intellectual life of eighteenth century Germany, in which Herder appears as a representative figure rather than as a creative originator.

It is eighteenth century France, not Germany, which has attracted the American scholar, perhaps because of the close connection between the French Enlightenment and the American Revolution. Short of devoting to it a special chapter, one cannot hope even to list American scholarly literature on the eighteenth century *philosophes.* That special chapter would not be justified, for very little of the mass of scholarly work is of philosophical interest, whatever its literary or historical importance.

One of the most substantial of American eighteenth century

studies, L. G. Crocker's *An Age of Crisis: Man and World in Eighteenth Century French Thought* (1959), begins, indeed, by frankly admitting that the *philosophes* were not "systematic philosophers in the usual sense, but were primarily combative social and moral thinkers, usually with a strong tinge of scientific dilettantism" (p. xv). When Crocker touches on a metaphysical issue he rapidly becomes impatient of it; thus, after a paragraph or so on determinism, he says, "it would be tedious, except for the reader who is interested in the play of dialectical logic, to pursue the argumentation further" (p. 159). Crocker's book is an important contribution to intellectual history, which nobody interested in eighteenth century culture ought to neglect, but it is not a contribution to the history of philosophy.

C. L. Becker's *The Heavenly City of the Eighteenth-Century Philosophers* (1932) has already attracted our attention as a lively and controversial example of intellectual history; Charles Frankel's *The Faith of Reason* (1948) is a slighter but scholarly monograph, of much the same general character as Crocker's *An Age of Crisis*. Frankel quotes Voltaire's dictum that "in the eighteenth century man cried 'all is well' in a mournful tone of voice"; writing as a historian, Henry Vyverberg emphasizes the mournful tone of voice in his *Historical Pessimism in the French Enlightenment* (1958). I. O. Wade's *The Clandestine Organization and Diffusion of Philosophic Ideas in France from 1700 to 1750* (1938) describes in such detail the devious means by which empirical and skeptical doctrines circulated in France that the main outlines of the story— an important one—never firmly emerge.

Of most of the books on individual *philosophes,* a single comment could be made: "interesting to any educated man, but of no special relevance to philosophy." One could spend a considerable time discussing the literature on Voltaire. M. S. Libby's *The Attitude of Voltaire to Magic and the Sciences* (1935) ranges beyond its title into a general study of eighteenth century attitudes to science; I. O. Wade's *Voltaire and Madame Du Châtelet* (1941) is not, as the title might suggest, of purely biographical interest, but has quite a little to say about Voltaire's relations to Newton; his connection with English thought has been brought out by N. L. Torrey—a professor of French—in *Voltaire and the English Deists*

(1930) and his general position described in the same author's *The Spirit of Voltaire* (1938). R. E. Fitch's *Voltaire's Philosophic Procedure* (1935) analyzes his method of thought. Would that so rich a story—although these works, of course, are not all of the same quality—could be told about a philosopher, as distinct from a *philosophe!* But in fact none of these books, even those whose titles might promise otherwise, provide much in the way of sustenance for the historian of philosophy.

A wave of enthusiasm for Diderot has produced a number of books and articles; the essays included in the two volumes of *Diderot Studies* (1949, 1952) include several on Diderot's more philosophical ideas, including one by Leland Thielemann, which makes out a case for the view that Diderot was exceptionally conscious of Hobbes; Crocker (Krakeur) has written a number of essays on Diderot including *Two Diderot Studies: Ethics and Aesthetics* (1952); Aram Vartanian in his *Diderot and Descartes: A Study of Naturalism in the Scientific Enlightenment* (1953) sets out to show in detail that Diderot belonged, in principle, to the Cartesian tradition.

Vartanian conceives his task in an interesting way. He has no illusions about the philosophical powers of Diderot; he thinks of him, primarily, as an ideologist, and the movement from Descartes to Diderot, therefore, as "the historical transition from a philosophy to an ideology" (p. 21). Thus it is not an episode in the history of philosophy as such; it is an episode in the history of human thought in which, as it happens, a philosopher has played an important part. In a manner characteristic of historians of ideas Vartanian places very considerable emphasis on a work which most philosophical commentators have very largely ignored, Descartes's *Recherche de la vérité*. This is not because Vartanian has discovered it to have a previously unperceived philosophical importance but because both in its popular method of presentation and in its general intention—as explained in its full title, *Recherche de la vérité par la lumière naturelle, qui toute pure, et sans emprunter le secours de la religion ni de la philosophie, détermine les opinions que doit avoir un honeste homme . . .* —it foreshadows the main tendencies of the Enlightenment. Vartanian's book is an important contribution to our knowledge of the development of Western culture, insofar as it helps to dispel the view that English sensationalism, rather than Cartesian rationalism, was the source of the French Enlightenment.

The transition from Descartes to Diderot—the growth of the idea of a man machine—has indeed by now been amply illustrated. Reference has already been made to Vartanian's splendid edition of *L'Homme machine,* to Balz's *Cartesian Studies* and to Rosenfield's *From Beast Machine to Man Machine;* one could add to that list Hester Hastings' *Man and Beast in French Thought of the Eighteenth Century* (1936). The French materialists have not otherwise attracted much attention, but there is one book on Helvétius, I. L. Horowitz' *Claude Helvétius: Philosopher of Democracy and Enlightenment* (1954), which takes as its theme Marx's comment that "in Helvétius materialism receives its real French character. He comprehended it at once in its relation to social life." In short, Horowitz passes judgment on Helvétius from a Marxist standpoint, which sees him as representing the progressive social forces of his time but failing to grasp adequately their significance.

Rousseau, perhaps a little oddly, has been less studied than Voltaire and Diderot. The accuracy in detail of C. W. Hendel's *Jean-Jacques Rousseau: Moralist* (1934), which relates the development of Rousseau's ideas up to 1765 to their biographical background, has been impugned, but Hendel has effectively brought out the ways in which Rousseau's ideas responded to changing political and intellectual circumstances. Interest in Montesquieu has been wholly restricted to his politics.

So much for the eighteenth century. Very little, to sum up, on British or German philosophy except what has been produced by modern language departments or historians; quite a lot, some of it relatively important, on the Enlightenment, but belonging to the history of ideas rather than the history of philosophy. The record of nineteenth century studies is scarcely more exciting.

6.   French nineteenth century philosophy played an important role in American thought through its influence on William James; so that commentators on James—most notably R. B. Perry in his *The Thought and Character of William James* (1935)—have devoted some attention to, for example, Renouvier. But in general French

nineteenth century philosophy has not interested philosophical scholars, especially the scholars of the last thirty years. P. P. Hallie's *Maine de Biran: Reformer of Empiricism* (1959) is an exception. This is a careful study of Biran's criticism of British empiricism, which, incidentally, helps to bring out why French interpretations of Berkeley—most recently Sartre's in *L'Etre et le néant*—have so often been both inadequate and misleading: the tradition dates back to Biran. Biran's work is, in important respects, a turning point in the history of French philosophy; Hallie brings out that fact, even if one might quarrel at times with his interpretation of the British empiricists.

M. H. Moore has translated and introduced Cournot's *Essay on the Foundations of Our Knowledge* (1956); and an occasional article or dissertation has taken as its theme some aspect of Cournot's thought—for example, C. T. Ruddick's "Cournot's Doctrine of Philosophical Probability" (*Phil. Rev.*, 1940). Comte's influence on American thought, as we shall see, has been exhaustively investigated; but his own philosophical views have been neglected. Reino Virtanen's *Claud Bernard and His Place in the History of Ideas* (1960) is a brief but somewhat repetitious study of a leading philosopher-scientist, in which the emphasis is on Bernard's influence and personal relationships rather than on the close analysis of his methodological ideas. Even Bergson has latterly been ignored; it is perhaps significant that B. A. Scharfstein in his *Roots of Bergson's Philosophy* (1943) arrives at the conclusion that "although most of his followers would regard this as a paradox, because they have learnt to prize the fertile intuition, he stands out chiefly as a summary and a symbol" (p. 138). Bergson, that is, is being prepared for a place in the history of ideas.

As for nineteenth century British philosophy, that has been almost entirely neglected by recent American scholarship. Even relatively slight articles such as Jack Kaminsky's expository "The Empirical Metaphysics of George Henry Lewes" (*JHI*, 1952) are few and far between. One looks in vain for work on Hamilton, Mansel, Spencer; Huxley, Clifford, Stephen; Grote and Ferrier; Jevons and Venn. A. W. Brown's *The Metaphysical Society* (1947) is one of the few exceptions, and it is concerned with the activities of a society rather than with the arguments of a philosopher, useful as it is in exploring the still surprisingly little-known institutional background of Victorian intellectual life.

Only the British idealists have in some measure escaped this wholesale neglect. Important essays on Coleridge's philosophical ideas include Lovejoy's "Coleridge and Kant's Two Worlds" (1940; now in *Essays in the History of Ideas*) and Rudolf Kagey's "Coleridge" (*Columbia Studies,* vol. 3, 1935). G. W. Cunningham's *The Idealistic Argument in Recent British and American Philosophy* (1933) is a good general introduction to idealist reasoning; and Bradley, unlike Green or Bosanquet or Caird, has not been entirely ignored. A good deal of the work on Bradley, however, has been at the "competent dissertation" level. Rudolf Kagey's *The Growth of F. H. Bradley's Logic* (1931) sets out to show that Bradley gradually developed away from the absolutism of *Appearance and Reality*—a view which has been somewhat critically greeted; R. G. Ross's *Scepticism and Dogma* (1940) sympathetically expounds Bradley's metaphysical ideas. The most important work by an American on Bradley is R. W. Church's *Bradley's Dialectic* (1942), but Church tells us in his preface that the outlines of his book were laid down in England, and certainly there is nothing at all in its character or its controversial references to suggest that it originated in the United States. Church's defense of Bradley shows the influence of the sort of Italian idealism espoused in Oxford by J. A. Smith; but it takes surprisingly little account of the controversial context in which Bradley was writing. Herein it exemplifies the defects of a great deal of British philosophical scholarship; in compensation, it is through-and-through philosophical in spirit.

Nineteenth century Italian philosophy, as represented in Rosmini and Spaventa, has been left to Italian and Spanish scholars. German philosophy has excited a little, but only a little, more interest. R. B. Brandt's *The Philosophy of Schleiermacher* (1941) is an extremely thorough study of a thinker who is rarely taken seriously as a philosopher in Anglo-Saxon countries. Brandt brings out the connection between Schleiermacher's philosophical ideas and his theology, puts him, if not quite sufficiently, in his historical setting, and adds a few brief comments on his influence. He makes no extravagant claims for Schleiermacher and does not attempt to conceal the obscurity and inconsistency of his thinking; in short, his book is a good example of a sober study of a secondary philosopher.

The controversial figure of Nietzsche has aroused as much partisanship in America as elsewhere; much of the work on Nietzsche, as we have already said in discussing Brinton's *Nietzsche* (1941), is of biographical or historical rather than philosophical interest. But G. A. Morgan's *What Nietzsche Means* (1941) attempts to accomplish what is badly needed; he sets out to give a coherent account, so far as that is possible, of Nietzsche's leading philosophical ideas. Whether he has completely succeeded is a matter on which there can be more than one opinion; W. A. Kaufmann in his *Nietzsche: Philosopher, Psychologist, Antichrist* (1950) is critical in important respects of Morgan's interpretation. Kaufmann's *Nietzsche* "aims at a comprehensive reconstruction of Nietzsche's thought and is addressed to the general reader no less than to scholars" (p. vii). His central thesis is that "Nietzsche confronts us primarily as an educator, his primary concern is with the attainment of culture" (p. 365). Not surprisingly, then, Kaufmann's Nietzsche is philosophically a good deal less interesting than Morgan's; the very comprehensiveness of Kaufmann's book, to say nothing of the fact that it is addressed to the general reader somewhat blunts the impression it makes. Nevertheless, Morgan and Kaufmann between them have made a notable contribution to the understanding of Nietzsche.

Schopenhauer, on the other hand, has not recently aroused a great deal of interest, although Israel Knox gives a brief account of his aesthetic views in *The Aesthetic Theories of Kant, Hegel, and Schopenhauer* (1936). There have been two translations of Schelling, J. J. Gutmann's *Of Human Freedom* (1936) and Frederick de Wolfe Bolman's *The Ages of the World* (1942) and an occasional dissertation on Fichte and Schelling. For the most part, however, nineteenth century German metaphysics has been very little studied, except insofar as it has a theological concern.

Husserl is the exception; he has been much read and discussed, although often in a spirit of discipleship rather than a spirit of scholarship; in writing of Husserl we are at the border line which separates scholarship from the ordinary give-and-take of philosophical explanation and controversy. Marvin Farber's *The Foundation of Phenomenology* (1943) includes a paraphrase of the *Logische Untersuchungen* as well as a historical and explanatory study of the general development of Husserl's thought up to those later, more metaphysical stages where Farber is not prepared to follow him. This is in many respects an admirable work of scholarship. Other American works on Husserl include E. P. Welch's *The Philosophy of Edmund Husserl* (1941), which is based on only a partial selection from Husserl's writings, and *Philosophical Essays in Memory of Edmund Husserl* (1940) edited by Farber. But for all this explanation, to say nothing of innumerable articles in *Philosophy and Phenomenological Research,* many philosophers have been wont to complain that what Husserl taught is even more obscure than it was before his disciples began to explain him.

More recently, however, Herbert Spiegelberg has produced a notable two-volume study of *The Phenomenological Movement* (1960) which casts a great deal of light into exceptionally dark places. In part, this book lies outside our province; the second volume wholly concerns itself with contemporary writers, most of them French or German existentialists. The first volume, however, contains admirable studies of Brentano, Stumpf, and Husserl and their relation to phenomenology. Spiegelberg writes not as a partisan, but as a critical adherent, prepared to be frank about gaps and weaknesses; his account of phenomenology is both philosophically interesting and highly informative about the simple historical facts. The adjective "indispensable" has, through overwork, lost much of its original force; for once, however, it can be applied with genuine conviction—for anybody who hopes to understand recent European philosophy, Spiegelberg's *The Phenomenological Movement* is indispensable.

Husserl described Bolzano as "the best of logicians" and Russell referred to him with admiration, but in English there is no study of Bolzano which is at all adequate; H. R. Smart's "Bolzano's Logic" (*Phil. Rev.,* 1944) is, however, a step on the way. Those philosophers whom only a philosopher can hope to understand or to explain are liable to be badly neglected in an atmosphere in which the history of philosophy is left to historians.

Thus, too, of Scandinavian thinkers, only Kierkegaard has been at all seriously considered, and one can reasonably doubt whether he is properly to be described as a philosopher. Walter Lowrie's biographical *Kierkegaard* (1938) and James Collins' *The Mind of Kierkegaard* (1953) at least provide the materials on which a judgment can be made, and Lowrie has done noble work in translating and editing Kierkegaard's difficult and voluminous writings. Collins sets out to discuss the "philosophically relevant aspects of his thought"; he grants that Kierkegaard was neither a philosopher nor a theologian but "belonged to the borderline category of the 'religious thinker.'" Collins goes on to justify his writing a book on Kierkegaard by remarking that "unless it pays due attention to the deliverances of Galileo and Newton, Boehme and Pascal, Shakespeare and Baudelaire, Jefferson and Marx, the history of philosophy is immeasureably impoverished, and tends to shrivel up from excessive inbreeding" (p. ix). This judgment, as will already be apparent, I should wish to combat; philosophy is not, it seems to me, interested in "deliverances" unless they are backed by argument. No doubt something Shakespeare says might set a philosopher's mind moving, and if that fact were known it could be of interest to the historian of philosophy, but to introduce into a history of philosophy a chapter on "the philosophy of Shakespeare" is merely to produce confusion. Galileo and Newton are in a rather different position from Shakespeare and Baudelaire, and so are Jefferson and Marx, insofar as they sometimes argue philosophically. But however firmly one might believe that a philosopher should read widely outside philosophy—and major contributions to philosophy have arisen out of reflection on such "outside reading"— or even that philosophy can "shrivel up from excessive inbreeding," it is quite another matter to conclude that a *history* of philosophy should set out to be a history of thinking. There is no reason why a philosopher, if he is prepared to do the work involved, should not write a general book on Shakespeare, or Baudelaire, or Kierkegaard—a book which particularly emphasized the character of their thinking—but he is not, in so doing, writing a book on a philosopher.

7. When we come nearer to our time, the situation is confused by the fact that scholarly elucidation fades imperceptibly into the

ordinary controversial life of philosophy. Most of the contributors to, for example, P. A. Schilpp's "Library of Living Philosophers" are carrying on an argument with the author about whom they are writing, and they are able to—or believe they are able to—take for granted the sort of background which a scholar ordinarily has to establish. In a sense, the autobiographies in Schilpp's volumes are themselves contributions to the history of philosophy but it would be somewhat embarrassing to press matters so far as to consider them thus. Quite arbitrarily, I shall make no reference to works on philosophers who are still alive, or but recently dead.

In fact, I shall do no more than indicate the early twentieth century European philosophers who have been considered in a scholarly way; the list will not be a long one. So far as British philosophy is concerned, Samuel Alexander is a rare case. There is a continuing interest in Alexander's philosophy in the United States—revealed in such books as J. W. McCarthy's *The Naturalism of Samuel Alexander* (1948) and A. P. Stiernotte's *God and Space-Time in the Philosophy of Alexander* (1954)—as there scarcely is in Great Britain. The same is even more strikingly true of Whitehead; one hardly knows, indeed, whether to call Whitehead a British or an American philosopher, especially as American scholars have so largely concentrated on the metaphysical works which he wrote after he took up his Chair at Harvard in 1924. The volume and range of American scholarly writings on Whitehead is, in the light of the story we have told of gaps and meagerness, nothing short of fantastic. It ranges from scholarly studies like Victor Lowe's "The Development of Whitehead's Philosophy" in *The Philosophy of Alfred North Whitehead* ("Library of Living Philosophers," 1941) to S. L. Ely's *The Religious Availability of Whitehead's God* (1942) by way of books on *The Philosophy of A. N. Whitehead* (D. L. Miller and George V. Gentry, 1938), *Whitehead's Theory of Experience* (E. P. Shahan, 1950), *Whitehead's Theory of Reality* (A. H. Johnson, 1952), *Whitehead's Philosophy of Time* (W. W. Hammerschmidt, 1947), *Whitehead's Philosophical Development* (Nathaniel Lawrence, 1956), and W. A. Christian's *An Interpretation of Whitehead's Metaphysics* (1959). One should add the substantial essays by American scholars in Ivor Leclerc's *The Relevance of Whitehead* (1961) and a long stream of periodical articles. Even briefly to discriminate within, and to discuss, the literature on Whitehead would throw completely out of proportion this whole account of American scholarship—in itself, a quite extraordinary fact. Some of these books, I shall be content to say, are distressingly uncommunicative, some cast a degree of light on their exceedingly, and, indeed, excessively, obscure subject. Without wishing to anticipate the judgment of history, and without sharing the convictions of those who complain if scholars spend any time at all on Whitehead, it is still difficult not to feel that some of this scholarly energy could have been more fruitfully—not to make too sudden a break—diverted to the study of Hegel.

With the exception of Alexander—and Whitehead if one regards him as British—British philosophy of the last half-century has aroused very little scholarly, as distinct from polemical, interest in the United States. There has been some useful work on Russell, but in general one looks rather to Italy or to Scandinavia or to England itself than to the United States for a detailed commentary on British philosophy of the recent past.

Of work on the German existentialists, I shall say nothing, since they are still alive—except to note that the attempt to explain what existentialism is and what Heidegger's philosophy is about has been quite vigorously undertaken in the United States, as in Thomas Langan's not uncritical *The Meaning of Heidegger* (1959). Otto Samuel has written an essay on *A Foundation of Ontology: A Critical Analysis of Nicolai Hartmann* (1954), but otherwise German metaphysics of the early decades of the present century has not been intensively explored, although a recent (1959) volume of essays on George Simmel, edited by K. H. Wolff, does something to introduce the English speaking reader to Simmel's philosophical ideas.

There is, however, one scholarly book on the German—or more accurately the Austrian—antimetaphysicians, J. R. Weinberg's *An Examination of Logical Positivism* (1936). This is a gallant pioneer attempt to analyze critically and historically the teachings of the Vienna positivists—a task difficult enough to bring to successful completion even now, which Weinberg carried out, all things considered, with considerable success.

The Italian idealism of Croce and Gentile has not come in for a great deal of attention. R. A. Caponigri's *History and Liberty*

(1955) concerns itself with Croce the historian rather than with Croce the philosopher. R. W. Holmes's *The Idealism of Giovanni Gentile* (1937), on the other hand, tries to lead us into the very heart of Gentile's philosophy; if the anatomy of that heart is still not wholly clear to us, it would be too severe to judge that Holmes is always at fault.

Of relatively recent French philosophers—excluding, once again, the existentialists—only Meyerson and Duhem have attracted any considerable attention. George Boas' *A Critical Analysis of the Philosophy of Emile Meyerson* (1930) critically examines some of the main themes in *Idéalité et réalité*, but in a manner which would lead one to consider it as a contribution to philosophical controversy rather than to scholarship; T. R. Kelly's *Explanation and Reality in the Philosophy of Emile Meyerson* (1937) brings out, in a more scholarly fashion, the internal tensions in Meyerson's theory of explanation; a number of philosophers have written critical essays on one aspect or another of Meyerson's teachings. Armand Lowinger's *The Methodology of Pierre Duhem* (1941) and Tobias Dantzig's *Henri Poincaré* (1954) usefully contribute—Lowinger's book especially—to our knowledge of an important period in the history of the philosophy of science. But there is still room for a general study of the conventionalist movement of ideas, to say nothing of other movements of thought in the recent past. Scholars tend to call a halt around about 1900; controversialists are only interested in the present or the very immediate past. As a result the recent past is often more obscure to the younger generation of philosophers than is the eighteenth century.

AMERICAN PHILOSOPHY

1. General histories.   2. The secondary philosophers.   3. The major writers.

1. America now has a rich philosophical tradition and, not unnaturally, American scholars have set to work to explore that tradition. From the point of view of the European observer, however, the American philosophical tradition begins, for all practical purposes, in the latter half of the nineteenth century, with Peirce, Royce, James, and Santayana; American scholars, on the other hand, have sought to trace it back to its beginnings in American intellectual life, somewhat as if historians of British philosophy were to begin their story with the Venerable Bede, and include chapters on Thomas More, Wycliffe, Digby, and Temple.

Two general tendencies which we noted in American scholarship are in the case of American studies at their peak: the tendency to engage in justice-doing rescue operations, and the tendency so to extend the limits of philosophy that the history of philosophy comes to be identified with the history of reflection—or at least of such reflections as do not belong to any specialized discipline. To put it crudely, many scholars proceed as if philosophy could be defined as "reflective thinking which is not backed by experimental nor mathematical reasoning, whatever its problems and however little disciplined in argument it might be." That view I have supposed to be mistaken. To put the matter in terms of nineteenth century Great Britain, I have presumed that Carlyle, Ruskin, Browning, and Tennyson were not philosophers, but rather, to appropriate the title of John Holloway's book, Victorian sages.

No such presumption underlies J. L. Blau's anthology *American Philosophic Addresses, 1700-1900* (1946), which is designed to be read as a companion piece to H. W. Schneider's *History of American Philosophy* (1946). Blau has chosen to reprint, he tells us, such addresses as are "a carefully prepared and clearly expressed formulation of a characteristic philosophical position" (p. vii). One can agree that the addresses he includes are "carefully prepared"; such rhetoric comes spontaneously to a very few men. And, in certain cases, one might also agree that the addresses contain a statement of a "philosophical position," in the sense that the position which they state is one at which a philosopher might, after argument, arrive. They state a philosophical position, that is, in the sense in which if I were to insist that the earth is six thousand years old I should be stating a scientific position—affirming a proposition which could conceivably appear at the conclusion of a scientific argument. But whether I was doing science or not would depend on how I went on to support my position, by geological evidence or by scriptural authority. There is occasionally, very occasionally, a little genuine philosophizing in Blau's volume, as in the latter part of Cadwallader Colden's *Introduction to the Study of Philosophy,* but the small ingredient of very minor philosophizing is submerged within seven hundred pages of sententious rhetoric. The working philosopher who finds himself confronted by these addresses will certainly impatiently ask himself what all this has to do with philosophy. Should he already be inclined to believe that the history of philosophy is of no relevance to philosophy, his prejudice will be confirmed. The ordinary reader, for his part, will feel justified in contending that since all men are entitled to have and express opinions, it follows that all men are entitled to describe themselves as philosophers, and that the writing of philosophy involves no more intellectual discipline than is necessary to prepare a reasonably coherent commemoration address, sermon, or leading article.

Schneider's *History of American Philosophy* is quite properly described on its jacket as "a much-needed contribution to the history of American culture—especially American literature, social theory, political theory and religion." Considered from this point of view, it fully deserves, for once, the laudatory description—"this brilliant volume"—which the jacket also applies to it. Well illustrated by quotations, carefully and clearly written, lavishly supplied with bibliographies, Schneider's *History* incorporates a good brief account of what is certainly American *philosophy* within a general history of "American thought." But the non-American reader, at least, is likely to be so overwhelmed by the mass of excessively minor thinkers that the philosophical core of Schneider's *History* will escape him.

The American historian of American philosophy, then, has been particularly unwilling to make a sharp distinction between the history of philosophy and intellectual history. This is true even of so good a philosopher as Morris Cohen. His *American Thought* (1954)—a posthumous publication—is at its lively best as a vigorous critical account of American university life; his summary version of American philosophers is scrappy and inadequate. Were I to accept the general American judgment, then, I should be obliged now to explore and comment on a very considerable literature, most of which makes some reference to what—in the eyes of Schneider and Blau—are certainly philosophers. Schneider himself refers the reader to, for example, S. E. Morison's *Builders of the Bay Colony* (1930) for the account it gives of Winthrop, Shepard, Ward, and Eliot. Books like Perry Miller's *The New England Mind* (1939) come closer to our purpose, insofar as Miller describes the Ramist ingredients in "Puritan philosophy," but Ramus himself is scarcely a major philosopher, and by the time his ideas are diffused through the minds of Puritan preachers whatever was philosophically solid in them has been filtered out.

In a critical notice of Sidney Warren's *American Freethought, 1860-1914* (1943) M. H. Fisch wrote as follows: "Merle Curti in his *Growth of American Thought* has recently provided a synthesis of the background, absorbing the major achievements into it so skilfully that they take on its protective colouring and lose all distinction" (*Phil. Rev.*, 1945, p. 614). This is my own judgment precisely: in such volumes not only the distinction of major writers but even the distinction of philosophy itself quite disappears. Curti, of course, is a historian, not a philosopher, and he admits that he does not "purport to provide an exhaustive analysis of the 'insides' of the ideas and system of thought chosen for consideration" (p. x). To put the matter less politely, ideas as Curti describes them are gutless. I propose to say no more of such histories of "American thought," whether or not they bear the title "American philosophy"; they may, in some case, interest the philosophical scholar, but they are not, in my judgment, examples of philosophical scholarship.

There are one or two books, however, in which the emphasis, so far as can be, is on what is philosophical in America's earlier writers. This is true, for example, of H. G. Townsend's *Philosophical Ideas in the United States* (1934), which concentrates, as to the earlier period, on men like Jonathan Edwards and the St. Louis idealists— philosophers who deserve some measure of commemoration—and brings out the metaphysical ingredients in their thinking. Many, perhaps most, of Townsend's readers will certainly disagree with his sharp judgments, for his book is written from a strongly felt point of view; but at least it is a philosophical book about philosophy, describing in detail philosophy since James and treating American thought before James only as the process through which America was "becoming philosophically literate," rather than as an independent contribution to philosophy.

J. L. Blau's *Men and Movements in American Philosophy* (1952) begins depressingly with the statement that it should be possible "for many Americans to learn to take pride in our philosophical history" because "there has been a 'democratic' quality to American philosophizing; it has grown as much outside of academic circles as it has within the colleges and universities" (p. v). This is depressing for two reasons: first, because it suggests that what happens outside universities is more democratic, and more a source of pride, than what happens inside them, and second, because Blau has apparently failed to realize that the situation he describes is not at all peculiar to American philosophy—Bacon, Hobbes, Locke, Berkeley, Mill were none of them university teachers. This lack of comparison is, indeed, characteristic of Blau's book. The brief account he gives of Locke's philosophy (pp. 10-11) is quite inaccurate; he does not even mention the Cambridge Platonists in connection with Edwards, whom he describes as if he had worked out for himself the doctrines on which he differs from Locke; he fails to indicate that Creighton's variety of idealism is not of his own making—in short, he leaves the reader with no way of telling who were the creative thinkers in American philosophy and who did no more than acclimatize British or German ideas.

2. Non-Americans are sometimes accused by Americans, and sometimes rightly, of exaggerating the degree of uniformity in American life and thought; the emphasis of American historians on intrinsically minor eccentric figures has been most useful, perhaps, as a corrective to the foreigner's rash judgment. But Martha Pingel concludes her preface to *An American Utilitarian: Richard Hildreth as a Philosopher* (1948) with the general observation that "Hildreth was, and still is, as truly an expression of American principles and ideals as any man can ever hope to be" (p. 39). This study of Hildreth is a fairly characteristic piece of justice-doing, providing us with lengthy extracts from the writings of a largely unknown thinker. The extracts show that Hildreth was an intellectually vigorous man, who had read his Bentham and who was prepared to pursue, in the teeth of the society of his time, a fiercely independent line; that he was a philosopher of even minor importance is not, however, demonstrated. Whether, in fact, he expresses "American principles and ideals" it is not for me to say.

The philosopher-banker A. B. Johnson has been resuscitated by David Rynin, who has edited, published, and critically examined his *A Treatise on Language* (1947). Johnson was undoubtedly a philosopher, concerning himself with genuinely philosophical problems and dealing with them in a philosophical way; that he is, as Rynin claims, a major philosopher, is a good deal less certain. One would have liked Rynin to consider more carefully how far the views he ascribes as a novelty to Johnson were present in the writings of such philosophers as Brown and Stewart, to whom Johnson himself refers with respect; to place Johnson we need that information, and it is not easily accessible.

Other resurrected authors include the Texan Edmund Montgomery whose life is described by I. K. Stephens in *The Hermit Philosopher of Liendo* (1950) and whose work is characterized in M. T. Keeton's *The Philosophy of Edmund Montgomery* (1950)— two books which were designed to supplement one another. This philosopher-biologist interested Peirce, but one may doubt whether he has a secure place in the history of philosophy. Jonathan Edwards and Chauncey Wright are figures of much greater importance. The new edition of Edwards edited by Perry Miller will help to bring Edwards' philosophical writings before a wider audience;

the first volume, *Freedom of the Will* (ed. Paul Ramsey, 1957), is particularly important in this respect. It has already provoked, in A. E. Murphy's "Jonathan Edwards on Free Will and Moral Agency" (*Phil. Rev.,* 1959), a fundamental philosophical interpretation of a book which had—as Murphy puts it—"become the shopworn subject of much literary lecturing in a field not notable for precision of thought" (p. 181).

E. H. Madden's selections from the slight and scarce writings of Chauncey Wright (*The Philosophical Writings of Chauncey Wright,* 1958) are equally useful; Madden has industriously written about Wright in a considerable number of articles. Wright is likely always to be a controversial figure, but at least we are now nearer to understanding what he stood for. He also plays a prominent part in P. P. Wiener's *Evolution and the Founders of Pragmatism* (1949). This is an important study of a group of philosophers and jurisprudentialists, and of the effects on their thinking of evolutionary ideas. The theme is a good one, and Wiener develops it thoroughly and effectively; he is not describing the way in which a major idea comes to be diluted by minor thinkers, but rather the way in which a major idea makes an impact upon major thinkers, most of them philosophers in the strictest sense of the word.

On the other hand, R. L. Hawkins is a professor of French, not a philosopher, and his two volumes on American positivism, *Auguste Comte and the United States* (1936) and *Positivism in the United States* (1938), are of scarcely any philosophical interest. In a closely related field, Richard Hofstadter's *Social Darwinism in American Thought* (1944) is, except for a short chapter on the philosophers, wholly concerned with the impact of Darwin upon social and political ideas. Several essays on evolutionary philosophy are included in *Evolutionary Thought in America* (ed. Stow Persons, 1950), although, strangely enough, considering the title of the collection, only one of them, W. F. Quillian's "Evolution and Moral Theory in America," has anything to say about American philosophy in particular. (The names of Wright and Peirce are not to be found in the index.)

Other American philosophers or philosophical movements have come in for some slight measure of scrutiny. G. Watts Cunningham in his *The Idealistic Argument in Recent British and American*

Philosophy (1933) offers a sympathetic examination of idealistic arguments. G. H. Howison has been exhaustively treated, in a biographical and bibliographical sense, in J. W. Buckham and G. M. Stratton's *George Holmes Howison, Philosopher and Teacher* (1934); M. E. Jones's *George Sylvester Morris* (1948) is also biographical; and *William Torrey Harris* (ed. E. L. Schaub, 1936) is the usual collection of miscellaneous essays. One could also refer to articles and books on, for example, the "Vermont transcendentalists," but these have been written by students of literature and by intellectual historians, and may safely be left to be read by them.

G. H. Mead is a much more interesting figure, philosophically speaking, but he is in the Peirce tradition—dark and fragmentary—especially at those points at which the philosopher, as distinct from the psychologist and the sociologist, is likely to find him interesting. Much has been done to edit his scattered lecture notes into the form of books and a number of critics have critically considered, in periodical articles, his "philosophy of the present." One or two introductions to his general thought have also appeared, e.g., G. C. Lee's *George Mead: Philosopher of the Social Individual* (1945) —a segment of a dissertation. But the task of interpreting Mead is a very difficult one, which only a highly skilled philosopher could hope to bring to satisfactory completion. Maurice Natanson's *The Social Dynamics of George H. Mead* (1956) is perhaps the most ambitious English language study of Mead, brief though it is; it looks at Mead as an only partly successful phenomenologist rather than, as is conventional, a "social behaviorist." But he still leaves us puzzled, and perhaps we shall stay puzzled, about central points in Mead's thinking.

3. Commentators on the major American philosophers have shown a strong tendency to concentrate—if one excludes Whitehead—on two men, Peirce and Dewey. James, of course, has not been wholly ignored; no other single work on an American philosopher approaches R. B. Perry's *The Thought and Character of William James* (1935) in its completeness, penetration, and scholarly range, but the center of its interest is biographical, even though the biography emphasizes James's intellectual development. Perry's *In the Spirit of William James* (1938) is a set of reflections on the gen-

eral character of James's thought rather than a scholarly study; C. H. Grattan's *The Three Jameses* (1932) is a fascinating biographical study of one of the most intellectually remarkable families the world has ever known. Apart from occasional articles on such topics as "the right to believe," little else has been written on James; there is certainly room, at least, for a new commentary on *The Principles of Psychology*, especially now that philosophical psychology is experiencing a revival.

Royce, too, has latterly been neglected. Indeed, no American scholar has published studies of Royce to compare in interest and importance with Muirhead's or Marcel's. A number of anthologies from his works or collections of his essays have been published. D. S. Robinson has edited his *Logical Essays* (1951), S. G. Brown —interestingly enough, a Professor of Citizenship and American Culture, not a philosopher—has prepared two volumes of selections as *The Social Philosophy of Josiah Royce* (1950) and *The Religious Philosophy of Josiah Royce* (1952). Not even the patriotic appeal implicit in D. S. Robinson's article on "Josiah Royce—California's Gift to Philosophy" (*Personalist*, 1950) has provoked any substantial interest in Royce's logicometaphysical ideas, although scholars have produced rather slight studies of Royce's social theories (as in J. E. Smith's *Royce's Social Infinite*, 1950) and his theory of the self (as in J. H. Cotton's *Royce on the Human Self*, 1954). The special number of the *Journal of Philosophy* (1956) devoted to Royce is as uneven, discontinuous, scrappy, and generally unsatisfactory as are most such special numbers—or, indeed, commemorative volumes—written, it is clear, from a sense of duty rather than from an inner impulse.

The idea which lies behind commemorative volumes, I take it, is that each contributor should discuss some special "aspect" of the commemorated philosopher's work; in that respect, they are the ultimate outcome of the general American emphasis on specialization. Writing to the secretary of the Peirce Society, Lovejoy expressed the opinion, with which one may well agree, that Peirce's "philosophy *as a whole* or system (which we certainly conceive it to be) has never been subjected to a sufficiently methodical and searching criticism" and went on to suggest—by what, I should say, is a manifest non sequitur—that "what is needed, then, is the preparation of a cooperative volume." The outcome of this suggestion was *Studies in the Philosophy of Charles Sanders Peirce* (1952), edited by P. P. Wiener and F. H. Young. It is, on the face of it, a strange notion that a man's philosophy can best be studied as a whole by persuading a long series of interpreters—there are twenty-four contributors to this volume—to write essays on some aspect of it, so that, for example, an article by I. S. Stearns on "Firstness, Secondness and Thirdness" is followed by an article by H. W. Schneider on "Fourthness." The sudden transitions of style and method from one essay to another inevitably have the effect of increasing, rather than diminishing, the fragmentary effect of Peirce's philosophy. No doubt an interpreter who tries to cope with the whole extent of Peirce's work will sometimes go badly astray, but we may possibly come to understand Peirce by reading a series of attempts to come to terms with his philosophy, even if no one of them is quite successful. All we can do with the Wiener-Young volume is to consult it for detailed information on a particular point; from that narrower point of view a good many of the essays are undoubtedly of high quality.

Fortunately, in Peirce's case, one can also refer to more continuous and substantial studies; quite properly, his elusive but undeniable genius has aroused a considerable degree of scholarly interest, inside as well as outside the United States. He is one of those philosophers, like Kant, whom different commentators will read in very different ways, according as they value this or that side of his philosophizing. That fact comes out with particular clarity in a controversy (*Journal of Philosophy*, 1940) between Paul Weiss and Justus Buchler, both of them serious students of Peirce, on the degree to which Peirce's more metaphysical utterances are "essential" to his system. Buchler's *Charles Peirce's Empiricism* (1939) is wholly concerned with Peirce the empiricist. Peirce's empiricism, Buchler argues "can stand on its own feet as a self-sufficient philosophy" (p. x); Buchler helps it to do so, by a careful and critical elucidative analysis. Manley Thompson in *The Pragmatic Philosophy of C. S. Peirce* (1953) sets out to show—as "an essential propaedeutic to the determination of Peirce's place in the history of ideas and to any evaluation of his contribution to specific issues" (p. xvii)—that pragmatic modes of thinking are continuous throughout the development of Peirce's philosophy. On the other hand, James Feibleman, in his *An Introduction to Peirce's Philosophy, Interpreted as a System* (1946), succeeds in finding a metaphysical and ethical system in Peirce by adopting a somewhat startling principle of scholarly interpretation: "Where statements conflict (and this situation is not at all uncommon) a choice has been made of the one which is most consistent with his [Peirce's] leading principles and the others abandoned" (p. xix).

Peirce is very much a philosopher's philosopher. John Dewey in contrast, is, to take over the title of a volume of commemorative essays (1940), "the philosopher of the Common Man," combining in one person the roles of metaphysician and sage. Much of the literature on Dewey is written by nonphilosophers and is of very slight philosophical interest: into that class falls, for example, the volume of addresses *John Dewey: The Man and His Philosophy* (1930), introduced by H. W. Holmes. The symposium edited by Sidney Hook on *John Dewey: Philosopher of Science and Freedom* (1950) is in a rather different position; it contains a number of essays of philosophical importance, and one or two which are also of scholarly interest. M. G. White's *The Origins of Dewey's Instrumentalism* (1943) is a good example of a work which is illuminating in both a scholarly and a philosophical sense; by bringing out the Hegelian roots of Dewey's thinking, it helps to make intelligible what is wholly puzzling if we approach Dewey with the presumption that he was a disciple of James. A number of volumes of selections, such as Irwin Edman's *John Dewey: His Contribution to the American Tradition* (1955) and Joseph Ratner's *Intelligence in the Modern World* (1939), have done something to make Dewey's work more accessible. But the fact remains that Dewey's great American reputation is still a mystery to the philosophical world outside the United States, and more especially in England. No Englishman has written, or is likely to write, about Dewey as Gallie has written about Peirce; Bertrand Russell is the only Englishman to contribute—in a highly critical essay—to P. A. Schilpp's *The Philosophy of John Dewey* (1939). Russell begins by remarking that "Dewey is the foremost representative of a philosophy which, whether one accepts or rejects it, must undoubtedly be judged to have great importance as a social phenomenon" (p. 137);

many British philosophers would think of Dewey's American reputation as a puzzling form of intellectual aberration, sociologically intelligible but philosophically mysterious, especially as he is well spoken of and seriously discussed by American philosophers about whose ability there is no question.

Nobody has yet written a clear coherent account of Dewey's logical and metaphysical views which might persuade Dewey's critics that they are wrong. Neither H. S. Thayer's *The Logic of Pragmatism: An Examination of John Dewey's Logic* (1952) nor Sidney Hook's *John Dewey: An Intellectual Portrait* (1939) nor G. R. Geiger's *John Dewey in Perspective* (1958) nor Jerome Nathanson's *John Dewey* (1951) supplies what is needed. A commentator on Dewey must combine passionate concern and cool judgment. He must possess historical insight to appreciate the problems from which Dewey set out, and a good understanding of the contemporary philosophical scene in order to understand just why what Dewey says is, to so many philosophers, quite unintelligible. Hook and Geiger stand too close to Dewey to see the problems of interpreting him, and their work is only a sketch; Thayer's work is a substantial piece of philosophical criticism, but does nothing to set Dewey in his historical context.

No one doubts, however, that Dewey is a philosopher; the question, only, is whether he is a good one. In Santayana's case, the doubt cuts deeper; whether with his distaste for and neglect of argument he should not be regarded as a remarkably penetrating sage rather than as a philosopher. Once again, the task of interpreting him has been wholly left to Americans; once again the record of their interpretations is not a wholly satisfactory one. A volume on *The Philosophy of George Santayana* (ed. P. A. Schilpp, 1940) in the "Library of Living Philosophers" and a special number of the *Journal of Philosophy* (1954) contain the usual array of articles, some well informed and illuminating, others, in a bad sense, obvious *pièces d'occasion*. A number of critical articles have brought out the manifold conflicts of purpose and doctrine within Santayana's writings: one may mention J. H. Randall's "The Latent Idealism of a Materialist," S. P. Lamprecht's "Naturalism and Agnosticism in Santayana," Justus Buchler's "*One* Santayana or Two" (*Journal of Philosophy*, 1931, 1933, 1954). Santayana's diverse intentions are also the theme of Milton Munitz' *The Moral Philosophy of Santayana* (1939), in which Munitz detects within Santayana's moral philosophy a worldly humane strain and an unworldly ascetic strain. For Munitz it is the naturalistic and humanistic side of Santayana's thought on which his reputation as a philosopher must depend—"for the rest, it [his philosophy] may be appreciated as a work of the imagination" (p. 104). This is, indeed, the general view of American expositors of Santayana, most of whom are a good deal more interested in *The Life of Reason* than in, especially, *The Realm of Essence*. Richard Butler's *The Mind of Santayana* (1956) is at one with them insofar as he describes essentialism as "a speculative luxury for Romanticists," but his curious book—a strange mixture of personal anecdotes, elementary information and weirdly phrased "explanations"—"The clenched mind, closed to the claim of fact, is prised persistently by one unavoidable pressure" (p. 64)—is mainly directed against "a philosophical structure that is composed of an impossible scepticism, an unnatural transcendentalism, and an irrational presupposition of materialism" (p. xi). G. W. Howgate's *George Santayana* (1938) is a kind of philosophical and literary biography; Willard Arnett's *Santayana and the Sense of Beauty* (1955) brings out the influence of Santayana's aesthetic outlook on his later, more metaphysical, writings.

To sum up, American philosophy has in a sense been very extensively written about; a great many not unjustifiably dusty works have been taken down from the shelves and discovered to have a place in "the development of American thought," but there is still room for careful formal studies of what has come to be called "the classic period in American philosophy." These studies, however, will have to be undertaken by historically minded philosophers, not by intellectual historians, if the philosophical importance of the "classic" philosophers is to be adequately brought out and their place in the history of philosophy more firmly fixed. Thanks to the work of the intellectual historians, we are now in a better position to understand and depict the intellectual environment in which the "classical" American philosophers lived and worked—or at least that segment of their environment which was represented in the intellectual life of the United States—but their own character as independent contributors to Western philosophy has still to be accurately delineated.

METAPHYSICS

MANLEY THOMPSON

PROFESSOR OF PHILOSOPHY
UNIVERSITY OF CHICAGO

INTRODUCTION

In bookstores and libraries one is likely to find the single heading "Metaphysics and the Occult," but hardly the heading "Metaphysics and Science." Literary critics and intellectual historians may devote considerable attention to metaphysical poets, artists, and theologians, but not to metaphysical scientists. If the word "metaphysical" occurs in present-day scientific literature it is almost surely to be for the sake of branding some theory, hypothesis, or entity "scientifically unacceptable"—not "unacceptable" in the sense of "too controversial" or "insufficiently established by all available evidence," but "unacceptable" in the fundamental sense of "unscientific in principle because incapable of either confirmation or disconfirmation by any recognized scientific procedure." American philosophy from 1930 to 1960 has acknowledged this common dissociation of the terms "metaphysics" and "science" and yet has continued to associate them. The relation between the endeavors signified by the two terms is a frequent topic in the philosophical literature of the period and in philosophy courses offered by colleges and universities. While the phrase "metaphysics and science" is rare in the catalogs of booksellers and librarians, it often occurs in the description of the contents or even as the title of a philosophy course. Yet it is fairly certain that in any such course it is acknowledged that metaphysics is not a science in the current sense of "science" and is not established by currently recognized methods of science, even though it may be something presupposed by science.

Any discussion of metaphysics as a respectable part of philosophy must begin by isolating what is properly called "metaphysics" and distinguishing it from the rest of philosophy. This is an indispensable first step without which a discussion of metaphysics could very well turn out to be a discussion of philosophy generally, or even primarily of parts of philosophy which can be distinguished from metaphysics. The trouble is that many questions and problems which are properly assigned to other parts of philosophy are also frequently taken as metaphysical and discussed in treatises on metaphysics. The question, for example, of whether we can know physical objects or only our own perceptions is a stock illustration of an epistemological question, although it may also be the central issue in a work purportedly on metaphysics. "Can goodness be an objective quality of an action?" is readily assigned to ethics but has often been discussed as a problem to be settled by metaphysics. "Is the distinction between cause and effect determined by an order in nature or merely by what we choose to regard as the independent variable?" falls equally well under what is now called "philosophy of science" and what is still called "metaphysics." "Must every proposition have a subject and predicate?" is answered by most logicians of our period on grounds which they take as purely logical and in no need of support from metaphysics, yet those who still call themselves "metaphysicians" may claim that this question too is one for which their study alone can provide the final answer.

We can succeed in isolating metaphysics only if we can locate questions which belong indisputably to it and not to any other part of philosophy. We may then account for the tendency of metaphysical speculation to appropriate problems belonging to other parts of philosophy if we can show that the questions which belong only to metaphysics are so general that in answering them one is also answering (or seems to be answering) questions which are proper to epistemology, ethics, the philosophy of science, or logic. It is not difficult, at least at the verbal level, to find questions which belong to metaphysics alone if they belong to any part of philosophy. One need go no further than the opening chapters of a work that must be given a central role in any discussion of the metaphysical literature of our period. I mean the late A. N. Whitehead's monumental *Process and Reality,* first published in 1929. After the introduction, Whitehead commences in the second chapter to unfold the "categorial scheme" which forms the structure of his elaborate metaphysical system. The unfolding begins with the sentence " 'Actual entities'—also termed 'actual occasions'—are the final real things of which the world is made up." Verbally this constitutes an answer to the question "What are the final real things of which the world is made up?"

If this question is accepted as proper to philosophy, it can only be assigned to metaphysics—to what has also traditionally been called "first philosophy." Ethicists and logicians can readily claim that the question forms no part of their special concerns. The epistemologist may be expected to tell us whether we can or cannot be said to know physical objects as well as our own perceptions, but as epistemologist he is not required to affirm or deny that either or both of these constitute the final real things of which the world is made up. The philosophy of science may seem especially concerned with the question of the final real things, since science itself seems to be concerned with them. In popular accounts of science, one is likely to be told that scientists from the Greek atomists to present-day nuclear physicists have been searching for the final real things of which the world is made up. Yet the search of the scientists is not the same as the search of the metaphysicians. The difference becomes apparent if we note the effect of placing the adjective "physical" before "world" in our original question. This addition means little or nothing to the physicist. It is a trivial truism to say that the physicist or physical cosmologist is seeking the final real things of which the physical world is made up. Why bother to add "physical," since who would think that the physicist as physicist is concerned with any world but the physical world? Yet the addition of "physical" is of extreme importance for the metaphysician. He cannot accept this addition without committing himself to a particular metaphysical position, since, unlike the physicist, the metaphysician cannot admit that there may be reality not included in the world which he studies.

If one were to object to the physicist that his theories do not account for human freedom, for human suffering, for man's faith in God, the physicist can reply quite properly that such matters are beyond the scope of his inquiry. Whether at some time in the remote future physics will have advanced to the point where it can be shown that man's physical nature compels him to maintain that he is free, compels him to suffer, and to have faith in God, or whether this side of human nature can never be accounted for by physics, is a question which does not concern the physicist at any point in his inquiry. His job is simply to develop his theories as best he can without attempting to decide beforehand what the theories can and what they cannot account for in their final development.

But the metaphysician, on the contrary, is committed at the outset to the development of theories which account for everything—for a world which includes all the reality there is. To characterize metaphysics as a quest for the final real things of which the *physical* world is made up is to adopt the metaphysical position traditionally known as "materialism," which holds that all final real things are physical things. The defense of this position is then the special job of the metaphysician; the actual determination of the final real things of the physical world may be left to the physicist. The crucial point is that the metaphysician at the very start goes beyond anything the physicist says about the physical world. It is always as metaphysician and not as physicist that one tries to show that the physical world includes all reality.

The philosophy of science and metaphysics thus differ in that the former need say nothing about the world which is not said or implied by science itself. The philosopher of science attempts to analyze and thereby to clarify the concepts and methods actually employed by scientists. If on the basis of his analysis he maintains, for example, that cause and effect are distinguished only by our choice of an independent variable and not by an order in nature, he may claim to be asserting nothing about the world except what is in fact already, if only implicitly, asserted by science. The metaphysician may take the same view of cause and effect, but as metaphysician he presents the view as resulting from an account of the final real things in the world rather than from an analysis of what science itself has already asserted or presupposed. The difference is easily obscured, but it is just as great as the difference between physics and metaphysics. The philosopher of science like the physicist can remain skeptical toward or even flatly deny the possibility of a single rational system which determines the final real things—the ultimately real for science, poetry, art, theology, and every other phase of human activity. Yet the construction of such a system is precisely the aim of metaphysics.

The distinction between metaphysics and the other parts of philosophy is especially important for understanding the philosophical literature written in the United States during the past thirty years. A sizeable and influential portion of this literature contains outright attacks on the possibility of metaphysics. It would be a fatal misunderstanding to construe these attacks as directed against the possibility of philosophy itself. The metaphysician in his quest for the final real things of which the world is made up is almost inevitably led to pronouncements on the knowability, goodness, and rationality of what is ultimately real, and he thus appears to be answering questions which are proper to epistemology, ethics, logic, or the philosophy of science. Yet this does not mean that one who rejects the quest of the metaphysician as meaningless must also similarly reject all the questions belonging to the rest of philosophy. To ask what things are knowable, good, or determinative of rational order is not also to ask what things are the final realities of which the world is made up. This last question belongs exclusively to the inquiry of the metaphysician and not to every inquiry which would usually be called "philosophical."

One final remark about the relation between metaphysics and the rest of philosophy seems in order at this point. It has been held that metaphysics is unavoidable, that everyone has a metaphysics whether he knows it or not. To deny the possibility of metaphysics is from this point of view to adopt a particular metaphysics. Needless to say this is a point of view shared only by those who themselves claim to have a metaphysics, and it is possible only with a latitude in the use of the term which is by no means sanctioned by all metaphysicians. It is like the contention that even atheism must be a religion. Something will be said about this point of view later in this essay, and it is mentioned here only to call attention to the fact that the characterization of metaphysics given thus far is not strictly in accord with the widest use which the term sometimes acquires in contemporary philosophy. Later there will be occasion to distinguish between presenting a metaphysics and presenting a view of the world, a Weltanschauung, or a philosophy of life. This distinction is possible when "metaphysics" is understood as already indicated, but hardly possible if metaphysics, like a philosophy of life, is something which everyone may be said to have.

The philosophical literature falling within the scope of this essay divides roughly (and with important qualifications to be added later) into four main types. There are first those works, like Whitehead's *Process and Reality,* which claim to present a metaphysics, to undertake the formulation of ultimate generalities—generalities which concern the final real things of which the world is made up. In opposition to these works are those which offer theories about attempts to formulate ultimate generalities, theories which allege the limited success or total lack of success of all such attempts. Again, there are works which, though they disavow any attempt at ultimate generalities, may still be called "metaphysical" in a broad sense because their primary concern is to present a view of the world—to uncover the ultimate presuppositions we make about the world. Finally, there are works which try to dispose of or to solve philosophical problems through an analysis of the language used in the formulation of the problems. These four types of philosophical literature are considered in the order mentioned in the four chapters which follow.

This way of classifying the literature focuses attention primarily on ways of conceiving the task of metaphysics rather than on ways of dealing with specific metaphysical issues. Such an approach is to some extent justified by the fact that discussions of the nature and the possibility of metaphysical inquiry fill more pages in the literature of our period than of any other in the history of philosophy. But the approach is fully justified only if these discussions have contributed significantly to the clarification of metaphysical issues and are not to be dismissed as symptoms of an age so preoccupied with natural science as to have lost touch with the metaphysical wisdom of the past. As I take this view of the discussions I feel justified in the approach, but then I am obliged to warn the reader that my essay is in its way as biased as it would be if I had written throughout as a partisan of one of the systems of speculative metaphysics I discuss. In particular my approach has led me to devote a fair amount of space to some philosophers only because they have written rather extensively, if not always profoundly, on the nature of metaphysics and to slight others who have much to say of importance on specific issues. While I have always tried to indicate this bias at the relevant places in the essay, it seems appropriate to close the introduction with an explicit statement of the general point.

METAPHYSICS AS SPECULATIVE PHILOSOPHY

1. The meaning of "speculative philosophy." 2. The problem of evidence. 3. The support of science. 4. The support of special appeal. 5. The support of rationalistic arguments. 6. The support of the inclusiveness of a system. 7. The goal of human reason.

1. *The meaning of "speculative philosophy."* In the preface to *Process and Reality*[1] Whitehead lists nine "prevalent habits of thought" which are "repudiated" in his philosophy. The first of these habits is "the distrust of speculative philosophy." The importance of this repudiation for Whitehead's undertaking is obvious from the discussion in his opening chapter, which bears the title "Speculative Philosophy." The sort of position Whitehead wished to repudiate is also obvious from the opening chapter of another work, *Mind and the World-Order*,[2] which appeared in the same year as *Process and Reality* and which was written by Whitehead's distinguished Harvard colleague, C. I. Lewis. Whitehead is in full agreement with Lewis's contention that "metaphysics studies the nature of reality in general" (*MWO*, p. 4),[3] but he is in radical disagreement with Lewis concerning the method proper to such a study.

Whitehead speaks of his method as "the method of generalization." The main contrasting method is "the method of difference," a procedure which presupposes that discriminations can be fixed prior to an inquiry without prejudicing the results of the inquiry. We do not, for example, prejudice the outcome when we determine the effectiveness of a vaccine by the difference between those who

---

[1] A. N. Whitehead, *Process and Reality* (Macmillan, 1929). Abbreviation, *PR*.
[2] C. I. Lewis, *Mind and the World-Order* (Scribner, 1929). Abbreviation, *MWO*.
[3] When an abbreviation for the title of a work is given in a footnote, references to that work will thereafter be given in the text, using the abbreviation.

have and those who have not been inoculated, though we adopt this difference as the criterion before we begin the inquiry. The point is that the difference in this case is independent of any assumptions about what is to be recognized as an effect of the vaccine. But we obviously prejudice the outcome when we determine the effects of gravity by the difference between the motions of celestial and terrestrial bodies, since the difference in this case depends on assumptions about what is to be recognized as an effect of gravity. The "rigid empiricism" of the method of difference "collapses," Whitehead contends, whenever we seek "the larger generalities." The latter call for "the play of a free imagination, controlled by the requirements of coherence and logic" (*PR*, p. 7). The imaginative construction, however, "must have its origin in the generalization of particular factors discerned in particular topics of human interest" (*ibid.*), and "the success of the imaginative experiment is always to be tested by the applicability of its results beyond the restricted locus from which it originated" (*PR*, p. 8). Thus, the generalization that all bodies are subject to gravitational attraction may have had its origin in Galileo's experiments with falling bodies, and the success of the generalization was then tested by its applicability to the motions of celestial as well as terrestrial bodies. But if scientists after Aristotle had insisted on pursuing only the method of difference, they would never have been able to break away from the Aristotelian doctrine that terrestrial motions alone are effects of gravity.

The foregoing examples are not Whitehead's, but they illustrate the sort of thing he seems to have meant by "the method of generalization." This method is not only the one used largely in the development of physics; it is also the one used exclusively in the development of metaphysics, where ultimate generalities are sought. "Philosophical generalization," Whitehead explains, is "the utilization of specific notions, applying to a restricted group of facts, for the divination of the generic notions which apply to all facts" (*ibid.*). Initially the hypothesis of universal gravitation was of course speculative, but gradually it ceased to be so as Newton and others systematized the relevant generalizations and made precise the conditions of their application. The generalizations of metaphysics, on the other hand, were not only speculative at the start but seem to have remained so. Whitehead gives little indication of hope for a metaphysics that is other than speculative, and his use of the label "speculative philosophy" for his own endeavors is clear indication of the claims he wishes to make for the latter. He often speaks as though metaphysics could never be anything but speculative, as when he declares: "Philosophers can never hope finally to formulate these metaphysical first principles. Weakness of insight and deficiencies of language stand in the way inexorably" (*PR*, p. 6). Yet he also makes it clear that we may hope for progress in metaphysics—progress which, if it will never entirely remove metaphysics from the realm of speculation, will at least advance us to closer approximations of the true ultimate generalities. At times he speaks of this progress in terms which could also be used to characterize progress in science, as when he says that it is "the purpose of research to conciliate the differences" among rival metaphysical systems which are "inconsistent among themselves," "each with its own merits and its own failures" (*PR*, p. 12).

An enumeration of the ways in which metaphysics for Whitehead is like and unlike science is far too complicated a matter for the present discussion, but there is the one likeness which stands out clearly and is crucial for any discussion of his philosophy. Metaphysics and science both seek knowledge of the actual world by the method of generalization. *Process and Reality* bears the subtitle *An Essay in Cosmology*. While Whitehead clearly does not mean only or primarily the sort of thing which physicists today call cosmology, he seems to mean something which differs from this only in the form and extent of its generality. Cosmology for him goes well beyond what can be said of the universe as a whole in terms of the most advanced physical science; it must recognize aesthetic, moral, and religious values as ingredients of the cosmos. Yet like the cosmology of the physicist it remains an account of the actual world. These remarks suggest that for Whitehead metaphysics and science differ mainly in degree of generality, but the suggestion is misleading. For one is thus led to expect that since the generalizations of metaphysics are the widest in scope they are also the most abstract, so that we must depend on the special sciences for an account of the world in its concreteness; yet the reverse is the case with Whitehead. Metaphysics alone is capable of accounting for the world in its full concreteness. An explanation of this point is impossible without a detailed consideration of Whitehead's complicated doctrine of abstraction, but such an explanation is unnecessary for the basic point that science and metaphysics alike seek knowledge of the actual world by the method of generalization.

According to Lewis the method of philosophy is best characterized as "critical" and "reflective," since the problems of philosophy call for criticism and reflection as opposed to speculation. Lewis admits that the term "metaphysics" is applied with some justification "to those cosmological and ontological problems" which have a "partly speculative and partly critical character" (*MWO*, p. 7). But insofar as the problems are speculative, they concern "undetermined scientific fact" rather than philosophy (*ibid.*), and for their solution "we can do nothing but wait upon the progress of the special sciences" (*MWO*, p. 8). "Speculative" philosophy for Lewis, then, is simply not philosophy at all, and if at times his remarks imply distrust of speculation, he makes it clear that he does not mean to imply distrust of philosophy. After cautioning that we must wait upon the progress of the special sciences, he adds: "Or if speculate we must, at least such speculation is in no special sense the philosopher's affair" (*MWO*, p. 4).

In the preface to *Process and Reality* Whitehead observes that "in the main" his philosophy "is a recurrence to pre-Kantian modes of thought," [4] and Lewis's restriction of philosophy to criticism and reflection is obviously post-Kantian. The metaphysician's quest for the final real things of which the world is made up is reformulated in Kantian modes of thought as a quest for the final categories of thought and language. The metaphysician is then (if he is still called a metaphysician and not simply a critical or analytical philosopher) not in search of generalizations which apply to the actual world in its full concreteness. If he is said to seek generalizations at all (rather than the structure of thought and language) they are formal and not material. That is, they are generalizations which express structural patterns to which rational thought or discourse

---

[4] For Whitehead, Kant's attempt to make criticism and reflection concerning thought and language take the place of speculation about ultimate reality leads inevitably to some form of subjectivism. Thus, Whitehead repudiates what he calls "the Kantian doctrine of the objective world as a construct from subjective experience" (*PR*, p. 237). It will be argued in later chapters of this essay that the important issue here is not that of subjectivism.

must conform whatever its content. The term "speculative philosophy" is generally associated with the Hegelian tradition and is thus historically post-Kantian,[5] but inasmuch as it reflects Hegel's opposition to the radical separation of form and content initiated by Kant, Whitehead is speaking quite accurately when he calls his own philosophy "speculative" and "in the main pre-Kantian." For Whitehead as for Aristotle, Leibniz, and other traditional metaphysicians, the generalizations of metaphysics concern the ultimate content of the actual world as well as the form of any discourse about it.

Lewis's *Mind and the World-Order* belongs with the literature to be considered in a later chapter, and it has been mentioned here only to help bring out the significance of the term "speculative philosophy" as Whitehead uses it. The remainder of this chapter will be concerned with metaphysical writings like *Process and Reality* which are speculative in the sense just indicated. Unless otherwise specified, "metaphysics" is used in this chapter as a synonym for "speculative philosophy."

2. *The problem of evidence.* Speculative philosophy since its beginning in Greek cosmology has been distinguished by the radical disagreement of its practitioners. By the time of Kant it was apparent that agreement had been reached only in those areas of investigation which had ceased to be speculative and had become established branches of mathematics or natural science. It is apparent today that the important difference in this respect between science and metaphysics is not the extent of agreement but the circumstances within which agreement is sought. Turning from the method of difference to the method of generalization (to use Whitehead's terms) does not mean in the practice of science calling into question all the circumstances in which agreement is sought. While the seventeenth century physicists, who looked for the effects of gravity in celestial as well as terrestrial motions, may be said to have called into question the circumstances in which Aristotelian

---

[5] Medieval philosophers usually referred to Aristotle's theoretic sciences, metaphysics, mathematics, and natural science, as *scientiae speculativae,* and the use of "speculative" as a synonym for "theoretic" is common today among neo-Thomistic writers. This use of "speculative" is not to be confused with its post-Kantian use in this essay, where it serves to distinguish metaphysics from mathematics and natural science.

physicists had sought agreement on the effects of gravity, the important thing is that prior to their inquiry the new physicists found new circumstances in which to seek agreement. Science cannot advance by the method of generalization so long as the circumstances in which generalizations might be tested are in dispute. Scientists in practice take it for granted that such factors as particular instruments, specimens, data sheets, operations, and techniques define circumstances within which they seek agreement. If the admissibility of some of these factors is questioned, the issue can be resolved only by turning to those circumstances which are recognized without question. Without some such circumstances there is not even a scientific issue. In short, scientists always seek agreement within circumstances and never give themselves up entirely to disputes concerning what circumstances must be recognized as those within which to seek agreement. Yet major disputes among metaphysicians are perforce of the latter sort. In the metaphysical quest for the final real things of which the world is made up, there are no instruments, techniques, operations, or data which, prior to the inquiry itself, define circumstances within which rather than material about which agreement is to be sought. Each metaphysical system defines for itself the circumstances within which all metaphysical systems are to be tested, so that proponents of rival systems can hardly expect to find circumstances within which they can seek agreement without prejudice to the issues. The metaphysician is thus confronted with a unique problem, unlike any faced by the scientist, when he tries to convince his fellow metaphysicians of the plausibility, truth, and evidence of his own system.

This problem of giving evidence for a metaphysical system is at least one problem common to all speculative philosophers and one which readily becomes central in any discussion of the diverse metaphysical literature of a period. It will emerge in its various aspects as the central problem throughout the remainder of this essay.

3. *The support of science.* The metaphysics presented in Whitehead's *Process and Reality* is original and unique in many respects, but perhaps the most impressive point is the extent to which Whitehead's metaphysics evinces an intimate knowledge of contemporary

physics. With a few notable exceptions (such as C. S. Peirce and Josiah Royce) the speculative philosophers in the United States during the first quarter of the present century had little or no first-hand acquaintance with science. They continued an idealistic and primarily Hegelian tradition and remained, as Peirce had characterized them in the nineteenth century, "seminary" rather than "laboratory" philosophers. By and large the scientifically minded philosophers were associated (as was indeed Peirce himself for the most part) with antimetaphysical movements—with various forms of empiricism, positivism, and pragmatism. As the twentieth century advanced these movements threatened to take over the main stream of American philosophy, and by 1929 Whitehead had "the distrust of speculative philosophy" first on the list of "prevalent habits of thought" which he wished to reject.

Process and Reality promised new life for the waning cause of speculative philosophy. Here was a book boldly speculative and metaphysical in its undertaking and yet written by a man already distinguished as a mathematician, philosopher of science, and logician—a book which professed to follow the very method so essential in the development of the sciences themselves, the method of generalization. Here indeed was an elaborate system of speculative philosophy with impressive credentials of scientific respectability. While these credentials can hardly be taken as positive evidence for the truth of the system, it seems difficult at first to dismiss them as entirely irrelevant to the question of evidence. According to W. E. Hocking, one of Whitehead's Harvard colleagues who joined him in repudiating the distrust of speculative philosophy: "Every future philosophic era will be, like our modern era, for better or for worse 'scientific' in the sense that whatever science reveals belongs integrally to the philosophical world picture." [6] Metaphysical generalizations which fail to integrate the latest findings of science can never, it would seem, be wholly adequate expressions of metaphysical truth. Insofar as Whitehead's metaphysical generalizations achieve this integration more completely than any others they appear to be more true and adequate.

But unfortunately, the matter is by no means so simple as these

[6] In the foreword to *Reality as Social Process,* by Charles Hartshorne (Free Press of Glencoe, 1953), p. 12.

139

remarks suggest. Hocking continues in the next sentence after the one just quoted: "But the era now opening has the special task of putting science into its place. . . . But to put science into its place requires a *pou sto* beyond science: that is the task of metaphysics." In achieving this task metaphysics of course ceases to be a science— it must venture into the no man's land outside the circumstances in which scientists themselves work and seek agreement. In *Process and Reality* and later writings Whitehead gives many descriptions of this metaphysical task; one of the most concise descriptions and one which clearly points up the central features of his position occurs in the closing remarks of his lecture "Mathematics and the Good," delivered at Harvard in 1939. "The basis of science," he explains, is an "order of abstraction whereby finite constituents of the actual thing are abstracted from that thing." The lecture closes with the sentences "The task of philosophy is to reverse this process and thus to exhibit the fusion of analysis with actuality. It follows that philosophy is not a science."[7] While metaphysics pursues the method of generalization its aim is not, as in science, the abstraction of finite constituents from the infinite complexity of actual things. On the contrary, metaphysics seeks generalizations which direct the mind back to a grasp of each actual thing in its full concreteness, in all its infinite variety. It is only with this grasp of complete actuality that the mind can succeed in putting science into its place.

If the task of metaphysics is conceived in this manner, it is misleading to speak of metaphysical generalizations as integrating the latest findings of science. What is sought is not an integration within science which interrelates the various fields of science, but an integration outside science which puts science as such into its place, however diverse its varieties, and opposes it to true metaphysical knowledge which alone can lay claim to a grasp of ultimate reality. But then the extent to which this metaphysical integration requires detailed knowledge of and firsthand acquaintance with the latest findings of science remains problematic. One may even claim that such knowledge and acquaintance constitutes a block to metaphysical understanding because the more a man is

[7] Cf. *The Philosophy of Alfred North Whitehead,* 2nd ed., ed. P. A. Schilpp (Tudor, 1951), p. 681.

immersed in modern science the more difficult it is for him to step outside this science and put it into its place. Substantially this claim has been made by the French philosopher Jacques Maritain, who appears on the American scene as an outstanding contemporary exponent of Thomistic philosophy, not only through English translations of his writings but more directly through his teaching and lecturing in American universities. According to Maritain,

> It is only too true that eternal metaphysic does not fit in with the modern mind, or more exactly that the latter does not fit in with the former. Three centuries of mathematical empiricism have so bent the modern mind to a single interest in the invention of engines for the control of phenomena—a conceptual network, which procures for the mind a certain practical domination over and a deceptive understanding of nature, where thought is not resolved in being but in the sensible itself.[8]

From this point of view, the fact that *Process and Reality* appeared with impressive credentials of scientific respectability lessens rather than enhances the hope of finding metaphysical truth and adequacy in the work, and at best the fact is irrelevant to the evidence of truth and adequacy. This irrelevance must be accepted to some extent by Whitehead himself, since he insists so emphatically that metaphysics, despite its use of the method of generalization, is not a continuation of science but something essentially different— something as close to art and poetry as to science. There remains of course the question "How much and in what way must one know science in order to put science into its place?"—but this is a question for Maritain as well as for Whitehead. Each provides an answer in terms of his own metaphysics, yet one thing is clear: truth and adequacy as decided within science are irrelevant to the truth and adequacy of a metaphysics. It is no argument for the truth of Whitehead's process metaphysics to point out that it was framed by a man who possessed a profound knowledge of relativity physics, while Maritain's substance metaphysics was derived from pre-Newtonian and largely Aristotelian sources and was framed by a man who possessed at most an educated layman's knowledge of relativity physics. Relativity physics may be scientifically true and

[8] Jacques Maritain, *The Degrees of Knowledge,* trans. Bernard Wall and Margot R. Adamson (Geoffrey Bles/Centenary, 1937), p. 3.

Aristotelian physics scientifically false, but this has nothing to do with the truth of metaphysical statements which purport to put all science into its place.

Whitehead's scientific respectability, then, offers the cause of speculative philosophy nothing but *ad hominem* arguments. The scientifically minded who dismiss metaphysics because it is the work of seminary philosophers may be answered with a like argument simply by pointing to Whitehead, but the argument is in no sense evidence for the truth and adequacy of Whitehead's metaphysics.

4. *The support of special appeal.* In *Process and Reality* Whitehead declares of speculative philosophy:

> Its ultimate appeal is to the general consciousness of what in practice we experience. Whatever thread of presupposition characterizes social expression throughout the various epochs of rational society, must find its place in philosophic theory. Speculative boldness must be balanced by complete humility before logic, and before fact. It is a disease of philosophy when it is neither bold nor humble, but merely a reflection of the temperamental presuppositions of exceptional personalities [*PR*, p. 25].

This passage suggests that the circumstances in which metaphysicians must seek agreement may be defined by "threads of presupposition" which characterize "social expression throughout the various epochs of rational society." The appeal to facts which is essential to metaphysics should thus be determined by these threads of presupposition as opposed to "the temperamental presuppositions of exceptional personalities." One would expect that threads of presupposition which characterize social expression and define circumstances within which men can make ultimate appeal to facts are to be found primarily in forms of language. Whitehead is explicit on the point a few pages before the passage just quoted.

> Every science must devise its own instruments. The tool required for philosophy is language. Thus philosophy redesigns language in the same way that, in a physical science, pre-existing appliances are redesigned. It is exactly at this point that the appeal to facts is a difficult operation. This appeal is not solely to the expression of facts in current verbal statements. The adequacy of such sentences is the main question at issue. It is true that the general agreement

of mankind as to experienced facts is best expressed in language. But the language of literature breaks down precisely at the task of expressing in explicit form the larger generalities—the very generalities which metaphysics seeks to express [*PR*, p. 16].

Speculative philosophy thus seeks to put not only science but also ordinary language into its place. Metaphysicians in their ultimate appeal to facts must dispense with the ordinary common-sense expression of facts as well as with the technical formulations of science. The appeal must be, in Whitehead's phrase, "to the general consciousness of what in practice we experience," and this consciousness must be undistorted by language, common or technical. Yet Whitehead does not go to the extreme of proposing that metaphysicians should begin by dispensing with ordinary language altogether. On the contrary, he declares that "the only possible procedure is to start from verbal expressions which, when taken by themselves with the current meaning of their words, are ill-defined and ambiguous" (*PR*, p. 19). But then one must remember that "no language can be anything but elliptical, requiring a leap of the imagination to understand its meaning in its relevance to immediate experience" (*PR*, p. 20). As an example of the way inadequate metaphysics results from failure to go beyond ordinary language by a leap of the imagination, Whitehead asks the reader to consider "the type of propositions such as 'The grass is green,' and 'The whale is big.'" He then remarks, "This subject-predicate form of statement seems so simple, leading straight to a metaphysical first principle; and yet in these examples it conceals such complex, diverse meanings" (*PR*, p. 20).

The metaphysical first principle which Whitehead has in mind here is obviously some form of the substance-accident principle which is central in many philosophies, including Thomism. Yet it is doubtful if any philosopher of note who held this principle would admit that he arrived at it simply by generalizing the common subject-predicate form of statement exhibited in sentences like "The grass is green" and "The whale is big." Certainly this is not true of Maritain. Whitehead's remark is appropriate only when it is first decided on *nonlinguistic* grounds that the substance-accident principle is false or inadequate. That so many philosophers have fallen into the error of subscribing to this principle may then be explained by the contention that they were misled by language. But what are the nonlinguistic grounds on which the issue is to be decided? As Whitehead's answer, we have only the sort of thing indicated by the phrase "the general consciousness of what in practice we experience"; this is all there is to appeal to in the "research" which Whitehead speaks of as conciliating the difference between rival metaphysical systems (see *PR*, p. 12). And Maritain too has a similar if somewhat more specific answer. "How is it possible to dissertate on metaphysics," he asks, "if one does not *see* the quiddities in the intelligible?" [9] This seeing, he goes on to say, requires "a certain original talent."

The final issue between these two speculative philosophers, then, concerns what there is to be conscious of or to be seen intellectually. According to Whitehead, we must say that Maritain fails at a crucial point in his grasp of "the general consciousness of what in practice we experience" because he is a victim of that "prevalent habit of thought," "the subject-predicate form of expression." (This habit is another of the nine repudiated at the outset of *Process and Reality*.) According to Maritain, we must say that Whitehead either lacks "a certain original talent" for intellectual seeing or is inhibited in his exercise of this talent by those prevalent habits of thought which have "so bent the modern mind" through "three centuries of mathematical empiricism." Each philosopher (Maritain no less than Whitehead) strives for language that will direct the attention of his readers to those factors of experience or intellectual insight which he feels disclose the ultimate characters of reality—characters which he finds obscured by both ordinary language and the technical language of science. The philosophers thus differ not only in the language they use but also in what they seek to reveal in their use of language. The second difference is clearly the fundamental one, yet it is lost in the verbalism that as metaphysicians both men are seeking in their use of language to reveal the same thing—ultimate reality. The difference reappears when one remembers that the phrase "ultimate reality" has a different meaning in the language of each philosopher.

Neither Whitehead nor Maritain address arguments specifically to the hostile reader who lacks the requisite consciousness or intel-

9 *Ibid.*, p. 2, Maritain's italics.

lectual insight. Both begin by rejecting prevalent habits of thought and thus make no claim to communicate with the reader who refuses even to entertain the rejections. From what has been said thus far about speculative philosophy this situation seems to be unavoidable. There are no common circumstances for rival metaphysicians to accept as those within which they should all conduct their inquiries and seek agreement; each begins within the circumstances of his own inquiry and rejects all others. If the reader is to understand, he must be amenable to orientation—ready to go along with Thomistic, Whiteheadian, or whatever the appropriate mode of thought.[10] Yet there have been and still are speculative philosophers who profess to support metaphysical principles by arguments that require no special orientation on the part of the reader. The appeal is only to what is necessary for rational thought itself so that the arguments are to command assent from any reader capable of following the steps in a rational account. The arguments in this case are appropriately called rationalistic.

5. *The support of rationalistic arguments.* A central doctrine in Whitehead's metaphysics is that each of the final real things of which the world is made up—each actual entity or actual occasion —is a social entity. We say that man is a social entity because human beings characteristically maintain their existence in social groups, and with Whitehead the generalization is extended to every actual entity. A social group, one may say, is a group of individuals with sympathetic feelings and this property of sympathetic feeling applies not only to men in societies but also to stars in galaxies, planets in solar systems, cells in plants and animals, molecules in cells, atoms in molecules, and elementary particles in atoms. This seems to be at least part of what Whitehead means to assert by his generalization and it helps one to see why he referred to his metaphysics as "the philosophy of organism." The important point for the present discussion is that Whitehead nowhere attempts to sup-

---

[10] An excellent, penetrating, and critical discussion of Whitehead's speculative philosophy and the extent to which its evidence presupposes a properly oriented reader is given by Arthur E. Murphy, "Whitehead and the Method of Speculative Philosophy," in *The Philosophy of Alfred North Whitehead*, ed. Schilpp, pp. 353-80.

port his generalization by rationalistic arguments considered in isolation from the rest of his metaphysics. The skeptical reader who suspects that the attribution of sympathetic feelings to such diverse entities as men, cells, and atoms rests on too far-fetched an analogy to be of philosophic significance is not confronted with an isolated argument designed to refute his skepticism once and for all. On the contrary, in order to be convinced the reader must be willing to entertain new modes of thought and to endeavor to understand the generalization as an integral part of Whitehead's entire metaphysical scheme. Without this understanding it is pointless to dispute the significance of the analogy. Yet the understanding is by no means easy to achieve and the risk of philosophic misunderstanding and controversy might be avoided altogether if the skeptic could be demolished in a single blow by rationalistic argument.

This way of nipping issues in the bud has been undertaken by Charles Hartshorne, one of Whitehead's former students and a prominent defender and expositor of the philosophy of organism. At the outset of his *Reality as Social Process*[11] Hartshorne offers an argument for Whitehead's social principle. The argument is admirably brief and is designed to convince the skeptical reader once and for all that the generalization is probably true and cannot conceivably be shown false. "The situation," Hartshorne declares, "is that nothing could conceivably be known by any observer not to be social; whereas the social character of some things, such as human groups, can be and is known," for "at least we can know that human beings are social in the sense of having sympathetic feelings" (*RSP*, p. 32). The crucial point is then that "it cannot be known that any part of nature is without such feelings" (*ibid.*). "Critics of the social philosophy," Hartshorne explains, "who complain that we cannot detect definite social character in all portions of nature are missing the main point, which is that an idea actually known to be true in some cases, but not even potentially known to

---

11 Abbreviation, *RSP*. For a critical discussion of the method of supporting speculative philosophy by rationalistic arguments, see the section entitled "Urban on Philosophical Method" in C. J. Ducasse, *Philosophy as a Science* (Oskar Piest, 1941), pp. 26-30. Ducasse is discussing the work of C. M. Urban, another speculative philosopher of our period. See also C. M. Urban, *The Intelligible World* (Macmillan, 1929). For further comments on Ducasse's criticisms of speculative philosophy, see below, note 16.

be false in any *conceivable* case, is for all purposes an ultimate idea" (*RSP*, p. 33, Hartshorne's italics). Thus, Whitehead's generalization that all actual entities are social is supported by what we know of some things and cannot conceivably be contradicted by what we can know of anything.

The force of this argument depends on the assumption that it makes sense to ask of everything whether it has sympathetic feelings. The argument rules out the common-sense view that one asks whether two beings sympathize with each other only when one assumes that the two beings are capable of sympathetic feelings— that they are human beings or other animals and not inanimate things like sticks and stones. The argument, in other words, assumes at the start that all things are capable of sympathetic feelings. Yet surely this leap of imagination beyond ordinary language is the very point at issue for the skeptical reader and in assuming it the argument begs the question. The logical point—the point which any rational reader must admit—is only that whatever is capable of sympathetic feelings may actually have them. It will not do to retort "But one can never know that anything is really incapable of such feelings." The issue is whether we should retain our common practice of not regarding a thing as capable of sympathetic feelings unless we know that other things of the same kind actually have these feelings, or whether we should give up this practice. The statement that we can never know whether something is really incapable of sympathetic feelings is thus true only if we have abandoned the practice in question, so the statement by itself does not give a reason for the abandonment.

Hartshorne's argument, then, provides no escape from the necessity of asking the reader to go along with a certain mode of thought, and thus to consider Whitehead's generalization as an integral part of a whole metaphysical system and not as a single proposition which stands or falls by itself. Since a metaphysical first principle purports to be a generalization in accord with everything conceivable, it is of course regarded by one already convinced of its truth as a proposition which cannot conceivably be falsified. It is thus tempting to think that anyone capable of rational thought can be convinced that the principle is true by a simple argument demonstrating the impossibility of falsifying it. To yield to this temptation is inevitably to beg the question. Any such demonstration presupposes a decision regarding what is and what is not conceivable, and anyone who doubts the principle does so only by denying exactly what the demonstration presupposes. In this sense of "demonstration" incompatible metaphysical principles are easily demonstrated. An argument for the contrary of Whitehead's generalization might run as follows. We know that at least some things (e.g., sticks and stones) do not have sympathetic feelings. While we commonly assume that men and certain animals have such feelings, we also know that on occasion this assumption turns out to be wrong. What appears to be an expression of sympathetic feeling is later found not to be so, and this happens even when we are appraising our own feelings. We are thus forced to the conclusion that no being can conceivably be known by any observer (even when the being is oneself) to have sympathetic feelings rather than merely to appear to have them. Hence, the generalization that no actual entities are social in the sense of having sympathetic feelings is supported by what we know of some things and cannot conceivably be contradicted by what we can know of anything.

For one convinced by Hartshorne's demonstration the above argument begins with the false assumption that we can conceivably know sticks and stones lack sympathetic feelings. Yet from a common-sense point of view this assumption is perhaps the only sound point in the whole argument. The metaphysical opposition between the two arguments is indicated by the propositions: "No observer can conceivably know that anything whatsoever lacks sympathetic feelings entirely" and "No observer can conceivably know that any being (including himself) really has sympathetic feelings and does not merely appear to have them." Either of these propositions is easily construed in a variety of ways as an absurd departure from common sense, but with a little ingenuity in dialectic one may defend each of them as true and as compatible with the other. Yet no such refutation or defense will settle the metaphysical opposition. This opposition does not arise until the propositions are taken as starting points for rival metaphysical systems and hence as presenting incompatible views of what is conceivable. The opposition, in other words, has to be created by accepting each proposition as presupposing the conceivability of what the other declares to be inconceivable. In this situation there is no alternative to asking that the reader begin with the orientation of consciousness or insight required by the metaphysical system to be defended.

Yet surely this seems an unsatisfactory state of affairs. A metaphysical principle is construed as in effect determining what is conceivable and as thereby rendering inconceivable any evidence against itself. If the metaphysician, as Hocking has said (§ 3), seeks a *pou sto* beyond science where science can be put into its place, the critic of metaphysics cannot likewise be said to take a stand beyond metaphysics. To stand outside one metaphysical system and criticize its principles is inevitably, it seems, to take a stand inside another system. Appeal to a common-sense practice like that of not regarding a thing as capable of sympathetic feelings unless we know that other things of the same kind actually have these feelings can never in itself settle a metaphysical issue. Opposing metaphysical systems may each recognize the practice as a fact and each dismiss it for different reasons as a failure to achieve proper insight into what is conceivable. What appears at first sight to be an opposition between contrary propositions thus turns out to be an opposition between incompatible metaphysical systems. Any attempt to resolve the opposition by arguing for the truth of one of the propositions without begging the question, i.e., without presupposing the system within which that proposition is a principle, seems doomed to failure.

6. *The support of the inclusiveness of a system.* The apparent impossibility of defending or criticizing a metaphysical principle without presupposing a system of metaphysics is the subject of considerable attention in an impressive work of speculative philosophy which has just appeared on the American scene. Paul Weiss, a distinguished speculative philosopher and editor of the *Review of Metaphysics,* devotes a chapter of his recent *Modes of Being* [12] to the question of determining the adequacy of a metaphysical system. "The polemics which dot the history of philosophy," Weiss contends, "are bitter but ineffective" (*MB,* p. 380). For each metaphysician "finds himself refuted inside another system which has

[12] Paul Weiss, *Modes of Being* (Southern Illinois U., 1958). Abbreviation, *MB.*

no way of allowing him to be over against that system," yet *in* his own system he is *outside* the system in which he is refuted, and this is "even where that other system claims him to be" while refuting him (*MB*, pp. 380-81). In this clash of systems, according to Weiss, what passes for metaphysical truth is variously viewed as *whole* and *partial*. Each speculative philosopher in refuting the principles of another system unavoidably makes the claim that the system in which he achieves his refutation is closer to the whole truth than the system determined by the principles he refutes. Such truth as the refutation grants to the other system must be construed as part of the truth expressed in the system through which the refutation is effected. An adequate metaphysical system must thus include all truth within itself.

"The existence of warring philosophic systems," Weiss declares, "is proof enough that no one of them says all that needs be said," and "rejection of the rest by each is what one might expect from partial systems falsely claiming to be all-inclusive" (*MB*, p. 381). The crucial point in Weiss's proposed way out of the struggle is the contention that an adequate metaphysical system will not reject the rest but will include them all "as partial illustrations of itself" (*ibid.*). By rejecting the principles of rival systems as false or meaningless a metaphysician accomplishes nothing but the dogmatic reaffirmation of his own principles. In order to argue for his principles he must show, Weiss feels, that each of the other systems is actually a part of his own system mistakenly viewed as presenting the whole truth. By aiming at inclusion rather than refutation one may claim to criticize from within and thus seem to escape the dilemma of having either to accept a metaphysical system as it stands or to beg the question by offering a refutation which presupposes an incompatible system. A good portion of Weiss's *Modes of Being* is designed to show that his system includes and is illustrated by rather than refutes other systems, and the purported success of this venture is intended to demonstrate the adequacy of the metaphysics expounded in the rest of the book.

Weiss's essay in defense of speculative philosophy generally and of his own metaphysics in particular is open to certain fundamental objections which have been urged in a critical study of his book by John Wild, another American philosopher prominent in the field of metaphysics.[13] Wild's objections are based on the claim that "basic philosophical disagreement penetrates to the very roots of meaning" (*WFU*, p. 621). Such disagreement "involves not merely a clash of doctrines or opinions, but a clash between divergent worlds of meaning" (*WFU*, pp. 621-22). If this is the case, Weiss's efforts at inclusion rather than refutation can have no effect on basic disagreement. For inclusion just as much as refutation can take place only within a single world of meaning—a single way of determining what is conceivable. A Whiteheadian metaphysician presupposes a Whiteheadian world of meaning whether he claims to include or to refute his opponent's denial that sticks and stones conceivably have sympathetic feelings. In fact, "inclusion" in this case is but a polite word for "refutation," since the Whiteheadian's "inclusion" of his opponent's denial omits precisely that factor which makes the denial metaphysical—its claim to express the whole truth. Weiss tries to cope with this point by insisting that a metaphysician in effecting an inclusion "must enter sympathetically into the spirit" of his opponent's views "and come to understand how they also must claim to be adequate" (*MB*, p. 380). Sympathy for an opponent's views, however, in the end is no more than balm for the sting of refutation. It enables the "including" metaphysician to say to his "included" opponent, "I fully understand how you came to your conclusions, and your claims are entirely plausible from your limited point of view." The sting is soothed, but is nevertheless there in the last five words.

Wild points out that the device of inclusion may settle a philosophical disagreement that occurs within "the limits of a single school," but such disagreement, he remarks, "is only one relatively trivial type" (*WFU*, p. 622). The matter is quite different when one turns to the basic disagreements which divide metaphysical systems rather than the opinions of those who work within a single system. Wild distinguishes three types of basic disagreement. There is first the case where a metaphysician finds "no factual evidence in the phenomena" for the existence of certain "entities and relations" affirmed by his opponent; second, the metaphysician may find that phenomena he clearly discerns are ruled out by "negative asser-

[13] John Wild, "Weiss's Four-fold Universe," *Review of Metaphysics*, XI (1958), 610-36. Abbreviation, *WFU*.

tions" in his opponent's system. "There is hope," Wild says, "of resolving such disagreements by phenomenological description and analysis" (*WFU*, p. 623). However, the third type of disagreement is "even more serious." Two metaphysicians "may agree ostensively that something is the case" and yet "finally interpret it in terms of radically divergent structures of meaning." The issues in this case, Wild feels, can at most "be moderated and reduced by phenomenological description and by disciplined argument"; "to hope that they can ever be finally resolved, as long as man retains his freedom, is to ignore the facts of human finitude and history" (*ibid.*).

Wild's criticisms of Weiss leave the problem of giving evidence for a system of speculative philosophy virtually where it was with Whitehead and Maritain. A reader who lacks the requisite orientation of consciousness or insight can never be convinced by phenomenological description and analysis, and, unless he is convinced of the premises, disciplined argument will not help to produce agreement. Wild's reference to man's freedom and the facts of human finitude and history add a pessimistic note not explicit in Whitehead or Maritain. If history offers no hope for final agreement among metaphysicians except by attainment of omniscience or submission to intellectual authority, one may not wish to begin with Whitehead by repudiating the distrust of speculative philosophy. In any event, it seems apparent from the foregoing samples of recent literature in speculative philosophy that neither scientific respectability nor rationalistic argument in defense of isolated principles nor inclusion rather than refutation of rival systems will suffice as evidence for a particular metaphysics. There appears to be no alternative to speculative philosophy supported by special appeal, even though the difficulties of reaching agreement through such appeal generate distrust of speculative philosophy.

7. *The goal of human reason.* I have remarked (§ 1) that the phrase "speculative philosophy" as used by Whitehead was post-Kantian in origin and reflected Hegel's opposition to Kant's radical separation of form and content. According to Hegel the succession of incompatible systems of speculative philosophy that comprises the history of metaphysics provides no occasion for distrust of speculative philosophy. The conflict of systems is an inevitable

product of the efforts of human reason to realize its final goal, the ultimate synthesis of all oppositions in the absolute ideal of reason. Distrust of speculative philosophy arises from a false separation of form and content, from the mistaken view that contradictions between systems unavoidably arise because of the way the systems were formed by their authors and not also because of the content that led to their formation. For Hegel, the contradictions are in the content, in the world, as well as in man's endeavors to comprehend the world. Just as in the actual course of world history oppositions continually arise and are continually reconciled in higher syntheses, so in the history of speculative philosophy contradictory systems continually appear and are continually brought together in more comprehensive systems.

As noted (§ 3), speculative philosophy in the first quarter of the twentieth century was largely dominated by Hegelian modes of thought. Hegel had written as though his own system achieved the final synthesis, but Hegelians of later generations could claim that Hegel like all speculative philosophers was limited by his own historical perspective. History has moved on since Hegel, science has advanced, and the need for a higher synthesis inevitably arises, but this very point suggests an important modification of Hegel. Hegel's claim that the final synthesis could actually be achieved in the system of a single philosopher may be replaced by the claim that while rational man inevitably seeks the final synthesis and indeed may continually advance in his history to ever higher syntheses, he still as finite man remains infinitely removed from his ultimate goal.

This modification of Hegel gives renewed intellectual respectability to absolute idealism, to the continuation of speculative philosophy within what is still broadly a Hegelian framework. It is unnecessary to claim with Whitehead that speculative philosophy is intellectually respectable because like science it is developed by the method of generalization. The method may remain the dialectical method of Hegel, a method that continually develops and reconciles contradictions. Intellectual respectability is restored with the abandonment of the dogmatic claim that pursuit of the method can lead finite man to a goal from which he is infinitely removed.

At the same time that Whitehead was promising new hope for

the cause of speculative philosophy by freeing it from its associations with Hegelian idealism, other American philosophers were laboring to free the old idealism from its associations with antiscientific dogmatism. In 1939 Brand Blanshard consummated the work of some twelve years with the publication of a two-volume treatise, *The Nature of Thought*.[14] Blanshard moves from a concern in the early chapters with empirical psychology to an exploration of metaphysical views concerning the nature of thought in Volume II. He concludes, "Throughout the career of thought, from its first tentative appearance in perception to the flights of speculative reason, there is a single continuous drive toward intelligible system, a system which, as all-comprehensive, is logically stable, and, as perfectly integrated, leaves no loose ends" (*NT*, p. 429). This essentially Hegelian view of the goal of thought is accompanied by a modified Hegelian view of the achievement of the final synthesis. "The test of any conclusion," Blanshard writes, "is whether or not it coheres with such system as we have; but that system itself must be revised, and revised perpetually, under the correction of the immanent end that is working through it" (*NT*, pp. 428-29).

The modification of Hegel is in the phrases "with such system as we have" and "must be revised, and revised perpetually." Unlike Hegel, Blanshard carefully avoids the appearance of claiming to present the final system as opposed to arguing for the necessity of accepting the ideal of such a system as the ultimate goal of thought. The conclusion that finite man is forever doomed to fall short of the goal his thought presses him toward is not emphasized by Blanshard, though it is suggested by the phrase "revised perpetually." Emphasis on this conclusion raises at once a question that has become paramount for other American philosophers who have continued after the appearance of Blanshard's *The Nature of Thought* to write in the tradition of absolute idealism. If man is compelled by his reason to seek an unobtainable goal, is he condemned to live in despair and frustration or can he hope to achieve his goal by means other than his reason?

The obvious alternative to reason is some form of mystical in-

14 Brand Blanshard, *The Nature of Thought*, 2 vols. (George Allen, 1939). Abbreviation, *NT*. All page references in the text are to Volume II.

sight or religious faith. Hegel himself held that religion achieves in concrete imagery the very synthesis which philosophy achieves in a higher form, in abstract thought. But any attempt to place mysticism or religion above reason as providing man's final hope for ultimate synthesis seems to leave us virtually where we were with speculative philosophy supported by special appeal. At best we have specified the kind of appeal called for, but we have not justified the specification.

One way of justifying it is found in the position taken by W. T. Stace, an American philosopher known for his work in Hegel scholarship as well as in metaphysics and the philosophy of religion. In his *Time and Eternity*,[15] Stace argues that human efforts to know God culminate in both a negative and a positive divine. The negative divine appears in the mystic's pronouncements that God is nothing, that God is nonbeing and eternal darkness. The meaning of these pronouncements, according to Stace, is that no predicate is literally true of God. All attempts to state literally what God is, or even that he is, end in falsity. Yet the negative divine, according to Stace, does not mean that "God is unqualifiedly nothing." It means only that "God is nothing *to the conceptual intellect*. It does not mean that He has no positive being, but only that His positive being, though revealed to intuition, is hidden from intellect" (*TE*, p. 49, Stace's italics).

What Stace calls the "positive divine," on the other hand, appears when positive statements about God are interpreted symbolically rather than literally. Even though the statements are literally false, they may "evoke in us some intuition of the divine nature" (*TE*, p. 52), but this does not mean that, in the apprehension of the positive divine, reason must be abandoned altogether in favor of intuition. Stace holds that "faith and intuition are one and the same thing. To discover God is the function of faith. But, reason too has its function in the religious sphere. It has to interpret to the intellect the discoveries of faith in the only possible way, by means of symbolic propositions, and also to ensure that these symbolic propositions are mutually consistent and fall into an ordered system" (*TE*, p. 152).

According to Stace's position, then, systems of speculative phi-
15 W. T. Stace, *Time and Eternity* (Princeton, 1952). Abbreviation, *TE*.

losophy in their efforts to achieve a final synthesis of all reality in God, the absolute, or whatever it may be called, must be understood as attempts of reason to interpret to the intellect the discoveries of faith. Contradictions within systems and among systems are unavoidable as long as statements are taken literally. The aim of reason is to avoid contradictions when the propositions are symbolically interpreted, and this is a goal obtainable only by a mind in which reason is properly oriented by faith or intuition. As Stace remarks, "This is the truth of the medieval view that reason operates within the framework set by faith and revelation" (*ibid.*).

The specification of mystical insight and religious faith as the special appeal required for the support of a system of speculative philosophy is thus justified by an account of the goal that any such system strives to obtain. Stace holds that "the objectivity of science is due to the fact that sense experiences are basically the same in all men," and that "in principle, exactly the same can be said of religion"; but he adds that this is not to say "the similarity of religious experience in all men is either as great, or as clearly verifiable, as are the similarities of their sense experiences" (*TE*, p. 146). But then the question is whether the similarity of religious experience is sufficiently great to provide a system of speculative philosophy with anything like the support that sense experience provides a system of science. Stace feels that the existence of such similarity is shown by a study of the great religions of the world, such as Christianity, Judaism, Islam, Hinduism, and Buddhism.

This position is open to the objection that any such study of the great religions is made by individual men, each of whom is bound by his own religious faith as he uses his reason to interpret the symbolic statements of religious literature. It is difficult to see how the study can produce any more evidence for a similarity of religious feeling among all men than that which already exists in the numerous systems of speculative philosophy that have been advanced by individual men as providing the universal framework within which to interpret all religious experience. Since the dissimilarity of these systems is the very point at issue, Stace's appeal to the ultimacy of religious faith hardly provides a means of resolving the issue. Indeed, this appeal to religious faith in support of metaphysics has been viewed by philosophers unfriendly to Hegelian modes of thought as tantamount to the abandonment of philosophy—as the reduction of philosophy to nothing more than "logically articulated faith." [16]

A position similar to Stace's but one that contains an answer to the above objection has been developed at length by an American scholar who is known primarily as one of the leading theologians of our time. In his two-volume treatise *Systematic Theology*,[17] Paul Tillich holds that philosophy and theology ask the same question, "the question of the structure of being" (*ST*, pp. 20-21). But the philosopher approaches the question "through rational detachment," looking at "the universal *logos*," "the *logos* of reality as a whole," the "common" *logos* that "every reasonable being participates in" and "uses" "in asking questions and criticizing the answers received." The theologian, on the other hand, approaches the question "through believing commitment," looking at "the concrete *logos*," the "Logos 'who became flesh,'" that is, the *logos* manifesting itself in a particular historical event. And the medium through which he receives the manifestation of the *logos* is not common rationality but the church, its traditions and its present reality" (*ST*, pp. 23-24).

This divergence between philosophy and theology "is counterbalanced," according to Tillich, "by an equally obvious convergence" (*ST*, p. 24). The crucial point is that the ideal of rational detachment is never completely obtainable by the philosopher. As a finite being existing in particular circumstances no philosopher can look simply at the universal *logos;* his vision is always colored by the conditions of his particular existence. This means, for Tillich, that "every creative philosopher is a hidden theologian (sometimes even a declared theologian)" (*ST*, p. 25). "He is a theologian in

---

[16] Cf. C. J. Ducasse, *Philosophy as a Science,* chap. II, "Philosophy as Logically Articulated Faith." The radical difference between Stace's and Ducasse's views on religion is indicated by the title of Ducasse's later book, *A Philosophical Scrutiny of Religion* (Ronald, 1953). For Ducasse, religion is a phenomenon to be investigated by social scientists, psychologists, and parapsychologists and to be scrutinized by the philosopher for its claims to knowledge and moral value. In no sense does it provide, as it does for Stace, the framework within which human reason is forced to operate.

[17] Paul Tillich, *Systematic Theology,* 2 vols. (U. of Chicago, 1951). Abbreviation, *ST*. All page references in the text are to Volume I.

the degree to which his intuition of the universal *logos* of the structure of reality as a whole is formed by a particular *logos* which appears to him on his particular place and reveals to him the meaning of the whole" (*ibid.*).

Unlike Stace, Tillich does not imply that the particular orientation of the mind of an individual speculative philosopher is simply a matter of individual religious experience. The fundamental question is not whether the religious experience of all men is sufficiently similar. Tillich is emphatic on the point that Christian theology, as he views it, "implies the claim that it is *the* theology." "The basis of this claim," he continues, "is the Christian doctrine that the Logos became flesh, that the principle of the divine self-revelation has become manifest in the event 'Jesus as the Christ'" (*ST*, p. 16, Tillich's italics). A few sentences later he sums up the point: "Christian theology is *the* theology in so far as it is based on the tension between the absolutely concrete and the absolutely universal" (*ibid.,* Tillich's italics).

Tillich thus sees in Christian theology the final answer to the neo-Hegelian problem of how man can achieve the infinite goal he sets for his finite intellect. The conflicts between different systems of speculative philosophy are not to be reconciled, as Blanshard recommended, by each man perpetually revising such system as he has, nor, as Stace held, by appealing to the similarity of the religious experience of all men. This is not to say that Tillich simply rejects either the need for perpetual revision of a metaphysical system or the claim that there is a similarity in all religious experience. Both points are recognized by Tillich and have their place in his thought, but both are secondary to the central point that Christianity provides *the* way for finite man to approach his infinite goal. As a creative philosopher every man is a theologian whether he is aware of it or not, and he can hope to develop an adequate system of speculative philosophy only if his theology is *the* theology, Christian theology. As philosopher man is perpetually revising his system, struggling to look only at the universal *logos* of reality and to interpret his own theological answer—his own grasp of the concrete *logos,* his own religious experience—by what he sees. "If he sees something he did not expect to see in the light of his theological answer, he holds fast to what he has seen and reformulates his theological answer" (*ST*, p. 64). But, Tillich adds, "he is certain that nothing he sees can change the substance of his answer, because this substance is the *logos* of being, manifest in Jesus as the Christ. If this were not his presupposition, he would have to sacrifice either his philosophical honesty or his theological concern." The ultimate appeal for speculative philosophers when their reason cannot bring them to agreement is thus to be found in their believing commitment as Christians.

The three philosophers discussed in this section share the view of absolute idealism that the ultimate goal of human reason is to comprehend all reality in a single coherent system. While our philosophers differ in their attempts to cope with the fact that this goal seems forever unobtainable, the value of their attempts depends first of all on the correctness of their common assumption that the ideal of an all-inclusive, completely coherent system is indeed the goal of human thought. Blanshard alone of the three philosophers places primary emphasis on the correctness of this assumption and argues for it with admirable subtlety and persuasion. The failure to consider here his arguments on this score is in no sense a judgment of them and is dictated solely by the brevity of this essay.

We should note in conclusion that while Whitehead and the other speculative philosophers mentioned earlier in this chapter do not embrace the goal of ultimate systematization in exactly the manner of the absolute idealists, still, as speculative philosophers, they all assume in one way or another that the comprehension of everything real in a single coherent system is the legitimate goal of metaphysics. In this respect all our speculative philosophers represent pre-Kantian modes of thought, whether they return to such modes more in the manner of Whitehead, with his method of generalization, or of Hegel, with his dialectical method of uniting opposites. On the other hand, all the philosophers of our period who write in distrust of speculative philosophy are post-Kantian in that they reject in one way or another the assumption that ultimate systematization of all reality is the legitimate aim of philosophy. This does not mean, of course, that these philosophers necessarily reject metaphysics altogether. Prominent writers on the American scene like C. I. Lewis, John Dewey, and George Santayana have developed varieties of a naturalistic philosophy which may be called both "metaphysical" and "post-Kantian," but before turning to these philosophers it is well to consider those who have written at some length on the possibility of speculative philosophy—of ultimate systematization—and either flatly deny its possibility as the legitimate goal of thought or at least deny the claims to truth made by speculative philosophers. As diagnosticians of metaphysics, they are in the main sympathetic to naturalism and their diagnoses prepare the way for naturalistic philosophy.

2

THE POSSIBILITY OF
SPECULATIVE PHILOSOPHY

8. Logical positivism. 9. Carnap's statement of the case against metaphysics. 10. Toward a satisfactory diagnosis. 11. Alternative world hypotheses. 12. Diagnosis and the possibility of speculative philosophy. 13. Metaphysical theories as linguistic innovations. 14. Diagnosis and philosophical analysis.

8. *Logical positivism.* American philosophers who had been writing in distrust of speculative philosophy received new and strong support from European allies at the same time that their metaphysically minded colleagues were welcoming Whitehead as a new leader of speculative thought in the United States. During the Twenties a group of Continental philosophers began a movement which soon became known as "logical positivism" or "logical empiricism." While the primary interest of these philosophers was mathematical logic and the philosophy of science, the strong anti-metaphysical stand of their movement readily became its most distinguishing feature for the rest of the philosophical world. Several prominent members of the movement accepted regular teaching positions in American universities during the Thirties and by the end of the decade the positivists' attack on metaphysics had become the source of the most lively philosophical issues of the day.

The logical positivists generally claimed affinity with British empiricism and there was also much in their position which seemed at first sight close to the views of American pragmatists and naturalists.[1] Yet a rapprochement between the latter and the positivists

[1] An excellent brief account of the history of logical positivism and its relations to other movements in contemporary philosophy is given in *The Development of Logical Empiricism*, by Joergen Joergensen (U. of Chicago, 1951). A more extensive account written from the point of view of the author's own positivistic philosophy appears in *Positivism: A Study in Human Understanding*, by Richard von Mises (Braziller, 1956).

MANLEY THOMPSON

never materialized, at least never to anything like the extent anticipated in the Thirties.[2] Leading American naturalists like Dewey and Lewis continued to develop their own philosophies as alternatives to speculative metaphysics, and found themselves in disagreement with the positivists on important issues in the philosophy of science and epistemology.[3] The positivists, on the other hand, were generally not content to offer their own constructive work in philosophy as an alternative to metaphysics, as something which would do the job which metaphysics had failed to do. While the pragmatists, especially Dewey, were inclined to explain in sociological and biological terms both the appearance and the failure of speculative philosophy, the positivists sought a logical explanation—an explanation which would show on logical grounds alone that metaphysics could be nothing but pretense and illusion.

The logical explanation offered by the positivists, particularly in its early forms, is easily made to appear dogmatic and shallow, and the defenders of speculative philosophy were quick to seize upon this weakness in the positivists' position. As generally represented in semipopular accounts, the positivists' logical explanation was nothing more than the dogmatic claim (unsupported by reasons) that any sentence which fails to express either a tautology or a proposition capable of verification or falsification by the methods of natural science is devoid of literal significance. Since the speculative philosophers held that their sentences were of neither of these types and yet expressed true statements and not mere poetic fantasies, it could only follow that they were talking nonsense.

While the positivists' position thus appeared dogmatic when viewed from the outside, there were developments going on within the movement which were soon to prove even more embarrassing. Serious difficulties were encountered in the attempt to exhibit all

2 See C. W. Morris, "The Concept of Meaning in Pragmatism and Logical Positivism," *Actes du huitième congrès international de philosophie à Prague*, 2-7 septembre 1934 (Prague; 1936); *Logical Positivism, Pragmatism, and Scientific Empiricism* (Paris; 1937).
3 See John Dewey, "Peirce's Theory of Linguistic Signs, Thought, and Meaning," *Journal of Philosophy*, XLIII (1946), 85-95; John Dewey and Arthur F. Bentley, *Knowing and the Known* (Beacon, 1949). C. I. Lewis's disagreements with the positivists are clearly indicated in the preface to his *Analysis of Knowledge and Valuation* (Open Court, 1946).

the propositions of logic and pure mathematics as tautologies, and also in the attempt to show that all literally significant nontautological propositions were capable of verification or falsification by the methods of natural science. Both attempts seemed to require assumptions that were neither tautologous nor scientifically verifiable or falsifiable. In the first case the positivists found themselves debating the existence of entities other than individuals and calling each other "nominalists" or "realists." In the second case they debated whether the objects studied by natural science were ultimately phenomenal or physical and called each other "phenomenalists" or "physicalists." As this internal strife came to the attention of speculative philosophers, cries of *tu quoque* seemed obviously in order. The positivists had become metaphysicians in spite of themselves. What more effective *reductio ad absurdum* of their original anti-metaphysical stand could be given? By the late Forties, it was easy to conclude that the positivists' attack on metaphysics had run its course and that the result had been to increase respect for metaphysics.

Yet the most mature and subtle statement of the positivists' case against metaphysics was still to appear. This statement came in 1950 in a paper by Rudolf Carnap entitled "Empiricism, Semantics, and Ontology." [4] Carnap was already well known as a leader in the positivists' assault on metaphysics when he began his American career in 1935 and his paper of 1950 reflects clearly the changes his thought had undergone during the preceding fifteen years. "Empiricism, Semantics, and Ontology" offers an explanation of the fact that the appearance of metaphysical disputes had occurred within the positivists' movement itself and that even Carnap's own later works had been criticized by American naturalists as advocating a naïve metaphysics.[5] For the purposes of the present discussion this one paper by Carnap will serve admirably as a definitive, mature summary of the positivists' case against metaphysics. The concern in the present chapter will be limited to general ques-

---

[4] The paper first appeared in the *Revue internationale de philosophie,* IV, 11 (1950), 20-40. When the paper is subsequently referred to, page references will be to this publication. The paper is reprinted as a supplement to the second (1956) and later editions of Carnap's *Meaning and Necessity* (U. of Chicago).
[5] See Ernest Nagel's review of Carnap's *Meaning and Necessity* in the *Journal of Philosophy,* XLV (1948), 467-72.

tions about the nature of metaphysics; specific questions about the relation of language to metaphysics, though central to Carnap's position, will be postponed until Chapter 4.

9. *Carnap's statement of the case against metaphysics.* The key notion in Carnap's paper is what he refers to as "a framework." This notion is analogous in many respects to what was called in the preceding chapter "a metaphysical system." In fact, Carnap's frameworks are simply metaphysical systems or parts of such systems considered from a certain point of view—a point of view which focuses attention on just those features of metaphysical systems which generate seemingly interminable controversies. A metaphysical system provides a means of determining what is and what is not conceivable. In Carnap's terms this point is summed up in the contention that each framework represents a determination of the conditions of meaning. Consider, for example, a question which sharply divides the metaphysics of Whitehead and Maritain, "Are the final real things in the world events or substances?" Within the framework of each this question is given a meaning which at once determines its answer. The question is so general and fundamental that it is customary to characterize each framework as a whole by the answer given—Maritain's metaphysics is often referred to as a "substance metaphysics" and Whitehead's as a "process metaphysics." Within each framework there is no problem in answering the question; the answer is given immediately by the framework. The only problem within the framework is that of explaining how any intelligent person could fail to see the truth of the answer; and, as we have seen, in Whitehead there is the suggestion that Maritain was misled by the common subject-predicate form of statement, while in Maritain there is the suggestion that Whitehead was misled by the attitude of mathematical empiricism which has so dominated the modern mind.

From Carnap's point of view, when this question of substance or events is taken as answered within a framework, it is an *internal* question, and as internal it has as many different answers as there are different frameworks which provide an answer. Actually, of course, it is then a different question each time it is asked in a different framework. If we insist that it is but one question with one true answer we have made it an *external* question, a question which cannot be answered within a framework because it calls into question all frameworks. In effect, it has become the question "What is the one framework which supplies the true answer?" In this form, according to Carnap, the question is unanswerable, for any determination of truth presupposes the criteria and methods supplied by a particular framework. There is no alternative but to choose a framework; and since one can choose between truth and falsity only when one employs the criteria and methods of an already chosen framework, the choice of one framework rather than another is not itself a choice between truth and falsity. In its answerable form the question is thus "What is the one framework which best serves certain purposes?" Once philosophers agree on the purpose, they can, Carnap feels, reach agreement on the choice of a framework. Metaphysical disputes become interminable when philosophers fail to recognize that frameworks differ as tools which are more or less satisfactory for certain purposes and not as propositions which are objectively true or false. The claim of speculative philosophers that there is one true framework for all determination of truth is sheer illusion. Maritain and Whitehead, instead of accusing each other of being blinded by prevalent habits of thought, should recognize that the external questions which divide them are not questions concerning the one true framework of speculative philosophy.

Carnap contends that the apparent metaphysical disputes within the logical positivists' movement should be understood (though they have not always been so, even by the positivists themselves) as questions concerning what frameworks best serve certain purposes. The issue of nominalism and realism is not a question of the existence of universals but of the extent to which the foundations of mathematics can be presented within certain frameworks. Physicalists and phenomenalists are not debating whether the final real things in the world are in point of truth physical or phenomenal; they are debating whether, for the purposes of understanding how the propositions of natural science are empirically verifiable, a physicalistic or phenomenalistic framework is in general more fruitful. Yet situations inevitably arise in which one can do nothing but say "I want this rather than that." While in principle it is always objectively demonstrable that a given framework is more fruitful than another for a given purpose, there is in principle no way of demonstrating objectively that a certain purpose should be adopted. A philosopher may persuade others that this purpose rather than that is the one to be achieved by an account of the foundations of mathematics or the verification of scientific laws, but he cannot demonstrate objectively that his purpose is *the* one which has to be adopted. The choice of purposes thus presents, in Carnap's terms, a *noncognitive* issue, an issue which may be settled by persuasion but not by discovery of what is objectively true or false.

The noncognitive character of these ultimate issues is the substance of the positivists' case against metaphysics, as this case is summed up in Carnap's paper. Metaphysicians talk nonsense when they declare the truth of a framework. The original contention of the logical positivists, that sentences are devoid of literal significance if they express neither a tautology nor a proposition verifiable or falsifiable by the methods of natural science, must be replaced by the contention that sentences are devoid of literal significance when they purport to be true of the world apart from the conditions of any framework.

This new contention is not a fiat unsupported by reasons. It rests, according to Carnap, on semantical analysis—on an analysis of the conditions which make literal significance possible. Semantical rules which relate linguistic expressions to entities are necessary conditions for discourse about what is in the world. The crucial point is that one can specify a semantical rule only by specifying a type of entity to which linguistic expressions are to be related. In specifying a type of entity one is not asserting that entities of that type exist, since such an assertion presupposes a framework within which existential statements can be made. When one stipulates that expressions of a certain sort are to designate physical objects, phenomena, substances, numbers, processes, or some other type of entity, one is proposing that a certain semantical rule be incorporated in the framework we adopt for our discourse about the world. The proposal can be debated as desirable or undesirable, but not as true or false. Once the proposal is accepted, it is of course necessarily true within the framework that some entities of the type in question exist; and this is the point where confusion easily arises. A person speaking outside the framework may object to a truth which is necessary within the framework and believe that he is making a counterassertion about reality. He may say "This metaphysical system rests on a false premise because no entities of the type assumed exist." This sentence for Carnap is metaphysical nonsense; it speaks of an external as if it were an internal question.[6]

Semantical analysis, then, supplies the answer when one asks "On what does Carnap base his claim that metaphysical disputes turn on external questions and cannot be debated ultimately as matters of truth or falsity?" Semantical analysis is not concerned with what is true of the world but only with what is said to be true of the world. There are thus, Carnap maintains, no metaphysical prejudices in semantical analysis; it applies impartially to any discourse, metaphysical or otherwise, which purports to be true of the world. The necessity of adopting a framework, if only implicitly, in order to talk about the world, and the impossibility of talking sense about the world when one confuses an external with an internal question, are disclosures of semantical analysis with obviously fundamental philosophical import. If these disclosures render senseless any quest for the one true framework and thus demonstrate the impossibility of speculative philosophy, they at the same time provide philosophy with a new task and new possibilities.

The new task is the further development of semantical analysis; the new possibilities lie in the use of this analysis in other parts of philosophy, in logic, epistemology, the philosophy of science, and ethics. In the Thirties Carnap held that philosophy is the logical syntax of the language of science;[7] in the subsequent development of his position he came to hold that philosophical problems for the most part, if not always, require semantical as well as syntactical analysis. But he never came to the position that philosophy is semantical analysis. Along with the need for semantics as well as syntax, he also recognized the need for still another analysis of language, an analysis dealing with the relations of signs to the people

---

[6] This confusion of external and internal questions, according to Carnap, is precisely the error of his critics. See Carnap's "Empiricism, Semantics, and Ontology," esp. pp. 33-36.
[7] See Rudolf Carnap, *The Logical Syntax of Language* (Kegan Paul, 1937), pp. 277-333.

who use them rather than to entities designated. Carnap called this third analysis "pragmatics," following the lead of his Chicago colleague Charles W. Morris. (The implication that American pragmatists had been working primarily within the area of this third analysis was soon repudiated in print by John Dewey.[8]) All three analyses form a single science called "semiotic," and in Carnap's later view philosophy is thus semiotical analysis. As he sums it up at the end of his *Introduction to Semantics,* "the problems of philosophy concern—not the ultimate nature of being but—the semiotical structure of the language of science, including the theoretical part of everyday language." [9]

The phrase "ultimate nature of being" may suggest that Carnap has in mind speculative philosophy and that he is proposing semiotical analysis as a science designed to do the job attempted by metaphysicians. But it should be clear from the foregoing discussion that this is decidedly not what Carnap is proposing. It has already been remarked that metaphysics as speculative philosophy seeks an ultimate foundation for all the other parts of philosophy, since it seeks what is ultimate for knowledge, inquiry, moral action, and everything else when it seeks the ultimate nature of being. Insofar as this quest is shown to be impossible by semiotical analysis (specifically by that part of the latter comprising semantical analysis), it is of course senseless to speak of anything as doing the job of metaphysics. But this is not to say that problems in the other parts of philosophy, as they arise without the illusion that they concern the ultimate nature of being, are senseless. These are the philosophical problems, according to Carnap, which remain as genuine problems capable of resolution by semiotical analysis.

10. *Toward a satisfactory diagnosis.* Carnap's diagnosis of speculative philosophy is subject to criticism from two directions. Technical objections may be urged against his semantical analysis, in particular against his basic contention that all the true sentences which can be formulated within a given framework are either *analytic* (true solely by virtue of the rules of the framework) or

---

8 John Dewey, "Peirce's Theory of Linguistic Signs, Thought, and Meaning," *Journal of Philosophy,* XLIII (1946), 85-95.
9 Rudolf Carnap, *Introduction to Semantics* (Harvard, 1948), p. 250.

synthetic (true with reference to experience).[10] This contention is crucial for the diagnosis. Metaphysical disputes arise when seemingly incompatible statements are held by different metaphysicians to be necessary truths, and if necessary truths cannot always be identified with sentences analytic in some particular framework the disputes cannot always be diagnosed as the result of a difference in the choice of frameworks. The problems entailed by Carnap's contention, however, are not only too technical for the present discussion, they are also secondary to the central issue. Even if Carnap's semantical analysis were entirely free of technical difficulties, one could still ask whether it supplies a satisfactory diagnosis of the apparently interminable disputes of speculative metaphysics.

As I have already remarked, Carnap's diagnosis carries the disputes back to the point where each contestant must say merely "I want this and not that." This is the point at which the issues become noncognitive and the diagnosis presumably is complete. The interminable character of the disputes is explained by the fact that individual preference and not truth is at stake. This means that all terminable disputes—all those which have truth at stake—presuppose agreement in individual preferences, for disputes can be terminated only within a framework accepted by the disputants; and this acceptance, according to Carnap, is ultimately a matter of individual preferences. In the context of these remarks there is no going beyond preferences and giving a justification for them; they are ultimate. Within a chosen framework factors which justify preferences can of course be specified, but this specification in no way justifies the initial preferences which led to the choice of the framework in the first place.

If the logical positivists' case against metaphysics started as a kind of dogmatism, in its final formulation by Carnap it comes precariously close to utter skepticism. Instead of saying dogmatically that metaphysicians talk cognitive nonsense because their sentences fail to express either tautologies or propositions capable of verification or falsification by the methods of natural science, Carnap seems to

[10] For a statement of technical objections to Carnap's semantics with particular reference to his distinction between analytic and synthetic sentences, see W. V. Quine, *From a Logical Point of View* (Harvard, 1953), pp. 33-36. See also by the same author, "On Carnap's Views on Ontology," *Philosophical Studies*, II (1951), 65-72.

be saying that they are talking cognitive nonsense because they hold that their claims to truth can be justified by something more ultimate than individual preference. This looks like skepticism, not in the qualified sense of denying certain claims to knowledge, but in the unqualified sense of denying that knowledge is ever anything more than what each individual wants to believe. While Carnap's skepticism may appear to be mitigated by the fact that within a framework one can speak of objectively determined truth, it must be remembered that what is decided within a framework is objective only for those who choose that framework and need not be so for those who prefer another framework.

Carnap has given no indication of concern for the skepticism implicit in his diagnosis of metaphysical disputes, and perhaps he would say that the skepticism is harmless because it does not license an individual to believe whatever he pleases but only to believe whatever he can in the face of his experiences.[11] Then the manner in which each individual is able to face his experience will determine to a large extent his framework and hence what he is entitled to accept as knowledge. A satisfactory diagnosis must thus distinguish carefully between what one is able to believe in the face of experience and what one prefers to believe. Carnap's diagnosis becomes sidetracked by the distinction of questions internal and external to a framework and takes no explicit notice of the distinction between what experience forces one to believe and what one prefers to believe. The latter distinction, however, has received considerable attention in two other attempts by American philosophers to go beyond the diagnosis originally offered by the logical positivists.

11. *Alternative world hypotheses.* Stephen Pepper's *World Hypotheses*[12] is an attempt by a native American philosopher to ac-

---

[11] This clearly suggests a kind of pragmatism, in particular that of William James. James held that "the circumpressure of experience itself" was a sufficient answer to the charge that "pragmatism is believing anything one pleases and calling it truth." See James's *Selected Papers on Philosophy* (Dutton, 1917), pp. 228-29. The pragmatic character of Carnap's position has been pointed out by W. V. Quine in his *From a Logical Point of View*, pp. 45-46. The relation between this sort of pragmatism and the naturalism of Dewey is discussed in the next chapter (§ 17).

[12] Stephen C. Pepper, *World Hypotheses* (U. of California, 1942). Abbreviation, *WH*.

count for the seemingly endless disputes of metaphysicians without going to the positivistic extreme of dismissing metaphysics as cognitive nonsense. Pepper's philosophic background is strictly American; according to the autobiographical remarks in his preface, he began philosophizing under the influence of American idealists but soon came under the sway of the naturalists and pragmatists. He was at first hostile toward the positivists, though their attack on metaphysics eventually convinced him that physics was less dependent on speculative philosophy than he had been willing to allow. He feels that the diverse material in his background reaches "a sort of stability" in *World Hypotheses.*

Pepper argues in his two opening chapters that utter skepticism and dogmatism amount to the same thing. The "doctrine of utter skepticism" reduces to the dogma that "all grounds of belief are equally good" (*WH*, p. 16). While the dogmatist begins with the claim that certain grounds of belief are absolutely right and all others wrong, he is forced into skepticism by the fact that contrary beliefs are advanced by those who claim to share his grounds of belief. The common fault of all dogmatisms is the production of belief "in excess of the available evidence" (*WH*, p. 36); in this excess all controls of evidence are lost, contrary beliefs become equally tenable, and the way is paved for skepticism.

In opposition to Weiss and the other speculative philosophers considered in the preceding chapter, Pepper denies that there is in principle but one true and adequate world theory which all metaphysicians should strive to articulate. A plurality of world theories seems absolutely unavoidable; metaphysics must remain hypothetical in principle and Pepper thus prefers the phrase "world hypothesis" to "world theory." On the other hand, in opposition to Carnap, Pepper denies that the choice of a world hypothesis is ultimately always a matter of individual preference. There are many world hypotheses, Pepper maintains, which convict themselves of inadequacy, and anyone who chooses such a hypothesis can be shown to be wrong on his own terms. He cannot defend himself by claiming that the charges against him presuppose a world hypothesis he chooses to reject.

Each world hypothesis may be considered as generated by a single "root-metaphor," a basic analogy which serves to bind together all the facts. Pepper finds four different root-metaphors which may generate adequate world hypotheses. Each of these four hypotheses can account for all the facts accounted for by any of the others; none of them is forced—as mysticism, as Pepper interprets it, is—to put some facts aside as unreal, nor does any of them fail—as what Pepper calls "animism" does—to yield the means "for settling upon a determinate interpretation of facts" (*WH*, p. 122). Pepper refers to the four adequate world hypotheses as "formism," "mechanism," "contextualism," and "organicism." Though each is adequate and can absorb the others, this does not mean that we can get along with only one of them. "We need all world hypotheses, so far as they are adequate," Pepper contends, "for mutual comparison and correction of interpretative bias" (*WH*, p. 101). One is thus not faced with the necessity of choosing finally between different and competing but equally adequate world theories. While a metaphysician may concentrate on developing a single root-metaphor, he should not view other hypotheses as erroneous theories which he may either ignore or, if he thinks they are important enough, refute; he should view them as more or less adequate alternatives which provide a test for the adequacy of his own theory. Failure to heed this injunction is what has produced the perennial disputes of metaphysicians and obstructed the progress of science and philosophy.

While the metaphysician, then, is free to develop the root-metaphor of his choice, he can avoid dogmatism (and, by implication, skepticism) only if he refrains from allowing his preference for a particular metaphor to become the sole factor in determining his beliefs. If it becomes the sole factor, he is blind to any inadequacies which his theory may convict itself of and, even if his theory is adequate, his development of it is bound to suffer from lack of comparison with other adequate theories. To sum up Pepper's diagnosis: While strictly we can say that one is forced by experience to believe only the data of experience, we cannot say (without running into dogmatism and skepticism) either that one is free to interpret the data as one pleases or that one must accept a single interpretation to the exclusion of all others. Dogmatism and skepticism are avoided only by constantly tempering our preferences with the recognition that there are alternative world hypotheses.

12. *Diagnosis and the possibility of speculative philosophy.* Pepper's diagnosis is more open to technical objections than Carnap's. Pepper's distinction between what he calls "multiplicative and structural corroboration" gives rise to many technical issues in the analysis of scientific theories. While these issues are outside the scope of the present discussion, they are fortunately also, as are the technical issues in Carnap, secondary to the central issue. Even if Pepper's distinctions were free of technical difficulties, would his theory provide a satisfactory diagnosis of metaphysical disputes?

In sharp contrast with Carnap, Pepper regards his diagnosis—his root-metaphor theory—as itself a metaphysical theory. Its evidence lies in the adequacy of the world theories it characterizes, and insofar as these theories are adequate the root-metaphor theory becomes "absorbed in its own evidence" (*WH*, p. 85). Pepper seems to mean, in other words, that his diagnosis is ultimately a theory about the world, a theory that the facts of the world are adequately interpreted by different root-metaphors. Yet this theory says nothing about the world that is not already said by the conjunction of the different theories it proclaims adequate, and in this respect it becomes absorbed in its own evidence. The point might be put another way by saying that Pepper's diagnosis calls for a homeopathic cure. An apparently interminable dispute between proponents of different but adequate world hypotheses is settled, not as with the positivists by getting rid of metaphysics, but by administering more metaphysics. Each disputant must be led to see not that metaphysics is cognitive nonsense but that more metaphysics is true than he was prepared to allow. The further metaphysics administered is on the one hand a new theory different from the theories held by any of the disputants, and yet on its substantive side it is not a new theory but rather a conjunction of the theories already in question.

If Pepper succeeds in avoiding dogmatism and skepticism, it would seem that he does so only by embracing an eclecticism, and he is at some pains to deny this charge. His denial rests, first, on the contention that since an eclectic theory inevitably mixes metaphors it is excluded by his root-metaphor theory (see *WH*, pp. 104-13); and, second, on the claim that while his theory calls for "reasonable eclecticism in practice" it is not itself an eclectic theory (see *WH*, pp. 330-32). Yet Pepper does not explain how with this eclecticism in practice one avoids affirming conjunctively several different world theories, and unless one avoids such affirmation it is difficult to see how one avoids the charge of eclecticism. More important, it is difficult to see how eclecticism can provide a satisfactory diagnosis of metaphysical disputes, since it seems to afford nothing but the truism that metaphysicians would not dispute if they embraced each other's theories. At best this is a proposal which would effect a cure, but it is not a diagnosis. The root-metaphor theory can afford a diagnosis only to the extent that it rests on evidence distinct from the evidence for the theories in dispute, yet this is unacceptable to Pepper because it means giving up the traditional cognitive priority of metaphysics. It would give the root-metaphor theory a status comparable to that of Carnap's semantics—the status of an analysis which judges metaphysics on cognitive grounds not appealed to by metaphysicians. Pepper insists that "there is no reliable cognitive appeal beyond an adequate world theory" (*WH*, p. 86).

If Pepper fails in the end to provide a satisfactory diagnosis, he succeeds very well in pointing out that a diagnosis is impossible without denying, as the positivists do, the traditional cognitive priority of metaphysics. This denial is of course tantamount to the outright rejection of metaphysics as speculative philosophy, since a science incapable of diagnosing its own disputes would not be what speculative metaphysicians mean by "metaphysics." One might say that Carnap elevates semantical (or semiotical) analysis to the status of metaphysics, since he regards this analysis alone as one capable of diagnosing its own disputes, but there is the important difference that semantical analysis is not a theory true of the world but only of what is said about the world. It is just this fact that produces the appearance of skepticism in Carnap, since he seems to make knowledge depend ultimately on what one prefers to say about the world. By contrast, Pepper tries in his root-metaphor theory to make knowledge depend on what is true of the world, but only at the expense of making his theory itself an eclectic metaphysics rather than a diagnosis of metaphysical disputes. A further alternative would be a diagnosis which purports to appeal to what is true of the world and yet free of any metaphysics, eclectic or otherwise.

13. *Metaphysical theories as linguistic innovations.* This further alternative is the one taken by another American philosopher, Morris Lazerowitz, in his *The Structure of Metaphysics.*[13] Lazerowitz's philosophic background, unlike Pepper's, is not strictly American. He belongs to a group of American philosophers, for the most part a generation after Pepper, who write primarily under the influence of British analytical philosophy. While it is characteristic of these philosophers, as I shall remark at greater length in Chapter 4, to offer diagnoses of metaphysical disputes, they do not, like the logical positivists, have a common antimetaphysical position. While Carnap's diagnosis can be construed as a mature statement of a case already urged against metaphysics, the same cannot be said of Lazerowitz's. The latter is rather a development of analytical philosophy in one direction, a direction which, though not peculiar to Lazerowitz, is by no means typical. Lazerowitz's book is considered in the present chapter because, along with the works of Carnap and Pepper, it is primarily a defense of a single thesis or theory concerning the nature of metaphysics; it is not, as is more typical of British analytical philosophy, primarily an analysis of particular philosophic problems with a conception of philosophizing illustrated rather than explicitly argued.[14]

In brief, Lazerowitz's thesis is that metaphysical theories are "linguistic innovations." The thesis can be illustrated very well by Whitehead's proposition that all actual entities have sympathetic feelings, although this is not an example used by Lazerowitz. I remarked (§ 5) that Whitehead's proposition represents an obvious departure from ordinary linguistic usage. To speak of all things as sympathizing with each other in essentially the way that human beings do constitutes a radical innovation in the use of the phrase

[13] Morris Lazerowitz, *The Structure of Metaphysics* (Routledge, 1955). Abbreviation, *SM.*
[14] For recent criticism of Lazerowitz's position and an indication of its departures from analytical philosophy, see the essays by Antony Flew and Donald C. Williams in *Psychoanalysis, Scientific Method, and Philosophy,* ed. Sidney Hook (New York U., 1959).

"capable of sympathetic feeling." For Whitehead the innovation results from an imaginative generalization, the grounds for which can be seen only in the context of his entire metaphysical system. In isolation from this context the generalization can be neither established nor refuted because it cannot be understood. In order to see any grounds for the generalization the reader of Whitehead must be oriented in a certain way, willing to go along with certain modes of thought. As Lazerowitz puts the point, the reader must wear the proper "metaphysical spectacles" (SM, p. 62). Through these spectacles the generalization will be seen as only incidentally a linguistic innovation and primarily as the expression of a profound truth about ultimate reality. The aspect of linguistic innovation begins to seem important only when one notes that there are many pairs of metaphysical spectacles and that while the truth-value and significance of the generalization varies with the spectacles its apparently incidental character of linguistic innovation always remains.

Yet metaphysical generalizations on Lazerowitz's analysis turn out to be linguistic innovations of a very special kind. With Whitehead's generalization the descriptive force of the phrase "capable of sympathetic feeling" is not altered but totally obliterated. If all things—all actual entities—are capable of sympathetic feeling one does not succeed in describing something, in distinguishing it from anything else, by saying it is capable of sympathetic feeling. In this context the phrase "capable of sympathetic feeling" has no more descriptive force than the phrase "actual entity." The linguistic innovation thus neither enriches language nor renders it more precise, but actually impoverishes it. A phrase which previously had a definite descriptive function is deprived of this function and nothing is put in its place. With the innovation one can no longer say what one would ordinarily say by describing something as a being (an actual entity) which is capable of sympathetic feeling. It does not help matters to point out that with Whitehead's innovation one can still say that some beings are more and others less capable of sympathetic feeling. These comparative statements do not take the place of the simple descriptive statement in question. On the other hand, Whitehead's generalization loses its metaphysical import if it is taken metaphorically. It makes sense to say that all things are *like*

176

beings with sympathetic feeling only when not all things are in fact beings of this sort, and yet a generalization is metaphysical only to the extent that it purports to state what things are really as opposed to what they are like. As a final maneuver one may claim that reality can only be revealed through metaphorical language and that literal descriptions always refer to appearance. But with Lazerowitz's analysis this claim is itself a further metaphysical theory; it proposes an innovation in the use of "appearance" and "reality" which further impoverishes language by depriving it of the customary contrast between these two terms as they function in literal description.

Metaphysical generalizations thus turn out to be linguistic innovations which bring about incomplete reforms of language. Certain expressions are no longer allowed to perform their ordinary functions and no new expressions are provided to take over these functions. This failure to carry through linguistic reform is, according to Lazerowitz, an unconscious intention on the part of the metaphysician (see *SM*, pp. 225-26). The reform is "intentionally left unfinished" because its completion would destroy the metaphysician's illusion of having made a profound statement about the world. If Whitehead had proposed a new expression to perform the descriptive function ordinarily performed by "capable of sympathetic feeling," his proposal to use "capable of sympathetic feeling" coextensive with "actual entity" would appear to be a pointless and utterly confusing innovation. In the absence of such a new expression, however, what is proposed appears to be an extension rather than an obliteration of the descriptive function. In Whitehead's terms what is proposed is an imaginative generalization which greatly extends the range of actual entities described by the phrase "capable of sympathetic feeling." This claim passes over the fact that the range of actual entities is not merely extended but is made all-inclusive, so that the phrase is no longer able to perform its descriptive function, to distinguish some actual entities from others. While the metaphysician intends to pass over this fact in order to preserve his illusion, he succeeds in the preservation only as long as he is not conscious of his intention.

The final step in Lazerowitz's diagnosis is the claim that this unconscious intention constitutes a "flight from reality" (*SM*, p.

228). In his conscious mind the metaphysician seeks what is universally true of reality, but unconsciously he is fleeing from reality and constructing a world for himself which satisfies his unconscious needs much better than the real world. It is thus that metaphysicians remain in a chronic state of disagreement and dispute with each other. A fanciful world which satisfies the unconscious needs of one metaphysician proves so disquieting to another that the latter feels the need to demonstrate its logical impossibility, and to this end he makes further linguistic innovations. Lazerowitz offers no clinical evidence in support of this psychiatric hypothesis, and while he emphasizes its tentative character he admits that it points to the kind of investigation required to complete his diagnosis (see *SM, p.* 69). It is just with this claim that Lazerowitz's diagnosis, unlike those of Pepper and Carnap, purports to appeal to what is true of the world—to what is forced upon us by experience—and yet purports to be free of any metaphysics. While psychiatry deals with what is said of the world, unlike Carnap's semantics it is not a theory which remains indifferent to what is true of the world; and unlike Pepper's root-metaphor theory its claim to be about the world does not rest on evidence for the truth of statements about the world which it examines.

It might be charged that in appealing to psychiatry Lazerowitz fails to avoid metaphysics; he merely assumes that what psychiatry can say about reality and men's efforts to flee from it provides the true theory of reality, and he thereby elevates psychiatry to the status of metaphysics. But the charge in this form represents a gross misunderstanding of Lazerowitz's diagnosis. He does not appeal to psychiatry for a theory of reality but only for an explanation of the fact that metaphysical theories are unfinished linguistic reforms presented in the guise of profound truths. According to this linguistic analysis of metaphysical theories, a theory of reality can only be a linguistic illusion. A psychiatric hypothesis may explain why men become ready victims of this illusion, and while such a hypothesis is correctly called a theory concerned *with* reality—with what is true of the world—it is not a theory *of* reality.

On the other hand, Lazerowitz does claim to have a philosophical theory in the form of a hypothesis about the nature of metaphysics, and for him this theory provides a philosophical analysis of metaphysical theories more satisfactory than any analysis previously offered (see *SM*, pp. 57-58). Yet what is the subject matter of this theory which Lazerowitz claims to have? It is presumably a theory of metaphysical theories, or, more exactly, of the sentences which produce the illusion of belonging to a metaphysical theory. These sentences constitute subject matter for a theory in exactly the way that dreams constitute subject matter for psychiatry—Lazerowitz calls a metaphysical theory "a verbal dream" (*SM*, p. 26). His philosophical theory about the nature of metaphysics is actually a psychiatric theory about the satisfaction of unconscious needs. While this does not elevate psychiatry to the status of metaphysics it makes at least a considerable part of philosophical analysis part of psychiatry. With philosophical analysis alone Lazerowitz cannot claim to have a theory about metaphysics. He can claim only to have shown that many sentences which have been taken to express metaphysical theories turn out on analysis to be linguistic illusions exhibiting a common pattern. This analysis is not itself a theory but only an endeavor to make sense out of what has been offered as a theory. To regard the analysis as itself a theory turns the understanding of any theory into an infinite regress: every attempt to understand what has been offered as a theory constitutes another theory which requires still another theory to understand it, and so on *ad infinitum*. The analysis gives rise to a theory only when a hypothesis is advanced to explain why men continue to produce these linguistic illusions and to be deceived by them. When Lazerowitz refers to his analysis of metaphysical theories as an analysis of "verbal dreams" he has tacitly introduced his psychiatric hypothesis into his philosophical analysis. He thus obtains a theory about metaphysics, but it is a psychiatric and not a philosophical theory and it is not an alternative philosophical analysis of metaphysical theories.

It is this fusion of philosophical analysis with psychiatry that makes Lazerowitz's diagnosis of metaphysical disputes an atypical development of contemporary analytical philosophy. Only with the fusion can he claim to have a single diagnosis applying to all metaphysical disputes as opposed to separate diagnoses of particular disputes. Separate diagnoses can be achieved through philosophical analysis alone, and more will be said about this analysis in the next section and in the remaining two chapters of this essay. The single diagnosis which Lazerowitz obtains with the aid of a psychiatric hypothesis is similar in scope to the diagnoses offered by Carnap and Pepper, and it is open to similar objections.

14. *Diagnosis and philosophical analysis.* On the technical side, the objections to Lazerowitz's diagnosis can hardly be made specific even if this were the place to discuss them. The objections concern the lack of psychiatric evidence in favor of his hypothesis; he gives no case histories of individual metaphysicians in flight from reality, no clinical evidence at all, but cites examples from literature, mythology, and the more speculative parts of Freud which suggest imaginative creations similar to those suggested by certain metaphysical theories. Leaving aside technical issues, we may ask a question similar to the one we asked of Carnap and Pepper. Even if there were ample psychiatric evidence to show that men construct metaphysical theories to flee from reality and to satisfy their unconscious needs, would this evidence provide a satisfactory diagnosis of the endless disputes of metaphysicians?

Surely the answer is no. The fact that a man is fleeing from reality when he constructs a theory has nothing whatsoever to do with the truth or falsity of the theory, or even with whether it is a theory at all and not merely the verbal appearance of one. A theoretical physicist may be fleeing from reality—from his arduous life as a citizen, husband, and father—when he loses himself in the construction of theories and sees the world as reduced to a mass of elementary physical particles. His theories from this point of view may be verbal dreams, but this does not prevent them from being judged by his fellow physicists as true or false. For they are theories, and that they are is established through the linguistic analysis necessary to understand them. This linguistic analysis by which theories are distinguished from verbal appearances of theories is also philosophical (or conceptual) analysis, and only insofar as Lazerowitz carries on such analysis (as he does in some of his essays) can he claim to have given diagnoses of certain metaphysical disputes. The psychiatric hypothesis contributes nothing to these diagnoses, but its intrusion creates the appearance of a single theory concerning the nature of metaphysics. The appearance arises from the mistaken notion that a theory about the motives which lead men to construct theories is also a theory about the theories constructed.

It should now be clear that the possibility of diagnosing metaphysical disputes depends on the possibility of philosophical analysis, and that a single diagnosis in the form of a theory about the nature of metaphysics appears as a possibility only when philosophical analysis is itself merged with a particular theory. In Carnap the analysis is merged with a semantical (ultimately semiotical) theory about the nature of language; in Pepper it is merged with the metaphysical theories it analyzes so that instead of a single diagnosis the end result appears to be an eclectic metaphysics; finally, with Lazerowitz it is merged with psychiatry. In each case technical difficulties arise in connection with the theories propounded, and on the philosophical side the diagnoses prove unsatisfactory. Carnap's diagnosis appears philosophically as skepticism; Pepper's evaporates into eclecticism; and Lazerowitz's remains ambiguous, appearing to be both philosophical analysis and psychiatric theory.

The two chapters thus far have dealt with metaphysics as speculative philosophy, as a theory of the world—of everything that is. The metaphysical disputes mentioned in Chapter 1 and considered under diagnosis in the present chapter represent clashes between different metaphysical systems taken as single theories, and the persistency of these disputes seems good reason for distrusting speculative philosophy, for questioning its possibility, even though this question cannot be settled by a theory which provides a diagnosis of all the disputes. This distrust of speculative philosophy is not distrust of philosophy generally, but, as Kant put it, distrust of the ability of reason "to soar above the world of sense by the mere power of speculation" (see § 7). Kant had argued that the transcendental philosophy of his first critique supplies a theory which gives a demonstration of the impossibility of speculative philosophy as well as a diagnosis of its disputes. The philosophers considered in the present chapter have by and large followed the footsteps of Kant, seeking to settle the issues by a single theory, though Pepper turns the tables and tries to demonstrate the possibility of speculative philosophy. Lazerowitz's theory more than the others brings into prominence the crucial role of philosophical analysis and points up the question of whether such analysis can be merged with a theory. We shall return to this question of philosophical analysis in Chapter 4.

It was remarked at the close of Chapter 1 that the diagnosticians of metaphysics to be considered in the present chapter are in the main sympathetic to naturalism and that their diagnoses prepare the way for naturalistic philosophy. This remark is not to be taken to imply that any of the three diagnoses I have considered has any special affinity with naturalism. The fundamental point of agreement is rejection of speculative philosophy as an endeavor to formulate the true world theory, the one true and adequate account of everything that is. Naturalists have their own reasons for this rejection and it does not become with them as with the diagnosticians a central thesis to be argued separately and at length. Naturalism is basically a world view as opposed to a world theory and the rejection of speculative philosophy is part of the view and not the result of a theory.

◄§ 3 §►

NATURALISTIC METAPHYSICS

*15. Naturalism.   16. Naturalistic conceptions of metaphysics.
17. Pragmatic naturalism.   18. Lewis's pragmatic conception
of the a priori.   19. Philosophical analysis and the a priori.
20. Contextualism and contextual analysis.   21. Linguistic
contexts.*

15.   *Naturalism.* "Naturalism" more than most "ism"-terms in philosophy has been the label of a variety of different theories and attitudes. The closest thing to a common core of meaning is probably the view that the methods of natural science provide the only avenue to truth. The varieties appear as soon as one turns to an account of these methods and of the subject matters to which they are applicable. Naturalism is frequently presented as a set of theses or tenets which characterize but by no means precisely define a philosophical attitude. To qualify as a naturalist a philosopher need not accept all the tenets or agree fully with other naturalists in the interpretation of the tenets he does accept. This situation has inevitably led some self-styled naturalists to accuse each other of espousing a "half-hearted," "short-winded," "broken-backed," and "specious" kind of naturalism.

While one expects to find naturalists claiming to have naturalistic ethics, epistemology, and logic, "naturalistic metaphysics" seems paradoxical. However broadly one construes the tenets of naturalism, one cannot make them compatible with speculative metaphysics, with a discipline which claims to discover what is true of the world from a vantage point beyond that of natural science. Unlike the logical positivists, many naturalists closely ally (often identify) themselves with pragmatism, and following the lead of William James they have given new and pragmatic interpretations of ancient philosophical terms. Instead of looking to the truth-claims made by systems of speculative metaphysics, these pragmatic naturalists look to the ends which men have had in constructing such

183

systems. Insofar as these ends embrace a world view incorporating the most general truths established by the best available methods rather than a world theory specifically claiming to go beyond the methods of natural science, metaphysics remains a legitimate undertaking for the naturalists themselves.[1]

16. *Naturalistic conceptions of metaphysics.* Differences among the naturalists in their interpretations of naturalistic theses and in their use of the term "metaphysics" stand out clearly in a well-known exchange between two of the most prominent naturalists on the American scene. In 1925 George Santayana published a long review of John Dewey's *Experience and Nature* to which Dewey replied in an article which appeared a little over a year later.[2] Santayana's review was republished with a few minor changes in 1939 in *The Philosophy of John Dewey* as his still valid criticisms of Dewey's philosophy, and Dewey replied in the same volume by reaffirming his earlier stand.[3] Santayana called his review "Dewey's Naturalistic Metaphysics," and he explained in the opening paragraph that while for him the terms "naturalistic" and "metaphysical" appeared to represent contradictory characters, Dewey applied them both to his philosophy. Santayana found no alternative to the conclusion that if Dewey's philosophy was metaphysical, his naturalism was "half-hearted," "short-winded," and of a "specious" kind. Dewey called his reply " 'Half-hearted Naturalism' " and argued that it was Santayana who failed to be a true naturalist, and

[1] Rather than reinterpreting old terms, naturalists sometimes claim that they are preserving the sound conception of metaphysics which had its beginnings in Aristotle and are opposing only the misconceptions and confusions which stem from a Platonic and dialectical tradition that made metaphysics "speculative" rather than "empirical and scientific." See John H. Randall Jr., "Metaphysics: Its Function, Consequences, and Criteria," *Journal of Philosophy*, XLIII (1946), 401-12. For expressions of naturalistic views the reader may consult the essays by various authors in *Naturalism and the Human Spirit*, ed. Y. H. Krikorian (Columbia, 1944).
[2] John Dewey, *Experience and Nature*, 1st ed. (Open Court, 1925); 2nd ed. (Norton, 1929). Page references are to the second edition. Abbreviation, *EN*. George Santayana, "Dewey's Naturalistic Metaphysics," *Journal of Philosophy*, XXII (1925), 673-88. Abbreviation, *DNM*. John Dewey, " 'Half-hearted Naturalism,' " *Journal of Philosophy*, XXIV (1927), 57-64. Abbreviation, *HN*.
[3] *The Philosophy of John Dewey*, ed. P. A. Schilpp (Tudor, 1939; 2nd ed., 1951). Abbreviation, *PD*.

that Santayana's philosophy was merely a "broken-backed naturalism."

The basic issue between Santayana and Dewey is primarily the question of how naturalism is to be supported. The issue concerns the status of strictly human, conventional, and social factors in the acquisition of knowledge. Santayana refers to these factors as "the foreground" and insists that they are always relative to a particular point of view. In nature there is neither foreground nor background; these arise only when a view of nature is taken. Halfhearted naturalism or some other objectionable form of metaphysics is inevitable when the foreground factors determine a philosophy. The naturalism must be halfhearted because it arises not from philosophic understanding but from the social and cultural conditions which comprise a particular foreground. "The pragmatist," Santayana declares (explicitly mentioning Dewey as a pragmatist), "becomes, or seems to become, a naturalist only by accident, when as in the present age and in America the dominant foreground is monopolized by material activity . . ." (*DNM*, p. 679). Under different social and cultural conditions the pragmatist would become an idealist or transcendentalist rather than a naturalist.

Santayana's main point here is one that he has frequently urged elsewhere in his writings (without regard to criticism of Dewey). The following passage from his "Apologia pro mente sua" is a good illustration.

> My philosophy is not an academic opinion adopted because academic tendencies seemed at any moment to favour it. I care very little whether, at any moment, academic tendencies favour one unnecessary opinion or another. I ask myself only what are the fundamental presuppositions that I cannot live without making. And I find that they are summed up in the word materialism.[4]

A few pages later Santayana explains that while he has sometimes used the word "naturalism" rather than "materialism" to characterize his philosophy, he generally prefers the latter as being "safer, precisely because more disliked"; "the cruder notions of it are so crude that they may be easily distinguished and discarded" (*PS*, p.

---

[4] *The Philosophy of George Santayana*, ed. P. A. Schilpp (Tudor, 1940 and 1951), pp. 504-05. Abbreviation, *PS*.

508). In the terms Santayana used in his review of Dewey, "naturalism" is currently a word more in the foreground and therefore more freighted with accidental associations.

The point, then, is that a philosophy is wholeheartedly naturalistic or materialistic only when it arises from an individual's awareness of the presuppositions which he cannot live without making. And Santayana clearly means "without making in any environment whatsoever" and not "without making in some particular environment—some particular foreground." Dewey's naturalism is thus halfhearted on two counts. Not only is Dewey led to naturalism because it happens to be dominant in the foreground in which he lives, but also because he subscribes to a theory of knowledge—a pragmatic epistemology—which makes the foreground factors the ultimate determination of knowledge. In other words, Dewey's pragmatic philosophy explicitly advocates domination by the foreground as well as being itself dominated by a particular foreground. This means, moreover, that Dewey's philosophy is "metaphysical" in the bad sense—in the sense in which Santayana prefers to use the term. "Dominance of the foreground," Santayana argues in his review of Dewey, "has always been the source of metaphysics" (*DNM,* p. 678); and in his "Apologia" he characterizes metaphysics in this bad sense as "humanism materialized" (*PS,* p. 519). The human factors which make up the foreground are assumed to have the power, the efficacy, which can belong only to matter or nature.

It is just in this separation of the human and the natural that Dewey finds one of the primary sources of philosophical error. Human affairs, "associative and personal," Dewey contends in his reply to Santayana, "are projections, continuations, complications, of the nature which exists in the physical and pre-human world" (*HN,* p. 58). The foregrounds are thus in nature, part of nature, and in opposing them to nature Santayana has created an unnatural gulf, a "bifurcation" of nature which can only result in "a broken-backed naturalism." The fundamental question as Dewey sees it is whether immediate experience in the foreground "conducts our thought to the background" or whether, as Santayana seems to hold, it is "a screen which conceals the background" (*HN,* p. 60). Dewey has no objection to calling this a "metaphysical" question.

186

He remarks in a footnote on the same page, "my 'metaphysical principle' is that the related foreground may be taken as a method for determining the traits of the background."

The sense of "metaphysical" intended here is presumably the broad pragmatic one of a world view; the sense summed up in Dewey's remark of 1939: " 'metaphysical' in the sense in which an empirical naturalist may give that name to the more generalized statements about Nature which he finds to be justified" (PD, p. 597). But then there is a double meaning to the "metaphysical principle" just mentioned. On the one hand, as "metaphysical" and naturalistic it is a generalization concerning man in relation to his environment, a generalization about natural objects. Human organisms are asserted to be so related to their environment that their immediate experience of the latter provides them with a method for determining its traits which they cannot immediately experience. On the other hand, the principle in another sense may be understood as presupposed in the very process by which it itself along with all other generalizations of science and naturalistic metaphysics is established. For unless men are related to their environment as the principle declares, they are cut off from all science including that knowledge of themselves as human organisms which is expressed in the principle.

In this second sense the principle qualifies as one of Santayana's "fundamental presuppositions" that one cannot live without making. In this sense too the principle has sometimes been called "metaphysical," and Santayana recognizes this sense of "metaphysical," though he does not prefer it, as a nonpejorative use of the term. He remarks in his "Apologia" that if we adopt this use, "I should indeed have a metaphysics; not my materialism, for that would be only my physics or scientific speculation; but my metaphysics would be the belated history or analysis of my presuppositions contained in this very Apology" (PS, pp. 519-20). The principle in the first sense mentioned above, the sense in which it is metaphysical for Dewey, would now not be metaphysical but would be a generalization about the world, supported by scientific evidence, and comprising one of the tenets of materialism or naturalism.

The issue between Dewey and Santayana arises because Dewey does not recognize this double meaning of his principle. The recognition for him would lead to a bifurcation of nature. As presupposition the principle is made prior to all knowledge of nature and cannot be part of such knowledge; a part of nature is thus severed from the rest and the back of naturalism is broken. Santayana's point is then that Dewey has nothing on which to base his naturalism except the fact that the scientific attitude is currently in the foreground. By taking the principle only as part of our knowledge of nature Dewey can offer in support of his naturalism only the evidence of natural science. But why must one accept this evidence? Dewey cannot say "Because of presuppositions which one cannot live without making." The presuppositions of naturalism would be for Dewey part of our knowledge of nature and would therefore stand in need of scientific evidence rather than behind it as a reason for accepting it. The evidence thus has no force except that derived from the dominance of the foreground; Dewey's naturalism is halfhearted and "metaphysical" in the bad sense for Santayana.

But how do Santayana's presuppositions supply any evidence? At the outset of his review of Dewey he says that naturalism "is not a special system at all, but the spontaneous and inevitable body of beliefs involved in animal life" (*DNM,* p. 673). His presuppositions thus seem to reduce to an expression of what he calls elsewhere "animal faith." While this is admittedly not evidence in the sense of scientific evidence, it is the only kind of evidence possible for naturalism as Santayana understands it. One sees the reason for accepting naturalism when one recognizes it as an unavoidable body of beliefs, and with this recognition one acknowledges the force of scientific evidence. One also acknowledges in particular that the very animal faith which underlies naturalism is itself subject matter to be explained by a sufficiently developed science of animal life. With this explanation science, in Santayana's phrase, "would come round full circle," [5] but it would not thereby establish naturalism or provide evidence for it in any way. Naturalism remains unavoidable even though this scientific explanation is never achieved. But when the possibility of such explanation is in the dominant foreground it can give rise to a halfhearted naturalism—a naturalism

[5] George Santayana, *The Realms of Being* (Scribner, 1942), p. 194. Abbreviation, *RB.*

accepted without the philosophic understanding that comes with recognition of its inevitability.

I remarked above that Santayana in his "Apologia" spoke of metaphysics in the nonpejorative sense as a "history or analysis" of his presuppositions. He went on in the next sentence to call such an undertaking "self-criticism or the pursuit of self-knowledge" rather than "metaphysics." It is just this analysis, this self-criticism, that discloses the inevitability of naturalism, and the issue between Dewey and Santayana may now be seen as one concerning the status of philosophical analysis and criticism. In the final chapter of *Experience and Nature* Dewey speaks of philosophy as criticism, but not so much of oneself as of human life in all its manifestations. Metaphysics is described as "but a ground-map of the province of criticism, establishing base lines to be employed in more intricate triangulations" (*EN,* p. 413). This conception of metaphysics as the foundation of criticism is summarized clearly in Dewey's reply to Santayana.

> This is the extent and method of my 'metaphysics':—the large and constant features of human sufferings, enjoyments, trials, failures, and successes together with the institutions of art, science, technology, politics, and religion which mark them, communicate genuine features of the world within which man lives. The method differs no whit from that of any investigator who, by making certain observations and experiments, and by utilizing the existing body of ideas available for calculation and interpretation, concludes that he really succeeds in finding out something about some limited aspect of nature [*HN,* p. 59].

In *Experience and Nature* Dewey remarks that metaphysics "begins and ends with analysis and definition" (*EN,* p. 413), but the above statement makes it clear he does not intend to distinguish the method of metaphysics from that of natural science. The analyses and definitions in metaphysics and science may differ in degree of generality but they result from essentially the same kind of inquiry. Thus, with Dewey, as with the diagnosticians considered in the preceding chapter, philosophical analysis appears to be merged with theory. But now the theory itself is merged with all of science, natural and social, instead of remaining a particular theory for the diagnosis of metaphysical disputes. For Santayana, on the other hand, philosophical analysis remains a distinct kind of inquiry, reflective and self-critical rather than theoretical, and inappropriately called "metaphysics" precisely because this name has traditionally meant a kind of theory. Santayana's naturalism—his faith in the ultimacy of the methods of natural science—is supported by or arises from his philosophical analysis. Dewey's faith in the same methods receives support only from a theory purportedly established by the methods themselves.

We shall return presently to this question of philosophical analysis, but it is well to note first some questions about Dewey's naturalism in relation to speculative philosophy.

17. *Pragmatic naturalism.* It is easy to construe Dewey's naturalistic metaphysics as very much the same sort of thing as Whitehead's speculative philosophy. Whitehead's method of generalization is the method employed whenever "the higher generalities" are sought, in science or in metaphysics, and his speculative philosophy thus appears as a continuation of science. But there is one fundamental point of difference between Whitehead and Dewey on the relation of science to metaphysics. While Whitehead regards metaphysics as differing from science in degree of generality, this does not mean that science rather than metaphysics deals with the world in its concreteness. On the contrary, metaphysics alone approaches reality in its full concreteness while science is always an abstraction from the concrete (see § 1). Though in method metaphysics appears as a continuation of science, in content and purpose it is not science but something beyond science which redirects the mind from abstractions back to the concrete (see § 3).

Dewey notes his disagreement with Whitehead on this point in his essay "The Philosophy of Whitehead." [6] After agreeing with Whitehead that "physical science is an abstraction" and that "rational thought" must "describe the more concrete fact from which that abstraction is derivable," Dewey objects to Whitehead's further contention that actual entities in their full concreteness express "emotional and purposeful" energy (*PW*, p. 660). The objection is

[6] In *The Philosophy of Alfred North Whitehead,* ed. Schilpp. Abbreviation, *PW.*

not to the claim that such energy has a place in the concreteness of things, but to the claim that any determination of concreteness can be final or ultimate. Dewey sees this second claim as contrary to what he finds most congenial in Whitehead's philosophy, its emphasis on process, growth, and development. For Dewey this emphasis means not only that the actual results of inquiry are never final and beyond need of revision, but also that inquiry itself is practical and instrumental—always means to further ends—and is not to be conceived as striving to approximate final determinations of an ultimate reality. Whiteheadian metaphysics as an attempt to formulate ultimate generalities which expose the full concreteness of actual entities appears to be an inquiry so conceived; and it appears all the more so in view of Whitehead's further claim that metaphysics is fundamentally unlike science in content and purpose. Dewey is forced to conclude that Whitehead's metaphysics, at least in certain of its formal statements, represents a return to the "conversion of moral idealism, the idealism of action, into ontological idealism or 'spiritualism'" (*PW*, p. 661). The presence of fixed ideals in particular situations of moral action is converted into the presence of ultimate purposefulness in the nature of reality.

In this opposition to Whitehead Dewey stands with the logical positivists. There is no knowledge of the world beyond natural science and a science of ultimate reality is illusion. Yet Dewey differs radically from the positivists as well as from Santayana in basing his rejection of speculative metaphysics on inquiry continuous with and following the methods of natural science. He recognizes no form of critical or analytical inquiry with a different method. Instead, he professes to have a "metaphysics" which follows the method of natural science, seeks the "common traits of all existence" (*EN*, p. 413), and provides a ground map of the province of criticism. It is this circumstance that makes it easy to construe Dewey's naturalistic metaphysics as essentially like Whitehead's speculative philosophy. His opposition to Whitehead then appears simply as a disagreement of one speculative philosopher with another. One may of course reply that unlike the speculative philosophers Dewey insists that his inquiry is not conceived as approximating ultimate determinations. But then why does he call it "metaphysics"? The answer can only be that he has given a pragmatic reinterpretation of

191

old terminology and is trying to make clear the function which men have often thought metaphysics should perform. The situation, after all, is the same with natural science, which has been traditionally conceived, not as instrumental, but as a quest for final determinations of nature. "Physics" is no less in need of pragmatic reinterpretation than "metaphysics," and if the former term is retained, why not the latter?

Dewey's naturalism, then, is a pragmatic naturalism, a naturalism in which there is no final distinction between philosophical analysis and theory. For all theories are ultimately practical and instrumental and are no more true of a fixed subject matter determined independently of inquiry than is philosophical analysis. The kind of practically compelling evidence, the animal faith, disclosed by Santayana's philosophical analysis is for Dewey not different in kind from the evidence disclosed by the methods of natural science. Rather than merging philosophical analysis with theory, as the diagnosticians, Dewey thus comes closer to construing all theory as essentially like philosophical analysis.

It is this union of pragmatism and naturalism that makes Dewey's philosophy susceptible to such contrary interpretations—that makes Dewey appear to belong both with the logical positivists and with the speculative metaphysicians, to be a halfhearted naturalist because of his pragmatism and yet to be opposed to pragmatism. Dewey objects to the thoroughgoing pragmatism of William James insofar as it seems to recognize individual preference and satisfaction as ultimate criteria of truth. The objection is essentially that in James's pragmatism the individual is conceived personally and humanistically and not (as naturalism would require) biologically and sociologically.[7] Yet Dewey does not intend (as strict logical

[7] See Dewey's review of James's *Pragmatism,* reprinted in John Dewey, *Essays in Experimental Logic* (Dover, 1953), pp. 303-29. Nonnaturalistic philosophers often find a metaphysical thesis in the naturalists' restriction to a biological, sociological, and essentially behavioristic view of man. DeWitt Parker, for example, contends that "even the materialist, in his nonacademic moments, accepts a nonnaturalistic—one might almost say a religious—interpretation of at least one part of his environment, namely the social part. Here at least is a portion of reality the behavior of which he tries to affect by an appeal to desire and reason, rather than by the purely technological methods employed to affect 'things.' Whoever believes in his fellowmen believes in the supernatural" (DeWitt H. Parker, *Experience and Substance* [U. of Mich., 1941], pp. 336-37).

positivism and naturalism would) to deny theoretic meaning to a personal and humanistic account; he means only to oppose any sharp break between the human and the natural, the personal and the biological, action and theory. He is thus opposed both to outright pragmatism and to outright naturalism, though the two are amalgamated in his philosophy.

The virtues of this amalgamation are open to serious question, but the present essay is not the place to discuss them. Reasons for distinguishing philosophical analysis from scientific theory should become apparent from a consideration of naturalistic philosophies in which the distinction is drawn.

18. *Lewis's pragmatic conception of the a priori.* C. I. Lewis was mentioned in Chapter 1 as a philosopher who maintained in opposition to Whitehead that metaphysics should be critical and reflective rather than speculative. Lewis's *Mind and the World-Order* was cited as a work written with that distrust of speculative philosophy which Whitehead repudiated at the outset of his *Process and Reality.* "Philosophy," according to Lewis, "is the study of the a priori," and "is thus the mind's formulation of its own active attitudes" (*MWO,* pp. 24, 36). It is "the mind's own study of itself in action" and it "seeks to formulate explicitly what from the beginning is our own creation and possession" (*MWO,* p. 18). The part of philosophy which comprises metaphysics is the part addressed to "the problem of the categories"; more specifically, "the categories of reality" as distinct from "the categories of value" (*MWO,* pp. 10-11).

The problem of the categories is a priori because "we cannot even interrogate experience without a network of categories and definitive concepts" (*MWO,* p. 259). Scientific experiment and ob-

---

From the standpoint of either Santayana or Dewey, Parker makes the mistake of regarding naturalism or materialism as a thesis concerning what ultimately exists—as an ontological thesis of speculative philosophy—rather than a presupposition unavoidable in the practice of science. Parker's view, however, can be found in the writings of some professed naturalists. Parker's Michigan colleague, Roy Wood Sellars, for example, espouses naturalism as a thesis concerning what is ultimately real and remarks that Dewey has a naturalism "dominated by the term *experience,* a very human term which is thin in its ontological possibilities" (Roy Wood Sellars, *The Philosophy of Physical Realism* [Macmillan, 1932], p. 4; Sellars' italics).

servation as well as the simplest empirical inquiries of our everyday practice presuppose criteria by which we distinguish the real
from the illusory. Empirical inquiry is never mere instinctive response or conditioned reflex; it is always conscious activity, discriminating and paying attention to some factors of experience rather
than others. The initial direction of attention, the discrimination
without which empirical inquiry can never get underway, cannot
itself be accounted for as a further result of such inquiry. It must
be the result of something we know prior to all empirical inquiry, something we know a priori, and this something, according
to Lewis, is a network of categories and definitive concepts which
provides the criteria for the initial discrimination and direction of
attention.

In opposition to Kant, Lewis holds that the network of categories is not fixed and unalterable. But then what is known a priori must meet "the apparently contradictory requirements that it
may be known in advance to hold good for all experience and that
it have alternatives" (*MWO*, p. 232). Lewis contends that a definition or rule of classification and interpretation meets these requirements. For example, the principle that all physical objects have
mass is known to be true in advance of all experience insofar as it
serves only to define "physical object." In this sense no experience
could conceivably falsify the principle, because anything found not
to have mass would not be called "a physical object." Yet the
principle has alternatives for we may conceivably reach a situation
where we discover that the principle is no longer useful as a rule
for classification and interpretation of our experience. We may find
something we want to call "a physical object" even though it does
not have mass. But then we would not say that the principle in
question is false but only that it should be abandoned in favor of
an alternative principle—that our old concept of "physical object"
should be dropped from our network of categories (see *MWO*, pp.
26-27, 232). Lewis thus concludes that "the determination of the a
priori is in some sense like free choice and deliberate action" (see
MWO, pp. 232-33).

This does not mean that the a priori is "arbitrary in the sense of
being capriciously determined" (*MWO*, p. 237). In pure mathe-

matics the determination is given by criteria of self-consistency, but something more is needed when concepts are used in classification and interpretation of experience. In this second case we must recognize the fact that "man, being a species of animal, has characteristics which mark him as such, and some of these at least are reflected in the bent of human thought" (*MWO*, p. 238). Some modes of thought are thus simpler and more natural for us than others which are still possible. The point is that "knowledge has a practical business to perform" and what we take as the a priori basis of knowledge is limited by the way in which our animal nature enables us to cope with the facts of our environment. The a priori element in knowledge, then, is pragmatic, and as such it is to be distinguished from the empirical element. Failure to draw this distinction is a serious mistake of pragmatism. Lewis remarks: "The pragmatists generally have neglected to make the separation of concept and immediacy, with the result that they seem to put all truth at once at the mercy of experience and within the power of human decision or in a relation of dependence upon the human mind" (*MWO*, p. 266). The trouble with this view is that "the sense in which facts are brute and given cannot be the sense in which the truth about them is made by the mind or alterable to human needs" (*ibid.*).

19. *Philosophical analysis and the a priori.* In sharp opposition to Dewey, Lewis thus draws a fundamental distinction between philosophical analysis, in which we study our own creations, and natural science, in which we study interrelations of brute fact. Yet Lewis remains a naturalist because he holds that when it comes to what is true of the world as distinct from what is true of our own creations, natural science is the sole arbiter. While there is much in Lewis that seems close to Santayana, especially the reference to animal nature as determining our categorial scheme, there are also important differences between the two philosophers. The opening chapter of Santayana's *The Realm of Truth* bears the title "There Are No Necessary Truths." This is in explicit opposition to Lewis, for whom as for Santayana "necessary truth" and "a priori truth" are equivalent expressions. Santayana contends that the rea-

sons for saying that a proposition is necessary must be distinguished from the reasons for saying that it is true. Many propositions, he explains, "may be necessary, by virtue of the definitions given to their terms; many may be true, in that the facts of nature confirm them; and some may be both necessary logically and true materially, but even then the necessity will come from one quarter and the truth from another" (*RB*, p. 407). The determination of truth is always contingent; it depends on what happens to be the fact and not, like the determination of necessity, on what we create through our definitions.

The technical expressions "necessary truth" and "a priori truth" thus have no application in Santayana's philosophy, but he remarks at the start of his third chapter that, having shown that truth as he defines it is "wholly contingent," he has "no desire to quarrel with mankind for using words as they choose, and talking of truth also in cases where there is only consistency" (*RB*, p. 426). This "idiomatic use of the word true," he continues, "is semi-moral. It turns on not belying one's professions and being constant to a plighted troth. Serious thought requires this sort of fidelity." The common phrase "true to one's principles" illustrates the sort of thing Santayana has in mind, though he does not mention this example. We say that a proposition of some part of pure mathematics is "true" when it is either an axiom (a principle to which we must be true if we are to have this part of pure mathematics at all) or a theorem logically implied by the axioms, and hence a proposition which we must accept if we remain true to the axioms. Likewise, in philosophical analysis we say that a certain presupposition is "true" when we find that we cannot live without making it—that we must accept it if we are true to ourselves.

On the surface, it may seem that Santayana is in substantial agreement with Lewis's pragmatic view of the a priori and that the main difference is only verbal—Santayana simply refuses to dignify truth limited only by the demands of consistency and our animal nature with the philosophical title "necessary truth" or "a priori truth"—but there is much more than this verbal difference. The refusal to use the philosophical title is due to Santayana's conviction that philosophical analysis is not a theory—not an investigation of an actual subject matter; the refusal is not due to any prejudice against philosophical jargon. Santayana does not hesitate to use the latter when he feels it is needed.

We have already noted (§ 1) that Lewis is in verbal agreement with the speculative philosophers when he says that metaphysics "studies the nature of reality in general," but then by "reality" Lewis means experience "categorially interpreted" (see, e.g., *MWO*, p. 197). Metaphysics studies only the principles of interpretation, the a priori element in reality and not the element given in experience. There is thus no actual subject matter for metaphysics determined both by what is given in experience and by principles of interpretation. Yet metaphysics studies something; it is a critical and reflective examination of principles, but it is also a study of what is necessarily true of reality—of the nature of reality in general. Metaphysics thus appears to be both philosophical analysis and a theory.

I have remarked (§ 13) that the attempt to regard philosophical analysis as a theory turns the understanding of any theory into an infinite regress. There is then always a further theory to understand in the process of trying to understand any theory. Lewis in effect proposes to break the regress with his distinction between a priori and empirical knowledge. The understanding of any theory concerning an actual subject matter requires the understanding of a further "theory," the theory comprising the a priori principles which the first theory presupposes. But then since this second "theory" concerns all possible reality and has no actual subject matter, there are no further a priori principles—no further theory—required to understand it. The discovery and analysis of presuppositions or a priori principles is, so to speak, self-illuminating, self-explanatory. The regress is stopped. But is it stopped by the discovery of a priori truth—truth concerning all possible reality—or by the fact that we have accomplished what we set out to accomplish, an understanding of the theory in question, including its presuppositions?

Santayana takes the second alternative. In our understanding of the presuppositions we do not discover principles true a priori, but rather principles to which we must be true if we are to have theories at all. As true of the world, these principles like all other truths are contingent; yet they are peculiar in that we must be true

197

to them now (even though we admit that subsequent experience may show them not to be true of the world) because we find them to be presuppositions we cannot live without making.

By taking the first alternative and speaking of the principles as a priori knowledge Lewis is faced with the problem of explaining how the principles are necessarily and not just contingently true of the world. This is precisely the problem Kant faced and professed to solve in his transcendental philosophy by maintaining that while the world in itself, apart from its appearances to us, is unknown and unknowable, we can discover through philosophical analysis how the world must appear to us and thus obtain principles which for us are necessarily true of the world. But this conversion of philosophical analysis into a transcendental theory—a theory which transcends everything given in experience and determines the necessary preconditions of experience—is as unacceptable to Lewis as to any other naturalist. Yet Lewis can accept neither the more thoroughgoing naturalism of Santayana, in which philosophical analysis is not a theory at all, nor the more thoroughgoing pragmatism of Dewey in which philosophical analysis is merged with natural science and all theory is made ultimately practical. The sense in which Lewis's pragmatic theory of the a priori is a theory remains puzzling; it is not a transcendental theory and to construe it as a theory of natural science would be to make the presuppositions of all natural science depend on a particular theory of natural science. The latter is hardly what Lewis intends—the adjective "pragmatic" characterizes what the theory is about—the nature of the a priori— rather than the theory itself; the theory is not pragmatic in the sense that it itself is instrumental and merged with practice.

A further remark may help to clarify the status of Lewis's theory and the issues it raises. The propositions of pure mathematics are prominent examples of a priori truth for Lewis and his point seems to be that since we recognize these propositions as true of a subject matter, as necessarily true of something, the same should hold for a priori propositions occurring outside mathematics, including those occurring in philosophical analysis. Santayana too regards philosophical analysis and pure mathematics as having the same status with respect to truth, but he draws the opposite conclusion. The propositions of pure mathematics like the presuppositions disclosed in philosophical analysis can be true of something only in the sense of being contingently true of the world. Yet both are "true" in the semimoral sense that we must be true to them if we are to realize certain conditions. Santayana unlike Lewis is thus forced to reject the apparently reasonable view, that mathematical propositions are necessarily true in themselves and are not merely assumptions necessary for certain conclusions or conclusions necessitated by certain assumptions. But, on the other hand, Santayana avoids the difficulties of having to explain the status of a general theory of the a priori and to account for philosophical analysis as a kind of theoretical knowledge. Another alternative, taken by neither Santayana nor Lewis, is to maintain that pure mathematics and philosophical analysis are concerned with truth in fundamentally different ways. One form of this alternative is represented by the position sometimes called "contextualism."

20. *Contextualism and contextual analysis.* Various naturalists have adopted the label "contextualism" as a mark of their opposition to any form of absolutism, to any attempt to fix the meanings of key terms absolutely without regard for context. But these naturalists by no means always agree in what they regard as a context or in the extent to which the notion of context should be relativized and pluralized. Arthur Murphy, for example, in his essay in *The Philosophy of John Dewey* charges that Dewey's instrumentalism rests on the mistaken assumption that a single context is ultimate. While science has an instrumental function, "to suppose," as Dewey does, "that the whole meaning of what science tells us about the physical environment is reducible to this instrumental function is to treat one context in which things come to us as ultimate for metaphysics, and this is an irreparable mistake" (*PD,* p. 223). In his reply to Murphy in the same volume Dewey frankly acknowledges that "the problematic situation is *the* context in which everything I say about knowing is placed and by reference to which it is to be understood" (*PD,* p. 560, Dewey's italics). He remarks later in the same paragraph that Murphy has failed "to note the context which actually controls my theory, both in general and in all its constituent details."

Dewey's contextualism, apparently accepting a single context as ultimate, is easily construed as a piece of speculative metaphysics. We noted that Pepper lists contextualism as one of the four adequate world hypotheses, and his descriptions of this hypothesis apply readily to Dewey's philosophy. That the problematic situation provides *the* context for metaphysics can be taken as an imaginative generalization about all reality—the ultimately real comprises a continuum of problematic situations and not a continuum of events or a series of independent substances. Acceptance of this generalization is appropriately called "contextualism" because it makes terms like "substance" and "event," which are ultimate in other metaphysical generalizations, relative to the context of a given problematic situation. By taking problematic situations as ultimate one appears to avoid the usual metaphysical questions "What is reality in its full concreteness?" and "What are the final real things of which the world is made up?" These questions, one may claim, make sense only within the context of a problematic situation; they have no final or metaphysical answer. But there remains the problem of explaining how problematic situations themselves are ultimate. At this point terms like "organism," "environment," and "experience" seem to take on the ultimacy of metaphysical terms for Dewey and he seems to end by making generalizations of biology and sociology generalizations of speculative metaphysics.

Dewey persistently denied this charge of speculative metaphysics and insisted that his metaphysics remains naturalistic and empirical, just as tentative in principle as any generalization in the natural sciences. Yet what conceivable circumstance would have led Dewey to abandon the assumption he seems to make that the problematic situation provides *the* context for metaphysics? This is a serious question for Dewey if, with Murphy, one regards the problematic situation as one context among others. But if the phrase "problematic situation" serves simply as an elucidation of what is meant by "context" in philosophical analysis, the assumption in question is not that one context alone is ultimate for metaphysics. It is rather that no generalizations about the world are intelligible apart from the contexts of inquiry, apart from the problematic situations which give rise to them. Ernest Nagel inclines to this interpretation of Dewey and construes Dewey's assumption as one "unavoidable in any responsible analysis." [8] Metaphysics, according to Nagel, is something that arises only when this assumption is not made and generalizations about the world are attempted without reference to contexts of inquiry. To interpret Dewey as holding that the ultimately real comprises a continuum of problematic situations, or that the problematic situation provides *the* context for metaphysics, is in Nagel's view contrary to the spirit of Dewey's philosophy despite the fact that at times it seems to be what Dewey is saying.

Nagel's point is that contexts or situations for the philosophical analyst are not realities about which one generalizes but rather circumstances within which one conducts inquiries and seeks to reach agreement with one's fellow inquirers. I remarked (§ 2) in Chapter 1 that agreement among speculative philosophers seems impossible because each system of speculative metaphysics defines for itself the circumstances within which agreement can be sought. In the language of the present chapter, each system of speculative metaphysics puts forth a single context or set of circumstances as the context within which all cognitive issues can be settled. Nagel's "contextualistic naturalism" accepts an irreducible plurality of contexts or situations and insists that cognitive issues can be settled only within the specific contexts that give rise to them. This insistence is not intended to constitute an assumption about the world; it is intended simply as a recognition of what is necessary for the analysis and understanding of cognitive issues. While of course the contexts or situations of inquiry provide subject matter for biological and sociological investigations, this subject matter is no more or less ultimate than any other. Contextualistic naturalism accords no special ultimacy to biological and sociological generalizations unless it is interpreted as speculative metaphysics. Nagel unlike Dewey guards against this interpretation by rejecting the term "metaphysics" or even the phrase "naturalistic metaphysics" as a label for any part of his philosophy. The ultimately real for contextualistic naturalism is not a continuum or series of contexts, problematic situations, substances or events, or anything else; there is no ultimate reality behind the diverse realities which different contexts take as ultimate.

[8] Ernest Nagel, *Sovereign Reason* (Free Press of Glencoe, 1954), p. 105.

There remains the difficulty of deciding what constitutes a context. Murphy, as we have noted, regards the problematic situation in which the whole meaning of science is reducible to an instrumental function as constituting one context of inquiry among others, while Dewey (and probably Nagel) regards any context of inquiry as a problematic situation. It was said at the close of the preceding section that an alternative to the views of both Lewis and Santayana on a priori truth was represented by contextualism. The alternative was that pure mathematics and philosophical analysis are concerned with truth in fundamentally different ways, or, as we may say now, that the contexts of inquiry in the two cases are fundamentally different. Even if the truth sought in both contexts is instrumental, it is not instrumental in the same way. Pure mathematics is instrumental in an obvious sense: it provides tools indispensable for further inquiries, including, perhaps, inquiries in philosophical analysis as well as in natural science. Philosophical analysis uses tools rather than provides them, and it is instrumental only in the sense that a critical analysis and understanding of one's objectives facilitates their attainment. But if contextualism thus avoids the difficulties of construing pure mathematics and philosophical analysis as seeking necessary truth, it is faced with the task of presenting a clear conception of philosophical analysis as contextual analysis. This task can hardly be fulfilled as long as what constitutes a context remains unclear.

21. *Linguistic contexts.* Philosophical analysis, whether practiced by speculative philosophers, diagnosticians of metaphysics, or naturalists, is addressed to the explication of certain key terms or concepts. The latter are of course represented by words, sometimes by words coined especially for the purpose by the philosophical analyst and sometimes by words borrowed from ordinary language or science. But the newly coined words are always introduced and defined with the help of words already familiar. One obvious sense of "context" stands out in this process. The different functions of a given word become clear through its associations with other words, through its linguistic contexts. The word "substance," for example, functions in one way in the sentence "Water is a substance composed of hydrogen and oxygen" and in another way in the sentence

NATURALISTIC METAPHYSICS

"The substance of his proposal is unacceptable." Contextual analysis thus begins as an analysis of the use of linguistic expressions, but how it should proceed after this beginning is another matter.

The earlier naturalists of our period, like Dewey and Santayana, turned to the biological and sociological conditions which make inquiry possible and sought in these conditions the ultimate factors governing the use of the linguistic expressions in question. Lewis's pragmatic theory of the a priori accords a quasi-Kantian status to these factors, a status intended to accommodate the circumstance that such factors, after all, are ultimate for any inquiry, including the inquiries of biology and sociology. Such positions thus represent attempts to locate unifying conditions behind the initial plurality of linguistic contexts.

Second generation American naturalists such as Murphy and Nagel tend to accept the plurality as ultimate and to seek piecemeal, context by context, resolutions of philosophical issues rather than a set of unifying conditions that provides the key to all resolutions. There is still the unity afforded by naturalism as a view of the world, but the ultimate plurality of the issues is then part of the view. This emphasis on pluralism focuses attention on the linguistic context itself rather than its underlying conditions; the end of philosophical investigation and analysis then tends to be an understanding of what is meant by statements of scientific inquiry and everyday life rather than an account of ultimate presuppositions. This tendency has become even more pronounced in the younger generation of American philosophers today who may be said to write in the tradition of American naturalism, and the tendency produces affinities not only with British analytical philosophy, as remarked above (§ 13), but also with certain features of logical positivism.[9]

Philosophy for Carnap, as we have noted, becomes semiotical analysis, a kind of general investigation of language, its structure and functions (§ 10). In contrast to what has become characteristic of British analytical philosophy, Carnap's analysis proceeds by

[9] This type of philosophizing is well illustrated by the essays in *Philosophical Analysis*, ed. Max Black (Cornell, 1950), and also by Black's own books *Language and Philosophy* and *Problems of Analysis* (Cornell, 1949 and 1954). Morton G. White in his *Toward Reunion in Philosophy* (Harvard, 1956) explores ways of uniting different strands in pragmatism, naturalism, positivism, and contextualism.

translating the sentences of an ordinary language like English into sentences of an artificial language like one of the calculi developed in mathematical logic. The extent to which these translations are possible or desirable becomes a central issue when philosophical analysis is focused on the linguistic context, and, as we shall see in the next chapter, concentration on this issue places the relation between speculative and analytical philosophy in a new perspective.

METAPHYSICS AND LINGUISTIC ANALYSIS

22. The turn to language. 23. Speculative philosophy and the ideal language. 24. Semantic ascent. 25. Contextualism and "holism." 26. Mathematical logic and philosophical analysis. 27. "Casuism" and philosophical analysis. 28. "Casuism," naturalism, and speculative philosophy. 29. A glance at the future.

22. *The turn to language.* The view that language is fundamental in philosophical investigation is not confined to those who write in distrust of speculative philosophy. We have already noted (§ 4) that Whitehead regarded language as "the tool required for philosophy." The continual improvement of this tool, according to Whitehead, is as crucial for the advance of philosophical inquiry as the continual improvement of physical instruments is for the advance of physical inquiry. Yet the analogy is not intended to imply that linguistic expressions are part of the subject matter of philosophy in the way that physical instruments are part of the subject matter of physics. The generalizations of physics apply indiscriminately to physical instruments of observation and physical objects observed, but the generalizations of metaphysics do not apply indiscriminately to linguistic expressions and the ultimate realities symbolized. The Whiteheadian metaphysician uses linguistic tools to investigate what is not linguistic while the physicist uses physical tools to investigate what is physical. The analogy holds only for the point that increased metaphysical knowledge makes possible an improvement of linguistic tools essential for further metaphysical knowledge, just as increased physical knowledge makes possible an improvement of physical tools essential for further physical knowledge.

In contrast to this conception of language and philosophy many opponents of speculative metaphysics tend to view language as providing the subject matter as well as the tool of philosophical inquiry. While such a view avoids the problem of giving evidence for generalizations about ultimate reality, it seems to do so at the expense of reducing philosophy to a study of linguistic usage. This appears to be the case, whether the philosophical analysis of linguistic contexts is unified by a general theory of language such as that given in semiotics or remains ultimately pluralistic and piecemeal. A position which claims to avoid the difficulties of either of these extremes and still maintains that philosophy is about language has been championed in America by a philosopher who began his career in Europe with the logical positivists.

Gustav Bergmann came to the United States in the late Thirties, and while he continued to share with the positivists a strong interest in the development of mathematical logic and the philosophy of science he refused to join the attack on metaphysics. The positivists, according to Bergmann, were developing a metaphysics without being aware of it, and their philosophical program was severely handicapped by their failure to recognize what they were doing. Bergmann's own position appears in a collection of essays published in 1954, *The Metaphysics of Logical Positivism*, and in a second collection, *Meaning and Existence*, published in 1960.[1]

While Bergmann sees contemporary philosophy as taking what he calls a "linguistic turn," he contends that this turn properly executed in no way reduces philosophy to a study of linguistic usage. His central thesis is that language is related to the world much as a picture is related to what it pictures. "To say that a picture, to be a picture, must have certain features is, clearly, to say something about what it is a picture of"; and, analogously, to say that a language, to be a language, must have certain features is to say something about the world the language represents (*MP*, p. 41). "I know no other way," Bergmann adds, "to speak of the world's categorial features without falling into the snares the linguistic turn avoids" (*ibid.*). Instead of asking about the final real things of which the world is made up and thus becoming ensnared in a maze of conflicting world hypotheses, one asks, with Bergmann's linguistic turn, about the categories of primitive signs in "the ideal

[1] Gustav Bergmann, *The Metaphysics of Logical Positivism* (Longmans, 1954). Abbreviation, *MP*. *Meaning and Existence* (U. of Wisconsin, 1960). Abbreviation, *ME*.

language." The latter is simply that language which contains all the features, and only the features, which any language must contain in order to provide an adequate representation of the world. The subject matter of philosophy is thus language in the sense that philosophical discourse consists of talk in an ordinary language like English about the ideal language; but the subject matter is not language in the sense that philosophy is the study of actual linguistic usage. And even this proviso is not quite enough. For Bergmann "philosophical discourse is not just about the ideal language but rather, by means of it, about the world" (ME, p. 93). The aim of metaphysics, in other words, is knowledge of the world and not of language, even though the proper method of philosophizing is to talk about the world only by talking about language.

Bergmann's ideal language always remains a language spoken about but not spoken. In fact, it is not a language we can speak as we can an ordinary language; it is only "the blueprint or schema" of a language, "complete only in the sense that it shows, in principle, the structure and systematic arrangement of all areas of our experience" (MP, p. 8). The construction of such a schema makes possible what Bergmann calls "the reconstruction of metaphysics"; the traditional problems of speculative philosophy can be reformulated with clarity and precision as questions concerning the syntactical categories of the ideal language. Instead of seeking evidence for the truth of imaginative generalizations about ultimate realities, the task of the metaphysician is to discover what kinds of primitive terms belong in the ideal language. In this way language becomes both the subject matter and the tool of philosophy. It is subject matter in the sense of being what the metaphysician explicitly talks about, and yet it is a tool in the sense of being a formalism or schema constructed for the purpose of discovering what we can know to be true of the world because of what must be true of any language which adequately represents the world.

Bergmann's conception of philosophizing via the ideal language owes much to the early teaching of Ludwig Wittgenstein. The same is true of Carnap's conception of metaphysics as the expression of preference for a linguistic framework. Both philosophers started with the Wittgensteinian dictum that philosophy is logical syntax. With Carnap, as we have seen, the dictum eventually comes to mean that the task of philosophy is to analyze the structure of different linguistic frameworks and thus to provide a basis for choosing the framework best adapted for one's purposes. The traditional disputes of metaphysics are dismissed as confusions arising from attempts to construe declarations of choice as pronouncements of truth or falsity. Bergmann, on the other hand, says "One does not, in any intelligible sense, choose the ideal language" (*MP,* p. 43). One discovers that a certain schema is adequate for the systematic arrangement of all areas of our experience. With their attack on metaphysics the logical positivists lose sight of this need for critical examination of what they offer as the ideal language. Whatever has no place in their schema is dogmatically cast aside as nonsense, as seems to be the case with their early position, or is dismissed as part of a framework they prefer not to use, as in Carnap's later statement of the position. In either case, according to Bergmann, the positivists uncritically adopt an implicit metaphysics and shut themselves off from any means of detecting its inadequacies.

The way in which a positivist might rebut Bergmann's charge of implicit metaphysics appears in Nelson Goodman's *The Structure of Appearance,*[2] a work by a native American philosopher continuing in the vein of Carnap's early *Der logische Aufbau der Welt.* Goodman argues in effect that we cannot say a positivist who constructs a phenomenalistic or a physicalistic system has an implicit metaphysics, because it is not clear what a metaphysics of phenomenalism or physicalism would be if it were made explicit. In the attempt to make it explicit we come back to sentences like "The final real things of which the world is made up are phenomenal and not physical." But the whole point of the positivists' attack on metaphysics is that we do not know how to decide whether what is expressed by such sentences is true or false. Bergmann's translation into sentences like "The primitive terms of the ideal language are phenomenalistic and not physicalistic" makes sense as a way of characterizing the language constructed by a particular philosopher, but in order to bring in metaphysics the phrase "ideal language" must mean more than this. It must mean something like "that language the primitive terms of which correspond to the final real

2 Nelson Goodman, *The Structure of Appearance* (Harvard, 1951). For the points discussed here, see esp. pp. 101-07.

208

things of which the world is made up," and it is just this extension of meaning that Goodman finds unclear.

Goodman limits himself to an investigation of what can be formulated within particular systems and neither makes nor recognizes any claims concerning the metaphysical ultimacy of various systems. Yet as we shall see (§ 26) the question of an implicit metaphysics may be raised in a different sense in connection with Goodman's work. Like Bergmann, Carnap, and others, Goodman uses the same mathematical logic in all his investigations. One may ask whether this use itself constitutes a kind of implicit metaphysics, but before commenting on this question we must note some further points in connection with the linguistic turn and the notion of an ideal language.

23. *Speculative philosophy and the ideal language.* The crucial question for Bergmann's ideal language philosophizing is whether it avoids becoming just another essay in speculative metaphysics. Is there any fundamental difference between asking, for example, whether feelings are primitive ingredients of reality, inexplicable as complex physical events, and whether the word "feeling" is represented in the ideal language by a primitive, undefined symbol? Even if we grant Bergmann's claim that the linguistic turn marks an advance in clarity, does this bring the original question about feelings any closer to resolution or merely expose it as a non-cognitive question concerning the choice of a linguistic framework? On this score, the issue between Bergmann and Carnap seems just as difficult to decide as that between Whitehead and a traditional materialist. Once again we are driven to ask about the status of philosophical analysis. All four parties in the case just mentioned, Bergmann, Carnap, Whitehead, and the materialist in one form or another merge philosophical analysis with theory—view it as yielding generalizations about a subject matter.

I have already remarked (§ 13) that when philosophical analysis is merged with theory there is the problem of avoiding an infinite regress of theories in the understanding of any one theory. We noted (§ 19) that Lewis in effect proposes to stop the regress by distinguishing a priori from empirical knowledge and identifying philosophical analysis with a species of the former. The result is to make philosophical analysis in this respect like pure mathematics as opposed to natural science. Bergmann does not follow Lewis's procedure. The discovery of a formalism adequate for the ideal language is an empirical matter (see *MP,* p. 43) and the task of philosophical analysis is thus like that of applied rather than pure mathematics. Just as the natural scientist may turn to an already developed pure mathematics for formulas which apply to the phenomena he is investigating, so the philosophical analyst may turn to an already developed formalism for formulas which provide the systematic arrangement of all areas of experience and hence comprise the ideal language. The already developed formalism in the latter case, according to Bergmann, is supplied by contemporary mathematical logic, especially that developed in Whitehead and Russell's *Principia mathematica.* While the philosophical analyst by means of his formalism explicates the notion of a priori or necessary truth and shows that the propositions of pure mathematics fall within this category, there is nothing to make the statements about the ideal language which occur in his explication themselves instances of the kind of truth being explicated. The distinction in kind which is to stop the regress of theories is afforded by the linguistic turn itself, by the fact that since the philosopher alone discourses in ordinary language about an ideal language his discourse unlike that of the natural scientist does not provide another theory about the world which the ideal language must accommodate.

Yet Bergmann seems to merge philosophical analysis with theory when he declares that philosophical discourse is not just about the ideal language but by means of the latter also about the world, and that the question of which formalism is adequate for the ideal language is a matter of fact rather than of preference. While this view avoids reduction of philosophical analysis to a study of linguistic usage, it does not seem to escape the problem of giving evidence for generalizations about ultimate reality. Questions concerning the adequacy of different formalisms can become questions of fact only if we can make true generalizations about the reality the formalisms are supposed to represent. In other words, only if we can hope to establish the truth of one world hypothesis and the falsity of others. Bergmann's reconstruction of metaphysics by his linguistic turn affords a new way of putting the issues, but it hardly alters the fundamental nature of the problems. The disagreements, say, between Bergmann and Whitehead over the character of the ideal language (over the categories of reality) seem in principle no different from the disagreements between Whitehead and Maritain or any other speculative philosopher.

24. *Semantic ascent.* Another interpretation of the linguistic turn in contemporary philosophy is given by W. V. Quine, an American philosopher distinguished as a mathematical logician. Quine regards the difference between asking about feelings and the use of the word "feeling" as illustrating what he calls "semantic ascent." [3] Often the ascent is pointless, unless for special rhetorical effects, as when one asks whether the word "man" applies to anything on Mars instead of asking simply "Are there men on Mars?" But sometimes the ascent is implicit in the question, as when a child protests "But people aren't really animals, are they?" We think that the child is confused by different uses of the word "animal" and we thus understand him as questioning whether this word applies to people and not whether men biologically are animals. The semantic ascent makes our answer much simpler and without it we might do nothing but add to the child's confusion.

While semantic ascent may be implicit in most philosophical questions—at least in the most troublesome ones—Quine holds in opposition to Carnap and Bergmann that this fact does not yield a distinguishing mark of philosophical questions. In order to make it yield such a mark one must assume something like Carnap's linguistic frameworks or Bergmann's ideal language. Semantic ascent then divides into two sorts. The question may be about usage within either a particular framework or a particular formalism offered as the ideal language. On the other hand, the adequacy of the framework or formalism may be questioned. To illustrate: in the one case we understand the child as asking merely "Is it good English usage to apply the word 'animal' to people?" In the second case, we have the peculiar sort of question, "Does the use of 'animal' in English afford an adequate representation of reality?" Philosophical questions for Carnap and Bergmann are always like the latter. For

[3] See W. V. Quine, *Word and Object* (Wiley, 1960), pp. 270 ff. Abbreviation, *WO.*

Carnap they are external questions (§ 9) and their answer depends on the purpose for which the usage is to be adequate—on the way one prefers to regard the task of representing reality. Taken as metaphysical questions about the ultimate nature of reality, they are cognitive nonsense. With Bergmann of course the language in question is always a formalism proposed for the ideal language and not an ordinary language such as English. The philosophical question for him would be something like "Does this formalism provide adequate means for the systematic arrangement of our knowledge of animals?"

Quine does not make a sharp division between these two sorts of semantic ascent. The important thing for him is that one ascends from talk about objects to talk about words or symbols, whether one is interested only in the fact or also the adequacy of usage. There is no sharp division because there is neither the need nor the possibility of calling into question and reconstructing our conceptual scheme as a whole. One can only question a part of the scheme while retaining another part, and this sort of questioning occurs continually in the practice of natural science as well as in philosophy. Quine concludes that the philosopher's task differs from others' "in no such drastic way as those suppose who imagine for the philosopher a vantage point outside the conceptual scheme that he takes in charge" (WO, p. 275).

Both Carnap and Bergmann retain the notion, indigenous to speculative metaphysics, that the philosopher seeks a single system which defines the limits of conceivability (see § 5). Carnap then uses semantic ascent to show the impossibility of construing this philosophical quest as a cognitive inquiry. Since the philosopher as Carnap sees him ascends to a vantage point outside the total conceptual scheme which he propounds, there is nothing conceivable left to which he can appeal in support of what he propounds. He can do nothing but state preferences. Bergmann takes another turn. The philosopher as Bergmann sees him stands outside the ideal language he constructs but not outside the conceptual scheme of common sense and ordinary language which he is trying to reconstruct in the ideal language (see MP, p. 156). All might be well if Bergmann's reconstruction offered in the end anything different in principle from what speculative metaphysicians have always tried to do. Insofar as this fails to be the case, Bergmann does not afford relief from the perennial disputes of metaphysics.

By insisting that the philosopher never stands wholly outside the conceptual scheme which claims his attention as a philosopher, Quine can hold that the disputes of speculative metaphysicians are cognitively meaningless without having to affirm with Carnap that science as a whole therefore depends on an individual's choice of a single framework. Various parts of science in Quine's view depend on various limited frameworks which are chosen while one works within the larger framework of science and common sense. The choice of these limited frameworks is never merely a matter of preference, since one always has the criteria afforded by the larger framework. Criticism and revision of limited frameworks are tasks for the scientist and philosopher alike, and the latter is distinguished by the detail and extent but not the nature of his critical activity.

25. *Contextualism and "holism."* Quine thus appears close to a form of contextualistic naturalism. Philosophical analysis is not merged with a general theory of language or reality; philosophical problems are resolved piecemeal as they arise within contexts of limited frameworks, and there is no truth about the world beyond that of natural science. This contextualism does not conflict with Quine's "holism," with his view of language as a single whole. His holism takes account of the fact that a linguistic context in some sense always includes more than the sentences actually spoken (or written); certain unspoken sentences are "understood" and are just as truly part of the context as the former. When the child asks "Are people really animals?" we understand the context of his question to include sentences contrasting people and animals and other sentences referring to people as animals. Without recognizing these unspoken sentences as part of the context we cannot understand the child's bewilderment. And not even this is enough; the child must also have in the back of his mind something equivalent to what we would express by a sentence declaring that people cannot be without qualification both animals and not animals. This further sentence is in effect an instance of the general principle that the same thing cannot without qualification both be and not be such

and such. The child understands this principle (even though he does not articulate it) as an unspoken sentence forming part of any linguistic context in which the truth or falsity of sentences is an issue. Because of this universal relevance the principle represents what the child is least prepared to give up—what he cannot give up without the most far-reaching changes in his beliefs. He finds the sentences about people and animals disturbing precisely because they seem to imply rejection of the principle, and his first reaction understandably is that he has been misinformed about people and animals and not that the principle is wrong.

Quine's holism is then the contention that all the sentences of science and of ordinary discourse about the world form a "single connected fabric" linked by various sentences like the one expressing the principle in our example (see *WO,* pp. 12-13). With this point of view one acknowledges that some principles are universally relevant without claiming that these principles constitute a priori truth. The fact that sentences expressing the principles form a part, usually unspoken and unquestioned, of the context of any cognitive discourse is not incompatible with the claim that in particular contexts any of the principles may be made explicit and questioned. When Quine's holism is interpreted as contrary to a thoroughgoing contextualism, the point is similar to that urged against Dewey by Murphy (§ 20): a single context seems to be taken as ultimate for all philosophical analysis. But Quine makes clear in the later statement of his position that he definitely does not intend this sort of holism. His concern is to reject a position like Lewis's in which the aim of philosophical analysis is to establish a priori truth, or even Bergmann's in which the aim is to reconstruct such truth in the ideal language. With either of these positions the universal relevance of principles is not accounted for by their implicit inclusion in every context but by their supposed a priori and necessary character which makes them true and immune to criticism in any context.

Far from being opposed to a thoroughgoing contextualism Quine's holism is thus a position which attempts to reconcile contextualism with the fact of universally relevant principles. The philosophical analyst, according to this holism, does not work within a single all-inclusive context as he must claim to do when he tries to establish a priori truth; rather, he works within various contexts and criticizes limited frameworks, even if what he criticizes within a given context might be an unspoken part of every context.

26. *Mathematical logic and philosophical analysis.* There is another side of Quine's philosophy which is more difficult to construe as contextualism. Quine takes mathematical logic as providing the philosopher with a "canonical notation." While this phrase suggests something less than an ideal language, it means something more for Quine than a convenient notation which the philosopher may take or leave as he pleases. The notation, which Quine also calls "a canonical idiom," quite aside from questions of convenience, provides "a scheme for systems of the world"—a logical structure for all cognitive discourse (*WO,* p. 228). To adopt the idiom is thus to accept a philosophical doctrine about reality. In Quine's words, "The doctrine is that all traits of reality worthy of the name can be set down in an idiom of this austere form if in any idiom" (*ibid.*).

The most obvious use of canonical notation in the resolution of philosophical problems appears in connection with ontology, with questions concerning what Quine calls "ontic content." The traditional problem is the issue of nominalism versus realism. The nominalist holds that the ontic content of any significant sentence need contain no entities except individuals; the realist holds that in addition to individuals other entities, often referred to as "abstract entities," must be included. The problem as Quine sees it can never be resolved as long as the philosophical analyst lacks the linguistic tools needed to make the ontic content of sentences explicit. The nominalist will claim, for example, that the content of "Saint Peter has apostolic successors" includes nothing but individual men; the phrase "apostolic successors" refers only to these men and not also to a further entity, the apostolic succession, as the realist would have it. How is one to decide what is actually the ontic content? "To paraphrase a sentence into the canonical notation," Quine maintains, "is, first and foremost, to make its ontic content explicit" (*WO,* p. 242). Paraphrasing in English but using the canonical notation as a guide, we have, for the nominalist, "There is an entity which is Saint Peter and apostolic and at least a second and a third entity, each of which is apostolic, and such that the second entity succeeds the entity which is Saint Peter and the third entity succeeds the second"; for the realist, "There is an entity which is Saint Peter and another entity which is the apostolic succession, and the first entity is a member of the second."

While the paraphrasing alone is not a solution, it is for Quine an indispensable step toward one. Having constructed the sentences in which the ontic content is explicit, the philosophical analyst may inquire which of these sentences, if either, expresses what is expressed by the original sentence in its context. Strict nominalism is the position that the nominalistic paraphrase provides an adequate expression in every case, and since ontic content is reduced to an absolute minimum with this position the philosophical analyst begins as a nominalist and asks when if ever further content is necessary. This procedure leads Quine to argue for nominalism as far as he possibly can and some of his critics have come to interpret his position as strict nominalism. In answer to these critics Quine replies that he never meant to argue for the adequacy of nominalism in all cases and that in some cases, especially in mathematics, he has acknowledged its limitations (see *WO,* p. 243n). He is of course opposed to extreme realism, the position that the nominalistic paraphrase is never adequate, but this opposition is not enough to make one a nominalist.[4]

A great deal of what Quine says about resolving questions of ontic content seems to accord with contextualism. The issue of nominalism versus realism is not to be decided once and for all, as a speculative metaphysician would hold; the issue conceals many questions which must be decided piecemeal by determining the adequacy of a nominalistic paraphrase in individual contexts. What

[4] Similar qualifications with regard to claims for the adequacy of nominalism do not apply to the work of Nelson Goodman, who has worked closely with Quine in the project of developing nominalistic paraphrases. Goodman's *The Structure of Appearance* (see § 22) is unquestionably the outstanding contribution of American philosophy to the task of systematically exploring the extent to which we can characterize our world in nominalistic paraphrases conforming to the austere pattern of what Quine later called a "canonical idiom." The question of an implicit metaphysics in Goodman's use of mathematical logic is to be answered in the same way as the corresponding question about Quine's use of a canonical idiom; however, the suggested interpretation of Quine (§ 28) is not so easily applied to Goodman.

seems incompatible with a thoroughgoing contextualism is Quine's use of canonical notation. His philosophical doctrine that this notation is adequate for the expression of all traits of reality seems more like a principle of speculative philosophy than a universally relevant principle compatible with contextualism. A principle of the latter sort, though implicitly part of every context of cognitive discourse, is still subject to criticism within any particular context. Yet Quine appears to recognize no context in which his doctrine of canonical notation is subject to criticism; the doctrine seems to rest on a claim about all possible reality and thus to transcend anything that might be decided in a particular context. The notation, then, is not only a linguistic tool of philosophical analysis but also the source of a principle determining the structure of reality. At this point Quine seems to merge philosophical analysis with theory, in particular, with speculative metaphysics, and hence to have what might be called an "implicit metaphysics." His claim that the philosopher can never stand wholly outside of and generalize about the total conceptual scheme of science and common sense seems incompatible with his doctrine of canonical notation, though as we shall see (§ 28) it is possible to interpret Quine in a way that removes the incompatibility.

The similarities between Quine's doctrine of canonical notation and Bergmann's doctrine of the ideal language are obvious; the differences are complicated. On the question of necessary truth Quine rather than Bergmann appears as a contextualist. Bergmann holds and Quine denies that in ordinary language there are certain sentences which express necessary truths—necessary in the sense of being immune to criticism in any context—and that the philosophical analyst explicates this necessity when he shows that these sentences transcribed into the formalism of the ideal language become analytic, i.e., have their truth guaranteed by the rules of the formalism. For Quine there are universally relevant principles but none immune to criticism in every context, so that there are no context-independent truths to be explicated by a formalism. On the other hand, on the question of ontic content Bergmann appears closer to contextualism. Quine holds and Bergmann denies that the difference between "Saint Peter has apostolic successors" and a paraphrase of this sentence in canonical notation is that the ontic content of the latter but not the former is explicit. The question of ontic content for Bergmann is the question of what is simple and elementary and thus exists in the strict sense, and what is composite and thus exists in a derivative sense (see *ME*, p. 156). The fact that a person says "There is an entity which is the apostolic succession" need not mean, according to Bergmann, that the person intends to say that the apostolic succession is a simple existent. The succession may be an entity, but a complex one composed of the individual apostles. The difference between simple and complex existence, Bergmann contends, is apparent in contexts of ordinary language and is completely obscured by the "there is" idiom of Quine's canonical notation. The question of ontic content for Bergmann may be put as "What are the primitive (simple) descriptive signs of the ideal language?" This question is to be answered in ordinary discourse about the ideal language (see *ME*, p. 93); the formal properties of the latter indicated by its counterpart of "there is" are irrelevant.

Quine and Bergmann, then, agree on the general point that the formalism of mathematical logic constitutes for philosophical analysis both an indispensable linguistic tool and also a source of principles which are immune to criticism in any linguistic context, but they differ radically in what they identify as principles. The difference lies in what each claims to find in ordinary language. Bergmann finds necessary truths which can be explicated only by the principle that such truths are represented in the formalism by analytic sentences. Quine finds ontic contents which can be made explicit only with the principle that any possible structure of ontic content is represented by uses of the phrase "there is" properly transcribed into the formalism. Inasmuch as this difference over principles concerns what is held to be universally true, not just of ordinary language but of whatever ordinary language is about, it seems very much like a difference between two rival theories of speculative philosophy. Yet unlike many differences between speculative philosophers this difference directs attention to the role of mathematical logic as a linguistic tool of philosophical analysis. In opposition to both Quine and Bergmann there are those who maintain that any use in philosophical analysis of a formalism such as that provided by mathematical logic must be justified by the peculiar conditions of a given context. There is no single linguistic formalism which we can expect to apply in every context, and hence none that can supply principles for all philosophical analysis.

27. *"Casuism" and philosophical analysis.* Bergmann refers to philosophers who take the linguistic turn and yet recognize no universal formalism in philosophical analysis as "linguistic casuists." The word "casuism" is appropriate, he contends, because these philosophers appear to hold that "all one can do is to do the job in each case exactly as the circumstances of the case require" (*MP,* p. 70). The philosophers are the British analysts and their American associates referred to earlier (§§ 13, 21). "Casuism" as opposed to "contextualism" has pejorative connotations, and Bergmann makes it clear he has this point in mind when he uses the former. One is a casuist in a bad sense when one stays with particular cases and refuses to accept warranted generalizations.

But how does the doctrine that mathematical logic supplies a linguistic formalism for all philosophical analysis become a warranted generalization? Our considerations thus far suggest that this generalization is basically no different from those made by speculative metaphysicians—it is a generalization which rests on a claim about the ultimate structure of reality. In denying that any such generalization is warranted Bergmann's casuists display their affinity with Carnap and the logical positivists. But unlike Carnap the casuistic analysts do not draw the conclusion that one can do nothing but choose the universal formalism one prefers to use. Why must there be a universal formalism at all? Carnap's answer is given by his semantical (or semiotical) analysis, which purportedly shows that any cognitive discourse must exhibit a formalism which can be represented by the general formalism of mathematical logic. In this analysis of language Carnap does not profess to choose the formalism of mathematical logic, he claims to find it dictated by the subject matter; what one has to decide, according to Carnap, is which formalism among those shown to be possible by mathematical logic is to be taken as the universal formalism for discourse about the world. I have already remarked (§ 10) that as a theory concerning the nature of language Carnap's position encounters serious technical difficulties, and that as a philosophical position it seems tantamount to skepticism. Quine endeavors to avoid these troubles by making the only question that of accepting a doctrine of canonical notation—a doctrine which seems to mark a return to speculative metaphysics.

On the fundamental question of the nature of philosophical analysis, the casuists show affinities with Santayana and the contextualistic naturalists rather than with Carnap and the positivists. Metaphysical generalizations are unwarranted not because a theory of language shows them to be impossible but because philosophical analysis itself is not a theory. The pejorative connotations of "casuism" are rebutted by the fact that the aim of philosophical analysis for the casuists is an understanding of generalizations already made and not establishment of new generalizations. Santayana, as we have noted (§ 16), regarded philosophical principles as presuppositions he found he could not live without making and not as generalizations which philosophy establishes as necessary truths of reality. By analyzing what is meant in given contexts the philosophical analyst achieves an understanding of generalizations already made, particularly those made only implicitly in the course of making sense in a given context.

The casuists differ from the contextualistic naturalists and especially from Santayana in the emphasis they place on language itself, but the difference is not as great as it may seem. Santayana spoke of philosophical analysis as self-analysis and self-criticism, and for him this meant a critical examination of one's own fundamental beliefs —of the beliefs which shape one's world view and which, in his case, led to naturalism. With the casuists this self-analysis is conceived as beginning with reflection on one's language rather than one's beliefs—on the common everyday language which one cannot live without using. Implicit in this language are cognitive presuppositions which one cannot avoid making without talking nonsense, and the aim of philosophical analysis is to uncover, not to establish, these presuppositions. In this respect language becomes the subject matter of philosophy, but it would be incorrect to say that philosophy is thereby reduced to a study of linguistic usage. Such a statement implies that the aim of philosophy is a theory or at least a catalog of facts concerning linguistic usage, but for the linguistic casuists philosophy does not aim at a theory of anything and linguistic facts are only a means and not an end of philosophizing. While philosophy with the casuists is not as with Bergmann discourse about the world by means of discourse about the ideal language, it still seems close (despite the greater emphasis on language) to philosophy in the tradition of Socrates and Santayana, which is discourse about oneself by means of discourse about the things one says and believes.

This emphasis on oneself and one's language makes philosophy in a fundamental sense therapeutic. The self-knowledge which accompanies a deeper understanding of sentences one has long been accustomed to utter has the effect of dispelling intellectual confusion and worry rather than of imparting new information about the world. Troublesome problems vanish not because the answers are given but because the confusions which produced the appearance of a genuine question are exposed. In particular, with the casuists this disposes of questions which produce the interminable disputes of metaphysics. But the endeavor is successful only to the extent that with each question the exposé emerges from the language of the given context and does not depend on a formalism which is imported into the context without its relevance being exhibited. To Bergmann and many others the casuists seem to abandon the pursuit of philosophy when they impute a therapeutic function to philosophical analysis. But if in philosophy as opposed to speculative metaphysics and natural science one undertakes self-criticism and self-analysis, the aim is self-improvement rather than information about the world. Socrates too spoke of himself as a physician of the soul, helping men to cure themselves of ignorance and confusion.

Earlier (§§ 13, 14) I mentioned the difference between a diagnosis that emerges from a critical analysis of the linguistic contexts in which the apparently conflicting metaphysical propositions are expressed, and a diagnosis of metaphysical disputes in general based on a theory, psychiatric, semantical, or simply speculative, about metaphysical theories. I remarked some of the difficulties confronting the second kind of diagnosis; similar remarks cannot be made concerning the diagnoses offered by the casuists, since there is no single theory underlying them all which can be made the subject of criticism. The only general charge is that the casuists are not doing philosophy at all, that they have forsaken altogether the truly philosophical task of presenting a unified picture of the whole of things. Such a charge has force only if one assumes that unity of vision is incompatible with a plurality of pictures, that the whole must fit into a single picture. With the casuists the situation is rather the reverse. The unity is already given in man, the viewer, and the problem is not to objectify the unity in a single picture, a single verbal structure, but to avoid losing unity of vision in a maze of conflicting verbalizations. With each exposé of the verbal confusions which generate a particular metaphysical dispute, one achieves a deeper understanding of one's language and thereby of oneself. Unity of vision then comes from the ability to distinguish sense from nonsense rather than from anything in particular that has been said.

28. *"Casuism," naturalism, and speculative philosophy.* It would be a mistake to view the tendencies in American philosophy that Bergmann labels "linguistic casuism" as exclusively a recent British import. I pointed out at the close of Chapter 3 that piecemeal resolutions of particular problems and rejection of the ultimate generalities of speculative philosophy have been prominent tendencies in the development of American naturalism. These tendencies may be called "casuistic" but they cannot be written off as British imports. While the attempt to dispose of philosophical problems by showing how they arise from a misunderstanding of our ordinary language is characteristic of recent British analytical philosophy, on the American scene this appears as a refinement and development of the "casuism" in one direction rather than its introduction. The basic point of the "casuism" is that since the ultimate generalities of speculative metaphysics cannot help us to explain why any part of the world is the way it is and not some other way they cannot form part of our knowledge of the world. This point can be argued without reference to linguistic confusions that may make it seem as though the generalizations added to our knowledge of the world; for whether they really add anything is independent of linguistic or other confusions that make them seem to do so.

The point is well illustrated in "A Symposium on the Relation of Logic to Metaphysics," which appeared in the *Philosophical Review,*

LVIII (1949). The four symposiasts, all American philosophers, are divided evenly on the two sides of the question. Everett J. Nelson and Everett W. Hall argue for the position that logic requires the support of metaphysics; Alice Ambrose and Ernest Nagel criticize their arguments. Miss Ambrose confines herself to a few technical difficulties and obscurities she finds in Nelson's paper; Nagel, on the other hand, argues at some length against the basic tenets of the position taken by Nelson and Hall. Since the latter present their position as the alternative to what they argue is an untenable view defended in Nagel's earlier paper, "Logic without Ontology," [5] Nagel's symposium paper is also a defense of a position he has already advanced.

Nelson and Hall argue that a logical law such as the principle of contradiction cannot be viewed as Nagel seems to view it in his earlier paper, as a linguistic rule we accept in the conduct of inquiry. This view fails to distinguish linguistic conventions, which are accidents of a particular language, from regulative principles of inquiry that cannot be changed as linguistic conventions can. The logical law that we must not contradict ourselves is fundamentally different from the linguistic convention that we must not use "he runed" as the past tense of "he runs." If we ignore the convention and say "He runed across the field," we use bad grammar but we may still succeed in making a true statement. Yet if we ignore the logical law and say "At the same time and in the same respect he is both running and not running across the field," we use correct grammar but we cannot possibly succeed in making a true statement. One may be running and not running across the field at different times or at the same time in different respects, but if the time and the respect are the same it is never true to say one is both running and not running across the field. Violation of the logical law unlike violation of the linguistic convention precludes our making a true statement about the world.

We are thus forced to conclude, according to Nelson and Hall, that the logical law itself is a truth about the world. That to which

---

[5] This paper first appeared in *Naturalism and the Human Spirit*, ed. Y. H. Krikorian (Columbia, 1944). The paper is reprinted along with the symposium paper, "In Defense of Logic without Metaphysics," in a volume of Nagel's essays, *Logic without Metaphysics* (Free Press of Glencoe, 1956).

we must conform if we are to make true statements is characteristic of the world and is not a convention to which we conform only when we talk about the world in a particular language. Yet, as Nelson and Hall recognize, if the logical law is a truth about the world it is a special kind of truth. It is not a truth like those expressed by laws of physics and biology, or by the statement of a particular fact, such as "Jones is now running across the field." In the case of these truths we can specify a subject matter, an object or class of objects with respect to which the truth in question holds, but we cannot thus specify a subject matter for the logical law. No matter what sort of object x may be, physical, biological, or neither, and no matter what object it may be in particular, an individual man or a prime number, it remains true to say that x cannot both have and not have a given characteristic at the same time and in the same respect. The logical law has no specific subject matter; it holds with respect to any object whatsoever. It is a metaphysical principle, a principle true of all reality, of being *qua* being.

But then our knowledge of such a principle is quite different from our knowledge of a law of science or a statement of particular fact. We can always specify conditions that would make the scientific law or the factual statement false, and we believe that either of them is true only insofar as we believe that the falsifying conditions do not obtain. Our knowledge in this case is thus a posteriori, posterior to the experience necessary to convince us of the absence of falsifying conditions. But we cannot likewise specify conditions that would make the logical law false. We may say that the law is falsified if we find a single object that at the same time and in the same respect both has and does not have a given characteristic. But if we are thus to succeed in specifying conditions that make the law false, we must render more precise the crucial phrases "at the same time" and "in the same respect." Given sufficient latitude in the use of these phrases we can easily find cases that falsify the principle— e.g., "During the same week and in the same respect Johnny was both good and not good"—but we make the principle so obviously false that we can hardly claim to be talking about the same principle that philosophers from Aristotle to the present have seriously defended as a logical law holding without exception.

On the other hand, if we are free to limit the time and the respect as we please we can easily explain away any possible exception to the law. This procedure leads to what Nagel calls a "self-protective formulation" of the principle. The principle holds without exception simply because we have so formulated it that we know in advance how to explain away any apparently falsifying instance. In this case if the principle forms part of our knowledge of the world the knowledge is a priori, knowledge that we may have prior to any particular experience of objects in the world. Nelson and Hall admit that as a logical law the principle may be said to have a self-protective formulation and that the knowledge it yields is a priori, but they oppose Nagel's conclusion that the law, having a self-protective formulation, is simply a regulative principle of language and that the a priori knowledge it yields is knowledge only of what is to constitute correct linguistic usage and not of what must be characteristic of all reality.

Nelson and Hall, then, align themselves with the speculative metaphysicians who, since Aristotle, have held that it is the job of metaphysics to explain how all reality, how being *qua* being, is such that logical laws hold without exception. The alternative to having logical laws supported by metaphysics is taken to be the view that the laws are mere linguistic conventions, that the principle of contradiction is essentially like the convention we follow when we form the past tense of the verb "to run." Each system of speculative metaphysics, each account of the final real things of which the world is made up, of course supplies its own peculiar support for the laws of logic. With Maritain, for example, the support is found in the substance-accident structure of all reality, with Whitehead in the structure of events and societies of events that comprise the actual entities of the world. Nelson and Hall are not concerned in their papers to argue for a particular system of metaphysics, but only for the general point that without a metaphysical system we cannot hope to give a satisfactory account of the laws of logic.

Nagel argues that Nelson and Hall fail to take account of the fact that we discover logical laws by reflecting on what we do with language in the course of inquiry and that we distinguish logical laws from other linguistic conventions by their indispensability for the functions of inquiry. It should not take much reflection to convince us that the convention by which we form the past tense of "to run" is not and that the principle of contradiction is indispensable for making true statements. As conventions both have self-protective formulations—they may be abandoned but they cannot be shown false. While we can easily imagine that in the future evolution of English "he runed" or some other form may become standard for the past of "to run," we seem unable to imagine an alternative to the principle of contradiction or to any of numerous other logical laws. However, as Nagel points out in his paper "Logic without Ontology," some scientists have given serious consideration to the proposal that a more satisfactory theoretical treatment of certain subatomic phenomena can be achieved by abandoning logical laws that seem as indispensable as the principle of contradiction. While it is too early to assess the merits of this proposal the fact that it has received serious consideration by distinguished scientists indicates that logical laws may not be as unalterable as speculative metaphysicians assume.

On the other hand, even if there are some logical laws that are absolutely indispensable and can never be altered without disastrous consequences, still, Nagel argues, systems of speculative metaphysics do not help to explain this fact. Logical laws are discovered in contexts of language and inquiry and their indispensability is limited to such contexts. Any explanation of the indispensability is to be achieved by a further understanding of specific conditions within these contexts and not, as is done in speculative metaphysics, by ignoring the contexts and elevating logical laws to the status of principles true a priori of all reality. While we may say a priori that the same thing, whatever it is, cannot both be and not be at the same time and in the same respect, we have uttered merely a trivial truth guaranteed to be true by a self-protective formulation. We have not said anything that will help us in any way to explain why some part of reality is the way it is and not some other way, nor in particular why in contexts of language and inquiry the law of contradiction is an indispensable regulative principle.

To a speculative metaphysician Nagel's contextualism opens the way to intellectual anarchy. By restricting logical laws to contexts of language and inquiry Nagel leaves undertermined the question of whether the world itself is rational or irrational, logical or illogical. The mere fact that we find certain logical laws indispensable in our inquiries does not mean that the world itself is logical, though if it is not there is no ultimate sanction for logical laws. Nagel's explanation of logical laws thus seems no more satisfactory than the ethical casuist's explanation of moral laws. To hold that moral laws are justified only as they seem indispensable in particular contexts of human action and not because the world itself is moral and embodies moral values is to deny ultimate sanctions for moral laws, and Nagel takes the analogous position with regard to logical laws.

Nagel's contextualism, then, appears casuistic to a speculative metaphysician because it embraces a post-Kantian distrust of speculative philosophy and questions the legitimacy of all claims to have shown how the world in itself really is. Kant professed to avoid intellectual anarchy with his peculiar view of synthetic a priori propositions. Nelson and Hall are inclined to reject this Kantian view and to return to a pre-Kantian trust in speculative philosophy. Nagel rejects the synthetic a priori as well as the trust in speculative philosophy, but finds no danger of intellectual anarchy unless one makes the foolish assumption that we can arbitrarily dispense with (and not merely experiment with possible alterations in) the regulative principles we have thus far found indispensable for language and inquiry. The cure for anyone making this foolish assumption is confrontation with contexts of language and inquiry that compel recognition of the indispensability of the principles. While one will of course abandon the assumption when one believes that logical laws are ultimately sanctioned by the logical nature of the world itself, the cure in this case is hardly an improvement over the disease. Regulative principles incapable of being falsified because of their self-protective formulation are mistaken for a priori truths revealing the logical structure of the world, and, what is worse, this confusion is taken as the price one has to pay to avoid intellectual anarchy.

Logical laws as Nagel views them are obviously similar to Quine's universally relevant principles discussed above (§ 25). Quine has referred to his position on this score as a form of pragmatism, and in the context of the present discussion it is also clearly a form of "casuism." Both labels are justified because Quine like Nagel rejects the view that logical laws must express a priori truths about the world and hence must receive a sanction beyond that which they receive as principles indispensable in contexts of language and inquiry. But this is a "casuism" easily traceable to doctrines in Peirce, James, and Dewey, a casuism that goes hand in hand with the development of American naturalism and pragmatism.

I remarked (§ 26) that in his doctrine of canonical notation Quine seems to merge philosophical analysis with speculative philosophy and hence to embrace an "implicit metaphysics." Philosophical analysis exhibits the indispensability of logical laws in contexts of language and inquiry, and the canonical notation is taken as a tool indispensable for the analysis. The alternative tool is what we know of the grammar of our ordinary language and the need for a sharper tool becomes apparent as the analysis proceeds. The issue that places Quine, Carnap, Goodman, and Bergmann more or less in opposition to the "ordinary language" analysts is then that of the grounds one has for accepting mathematical logic as *the* sharper tool required for philosophical analysis. Bergmann's doctrine of the ideal language and Carnap's semantics justify the acceptance by a theory, in the one case a theory about the world and in the other a theory about language. In both cases philosophical analysis ceases to be simply an activity in which we discern principles indispensable in contexts of language and inquiry; it becomes the application of a theory concerning what we talk about or how we talk.

Insofar as Quine intends the acceptance of his canonical notation to be justified by a doctrine about the nature of reality, he stands on this point with Carnap and Bergmann. However, in view of Quine's contextualism with regard to logical principles one might take his remarks that seem to imply a doctrine of reality as expressing only an attitude to be adopted provisionally at the start of philosophical analysis. In this case the canonical notation itself like the logical laws formulated by means of it is constantly on trial and remains canonical only so long as we find no context in which we are compelled to search for other means to express what we want to say. Philosophical analysis then remains critical reflection on language, inquiry, and action and the principles we thus seek to test and use are the principles we presuppose in the effective use of our ordinary language, though by no means necessarily these principles as they have already been formulated in works of grammar and logic. That the formalism of mathematical logic may provide the best analytical tool available does not mean that we must elevate the formalism, any more than ordinary grammar, to the status of principles revealing the structure of all reality, nor does it mean that we must always discard ordinary grammar when it conflicts with the formalism. Quine's canonical notation thus need not represent a position incompatible with contextualism or with the "casuism" of recent British analytical philosophy. Compatibility is possible because of the extent to which Quine continues in the tradition of American pragmatism and naturalism and not because of anything he may be said to have imported from England.

Nagel makes no claims concerning the formalism of mathematical logic that might be construed as having implications concerning the metaphysical structure of reality, but he also makes no attempt to explain how what he takes to be the erroneous views of Nelson and Hall arise from linguistic confusions. He is content to remark that the argument of Nelson and Hall seems to him "to illustrate the subtle but common error of attributing to things as inherent possessions properties which they manifest only under certain conditions." Because contradictions, entailments, and other logical properties are manifested in contexts of language and inquiry Nelson and Hall assume that these are inherent properties of all reality. Nagel does not consider whether the erroneous assumption may depend on misleading grammatical analogies between phrases like "inherent properties of all reality" and "inherent properties of all iron." If he had argued in this vein one could easily allege the influence of an imported "linguistic casuism," though the fact that he did not so argue does not make his philosophy any the less "casuistic."

29. *A glance at the future.* American casuists who write in the vein discussed above are not named and their writings are not cited because at present their work is primarily work in progress. Their most important writings thus far have appeared in volumes of col-

lected essays and in philosophical periodicals.[6] The authors and the contributions are many and any attempt to select a few for mention here would be arbitrary and pointless. While the main inspiration may come from recent philosophical writing in Great Britain, the affinities with contextualistic naturalism are obvious. I remarked in Chapter 2 that the rapprochement anticipated in the Thirties between logical positivism and native American pragmatism and naturalism did not materialize. As the naturalists moved toward contextualism, positivists in America continued to sanction the formalism of mathematical logic by metaphysical and semantical theories. Yet in England where positivists themselves began turning away from formalism and began philosophizing within contexts of ordinary language, the way was prepared for a rapprochement between descendents of positivism and naturalism. It is much too early to say whether the new American casuists will develop a philosophy with an identity distinct from that of its British counterpart, but if such a development should occur it is likely that the new philosophy will seem almost as much the offspring of American naturalism as of British analytical philosophy.

One influence in current American philosophy which has been omitted entirely from the present discussion must be taken into account in any attempt to guess the future. Phenomenology and existentialism have been in the forefront of philosophical activity on the continent of Europe since World War II, and these movements, still virtually ignored by professional philosophers in England, now occupy a place of some prominence on the American philosophical scene. But the American philosophers working in this area, even more than the linguistic casuists, display only work in progress.[7] Their work is also more difficult to construe as a manifestation of one view of how to philosophize. While most of them appear to share with the casuists an opposition to speculative philosophy, they remain so far apart from the casuists in other respects that eventual agreement on fundamental issues seems out of the question. If a dis-

---

[6] The volume of essays edited by Max Black and Black's own works mentioned in Chapter 3, note 9, provide some illustrations.

[7] A possible exception is Paul Tillich, whose views have been discussed briefly (§ 7). Tillich has definitely been influenced by phenomenology and existentialism, but to what extent he belongs in this group of philosophers is questionable.

tinctly American version of phenomenology and existentialism should emerge, it will certainly not appear as an offspring of American naturalism. The most likely guess is that in the immediate future American metaphysical writing will proceed largely along two independent lines, naturalists and linguistic analysts on the one hand, phenomenologists and existentialists on the other.

This is not to imply that speculative metaphysics in the grand manner of Whitehead and Weiss will disappear altogether, but it seems safe to say that pre-Kantian modes of thought have about run their course. A similar remark seems almost as safe for the post-Kantian endeavors to merge philosophical analysis with a theory about metaphysics, whether the theory is psychiatric, semantical, or of some other sort. The claim to have given a theoretical account of the interminable disputes peculiar to metaphysics seems just as difficult to establish as any of the claims about ultimate reality made in the metaphysical systems under diagnosis. The theoretical diagnosticians of metaphysics as well as the metaphysicians themselves are more likely to be read in the future for their contributions to the analysis of particular problems than for the theoretical account of philosophy each professes to give.

Contemporary professional philosophers have been criticized for their failure to assume the traditional role of philosophers. Living in a time of desperate need for a synthesis of scientific, artistic, political, and religious values they are accused of undermining these values or at least of becoming lost in analyses of their own artificial problems and of expending their energy in idle disputes over the existence of values they all recognize. Genuine philosophizing in our age is said to come more and more from outside the philosophical profession, from physicists, poets, novelists, social scientists, literary journalists, and theologians. It is hoped that the present essay has helped to create a more philosophical understanding of this charge, of why it almost has to be made and of how it is rebutted. It is hardly a great achievement to form a vision of the whole which synthesizes all recognized values and is irresistible to a properly oriented mind—such visions are found in all but the most primitive forms of human culture. Yet nothing is more difficult (if indeed it is possible at all) than to form a vision of this sort which is irresistible to all minds however they may be oriented. Philosophy in its infancy begins with such visions, even in a culture as developed and as complex as ours. Philosophy in its maturity becomes infected with Socratic questioning even while it remains speculative, and it inevitably appears dangerous or useless to those who do not question. Such has been and will continue to be the fate of all the varieties of metaphysical thought considered in this essay.

THEORY OF KNOWLEDGE

❧

RODERICK M. CHISHOLM

PROFESSOR OF PHILOSOPHY AND ROMEO ELTON
PROFESSOR OF NATURAL THEOLOGY
BROWN UNIVERSITY

ANALYTIC TABLE OF CONTENTS

Introduction

Summary statement of tendencies in American epistemology since 1930. Most of the important contributions to the subject have been in works devoted primarily to other subjects.

1

The Problem of Skepticism

1. The relations between "What do we know?" and "How are we to tell whether we know?" Three approaches: "commonsensism" presupposes an answer to the first question, "empiricism" to the second, and "skepticism" to neither. Some American philosophers have taken the first approach to one subject matter, the second to another, the third to still another.

2. Traditionally both "experience" and "reason" have been cited as "sources" of knowing; the former have usually been taken to comprise perception, memory, and "inner consciousness." But appeal to the "sources" of knowledge transfers the epistemological problem to "How are we to tell what is a proper source of knowing?" and "How are we to tell what is yielded by such a source?"

3. Some ethical and religious cognitivists ("intuitionists" and "mystics") have been liberal in answering the first of the latter two questions, others have been liberal in answering the second. Examples from recent American philosophy. The general problem is also illustrated by the great variety of views about "reason" and the status of our knowledge of logic and mathematics.

4. Some philosophers tried to resolve these predicaments by "correcting" the language of other philosophers. But these attempts were only partly successful.

5. The hope to prove that certain characteristically philosophical sentences, including those in which the epistemological problem is formulated, are sentences which "make no sense" involved similar predicaments. And the belief that significant and relevant philosophical conclusions

may be derived from investigations of the nature and use of language seems to be unfounded.

2

The "Myth of the Given"

1. The doctrine of "the given," as set forth by Lewis and others, involved the theses that our knowledge is an "edifice" having a "foundation" and that this foundation consists in part of the apprehension of "appearances."

2. These theses are properly construed as answering certain Socratic questions about justification; e.g., "What justification do you have for thinking you know that such and such a proposition is true?"

3. But they are only some of several possible answers to such questions.

4. Some philosophers seemed to misinterpret the questions and to assume, mistakenly, that they presupposed, with respect to those propositions we know to be true, that they are not propositions we know to be true.

5. Other philosophers seemed to suggest, with respect to every proposition, that we are not justified in thinking we know that it is true, unless we can justify it by reference to some other proposition which cannot, in turn, be justified by reference to it. Criticism of this suggestion.

6. Others seemed to suggest that no proposition A would be justified unless it were justified by some other justified proposition B which would not be justified unless it were justified in turn by A. Criticism of this suggestion.

7. Others seemed to suggest that there is a kind of "proper stopping place" for the Socratic questions about justification. Carnap suggested that statements expressing what we perceive might provide such a stopping place. Criticism of this suggestion. Others—e.g., Ducasse, Hempel —suggested that there is a class of statements the justification for which we may express by asserting the statements themselves.

8. The doctrine of "the given" may be construed as saying, in part, that there are such "self-justifying" statements. Some philosophers objected that such terms as "justified" are not properly applicable to the statements in question. But this part of the doctrine of "the given" may be re-expressed, in language more acceptable to these philosophers, by saying that there are statements which are such that (a) they are "neither justified nor unjustified," or it "makes no sense" to say that they are

237

4. One form of "the revolt against dualism": the attempt to construe "appearances," or "ways of appearing," as "objective" entities; Murphy's "objective relativism" and McGilvary's "perspective realism."

5. Discussion of the question whether, in order to know that an object has certain characteristics, the knower—or the "appearances" which he senses—must take on these characteristics. Discussion of variants of "critical realism," "Thomistic realism," and other "identity" theories.

6. The "phenomenalistic" alternative to such theories, as suggested by Lewis and Stace. Criticism of "phenomenalism."

7. Dewey's "transactional" alternative. Criticism.

8. The "specific response" theory of Perry and Holt and other attempts to construe knowing in terms of "behavior." Criticism.

9. The present status of the problem of "intentionality," or "objective reference."

10. The thesis, of Santayana and Lovejoy, that knowledge involves "animal faith." The thesis is true if it means that the statements expressing our knowledge cannot be derived deductively from what is a priori and what is "self-justifying." It is problematic whether such statements can be derived inductively from what is a priori or what is "self-justifying."

11. A dilemma for the theory of knowledge: if evidence implies truth, then "skepticism with regard to the senses" and other types of skepticism are justified; if evidence does not imply truth, then there is still another true interpretation of "knowledge involves animal faith."

12. *Conditions of truth* should be distinguished from *criteria of evidence;* these two coincide only in the case of what is "self-justifying." Some "theories of truth" in recent American philosophy—e.g., some versions of the "coherence theory" and some versions of "instrumentalism" —apparently confuse conditions of truth with criteria of evidence. The dilemma cited above cannot be satisfactorily avoided by defining "evidence" in terms of "truth," or "truth" in terms of "evidence."

INTRODUCTION

Most of the problems and issues constituting the "theory of knowledge" were discussed in detail by Plato and Aristotle and by the Greek skeptics. There is some justification, I am afraid, for saying that the subject has made very little progress in the past two thousand years. Perhaps it is unreasonable, therefore, to expect much to have happened within a thirty-year period in twentieth century America.

In the late 1920's and early 1930's—the beginning of the period with which this study is concerned—the principal emphasis in American epistemology was metaphysical or cosmological. The problem was that of the status of "appearances" and the controversy concerned the two basic theses of "dualism." These theses, which received their classic statement in A. O. Lovejoy's *The Revolt Against Dualism* (1930), were, first, that our knowledge of reality is derived from the inspection of the "appearances" of reality and, second, that "appearances" are mental entities composed of a different metaphysical stuff from that of physical objects.

The "revolt against dualism," which had taken many forms, became the attempt to reconcile the first of the two dualistic theses with the denial of the second. This involved constructing metaphysical systems in which "appearances" were treated as a part of the stuff of physical reality. In C. A. Strong's *Essays on the Natural Origin of Mind* (1930), physical objects were said to have a "double aspect," one aspect of which was made up of appearances; in Roy Wood Sellars' *The Philosophy of Physical Realism* (1932), physical objects were said to have sensible appearances as their "qualitative dimensions," or, as some put it, as their "metaphysical insides"; and in the "objective relativism" of Arthur Murphy and the "perspective realism" of E. B. McGilvary, the *ways* in which physical objects appear were taken to be a kind of constituent of the objects themselves. "Objective relativism" and "perspective realism" had been influenced by similar views, developed in the 1920's by

239

the British philosophers Samuel Alexander and A. N. Whitehead, and also suggested in John Dewey's *Experience and Nature* (1925). Perhaps the last great work of this phase of American epistemology was George Santayana's *The Realms of Being,* first published as a single volume in 1942; Santayana's epistemology was a version of "dualism." But by the end of the 1930's the live issues in epistemology had changed.

The change of interest was due, in part, to "logical positivism," or "logical empiricism," an approach to philosophy which is generally associated with the Vienna Circle of the late 1920's. The members of the original circle were logicians and philosophers of science who hoped to make philosophical use of the techniques of mathematical logic. The philosophical work of the "logical positivists" was partly constructive and partly destructive. The constructive work was done in mathematical logic, in the logic of probability and confirmation, and in the attempt to describe what an adequate "language of science" would be. Most of this work was not primarily epistemological and hence does not fall within our survey, but it touched upon epistemology in various places. Discussions of probability and confirmation, for example, presupposed the concept of *evidence,* or that of a proposition or statement being *evident;* what little that has been said, in these discussions, about the concept of evidence seems to me to be inadequate, but it has served to bring this essentially epistemological concept into clear focus. Investigations of what would constitute an adequate "language of science" touched upon the first of the two theses of "dualism" noted above, upon the thesis that our knowledge of reality is derived from the inspection of the "appearances" of reality. The status of "the given"—including the "appearances" which were thought by many to be at the basis of the "edifice of knowledge"— became one of the dominant epistemological questions of the late 1930's and early 1940's. "Logical empiricists" touched upon other epistemological questions in discussions of the place of psychology, or "behavioristics," in the system of sciences.

The destructive side of "logical empiricism"—an attempt to dismiss the traditional questions of philosophy as deriving from statements which are "meaningless" or which "make no sense"—is of much less significance, it seems to me. There are now indications that the metaphysical discussion of the late 1920's and early 1930's is being resumed—for example, in recent discussions of the "physical status" of sensations—and that these discussions will be characterized by the clarity, precision, and objectivity which are typical of the constructive writings of "logical empiricism."

Among the American philosophers who have come to be known as "logical empiricists," some but not all of whom were associated with the original Vienna Circle, are Gustav Bergmann, Rudolf Carnap, Herbert Feigl, C. G. Hempel, and the late Hans Reichenbach. Philosophers having similar interests, but not properly called "logical empiricists," are Nelson Goodman, Ernest Nagel, W. V. Quine, and Wilfrid Sellars. The writings of these philosophers are not primarily concerned with the theory of knowledge. Indeed, not many American philosophers, during the period of this survey, have thought of themselves as being primarily epistemologists, or specialists in the theory of knowledge. Most of the important contributions to the subject have come from philosophers specializing in other areas—in logic, in the philosophy of language, in the philosophy of science, and in metaphysics—and most of these contributions have appeared in works which are concerned with these other areas and which only touch upon the theory of knowledge.

The dominant influence in the 1940's and early 1950's came to be the later philosophy of Ludwig Wittgenstein and the writings of Gilbert Ryle, J. L. Austin, and other philosophers teaching at Oxford. Wittgenstein, whose *Tractatus logico-philosophicus* (1922) is one of the most important philosophical writings of the present century, later developed quite different views which, for a while, he preferred not to publish. These views, which were thought to be revolutionary, were first made known to American philosophers through copies of his lectures; through the writings of Max Black, Alice Ambrose Lazerowitz, Morris Lazerowitz, Norman Malcolm, and others; and after 1953 through the publication of Wittgenstein's own work. These writings and those of the Oxford philosophers have made philosophers sensitive to language and have served to sharpen and clarify many philosophical questions. But, if I am not mistaken, they have also led some philosophers to exaggerate the relevance of linguistic facts to philosophy.

"Idealism" and "neo-Kantianism" are represented in the works of

Brand Blanshard, W. H. Werkmeister, and others. "Thomistic realism" is represented in John Wild's *Introduction to Realistic Philosophy* (1948), in writings of the members of the Association for Realistic Philosophy, and in the manuals on epistemology which are used in many Catholic universities. There is considerable literature by American philosophers on "phenomenology," "existentialism," and "existential psychiatry," but, as I interpret these works, they are not strictly relevant to the traditional questions of epistemology.

The "pragmatic" tradition in American philosophy persisted through this period, most notably in the writings of John Dewey. Dewey disclaimed being an epistemologist and most of his philosophical work was concerned with what others would call "philosophical anthropology." There are many who believe, however, that his views about human knowledge are relevant to the traditional questions of epistemology. In what follows I shall note where these views do seem to me to be relevant and important. "Pragmatism" is also represented, but only to a limited extent, in the writings of C. I. Lewis, whose first contributions to philosophy were in the field of modal logic. The important "pragmatic" element in his philosophy is his view of the cognitive function of "appearances" and their relation to action. Lewis's *An Analysis of Knowledge and Valuation* (1946) combines the clarity and precision of the positivistic writings with what I believe to be a proper respect for the problems of traditional philosophy.

This essay is itself offered as a contribution to the theory of knowledge, for I have attempted to justify my appraisals of the various works and views I have mentioned. The reader who is not familiar with contemporary philosophy should be told that, for almost every judgment I make here, there is some competent philosopher who would disagree with it, and that any other philosopher would probably discuss works quite different from those that I discuss.

In the first chapter, on "the problem of skepticism," I shall attempt to present one of the basic problems of the theory of knowledge and one which may well be incapable of solution; many of the views I shall consider in subsequent chapters can be understood only in terms of this problem. In the second chapter, on the "myth of the given," I shall consider the controversies about the "basis" of our knowledge; in the third chapter I shall consider what American philosophers have said about "reason and a priori knowledge"; and in the final chapter, I shall consider the problem of the relation of "appearances" to our knowledge of reality.

THE PROBLEM OF SKEPTICISM

1. Two of the traditional questions of the theory of knowledge, or epistemology, have been "*What* do we know?" and "How are we to decide *whether* we know?" The former question may also be put as "What is the *extent* of our knowledge?" and the latter as "What are the *criteria* of knowing?" If we happen to know the answer to either one of these questions, then we can set out to answer the other. If we can specify the *criteria* of knowledge and thus have a procedure for deciding whether we know, we may then be able to decide the extent of our knowledge. Or if we happen to know the *extent* of our knowledge and thus know what the things are that we know, we may then be able to formulate criteria enabling us to mark off the things we do know from those we do not. But if we do not have the answer to the first question, then, it would seem, we cannot determine the answer to the second, and if we do not have the answer to the second, then, it would seem, we cannot determine the answer to the first.

It is characteristic of "empiricism," as a philosophical tradition, to assume that we have certain criteria of evidence, or that we can identify a certain "source" of our knowledge, and then to apply these criteria, or to refer to this source, and thus determine what it is that we can know. It is characteristic of "commonsensism," as an alternative philosophical tradition, to assume that we do know, pretty much, those things that we think we know, and then, having identified this knowledge, to trace it back to its sources and formulate criteria which will set it off from those things that we do not know. And it is characteristic of "skepticism" *not* to assume either that we know or that we have any criteria of evidence. Each of these traditions has been represented in recent American philosophy.

The philosophers with whom we are here concerned have found it difficult to agree about these questions or even to understand each other. The reasons are, in part: the fundamental questions of epistemology have been approached, as it were, from three different directions; one and the same philosopher may approach one area of knowledge (say, "our knowledge of the external world") from the first of these three points of view, another area (say, logic and mathematics) from the second, and still another (say, ethics) from the third; and many philosophers seem not to realize that the approach they take to some of these questions may differ, not only from that which certain other philosophers take to these same questions, but also from that which they themselves take to other questions of a very similar sort.

2. A typical way of answering the second question—"How are we to decide *whether* we know?"—is to refer to the "sources" of our knowledge and say that an ostensible item of knowledge is genuine if and only if it is the product of a properly accredited source. It is traditional to say that there are four such sources:

(1) perception, by means of the external sense organs;

(2) memory;

(3) "inner consciousness," or the apprehension of our own states of mind—for example, our awareness of our own sensations, of our beliefs and desires, of how we feel, of what we are undertaking to do;

(4) reason, as the source of our a priori knowledge of necessity —our knowledge, for example, of some of the truths of logic and mathematics.

The first three sources on the list are sometimes grouped together and called simply "experience"; hence those who believe that our knowledge is restricted to whatever is yielded by these four sources say that our knowledge is "the product of reason and experience."

But if we are concerned with the question "How are we to decide whether we know?" we can hardly be satisfied with the answer that an ostensible item of knowledge is genuine if and only if it is the product of a properly accredited source of knowledge. For we are now led to ask "How are we to decide whether an ostensible source of knowledge *is* properly accredited?" and "How are we to decide just *what* it is that is yielded by a properly accredited source?"

We will best understand these questions if we recall that, according to some, there are three *additional* sources of knowing, other than reason and experience. These are:

(5) "moral consciousness";
(6) "intuitive understanding"; and
(7) "religious consciousness."

Among the things we know (according to philosophers who appeal to these additional sources) are certain facts about ethics, about human society and "other minds," and about God or "the Holy." It is controversial whether any such knowledge is yielded by (1), (2), (3), or (4); hence some of those who believe we do know such facts deduce that there are (5), (6), and (7). Those who are skeptical with respect to the type of fact in question deny that there *are* these additional sources of knowledge. Hence we arrive at the question "How are we to decide whether an ostensible source of knowledge is a source of knowledge?"

Some of those who believe that we do have knowledge about these controversial subjects—ethics, other minds and society, and God—*also* believe that there are no "sources of knowing" in addition to experience and reason, i.e., in addition to (1), (2), (3), and (4). And those who are more skeptical believe that experience and reason do not yield the kind of knowledge that is claimed. Hence we arrive at the question "How are we to decide what it is that we know by means of experience and reason?"

3. Some of the moral philosophers who believe that our sources of knowledge include a "moral consciousness" have reasoned in essentially this way: (P) We do have ethical knowledge; for example, we know that mercy is good and ingratitude is bad, whatever their consequences; but (Q) reason and experience do not yield such knowledge; hence (R) there is a source of knowledge in addition to reason and experience. The reasoning of such philosophers, who have been called "moral intuitionists," may be contrasted with that of certain other philosophers who believe that we have no strictly ethical knowledge and who may therefore be called "moral skeptics." The moral skeptic argues: (Not-R) There is no source of knowledge other than reason and experience; (Q) reason and experience do not yield any strictly ethical knowledge; therefore

(not-P) we do not have such knowledge. The intuitionist and the skeptic thus agree with respect to the second premise; the intuitionist takes as his first premise the contradictory of the skeptic's conclusion; and the skeptic takes as *his* first premise the contradictory of the intuitionist's conclusion.

The moral intuitionist may also be called a "moral cognitivist." But it is essential to note that there are moral cognitivists of a somewhat different sort—essential because the distinction will throw light upon the epistemological controversies to which our first four "sources" of knowledge give rise. This second type of cognitivist is like the skeptic in that he is *not* liberal with respect to what he will count as a proper source of knowledge; he will say with the skeptic that, for his part, he cannot find the moral intuitions to which the intuitionist appeals. But this second type of cognitivist is unlike the skeptic in that he *is* liberal with respect to what he will count as the legitimate product of a proper source of knowledge. Oversimplifying slightly, we may put his argument as follows: "Whatever we know we know through experience and reason; we do know that certain things are morally good and other things morally bad; the only experience that could yield such knowledge is our experience of moral feelings, e.g., of moral approval and disapproval; hence the experience of these moral feelings yields knowledge of what is morally good and morally bad." (This point of view is typical of "value theory" in the Austrian tradition, where our feeling for what is valuable, *das Wertgefühl,* is said to be something we know by means of our "inner consciousness" and to be the source of our knowledge of values.) The skeptic replies, of course, by saying that we do not have such moral knowledge, or knowledge of values, and that the moral cognitivist of our second sort has mistaken certain facts about his own state of mind for a knowledge of ethical truths.

The dispute between the skeptic and the cognitivist of the second sort is thus a dispute, not about the "sources of knowing," but about criteria of evidence: the cognitivist holds that our moral feelings justify us in believing something about the presence of value, or of good or evil; and the skeptic believes that they do not. (It is unfortunate that, in contemporary writings on ethics, the term "intuitionism" is used to designate both types of moral cognitivism. It would be more correctly used to designate only cognitivism of the first type, for some of the objections which hold of the first—e.g., the objection that such "intuitions" are not to be found—do not apply to the second.) The pattern of these disputes, as we shall see, is repeated in many different areas of epistemology.

The problem of religious knowledge, as many conceive it, is similar in essential respects to that of ethical knowledge. George Burch, who has seen the problem clearly, has recently written: "There are three coordinate sources of ordinary knowledge—reason, experience, and revelation. . . . Reason discloses relations among ideas and so shows what conclusions follow from premises already accepted. Experience, including perception and introspection, discloses the existence of those processes which we actually observe. Revelation, at the minimum, teaches the existence of the substantial deity which is the reality of the world and the substantial self which is the reality of the individual. . . . Experience has illusions, reason has fallacies, and faith has heresies. These errors can be corrected only within the faculty concerned." [1] Thus Burch argues: (P) Some people have metaphysical knowledge about God and the self; but (Q) such knowledge is not yielded by, or significantly confirmed by, reason or experience; hence (R) there is a source of knowledge—revelation—in addition to reason and experience. The "positivists" whom he criticizes argue, on the contrary: (Not-R) Reason and experience are the only sources of knowledge that there are; (Q) reason and experience do not supply, or significantly confirm, any information about God and the self; hence (not-P) no one has metaphysical knowledge about God and the self. The pattern of the argument is like that of the first argument over moral cognitivism: Burch and the positivist agree with respect to the second premise; Burch takes as his first premise the negation of the positivist's conclusion; and the positivist takes as *his* first premise the negation of Burch's conclusion.

But Burch also allows for the possibility of "religious cognitivism" of a second sort—parallel to our second type of moral cognitivism.

The source of revelation is an obscure problem. Quakers believe that God speaks directly to individuals; Protestants and Moslems,

[1] George Burch, "The Place of Revelation in Philosophical Thought," *Review of Metaphysics,* XV (1962), 396-408; the quotation is from p. 407.

that revelation is given once for all in the inspired scripture; Catholics, that it is given continuously in the living Church; Hindus, that it exists eternally in the Veda. The most naturalistic theory is that it has its source in the insight of mystics, men who have abnormal cognitive powers transcending both reason and perception, and who give to the rest of us verbal reports of these ineffable visions, reports which we are then free either to believe or disbelieve. Or it may be that revelation has no origin, but is handed down from an infinite regress of teachers, without any beginning. Ignorance of its source, however, does not affect our knowledge of its existence; we do not deny the moon's existence because we do not know where it came from.[2]

The controversies to which some of these possibilities give rise are like those of the second type of moral cognitivism we have considered, for they concern criteria of evidence. The religious cognitivist holds that certain facts of common experience are an indication that we know certain truths about religious matters, and the skeptic holds that they are not.

Of the three areas of skeptical controversy which we noted above —our ostensible knowledge of ethics, of religious truths, and of certain social and psychological facts—the third differs in one important respect from the other two. Although we find moral and religious cognitivists of two sorts—the first appealing to "sources" of knowing beyond reason and experience and the second confining themselves to reason and experience but appealing to special criteria of evidence—I think we find only the latter type of cognitivist in the third area. Wilhelm Dilthey and his followers have spoken of *Verstehen* as a "source" of our knowledge of certain psychological and social facts. But this *Verstehen*, or intuitive understanding, is not something which is unfamiliar to those who are skeptical about such facts; it is a feeling which is said to be familiar to everyone. The social cognitivist believes that the presence of this feeling is an indication of certain facts about societies and "other minds," and the skeptic believes that it is not.

2 *Ibid.*, p. 406. I think that John Hick's *Faith and Knowledge* (Cornell, 1957) may be interpreted as a defense of the second type of religious cognitivism. For a different point of view of the same problem, compare Morton White, "Reflections on Anti-Intellectualism," *Daedalus*, XCI (1962), 457-68.

RODERICK M. CHISHOLM

Maurice Mandelbaum has recently defended this type of social cognitivism. He argues, not implausibly, that the knowledge which most of us have of social facts (e.g., the fact that Mr. Jones has overdrawn his account at the bank) cannot be completely expressed in terms of those physical facts which we are ordinarily thought to perceive by means of the external senses. To those who would object that our experience does not yield any knowledge of "societal facts" and who are thus skeptical about such facts on the basis of a particular theory of knowledge, Mandelbaum replies: "Since those who would hold this theory of knowledge would presumably wish to show that we can be said to know something of the nature of human societies, and since they would also wish to hold that our means of gaining this knowledge is through the observation of the repeated patterns of activities of individuals, a proof that their theory of knowledge cannot account for our apprehensions of the nature of individual action is, in the present context, a sufficient disproof of the epistemological type of objection." [3]

We encounter similar controversies in connection with the knowledge that is sometimes attributed to "reason"—number (4) on our list. The "rationalists" of the seventeenth and eighteenth centuries emphasized "reason" as the most important of our sources of knowledge, but philosophers in the "empirical" tradition have tried, in various ways, to show that there is *no* such source of knowledge. Knowledge of metaphysics, as well as of logic and mathematics, has been attributed to reason. Most of those who now reject reason as a possible source of knowledge also deny that we have the kind of knowledge of metaphysics which has been attributed to this source; but instead of denying that we have the knowledge of logic and mathematics which has traditionally been attributed to reason, they attribute this knowledge to some one or another of the other sources listed here. John Stuart Mill tried to show that our knowledge of logic and mathematics is derived by induction from the perception of external things, and he might be

[3] Maurice Mandelbaum, "Societal Facts," *British Journal of Sociology*, VI, 307; reprinted in *The Structure of Scientific Thought*, ed. Edward Madden (Houghton, 1960). In an interesting monograph, *On the Epistemology of the Inexact Sciences* (Rand Corp., 1958), Olaf Helmer and Nicholas Rescher have defended making use of "experts' personal probability valuations" in a way which suggests that their view is close to the one I have attributed to Mandelbaum.

interpreted therefore as reducing (4) to (1). Theodore Lipps proposed, in 1880, that "logic is either the physics of thought or nothing at all" and tried to show that the truths of logic are in fact truths about the ways in which people think; the logical statement "If no Greeks are Romans, then no Romans are Greeks" tells us, really, that whoever believes that no Greeks are Romans cannot help believing also that no Romans are Greeks.[4] This "psychologistic" conception of the truths of logic, if it were tenable, would reduce "reason," as a source of knowledge, to our "inner consciousness"—i.e., reduce (4) to (3). Other philosophers proposed a modified "psychologistic" view, according to which the truths of logic and mathematics concern, not the ways in which people *do* think, but the ways in which they *ought* to think. On one interpretation, this modified view could be said to reduce "reason" to our "moral consciousness"—reducing (4) this time to (6)—and moral skepticism would then imply skepticism concerning logic and mathematics.

In recent years, "psychologism," as a view about the subject matter of logic and mathematics, has been replaced by a parallel view, which might be called "linguisticism." This view attempts to construe the statements of logic and mathematics as expressing certain facts about language, and hence might be thought to reduce (4) to (1), (2), and (3), or to some subclass of these. But the "rationalist" may say, as the American logician Alonzo Church has said: "The preference of (say) *seeing* over *understanding* as a method of observation seems to me capricious. For just as an opaque body may be seen, so a concept may be understood or grasped." [5]

The linguistic conception of logic and mathematics, like the "psychologistic" one, may seem also to have an ethical form; for the statements of logic and mathematics have also been associated with "rules" of language and hence might be thought to tell us something about the ways in which words *ought* to be used. If this view could be taken literally and were true, then (4) would be

[4] An excellent statement of the limitations of this view may be found in Rudolf Carnap, *The Logical Foundations of Probability* (U. of Chicago, 1950), pp. 37-51.
[5] Alonzo Church, "Abstract Entities in Semantic Analysis," *Proceedings of the American Academy of Arts and Sciences*, LXXX (1951), 100-12; the quotation is from p. 104.

reduced, again, to (6); but I believe the view cannot be taken this way and, as it happens, many of the philosophers who have accepted it have also been ethical skeptics. I shall consider some of the details of these questions in Chapter 3.

4. In discussing the issues of recent American epistemology, I shall assume, with respect to certain beliefs falling within the first four categories on our list, that we are justified in thinking they are instances of knowing; or, what comes to the same thing, I shall assume, with respect to these beliefs, that we have *adequate evidence* for them, or, better, that these beliefs pertain to what is evident. Then, given this assumption, I shall go on to ask certain further questions about the nature of this justification, or evidence.

The man who is more skeptical than we are will feel that we are assuming too much, and the man who is more credulous, that we are assuming too little. The skeptic may say, for example, "You should *not* assume that we have adequate evidence for any belief about the past" and the credulous man may say "You *should* assume that we have adequate evidence for certain beliefs about the relations between God and man." Perhaps we can show the skeptic that certain principles which he himself accepts imply that we *do* have adequate evidence for some of our beliefs about the past; and perhaps we can show the credulous man that certain principles which *he* accepts imply that we do *not* have adequate evidence for any beliefs about the relations between God and man. But if we cannot show the skeptic and the credulous man that they themselves have beliefs which imply that our assumptions are true, then we can only be dogmatic and say "We do have evidence for this, and we do not have evidence for that." But the skeptic and the credulous man may be equally dogmatic in their replies. To understand the issues of epistemology, it is essential to realize that there is no way of evaluating these conflicting dogmas until we have made certain assumptions concerning what it is that we know, or what it is that we are justified in thinking we know.

If two philosophers happen to make the same assumptions concerning what we are justified in thinking that we know, and if they also find themselves accepting common principles of justification, then they may be able to agree about other things that we can, or cannot, know. If they do not share any assumptions or principles, they may yet be able to agree concerning what each of them, given his own assumptions and principles, is justified in thinking that he knows; but there will be no way to reach an agreement concerning these assumptions or principles themselves. Here, then, we have a typically philosophical predicament.

Philosophers have come to realize—largely as a result of the work of G. E. Moore and Ludwig Wittgenstein—that many of their apparent disagreements are a result of linguistic difficulties, and some have attempted to trace the present predicament to a similar source. Occasionally we can deal with the skeptic merely by correcting his language. One such case of this, in recent American philosophy, is Paul Edwards' treatment of Bertrand Russell's doubts about induction.[6] Somewhat oversimplified, the situation was this: Russell had said that we have no good evidence for any of our beliefs about the future; Edwards pointed out, first, that Russell was using the words "we have no good evidence for any of our beliefs about the future" to mean *merely* that none of our beliefs about the future can be logically deduced from any of our beliefs about the past; he pointed out, second, that Russell's use of these words was hardly their ordinary use, and that when we put in a more correct way what it was that Russell was telling us, we see that his view is not a form of skepticism at all. Perhaps there are credulous men whose statements can be treated similarly: when they say "We have good evidence for believing that certain relations hold between God and man" they *may* mean merely that such beliefs are essential to a certain kind of peace of mind; and in such a case, perhaps, they do not disagree with us at all. But this way of resolving our ostensible disagreements is available only when the disagreements *are* thus verbal ones; if the skeptic, or the credulous man, happens to mean what we mean by "evidence,"

---

[6] Paul Edwards, "Bertrand Russell's Doubts about Induction," in *Essays on Logic and Language,* First Series, ed. A. G. N. Flew (Blackwell, 1951). Cf. F. L. Will, "Will the Future Be Like the Past?" *Mind,* LVI (1957), 332-47; Norman Malcolm, "Certainty and Empirical Statements," *Mind,* LI (1942), 18-46; O. K. Bouwsma, "Descartes' Skepticism of the Senses," *Mind,* LIV (1945), 313-22; Max Black, "Linguistic Method in Philosophy," *Philosophy and Phenomenological Research,* VIII (1948), 635-49; John Hospers, *An Introduction to Philosophical Analysis* (Prentice-Hall, 1953), chap. III.

"knowledge," and "justification," we are still in our predicament. (The importance of "correcting" the language of philosophers was, for a time, exaggerated, it seems to me. Norman Malcolm wrote, in 1942, that "any philosophical statement which violates ordinary language is false."[7] But it should be noted, concerning the example of Russell's supposed skepticism, above, that when Russell's statements, purporting to express doubts about the future, were "corrected" and translated into ordinary language, we learned that what he had been saying, incorrectly, was *true,* not false.)

There have been other "linguistic" attempts to deal with our predicament. One of these—aimed at the philosopher who professes to be skeptical about the existence of material things—may be put as follows. There are linguistic expressions, among them the expression "material thing," which we can understand only in virtue of the fact that we are acquainted with certain paradigm cases of their correct use; one cannot understand "material thing" unless one has been *shown* a material thing. Hence, from the fact that the expression "material thing" has a correct use, it follows that there are material things.[8] Or, somewhat more precisely: (1) Many people, both skeptics and nonskeptics, understand and are able to use correctly the expression "material thing"; but (2) the meaning and use of this expression could not have been explained to these people in terms merely of other expressions; hence (3) the people could not have learned the meaning and use of the expression unless they had been confronted with instances of what it denotes or truly applies to—i.e., unless they were confronted with some material things; and therefore (4) there are material things.

The weakest point of the argument, obviously, is the step from (2) to (3). For the skeptic—even if he has conceded (1) and (2)

---

[7] Norman Malcolm, "Moore and Ordinary Language," *The Philosophy of G. E. Moore,* ed. P. A. Schilpp (Northwestern, 1942). Malcolm subsequently conceded that this view was mistaken; cf. Malcolm's symposium with the present author, "Philosophy and Ordinary Language," *Philosophical Review,* LX (1951), 317-40.
[8] "In the case of all expressions the meanings of which must be *shown* and cannot be explained . . . , it follows, from the fact that they are ordinary expressions in the language, that there have been *many* situations of the kind which they describe; otherwise so many people could not have learned the correct use of those expressions." (Norman Malcolm in "Moore and Ordinary Language," p. 361.)

—has only to point out that people could learn the meaning and correct use of the expression "material thing" by being shown instances of what, as it happens, they *mistakenly,* though perhaps quite reasonably, *believe* to be material things. (Just as a man might learn the meaning of the word "rabbit" by being shown a toy which he mistakenly believes to be alive.) But if (3) is a non sequitur, then the conclusion (4) has not been established.

Other versions of this argument, which in some of its forms has come to be known as the "paradigm case argument" have been applied in other areas of recent philosophy.[9]

5. In the 1930's, and for a while after, it was thought that a certain doctrine about what types of statement are "meaningless," or "make no sense," would help us in dealing with some aspects of the kind of epistemological predicament we have been considering. But, I think, the doctrine itself involved a similar predicament.

During the writing of the *Principles of Mathematics* (1903), Bertrand Russell discovered the following logical paradox. Suppose W is the class of all those classes which are not members of themselves; then the statement *"W* is *not* a member of itself" implies *"W is* a member of itself," and *"W* is a member of itself" implies *"W* is not a member of itself." To enable logic to escape this and similar paradoxes, Russell proposed the "theory of types." This theory, which was incorporated into Russell and Whitehead's *Principia mathematica,* implied, among other things, that some of the sentences giving rise to the paradoxes belong to a class of sentences which are "meaningless"—in a sense of the term "meaningless" which implies that a "meaningless" sentence is neither true nor false. If a sentence can be shown thus to be "meaningless," then the theoretical difficulties which would be involved in supposing it to be true, or in supposing it to be false, need not be faced. And this suggests the possibility of setting aside many of the traditional problems of philosophy—if we can show that the philosophically puzzling sentences which give rise to these problems are "meaningless," in the present technical sense of the term. But how are we to

[9] In recent American philosophy, for example, by Max Black, *Language and Philosophy* (Cornell, 1949), chap. 1, and *Problems of Analysis* (Cornell, 1954), chap. 2.

show, with respect to sentences which sophisticated people think they understand, that the sentences are neither true or false? One answer to this question had been proposed by Charles Saunders Peirce in an article entitled "How to Make Our Ideas Clear," which first appeared in the *Popular Science Monthly* in 1878—an article which, according to William James, constituted the beginning of "pragmatism" in American philosophy.[10] "Our idea of anything," Peirce said, "is our idea of its sensible effects." Hence to ascertain the meaning, for us, of any particular concept, we have only to apply the following maxim: "Consider what effects, that might conceivably have practical bearings, we conceive the object of our conception to have. Then our conception of these effects is the whole of our conception of the object." If a sentence, purporting to express some concept, tells us nothing about any possible experience, then the sentence does not really express any concept at all. To talk of something, for example, "as having all the sensible characters of wine, yet being in reality blood, is senseless jargon."

This doctrine was set forth in somewhat more precise terms in the 1929 manifesto of the Vienna Circle and defended in various forms by subsequent "logical positivists," or "logical empiricists."[11] The "verifiability theory of meaning," as the doctrine came to be called, was essentially this: (1) the more puzzling sentences of traditional philosophy differ from the sentences of the empirical sciences in that the latter but not the former are *verifiable;* and (2) a sentence (other than one expressing a truth or a falsehood of logic or mathematics) is *meaningful,* and therefore either true or false, if and only if it is *verifiable.* Some philosophers objected that (2) was arbitrary, as of course it was, and that it was implausible.[12]

---

10 Peirce's article is reprinted in Volume V of his *Collected Papers* (Harvard, 1934); the quotations are from p. 258. Cf. William James's *Pragmatism* (Longmans, 1907), chap. 2.
11 *Wissenschaftliche Weltauffassung: Der wiener Kreis* (1929); see esp. pp. 15-20. The classic statement of the development of this doctrine is Carl G. Hempel's "Problems and Changes in the Empiricist Criterion of Meaning," *Revue internationale de philosophie,* quatrième année, no. 11 (1950), pp. 41-63; reprinted in *Semantics and the Philosophy of Language,* ed. Leonard Linsky (U. of Ill., 1952), and in *Logical Positivism,* ed. A. J. Ayer (Free Press of Glencoe, 1959).
12 Cf. R. M. Blake, "Can Speculative Philosophy Be Defended?" *Philosophical Review,* LII (1943), 127-34; W. T. Stace, "Positivism," *Mind,* LIII (1944), 215-37.

Others noted that the criteria of *verifiability* which had been offered did not in fact preserve the truth of (1): on some of the criteria, the sentences, neither of philosophy nor of the physical sciences, could be counted as verifiable; on others, the sentences *both* of philosophy and the sciences could be counted as verifiable. Which sentences, moreover, *are* sentences of "science"? Some philosophers had hoped to count, among the sentences which are meaningless, those expressing "the neo-vitalist speculations about entelechies or vital forces" and "the 'telefinalist hypothesis' proposed by Lecomte du Nöuy" and hence it was essential to say that these are not sentences of science.[13] But those scientists—or those people believing themselves to be scientists—who accepted such sentences preferred to say that the sentences *are* sentences of science; and hence that if there is a sense in which their sentences are "unverifiable," then there is a sense in which some of the sentences of science are "unverifiable."

The kind of predicament we have encountered in connection with skepticism and its alternatives has its analogues, then, when we attempt to answer such questions as "What sentences are meaningless?" and "What sentences are sentences of science?" (The questions "What sentences are descriptive?" "What sentences are factual?" and "What sentences are capable of being settled by recourse to empirical matters of fact?" involve a similar predicament.) This fact and, more generally, the kind of answer that was available to the question "What reason is there for believing that the sentences of traditional philosophy are neither true nor false?" suggested to many that problems of philosophy could not be so easily set aside.

Other philosophers, influenced by Wittgenstein, believe there are certain facts about our language—about how it is acquired and taught and about the ways in which it is ordinarily used—which *do* indicate that certain philosophical sentences "make no sense" and hence that some of the problems which these sentences are used to express can be dealt with by reference to linguistic considerations. Here, too, there is a conflict of approaches which seems incapable of being resolved. One philosopher may assume, con-

[13] C. G. Hempel, "Problems and Changes in the Empiricist Criterion of Meaning," *op. cit.*, p. 42.

cerning certain troublesome philosophical sentences, that enough is now known about language for us to infer, from linguistic facts, that the troublesome sentences are neither true nor false and hence that they are not really understood. Another philosopher may assume that not enough is yet known about language to warrant such inferences and that, since the sentences *are* understood and are either true or false, any theory of language which implies that they are not is, *ipso facto,* inadequate.

An interesting example of the first approach is Norman Malcolm's *Dreaming* (Humanities, 1959). Most philosophers, from Aristotle on, have assumed that dreams are "the activity of the mind during sleep"—that is to say, that thinking, judging, fearing, desiring, and the other activities commonly called "mental" take place during our dreams just as they do during our waking life. This view seems obvious enough (consider "In my dream last night I remembered that I had promised to meet you today"), but if we could show it to be false, we could simplify the work both of the theory of knowledge and of the philosophy of mind. The point of Malcolm's book is to show, by reference to certain facts about language, that the view is not only false but "unintelligible" as well.

Malcolm claimed to offer "a proof that thinking in sleep, reasoning in sleep, imagining in sleep, and so on, are all unintelligible notions," a proof that would also apply, mutatis mutandis, to judging in sleep, to having imagery in sleep, and to feeling emotions such as fear, joy, and anxiety in sleep (p. 45). To illustrate this approach to the problems of philosophy, I shall set forth in a series of separate steps what I take to be Malcolm's proof that judging in sleep is an "unintelligible concept." It should be noted, however, that he does not set forth his reasoning in this explicit fashion and that there is a problem of interpretation concerning what I shall list as the second step of the proof.

The argument, then, seems to be this: (1) It is theoretically impossible for me, or for anyone else, to find out, or to verify, that "the state of myself that I claim to describe by the sentence 'I am asleep' really is the state of being asleep." (2) No one can understand a sentence unless, for the most part, when he utters the sentence what he says is true. Hence (3) no one can understand the sentence "I am asleep" unless "for the most part when he says 'I am asleep' what he says is true." And therefore (4) it is theoretically impossible for anyone to verify the sentence "I am asleep." But (5) if it is theoretically impossible for anyone to verify a given sentence, then that sentence is "without sense and necessarily so." Therefore (6) the sentence "I am asleep" is without sense and necessarily so. Hence (7) the notion of a person judging that he is asleep is absurd. But (8) if it is absurd to speak of a sleeping person judging that he is asleep, then it is also absurd to speak of him making any *other* judgment in his sleep. And therefore (9) judging in sleep is an unintelligible concept.

A similar argument may be applied in the case of those other mental activities which, we ordinarily suppose, sometimes take place while we dream.[14]

I have presented the argument in such a way that the conclusion does follow from the premises. Premises (2), (5), and (8) are, of course, the ones that are controversial. In defense of (2), or of something like (2), Malcolm says: "In order for the sentence to have a *correct* use, one would sometimes have to say it when the thing one said was true. . . . You would have no right to say that someone understood the sentence 'He is asleep' unless, for the most part, when he applied those words to some person that person was indeed asleep. The same thing would have to hold for the sentence 'I am asleep'" (pp. 36, 10). He also refers to a passage in Wittgenstein's *Philosophical Investigations* which he interprets as saying something similar.[15] Yet Malcolm does not quite commit himself to (2), and it may be doubted whether he would wish to. For (2) implies, implausibly, that no one can understand the sentences "There are people on the moon," "Nixon is President of the United States," and "I am sitting perfectly still."[16] Some version of (2), however, is required in order to justify (3) and therefore (9), but it is extraordinarily difficult to imagine how such a premise might it-

---

[14] Assuming that his argument was sound, Malcolm proposed a theory concerning the "uses" of those sentences which ostensibly attribute mental activities to sleeping persons. This theory falls outside the scope of this essay.

[15] "If language is to be a means of communication, there must be agreement not only in definitions but also (queer as this may sound) in judgments." (Ludwig Wittgenstein, *Philosophical Investigations* [Blackwell, 1953], p. 88e.)

[16] The third quoted example is taken from John Canfield, "Judgments in Sleep," *Philosophical Review*, LXX (1961), 224-30.

self be justified. Even if such a premise *could* be found and justified, we could still avoid the implausible conclusion of the argument merely by rejecting (8), or by rejecting that version of the "verifiability theory of meaning" which survives in (5). And this takes us back to the kind of predicament with which we began.

THE "MYTH OF THE GIVEN"

1. The doctrine of "the given" involved two theses about our knowledge. We may introduce them by means of a traditional metaphor:

 (A) The knowledge which a person has at any time is a structure or edifice, many parts and stages of which help to support each other, but which as a whole is supported by its own foundation.

The second thesis is a specification of the first:

 (B) The foundation of one's knowledge consists (at least in part) of the apprehension of what have been called, variously, "sensations," "sense-impressions," "appearances," "sensa," "sense-qualia," and "phenomena."

These phenomenal entities, said to be at the base of the structure of knowledge, are what was called "the given." A third thesis is sometimes associated with the doctrine of the given, but the first two theses do not imply it. We may formulate it in the terms of the same metaphor:

 (C) The *only* apprehension which is thus basic to the structure of knowledge is our apprehension of "appearances" (etc.) —our apprehension of the given.

Theses (A) and (B) constitute the "doctrine of the given"; thesis (C), if a label were necessary, might be called "the phenomenalistic version" of the doctrine. The first two theses are essential to the empirical tradition in Western philosophy. The third is problematic for traditional empiricism and depends in part, but only in part, upon the way in which the metaphor of the edifice and its foundation is spelled out.

I believe it is accurate to say that, at the time at which our study begins, most American epistemologists accepted the first two theses and thus accepted the doctrine of the given. The expression "the given" became a term of contemporary philosophical vocabulary partly because of its use by C. I. Lewis in his *Mind and the World-*

Order (Scribner, 1929). Many of the philosophers who accepted the doctrine avoided the expression because of its association with other more controversial parts of Lewis's book—a book which might be taken (though mistakenly, I think) also to endorse thesis (C), the "phenomenalistic version" of the doctrine. The doctrine itself—theses (A) and (B)—became a matter of general controversy during the period of our survey.

Thesis (A) was criticized as being "absolute" and thesis (B) as being overly "subjective." Both criticisms may be found in some of the "instrumentalistic" writings of John Dewey and philosophers associated with him. They may also be found in the writings of those philosophers of science ("logical empiricists") writing in the tradition of the Vienna Circle. (At an early stage of this tradition, however, some of these same philosophers seem to have accepted all three theses.) Discussion became entangled in verbal confusions—especially in connection with the uses of such terms as "doubt," "certainty," "appearance," and "immediate experience." Philosophers, influenced by the work that Ludwig Wittgenstein had been doing in the 1930's, noted such confusions in detail, and some of them seem to have taken the existence of such confusions to indicate that (A) and (B) are false.[1] Many have rejected both theses as being inconsistent with a certain theory of thought and reference; among them, in addition to some of the critics just referred to, we find philosophers in the tradition of nineteenth century "idealism."

Philosophers of widely diverging schools now believe that "the myth of the given" has finally been dispelled.[2] I suggest, however, that, although thesis (C), "the phenomenalistic version," is false, the two theses, (A) and (B), which constitute the doctrine of the given are true.

The doctrine is not merely the consequence of a metaphor. We

[1] Philosophers in other traditions also noted these confusions. See, for example, John Wild, "The Concept of the Given in Contemporary Philosophy," *Philosophy and Phenomenological Research,* I (1940), 70-82.
[2] The expression "myth of the given" was used by Wilfrid Sellars in "Empiricism and the Philosophy of Mind," in *Foundations of Science and the Concepts of Psychology and Psychoanalysis,* ed. Herbert Feigl and Michael Scriven, Minnesota Studies in the Philosophy of Science, vol. I (U. of Minn., 1956), pp. 253-329.

are led to it when we attempt to answer certain questions about *justification*—our justification for supposing, in connection with any one of the things that we know to be true, that it is something that we know to be true.

2. To the question "What justification do I have for thinking I know that *a* is true?" one may reply: "I know that *b* is true, and if I know that *b* is true then I also know that *a* is true." And to the question "What justification do I have for thinking I know that *b* is true?" one may reply: "I know that *c* is true, and if I know that *c* is true then I also know that *b* is true." Are we thus led, sooner or later, to something *n* of which one may say: "What justifies me in thinking I know that *n* is true is simply the fact that *n* is true." If there is such an *n,* then the belief or statement that *n* is true may be thought of either as a belief or statement which "justifies itself" or as a belief or statement which is itself "neither justified nor unjustified." The distinction—unlike that between a Prime Mover which moves itself and a Prime Mover which is neither in motion nor at rest—is largely a verbal one; the essential thing, if there is such an *n,* is that it provides a stopping place in the process, or dialectic, of justification.

We may now re-express, somewhat less metaphorically, the two theses which I have called the "doctrine of the given." The first thesis, that our knowledge is an edifice or structure having its own foundation, becomes (A) "every statement, which we are justified in thinking that we know, is justified in part by some statement which justifies itself." The second thesis, that there are appearances ("the given") at the foundation of our knowledge, becomes (B) "there are statements about appearances which thus justify themselves." (The third thesis—the "phenomenalistic version" of the doctrine of the given—becomes (C) "there are no self-justifying statements which are not statements about appearances.") Let us now turn to the first of the two theses constituting the doctrine of the given.

3. "Every justified statement is justified in part by some statement which justifies itself." Could it be that the question which this thesis is supposed to answer is a question which arises only because of

some mistaken assumption? If not, what are the alternative ways of answering it? And did any of the philosophers with whom we are concerned actually accept any of these alternatives? The first two questions are less difficult to answer than the third.

There are the following points of view to be considered, each of which *seems* to have been taken by some of the philosophers in the period of our survey.

(1) One may believe that the questions about justification which give rise to our problem are based upon false assumptions and hence that they *should not be asked* at all.

(2) One may believe that no statement or claim is justified unless it is justified, at least in part, by some other justified statement or claim which it does not justify; this belief may suggest that one should continue the process of justifying *ad indefinitum,* justifying each claim by reference to some additional claim.

(3) One may believe that no statement or claim *a* is justified unless it is justified by some other justified statement or claim *b,* and that *b* is not justified unless it in turn is justified by *a;* this would suggest that the process of justifying is, or should be, *circular.*

(4) One may believe that there are some particular claims *n* at which the process of justifying should stop, and one may then hold of any such claim *n* either: (a) *n* is justified by something—viz., *experience* or *observation*—which is not itself a claim and which therefore cannot be said itself either to be justified or unjustified; (b) *n* is itself *unjustified;* (c) *n justifies itself;* or (d) *n* is *neither justified nor unjustified.*

These possibilities, I think, exhaust the significant points of view; let us now consider them in turn.

4. "The questions about justification which give rise to the problem are based upon false assumptions and therefore should not be asked at all."

The questions are *not* based upon false assumptions; but most of the philosophers who discussed the questions put them in such a misleading way that one is very easily misled into supposing that they *are* based upon false assumptions.

Many philosophers, following Descartes, Russell, and Husserl, formulated the questions about justification by means of such terms as "doubt," "certainty," and "incorrigibility," and they used, or misused, these terms in such a way that, when their questions were taken in the way in which one would ordinarily take them, they could be shown to be based upon false assumptions. One may note, for example, that the statement "There is a clock on the mantelpiece" is not self-justifying—for to the question "What is your justification for thinking you know that there is a clock on the mantelpiece?" the proper reply would be to make some other statement (e.g., "I saw it there this morning and no one would have taken it away")—and one may then go on to ask "But are there any statements which can be said to justify themselves?" If we express these facts, as many philosophers did, by saying that the statement "There is a clock on the mantelpiece" is one which is not "certain," or one which may be "doubted," and if we then go on to ask "Does this doubtful statement rest upon other statements which are certain and incorrigible?" then we are using terms in an extraordinarily misleading way. The question "Does this doubtful statement rest upon statements which are certain and incorrigible?" —if taken as one would ordinarily take it—does rest upon a false assumption, for (we may assume) the statement that there is a clock on the mantelpiece is one which is not doubtful at all.

John Dewey, and some of the philosophers whose views were very similar to his, tended to suppose, mistakenly, that the philosophers who asked themselves "What justification do I have for thinking I know this?" were asking the quite different question "What more can I do to verify or confirm that this is so?" and they rejected answers to the first question on the ground that they were unsatisfactory answers to the second.[3] Philosophers influenced by Wittgenstein tended to suppose, also mistakenly, but quite understandably, that the question "What justification do I have for thinking I know this?" contains an implicit challenge and presupposes that one does not have the knowledge concerned. They then pointed out, correctly, that in most of the cases where the question was raised (e.g., "What justifies me in thinking I know that this is a

[3] Dewey also said that, instead of trying to provide "Foundations for Knowledge," the philosopher should apply "what is known to intelligent conduct of the affairs of human life" to "the problems of men." John Dewey, *Problems of Men* (Philosophical, 1946), pp. 6-7.

table?") there is no ground for challenging the claim to knowledge and that questions presupposing that the claim is false should not arise. But the question "What justifies me in thinking I know that this is a table?" does not challenge the claim to know that this is a table, much less presuppose that the claim is false.

The "critique of cogency," as Lewis described this concern of epistemology, presupposes that we *are* justified in thinking we know most of the things that we do think we know, and what it seeks to elicit is the nature of this justification. The enterprise is like that of ethics, logic, and aesthetics:

> The nature of the good can be learned from experience only if the content of experience be first classified into good and bad, or grades of better and worse. Such classification or grading already involves the legislative application of the same principle which is sought. In logic, principles can be elicited by generalization from examples only if cases of valid reasoning have first been segregated by some criterion. In esthetics, the laws of the beautiful may be derived from experience only if the criteria of beauty have first been correctly applied.[4]

When Aristotle considered an invalid mood of the syllogism and asked himself "What is wrong with this?" he was not suggesting to himself that perhaps nothing was wrong; he presupposed that the mood *was* invalid, just as he presupposed that others were not, and he attempted, successfully, to formulate criteria which would enable us to distinguish the two types of mood.

When we have answered the question "What justification do I have for thinking I know this?" what we learn, as Socrates taught, is something about ourselves. We learn, of course, what the justification happens to be for the particular claim with which the question is concerned. But we also learn, more generally, what the criteria are, if any, in terms of which we believe ourselves justified in counting one thing as an instance of knowing and another thing not. The truth which the philosopher seeks, when he asks about justification, is "already implicit in the mind which seeks it, and needs only to be elicited and brought to clear expression."[5]

[4] C. I. Lewis, *Mind and the World-Order* (Scribner, 1929), p. 29.
[5] *Ibid.,* p. 19. Cf. Hans Reichenbach, *Experience and Prediction* (U. of Chicago,

Let us turn, then, to the other approaches to the problem of "the given."

5. "No statement or claim would be justified unless it were justified, at least in part, by some other justified claim or statement which it does not justify."

This regressive principle might be suggested by the figure of the building and its supports: no stage supports another unless it is itself supported by some other stage beneath it—a truth which holds not only of the upper portions of the building but also of what we call its foundation. And the principle follows if, as some of the philosophers in the tradition of logical empiricism seemed to believe, we should combine a frequency theory of probability with a probability theory of justification.

In *Experience and Prediction* (U. of Chicago, 1938) and in other writings, Hans Reichenbach defended a "probability theory of knowledge" which seemed to involve the following contentions:

(1) To justify accepting a statement, it is necessary to show that the statement is probable.

(2) To say of a statement that it is probable is to say something about statistical frequencies. Somewhat more accurately, a statement of the form "It is *probable* that any particular *a* is a *b*" may be explicated as saying "Most *a*'s are *b*'s." Or, still more accurately, to say "The probability is *n* that a particular *a* is a *b*" is to say "The limit of the relative frequency with the property of being a *b* occurs in the class of things having the property *a* is *n*."

(3) Hence, by (2), to show that a proposition is probable it is necessary to show that a certain statistical frequency obtains; and, by (1), to show that a certain statistical frequency obtains it is necessary to show that it is probable that the statistical frequency obtains; and therefore, by (2), to show that it is probable that a certain statistical frequency obtains, it is necessary to show that a certain frequency of frequencies obtains. . . .

(4) And therefore "there is no Archimedean point of absolute certainty left to which to attach our knowledge of the world; all we

1938), p. 6; C. J. Ducasse, "Some Observations Concerning the Nature of Probability," *Journal of Philosophy*, XXXVIII (1941), esp. 400-01.

have is an elastic net of probability connections floating in open space" (p. 192).

This reasoning suggests that an infinite number of steps must be taken in order to justify acceptance of any statement. For, according to the reasoning, we cannot determine the probability of one statement until we have determined that of a second, and we cannot determine that of the second until we have determined that of a third, and so on. Reichenbach does not leave the matter here, however. He suggests that there is a way of "descending" from this "open space" of probability connections, but, if I am not mistaken, we can make the descent only by letting go of the concept of justification.

He says that, if we are to avoid the regress of probabilities of probabilities of probabilities . . . , we must be willing at some point merely to make a guess; "there will always be some blind posits on which the whole concatenation is based" (p. 367). The view that knowledge is to be identified with certainty and that probable knowledge must be "imbedded in a framework of certainty" is "a remnant of rationalism. An empiricist theory of probability can be constructed only if we are willing to regard knowledge as a system of posits." [6]

But if we begin by assuming, as we do, that there is a distinction between knowledge, on the one hand, and a lucky guess, on the other, then we must reject at least one of the premises of any argument purporting to demonstrate that knowledge is a system of "blind posits." The unacceptable conclusion of Reichenbach's argument may be so construed as to follow from premises (1) and (2); and premise (2) may be accepted as a kind of definition (though there are many who believe that this definition is not adequate to all of the uses of the term "probable" in science and everyday life). Premise (1), therefore, is the one we should reject, and there are good reasons, I think, for rejecting (1), the thesis that "to justify accepting a proposition it is necessary to show that the proposition is probable." In fairness to Reichenbach, it should be added that he never explicitly affirms premise (1); but some such premise is essential to his argument.

[6] Hans Reichenbach, "Are Phenomenal Reports Absolutely Certain?" *Philosophical Review,* LXI (1952), 147-59; the quotation is from p. 150.

6. "No statement or claim *a* would be justified unless it were justified by some other justified statement or claim *b* which would not be justified unless it were justified in turn by *a*."

The "coherence theory of truth," to which some philosophers committed themselves, is sometimes taken to imply that justification may thus be circular; I believe, however, that the theory does not have this implication. It does define "truth" as a kind of systematic consistency of beliefs or propositions. The truth of a proposition is said to consist, not in the fact that the proposition "corresponds" with something which is not itself a proposition, but in the fact that it fits consistently into a certain more general system of propositions. This view may even be suggested by the figure of the building and its foundations. There is no difference in principle between the way in which the upper stories are supported by the lower, and that in which the cellar is supported by the earth just below it, or the way in which that stratum of earth is supported by various substrata farther below; a good building appears to be a part of the terrain on which it stands and a good system of propositions is a part of the wider system which gives it its truth. But these metaphors do not solve philosophical problems.

The coherence theory did in fact appeal to something other than logical consistency; its proponents conceded that a system of false propositions may be internally consistent and hence that logical consistency alone is no guarantee of truth. Brand Blanshard, who defended the coherence theory in *The Nature of Thought,* said that a proposition is true provided it is a member of an internally consistent system of propositions and *provided further* this system is "the system in which everything real and possible is coherently included." [7] In one phase of the development of "logical empiricism" its proponents seem to have held a similar view: a proposition—or, in this case, a statement—is true provided it is a member of an internally consistent system of statements and *provided further* this system is "the system which is actually adopted by mankind, and especially by the scientists in our culture circle." [8]

A theory of truth is not, as such, a theory of justification. To say

[7] Brand Blanshard, *The Nature of Thought,* vol. II (Macmillan, 1940), p. 276.
[8] C. G. Hempel, "On the Logical Positivists' Theory of Truth," *Analysis,* II (1935), 49-59; the quotation is from p. 57.

that a proposition is true is not to say that we are justified in accepting it as true, and to say that we are justified in accepting it as true is not to say that it is true. (I shall return to this point in my final chapter.) Whatever merits the coherence theory may have as an answer to certain questions about truth, it throws no light upon our present epistemological question. If we accept the coherence theory, we may still ask, concerning any proposition *a* which we think we know to be true, "What is my justification for thinking I know that *a* is a member of the system of propositions in which everything real and possible is coherently included, or that *a* is a member of the system of propositions which is actually adopted by mankind and by the scientists of our culture circle?" And when we ask such a question, we are confronted, once again, with our original alternatives.

7. If our questions about justification do have a proper stopping place, then, as I have said, there are still four significant possibilities to consider. We may stop with some particular claim and say of it that either:

(a) it is justified by something—by experience, or by observation—which is not itself a claim and which, therefore, cannot be said either to be justified or to be unjustified;

(b) it is justified by some claim which refers to our experience or observation, and the claim referring to our experience or observation has *no* justification;

(c) it justifies itself; or

(d) it is itself neither justified nor unjustified.

The first of these alternatives leads readily to the second, and the second to the third or to the fourth. The third and the fourth—which differ only verbally, I think—involve the doctrine of "the given."

Carnap wrote, in 1936, that the procedure of scientific testing involves two operations: the "confrontation of a statement with observation" and the "confrontation of a statement with previously accepted statements." He suggested that those logical empiricists who were attracted to the coherence theory of truth tended to lose sight of the first of these operations—the confrontation of a statement with observation. He proposed a way of formulating simple "acceptance rules" for such confrontation and he seemed to believe that, merely by applying such rules, we could avoid the epistemological questions with which the adherents of "the given" had become involved.

Carnap said this about his acceptance rules: "If no foreign language or introduction of new terms is involved, the rules are trivial. For example: 'If one is hungry, the statement "I am hungry" may be accepted'; or: 'If one sees a key one may accept the statement "there lies a key." ' " [9] As we shall note later, the first of these rules differs in an important way from the second. Confining ourselves for the moment to rules of the second sort—"If one sees a key one may accept the statement 'there lies a key' "—let us ask ourselves whether the appeal to such rules enables us to solve our problem of the stopping place.

When we have made the statement "There lies a key," we can, of course, raise the question "What is my justification for thinking I know, or for believing, that there lies a key?" The answer would be "I see the key." We cannot ask "What is my justification for seeing a key?" But we can ask "What is my justification for thinking that it is a key that I see?" and, if we do see that the thing is a key, the question will have an answer. The answer might be "I see that it's shaped like a key and that it's in the lock, and I remember that a key is usually here." The possibility of this question, and its answer, indicates that we cannot stop our questions about justification merely by appealing to observation or experience. For, of the statement "I observe that that is an A," we can ask, and answer, the question "What is my justification for thinking that I observe that there is an A?"

It is relevant to note, moreover, that there may be conditions under which seeing a key does not justify one in accepting the statement "There is a key" or in believing that one sees a key. If the key were so disguised or concealed that the man who saw it did not recognize it to be a key, then he might not be justified in accepting

[9] Rudolf Carnap, "Truth and Confirmation," in *Readings in Philosophical Analysis,* ed. Herbert Feigl and W. S. Sellars (Appleton, 1949), p. 125. The portions of the article quoted above first appeared in "Wahrheit und Bewährung," *Actes du congrès internationale de philosophie scientifique,* IV (Paris; 1936), 18-23.

RODERICK M. CHISHOLM

the statement "There is a key." Just as, if Mr. Jones unknown to anyone but himself is a thief, then the people who see him may be said to see a thief—but none of those who thus sees a thief is justified in accepting the statement "There is a thief." [10]

Some of the writings of logical empiricists suggest that, although some statements may be justified by reference to other statements, those statements which involve "confrontation with observation" are not justified at all. C. G. Hempel, for example, wrote that "the acknowledgement of an experiential statement as true is psychologically motivated by certain experiences; but within the system of statements which express scientific knowledge or one's beliefs at a given time, they function in the manner of postulates for which no grounds are offered." [11] Hempel conceded, however, that this use of the term "postulate" is misleading and he added the following note of clarification: "When an experiential sentence is accepted 'on the basis of direct experiential evidence,' it is indeed not asserted arbitrarily; but to describe the evidence in question would simply mean to repeat the experiential statement itself. Hence, in the context of cognitive justification, the statement functions in the manner of a primitive sentence." [12]

When we reach a statement having the property just referred to —an experiential statement such that to describe its evidence "would simply mean to repeat the experiential statement itself"— we have reached a proper stopping place in the process of justification.

8. We are thus led to the concept of a belief, statement, claim, proposition, or hypothesis, which justifies itself. To be clear about the concept, let us note the way in which we would justify the state-

10 Cf. Nelson Goodman, *The Structure of Appearance* (Harvard, 1951), p. 104. If Goodman's book, incidentally, is not discussed in this collection of essays, the fault is with our conventional classification of philosophical disciplines. The book, which is concerned with an area falling between logic and metaphysics, is one of the most important philosophical works written by an American during the period being surveyed.
11 C. G. Hempel, "Some Theses on Empirical Certainty," *Review of Metaphysics*, V (1952), 621-29; the quotation is from p. 621.
12 *Ibid.*, p. 628. Hempel's remarks were made in an "Exploration" in which he set forth several theses about "empirical certainty" and then replied to objections by Paul Weiss, Roderick Firth, Wilfrid Sellars, and myself.

272

ment that we have a certain belief. It is essential, of course, that we distinguish justifying the statement *that* we have a certain belief from justifying the belief itself.

Suppose, then, a man is led to say "I believe that Socrates is mortal" and we ask him "What is your justification for thinking that you believe, or for thinking that you know that you believe, that Socrates is mortal?" To this strange question, the only appropriate reply would be "My justification for thinking I believe, or for thinking that I know that I believe, that Socrates is mortal is simply the fact that I *do* believe that Socrates is mortal." One justifies the statement simply by reiterating it; the statement's justification is what the statement says. Here, then, we have a case which satisfies Hempel's remark quoted above; we describe the evidence for a statement merely by repeating the statement. We could say, as C. J. Ducasse did, that "the occurrence of belief is its own evidence." [13]

Normally, as I have suggested, one cannot justify a statement merely by reiterating it. To the question "What justification do you have for thinking you know that there can be no life on the moon?" it would be inappropriate, and impertinent, to reply by saying simply "There *can* be no life on the moon," thus reiterating the fact at issue. An appropriate answer would be one referring to certain *other* facts—for example, the fact that we know there is insufficient oxygen on the moon to support any kind of life. But to the question "What is your justification for thinking you know that you believe so and so?" there is nothing to say other than "I *do* believe so and so."

We may say, then, that there are some statements which are self-justifying, or which justify themselves. And we may say, analogously, that there are certain beliefs, claims, propositions, or hypotheses which are self-justifying, or which justify themselves. A statement, belief, claim, proposition, or hypothesis may be said to be self-justifying for a person, if the person's justification for thinking he knows it to be true is simply the fact that it *is* true.

Paradoxically, these things I have described by saying that

[13] C. J. Ducasse, "Propositions, Truth, and the Ultimate Criterion of Truth," *Philosophy and Phenomenological Research*, IV (1939), 317-40; the quotation is from p. 339.

they "justify themselves" may *also* be described by saying they are "neither justified nor unjustified." The two modes of description are two different ways of saying the same thing.

If we are sensitive to ordinary usage, we may note that the expression "I believe that I believe" is ordinarily used, not to refer to a second-order belief about the speaker's own beliefs, but to indicate that the speaker has not yet made up his mind. "I *believe that I believe* that Johnson is a good president" might properly be taken to indicate that, if the speaker *does* believe that Johnson is a good president, he is not yet firm in that belief. Hence there is a temptation to infer that, if we say of a man who is firm in his belief that Socrates is mortal, that he is "justified in believing that he believes that Socrates is mortal," our statement "makes no sense." And there is also a temptation to go on and say that it "makes no sense" even to say of such a man, that his *statement* "I believe that Socrates is mortal" is one which is "justified" for him.[14] After all, what would it mean to say of a man's statement about his own belief, that he is *not* justified in accepting it? [15]

The questions about what does or does not "make any sense" need not, however, be argued. We *may* say, if we prefer, that the statements about the beliefs in question are "neither justified nor unjustified." Whatever mode of description we use, the essential points are two. First, we may appeal to such statements in the process of justifying some *other* statement or belief. If they *have* no justification they may yet *be* a justification—for something other than themselves. ("What justifies me in thinking that he and I are not likely to agree? The fact that I believe that Socrates is mortal and he does not.") Second, the making of such a statement does provide what I have been calling a "stopping place" in the dialectic of justification; but now, instead of signalizing the stopping place by reiterating the questioned statement, we do it by saying that the question of its justification is one which "should not arise."

---

14 Cf. Norman Malcolm, "Knowledge of Other Minds," *Journal of Philosophy,* LV (1958), 969-78. Reprinted in Malcolm, *Knowledge and Certainty: Essays and Lectures* (Prentice-Hall, 1963).
15 The principle behind this way of looking at the matter is defended in detail by Max Black in *Language and Philosophy* (Cornell, 1949), p. 16 ff.

It does not matter, then, whether we speak of certain statements which "justify themselves" or of certain statements which are "neither justified nor unjustified," for in either case we will be referring to the same set of statements. I shall continue to use the former phrase.

There are, then, statements about one's own beliefs ("I believe that Socrates is mortal")—and for statements about many other psychological attitudes—which are self-justifying. "What justifies me in believing, or in thinking I know, that I *hope* to come tomorrow? Simply the fact that I *do* hope to come tomorrow." Thinking, desiring, wondering, loving, hating, and other such attitudes are similar. Some, but by no means all, of the statements we can make about such attitudes, when the attitudes are our own, are self-justifying—as are statements containing such phrases as "I think I remember" or "I seem to remember" (as distinguished from "I remember"), and "I think that I see" and "I think that I perceive" (as distinguished from "I see" and "I perceive"). Thus, of the two examples which Carnap introduced in connection with his "acceptance rules" discussed above, viz., "I am hungry" and "I see a key," we may say that the first is self-justifying and the second not.

The "doctrine of the given," it will be recalled, tells us (A) that every justified statement, about what we think we know, is justified in part by some statement which justifies itself and (B) that there are statements about appearances which thus justify themselves. The "phenomenalistic version" of the theory adds (C) that statements about appearances are the *only* statements which justify themselves. What we have been saying is that the first thesis, (A), of the doctrine of the given is true and that the "phenomenalistic version," (C), is false; let us turn now to thesis (B).

9. In addition to the self-justifying statements about psychological attitudes, are there self-justifying statements about "appearances"? Now we encounter difficulties involving the word "appearance" and its cognates.

Sometimes such words as "appears," "looks," and "seems" are used to convey what one might also convey by such terms as "believe." For example, if I say "It appears to me that General de Gaulle was successful," or "General de Gaulle seems to have been

275

successful," I am likely to mean only that I believe, or incline to believe, that he has been successful; the words "appears" and "seems" serve as useful hedges, giving me an out, should I find out later that de Gaulle was not successful. When "appear"-words are used in this way, the statements in which they occur add nothing significant to the class of "self-justifying" statements we have just provided. Philosophers have traditionally assumed, however, that such terms as "appear" may also be used in a quite different way. If this assumption is correct, as I believe it is, then this additional use does lead us to another type of self-justifying statement.

In the final chapter we shall have occasion to note some of the confusions to which the substantival expression "appearance" gave rise. The philosophers who exposed these confusions were sometimes inclined to forget, I think, that things do appear to us in various ways.[16] We can alter the appearance of anything we like merely by doing something which will affect our sense organs or the conditions of observation. One of the important epistemological questions about appearances is "Are there self-justifying statements about the ways in which things appear?"

Augustine, refuting the skeptics of the late Platonic Academy, wrote: "I do not see how the Academician can refute him who says: 'I know that this appears white to me, I know that my hearing is delighted with this, I know this has an agreeable odor, I know this tastes sweet to me, I know that this feels cold to me.' . . . When a person tastes something, he can honestly swear that he knows it is sweet to his palate or the contrary, and that no trickery of the Greeks can dispossess him of that knowledge."[17] Suppose, now, one were to ask "What justification do you have for believing, or thinking you know, that this appears white to you, or that that tastes bitter to you?" Here, too, we can only reiterate the statement: "What justifies me in believing, or in thinking I know,

---

[16] One of the best criticisms of the "appearance" (or "sense-datum") terminology was O. K. Bouwsma's "Moore's Theory of Sense-Data," in *The Philosophy of G. E. Moore,* ed. Schilpp, pp. 201-21. In *Perceiving: A Philosophical Study* (Cornell, 1957), I tried to call attention to certain facts about appearing which, I believe, Bouwsma may have overlooked.

[17] Augustine, *Contra academicos,* xi, 26; translated by Sister Mary Patricia Garvey as *Saint Augustine Against the Academicians* (Marquette, 1942); the quotations are from pp. 68-69.

that this appears white to me and that that tastes bitter to me is the fact that this *does* appear white to me and that *does* taste bitter."

An advantage of the misleading substantive "appearance," as distinguished from the verb "appears," is that the former may be applied to those sensuous experiences which, though capable of being appearances of things, are actually not appearances of anything. Feelings, imagery, and the sensuous content of dreams and hallucination are very much like the appearances of things and they are such that, under some circumstances, they could be appearances of things. But if we do not wish to say that they are experiences wherein some external physical thing *appears* to us, we must use some expression other than "appear." For "appear," in its active voice, requires a grammatical subject and thus requires a term which refers, not merely to a way of appearing, but also to something *which* appears.

But we may avoid *both* the objective *"Something* appears blue to me," and the substantival "I sense a blue *appearance."* We may use another verb, say "sense," in a technical way, as many philosophers did, and equate it in meaning with the passive voice of "appear," thus saying simply "I *sense* blue," or the like. Or better still, it seems to me, and at the expense only of a little awkwardness, we can use "appear" in its passive voice and say "I am *appeared to* blue."

Summing up, in our new vocabulary, we may say that the philosophers who talked of the "empirically given" were referring, not to "self-justifying" statements and beliefs generally, but only to those pertaining to certain "ways of being appeared to." And the philosophers who objected to the doctrine of the given, or some of them, argued that no statement about "a way of being appeared to" can be "self-justifying."

10. Why would one suppose that "This appears white" (or, more exactly, "I am now appeared white to") is not self-justifying? The most convincing argument was this: If I say "This appears white," then, as Reichenbach put it, I am making a "comparison between a present object and a formerly seen object." [18] What I am saying *could* have been expressed by "The present way of appearing is the

[18] *Experience and Prediction,* p. 176.

way in which white objects, or objects which I believe to be white, ordinarily appear." And this new statement, clearly, is not self-justifying; to justify it, as Reichenbach intimated, I must go on and say something further—something about the way in which I remember white objects to have appeared.

"Appears white" *may* thus be used to abbreviate "appears the way in which white things normally appear." Or "white thing," on the other hand, *may* be used to abbreviate "thing having the color of things which ordinarily appear white." The phrase "appear white" as it is used in the second quoted expression cannot be spelled out in the manner of the first; for the point of the second can hardly be put by saying that "white thing" may be used to abbreviate "thing having the color of things which ordinarily appear the way in which *white things* normally appear." In the second expression, the point of "appears white" is not to *compare* a way of appearing with something else; the point is to say something about the way of appearing itself. It is in terms of this second sense of "appears white"—that in which one may say significantly and without redundancy "Things that are white may normally be expected to appear white"—that we are to interpret the quotation from Augustine above. And, more generally, when it was said that "appear"-statements constitute the foundation of the edifice of knowledge, it was not intended that the "appear"-statements be interpreted as statements asserting a comparison between a present object and any other object or set of objects.

The question now becomes "Can we formulate any significant 'appear'-statements *without* thus comparing the way in which some object appears with the way in which some other object appears, or with the way in which the object in question has appeared at some other time? Can we interpret 'This appears white' in such a way that it may be understood to refer to a present way of appearing *without* relating that way of appearing to any other object?" In *Experience and Prediction*, Reichenbach defended his own view (and that of a good many others) in this way:

> The objection may be raised that a comparison with formerly seen physical objects should be avoided, and that a basic statement is to concern the present fact only, as it is. But such a reduction would make the basic statement empty. Its content is just that there is a

similarity between the present object and one formerly seen; it is by means of this relation that the present object is described. Otherwise the basic statement would consist in attaching an individual symbol, say a number, to the present object; but the introduction of such a symbol would help us in no way, since we could not make use of it to construct a comparison with other things. Only in attaching the same symbols to different objects, do we arrive at the possibility of constructing relations between the objects [pp. 176-77].

It is true that, if an "appear"-statement is to be used successfully in communication, it must assert some comparison of objects. Clearly, if I wish *you* to know the way things are now appearing to me, I must relate these ways of appearing to something that is familiar to you. But our present question is not "Can you understand me if I predicate something of the way in which something now appears to me without relating that way of appearing to something that is familiar to you?" The question is, more simply, "Can I predicate anything of the way in which something now appears to me without thereby comparing that way of appearing with something else?" From the fact that the first of these two questions must be answered in the negative it does not follow that the second must also be answered in the negative.[19]

The issue is not one about communication, nor is it, strictly speaking, an issue about language; it concerns, rather, the nature of thought itself. Common to both "pragmatism" and "idealism," as traditions in American philosophy, is the view that to *think* about a thing, or to *interpret* or *conceptualize* it, and hence to have a *belief* about it, is essentially to relate the thing to *other* things, actual or possible, and therefore to "refer beyond it." It is this view—and not any view about language or communication—that we must oppose if we are to say of some statements about appearing, or of any other statements, that they "justify themselves."

[19] It may follow, however, that "the vaunted incorrigibility of the sense-datum language can be achieved only at the cost of its perfect utility as a means of communication" (Max Black, *Problems of Analysis* [Cornell, 1954], p. 66), and doubtless, as Black added, it would be "misleading, to say the least" to speak of a "language that cannot be communicated"—cf. Wilfrid Sellars, "Empiricism and the Philosophy of Mind"—but these points do affect the epistemological question at issue.

To think about the way in which something is now appearing, according to the view in question, is to relate that way of appearing to something else, possibly to certain future experiences, possibly to the way in which things of a certain sort may be commonly expected to appear. According to the "conceptualistic pragmatism" of C. I. Lewis's *Mind and the World-Order* (1929), we grasp the present experience, any present way of appearing, only to the extent to which we relate it to some future experience.[20] According to one interpretation of John Dewey's "instrumentalistic" version of pragmatism, the present experience may be used to present or disclose something else but it does not present or disclose itself. And according to the idealistic view defended in Brand Blanshard's *The Nature of Thought,* we grasp our present experience only to the extent that we are able to include it in the one "intelligible system of universals" (vol. I, p. 632).

This theory of reference, it should be noted, applies not only to statements and beliefs about "ways of being appeared to" but also to those other statements and beliefs which I have called "self-justifying." If "This appears white," or "I am appeared white to," compares the present experience with something else, and thus depends for its justification upon what we are justified in believing about the something else, then so, too, does "I believe that Socrates is mortal" and "I hope that the peace will continue." This general conception of thought, therefore, would seem to imply that no belief or statement can be said to justify itself. But according to what we have been saying, if there is no belief or statement which justifies itself, then it is problematic whether any belief or statement is justified at all. And therefore, as we might expect, this conception of thought and reference has been associated with skepticism.

Blanshard conceded that his theory of thought "does involve a degree of scepticism regarding our present knowledge and probably all future knowledge. In all likelihood there will never be a proposition of which we can say, 'This that I am asserting, with precisely the meaning I now attach to it, is absolutely true."[21] On

[20] This doctrine was modified in Lewis's later *An Analysis of Knowledge and Valuation* (Open Court, 1946) in a way which enabled him to preserve the theory of the given.
[21] *The Nature of Thought,* vol. II, pp. 269-70. Blanshard added, however, that "for all the ordinary purposes of life" we *can* justify some beliefs by showing

Dewey's theory, or on one common interpretation of Dewey's theory, it is problematic whether anyone can now be said to *know* that Mr. Jones is working in his garden. A. O. Lovejoy is reported to have said that, for Dewey, "I am about to have known" is as close as we ever get to "I know." [22] C. I. Lewis, in his *An Analysis of Knowledge and Valuation* (Open Court, 1946) conceded in effect that the conception of thought suggested by his earlier *Mind and the World-Order* does lead to a kind of skepticism; according to the later work there *are* "apprehensions of the given" (cf. pp. 182-83) —and thus beliefs which justify themselves.

What is the plausibility of a theory of thought and reference which seems to imply that no one knows anything?

Perhaps it is correct to say that when we think about a thing we think about it as having certain properties. But why should one go on to say that to think about a thing must always involve thinking about some *other* thing as well? Does thinking about the other thing then involve thinking about some third thing? Or can we think about one thing in relation to a second thing without thereby thinking of a third thing? And if we can, then why can we not think of one thing—of one thing as having certain properties—without thereby relating it to another thing?

The linguistic analogue of this view of thought is similar. Why should one suppose—as Reichenbach supposed in the passage cited above and as many others have also supposed—that to *refer* to a thing, in this instance to refer to a way of appearing, is necessarily to relate the thing to some *other* thing?

Some philosophers seem to have been led to such a view of reference as a result of such considerations as the following: We have imagined a man saying, in agreement with Augustine, "It just does appear white—and that is the end of the matter." Let us consider

---

that they cohere "with the system of present knowledge"; and therefore, he said, his theory should not be described as being "simply sceptical" (vol. II, p. 271). Cf. W. H. Werkmeister, *The Basis and Structure of Knowledge* (Harper, 1948), part II.

[22] Quoted by A. E. Murphy in "Dewey's Epistemology and Metaphysics," in *The Philosophy of John Dewey,* ed. P. A. Schilpp (Northwestern, 1939), p. 203. Dewey's theory of inquiry, however, was not intended to be an epistemology and he did not directly address himself to the questions with which we are here concerned.

now the possible reply "That it is not the end of the matter. You are making certain assumptions about the language you are using; you are assuming, for example, that you are using the word 'white,' or the phrase 'appears white,' in the way in which you have formerly used it, or in the way in which it is ordinarily used, or in the way in which it would ordinarily be understood. And if you state your justification for this assumption, you *will* refer to certain other things—to yourself and to other people, to the word 'white,' or to the phrase 'appears white,' and to what the word or phrase has referred to or might refer to on other occasions. And therefore, when you say 'This appears white' you are saying something, not only about your present experience, but also about all of these other things as well."

The conclusion of this argument—the part that follows the "therefore"—does not follow from the premises. In supposing that the argument is valid, one fails to distinguish between (1) *what* it is that a man means to say when he uses certain words and (2) his assumptions concerning the adequacy of these words for *expressing* what it is that he means to say; one supposes, mistakenly, that what justifies (2) must be included in what justifies (1). A Frenchman, not yet sure of his English, may utter the words "There are apples in the basket," intending thereby to express his belief that there are potatoes in the basket. If we show him that he has used the word "apples" incorrectly, and hence that he is mistaken in his assumptions about the ways in which English speaking people use and understand the word "apples," we have not shown him anything relevant to his *belief* that there are apples in the basket.

Logicians now take care to distinguish between the *use* and *mention* of language (e.g., the English word "Socrates" is mentioned in the sentence " 'Socrates' has eight letters" and is used but not mentioned, in "Socrates is a Greek.") [23] As we shall have occasion to note further in the next chapter, the distinction has not always been observed in writings on epistemology.

11.   If we decide, then, that there is a class of beliefs or statements which are "self-justifying," and that this class is limited to certain

[23] Cf. W. V. Quine, *Mathematical Logic* (Norton, 1940; rev. ed., Harvard, 1951), sec. 4.

beliefs or statements about our own psychological states and about the ways in which we are "appeared to," we may be tempted to return to the figure of the edifice: our knowledge of the world is a structure supported entirely by a foundation of such self-justifying statements or beliefs. We should recall, however, that the answers to our original Socratic questions had *two* parts. When asked "What is your justification for thinking that you know *a?*" one may reply "I am justified in thinking I know *a,* because (1) I know *b* and (2) if I know *b* then I know *a.*" We considered our justification for the *first* part of this answer, saying "I am justified in thinking I know *b,* because (1) I know *c* and (2) if I know *c* then I know *b.*" And then we considered our justification for the first part of the second answer, and continued in this fashion until we reach the point of self-justification. In thus moving toward "the given," we accumulated, step by step, a backlog of claims that we did not attempt to justify—those claims constituting the *second* part of each of our answers. Hence our original claim—"I know that *a* is true" —does not rest upon "the given" alone; it also rests upon all of those other claims that we made *en route.* And it is not justified unless these other claims are justified.

A consideration of these other claims will lead us, I think, to at least three additional types of "stopping place," which are concerned, respectively, with memory, perception, and what Kant called the a priori. I shall comment briefly on the first two and turn to the third in the following chapter.

It is difficult to think of any claim to empirical knowledge, other than the self-justifying statements we have just considered, which does not to some extent rest upon an appeal to memory. But the appeal to memory—"I remember that A occurred"—is not self-justifying. One may ask "And what is your justification for thinking that you remember that A occurred?" and the question will have an answer—even if the answer is only the self-justifying "I think that I remember that A occurred." The statement "I remember that A occurred" does, of course, imply "A occurred"; but "I think that I remember that A occurred" does not imply "A occurred" and hence does not imply "I remember that A occurred." For we can remember occasions—at least we think we can remember them— when we learned, concerning some event we had thought we remembered, that the event had not occurred at all, and consequently that we had not really remembered it. When we thus find that one memory conflicts with another, or, more accurately, when we thus find that one thing that we think we remember conflicts with another thing that we think we remember, we may correct one or the other by making further inquiry; but the results of any such inquiry will always be justified in part by other memories, or by other things that we think that we remember. How then are we to choose between what seem to be conflicting memories? Under what conditions does "I think that I remember that A occurred" serve to justify "I remember that A occurred"?

The problem is one of formulating a rule of evidence—a rule specifying the conditions under which statements about what we think we remember can justify statements about what we do remember. A possible solution, in very general terms, is "When we think that we remember, then we are justified in believing that we do remember, provided that what we think we remember does not conflict with anything else that we think we remember; when what we think we remember does conflict with something else we think we remember, then, of the two conflicting memories (more accurately, ostensible memories) the one that is justified is the one that fits in better with the other things that we think we remember." Ledger Wood made the latter point by saying that the justified memory is the one which "coheres with the system of related memories"; C. I. Lewis used "congruence" instead of "coherence." [24] But we cannot say precisely what is meant by "fitting in," "coherence," or "congruence" until certain controversial questions of confirmation theory and the logic of probability have been answered. And it may be that the rule of evidence is too liberal; perhaps we should say, for example, that when two ostensible memories conflict neither one of them is justified. But these are questions which have not yet been satisfactorily answered.

If we substitute "perceive" for "remember" in the foregoing, we can formulate a similar set of problems about perception; these problems, too, must await solution.[25]

[24] Ledger Wood, *The Analysis of Knowledge* (Princeton, 1941), p. 81; C. I. Lewis, *An Analysis of Knowledge and Valuation*, p. 334.
[25] Important steps toward solving them were taken by Nelson Goodman in

The problems involved in formulating such rules of evidence, and in determining the validity of these rules, do not differ in any significant way from those which arise in connection with the formulation, and validity, of the rules of logic. Nor do they differ from the problems posed by the moral and religious "cognitivists" (the "nonintuitionistic cognitivists") mentioned in Chapter 1. The status of ostensible memories and perceptions, with respect to that experience which is their "source," is essentially like that which such "cognitivists" claim for judgments having an ethical or theological subject matter. Unfortunately, it is also like that which other "enthusiasts" claim for still other types of subject matter.

12.   What, then, is the status of the doctrine of "the given"—of the "myth of the given"? In my opinion, the doctrine is correct in saying that there are some beliefs or statements which are "self-justifying" and that among such beliefs and statements are some which concern appearances or "ways of being appeared to"; but the "phenomenalistic version" of the doctrine is mistaken in implying that our knowledge may be thought of as an edifice which is supported by appearances alone.[26] The cognitive significance of "the empirically given" was correctly described—in a vocabulary rather different from that which I have been using—by John Dewey:

> The alleged primacy of sensory meanings is mythical. They are primary only in logical status; they are primary as tests and confirmation of inferences concerning matters of fact, not as historic originals. For, while it is not usually needful to carry the check or test of theoretical calculations to the point of irreducible sensa, colors, sounds, etc., these sensa form a limit approached in careful analytic certifications, and upon critical occasions it is necessary to touch the limit. . . . Sensa are the class of irreducible meanings which are employed in verifying and correcting other meanings.

"Sense and Certainty," *Philosophical Review*, LXI (1952), 160-67, and by Israel Scheffler in "On Justification and Commitment," *Journal of Philosophy*, LI (1954), 180-90. The former paper is reprinted in *Philosophy of Knowledge*, ed. Roland Houde and J. P. Mullally (Lippincott, 1960), pp. 97-103.
[26] Alternatives to the general metaphor of the edifice are proposed by W. V. Quine in the introduction to *Methods of Logic* (Holt, 1950; rev. ed., 1959), in *From a Logical Point of View* (Harvard, 1953), and in *Word and Object* (Wiley, 1960).

We actually set out with much coarser and more inclusive meanings and not till we have met with failure from their use do we even set out to discover those ultimate and harder meanings which are sensory in character.[27]

The Socratic questions leading to the concept of "the given" also lead to the concept of "rules of evidence." Unfortunately some of the philosophers who stressed the importance of the former concept tended to overlook that of the latter.

[27] John Dewey, *Experience and Nature,* 2nd ed. (Norton, 1929), p. 327.

⋘ 3 ⋙

REASON AND THE A PRIORI

The identity of each essence with itself and difference from every other essence suffices to distinguish and define them all in eternity, where they form the Realm of Essence. True and false assertions may be made about any one of them, such for instance, as that it does not exist; or that it includes or excludes some other essence, or is included or excluded by it. [George Santayana, *The Realms of Being.*]

Pure reason is unable to produce any real knowledge, its only business is the arrangement of symbols which are used for the expression of knowledge. [Moritz Schlick, "A New Philosophy of Experience."]

Our apprehension of such truths as the following is traditionally ascribed to "reason": being a square includes being rectangular, and excludes being circular; being a man includes being an animal, and excludes being an angel. Or, what may come to the same thing, it is *necessarily true* that if anything is a square then it is a rectangle and not a circle, and that if anything is a man then it is an animal and not an angel. Or it is true, not only in this world but in *all possible worlds,* that all squares are rectangles and no squares are circles, and that all men are animals and no men are angels. But being a square neither includes nor excludes being red, and being a man neither includes nor excludes being a Greek. Again: some men being Greek includes some Greeks being men and excludes no Greeks being men; it is necessarily true, or true in all possible worlds, that if some men are Greek then some Greeks are men; but some men being Greek neither includes nor excludes some men being Roman.

The period of American philosophy with which we are here concerned has been dominated by an attitude of skepticism toward such truths and faculties. The keynote of this attitude was struck by Moritz Schlick in his second public lecture at the College of the Pacific: "Empiricism now has the right and power to claim the

287

whole field of knowledge. We know nothing except by experience, and experience is the only criterion of the truth or falsity of any real proposition." [1] Subsequent debate has indicated, I think, that Schlick's confidence was not justified.

To understand the debate and the issues which it involved, we must consider the following topics: (1) the Kantian distinction between analytic and synthetic judgments, its reinterpretation by recent philosophers as a distinction between types of *statement,* and the relation of "analytic statements" to statements which are sometimes said to be "logically true"; (2) the Kantian distinction between a priori and a posteriori knowledge; (3) the attempt to construe the a priori knowledge, which is expressed in analytic statements, as a type of knowledge which is intimately connected with language; and (4) the question whether there is any a priori knowledge which is not expressible in statements which are either analytic or logically true.

1. An analytic judgment, according to Kant, is a judgment in which "the predicate adds nothing to the concept of the subject." If I judge that all squares are rectangles, then, in Kant's terminology, the concept of the subject of my judgment is the property of being square, and the concept of the predicate is the property of being rectangular. The concept of the predicate—and this is the reason for using the term "analytic"—helps to "break up the concept of the subject into those constituent concepts that have all along been thought in it." [2] Kant would have said that the "constituent concepts" of being square are being equilateral and being rectangular; perhaps it would be clearer to say that being square is a "conjunctive property" the components of which are being equilateral and being rectangular. In either case, the predicate of the judgment that all squares are rectangles may be said to "analyze out" what is already contained in the subject.

Synthetic judgments, on the other hand, are those in which the concept of the predicate is *not* thus "contained in" that of the sub-

[1] Moritz Schlick, "A New Philosophy of Experience," in *Lectures* . . . , ed. P. A. Schilpp, Publications in Philosophy, The College of the Pacific (1932); reprinted in Schlick's *Gesammelte Aufsätze* (Vienna; 1938).
[2] *Critique of Pure Reason,* A 7.

ject. The judgment that all men are mortal is a synthetic judgment since the concept of being mortal is not included in that of being a man; hence, in the terminology of Leibniz, the judgment though true of this world is not true of "all possible worlds."

Anything that exemplifies the concept of the subject of an analytic judgment will, *ipso facto*, exemplify that of the predicate; anything that is a square is, *ipso facto*, a rectangle. To *deny* an analytic judgment—to judge that some squares are *not* rectangles—would be to contradict oneself, for it would be to judge that there are things which both do and do not have a certain property. Kant made this point by saying that "the common principle of all analytic judgments is the law of contradiction." [3]

All analytic judgments are true, but synthetic judgments may be either true or false. The synthetic judgment that all men are mortal is true; the synthetic judgment that all men are Greeks is false. If we deny the former judgment, holding that some men are not mortal, we go wrong but we do not contradict ourselves.

In recent philosophy, the terms "analytic" and "synthetic" are applied not to judgments but to statements or sentences. The linguistic concept of a *statement* is in some respects clearer than the psychological concept of a judgment; but the emphasis upon statements, particularly in recent American philosophy, has led some philosophers to confuse certain fundamental questions of epistemology with certain quite different questions of the philosophy of language.

One of the best contemporary accounts of the distinction between analytic and synthetic statements is that given in C. I. Lewis's Carus Lectures, *An Analysis of Knowledge and Valuation* (Open Court, 1946). His account is substantially the following:

The word "square" has as its meaning the property of being square; it denotes, or applies to, anything that happens to have that property. The word "rectangle," similarly, has for its meaning the property of being rectangular, and it denotes, or applies, to anything that happens to have that property. The property of being rectangular, we have noted, is included in that of being square— i.e., it is a component of the conjunctive property of being both equilateral and rectangular; hence the meaning of "rectangular" is

[3] *Prolegomena to Any Future Metaphysics*, sec. 2.

289

included in that of "square." We may say, then, that an affirmative subject-predicate statement, such as "All squares are rectangles," is *analytic* if the meaning of the predicate is included in that of the subject, and a negative subject-predicate statement, such as "No spinster is married," is analytic if the meaning of the negation of the predicate (in this case, the meaning of "nonmarried") is included in the meaning of the subject. A subject-predicate statement may be called *synthetic* if it is not analytic. "All men are mortal" is therefore synthetic, since the meaning of "mortal" is not included in that of "man"—even though, as it happens, the predicate applies to all those things that the subject applies to.[4]

The statement "Socrates is mortal or it is false that Socrates is mortal" is not analytic, as "analytic" has just been defined, for it is a compound statement and not a simple subject-predicate statement; but it is similar, in important respects, to those statements which are analytic. It is necessarily true, or true for all possible worlds, since Socrates being mortal excludes Socrates not being mortal. Kant would have said that it "has its principle in the law of contradiction" and we may express the same point by saying that it is a logical truth. W. V. Quine proposed a useful definition of "logically true," as a phrase which may be predicated of statements or sentences. After we have formulated his definition, we will be in a position to understand some of the philosophical questions which these concepts involve.

Quine first enumerates a list of words, to be called "logical words"; the list includes "or," "not," "if," "then," "and," "all," "every," "some." A sentence or statement is then said to be logically true if it is one in which only the logical words *occur essentially*. In "Socrates is mortal or it is false that Socrates is mortal," which is logically true, the expressions "or" and "it is false that" occur essentially, but the nonlogical words, "Socrates," "is," and "mortal," do not. What this means, put somewhat loosely, is that the truth of the statement is independent of the particular nonlogical words that happen to occur in it. Put somewhat more exactly: a logically true statement is one such that, if, for any nonlogical word in the sentence, we replace each of its occurrences by any

---

4 For refinement of detail, see Lewis, *op. cit.*, book I, and Rudolf Carnap, *Meaning and Necessity* (U. of Chicago, 1947), chap. I.

other "grammatically admissible" word (making sure that all occurrences of the old word are replaced by occurrences of the same new word), then the new statement we derive will also be true. If the word "Socrates," in "Socrates is mortal or it is false that Socrates is mortal," is replaced by "these stones," if "is" is replaced by "are," and "mortal" by "blue," then the result—"These stones are blue or it is false that these stones are blue"—will be true. On the other hand, if we replace the logical words by other grammatically admissible words, the result may be false—as it would be if, in our example, we replaced "or" by "and." A logical truth on this interpretation, then, is "a statement which is true and remains true under all reinterpretations of its components other than logical particles." [5] (But if, in the logical truth "All elderly thieves are thieves," the nonlogical term "elderly" is replaced by such a term as "suspected," "possible," or "potential," the result will be a false statement. Certain qualifications must be added to "grammatic admissibility" to preclude this type of result. Moreover, as Quine recognized, such a definition of "logical truth" has this limitation: the question of *which* statements thus remain true under all reinterpretations of their nonlogical words remains problematic. The following are often said to be logical truths: "If it is true that either I am now in Providence or I am not now in Providence, then either it is true that I am now in Providence or it is not true that I am now in Providence," and "If it is true that either Zeno is in Athens or Zeno is in Sparta, and if it is also true that Zeno is walking either one mile an hour or Zeno is walking two miles an hour, then it is true that either Zeno is in Athens and walking one mile an hour, or Zeno is in Athens and walking two miles an hour, or Zeno is in Sparta and walking one mile an hour, or Zeno is in Sparta and walking two miles an hour." But if we change the tense of the first of these statements from present to future, then, according to some philosophers, we must reject the result on the ground that it conflicts with certain doctrines about freedom and human agency.[6]

[5] W. V. Quine, *From a Logical Point of View* (Harvard, 1953). Quine first set forth this view in "Truth by Convention," in *Philosophical Essays for Alfred North Whitehead,* ed. Otis Lee (Longmans, 1936).
[6] Cf. Paul Weiss, *Nature and Man* (Holt, 1947), pp. 13, 203; Charles Hartshorne, *Man's Vision of God and the Logic of Theism* (Willett, 1941); Richard Taylor, "The Problem of Future Contingencies," *Philosophical Review,* LXVI

And if the second statement is revised, so as to refer to the position and velocity, not of Zeno, but of certain subatomic particles, then, according to some philosophers, we must reject the result on the ground that it conflicts with certain doctrines of contemporary quantum physics.[7] These issues involve epistemological questions similar to those discussed in Chapter 1. For the present discussion, we may assume that we have a general characterization of logical truth, even though we have no definite way of fixing the boundary between logical and nonlogical truth.)

The analytic statements "All squares are rectangles" and "No spinsters are married" are not themselves logical truths on the above account. If in the former we replace the nonlogical word "squares" by "circles," the resulting statement will be false; and if in the latter we replace the nonlogical word "married" by "happy," the result will be false. But we may paraphrase any analytic statement—we may re-express what it expresses—by means of statements which *are* logically true. The term "squares" has among its synonyms (i.e., those terms having the same meaning that it has) a term—viz., "equilateral rectangles"—which includes the predicate term of "All squares are rectangles"; if we replace "squares" by this synonym, then the result—"All equilateral rectangles are rectangles"—will be a logical truth. The term "spinster" has among its synonyms a term—viz., "adult lady who is nonmarried"—which includes the negation of the predicate of "No spinster is married"; replacement will thus yield the logical truth "No adult lady who is nonmarried is married." And similarly for other analytic statements; e.g., "All ornithologists are students of birds" and "All quadrupeds have feet." In each case by providing the proper synonyms and then substituting, we can turn the analytic statement into a logical truth. And we can recognize a logical truth, informally, by noting that it is a statement which is explicitly redundant

---

(1957), 1-28, and "Fatalism," *Philosophical Review*, LXXI (1962), 56-66; Donald C. Williams, "The Sea Fight Tomorrow," in *Structure, Method, and Meaning: Essays in Honor of Henry M. Sheffer*, ed. Paul Henle, Horace M. Kallen, and Susanne K. Langer (Liberal Arts, 1951).
[7] Cf. Garrett Birkhoff and John von Neumann, "The Logic of Quantum Mechanics," *Annals of Mathematics*, XXXVII (1936); Hilary Putnam, "Three Valued Logic," *Philosophical Studies*, VIII (1957).

—e.g., "All professional students of birds are students of birds," "No adult ladies who are nonmarried are married," and "All things that have four feet have feet." It will be convenient to describe both analytic statements and logical truths as redundancies— the former being sometimes implicit, and the latter always explicit.

In opposition to the view, mentioned at the beginning of this chapter, that these truths are concerned with relations among essences or properties, and relations among situations or possible states of affairs, and that they are apprehended by a kind of "rational insight," it has been maintained in recent years that they are expressions of our linguistic "rules" or "conventions" and, strictly speaking, not truths at all. It has also been held that the distinction between analytic and synthetic is untenable. These views exhibit that "insurgence against reason," which, according to Morris Cohen, "has its roots deep in the dominant temper of our age." What Cohen said about the limitations of "psychologism," "historicism," and "empiricism," may also be said, if I am not mistaken, about these more recent doctrines.

2. "In the realm of logic and pure mathematics," Cohen wrote in *Reason and Nature* (Harcourt, 1931), "we have absolute and a priori truth." Even if "the more objective classical philosophies have overreached themselves in their abuse of the tests of self-evidence and self-contradiction, and in their sanctioning of false and meaningless propositions as a priori, it still remains true that in the Platonic ideas they have recognized the objectivity of the logical and mathematical forms of nature" (pp. 144-45). We can understand the concept of the a priori if we return to our Socratic questions about justification. What if such questions were raised in connection with that knowledge that is expressed in statements that are analytic or logically true? (The reader is referred again to the type of dilemma discussed in Chapter 1. If there is doubt whether anyone *can* be said to know that all squares are rectangles, or that if some men are Greeks then some Greeks are men, it may well be that such doubt is incapable of being resolved. But we may still discuss the consequences of supposing that people *do* have such knowledge. And it will be well to note, so far as *this* question is con-

cerned, that skepticism with respect to what is thought to be such knowledge is not to the point.)

"What justification do you have for believing you know that all squares are rectangles, or for believing you know that if some men are Greeks then some Greeks are men?"

If a man *does* know, as most of us think we do, that all squares are rectangles, or that if some men are Greeks then some Greeks are men, then there are only two ways he could answer our Socratic question. (1) He could say, simply: "I *see* that all squares are rectangles—that whatever is a square must be a rectangle—that being a rectangle is part of what it is to be a square. And I *see* that if some men are Greeks then some Greeks are men, that some men being Greeks and some Greeks being men are one and the same thing." Here we have a stopping place again for our Socratic questioning—but a stopping place which differs in a significant way from those considered in the previous chapter. (2) He might justify his claim to know these statements, not by saying that he sees that they are true, but rather by showing how to deduce them logically from *other* statements which are analytic or which are logically true. And if we ask him what his justification is for believing he knows these other statements to be true, and if we continue our questioning, then sooner or later, he will stop with some such statements and say that he simply sees that they are true.

Let us now contrast the two statements "I see that Mr. Jones is in his garden" and "I see that all squares are rectangles." Both have subordinate statements as the objects of their principal verbs, and both are such that, if they are justified, then their subordinate statements are also justified. I may justify my claim to know that Mr. Jones is in his garden by saying "I see that he is" and I may justify my claim to know that all squares are rectangles by saying "I see that they are." And, as we have seen, if I am asked "What justification do you have for believing you *see* that Mr. Jones is in his garden?" then, if I do see that he is there, I can state my justification for believing that I see that he is there—and what I say will not merely reiterate the claim to see that he is there. But if I am asked "What justification do you have for claiming to see that all squares are rectangles?" and if my justification does not consist in the fact that I can deduce it logically from other analytic statements or from statements that are logically true, then I can *not* provide any further answer; in this case, unlike the case of Mr. Jones being in his garden, I can only reiterate that I *do* see it.

It is traditional to say, following Kant, that most, if not all, of the analytic statements and logical truths which express what we know are statements which express what we know a priori, and to say that what is known, but not known a priori, is known a posteriori. The point of using "a priori" and "a posteriori" may be suggested by this fact: we can know that all squares are rectangles *before* we have examined any particular square; but we cannot know that all men are mortal until *after* some particular men have been examined. One might speak of contemplating certain members of the realm of essence before examining any of their particular exemplifications in the realm of matter; this is the way that Santayana and Cohen expressed themselves. But we need not speak in this way, for one may also "contemplate" essences, or properties, in their particular exemplifications. As Aristotle said, "I may come to see that man is a rational animal—that the property of being rational and animal includes that of being rational—by considering some particular man, Callias; but what I thus learn will not be restricted to this particular fact, nor will it depend for its justification upon this particular fact." [8] And I may, by reflecting upon some particular situation (say, upon the fact that this apple is not, in the same part at the same time, both red and not red), come to know some more general fact that holds of all possible situations (say, that, for any possible object, being red excludes not being red). According to R. M. Eaton, this is the way we come to know some of the truths of logic.[9]

The statements we know a priori to be true differ in a number of respects from the "self-justifying" statements described in the previous chapter. For one thing, the "self-justifying" statements—e.g., "I believe that Socrates is mortal" and "That appears white"—are restricted to a psychological or subjective subject matter, but a

---

[8] *Posterior Analytics,* 100a-100b.
[9] R. M. Eaton, *General Logic* (Scribner, 1931), pp. 495-501. Cf. W. P. Montague, *The Ways of Knowing* (Macmillan, 1925), chap. XI; Charles A. Baylis, "Universals, Communicable Knowledge and Metaphysics," *Journal of Philosophy,* XLVIII (1951), 636-44; Donald Williams, "The Nature and Variety of the A Priori," *Analysis,* V (1938), 85-94.

priori statements are not so restricted. (The program of "psychologism," referred to in Chapter 1, might be described as an attempt to reduce the a priori to the self-justifying, by transforming the statements of logic and mathematics into statements about the way in which people think.) For another thing, as Kant pointed out, the statements which we know a priori are statements which are *necessarily* true. All squares are rectangles—in this world and in all possible worlds. But "I cannot help believing that if a thing is a square it is a rectangle" is contingent and not necessary. (Consequently the program of "psychologism" was not successful.) And finally, if what I suggested in the previous chapter is accurate, a man's statement may be said to be "self-justifying" for him provided that his justification for thinking he knows it to be true is simply the fact that it *is* true; the point may be put alternatively by saying that such statements are "neither justified nor unjustified" but may constitute one's justification for other statements. Whether we may speak similarly of a priori statements remains problematic.[10]

What it is that we thus know a priori may seem meager and not worthy of being called "knowledge" at all. Schlick said, in his California lectures, that the statements of logic are "empty" and even Santayana, who wrote about "the realm of essence," said that there can be no *knowledge* of essences, that "there are no necessary truths," and that truth "never enters the field of mathematics at all."[11] But Schlick was saying only that the statements of logic *are* statements of logic and are not synthetic, and so, too, apparently was Santayana. (When Santayana wrote about the "realm of truth," he restricted the adjective "true" to what can be truly said only about the "realm of matter," about *this* possible world, and he did not apply the adjective—as he did in the quotation at the beginning of this chapter—to what can be truly said about the "realm of essence." But he did truly say, of essences, and this is what matters, that "every essence involves its parts, considered as

---

10 "What we require is a picture of the employment of mathematical propositions and of sentences beginning 'I believe that . . .', where a mathematical proposition is the object of belief." (Ludwig Wittgenstein, *Remarks on the Foundations of Mathematics* [Blackwell, 1956], p. 33e.)
11 George Santayana, *The Realms of Being* (Scribner, 1942), pp. 407, 421.

the elements which integrate it," and "excludes everything not it-self." [12]) The interesting question is not whether analytic state-ments and the statements of logic are "empty truths," but whether they are truths at all.

3. Schlick had contended, and many still agree, that once we have exposed the relations between logic and language, we will be able to account for our "so-called 'rational knowledge.'" But just what relation between logic and language would account for such knowledge remained obscure.

Schlick said three quite different things in his California lecture: (1) that the so-called propositions of logic and mathematics are "nothing but certain rules which determine the use of language, i.e., of expression by combination of signs"; (2) that their "abso-lute truth" cannot be denied; and (3) that "they do not deal with any facts, but only with the symbols by means of which the facts are expressed." [13] Herbert Feigl and Albert Blumberg, reporting to America in 1931 on the speculations of the Vienna Circle (of which Schlick was one of the leading members), said substantially the same three things: (1) logic is "the system of conventions which determines the syntactical order required if we are to have a consistent language"; (2) the propositions of logic are "tautolog-ically true"; and (3) "all formal sciences are engaged, then, in elaborating symbol-patterns and assert nothing about experience." [14] What, then, is the relation between logic and language which pro-vides the key to our so-called rational knowledge? If we say, as in (1), that logical statements are *rules,* or *conventions,* then it may seem strange to go on to say, as in (2), that they are *true;* for we do not ordinarily think of rules, or of conventions, as being true, or as being false. Statements *about* rules, however, are either true or false; and what (3) suggests is, not that logical statements are themselves the rules or conventions of our language, but rather that they are statements *about* the rules or conventions of our lan-

---

[12] *Ibid.,* pp. 401, 82, 88.
[13] *Gesammelte Aufsätze,* pp. 146-47.
[14] Albert E. Blumberg and Herbert Feigl, "Logical Positivism," *Journal of Phi-losophy,* XXVIII (1931), 281-96. It was in this article that the name "logical positivism" was introduced.

guage, statements telling us *what* these rules or conventions happen to be. Statements *about* the rules or conventions of language, however, need not be "tautologically true" (consider, e.g., "In French, adjectives of color are customarily placed after the noun they modify")—and the statements of logic with which we are concerned (e.g., "Either Socrates is mortal or it is false that Socrates is mortal") *are* tautologically true, and are *not*, in any clear sense, statements *about* the rules or conventions of our language.

What is usually maintained, in the face of such objections, is that the statements of logic are true *because* of the rules or conventions of our language. Thus Feigl and Blumberg said: "For example, '*p* or not-*p*' is tautologically true because of the very definitions of 'or' and 'not'" (p. 284). Others have said that analytic statements are true *because* of the way in which we use the words that make them up. What does this mean?

The doctrine of "truth by convention" will seem most plausible in the case of analytic statements. It may be recalled that the concept of the meaning of the words which make up a statement is essential to the definition of "analytic statement." The statement "All squares are rectangles," as it is understood in ordinary English, is analytic, inasmuch as the meaning of the predicate term is included in that of the subject term. But, as Plato had argued in the *Cratylus*, it is "by custom" and "convention," and not "by nature," that our words have the meanings they happen to have. Had the English language developed in a different way, as it quite conceivably could have, then those statements which happen now to be analytic might not be analytic and might even be false. If the word "square" were used to denote, not the geometrical objects which it does happen to denote, but, say, those things we now call "horses," then the English statement "All squares are rectangles" would be synthetic and false. Therefore, one may say that the English statement "All squares are rectangles" is analytic—and thus true—because we happen to use words the way we do. Similarly for the class of logical truths: if the word "some," for example, were used in the way in which, as it happens, we now use "all," then the statement "If some men are Greeks then some Greeks are men" would not be logically true.

May we infer from all of this that statements which are analytic

298

or logically true are "true only by convention" and that the so-called rational contemplation of essence is merely knowledge or belief about our language? If such reasoning were valid, then we could infer, not only that analytic and logical statements are "true only by convention," but also that all of those *synthetic* statements that are true are "true only by convention." For, as Quine was to point out, "even so factual a sentence as 'Brutus killed Caesar' owes its truth, in part, to our using the component words the way we do." [15] Had "killed," for example, been given the use which the phrase "was survived by" came to have, then "Brutus killed Caesar" would be false—unless, of course, Brutus were called "Caesar" and Caesar "Brutus."

What if it is said that an analytic statement—e.g., "All squares are rectangles"—owes its truth *solely* to the fact that we use the component words the way we do, or, as the matter is sometimes put, that it is true "solely in virtue of the rules of our language"? We may suppose that the following is a "rule of English":

(a) When the word "square" is used in English to designate something, the thing it designates should be square.

The rule seems more significant, of course, when it is formulated in a language other than English, e.g., as "Wenn das Wort 'square' auf Englisch angewendet wird, um etwas zu bedeuten, muss das, was es bedeutet, quadratisch sein." The following, then, would also be a "rule of English":

(b) When the word "rectangular" is used in English to designate something, the thing it designates should be rectangular.

("'Rectangular' darf nur das bedeuten, was rechtwinkelig ist.") According to the thesis in question, the analytic statement "All squares are rectangles" owes its truth to the fact—and only to the fact—that the following is also a "rule of English":

(c) When the word "square" is used in English to designate something, the thing it designates should be rectangular.

But (c) is a rule of quite a different sort from either (a) or (b). This may be seen as follows. If we were to teach English to an educated man, say to a native German, and taught him that (a) and

[15] W. V. Quine, "Carnap e la verità logica," *Revista di filosofia*, XLVIII (1957), 4.

299

(c) are rules of English, he would not be able to find out on his own that (b) is also a rule of English; or if we were to teach him that (b) and (c) are rules of English, he would not be able to find out on his own that (a) is a rule of English. But if we were to teach him that (a) and (b) are rules of English, he *would* then be able to find out on his own, to see by himself, that (c) is, or ought to be, an additional rule of English. How is it, then, that his knowledge of (a) and (b) enables him to know that (c) is also a rule? The only answer that seems reasonable to me is that, since he knows that all squares are rectangles, he knows that if (a) and (b) are rules, then (c) ought to be a rule as well. And, *ex hypothesi,* his knowledge that all squares are rectangles is not knowledge about the rules of English. I would say, therefore, that "All squares are rectangles" does not "owe its truth" solely to the fact that we use the component words the way we do; it owes it also to the fact that the conjunctive property of being both equilateral and rectangular has the property of being rectangular as one of its components.

Lewis wrote, in *An Analysis of Knowledge and Valuation:* "The *mode of expression* of any analytic truth is . . . dependent on linguistic conventions; as is also the manner in which any empirical fact is to be formulated and *conveyed.* But the meanings which are conveyed by symbols, on account of a stipulated or a customary usage of them, and the relation of meanings conveyed by an order of symbols, on account of syntactic stipulations or customary syntactic usage, are matters antecedent to and independent of any conventions affecting the linguistic manner in which they are to be conveyed" (p. 148).[16] What this passage makes clear to us is the need of keeping the following two questions distinct:

(1) How does one find out whether the English statement "All squares are rectangles" is analytic?

(2) How does one find out whether all squares are rectangles?

We can answer the first question only by making a linguistic investigation of English speaking people; but the answer to the second refers to what is a priori and depends only upon the "contemplation of essences," or however else we wish to describe that

16 Cf. Gustav Bergmann, *The Metaphysics of Logical Positivism* (Longmans, 1954), p. 45 ff.

consideration of properties which is the source of our a priori knowledge. The linguistic study which is essential to the answer of (1) is not essential to the answer of (2); to realize this, we have only to consider the fact that there are many people who do not know English, and who do not, therefore, know the answer to (1), but who do know the answer to (2)—who do know that all squares are rectangles. We need not answer (1), then, in order to answer (2), but—and this is still another point—we *do* need to answer (2) in order to answer (1). For when we answer (1) we study the "linguistic behavior" of English speaking people and find out, as best we can, what properties constitute, for most such people, the meanings of the words "square" and "rectangle"; then, having found one property which we suppose to be the meaning of "square" and another which we suppose to be the meaning of "rectangle," we "look to see" whether the latter is included in the former—and this is something we can know a priori.[17]

To be sure, when I formulate question (2)—"How does one find out whether all squares are rectangles?"—I assume that the reader will understand what I have written; I assume, indeed, that I have used the words "squares" and "rectangles," as well as most of the other words that appear, in the way in which they are ordinarily used in English. But if the reader is tempted to infer from these facts that, when I write that all squares are rectangles, I am saying something *about* the English language, then he may be referred back to the possible confusion between "use" and "mention" noted at the end of the previous chapter.

In *Mind and the World-Order* (1929) and earlier, C. I. Lewis had defended a "pragmatic conception of the a priori," a view which was easily misread as being a kind of conventionalism. But this "pragmatic conception" was a view, not about the nature of a priori truth or our knowledge of it, but about our ways of classifying things. Whether, for example, it is better to use the word "fish"

---

[17] On the problem of finding a definition or a criterion of *sameness of meaning* which does *not* refer to relations between properties, see: Nelson Goodman, "On Likeness of Meaning," in *Semantics and the Philosophy of Language*, ed. Leonard Linsky (U. of Ill., 1952), pp. 67-74; Morton White, "The Analytic and the Synthetic: An Untenable Dualism," in the same book, pp. 272-86; W. V. Quine, *Word and Object* (Wiley, 1960), chap. II; and Paul Ziff, *Semantic Analysis* (Cornell, 1960).

in such a way that it will apply to whales, or in such a way that it will not apply to anything that is a mammal—such questions as these are to be decided wholly on the basis of practical utility. "I *may* categorize experience as I will; but what categorical distinctions will best serve my interests . . . ?" (p. 265). I *may* let properties A, B, and C be the properties which constitute the meaning of "fish," as I use the word, or I may choose properties B, C, and D instead; the choice is a matter of convenience. In the first use, but not the second, "All fish are A" will be analytic, and in the second, but not the first, "All fish are D" will be analytic. But (as Lewis recognized) the choice of these two classifications has no effect upon the two a priori truths—that the properties A, B, and C include the property A, and that the properties B, C, and D include the property D—truths which do not at all depend upon anyone's convenience. Thus Lewis said that "the pragmatic element in knowledge concerns the choice in application of conceptual modes of interpretation," but does not touch that "abstract a priori truth" which is "absolute and eternal (pp. 272-73).

I think it is fair to say that, for any clear interpretation that has been found for the phrase "true only by convention," the phrase cannot be said to refer to any merely *linguistic* characteristic that is peculiar to analytic statements and the truths of logic. There remains, however, the possibility that the statements *are* linguistic conventions—not that they are *true* "by convention" but that they are themselves conventions, rules, or stipulations, and are thus not true (or false) at all. This possibility, as we saw, was suggested by Schlick's California lecture and by Feigl and Blumberg's report; it was defended by Ernest Nagel, writing on "Logic without Ontology." Logical principles, he said, are "regulative principles," which are *"prescriptive* for the use of language"; the choice between alternative systems of such principles may be grounded "on the relatively greater adequacy of one of them as an instrument for achieving a certain systematization of knowledge." [18] But even if it be conceded that some logical statements are no more than rules or conventions, there is a difficulty of principle in saying that

[18] Ernest Nagel, "Logic without Ontology," in *Naturalism and the Human Spirit,* ed. Y. H. Krikorian (Columbia, 1944); reprinted in *Readings in Philosophical Analysis,* ed. Herbert Feigl and W. S. Sellars (Appleton, 1949).

all such statements are rules or conventions. "Briefly the objection is that whatever rules one may have initially stipulated, and however arbitrary such stipulations may be, one will thereafter have to *find out* what these rules entail, and the statement that such and such is entailed by the rules could hardly be characterized as itself a rule." [19] What we find out, when we discover with respect to two statements in our language that our rules allow us to derive one from the other, includes a logical truth—something that we can know a priori.

I think that Schlick and his followers were mistaken, then, in saying that there are certain facts about language which will enable us to set aside our "so-called rational knowledge." Other attacks upon the traditional conception of the a priori have proceeded from a skeptical position—a skepticism about our knowledge of properties and states of affairs. According to Lewis, as we have noted, if the word "square" is used to mean the property of being square and if the word "rectangular" is used to mean the property of being rectangular, then the statement "All squares are rectangular" is analytic; for, as he said, one can *see* by a kind of experiment in the imagination, that the property of being rectangular is included in that of being square (i.e., in that of being equilateral and rectangular). Morton White was skeptical about this kind of seeing or understanding: "One either sees or doesn't see the relationship and that is the end of the matter. It is very difficult to argue one's difficulties with such a position and I shall only say dogmatically that I do not find this early retreat to intuition satisfactory." [20] On the basis of a similar skepticism, Quine concluded

[19] Arthur Pap, *Semantics and Necessary Truth* (Yale, 1958), p. 184. Compare Quine's "Carnap e la verità logica," p. 11. The latter paper is an excellent statement of the entire problem. Quine's critique of conventionalism goes back to his "Truth by Convention" (1936), and "Is Logic a Matter of Words?" (1937), read at the Princeton meeting of the American Philosophical Association and abstracted in the *Journal of Philosophy*, XXXIV (1937), 674.

[20] Morton White, "The Analytic and the Synthetic: An Untenable Dualism," *op. cit.*, p. 280. White also noted that attempts to define "analytic statement" *without* reference to meaning and to relations between properties were inadequate; he took these facts to indicate that the traditional distinction between analytic and synthetic is "untenable." For a criticism of this reasoning, see Richard Taylor, "Disputes about Synonymy," *Philosophical Review*, LXIII (1954), 517-29.

that acceptance of the traditional distinction between analytic and synthetic is "an unempirical dogma of empiricists, a metaphysical article of faith." [21]

Here again I take the liberty of referring the reader to the discussion of skepticism in Chapter 1.

4. There remains the question of the synthetic a priori. Is anything that is known a priori to be true expressible only in statements that are synthetic, i.e., in statements that are neither analytic nor logically true? Or, as we may say for short, do we have any synthetic a priori knowledge? According to the tradition of British empiricism, which has dominated much of the philosophical thought of the period with which we are concerned, all of our a priori knowledge is "empty" and "nonfactual"—that is to say, all of our a priori knowledge is expressible in statements that are analytic or logically true. But some American philosophers have argued, with some plausibility, that some of our a priori knowledge can be expressed only in statements which are synthetic.

The concept of the synthetic a priori, however, has been taken in two quite different ways, with the result that our question—"Do we have any synthetic a priori knowledge?"—has a certain ambiguity which is frequently overlooked. The technical term "a priori" is sometimes taken in a positive sense, as it has been here, and "a posteriori" is then defined as what is not a priori. If, for the moment, we take "rational knowledge" as a synonym for this positive sense of "a priori," then we may say that our a posteriori knowledge is any knowledge that is not rational knowledge. But sometimes "a posteriori" is taken as the positive term and the "a priori" is then defined as what is not a posteriori. When "a posteriori" is taken in this positive sense it then becomes a synonym for "empirical knowledge." (Our empirical knowledge may be thought of, roughly, as comprising: first, what we know by means of the "external senses"; second, those facts about our own psychological states and about appearing, which were discussed in the previous

---

[21] *From a Logical Point of View*, p. 37. He also said, what is obviously true, that if the traditional distinction between a priori and a posteriori were replaced by a "behavioristic" contrast "between more or less firmly accepted statements," then the distinction might well turn out to be merely a matter of degree.

chapter; third, those facts of the first two types that we *remember;* and, last, whatever is inductively supported by any of the foregoing. The concepts of *empirical knowledge* and *rational knowledge* are thus exclusive but not necessarily exhaustive. If Burch's views about revelation, referred to in Chapter 1, are correct, then there is religious knowledge which is neither empirical nor rational.) Hence our question, "Do we have any synthetic a priori knowledge?", may be taken in these two ways:

(A) Is there any rational knowledge which is expressible only in synthetic statements?

(B) Is there any knowledge which is not empirical and which is expressible only in synthetic statements?

An affirmative answer to (A) would imply an affirmative answer to (B). An affirmative answer to (B), however, need not imply an affirmative answer to (A); for if there is knowledge which is neither empirical nor rational, and if that knowledge is the only nonempirical knowledge which must be expressed in synthetic statements, then (A) would be answered in the negative and (B) in the affirmative. In the present chapter, we are concerned with (A).

Our problem may be discussed by reference to the following six statements, each of which has been taken, by some American philosopher, to indicate an area of synthetic a priori knowledge:

(1) Anything that is red is colored.

(2) Nothing is both red and green.

(3) If anything is orange, then it has a color which is intermediate between red and yellow.

(4) Anything that is colored is extended.

(5) Anything that is a cube has twelve edges.

(6) Seven and five are twelve.

If we wish to show that there is no synthetic a priori knowledge, then we must show, with respect to each of these statements, either that it is analytic, or that it expresses what is known but not known a priori, or that it does not express what is known at all. The statements may thus be thought of as presenting us with six puzzles or riddles. The way in which we deal with these puzzles or riddles will obviously have important implications concerning the nature of our knowledge.

C. H. Langford has defended the thesis of the synthetic a priori with respect to statements (1), (2), (3), and (5); Hector Neri Castañeda, following Kant, has defended it with respect to (6); and various philosophers have defended it with respect to (4).[22]

Statement (1)—"Anything that is red is colored"—is very much like our earlier statement, "Anything that is square is rectangular." I think we may assume that, if the latter can be known a priori, then so, too, can the former; in each case, knowledge of a single instance of the generalization is enough, if not more than enough, to enable us to see that the generalization itself is true. To show that "Anything that is square is rectangular" is analytic, we may "analyze the predicate out of the subject" in such a way that we turn the statement into an explicit redundancy; that is to say, we replace the subject term "square" with a synonymous expression, "equilateral and rectangular," containing the original predicate, and the result—"Anything that is equilateral and rectangular is rectangular"—is a statement which is logically true. Can we similarly "analyze the predicate out of the subject" in the case of statement (1)? Can we find some term, which along with "colored" can be used to make up a synonym for "red," and which will then enable us to turn "Anything that is red is colored" into an explicit redundancy? I believe that no one has been able to find a term that will do.

Suppose, however, that we had a list of all the colors, and suppose (for simplicity) that the list comprised just the colors red, yellow, green, and blue. Could we then say that "colored" is synonymous with "either red, yellow, green, or blue"? If we could, then by replacing the *predicate* instead of the subject we could turn "Anything that is red is colored" into the following logical truth: "Anything that is red is either red, yellow, green, or blue." But if our list of colors is not complete, then, of course, we cannot say that "colored" is synonymous with "either red, yellow, green, or blue," for the color that our list omits will be a color and neither red,

22 C. H. Langford, "Moore's Notion of Analysis," in *The Philosophy of G. E. Moore*, ed. P. A. Schilpp (Northwestern, 1942), and "A Proof That Synthetic A Priori Propositions Exist," *Journal of Philosophy*, XLVI (1949), 20-24; Hector Neri Castañeda, " '7 + 5 = 12' as a Synthetic Proposition," *Philosophy and Phenomenological Research*, XXI (1960), 141-58. For a useful general discussion, see "Denial of the Synthetic *A Priori*" by Oliver A. Johnson, *Philosophy*, XXXV (1960), 1-10.

yellow, green, nor blue. And even if our list of colors should happen to be complete, we may, at least, speculate on the possibility that it is not: "Were we all in the position of those people we now call 'color-blind,' we would have been mistaken about the completeness of any list we might have made. Might it not be that we are also mistaken about this present list? Perhaps there is some color which none of us is acquainted with, and which therefore is not on our list, but which is such that if we were to become acquainted with it we would see that it is a further color to be added to our list." This speculation may be false, but, as Langford said (concerning a slightly different example), "it is logically and conceptually possible, which is all that is required for our purposes." [23] If it is logically and conceptually possible that a thing be colored and neither red, yellow, blue, nor green, then "colored" cannot mean "either red, yellow, blue, or green"; for there is *no* possibility that a thing could be either red, yellow, blue, or green, but neither red, yellow, blue, nor green. And so runs the principal objection to this method of showing that statement (1) is analytic.

But if the objection is unfounded and if we can say that the list "red, yellow, blue, and green" (possibly with some additions), constitutes a complete list of colors, then we may also be able to say that statement (2)—"Nothing is both red and green"—is analytic. We might say, for example, that "green" means the same as "colored, but neither red, yellow, nor blue," and statement (2) could then be transformed into the logical truth "Nothing is both red and colored but neither red, yellow, nor blue." But if the objection we have just considered is valid, then we will have to deny that "green" means the same as "colored, but neither red, yellow, nor blue," and this method of transforming (2) into a logical truth will have to be rejected.

More technical devices have been proposed: we might try to revise our color vocabulary in such a way that, in our revised vocabulary, we can say everything we need to say about colors but cannot formulate the troublesome statement (2). If we can do this—and the technique has been applied with considerable success elsewhere in philosophy and in logic—then perhaps we can

23 "A Proof That Synthetic A Priori Propositions Exist," *op. cit.*, p. 24.

say that our difficulties with (2) can be traced, not to the fact that (2) is synthetic a priori, but to the fact that our ordinary color vocabulary is defective. In applying this method, however, we must be on guard lest, when we use our new vocabulary, our difficulties reappear in connection with some other sentence. The following is a simple example of this method.

Think of two objects, A and B, which are red and green, respectively; define "is red" as "has the same color as A and does not have the same color as B," and define "is green" as "has the same color as B and does not have the same color as A"; then "Nothing is both red and green" may be replaced by "There is nothing which has the same color as A and does not have the same color as B and has the same color as B and does not have the same color as A," which latter statement is a logical truth. But, if I am not mistaken, we will have only transferred the problem of the synthetic a priori—transferred the problem from "Nothing is both red and green" to "If one object is red and another object is green, then the two objects do not have the same color." A method somewhat similar to this, though with added technical detail and refinement, was proposed by Hilary Putnam.[24] Arthur Pap subsequently suggested that the troublesome statements with which such an analysis leaves us—e.g., "Red and green are different colors"—*are* synthetic a priori, but that they are *also* statements which have "a linguistic origin" and therefore "may even be purely *verbal* and not 'about the world' at all! . . . What capital could a rationalist make of such synthetic a priori knowledge?"[25] We have noted, however, that there are serious difficulties involved in saying, of statements which do not mention language, that they are "purely verbal" or that they have their "origin in language." I think it is more plausible to say of statement (2)—"Nothing is both red and green"—that it has its "origin" in the relation of *exclusion,* which obtains between the properties of being red and being green, and

24 Hilary Putnam, "Reds, Green, and Logical Analysis," *Philosophical Review,* XLV (1956), 206-17.
25 Arthur Pap, "Once More: Colors and the Synthetic A Priori," *Philosophical Review,* LXVI (1957), 94-99. Pap's discussion of these questions in his *Semantics and Necessary Truth* is more in the spirit of what I have tried to say here than in that of the passage just quoted. His book is a useful account of the issues which the concept of the a priori has involved in recent philosophy.

to which Santayana referred in the quotation at the beginning of this chapter.

Statement (3) on our list—"If anything is orange, then it has a color which is intermediate between red and yellow"—raises no new questions of principle. Of (3), Langford wrote: "We may suppose a person who has never seen anything that was either red or yellow, but has seen all his life things that were orange in color. Such a person will easily be able to understand the antecedent of this proposition; but he will not be able to understand its consequent, and that will not be due merely to a defect in vocabulary."[26] And this Langford took to be evidence for saying that (3) is synthetic a priori.

Perhaps we may deal with statement (4)—"Anything that is colored is extended"—in a simpler way. Instead of trying to prove that it is analytic, we might suggest, on the ground that it is not known at all, that it is not known a priori. For how are we to tell, of things that are not extended, whether or not they are colored?

What of statement (5), "Anything that is a cube has twelve edges"? Langford proposed the following argument to show that this statement, which seems clearly a priori, is not analytic. There are many people, he said, who know *what* a cube is, who can recognize dice and other such objects as being cubes, and who do *not* realize that being a cube requires having twelve edges. From this he deduced that "the notion of having twelve edges can be no part of the notion of being a cube" and hence that the statement "Anything that is a cube has twelve edges" is not analytic.[27] The conclusion follows, however, only if we assume that a man cannot recognize an object as exemplifying a certain complex of properties unless he also recognizes it as exemplifying each of the components of that complex. But it is at least problematic, I think, whether this assumption is true; the theories of the Gestalt psychologists suggest that it may be false.[28]

---

[26] "A Proof That Synthetic A Priori Propositions Exist," *op. cit.,* p. 24.
[27] *Ibid.,* p. 21.
[28] Langford introduced this example in connection with what he called the "paradox of analysis": viz., if the philosophical analysis of a concept is such that "the verbal expression representing the analysandum has the same meaning as the verbal expression representing the analysans, the analysis states a bare

Our statement (6)—"Seven and five are twelve"—involves technical questions of logic and mathematics which fall outside the scope of the present survey. According to Kant and Castañeda, such mathematical statements are synthetic a priori; according to John Stuart Mill, they are synthetic but not a priori; and according to the "logistic thesis," defended in Russell and Whitehead's *Principia Mathematica* and elsewhere, such statements may be translated into the statements of logic and are therefore not synthetic. The status of (6) in contemporary controversy turns upon the question whether the "logistic thesis" is true. If the thesis is true, then the translations of (6) and the other statements of pure mathematics would turn out to be very long; Professor Quine told a Brazilian audience in 1942 that, if the binomial theorem were written out in the vocabulary of logic and in type the size of this, it would "extend from the North Pole to the South Pole." [29] But the objection to the "logistic thesis" is not, of course, to the length of the translations in question; the controversy concerns, first, whether these lengthy translations *would* be translations of such statements as (6), as these statements are ordinarily understood, and, second, whether all of the statements needed for the logistic translation or paraphrase of (6) are statements which are logically true. But these are not questions of epistemology.

Other statements sometimes thought to be synthetic a priori involve questions of ethics and of metaphysics; examples are "To the extent that an act is charitable it is good, whatever its conse-

---

identity and is trivial; but if the two verbal expressions do not have the same meaning, the analysis is incorrect" ("The Notion of Analysis in Moore's Philosophy," p. 323). For further discussion of this "paradox," see: Moore's reply to Langford, *The Philosophy of G. E. Moore,* pp. 660-67; Morton G. White, "A Note on the 'Paradox of Analysis,'" *Mind,* LIV (1945); Max Black, "The 'Paradox of Analysis' Again: A Reply," *ibid.,* pp. 272-73; Morton G. White, "Analysis and Identity: A Rejoinder," *ibid.,* pp. 357-61; Max Black, "How Can Analysis Be Informative?" *Philosophy and Phenomenological Research,* VI (1946), 628-31; a review of White's and Black's papers by Alonzo Church, *Journal of Symbolic Logic,* XI (1946), 132-33; and Arthur Pap, *Semantics and Necessary Truth,* pp. 275-82.

[29] W. V. Quine, "Os estados unidos e o ressurgimento da lógica," in *Vida intelectual nos estados unidos,* vol. II (União Cultural Brasil–Estados Unidos, São Paulo, 1946); the quotation is from p. 277. Quine's "Truth by Convention" is a clear discussion of some of the issues which the "logistic thesis" involves.

quences" and "If there are complexes, then there are simples."[30] The philosophical significance of the particular examples we have considered lies partly in this fact: if some of them must be acknowledged as exemplifying the synthetic a priori, then, in order to defend skepticism with respect to the statements of ethics and of metaphysics, it will not be sufficient merely to point out that some such statements, if they are known to be true, are synthetic a priori.

[30] On statements of the latter sort, see Henry Veatch, "Matrix, Matter, and Method in Metaphysics," *Review of Metaphysics,* XIV (1961), 581-600.

❧ 4 ❧

APPEARANCES AND REALITY

1. "No man doubts," wrote A. O. Lovejoy in his Carus Lectures, *The Revolt Against Dualism* (Norton, 1930), "that when he brings to mind the look of a dog he owned when a boy, there is something of a canine sort immediately present to and therefore compresent with his consciousness, but that it is quite certainly not that dog in the flesh" (p. 305). The image—the something of a canine sort that is immediately before the mind—is not itself a physical object, Lovejoy said; it is a private, psychological object, conditioned by a series of physiological and psychological events, reaching back to the earlier dog which it now reveals.

If the man now looks at his desk, then, according to Lovejoy, there is another series of physiological and psychological events, this time involving the activity of sense organs, but resulting as before in a private, psychological object—a sensation, this time something of a desk sort, a "visible desk" which in certain respects serves to duplicate the real, external, physical desk which it makes known to us. More generally, Lovejoy said, "the datum or character complex presented in the perception of a given moment" is never more than "the report, more or less tardy and more or less open to suspicion, from the original object which we are said to know by virtue of that perception" (p. 20).

Both of these examples—the earlier dog being now presented by a private and transitory mental dog and the external desk being presented by an inner visual desk—provide us with the essentials of two philosophical theories, which Lovejoy had referred to as "epistemological dualism" and "psychophysical dualism." According to "epistemological dualism," which is a thesis about our knowledge, we have direct or immediate knowledge only of certain private or subjective states of mind; some external objects, past or present, are duplicated in these states of mind and it is in virtue of this duplication that we know what we do about the rest of the world. Our knowledge of external things and of past events

312

involves a "cleavage" between the *object* of our knowing and the subjective *vehicle* which makes that object known. And according to "psychophysical dualism," which is a thesis about reality, the world is constituted out of at least two fundamentally different kinds of stuff—the physical or material things that are studied by physics, and the psychical or mental things that make up our states of mind. When asserted in conjunction, as they were by Lovejoy, and in the seventeenth century by Descartes and Locke, these two forms of dualism imply that our knowledge of physical or material things is derived from our knowledge of the mental or psychical duplicates of physical or material things.

2. Future historians of British and American philosophy, Lovejoy suggested, might well describe the period from 1905 to 1930 as the period of the "Great Revolt Against Dualism"—an age in which philosophers sought to avoid epistemological and psychophysical dualism without falling into the subjectivism or skepticism which seemed to be the only alternatives. The appearance of *The New Realism* (Macmillan, 1912) had been an early American contribution to this revolt. The six New Realists—E. B. Holt, Walter T. Marvin, William Pepperell Montague, Ralph Barton Perry, Walter B. Pitkin, and E. G. Spaulding—had proclaimed, in opposition to the thesis of "epistemological dualism" (and in opposition to the thesis of nineteenth century "idealism"), that the objects of external perception and of memory are "directly presented to consciousness" and are "precisely what they appear to be." No inner visual desk is needed to present the one that is outside, and the dog of thirty years ago can present itself again today. For "nothing intervenes between the knower and the world external to him. Objects are not presented to consciousness by ideas; they are directly presented" (p. 2).

The New Realists had formulated their objection to dualism in the following way. If the two forms of dualism are true, then, they said:

> The only external world is one that we can never experience, the only world that we can have any experience of is the internal world of ideas. When we attempt to justify the situation by appealing to inference as the guarantee of this unexperienceable externality, we

313

are met by the difficulty that the world we infer can only be made up of the matter of experience, that it can only be made up of mental pictures in new combinations. An inferred object is always a perceptible object, one that could be in some sense experienced; and, as we have seen, the only things that according to this view can be experienced are our mental states. Moreover, the world in which all our interests are centered is the world of experienced objects. Even if, *per impossible,* we could justify the belief in a world beyond that which we could experience, it would be but a barren achievement, for such a world would contain none of the things that we see and feel. Such a so-called real world would be more alien to us and more thoroughly queer than were the ghostland or dreamland which, as we remember, the primitive realist sought to use as a home for certain of the unrealities of life [p. 5].

This is an accurate statement, I think, of the absurdity which some of the versions of dualism involve. The New Realists rejected epistemological dualism outright (though Montague had misgivings), and at least two of them—Perry and Holt—seemed also to reject psychophysical dualism. Subsequent philosophers, both in England and in America, were to construct metaphysical systems in the interests of this "Great Revolt Against Dualism."

Lovejoy's own activity, as Arthur Murphy said, was thus counter-revolutionary. He was one of the seven Critical Realists who contributed to a second cooperative study, *Essays in Critical Realism* (Macmillan, 1920). The adjective "critical" was used in order to distinguish the realism of the seven from the admittedly "naïve" realism of the six. All of the Critical Realists—Durant Drake, J. B. Pratt, A. K. Rogers, George Santayana, Roy Wood Sellars, C. A. Strong, and Lovejoy—accepted something very close to the thesis of epistemological dualism; and all but Drake, Sellars, and Strong accepted the thesis of psychophysical dualism.

By 1930, Lovejoy thought, the matter was finally settled. He concluded his book by saying, concerning the two types of dualism, that "there is no conclusion of empirical science about the physical world—assuming that there in any sense *is* a physical world—which is better established" (p. 319).

3. "Epistemological dualism," as Lovejoy understood it, involved the following three theses:

(1) The only things that are ever *immediately given* to anyone are sensible appearances, memory images, and other such ideas.

(2) Sensible appearances, memory images, and ideas are *subjective* in that they depend for their existence upon the physiological and psychological state of the subject to whom they are immediately given.

(3) Perceiving a physical thing to have a certain characteristic consists, in part, of (a) being given a sensible appearance which has that characteristic and (b) attributing that characteristic to the physical thing; analogously, remembering something to have had a certain characteristic consists, in part, of (a) being given a memory-image which has that characteristic and (b) attributing the characteristic to a prior state of the thing.

I have discussed, in Chapter 2, the issues which the first of these three theses involves; we may now turn to the second and third.

I shall refer to the second thesis as the "subjective premise," since it asserts the "subjectivity" of appearances and images. Some of the metaphysical systems which were developed in the course of the "Great Revolt Against Dualism" depended upon denying the subjective premise.

I shall call the third thesis the "messenger premise." Lovejoy had used the word "messenger" in this connection (p. 20); in perceiving, he suggested, we read the message contained in the appearance and thus (we suppose) learn something about the stimulus objects from which the message was sent. At times Lovejoy and some of the other Critical Realists seemed to take the messenger premise in a literal sense: In perceiving and in remembering, we attribute to the object of knowledge *just those characteristics* which we directly apprehend in the subjective vehicle of knowledge. At other times, however, the messenger premise seems not to have been taken in a literal sense.

4. Of the three theses which epistemological dualism involved, the least objectionable might seem to be the one that I call the "subjective premise"—the thesis that appearances and images depend for their existence upon the physiological and psychological

315

state of the subject to whom they are given, and are thus "subjective." But to the New Realists, who had been the leaders in the American revolt against dualism, and to the "objective relativists" and "perspective realists" who were to oppose "Mr. Lovejoy's Counter-Revolution," the hope for a realistic account of our knowledge of the world seemed to depend upon denying, or at least qualifying, the subjective premise.

The New Realists had written: "The content of knowledge, that which lies in or before the mind when knowledge takes place is numerically identical with the thing known." [1] By the "content" of knowledge, they seemed to mean just those sensible appearances which Lovejoy was to describe as the "vehicles" of knowledge. But where Lovejoy, as an "epistemological dualist," distinguished the "vehicle" from the object it makes known, the New Realists said that the "content" and the object are one and the same. E. B. Holt had written that the sensible appearance of a physical object is "a part of the object." [2] Hence, according to the New Realism, the physiological and psychological processes involved in perception cannot be said to "create" or "generate" the sensible appearances which "lie before the mind" when perception takes place; these processes serve merely to "select" among appearances which already lie outside the mind and beyond the skin of the perceiver's body. "What is selected," Perry said, "is there to be selected, and is not instituted by the act of selection." [3] Where the dualist thought of perception as involving something like "a painter's canvas or photographic plate on which objects in themselves imperceptible are represented," the New Realists spoke of perception as "analogous to a light which shines out through the sense organs, illuminating the world outside the knower." [4]

In rejecting the subjective premise, the New Realists exposed themselves to the puzzling questions which are sometimes thought

---

[1] *The New Realism,* p. 34.
[2] *Ibid.,* p. 357. Holt's essay was entitled "The Place of Illusory Experience in a Realistic World."
[3] R. B. Perry, "A Note on Neutralism," in *Structure, Method, and Meaning: Essays in Honor of Henry M. Sheffer,* ed. Paul Henle, Horace M. Kallen, and Susanne K. Langer (Liberal Arts, 1951), p. 223. Cf. James K. Feibleman, *The Revival of Realism* (U. of N. C., 1946), *passim.*
[4] *The New Realism,* pp. 2, 4.

to constitute the subject matter of epistemology. What of the appearances of such objects as the straight stick which looks bent when partially immersed, the railroad tracks which appear to converge in the distance, the rectangular tabletop which looks diamond-shaped from the corner, the distant star which no longer exists but still appears in the heavens? Do the appearances of *these* objects exist along with the objects when no one is looking? Santayana wrote: "For the human system whiskey is truly more intoxicating than coffee, and the contrary opinion would be an error; but what a strange way of vindicating this real, though relative, distinction, to insist that whiskey is more intoxicating in itself, without reference to any animal; that it is pervaded, as it were, by an inherent intoxication, and stands dead drunk in its bottle!" [5] The plausibility of the subjective premise lies in the fact that the ways in which things appear depend in part upon the state of the observer.

Arthur E. Murphy proposed "objective relativism" as a way of meeting such difficulties. "Objective relativism" was both a metaphysics and an epistemology, and had been influenced by Samuel Alexander, A. N. Whitehead, and John Dewey.[6] Murphy summarized the view, in 1939, in the following words:

The experienced world is *at once* in some of its major features dependent on and conditioned by the special relations in which sentient (and more particularly human) organisms stand to their environment *and also* a direct presentation of that environment itself, or the order of natural events, as it is under such conditions. Nature is not something essentially beyond the range of perceptual inspection, having its exclusive being in characters independent of all relation to human responses to it. Far more in the natural world than we can ever experience there certainly is and must be. But unless what we experience *also* belongs to and is, under the special but entirely natural conditions of organic interaction, a sample of the

[5] *The Winds of Doctrine* (Scribner, 1913), p. 146.
[6] Cf. A. E. Murphy, "Objective Relativism in Dewey and Whitehead," *Philosophical Review*, XXXVI (1927), 212-44; "Mr. Lovejoy's Counter-Revolution," *Journal of Philosophy*, XXVIII (1931), 29-42, 57-71; "A Program for Philosophy," in *American Philosophy Today and Tomorrow,* ed. Horace M. Kallen and Sidney Hook (Furman, 1935). Reprinted in Murphy, W. H. Hay, and M. G. Singer, *Reason and the Common Good: Selected Essays of Arthur E. Murphy* (Prentice-Hall, 1963).

nature to which we claim to refer, then our relation to this ulterior nature becomes problematic, and the conditions of interaction which are in fact our means of getting in touch with it are treated as barriers to knowledge of what it is.[7]

It is an "objectively relative" characteristic of the distant star that, long after the star has ceased to exist, it still appears in a certain way to those who look toward its former place in the heavens— "objective" because it is an objective fact about the star that the star *does* appear in this way, but "relative" because the star would *not* appear in this way unless some sentient being were there to be appeared to. When he *is* thus appeared to, the sentient being has a "sample" of what is in the heavens. The term "sample" is appropriate because, if we can accept the Whiteheadian cosmology which had influenced this view, we can say that the star is made up of such "concrete events" as its appearing in certain ways under certain conditions.

E. B. McGilvary defended a similar thesis. The star is made up of its "perspectives" (among other things); some of these perspectives are conditioned by perceiving organisms; and every perceptual experience may be regarded "as the real objective world appearing in the perspective of an experiencing organism."[8] McGilvary called his view "perspectivism," or "perspective realism," but he also accepted Murphy's term "objective relativism." Lovejoy had argued that nothing that is past can be conditioned by anything that is present; we cannot say that the characteristics of a star which no longer exists may yet depend upon some observer who looks into the heavens tonight. McGilvary replied: "There is such a character as that of 'being an ancestor of a president of the United States.' Had Mr. Hoover not been elected president in 1928 an indefinitely large number of men and women of bygone days would not have acquired this character."[9]

But the epistemology, as distinguished from the cosmology, of

---

[7] "Dewey's Epistemology and Metaphysics," in *The Philosophy of John Dewey*, ed. P. A. Schilpp (Northwestern, 1939), pp. 219-20.
[8] E. B. McGilvary, *Toward a Perspective Realism*, ed. A. G. Ramsperger (Open Court, 1956), p. 6. This book, published posthumously, was prepared from the typescript of McGilvary's Carus Lectures, delivered in 1939, and from articles previously published.
[9] "The Revolt Against Dualism," *Philosophical Review*, XL (1931), 246-65.

"objective relativism" does not seem to differ significantly from that of "epistemological dualism." Let us compare the ways in which Lovejoy and Murphy described the experience of the astronomer. According to Lovejoy, the astronomer has an experience which is conditioned by his own organic state and which contains a "message" about a star; according to Murphy, the astronomer has an experience which is conditioned by his own organic state and which contains, or constitutes, a "sample" of the star. In each case, we seem to have a "vehicle" which informs us about an object; in the one case the vehicle contains a "message," in the other a "sample"; both the "sample" and the "message" tell us about something that is in the sky; and both the "sample" and the "message"—or that which contains the message—are dependent upon the state of the perceiver. Thus Montague said that "these relativistic objects" bear "a suspicious resemblance" to the sensible appearances of Lovejoy's dualism.[10]

What the revolt against dualism needed was an attack upon what I call the "messenger premise."

5. According to the messenger premise, perceiving a physical thing to have a certain characteristic consists in part of (a) being "given" a sensible appearance which has that characteristic and (b) attributing the characteristic to the physical thing; and analogously for remembering. Let us now consider the implications of (a).

The term "picture theory" which the New Realists had applied to dualism was not unacceptable to Lovejoy. If a man perceives a physical object or remembers one, Lovejoy said, the "transcendent reference" which his cognitive state involves consists in ascribing to the object of knowing a characteristic which the sense-datum "actually and certainly" possesses (p. 314); perceiving and remembering involve the "faith" that the object has, or had, this same characteristic. Some of the other Critical Realists had written in similar terms: the "immediate datum" which is "private" to the knower was said to have characteristics which the knower, acting in "animal faith," attributes to the object. C. A. Strong said that the perceiver "predicates the sense-datum of the external thing" and

10 W. P. Montague, "The Story of American Realism," *Philosophy*, XII (1937), 1-22.

Roy Wood Sellars said that the vehicle of knowing has "a sort of revelatory identity with the object." [11] But these philosophical statements, when interpreted literally, seem clearly false.

The error had been noted by Durant Drake in his contribution to *Essays in Critical Realism*. Suppose, he said, that I perceive "a round wheel about three feet in diameter, moving away from me and now between this house and the next." The messenger premise would have us say that the characteristics, which I thus perceive a group of material things to have, are characteristics which "actually and certainly" belong to a sensible appearance. But it is clear, Drake said, that the complex sensible appearance which I experience on this occasion "is not round (on any theory), since the wheel is endwise towards me; nor is it three feet in diameter, or moving away from me, or between this house and the next; nor does it have many, if any, of the qualities connoted by the word 'wheel'. . . ." [12] Lovejoy had said that his memory-image had the characteristics which he attributed to his dog. But *which* characteristics? Perhaps he remembered the dog to be wearing a collar, and to be friendly and obedient; but surely he did not experience a sensible appearance possessing any of *these* characteristics.

There are certain words which do seem to apply both to appearances and to physical things—for example, "red," "bitter," "hard," "cold." And one might wish to say that the messenger premise does apply when it is restricted to the characteristics which these words connote. But these words, as Aristotle had said, are ambiguous, meaning one thing when applied to appearances and another thing when applied to physical things.[13] The distinction between these two uses was clearly drawn by C. J. Ducasse. When we say of a tree that it is green, then the term "green" refers to a property which is causal, or dispositional, in the same sense in which such terms as "abrasive" and "corrosive" refer to properties which are causal, or dispositional. If we are physicists, we may mean that the tree is such that, when it is struck by light,

---

[11] C. A. Strong, *Essays on the Natural Origin of the Mind* (Macmillan, 1930), p. 93; Roy Wood Sellars, "Knowledge and Its Categories," in *Essays in Critical Realism*, p. 200.

[12] Durant Drake, "The Approach to Critical Realism," in *Essays in Critical Realism*, p. 29.

[13] *De anima*, III, ii, 426a; cf. *Metaphysics*, IV, v, 1010b.

it reflects light vibrations of one frequency and absorbs the others; but those of us who are not physicists are more likely to mean that "the tree, whether or not it be at the moment looked at, is such that under the conditions of observation that are the standard ones for such an object," it would cause a sentient observer to have the sensation of green.[14] And when we say of the sensation, or appearance, that *it* is green, we do not intend the adjective in this causal or dispositional sense. To understand the nondispositional sense of such adjectives, we must look more closely at such terms as "appearance," "sense-datum," and "sensation."

As the quotation from Durant Drake suggests, to see something which appears to be a wheel is not to experience an *appearance* which *is* a wheel; this fact alone should make us wary of transforming "Something appears green to me" into "I experience a green appearance of something." The latter expression, moreover, seems to complicate matters beyond necessity; where the former involves the one category of *appearing* the latter involves the two categories of *experiencing* and *appearance*. Ducasse proposed, in effect, that we retain the verb "to experience" (or use "to sense" as a synonym) and that we reject the implication that there are *appearances* which are objects of experience. When we use such adjectives as "green" and "blue" in the locutions "appears blue, or green" and "presents an appearance, or sensation, which is blue, or green," the adjectives

are names not of objects of experience, nor of species of objects of experience, but of *species of experience itself*. What this means is perhaps made clearest by saying that to sense blue is then to sense *bluely* just as to dance the waltz is to dance "waltzily" (i.e., in the manner called "to waltz"). . . . Sensing, that is to say, is a mental process having to sensing blue the same logical relation which obtains, for example, between the process in a string called "vibrating" and a particular mode in which it vibrates—say, the middle-C mode. . . . Sensing blue, I hold, is thus a species or modulation of sensing.[15]

14 C. J. Ducasse, "On the Attributes of Material Things," *Journal of Philosophy* (1934), pp. 57-72. Cf. "Introspection, Mental Acts, and Sensa," *Mind*, XLV (1936), 181-92.
15 C. J. Ducasse, *Nature, Mind, and Death* (Open Court, 1951), p. 259. The

It would hardly be fair to say that, when Lovejoy contrasted the "visible desk" with the "'real' desk" which it makes known (p. 16), he took the statement "Something *appears* to me to be a desk" to imply that something presents me with an appearance which *is* a desk. But once we see that the messenger premise cannot be taken literally, we also see, if I am not mistaken, that there is no reason to suppose that the "real desk" has *any* kind of "internal duplicate."

It should be noted, in passing, that if the picture theory of *epistemological* dualism is false, then *one* of Lovejoy's arguments for *psychophysical* dualism is inconclusive. For Lovejoy had argued: (1) we see desks and stars and other objects by means of internal desks and stars which are not identical with the objects they enable us to perceive; but (2) no place among physical objects can be found for such internal desks and stars; therefore (3) the latter objects inhabit "the world of the mind" and not "the world of matter." But if premise (1) is false, *this* argument for psychophysical dualism is no longer available. Since there *are* no internal desks and stars, the materialist need not be asked to find a place for them.[16]

Variants of the picture theory which were defended by other Critical Realists had similar limitations. Roy Wood Sellars said, in *Essays in Critical Realism,* that sensible appearances serve as "substitutes" for external things: "these sensible characteristics which are open to inspection and so readily taken to be literal aspects, surfaces, and inherent qualities of physical things are *subjective substitutes* for the corresponding parts of the physical world" (p. 191). And he said elsewhere, of external physical things, that "we tend to mistake our sensations *for* these things"; "a patch of color,

misleading character of "appearance" terminology has been discussed in detail by Martin Lean, in *Sense-Perception and Matter* (Humanities, 1953); see also the references in Chapter 2 above.

16 But he must, of course, fit the fact of *appearing* into his scheme of things; the metaphysical problems which this very difficult project involves fall beyond the scope of this essay. Cf. Herbert Feigl, "The 'Mental' and the 'Physical,'" in *Concepts, Theories, and the Mind-Body Problem,* ed. Herbert Feigl, Michael Scriven, and Grover Maxwell, Minnesota Studies in the Philosophy of Science, vol. II (U. of Minn., 1958), pp. 370-497; John T. Stevenson, "Sensations and Brain Processes" *Philosophical Review,* LXIX (1960), 505-10.

for instance, is *interpreted as* the surface of a thing"; and "analysis shows that the only literally intuited object is the sensory datum but that, in perceiving as such, it is given a context which makes the percipient *regard* it *as* an appearing thing." [17] Sellars did not say, as Lovejoy did, that there *are* two desks, one an appearance and the other an external thing; no appearance *is* a desk, according to Sellars, but people tend mistakenly to *believe* that certain appearances are desks. If what I have been saying is true, however, Sellars' account is also inadequate. People do not mistake appearances for desks; and when a man is mistaken in thinking that he perceives his desk, his mistake does not consist in believing, with respect to some appearance, that the appearance is his desk. The "transcendent reference" involved in perception—and in memory —does *not* consist in ascribing to a physical thing a characteristic or property which some sense appearance "actually and certainly" possesses, or even in ascribing to the thing a characteristic or property which the sense appearance is mistakenly supposed to possess.

Aristotle taught that, in knowing, the soul "receives the form of the object" and that "actual knowledge is identical with its object." [18] Subsequent Aristotelians attempted to compromise between epistemological dualism and epistemological monism by saying that what is "in the mind" is "formally identical" with, but "materially different" from, the object that is known. "The thing *is* in the mind intentionally; the mind is or becomes the thing intentionally. Thus the thing actually known and the mind actually knowing it are identical." [19] This doctrine, which was developed by Thomas Aquinas and his commentators, is expounded in Thomistic manuals of epistemology; it was also set forth in 1948 as part of the "Platform" of a group of American philosophers called the "Association for Realistic Philosophy." [20] Where Lovejoy might be inter-

---

[17] Roy Wood Sellars, "A Statement of Critical Realism," *Revue internationale de philosophie*, première année (1947), pp. 476, 478, 479.
[18] *De anima*, II, 4, 5.
[19] Gerald B. Phelan, "Verum sequitur esse rerum," in *Philosophy of Knowledge*, ed. Roland Houde and J. P. Mullally (Lippincott, 1960), p. 209.
[20] See the appendix to *The Return to Reason*, ed. John Wild (Regnery, 1953). Cf. John Wild, *Introduction to Realistic Philosophy* (Harper, 1948); Henry Veatch, *Intentional Logic* (Yale, 1952); Oliver Martin, *The Order and Inte-*

preted as saying that, when a man perceives a dog, an *appearance* takes on *some* of the characteristics of the dog, the Thomistic doctrine could be taken to say that, when the man perceives a dog, then the *man*, or his soul, takes on *all* the characteristics of the dog, though without becoming "identical with the matter" of the dog, and that when the man perceives a dog and a bird together, then the *man* becomes "formally identical" with the *dog* and *also* with the *bird*. There have been many attempts to make this doctrine intelligible, but I cannot feel that they have been successful.

In *The Degrees of Knowledge* (Scribner, 1959; translated from the fourth French edition) Jacques Maritain reasoned in the following way: (1) "By an apparent scandal to the principle of identity, to know is to be in a certain way something other than what one is: it is to become a thing other than the self." But (2) the man who perceives a bird does not become identical with a bird in the precise sense in which the feathered object in the tree is identical with a bird. Hence (3) "there is a kind of union, transcending every union of a material sort, between the knower and the known." And therefore (4) "there is a vigorous correspondence between knowledge and immateriality. A being is a knowing being to the extent that it is immaterial" (p. 112).

Nicholas of Cusa, opening his argument in a similar way ("Intellegere est esse similitudinem omnium"), and assuming that the principle of identity is true, deduced that knowledge is impossible —a conclusion which Maritain avoids only by means of the qualifying premises (2) and (3). What his first three premises tell us, it seems to me, is merely that the relation between knower and known is quite unlike any of those relations which hold among the objects of physical science. I prefer Lovejoy's statement of the latter point:

> To be known (except in the way in which immediate sensory content is sometimes, but, as I think, unfortunately said to be "known") things must—to use a happy phrase of Professor Dewey's—be "present-as-absent"; but since . . . a given bit of reality cannot

gration of Knowledge (U. of Mich., 1957); Francis H. Parker, "Realism, 'New' and 'Critical,' Reappraised," *Proceedings of the Association for Realistic Philosophy*, I (1952), 2-15.

be literally *both* present and absent, knowing must be a function of a unique and anomalous (but not a self-contradictory) sort. It must consist (partly) in the existence, at a given time and within an individuated field of consciousness, of particulars which do duty for other particulars, extraneous to that time and that field; and the former particulars must have associated with them in consciousness, the peculiar—but, as I submit, empirically the perfectly familiar—property which some of the Schoolmen termed "intentionality" and later dualistic epistemology has called "self-transcendent reference." The "intentional" or referential quality of a given bit of content present *now* in *my* cognitive experience is itself an item in the same present experience.[21]

The problem is, as Lovejoy suggests: in what way do certain particulars thus "do duty" for other particulars? Traditionally there have been two alternatives to the "identity," or "resemblance," theories of knowledge. These alternatives have also been defended by American philosophers.

6. Sextus Empiricus said, in his treatise *Against the Dogmatists,* that the function of appearances in perceiving is that of being *signs*—but signs only of *other* appearances. The appearances caused by smoke may signify those that are caused by fire; and they perform this sign function, not because they *resemble* the appearances that they signify, but because appearances of both kinds have been associated in the past. Indeed, according to Sextus, to say that appearances of smoke are a sign for some person of appearances of fire, is to say only that when that person experiences the smoke appearances he will be led to expect the fire appearances. Bishop Berkeley proposed, in his *Three Dialogues between Hylas and Philonous* (1713), that this relation between appearances gives us the clue to the nature of perception: the immediate apprehension "of ideas by one sense suggests to the mind others, perhaps belonging to another sense, which are wont to be connected with them." W. T. Stace, in *The Theory of Knowledge and Existence*

[21] A. O. Lovejoy, "A Temporalistic Realism," in *Contemporary American Philosophy,* ed. G. P. Adams and W. P. Montague, vol. II (Macmillan, 1930), pp. 85-105; the quotation is from p. 97.

(Oxford, 1932), and C. I. Lewis, in *An Analysis of Knowledge and Valuation* (Open Court, 1946), defended sophisticated versions of this theory.

Stace said that, when a man sees an apple, the man experiences certain visual appearances and "interprets" them by taking them to be signs of possible future appearances; "thus the reddish colour and the shape become signs to me that the visual experiences which I have of them will be followed in certain circumstances by another quite different experience, [for example] the sweet taste in the mouth" (p. 245). Lewis said, similarly, that the cognitive function of appearances is that of signifying *other* appearances. Stace described the "external world" as a "mental construction," and Lewis said that any meaningful statement about a physical thing is "translatable" into conditional statements about appearances (or, somewhat more accurately, into statements of the form "If I experience an S kind of appearance, then, if I undertake to do A, I will experience an E kind of appearance"). The relation of physical things to appearances, according to this "constructional" or "translation" thesis, is like that of "the average man" to particular men; statements ostensibly about the former may be translated, or paraphrased, into statements which mention the latter and do not mention the former. If it is true (1) that people do perceive external physical things and (2) that perception consists of appearances thus signifying *other* appearances, actual or possible, then some version of this translation, or construction, thesis must be true. But the thesis—which has come to be known as "phenomenalism"—involves serious difficulties.

The difficulties may be traced to the "perceptual relativity" which the Critical Realists had stressed—to the fact that the ways in which things appear depend, not only upon the objective properties of the thing, but also upon the conditions under which the thing is perceived and upon the state of the person who perceives it. To translate or paraphrase a simple thing statement into a collection of appearance statements, or even to find a single appearance statement which is implied by the thing statement, we must find some appearance or appearances which can be uniquely correlated with the physical fact described by the thing statement. But we are not able to correlate any group of appearances with any particular physical fact unless we specify those appearances by reference to some *other* physical fact—by reference to some set of observation conditions and to the state of the particular person who is to sense the appearances. For it is the joint operation of the things we perceive and of the conditions under which we perceive them that determines the ways in which the things are going to appear to us. And this constitutes a difficulty in principle for the attempt to translate thing statements into appearance statements; whenever we seem to reach such a translation, we find that our translation still includes some set of thing statements which describe physical observation conditions and which have not been translated into statements about appearances. The problem is not unlike that of trying to define "uncle" in terms only of "descendant" and without use of the terms "male" or "female." [22] If the translation thesis is false, and if, as I have been assuming, we are justified in our beliefs about our ability to perceive the world, it will follow, I think, that we cannot describe perceiving, as Sextus had thought, in terms of sign relations that hold among appearances.

7. Long before the publication of *Essays in Critical Realism* (1920), John Dewey had argued that the "messenger premise" is false. Perceiving, he said, does *not* consist in inspecting sensible appearances, reading off their characteristics, and then attributing these characteristics to physical things. For example, in *The Schools of To-morrow* (Dutton, 1915), he quoted with approval a passage from Rousseau's *Émile* and then observed:

> This passage . . . indicates how far ahead he was of the psychology of his own day in his conception of the relation of the senses to knowledge. The current idea (and one that prevails too much even in our time) was that the senses were a sort of gateway and avenue through which impressions traveled and then built up knowledge pictures of the world. Rousseau said that they are a part of the apparatus of action by which we adjust ourselves to our environment, and that instead of being passive receptacles they are directly

---

[22] Further aspects of the problem are discussed by Lewis in "Professor Chisholm and Empiricism," *Journal of Philosophy*, XLV (1948), 517-24. The translation thesis is defended by Roderick Firth in "Radical Empiricism and Perceptual Relativity," *Philosophical Review*, LIX (1950), 164-83, 319-31.

connected with motor activities—with the use of hands and legs. In this respect he was more advanced than some of his successors who emphasized the importance of sense contact with objects, for the latter thought of the senses simply as purveyors of information about objects instead of instruments of the necessary adjustments of human beings to the world around them [pp. 11-12].

Dewey's criticisms of "sensationalistic empiricism" and of other "spectator theories" of knowing are clear and penetrating; it is more difficult, however, to understand his positive account of perception or to put it into a precise terminology. A comparatively clear statement is the following, from the second edition of *Experience and Nature* (Norton, 1929):

> That a perception is cognitive means, accordingly, that it is used; it is treated as a sign of conditions that implicate other as yet unperceived consequences in addition to the perception itself. That a perception is *truly* cognitive means that its active use or treatment is followed by other consequences which follow independently of its being perceived. To discover that a perception or an idea is cognitively invalid is to find that the consequences which follow from acting upon it entangle and confuse the other consequences which follow from the causes of the perception, instead of integrating or coordinating harmoniously with them [pp. 323-24].

What Dewey meant, I think, may be illustrated as follows: If a driver now perceives that the road is clear before him, then the road that he perceives is for him a source of sensible stimulation; a "transaction" occurs with the result that the man acts, or becomes prepared to act, upon the belief that the road *is* clear before him. If the road were *not* clear, or if there *were* no road, these ways of acting would lead to a state of "disruption," "imbalance," or "disequilibration" and the man would find himself in an "indeterminate situation"—a situation which would then precipitate further inquiry. But since (on our assumption) the road *is* clear before him, such "disruption," "imbalance," or "disequilibration" will not result.[23]

---

23 See Dewey's *Logic: The Theory of Inquiry* (Holt, 1938), p. 105 and *passim*, and his *Knowing and the Known* (Beacon, 1949), written in collaboration with Arthur F. Bentley. Dewey's theory of inquiry is similar in many respects to the theory which Charles Sanders Peirce first set forth in 1877; see Volumes

Were it possible on any occasion to act *only* upon what one perceives, then it might also be possible to correlate the "cognitive validity" of the perception with the consequences of acting. But in everything we do, we act upon an indefinite number of propositions, many of them true, and, at times at least, some of them false. Our driver, in acting upon the proposition that the road is clear before him, is also acting upon the proposition that the road will take him where he wants to go, that the car will continue to be in working order, that he will continue to be able to drive it, and so on and on. If any one of these propositions is false, then the whole set of propositions—the true ones as well as the false ones—may lead to "disequilibration." The propositions which we know, or believe, to be true, as Quine has said in a somewhat different connection, face the tribunal of reality "not individually but as a corporate body." [24] Our driver, seeing that the road is clear, acts upon this "truly cognitive" perception; he sets out and then finds himself in a "doubtful situation" because the road, though clear enough, is not the road he thought it was. The perception was "truly cognitive," yet the consequences which followed from acting upon it "entangled and confused the other consequences which followed from the causes of the perception." To be sure, if he had not been mistaken about where the road would take him, he would not now be in his "doubtful situation." But this fact does not absolve the true belief; for it was *also* this "truly cognitive" perception of the road which led him to act in the way that he did.

Suppose, on the other hand, that his perception of the road has not been "truly cognitive." Because he thought, mistakenly, that the road was *not* clear, he took another road instead. The other road turned out to be shorter and better, with the consequence that the driver did not land in any state of "disequilibration," "imbalance," "disruption," or "shock."

II and V of Peirce's *Collected Papers* (Harvard, 1934). I regret that I am unable to determine the significance of Dewey's writings for epistemology; many believe, however, that they are of first importance. The following works were influenced by Dewey: Lewis E. Hahn, *A Contextualistic Theory of Perception*, University of California Publications in Philosophy, XXII (1942), 1-205; Justus Buchler, *Nature and Judgment* (Columbia, 1955); George Boas, *The Inquiring Mind* (Open Court, 1959).
[24] W. V. Quine, *Methods of Logic* (Holt, 1959), p. xii.

Action upon a "truly cognitive" perception, then, is no guarantee that "disequilibration" will *not* result, and action upon an *un*veridical perception is no guarantee that it will. For this reason, it seems to me, we cannot describe the "cognitive validity" of any perception, or of any belief, in terms merely of the consequences of deliberating and acting.

The "specific response" theory of Holt and Perry—two of the New Realists—was an attempt to construe *believing,* as well as perception, in terms of bodily adjustment and behavior. This theory, which is considerably simpler than Dewey's "transactional" account, also seems to be quite obviously inadequate. In recent years, however, Reichenbach and Carnap have defended it.

8. When psychologists talk about the behavior of animals, they may describe certain kinds of responses by reference to the stimuli with which such responses are usually associated. An animal's "food responses," for example, may be described in terms of what the animal does only when it is in the presence of food. A man's "fire responses," similarly, might be those things he does when and only when he is in the presence of a fire. Thus Perry wrote: "If, for example, I suppose or 'entertain the idea' that the barn is on fire, I in some measure set my fire-response in readiness. . . . An expectation, then, is an implicit response unreservedly set for a specific occasion; as when, believing that my train leaves the station at three o'clock, I correlate my readiness to depart, or my train-taking activities, with a place and time in my field of action." [25] If this way of talking is satisfactory, we might be able to define, by reference to a man's "X-responses," what it is for the man to believe that there is an X nearby; to say that a man believes that there is a horse nearby, for example, might be to say that he "puts his horse responses in readiness." By incorporating this account of believing into our description of perceiving, we might then hope to describe perceiving in terms merely of sensible stimulation, behavior, and adjustment.

[25] R. B. Perry, *General Theory of Value* (Longmans, 1926), pp. 313, 316; cf. E. B. Holt, *The Concept of Consciousness* (Macmillan, 1914), chap. IX, and "Eight Steps in Neuro-Muscular Integration," in *Problems of Nervous Physiology and of Behavior,* Symposium, Dedicated to Professor I. Beritashvili, The Academy of Science of USSR, Georgian Branch (Tiflis; 1936), pp. 25-36.

But what would a man's "horse responses" be? Would they be those ways in which he acts, or is prepared to act, *only* when he is in the presence of horses? If we described his "horse responses" in *this* way, then we would not be able to say that believing a horse to be in the vicinity consists in "putting one's horse responses in readiness." For suppose we were to say (1) that a man's "horse responses" are those responses he puts in readiness *only* when he is in the presence of horses, and (2) that when a man believes that there is a horse nearby, then—and only then—the man puts his "horse responses" in readiness. In such a case our definitions would have the unacceptable consequence that no one can ever *mistakenly* believe that there is a horse in the vicinity. Should we say, then, that a man's "horse responses" are responses which are *similar* to those he makes when he is in the presence of horses? Unfortunately, any two responses are similar in *some* respect or other; hence this account would have the consequence that *all* of the responses a man may make are "horse responses" and thus we could never say, of a man in action, that he does *not* believe there are horses nearby. A man's "horse responses," of course, are those responses which are similar in *relevant* respects to those he makes in the presence of horses. But what are the respects that are relevant?

The concept of *sign* does not help at this point. We could say, to be sure, that when a man perceives something to be a horse, then, as a result of sensible stimulation, something serves for him as a *sign* of the presence of a horse—or something *signifies* a horse. But when we attempt to say what it is for something to signify a horse, we find ourselves saying either that the something calls up the man's "horse responses," or that it leads to a "transaction" which would be "fulfilled" only by the presence of a horse, or, more simply, that it causes him to *believe* that he is in the presence of a horse.

In recent years philosophers investigating language have tried to construct more subtle versions of the specific response theory, in which "horse response" and the like have been replaced by more technical concepts. But each of these attempts, I believe, suffers from one or another of three defects. If one attempts to define "the belief that there is a horse" in terms of the concept of "horse response" (or its more recent equivalents), one will find: either (1) a man's "horse responses" become responses which *only* a horse could call up, in which case we cannot say that a man may believe falsely that he is in the presence of horses; or (2) they become responses he may make when he does *not* believe he is in the presence of horses, in which case we cannot define the belief in terms of the responses; or (3) the theory makes use, in the last resort, of some synonym for "believes," "takes," or "perceives," and thus leaves us at the point at which we began.[26]

9. What, then can we say positively about perception and the problem of "objective reference"?

When we perceive, with respect to some physical thing, that the thing has a certain property, then, because the thing does have that property and because it is a source of sensible stimulation, it appears to us in a certain characteristic way. If we are justified in our belief that what we call perception is a reliable source of knowledge, then we may say with Lewis:

> The given appearance may not be discernibly different from that of some other kind of object, under conditions other than those which affect this observation—so that the appearance could "deceive" us under conditions which, for all we know, may presently obtain— but because the condition which would lead to this "deception" is one which is exceptional, there is a high correlation between just this given character of the appearance and the objective property it leads us to ascribe to the thing observed.[27]

But it would be a mistake, I have suggested, to suppose that the appearance itself *has* the property—or at least that it has *all* the properties—which it leads us to ascribe to the thing. We are so constituted that, because the thing appears to us in just the way it does

---

[26] See, for example, Charles Morris, *Signs, Language, and Behavior* (Prentice-Hall, 1946); Hans Reichenbach, *Elements of Symbolic Logic* (Macmillan, 1947), esp. pp. 274-84; Rudolf Carnap, "Meaning and Synonymy in Natural Languages," *Philosophical Studies*, IV (1955), 33-47, and "On Some Concepts of Pragmatics," *Philosophical Studies*, VI (1957), 89-91; Wilfrid Sellars, "Mind, Meaning, and Behavior," *Philosophical Studies*, III (1952), 83-94. I have discussed some of these attempts in more detail in "Sentences about Believing," *Proceedings of the Aristotelian Society*, LVI (1955-56), 125-48; reprinted with alterations in Minnesota Studies in the Philosophy of Science, vol. II (U. of Minn., 1956), with an appendix consisting of correspondence with W. S. Sellars.

[27] C. I. Lewis, "Professor Chisholm and Empiricism," *op. cit.*, pp. 519-20.

appear, we have a kind of spontaneous belief about the thing.[28] We may be led to expect subsequent appearances of some definite sort, and doubtless, as a result of our perceptions, we set ourselves to act in various appropriate ways; but neither of these facts, if what I have been saying is correct, may be said to constitute the belief which the perception involves.

The problem of objective reference persists in the concept of belief. What is it for a psychological state—in the present instance, a belief—to be *about* some object other than itself? Franz Brentano held that "intentional reference" is a distinctive mark of the psychological and that it cannot be described in physical terms. "Intentionality" is characteristic not only of believing and perceiving, but also of remembering, thinking, loving, hating, and other such states or dispositions; each of these states or dispositions, Brentano suggested, may be said to "have an object" in a sense in which no nonpsychological thing may be said to have an object. This concept of "reference," or "intentionality," has now become a subject of intensive philosophical investigation; I think it is likely that there will be important developments in the next few years.[29]

Let us now return to the concept of *justified* belief—and consider its relation to truth.

10. "The true sceptic," Santayana said, "merely analyses belief, discovering the risk and the logical uncertainty inherent in it. He finds that alleged knowledge is always faith; he would not be a sceptic if he pretended to have proved that any belief, much less all belief, was wrong."[30] Let us suppose that we are no longer con-

---

[28] On the kind of "spontaneous belief" involved, compare Brand Blanshard's description of perceiving in *The Nature of Thought* (Macmillan, 1940), book I, chap. IV-VI, and my own account in *Perceiving: A Philosophical Study* (Cornell, 1957).

[29] Recent suggestive articles are: Alonzo Church, "Logic and Analysis," *Proceedings of the Twelfth International Congress of Philosophy*, pp. 77-81; Arthur Pap, "Belief and Propositions," *Philosophy of Science*, XXIV (1957), 123-36; Nicholas Rescher, "The Problem of a Logical Theory of Belief Statements," *Philosophy of Science*, XXVII (1960), 88-95; Nelson Goodman, "About," *Mind*, LXX (1961), 1-24.

[30] "Apologia pro mente sua," in *The Philosophy of George Santayana*, ed. P. A. Schilpp (Northwestern, 1940), p. 516. Fichte's term "posit" has come to replace Santayana's "animal faith" in recent writings (see the discussion of Reichenbach in Chapter 2). Quine writes, in the spirit of Santayana: "To call a

fused about bent sticks, distant stars, and converging railroad tracks, that we are sensitive to the risks which "appearance" and other philosophical terms involve, and that we are clear about the general epistemological predicament I have tried to describe in Chapter 1 of this essay. What may we say now for the claim that our knowledge, in particular that knowledge which we attribute to perception, involves an element of "animal faith"—for Lovejoy's assertion in *The Revolt Against Dualism* (p. 318) that "we know by faith?"

In its application to perception, the assertion is based, I think, upon the following considerations. (1) As we noted in Chapter 2, there are beliefs, or statements, about some of our own psychological states and about some of the ways we are "appeared to," which can be said to be "self-justifying" in a sense in which no other belief, or statement, can be said to be "self-justifying"; thus the statements expressing what we attribute to perception cannot, in this sense, be "self-justifying." (2) "Our senses do at times deceive us"; that is to say, there are occasions when we *think* we perceive that some state of affairs obtains and when, as a matter of fact, that state of affairs does *not* obtain. And (3) if we were to make use *only* of premises which are "self-justifying," in the present sense of this term, then we could not construct a good argument, deductive or inductive, for the thesis that any of the beliefs we normally attribute to perception are true.

The first two of these three points are incontrovertible, I believe. The third is more problematic, for we do not as yet have a generally accepted and clear account of what a good *inductive* argument might be. It is clear that we cannot construct a good *deductive* argument from directly justified premises to a conclusion saying that any of the beliefs we attribute to perception are true. And we cannot construct an *enumerative* inductive argument—an argument where the directly justified premises are of the form "Some A's are B's" and the conclusion is of the form "All A's are B's," or "Most A's are B's," or even "Some other A's are B's." For the A's

---

posit a posit is not to patronize it . . ." (*Word and Object* [Wiley, 1960], p. 22). In "Realism and the New Way of Words," Wilfrid Sellars speaks of "positing" languages and their subject matter; see *Readings in Philosophical Analysis,* ed. Herbert Feigl and W. S. Sellars (Appleton, 1949), pp. 424-56.

and B's in the conclusion must refer to certain properties of the kind we normally attribute to the things we think we perceive; but the A's and B's in the premises can refer only to our own psychological states and to certain ways of being appeared to. What remains problematic is the question whether we can construct a good argument by means of what is sometimes called *hypothetical induction*—an argument in which the conclusion (saying that some of the beliefs that we normally attribute to perception are true) is advanced as being the most likely explanation of the facts asserted in the self-justifying premises. Any controversy concerning this point is likely to turn on the questions "What constitutes a good argument by hypothetical induction?" and "What are the criteria for determining what constitutes the 'most likely explanation' for any set of data?" During the past twenty years an extraordinary amount of important work has been done in this area, especially by American philosophers, but most of it is still controversial. (In a series of articles in 1933 and 1934, Donald Williams defended "realism as an inductive hypothesis," but the premises he made use of were not restricted to those that I have called "self-justifying." [31] Much of what he wrote was a criticism of various forms of skepticism and subjectivism.)

The relevant epistemological question is this: If we suppose that the three considerations I have listed are true—if we suppose that our "self-justifying" beliefs are what I have said they are, that "our senses do sometimes deceive us," and that our "self-justified" beliefs do not warrant any inferences about the reliability of the senses—then, what implications does our supposition have concerning the knowledge that we attribute to perception? We should first note, as a point of logic, that the three considerations by themselves do not imply that we are *not* justified in putting our faith in the "ex-

---

[31] Donald Williams, "The *A Priori* Argument for Subjectivism," *The Monist,* XLIII (1933), 173-202; "The Inductive Argument for Subjectivism," *The Monist,* XLV (1934), 80-107; and "The Argument for Realism," *The Monist,* XLIV (1934), 186-209. Cf. Everett Nelson, "The Inductive Argument for an External World," *Philosophy of Science,* III (1936), 237-49, and "The External World," *Philosophy of Science,* IX (1942), 261-67; George Chatalian, "Induction and the Problem of the External World," *Journal of Philosophy,* XXXIX (1952), 601-07.

335

ternal senses." If the skeptic wished to *prove* to us logically that such faith is unreasonable, then he would need to find an additional premise which, when added to our three, would yield his conclusion—a premise describing the conditions under which the faith is justified. If we cannot accept his conclusion, then we may deny his additional premise while retaining our original three, and his proof that we are misguided will fail. Yet *we* cannot prove, on his grounds, that *he* is wrong; if we attempt to prove from some set of directly justified premises that the senses *are* generally reliable, then, as I have suggested, *our* proof will fail, too.[32] If the reader feels that I have done an injustice to our position, or to that of the skeptic, he is referred to Chapter 1.

Why *should* one suppose that to justify what we attribute to perception we should construct an argument using only "directly justified" statements as premises? The supposition proceeds, I think, from the tendency, discussed at the end of Chapter 2, to emphasize "the given" at the expense of the related concept of "rules of evidence." Since we find that our senses do sometimes deceive us, we cannot say that *every* belief we attribute to perception is true. But "if one who trusts his senses is sometimes deceived, he is more wretchedly deceived who never trusts them." [33] According to the assumptions we made at the beginning, we are justified in thinking, with respect to a large class of our beliefs, including those that we attribute to perception, that they are instances of knowing; or, what comes to the same thing, we are justified in thinking that we have adequate evidence for those beliefs. But since our senses do sometimes deceive us, it follows that some of the beliefs for which we have adequate evidence are in fact false—or, in other words, that some of the things we are justified in thinking that we know are *not* in fact things that we know. If this, as I believe, is what intended by the statement "Our knowledge involves an element of animal faith," then I think the statement is correct.

It is necessary, finally, to say something about the relations between evidence and truth.

---

32 The position of our hypothetical skeptic is taken by W. T. Stace, in "The Refutation of Realism," in *Readings in Philosophical Analysis,* ed. Feigl and Sellars, pp. 364-72; first published in *Mind* (1934).
33 Augustine, *The City of God,* book XIX, chap. XVIII.

11. In light of all of the foregoing, we may make some general observations about criteria of evidence. A man may be said to have adequate *evidence* for a given statement—or the statement may be said to be *evident* to him—provided it meets one of these three conditions: (1) it is "directly justified"; (2) it is "a priori"; or (3) it expresses what the man thinks he remembers and is not logically incompatible with any statement expressing what he thinks he remembers. I believe we should also specify a certain subclass of perceptual judgments and say that a statement may be evident provided (4) it expresses what the man thinks he perceives (where the perceptual judgment is of the kind specified). Possibly we should add, further, that a statement is evident provided (5) it is logically implied by anything that is evident in the first four senses; this addition would have the result that a man may have adequate evidence for certain statements (e.g., some of the theorems of logic and mathematics) which, in fact, are not among those statements that he believes to be true. If, moreover, we are justified in saying that some of the conclusions of modern science (e.g., "There are nine planets") have the status of being evident, we should add that a statement is evident provided (6) it is highly probable in relation to all of those statements which are evident in the first five senses. (Generally speaking, an inductive conclusion which is probable—even highly probable—in relation to what is evident cannot itself be added *to* the evidence and then used to compute the probability, in relation to what is evident, of other statements.[34] The statement "There are nine planets" is one which most scientists would wish to count as evident, but its justification lies in the fact that it is highly probable in relation *to* the evident. What degree of probability—of probability less than one and in relation to other statements which are evident—is necessary in order that a statement may itself be counted evident, is an unanswered question of the theory of induction.) And perhaps there are still other criteria of evidence—associated with some of the other "sources" of knowing mentioned in Chapter 1.

A fundamental dilemma for the theory of knowledge is the following. If (3), (4), and (6) are omitted from our list of criteria

[34] See Rudolf Carnap, *The Logical Foundations of Probability* (U. of Chicago, 1950), pp. 382-86.

of evidence—that is to say, if the only statements which are to be counted as evident are those which are "self-justifying" or "a priori" or are logical consequences of what is "self-justifying" or "a priori," then our knowledge is restricted to a much smaller class of statements than anyone, other than the skeptic, believes that it is. But if we include (3), (4), and (6) in our list, then we must say that, from the fact that a statement is evident it does not follow that the statement is true.

What follows is based upon the assumption that the second of these courses is the lesser evil.

12.   One can say of the belief that Socrates is mortal, or of any statement which says that Socrates is mortal, and hence of the English statement "Socrates is mortal," that it is *true* if and only if Socrates *is* mortal. But one cannot say, of the belief or of the statement, that it is *evident* if and only if Socrates is mortal; for the belief or statement that Socrates is mortal may be evident even though Socrates is not mortal, or may not be evident even though he is mortal. More generally, the *conditions of truth* and the *criteria of evidence* for most beliefs and statements do not coincide. To state the conditions of truth for any belief or statement, we have only to assert the belief or statement; to state the criteria of evidence, if any, for any belief or statement (other than one that is "self-justifying"), we ordinarily must assert many other beliefs or statements.

We should be prepared, then, for an ambiguity in the philosophical expression *"criteria of truth."* Sometimes the expression is used to mean *conditions of truth,* but at other times it is used to mean what I have called *criteria of evidence.*

Conflicting "theories of truth" result partly from the fact that some philosophers consider the concept of *truth* in terms of the problem of "objective reference" and others consider it in terms of the concept of *evidence.* Thus philosophers who seem to have conflicting theories of truth may agree with the traditional dictum that truth consists in the "adequacy" of the intellect and reality: Veritas est aedequatio rei et intellectus. Some consider this "adequacy" in terms merely of objective reference, as I believe they should, and are thus able to accept Aristotle's simple statement: "To say of what is that it is not, or of what is not that it is, is false, while to say of what is that it is, or of what is not that it is not is true." [35] (The term "believe," or "judge," may also be used where this passage uses "say.") Other philosophers, mistakenly I think, seem to consider "adequacy" in terms of evidence. Thus Dewey said that he accepted a "correspondence theory of truth" and that he took the term "correspondence" to have an "operational" meaning: "the meaning, namely, of *answering*, as a key answers to conditions imposed by a lock, or as two correspondents 'answer' each other; or, in general, as a reply is an adequate answer to a question or a criticism—as, in short, a *solution* answers the requirements of a problem." [36] If we consider correspondence, or adequacy, in this second way, we will be led to the false conclusion that where no "solution" is available, i.e., where adequate evidence is not available, there is no truth. It was in this way, I think, that Otto Neurath was led to make the following paradoxical statement: "We should be doubtful even in admitting a definition of 'true' which implies that the saying, 'There is an elephant here,' may be called true if and only if there is an elephant here. Even this sounds like an 'absolute' expression . . . which we do not know how to fit into a framework based on observation statements." [37]

An adequate theory of evidence, I have suggested, will not imply that the belief or statement that Socrates is mortal is a belief or statement which is *evident* if and only if Socrates is mortal. But an adequate theory of objective reference must be one which implies that any belief or statement, which is a belief or statement *that* Socrates is mortal, is a belief or statement which is *true* if and only if Socrates is mortal. (Thus the stoics, according to Sextus Empiricus, defined the truth of statements in terms of what the words making up the statements *refer* to: "As to this definite proposition 'This man is sitting' or 'This man is walking,' they declare it is true

[35] Aristotle, *Metaphysics*, III, 7, 27.
[36] John Dewey, *Problems of Men* (Philosophical, 1946), p. 343.
[37] Otto Neurath, *Foundations of the Social Sciences, International Encyclopedia of Unified Science*, vol. II, no. 1 (U. of Chicago, 1944), p. 12. Cf. C. G. Hempel, "Le Problème de la vérité," *Theoria*, II (1937), 206-44, esp. 243-44; Hans Reichenbach, *Experience and Prediction* (U. of Chicago, 1938), p. 188 ff.

when the thing predicated such as 'sitting' or 'walking' belongs to the object indicated.")[38]

Thus if we were to accept a "copy theory" of reference (e.g., "a state of mind refers to a thing if and only if it takes on the properties of that thing") then we might also accept a "copy theory" of truth (e.g., "a state of mind is *true* if and only if it does thus refer to a thing—if and only if it does succeed in copying what exists"). William James's so-called pragmatic theory of truth was, as he realized, essentially a theory of reference, a theory about the nature of belief. He said, in effect, that if a man *believes* that there are tigers in India, then the man is in a bodily state which is such that, if the man were to go to India, then the bodily state (1) would turn out to be disrupted, or frustrated, if and only if there were *no* tigers in India, and (2) would be fulfilled or satisfied, if and only if there *were* tigers in India; hence, on this theory, the man's belief is *true* if and only if the bodily state would be fulfilled or satisfied; and James thus concluded, somewhat misleadingly, that truth consists in "satisfaction." [39] The limitations of this theory of reference, and hence of the account of truth, are substantially those of the theory of reference attributed to Dewey, above.

In the nineteenth century, "idealistic" philosophers attempted to formulate a "coherence theory" of truth. Believing that everything is mental and hence that there is nothing nonmental for the intellect to be adequate to, they thought of truth as a kind of systematic consistency of beliefs, or "ideas." Many philosophers rejected the theory on the grounds (1) that since a system of false

[38] Sextus Empiricus, *Against the Dogmatists,* II, 100; Loeb Classical Library ed., vol. II, p. 289. In Tarski's and Carnap's studies of the semantics of formalized languages, "truth" is defined in terms of the concept of *fulfillment,* or *satisfaction*—a concept which is exemplified in the relation between Socrates and the expression "X is mortal." Both authors emphasize, in effect, that to the truth conditions for any statement we have only to assert the statement. See Alfred Tarski, "The Concept of Truth in Formalized Languages," in *Logic, Semantics, Metamathematics* (Oxford, 1956); the paper referred to was published in Polish in 1933 and in German in 1935; "The Semantic Conception of Truth," *Philosophy and Phenomenological Research,* IV (1944), 341-76 (reprinted in *Readings in Philosophical Analysis* ed. Feigl and Sellars); and Rudolf Carnap, *Introduction to Semantics* (Harvard, 1942).

[39] James's clearest statements are in *Pragmatism* (Longmans, 1907), lecture VI, and in *The Meaning of Truth* (Longmans, 1909), chap. II ("The Tigers in India"); the latter was written under the influence of Dickinson Miller.

propositions may be internally consistent, consistency alone is not a condition of truth, (2) that the theory did not give a clear account of the respect in which "coherence" differs from mere consistency, and (3) that the possible interpretations of "coherence" seemed to presuppose the kind of "adequacy" or "correspondence" which the theory was designed to avoid.

In the present century, "logical positivists" defended for a time a "restrained coherence theory of truth." Believing that statements can be "compared" only with other statements, and hence that "statements are never compared with a 'reality,' with 'facts,'" they concluded that the "cleavage between statements and reality" which the "correspondence theory" seemed to presuppose is "nothing but the result of a redoubling metaphysics, and all the problems connected with it are mere pseudo-problems." [40] They admitted that mere consistency is not enough, and said that what distinguishes a system of true statements from a consistent fairy tale is that the former, unlike the latter, agrees with the "protocol statements of science," i.e., with the observation statements of science. The "protocol statements" were characterized as "true" only in the sense of being those observation statements which, as it happens, are "actually adopted by mankind, by the scientists of our culture circle." [41] It was noted that any observation statement is subject to being revoked at some later time, and that "the adoption of any observation statement has, after all, the character of a *convention*." [42] The latter quotation suggests the "postulational" theory of evidence, or justification, which I mentioned in section 7 of Chapter 2. I believe it would now be conceded that this "restrained coherence theory of truth" resulted from failure to distinguish criteria of evidence from conditions of truth. [43]

The "coherence theory of truth" was also developed by Brand Blanshard, in *The Nature of Thought* (Macmillan, 1940), as part

[40] Carl G. Hempel, "On the Logical Positivists' Theory of Truth," *Analysis*, II (1935), 49-59; the quotations are from pp. 49, 50, 51.
[41] *Ibid.*, p. 57.
[42] Carl G. Hempel, "Some Remarks on 'Facts' and Propositions," *Analysis*, II (1935), 93-96; the quotation is from p. 96.
[43] Cf. Rudolf Carnap on "the neglect of the distinction between truth and knowledge of truth (verification, confirmation)" in "Truth and Confirmation," *Readings in Philosophical Analysis,* ed. Feigl and Sellars, pp. 119-27; and Tarski on truth and "provability" in "The Semantic Conception of Truth," p. 354.

of a general theory of reality, or a metaphysics.[44] Blanshard's theory of truth depends partly upon a theory of reference, partly upon a theory of evidence. Following Josiah Royce's *The World and the Individual* (Macmillan, 1899), Blanshard says that "the relation between idea and object must be conceived teleologically, as the relation of that which is partially realized to the same thing more fully realized" (vol. I, p. 473). Hence "the idea can then be *both* the same as its object *and* different; the same because it *is* the object *in posse;* different because that object, which is its end, is as yet incompletely realized" (vol. I, p. 494). The theory (which may recall the Thomistic attempt, mentioned above, to find a mean between literal identity and difference) implies, concerning what I take to be my idea of Julius Caesar, either (1) that the idea is *not* an idea of Julius Caesar, or (2) that it is capable of becoming Julius Caesar himself, or (3) that Julius Caesar is capable of becoming my idea of him, or (4) that both Julius Caesar and my idea have purposes which are such that, if these purposes were realized, then my idea and Julius Caesar would both become the same thing. It is clear that Blanshard took the fourth of these courses; the metaphysical system which such a view must involve does not lie within the scope of the present work.

But Blanshard's theory of truth depends also upon his theory of evidence. His procedure is as follows: he poses the question "What are the tests of truth?" and examines various possibilities—authority, mystic insight, correspondence, self-evidence, and coherence—rejecting all but the last; he then concludes (1) that "coherence is our sole criterion of truth" (vol. II, p. 259) and, given this conclusion, attempts to demonstrate (2) that truth *consists* in coherence. "Assume coherence as the test, and you will be driven by the incoherence of your alternatives to the conclusion that it is also the nature of truth" (vol. II, p. 269).

If what I have said about the nature of evidence and of justification is accurate, and if I have interpreted Blanshard correctly, then there would seem to be two errors in his account. He seems to sup-

[44] W. H. Werkmeister, in *The Basis and Structure of Knowledge* (Harper, 1948), presented a similar theory, but combined it with a view enabling him to "identify 'truth' with 'warranted belief' and, therefore, with 'knowledge' " (p. 152). Cf. E. S. Brightman, *An Introduction to Philosophy*, rev. ed. (Holt, 1951), pp. 80 ff.

pose that coherence is a sufficient condition of evidence; I discussed this supposition in Chapter 2. And he also seems to suppose that, if we have found necessary and sufficient conditions for saying that a proposition is evident, we have also found, *ipso facto,* necessary and sufficient conditions for saying that the proposition is true. This second supposition does indeed give us the mark of those psychological propositions which I have called "self-justifying"; but if there are any other propositions which are evident, then, according to what has been said, the supposition is false. "I think I remember" (with the qualifications noted earlier) may imply "I have adequate evidence for that which I think I remember," but it does not imply "I remember." And a good inductive argument may guarantee that we have adequate evidence for its conclusion, but it does not guarantee that the conclusion is true.

The thesis that evidence does not imply truth is doubtless discomfiting and we may be tempted to think, therefore, that by redefining our terms we can somehow avoid it. Franz Brentano held that a belief may be called true provided it is a belief which would be held by one who "judged with evidence." [45] C. J. Ducasse said, similarly, that truth "means capacity to compel belief in a rational person who has the relevant evidence." [46] Charles Saunders Peirce said that a true opinion is one which accords "with the ideal limit towards which endless investigation would tend to bring scientific belief"—a view which Dewey also accepted (though without accepting the "conditional idealism" which Peirce took his theory to imply.) [47] But any theory which defines "evidence," or "truth," in such a way that "evidence" may be said to imply "truth," may be interpreted either as *restricting* the concept of evidence in order to confine it to propositions which are true, or as *relaxing* the concept of truth in order that it might apply to any proposition which is evident. In the former case, we succeed only in making evidence as

[45] Franz Brentano, *Wahrheit und Evidenz* (Leipzig; 1930), p. 139.
[46] C. J. Ducasse, "Facts, Truth, and Knowledge," *Philosophy and Phenomenological Research,* V (1945), 330.
[47] Charles Saunders Peirce, *Collected Papers,* vol. V, 5.565, 5.494, 5.358n; John Dewey, *Logic: The Theory of Inquiry,* p. 345. Peirce also defined truth as follows: "For truth is neither more nor less than that character of a proposition which consists in this, that belief in the proposition would, with sufficient experience and reflection, lead us to such conduct as would tend to satisfy the desires we should then have" (5.375n).

remote as truth; we will not know whether a good inductive argument yields evidence unless we know that its conclusion is true. In the latter case, we succeed only in making truth as *relative* as evidence; the belief that there are nine planets could be true, in this relaxed sense of "true," even if there were not nine planets.

ETHICAL THEORY

୶ટ੬ঌ

WILLIAM K. FRANKENA

PROFESSOR OF PHILOSOPHY
UNIVERSITY OF MICHIGAN

PREFACE

The age with which we have to deal is the most labeled of all the ages of man. It has been called an Age of Anxiety, Crisis, Global War, Social Revolution, Science, Technology, Uncertainty, and Unreason, the End of the Age of Reason, the End of the Modern and the Beginning of the Post-Modern Eras. Our age has also been an eventful one. We have had the Depression, the New Deal, Nazism, Fascism, Communism, World War II, the Spanish and Hungarian revolutions, China, Korea, the Cold War, the end of the British and other empires, the A- and H-Bombs, the United Nations, the population explosion, anti-Semitism, McCarthy, civil rights agitation, other-direction, the organization man, television, moon rockets, and the Abominable Snow Man. It would be most interesting to study the effects of such an age on our morals, mores, and popular ethical thinking. However, this essay is not a review of ethics in America in that sense. It is an account of the thinking and research done by scholars who have concerned themselves with ethics and values, more specifically, by philosophers and near-philosophers, a study, in short, not of morals and mores, but of moral philosophy and value theory in this country since about 1930. Like the other essays in this series, however, it will seek to give a review and discussion of its subject that will be of interest and use, not only to philosophers, but to educators and scholars in other fields, and to educated readers generally.

Now, the main concern of ethical theory or moral philosophy in our period has been with so-called meta-ethical questions rather than with normative or practical ones. That is, the primary concern has been, not with propounding judgments about what is right or good, but with analyzing the meaning or nature of such judgments and the logic of their justification. Accordingly, with some notable exceptions, our moral philosophers in their professional writings reflect relatively little direct preoccupation with the developments and events referred to earlier, though they observed

347

and lived through them with the interest that any intelligent and serious person could be expected to feel. In this respect, their philosophizing is more like that of Britain than that of the Continent. In fact, the movement that is currently most in the ascendancy in Britain and America tends to deny that it is part of the proper task of philosophy to propound goals and principles or to propose solutions to normative and practical questions.

My review of ethics in America since 1930 must therefore center on meta-ethical questions of the sort indicated, though it will, of course, consider views on other matters to make the picture as full as possible. Even then there are many ways in which I might proceed—chronologically, topically, etc. My procedure will be to distinguish the main types of meta-ethical theory and to take them up one by one, going back in each case to about 1930. The types of theory to be distinguished and explained are, first, intuitionism; then two forms of ethical empiricism, naturalism and pragmatism; third, noncognitive theories; and finally, religious theories. Certain proposals for reunion between these rival movements will also be considered. In general, what separates these different points of view is their answers to questions about the meaning and justification of ethical or value judgments, but in this "Age of Science" these answers tend to take the form of views about the relation of ethics or morality to science, and so I shall also present them as variations on this theme.

Although my main subject will be American work in ethics and value theory during the last three decades, I shall on occasion also say something about developments in the related fields of legal, political, and social philosophy.

1

INTUITIONISM

General account. W. M. Urban; E. W. Hall; Maurice Mandelbaum. Thomist writers; Walter Lippmann.

One traditional type of ethical theory that has full and ready answers to questions of ethics is called intuitionism or nonnaturalism. Its proponents are most insistent that ethical judgments constitute a body of knowledge as truly as do the judgments of any other discipline. However, they insist that ethics is an autonomous discipline with its own peculiar subject matter. They hold that the basic propositions of morality and normative ethics are intuitive or self-evident insights of a unique kind, uninferable from the propositions of any other discipline, whether this be physics, psychology, sociology, history, metaphysics, or theology; that their central concepts are irreducible to and different in kind from those that are characteristic of any of these other fields; and that some of their central concepts are absolutely indefinable. In other words, they believe that ethical judgments are true or false statements about the presence or absence of certain simple nonnatural or nonempirical (and nonmetaphysical) qualities or relations, and that the most basic of them are intuitively known or self-evident, and hence neither susceptible of any logical justification nor in need of one.

Here is a "short and easy way" with the meta-ethical problems of our age, and the wonder is that it has not been more resorted to. In the early Thirties it was, in fact, dominant in Britain and Germany. But, while this intuitionism was dominant in our transcendentalism and our textbooks of the nineteenth century, it has not been strong in America in this century. In its first decades the chief philosophies, idealism, realism, and pragmatism, were against intuitionism even when they were not in favor of empiricism or naturalism. The more recent influences of science and of work in logic and mathematics, both much stronger in philosophy in America than in Europe, have also counted against intuitionism. In general, American philosophers have shied away from the logic, epistemology, ontology, and psychology of intuitionism, sometimes on Hegelian or instrumentalist grounds, but usually because of a basic scientific empiricism combined with a non-Euclidean conception of logic and mathematics. They admit that ethical intuitionism has a considerable fidelity to the facts and phenomena of our ordinary moral consciousness and discourse, but regard it as untenable in the light of the findings of science and philosophy.

Of course, some American philosophers in our period have been intuitionists—some still are. Of these some are phenomenologists who came over from Europe: Dietrich von Hildebrand, Maximilian Beck, and Herbert Spiegelberg; others are Mary E. Clarke, T. E. Hill, and O. A. Johnson. Of these von Hildebrand is easily the most important; though his work can hardly be called an American contribution, it is interesting and good moral philosophy. Brand Blanshard was for a time an intuitionist, but then wrote relatively little in ethics, and has now changed his position to a kind of naturalism more consonant with his idealism in general philosophy. One interesting and able group of writers, following G. E. Moore with adaptations, adopted a hedonistic theory of value in combination with a utilitarian theory of obligation: William Savery, R. M. Blake, C. A. Baylis, and Lucius Garvin. With all due respect properly allocated, however, we cannot claim that American intuitionists of this century have made any contributions to moral philosophy comparable to those of British and German writers.

This is true even of W. M. Urban who was important in the development of the so-called theory of value and the value point of view in this country. Urban argued resolutely against naturalism with arguments akin to those of the British intuitionist, G. E. Moore, and also sought to meet the positivist attack based on the principle of verifiability. His own position was essentially intuitionistic, even though he declined to regard value or oughtness as a quality or relation. He took it to be an "objective," a *that* not a *what,* on the ground that a value judgment always claims it to be good or fitting *that* a certain object or act exist or be done, or *that* it have or be given a certain property. In other words, it was for him a kind of ultimate category coordinate with, but involving an inherent reference to, existence. Indeed, his most interesting suggestion, borrowed from Plato, was that Value or the Good or the Ought is "beyond Being" in such a way that metaphysics and even science are dependent on the theory of value. In this manner he proposed to keep the autonomy of ethics without divorcing it from the theory of being! Interesting as some of his ideas are, however, they have not had much effect on subsequent discussion, with the possible exception of the work of E. W. Hall.[1]

Like Urban, Hall is critical of many of the typical theses of the intuitionists, for example, that value is a quality, relation, or property of whatever kind, and that it has a priori connections with other properties, but he is still a quasi-intuitionist since he holds that value is an indefinable, objective, and cognizable something or other. Unlike Urban, Hall insists on the bifurcation of fact and value, which he thinks is established by the whole movement of modern science and thought. In fact, he remarks that recent writers who advocate the use of scientific method in ethics "are simply trying to modernize medievalism." For the rest he carefully explores the view about the nature of value that was suggested by Urban through the use of all the machinery of ideal languages, metalinguistics, and analysis that has been developed in our period. His conclusion is that value is a structure or form of unity different from but coordinate with, and analogous to, that of fact. For every actual or possible fact expressed by "X has P" there is a value expressed by "It is good (fitting, right, etc.) that X have P," and their structures are different, though both structures may be at least partially revealed by linguistic analysis. Judgments of fact are true or false, judgments of value are not, but are legitimate or nonlegitimate in an objective sense. Value is also cognized in a different way from fact; our knowledge of it comes initially not through the senses but through our attitudes or emotions, which Hall regards as cognitive. The technique for establishing the legitimacy of value judgments, however, is still to be worked out. This, according to Hall, is the agendum for our age.

This view, which is similar to that of the Austrian and German

[1] For works by Urban and Hall, see the bibliography. In general throughout this essay, when works of American authors are not cited in the text or footnotes, they may be found listed in the bibliography.

intuitionists, is intriguing, and one regrets that Hall was unable to elaborate it further;[2] at the same time I must confess that his rather exhausting exploration leaves me unconvinced. Perhaps this is the line that intuitionism must try to exploit today, instead of the more rationalistic one characteristic of earlier Anglo-Saxon intuitionists, but, in view of the fate of its Austro-German versions, one finds it hard to be optimistic about its possibilities, even with the help of new techniques.

Another valuable quasi-intuitionist exploration is made by Maurice Mandelbaum in *The Phenomenology of Moral Experience* (1955). Some of the Gestalt psychologists themselves wrote essays in ethics and value theory after coming to this country, for example, Max Wertheimer, Kurt Koffka, and Karl Duncker; and Wolfgang Köhler wrote a book called *The Place of Value in a World of Facts* (1938) in which, beginning with the vectorial experience of a visual Gestalt that "requires" a certain fulfilment, he seeks to show that requiredness is an objective phenomenon with a basis in fact, even though it is not reducible to fact. Mandelbaum writes as a phenomenologist influenced by the Gestalt psychologists, as well as by Max Scheler and von Hildebrand.[3] He contends that a phenomenological description of moral experience and judgment is not only legitimate but necessary as a basis for ethical theory, and criticizes recent British and American moral philosophy as linguistic and as not having an adequate descriptive basis of this kind. His phenomenological description of the various kinds of moral judgment is the most complete in recent English speaking philosophy, unless we count that of von Hildebrand; its only near rival is the rather different work of Eliseo Vivas in *The Moral Life and the Ethical Life* (1950). Mandelbaum disowns the attempt to present a normative ethics of his own; in fact, he argues that the search for a universally valid "contentual" standard must founder on the reef of ultimate moral disagreement. His own study he thinks of as "structural" or neutral. Its main findings are: (1) We experience certain actions as being required by or fitting in certain situations, and pred-

[2] It has been elaborated somewhat in Hall's later works and in E. M. Adams's book.
[3] See also S. E. Asch, *Social Psychology* (1952). Briefly, a phenomenologist is one who seeks to describe something, e.g., obligation or responsibility, *as it is experienced.*

icate this requiredness or fittingness of them in our judgments. Mandelbaum regards it as an indefinable "phenomenally objective relational characteristic," but as a natural or empirical one. (2) What is basic in our moral reasoning is the intuition of particular fittingnesses, not general principles or a consideration of consequences. (3) There are universally acknowledged principles of what constitutes a valid moral judgment, namely, the principles of the primacy of the facts, of universality, and of ultimacy; and through the use of them many, but not all, of our moral controversies can be resolved. Mandelbaum's book contains descriptive materials and conclusions that are relevant to any further study. At the same time it also shows the limits of the phenomenological method to which it confines itself, for it makes clear that a purely phenomenological approach cannot yield either a normative ethics or a full-fledged meta-ethics.

Some Thomist writers and natural law theorists speak as if they regard the basic principles of natural ethics as intuitive or self-evident, even if they do not subscribe in full to the intuitionist position as described above. Thus, in *Catholic Principles of Politics* (1940), J. A. Ryan and F. J. Boland define "the natural law" as "a necessary rule of action, determined by rational nature, imposed by God as author of nature, and perceived intuitively" (p. 4). Now all intuitionists believe that there is such a thing as natural (as versus revealed and human) law, though they believe this in a sense that involves separating value and fact, which Thomists refuse to do. In fact, an intuitionist might accept the definition quoted as an account of the nature of moral law. In general, however, the Thomist natural law theory seems to me to be closer to naturalism than to intuitionism.

Walter Lippmann in refurbishing the doctrine of natural law in *The Good Society* (1950) and *The Public Philosophy* (1955), has also spoken of certain intuitions or self-evident truths, such as the inviolability of the human person, as the rock upon which we may build our ethics and politics, just as our ancestors did. But his account of their nature, like those of our ancestors, is not very clear. He seems mainly concerned to hold that there are principles of the good society that are not private, relative, created, invented, or based on human volitions or wishes, but objective and public, capable of being "discovered by rational enquiry" and of being "developed and adapted and refined by rational discussion." This thesis, however, does not necessarily entail intuitionism in our sense, and it is in fact compatible with the empiricist theories next to be reviewed.

2

ETHICAL NATURALISM

*General account and remarks. Interest theories of value:
R. B. Perry; D. H. Parker. Affective theories. Natural
norms and natural law theories: S. C. Pepper; J. D. Wild; neo-
Thomism; F. S. C. Northrop. Other theories: Brand Blanshard; A. C. Garnett; W. T. Stace.*

By and large American philosophers of our age have been empiricists, in a broad sense at least, in general philosophy, and so
they have rejected the nonempirical or nonnatural concepts, properties, or "unique categorical features of reality," as well as the self-
evident truths, of Urban, Hall, and the intuitionists. Instead, many
of them have tried to exhibit ethical and value judgments as functions of empirical inquiry, conceived sometimes more and sometimes
less after the manner of scientific inquiry. With Dewey they tend
to think of this as the great problem of the modern period: the integration of ethics, without remainder, into the body of our empirical knowledge. This endeavor was not entirely new, but it was
bound to reappear in a relatively scientific age such as ours. Indeed, some of its proponents regard such a "reconstruction of
morals" as simply the culminating phase of the whole modern scientific movement. For such writers ethics and value theory are or
are to become scientific, not just in the wide older sense in which
any intellectual discipline is a science, but in the new narrower
sense in which psychology and the social sciences are trying to be
sciences and the natural sciences already are. Other writers like
D. H. Parker and J. D. Wild are not scientifically minded, but
even they regard ethics and value theory as empirical inquiries in
some sense.

Views that seek to integrate our beliefs about the principles and
values that should direct our action with our empirical knowledge
of the world in this thoroughgoing manner I shall label "ethical
empiricism." Ethical empiricism, in other words, holds that ethical

355

judgments are themselves empirical assertions or at least that they are, may, or should be grounded wholly in such assertions—in short that ethical judgments are without exception to be justified entirely by some kind of empirical inquiry. That is, what is being maintained is not merely that we should use experience or science to tell us how to apply or realize our principles and goals, but that we should take them as a basis for determining these goals or principles themselves—not merely that science and experience can tell us how to get where we are going but that they can tell us where to go. Hence ethical empiricism is sometimes disparagingly referred to as "scientistic." However, while some ethical empiricists do believe in the "omnicompetence" of science, natural or social, not all of them do. Some of them do not identify the appeal to experience on which ethics is to rest with the use of scientific method, and some of them even remain supernaturalists.

In the latter part of the nineteenth century such empiricist views were generally evolutionistic, but more recently they have not usually taken this particular cast. Their proponents do usually accept the evolutionary biology, of course, but it finds little direct expression in their theories of morality and value. In fact, there has been rather little "evolutionary ethics" in this country in our period; almost the only exceptions are E. G. Conklin's *Man, Real and Ideal* (1943), S. J. Holmes's *Life and Morals* (1948), and one line of thought in S. C. Pepper's books.

It will be convenient to distinguish two forms of ethical empiricism. The first, ethical naturalism, will be the subject of this and the following chapters, the second, pragmatism, will be covered in Chapter 4.

One way in which the integration of ethical and value judgments with those of another field may be accomplished is to argue that the characteristic terms appearing in such judgments, e.g., "good," "right," "obligation," can be defined by reference to the terms used in that other field. This is the method of what G. E. Moore called "naturalism." By ethical naturalism he meant (and I shall mean) any view that holds that ethical properties can be analyzed into or defined in terms of "natural" ones. Thus such views as the following are naturalistic in this sense:

(1) That "good" means "pleasant."

(2) That being good is the same thing as being desired.

(3) That "right" means "being conducive to the greatest general happiness."

(4) That to say "I ought to do A" is to say that A promotes the fulfillment of my potentialities.

There are difficulties about defining the distinction between natural and nonnatural properties that is employed in Moore's definition of "naturalism," and there have been various ways of stating the naturalistic position because of changing styles of analysis, but we may think of naturalism as saying roughly that all statements containing ethical terms can be translated into statements that do not contain any such terms and that are verifiable by empirical observation. If any definitions like those cited are satisfactory for all ethical terms, then such translations will be possible, and then ethical judgments will belong to psychology, sociology, or some similar empirical inquiry, and will be testable empirically. On this kind of view, in short, the logical condition of the desired scientific treatment of morality is the tenability of some such set of definitions as will make these translations possible.

It is important to realize that when the term "naturalism" is used in this way in ethical discussions it is being used in a special sense, namely, to stand for a certain kind of theory about the meaning and justification of ethical judgments. "Naturalism" in this sense is to be distinguished from "naturalism" in the wider philosophical sense in which naturalism is opposed to supernaturalism, for in the narrower ethical sense it is compatible with supernaturalism. A supernaturalist may perfectly well regard ethical terms as definable in terms of interests and their satisfaction, as F. R. Tennant and J. B. Pratt do. Thomism, so far as I can see, is a form of ethical naturalism. On the other hand, a naturalist in the wider sense need not be a naturalist in the ethical sense; he may be an intuitionist in ethics, as Moore is and as Russell once was, or he may be an emotivist, as A. J. Ayer and W. R. Dennes are.

Forms of naturalism in ethics will, of course, vary in accordance with the character of the definitions they propose. According to every form of naturalism, however, all ethical judgments will be susceptible of being proved true or false by the use of empirical evidence. Thus, if "X is good" means "X is pleasant" and "Y is right" means "Y is conducive to the greatest general good," then "X is good" can be verified by looking to see if X is pleasant and "Y is right" by looking to see if Y is conducive to the greatest general pleasure. But also, each kind of naturalism limits the range of the empirical evidence that is relevant to ethical judgment. Thus, given the definitions just suggested, only the evidence that will show that X is pleasant will be relevant to the judgment "X is good," and only the evidence that will show that Y will promote the greatest general happiness will be relevant to the judgment "Y is right." In general, each naturalistic definition says that a certain kind or range of evidence is logically necessary and sufficient to establish a certain class of ethical judgments, and that all other evidence is logically irrelevant. It also says, of course, that the ethical judgments in question can be proved true or false, regardless of our emotional attitudes or desires, just as judgments about size and shape may be, though not by the same sort of evidence.

It will at once be apparent that in an enterprise of this nature everything hangs on the correctness or acceptability of the claim that ethical terms and sentences can be defined or analyzed in some such manner as naturalists propose. Each naturalist rejects the specific definitions or translations proposed by the others, and antinaturalists reject them all, some of them even going so far as to assert that they need not be examined carefully and one at a time, as one might think, since it can be pretty readily seen or shown that no such definition or translation can possibly be satisfactory. Of this latter thesis, which so many seem to find obvious, I am by no means convinced. It depends on the possibility of finding a way of defining the distinctions between ethical and nonethical terms or statements, and between natural and nonnatural predicates or properties, and, so far as I can see, no one has yet found a way of doing this that does not either beg the question at issue or leave the distinction so vague as to render the desired sweeping conclusion uncertain.

One variety of this easy and almost a priori way of disposing of naturalism involves the contention that no ethical conclusion can be drawn from premises that are purely factual or nonethical. Value cannot be deduced from fact, it is averred, or Ought from Is.

The need for definitions of "ethical" and "factual" is here readily apparent. Even if we put the contention by saying that a conclusion involving the word "ought" cannot be logically deduced from premises, none of which contains this word, then, though it will be true, it will not serve to refute the naturalist. For he is not maintaining that such a deduction is possible; but only that "ought" can be defined in other terms. He is saying, not that "I ought to do X" can be inferred from "X is conducive to the greatest general balance of pleasure over pain" *without any further conditions,* but that the former can be derived from the latter *with the help of a definition* according to which the two have the same meaning. The definition he is offering may not be correct, but this cannot be shown by citing the dogma about Ought and Is, for *if* his definition is correct, then "ought"-statements *can* be derived from "is"-statements in the only sense in which he is concerned to hold that they can.

The moral is that the tenability of naturalism cannot be decided in advance, but must wait until its forms have been thoroughly reviewed. A so-called naturalist may offer his definitions merely as arbitrary stipulations about how he intends to use words like "good" and "right." Then, of course, he need not be taken very seriously. He may also, however, offer his definitions as formulations of what we all mean when we use those words, or as elucidations of the ways in which we ordinarily use them. Then his definitions are claimed to be descriptive of conventional or accepted usage, and must be taken seriously, for he may be right. But, thirdly, he may offer his definitions neither as arbitrary devices nor as descriptions of actual use, but as proposals about how the words in question should be used, and he may then offer us serious reasons for accepting his proposals. It makes a good deal of difference whether a naturalist takes the second or the third line when it comes to understanding what he is doing and deciding to agree with it or not.

Thus naturalism takes two main forms, depending on whether its definitions are to be taken as descriptions or as proposals. It also has different forms according to the content of the definitions offered. One kind of naturalism is the so-called interest theory, which seeks to define all ethical and value terms wholly by reference to interests or needs, their kinds, their objects, or their satisfactions. Of the large variety of possible views that can be called interest theories, several have been important in America in the last three decades.

For the most part, American interest theories have taken the form, not of mere moral philosophies or ethical theories, but of so-called theories of value. The idea of the theory of value originated in Europe, but became especially popular in America, and in 1932 Urban could remark that the notion of value had become central in present-day thought. This vogue is at least partly responsible for the present loose and widespread use in our culture and social sciences of such general terms as "value," "values," "valuations," "value systems," etc. It had, however, a serious motive, namely, to elaborate a set of terms and concepts that could be applied not only in ethics, but also in aesthetics, economics, and many other fields that seemed to have something in common. The "notion of value" seemed to many to provide a clue to the understanding of the unity and differences of a number of disciplines, many of them humanities, that appeared not to belong among the more purely descriptive or explanatory sciences.

The *summa*s of this new axiology are two works by R. B. Perry: *General Theory of Value* (1926) and *Realms of Value* (1954). Perry urges the need for a general theory of value along the lines I have indicated. He distinguishes between "description" and "criticism," where "criticism" includes all of the various kinds of appraisals or critical judgments that men pass on what goes on within or without them. Assuming that these kinds of critical judgments, for all their variety, involve a common concept or predicate, he goes on to assign to it the word "value" in "the generic sense," and then seeks to define it. Here he is not concerned to be describing ordinary usage faithfully, for he takes the term "value" to be a technical term to which it is desirable to "give" a meaning. Perry then proceeds to offer, not only definitions of its cognates, such as "valuable," "values," "disvalues," etc., but also of the more ordinary words that occur in the various *species* of critical judgments: "good," "bad," "better," "best," "beautiful," "morally good," "economic value," "right," "rights," "ought," "useful," "true," etc.

Even in defining these terms, however, he does not think of himself as simply clarifying ordinary usage, though he appeals to such usage when he can. He says he is providing a conceptual theory much as a scientist does, and his "hypothesis" is that all of the terms indicated can be satisfactorily defined in terms of interests, their objects, kinds, intensity, inclusiveness, and number. By an "interest" Perry means roughly any liking, disliking, desire, aversion, need, or preference—any favorable or unfavorable attitude toward an object. More behavioristically, an interest is *"a train of events determined by expectation of its outcome"* (*Realms of Value*, p. 3). Taking "interest" in this sense, Perry proposes his famous definition of "value": *"a thing—anything—has value, or is valuable, in the original and generic sense when it is the object of an interest—any interest"* (*Realms of Value*, pp. 2-3). To have positive value is to be an object of someone's (anyone's) favorable interest; to have negative value is to be an object of someone's unfavorable interest. Since a thing may be an object both of a favorable interest and of an unfavorable one, it may have both positive and negative value, or be both good and bad. This seems paradoxical, Perry admits, but is not really so, since any difficulty involved can be cleared up by seeing how the object compares with others in value, or whether its goodness outweighs its badness or not—that is, by inquiring into the number, intensity, and inclusiveness of the desires, aversions, and preferences directed at the object, at its consequences, or at alternative objects and their consequences.

Perrys aim is to interpret all of the more limited "critical" predicates as species or functions of value in his generic sense. Thus, to those already stated, he adds such definitions as the following:

(1) X is good = X has positive value.

(2) X is good in itself = X is an object of favorable interest for its own sake.

(3) X is the highest good = X is the object of an all-inclusive and harmonious system of interests.

(4) X is morally good = X is the object of interests harmoniously organized by reflective agreement.

(5) The moral good = the morally good life = harmonious happiness = a condition of harmonized positive interests.

(6) X is morally right = X is conducive to the moral good.
(7) X is morally obligatory = X is called for by the end of the moral good, that is, by harmonious happiness.
(8) X is beautiful = X has attributes of the class which commends itself to the aesthetic interest.

It will be noticed that these are all definitions in terms of interest in one way or another. Now, Perry does not conceive of them as private stipulations or as descriptions of conventional public usage, but as proposals about what we should understand by the terms defined. What then does he say in defense of his proposals? First he cites *linguistic* considerations where he can for whatever they are worth. Next he urges certain *formal* considerations, namely, the clarity, consistency, definiteness, tenability, and fruitfulness of the concepts employed. Primarily, however, he claims a kind of *empirical* validity for his definitions. He argues that these definitions are "real" or "descriptive" in the sense that they best reflect the nature and structure of the facts in the region of the world that our value terms roughly indicate, which, as he sees it, is the area of interests and their objects. His definitions, he insists, are hypotheses justified by their adequacy and correctness as a description of the data in this region.

Against all such naturalistic definitions, Moore, Urban, and others have used the well-known open question argument. Briefly, as applied to Perry's basic definition, this is the claim that we can significantly ask of an object of interest "But is it good?" [1] To this Perry replies, first, that the reason we can ask this significantly is that "good" has several senses, all allowed for and taken care of by his set of definitions; second, that no good definition keeps all of the associations of the original term; and, third, that the argument assumes incorrectly that a definition must simply transcribe ordinary meanings. This line of reply, also used by D. H. Parker and S. C. Pepper, seems to me to be good as far as it goes and to dispose of

---

[1] In general the argument is that, whatever predicate P one seeks to substitute for "good" or "right", one can always say sensibly "This has P, but is it good (right)?" and "This has P, but it is not good (right)." But one could not say such things sensibly if P can be substituted for "good" or "right." Therefore no definition of such terms can be correct. For Perry's reply I depend partly on his articles.

the usual simple forms of the argument in question, whatever one may think of subsequent restatements of it.

In the course of working out his general theory Perry makes an elaborate and careful study, in rather behavioristic terms, of interests and their objects, kinds, interrelations, genesis and mutations, and relation to cognition and to personality. This psychological analysis, further pursued by Pepper and E. C. Tolman, among others, must surely be counted as one of his contributions—so too must his applications of his general theory to morality, politics, law, economics, education, international relations, and "the present conflict of ideals," both in *Realms of Value* and in a series of more popular books on the intellectual problems of a democracy engaged in hot and cold war and of a world struggling to become one.

Perry's theory, as a look at his definitions makes clear, has the consequence of making critical judgments of any kind whatsoever verifiably true or false in the sense of agreement or disagreement with fact. As is his object, it converts criticism (that is, normative judgment of all kinds, ethical, aesthetic, etc.) into an empirical science that takes as its data the facts about human interests to which the definitions point. In fact, it has the effect, which Perry does not notice but would be the first to welcome, of turning "criticism" into a species of "description," "humanities" into "sciences." Whether this should be taken as a virtue or as a vice is one of the main questions of the entire discussion being reviewed in this study.

Perry's views, while influential, have been much criticized. The main difficulties are, perhaps, those that relate to his view that the moral good or the moral standard is the "harmonious happiness" of all. Here he seems to trade on a shift from a conception of the good as the *object* of interest to one of the good as the *satisfaction* of interest, even though he seeks to avoid this in his definition of "harmonious happiness" and sees clearly the distinction between the object and the satisfaction of an interest. More basic is the question whether an essentially utilitarian moral standard or first principle can be introduced in the form of a definition, as it is by Perry, and, if so, whether it can be "proved" in the purely intellectual way in which Perry tries to justify his definitions. His discussion on this point is interesting, but not entirely convincing. He insists that to say "The moral standard is harmonious happiness" is not to make

363

"a moral judgment in the sense of assigning such predicates as 'good,' 'right,' and 'ought,'" and that "moral theory [i.e., meta-ethics] . . . stands outside the whole circle of [moral] judgments, and makes non-moral statements about them." I am myself not persuaded that he is mistaken in this, but, after C. L. Stevenson, it can hardly be taken for granted, especially by one who is not merely elucidating ordinary verbal meanings.

Other so-called realists besides Perry have expounded forms of ethical naturalism in recent decades, for example, J. B. Pratt, A. C. Garnett, J. D. Wild, and the neo-Thomists. But some of the idealists have also been naturalists, namely D. H. Parker, W. T. Stace, and, lately, Brand Blanshard. Parker's approach, while empirical, is literary rather than scientific. But, like Perry, he is committed throughout to "the 'value' point of view in ethics" and argues for a teleological position that makes standards of right and wrong dependent on the values they promote. He defines value, however, as the *satisfaction* of desire rather than as its *object,* on the ground that an object of desire may turn out not to be good when it is attained. A satisfaction of desire can be bad, he allows, but only when it entails the frustration of other more basic or inclusive desires. One's most basic or inclusive desire is one's "life-plan" and one's final values and obligations are determined by it and are relative to it. One cannot and need not recognize any value or obligation that is not part of this life-plan, or that transcends oneself, not even those of morality. This view is worked out with a wealth of detail in *Human Values* (1931) and again in *The Philosophy of Value* (1957), but in the latter work, under the influence of Stevenson, it is combined with a noncognitivist theory of value and moral judgments as "volitional expressions."

A number of naturalists and other philosophers have been unhappy, as Parker was, with Perry's (and Dewey's) behaviorism in psychology. Some—for example, Stace, P. B. Rice, and H. D. Aiken —have also attacked the whole notion that value is to be defined in terms of interest, as it is by Perry and Parker. For the *interest* theory of value, Stace, Rice, and Aiken substitute the *affective* theory, which identifies intrinsic goodness with some affective tone or dimension of our experience such as pleasure, enjoyment, felt satisfactoriness, or happiness, and extrinsic value with the property of being conducive to experiences that have intrinsic value in this sense. Syntheses of the two theories have been proposed by Garnett and Blanshard. Some critics are also dissatisfied with the accounts of moral obligation provided by interest theories, feeling that they do not deal adequately with or provide an adequate basis for our obligations to others when these conflict with our own interests. This inadequacy is apparent on the surface of Parker's theory, they would say, since he admits or even insists that moral demands are not supreme and may be superseded by personal ones, but it is also present in Perry's view, since it is not clear that he can "prove" his first principle of the harmonious happiness of all as the moral end.

It is just at this juncture that S. C. Pepper makes his contribution to the discussion, for he carries the interest theory and behaviorism as far as possible, then finds an important place for introspection and affective values, and ends by maintaining that morality involves norms that transcend the purposes of individuals even though they are still natural, norms that are ultimately biological, cosmic, and evolutionary (*A Digest of Purposive Values*, 1947; *The Sources of Value*, 1958). Together with the work of Perry, his work represents most fully the development both of the theory of value and of ethical naturalism. In one aspect it is simply an elaborate and interesting psychological and sociological theory, based on Perry, Tolman, Freud, Lewin, Mead, Dewey, Lewis, and Darwin, but showing considerable originality. Pepper's aim here is to work out a comprehensive hypothesis about the main lines of relationship among the facts bearing on human decisions, since, as he holds, it is these facts that are pointed to by our common-sense use of value terms. His central thesis is that there are a number of dynamic agencies in man and nature which he calls "selective systems" or "natural norms," each of which governs and legislates over certain acts, enterprises, institutions, etc., selecting among them, imposing sanctions, and eliminating errors. These selective systems are "normative processes" but they are nevertheless natural facts that can be described empirically. Each individual interest is such a selective system. Others that are more inclusive but still personal are one's "life-space," "personality structure," and what G. H. Mead calls "roles." Still others that are transindividual are the social situation, the cultural pattern, and finally natural selection itself. Some of these selective systems govern and legislate over others; roughly, those last mentioned are supreme over those first mentioned. The "irrational conscience" that figures in many moral judgments is also a selective system, one that gets its "dynamics" partly from within the individual and partly from society and from the evolutionary impetus itself.

Given all this, which he regards as purely descriptive and empirically verifiable, Pepper goes on to define or redefine such terms as "value," "good," "right," "ought," etc. by reference to what is sanctioned or rejected by some selective system or other. And he distinguishes different kinds or levels of values and obligations for each of the various selective systems, e.g., affective, conative, prudential, character, social, and survival values and obligations. For him, therefore, the different natural norms provide the justification of the different judgments of obligation and value we may make; the final appeal is to the more authoritative ones, which for Pepper are over-individual, as most nonnaturalists also hold moral norms to be.

In thus linking moral norms with over-individual demands Pepper seems to me to be on the right track, though he jeopardizes the autonomy of the moral individual (which he wishes to preserve) by making the evolutionary process the final tribunal. Many philosophers will regard his proposals for redefining our ethical terms as unsatisfactory, but since his definitions are offered as proposals that best reflect the contours of empirical facts, they cannot be refuted merely by appeals to ordinary usage or to Moore's open question argument. The crucial question for Pepper is his conception of a "natural norm," a factual process that is at once natural and normative. The notion of something natural that somehow provides a norm is an old one, and Pepper does about as well with it as anyone has, but it is fraught with familiar difficulties that he has not clearly obviated.

Pepper's phrase "natural norms" suggests another that has experienced a revived use in our period, namely, "natural law," the central term in Thomist philosophical ethics and in a good deal of recent legal and political philosophy. Certainly Pepper's natural norms represent natural laws or tendencies of a sort; moreover they represent tendencies that in some sense actually control behavior yet

366

are not always actually followed—else there would be no "trials" that turn out to be "errors"—and in both respects this difficult concept resembles that of Thomas Aquinas. In fact, it seems to me that Thomist ethics, or at least the natural law doctrine as it is there expressed, is a form of ethical naturalism much like Pepper's, though with God's eternal law taking the place of or legislating over that of natural selection. This is not true of von Hildebrand's position, for he trenchantly attacks the Thomist view from the standpoint of a phenomenological intuitionism. But it does seem to be true of Wild's neo-Thomist but non-Catholic philosophy of natural law in *Plato's Modern Enemies and the Theory of Natural Law* (1953). Wild prefers to think of his ethics as metaphysical or ontological rather than as naturalistic or scientific, but he defines "value" and "obligation" in terms that are broadly empirical. Value is what fulfills the tendencies that belong to a thing's nature. To have an obligation is to recognize that a certain action is required for the completion of one's nature. There seems to be very little difference here between Wild's "active tendency" as an ontological principle and Pepper's "selective system" as a dynamic agency. In these days when even the metaphysicians are claiming to be empirical it is difficult to draw a line between metaphysical ethics and ethical naturalism, if indeed there is one. In any case, Wild's book represents a valiant and suggestive attempt to establish nature as an ethical norm, partly because it restates the Thomist position in the light of the contemporary discussion we are reviewing, something that Catholic writers seldom try seriously to do.

I need not here review further the literature of recent Thomist moral and social philosophy,[2] since its basic doctrines are old and familiar, even though they have been given a considerable development lately and have attained some vogue outside of Catholic circles. Its most important spokesman for American readers has been Jacques Maritain, who may only doubtfully be thought of as an American philosopher, coming to this country as he did late in life after his main views had already been determined.

All such conceptions of natural laws or norms have been subject to a number of criticisms, not only from intuitionists and emotivists,

---

[2] See, e.g., V. J. Bourke, *Ethics* (1951), and J. A. Ryan and F. J. Boland, *Catholic Principles of Politics* (1940).

but also from other naturalists. The conception of a kind of normative fact is an intriguing one but is particularly difficult to make clear and plausible, whether in empirical, ontological, or even intuitionist terms, and many, among them Ernest Nagel, E. W. Hall, and Arnold Brecht, have attacked it or rejected it out of hand. A more sympathetic naturalistic critic is F. S. C. Northrop, in *The Complexity of Legal and Ethical Experience* (1959). "Natural law ethics," he writes, "is frequently described as the thesis that conduct and its fruits are good when they express 'man's essential nature.' Put in this way, a difficulty arises. Since man's essential nature is what it is, how can man . . . avoid expressing [his] essential nature?" (p. 256). Northrop then rejects the Wild-Thomist move to meet this difficulty by resorting to a "metaphysics of becoming in which potential entities are being modified by their ideal final causes" (p. 253), and indeed it is hard to see how this appeal to ontology does anything but generalize the difficulty. But he does not repudiate the natural law theory; he insists that there is a "standard, objectively determinable, and hence an 'is,' other than the positive and the living law" (p. 155), against which the goodness and badness of these, and of all conduct and institutions can be measured. Instead, he suggests a widened conception of the natural law theory, intended to cover all those who have believed in the existence of such a standard (except the intuitionists). Natural law is simply "the inner order of nature [including man] as revealed by natural science. . . . Natural law [ethics and] jurisprudence is the thesis that scientifically verified theory of the 'is' of first-order facts [i.e., raw data, antecedent to all theory and all cultures] provides the cognitive standard for measuring the goodness or badness of second-order artifacts [i.e., behavior, institutions, and so forth]" (p. 255).

What Northrop goes on to say is interesting, but he does little to show just how we may go about using scientifically verified theory as a basis for action and judgment, except to suggest some vague definitions of "good" and "ought" in terms of such theory. The example of Northrop makes clear that there is a sense in which any ethical naturalist or empiricist affirms a natural law theory, since he holds that all value and ethical judgments about acts, objects, or institutions are cognitive and empirically verifiable, at least in principle, by a study of man and the world. In a somewhat different sense, intuitionists also subscribe to a natural law theory, for they too believe that there is a "higher law" above human conventions and institutions that is true and can be known by man's natural faculties apart from divine grace or revelation. In fact, if by a "natural law" we mean only a standard that does not depend on authority or revelation or custom, and that serves as a basis for deciding what to do and for judging human institutions, then even an emotivist can believe in natural laws and natural rights; he may even accept the principle that men have certain universal rights and duties by virtue of their very natures. All he need deny is that such principles themselves somehow represent or correspond to facts about the world; and even he may still maintain that they may in a sense be supported by such facts. The point is that "the theory of natural law" contains a number of strains of thought that are not always carefully distinguished, so that its "proponents" and its "enemies" can be on the same side of the fence on some issues while being opposed on others. He who is not for it is, no doubt, against it, but "it" can be several different things. This is often forgotten in the sound and fury of recent discussions.

Well, I have moved from interest theories of value in the strict sense to related theories that go beyond these either by recognizing certain transindividual values and norms as Pepper does or by defining value and obligation in terms of human needs, potencies, or tendencies as Wild does. In *Reason and Goodness* (1961), after an articulate and searching review of most of them and indeed of most of the views yet to be covered here (as well as those of previous centuries), Brand Blanshard offers his own "way out" of "the impasse in ethics." The good, he maintains, is what fulfills impulse, drive, or need and in doing so gives pleasure or satisfaction. The right is dependent on the good; it is what tends to bring into being as much good experience as any alternative action, not just for oneself but for all men. Since Blanshard regards these statements as definitions, his position is a kind of naturalism; he does insist that the good and the right cannot be determined by an empirical study of what men actually desire at the time, but presumably does not mean to deny that any judgment about what will fulfill or satisfy must rest on and ultimately be verified by experience of some sort.

The work of A. C. Garnett and W. T. Stace deserves comment

here, albeit brief. For the lay reader without background their books are the clearest and most readable of all those noted in this essay. Both men are naturalists in ethics, defining all ethical terms by reference to psychological concepts. They identify the good with happiness, satisfactory life, or the expression of human nature, and obligation with what is required for the realization of one's own good. Yet they are utilitarians in their view of the standard or end of moral conduct. What one ought to do, according to them, is what will promote the welfare of all, but the reason one should do this is that it will most fully realize one's own potentialities and happiness. On such empirical grounds Garnett and Stace seek to establish both the Christian ethic and the Greek appeal to reason, as well as the democracy that is their offspring.

There is a kind of ethical egoism in the thinking of Garnett and Stace, since they rest the moral obligatoriness of the utilitarian principle on the fact that acting on it is conducive to the development or happiness of the individual. But it is an egoism that depends on the claim that he who loses his life for the sake of his neighbor shall gain it after all—a claim that is also made by Dewey and Niebuhr. A more thorough form of ethical egoism that does not make the general welfare even the *criterion* of morality, let alone its *ground,* is, of course, possible, but it has not been prominent in recent years.[3]

About the ethical theories of Garnett and Stace, as well as those of Parker and Wild—that is, about all theories that take the good of the individual either as the standard of morality or as the basis on which to establish the general welfare as the standard of morality—one is impelled to ask the question "Has an individual no moral obligation to others except insofar as his own good is promoted?" To answer in the negative, as such theories do, seems to me paradoxical, even when the answer is abetted by the contention that we are "social animals," are "made for society," or have an altruistic streak in our nature, or that we are so made that we shall "gain" our lives if and only if we first "lose" them. Here Blanshard, Perry, Pepper, and other writers yet to be discussed, appear to be closer to the truth.

[3] But see the writings of D. C. Williams and Gardner Williams in the bibliography.

≈§ 3 §≈

MORE NATURALISMS

Approval theories: F. C. Sharp. Ideal observer theories: Roderick Firth. R. B. Brandt.

A point of view from which criticisms of the above forms of ethical naturalism (and some other theories) may be developed is represented by at least some species of the second general type of naturalism that has been prevalent in the period from 1930 to 1960. So far I have covered naturalisms that define ethical terms by reference to such concepts as interests, needs, drives, tendencies, capacities, the urge to self-realization, etc. (except for Pepper's notion of over-individual dynamic agencies as determinants of norms and values). Naturalistic theories of the "approval" or "spectator" type are theories that define ethical concepts in terms of "approval." Approval is not thought of as just any favorable feeling or attitude but as one of a somewhat special kind, one in which we observe and pass judgment on actions and persons and the desires and needs that motivate them.

The authors of such theories stand more or less in the tradition of Francis Hutcheson, David Hume, and Adam Smith, or what used to be called the "ethics of sentiment," but, while these earlier writers seem to me to be emotivists, the present authors are or seem to mean to be naturalists, though they are not always clear on this point. I shall therefore interpret them all as holding that ethical judgments are empirical *assertions about* emotions or attitudes of approval, not mere *expressions* of such emotions or attitudes. In any case, they agree with their predecessors and with the interest theorists in holding that ethical predicates do not stand for intrinsic properties of actions or things but at most for some relation they have to human or other beings—in this case for the fact that they are or would be approved by the speaker or by some actual or hypothetical observer or group of observers.

The "approval" type of naturalism can take a number of forms, not all of which need be classified, for its recent American proponents have tended to advocate only one form of it—the form that defines the right and the good, not by reference to the *de facto* approvals of individuals or societies, but in terms of some kind of reflective and at least partly hypothetical desire or approval. The only fully worked out view of this kind (if we assume that A. K. Rogers' view is of a kind to be described later) is that of F. C. Sharp, an unexciting but able and solid moral philosopher, rather more practical and empirical than most, who deserves more attention than he now receives. In *Ethics* (1928) he begins by distinguishing moral judgments about right and wrong from judgments about what is good and what is bad in a nonmoral sense, or in short the right from the good. Then he takes up the right. After an interesting study of our actual moral approvals and disapprovals, he concludes that they are all teleological, that they have two sources, benevolence and malevolence, and hence that they are rooted not in reason but in sentiment. From this we might expect him to infer that moral judgments are simply *expressions* of these sentiments. Instead, since he offers a definition of "right," he seems to construe moral judgments as statements that assert something true or false. A right volition, he says, may be defined as one which I desire should govern the actions of all men in the situation in question, when I take an impersonal point of view, i.e., when I have reduced my desires concerning volitions to a consistent system. Sharp then argues that the kind of volition that we desire should govern men's actions, when we take this point of view, is the kind that aims at bringing into existence the greatest amount of good attainable under the circumstances for all concerned. Hence he concludes that the true or valid standard of morality is the utilitarian principle.

Coming thus to the question of the good, Sharp contends that the hedonists are right in taking pleasure to be the criterion or standard of goodness. But he does not define "good" in terms of pleasure. The definition of "intrinsic goodness," he says, is what we desire for its own sake when we reflect in a cool hour. Pleasure is the good only because it is what we then desire.

Sharp's kind of subjectivism allows him to claim a certain objectivity for moral judgments. To say that an action is right is to say that one approves it when one is reflective, impartial, and objective. Since he maintains that we will all approve of what promotes the general happiness when we are reflective, impartial, and objective, he can even claim to find that this is a universally valid standard. But still, whether he intends this or not, he keeps one element in the extreme subjectivist position, namely, that "X is right" entails only that the speaker approves it, and makes no claim that others do or that anyone who reflects impartially and with a knowledge of the relevant facts will also approve. This brings us to theories of the "ideal spectator" type, which have been revived in a naturalistic form, though not fully worked out, by Roderick Firth and R. B. Brandt.

Firth correctly points out that ideal observer theories have been neglected in this century. He also notes that Sharp's analysis, while it is dispositional, relational, objectivist, and empirical, still contains the residual relativism just mentioned. He then proposes to give a somewhat similar analysis that is absolutist and not relativist. Roughly, this analysis is that "X is right" means that if there were an ideal observer, he would have a certain emotion or experience (e.g., feel approval) on contemplating X. Firth defines an ideal observer as one who is omniscient, omnipercipient, disinterested, dispassionate, and consistent, but otherwise normal. Ethical judgments are absolute because they involve no reference to any particular person, society, place, or time; objective because they do not entail the existence of any actual observers; empirical because the concepts involved are similar to dispositional, empirical concepts in the natural sciences; true or false because it is either true or false that an ideal observer would have a certain kind of experience if he were to observe the object or act in question. What kind of experience? The kind of moral experience that we take to be evidence, under ideal conditions, for the truth of our ethical judgments. By finding that we have such moral experiences when we approximate ideal conditions, we verify the claim that an ideal observer would have them, and so verify our ethical judgments empirically.

In 1941 Brandt advocated an emotive theory of judgments of moral worth, but since then he has been its most devoted (and impartial) critic. In "The Status of Empirical Assertion Theories in Ethics," published in 1952, the same year in which Firth's

"Ethical Absolutism and the Ideal Observer" appeared, Brandt makes a stout defense of empirical assertion theories in ethics against the arguments of noncognitivists, appealing to general English usage, as he takes them to be doing. The particular naturalistic theory that he has primarily in mind as the most tenable is the "Ideal-type Attitudinal" theory. In a later article, "The Definition of an 'Ideal Observer' Theory in Ethics," he again stresses the virtues of such theories, but argues that a relativistic form of the ideal observer analysis like that of Sharp is preferable to Firth's absolutistic one, appealing to ethnological and psychological evidence as well as to correct English usage. In his book *Ethical Theory* (1959), which has useful chapters on anthropological studies relating to ethics, Brandt's attitude toward the ideal observer theory is tentative but critical. He thinks it the most plausible of all the historic forms of naturalism, but sees "difficulties of detail" in it, and denies that it is tenable as an account of what everyone means who uses the language correctly. Among the different forms of the theory he favors a modified relativistic one like Sharp's. On the whole, however, he feels that a new and somewhat different form of naturalism is more convincing, and he presents this theory after sketching a view of the justification of ethical beliefs which he believes many or most people either do accept or would accept on having it explained to them.

This theory of justification runs as follows. We justify particular moral judgments to some extent by subsuming them under rules or principles. But principles may themselves be imprecise, conflicting, and in need of revision or even abandonment. Something more must come in to supplement our principles, and to help us in filling them out, weighing them, or correcting them. This something else, Brandt suggests, must be our moral feelings or attitudes. To serve this purpose, however, these feelings or attitudes must be "qualified"; they must be informed, impartial, not due to abnormal states of mind, and compatible with a consistent set of principles that is not too complex. An ethical judgment is justified, then, if and only if it passes the test of an appeal to our (i.e., one's own) moral attitudes thus qualified. Brandt calls this the Qualified Attitude Method of Justification.

This method, Brandt points out, is entailed by the ideal observer theory, but it is also compatible with certain other kinds of view. His own proposed theory is that "X has ethical property E" means "E-corresponding attitudes toward X satisfy all the conditions that would be set, as a general policy, for the endorsement of attitudes governing or appraising choice or actions, by anyone who was intelligent and factually informed and had thought through the problems of the possible different general policies for the endorsement of such attitudes." This theory, he says, is properly classified as naturalistic but he prefers to call it "quasi-naturalist," because it does not require that the conditions to be met be empirical; presumably, however, it could be made wholly naturalistic by adding this requirement.

It seems to me that Brandt's theory of the meaning of "right," etc., as just stated, is still essentially a form of the ideal observer theory and not really a new position. As for the theory of justification that he suggests, I can only say that we do not seem to look to our moral feelings in order to determine what is right but to the facts about the situation and about the actions possible in it. Otherwise, like Brandt and Firth, I find a naturalism of the "approval" type more plausible, at least as an account of strictly moral judgments, than any other. Among other things, as Brandt points out, it does not make apparently substantive ethical principles true by definition, as other forms of naturalism seem to, and so it sidesteps this charge of Moore and his followers. But I find even more plausible a noncognitivist view that says something like this: moral judgments are *expressions* of attitudes taken when one tries to take the point of view of some such "ideal" or "qualified" observer with respect to one's own or other people's actions, and not *assertions* that such observers do or would have certain attitudes. Indeed, Brandt himself concludes his discussion by admitting that he sees "nothing to choose" between his quasi-naturalist analysis of ethical terms and this noncognitivist account, but expressing his preference for the former.

In any case it is clear that such theories as those just reviewed do make it possible for one to say that, even if a certain kind of life will satisfy an individual's life-plan or complete his nature or realize his self or his potentialities, it may still be wrong for him to live that way. To be able to say this seems to me to be one of the

375

desiderata of moral theory, and it is not possible for some of the views studied earlier or still to be studied. An ideal or qualified observer, however, or even oneself when one tries to take such an observer's point of view, may well come to the conclusion that one's way of life and the conduct it dictates are simply bad or wrong. Society must insist that this is so if in its corporate capacity it is to claim that it is ever morally justified in punishing an individual who is merely living out his nature and its needs.

৵ঌ 4 ৡ৵

PRAGMATIC ETHICS

*Dewey's form of ethical empiricism. Pragmatic naturalists
and noncognitivists. Sidney Hook. C. I. Lewis.*

Pragmatism has been said to be the characteristic American philosophy and America's only contribution to philosophy. This judgment is not true without qualification, but pragmatic ethics does
have a distinctive flavor, at least in the writings of Dewey and his
followers, that must be appreciated if the development of ethical
theory is to be understood. And it does represent an American contribution. It will appear that the ethical and value theories of
those who are pragmatists in general philosophy do not all follow
the line of ethical empiricism. Even so, it is best to consider them
all together, for only then can we see what pragmatism in general
has had to say about ethics. We must begin, of course, with John
Dewey, who was still writing actively and acutely during much
of the past three decades.

The general nature of Dewey's program may be described thus:
he stands for an experimentalist or instrumentalist conception of
inquiry and knowledge in a naturalistic framework that he takes
as established; accordingly he proposes to reconstruct philosophy in
such a way to make it practical, that is, he roughly identifies it
with ethics or value theory; and he proposes also to reconstruct
ethics and value theory completely along experimentalist and, in
the broad sense, naturalistic lines. This means, for him, that all
ethical and value judgments, without exception, are to be put on
a scientific footing. Not only are they to be put on an empirical
basis, as earlier empiricists have advocated; they are to be put on
an experimentalist basis. They are to be subjected to experimental
verification through being acted on so that one may see what consequences are entailed by so doing, and whether the problem in
hand is solved. No genuine valuation, on Dewey's program, is to
be verifiable simply by looking to see if the object or action is de-

377

sired, pleasant, or satisfying, as other empirical theories of value have allowed, or by looking to custom, authority, revelation, ontology, etc., as so many other views have insisted. Every judgment is to be made on the basis of the best available knowledge from the experimental sciences, and is to be regarded as corrigible in the light of further knowledge from such sources.

Now, anyone can allow or even insist on "the use of science in ethics" as a guide in the application of basic principles or in the realization of assumed ends, without allowing that the basic principles or value judgments are themselves empirically justifiable. But Dewey's position is that even our most basic principles and judgments about ends are not to be taken as ultimate, fixed, arbitrary, irrational, or self-evident; they too can and should be construed as rooted in and justifiable by experience organized scientifically. How then can he make out his case? Many would say a priori that he cannot do so at all, since no normative premise can be derived from such factual judgments as experience can verify. One answer is that principles containing "ought" or "good" *can* be derived from factual ones *if* "good" and "ought" can be defined by reference to the terms composing these factual statements. The point is that Dewey can make his case if he can give us defensible naturalistic definitions of "value," "right," "ought," etc., for such definitions would have exactly the consequence he desires. But does Dewey try to make his case in this way? The answer is by no means clear, as P. B. Rice has pointed out. Dewey is, of course, a naturalist in general philosophy; the question is whether he is one in ethics in the narrower sense. Most interpreters seem to have thought so. It must be noted, however, that the fact that Dewey wishes to provide valuations with a scientific underpinning does not by itself make him a naturalist. One might hold that ethical judgments are expressions of attitude, as an emotivist does, and yet insist that our attitudes are rooted in belief and that these beliefs may and should be based on science. One may distinguish between evaluations (or appraisals) and statements (or descriptions) and yet accept Dewey's claim that scientific method is as available for the control of the one as it is for the control of the other.

How then are we to construe Dewey's proposal that ethics be wholly based on science? Is it to be conceived naturalistically, as a proposal to take ethical judgments as equivalent to scientific statements of a certain kind, or more noncognitivistically, as a proposal to identify them with expressions of attitude that are rooted in empirical knowledge of a scientific sort? Some passages and discussions in Dewey seem to require the one interpretation, some the other. For example, in Chapter X of *The Quest for Certainty* (1929) we read some sentences which have largely determined the interpretation of Dewey as a naturalist:

> *Judgments about values are judgments about the conditions and the results of experienced objects.* . . . To call an object a value is to assert that it satisfies or fulfills certain conditions. . . . It involves a prediction. . . . Values . . . may be connected inherently with liking, and yet not with *every* liking but only those that judgment has approved, after examination of the relations upon which the object liked depends [pp. 260-65].

The last sentence is somewhat ambiguous on the point at issue but otherwise this quotation seems to say that "X is good" means "X fulfills certain conditions (not specified)" or "X is liked after examination of its conditions and results." These sentences were written before noncognitive theories became prominent, but even in 1944 Dewey wrote an article, "Some Questions About Value," which invites a naturalistic interpretation. On the whole, however, later writings like *Theory of Valuation* (1939) suggest a somewhat different view, for in them he seems to say that a valuation proper, being practical, is not identical with any scientific proposition such as may be the conclusion of a theoretical inquiry. Most interesting in this connection is an article that appeared in the *Journal of Philosophy,* XLII (1945), "Ethical Subject Matter and Language," in which Dewey both commends and criticizes the emotivist C. L. Stevenson. Here Dewey distinguishes between the content or subject matter of ethical sentences and their function, office, or purpose. He insists against Stevenson that the content of an ethical sentence, the means by which it accomplishes its purpose, must be wholly cognitive and rational if the sentence is "to possess distinctively and genuinely *ethical* properties" (p. 709). In particular, because of its purpose, the content of such a sentence must consist of facts about human emotions, interests, satisfactions, etc. So far Dewey seems to be a naturalist. But he agrees with

379

Stevenson that the purpose of ethical sentences is directive, normative, practical, or prescriptive in a way in which that of scientific ones (as such) is not. "In [this] sense . . . that moral and scientific issues differ is not just to be admitted . . . , but is to be insisted upon as characteristic of ethical sentences *qua* ethical" (p. 701). Accordingly, Dewey concludes his paper by saying:

> Whatever I have said about "will be," or of a "predictive sort," is of the same kind as what I have said, in connection with evaluations, about what *has* been and what is *now* going on; that is, it is concerned exclusively with giving reasons or grounds, of the matter-of-fact sort . . . for taking a specific ground about some *to be* in the sense of what *should* be done. . . . *Evaluative* statements [advise and recommend]. But it is morally necessary to state grounds or reasons for the course advised and recommended. These consist of matter-of-fact sentences reporting what has been and now is, as conditions, and of estimates of consequences that will ensue if certain of them are used as means [p. 711].

This seems to mean that evaluations are not themselves assertions or predictions about conditions and consequences, but are or should be prescriptions or recommendations for action based on such assertions or predictions. Then the only real difference between Dewey and Stevenson would concern the question whether nonscientific or nonrational means can or may be used to implement prescriptions and recommendations. (Dewey would admit that they can be and have been, but insist that they should not be, in fact, cannot be, if our approach is genuinely ethical or evaluative.) And then Dewey's apparently naturalistic view of the "content" of evaluations is simply a claim that they must be rooted in scientific judgments of certain kinds, not a claim that they are identical with such judgments.

This interpretation of Dewey fits in with what Sidney Hook and others have been saying in defending him against Stevenson, White, and other critics. On this view Dewey's account of what happens or should happen when one makes a proper value judgment will run as follows. One is in a problematic situation that contains unsatisfied interests and needs and hence calls for intelligent action. Factual knowledge, preferably scientific, is brought to bear, including predictions like "Such and such actions will have such and such effects on the interests and needs involved." Hook says that then this factual knowledge, which is not normative in itself, becomes normative because of the demands of the situation. But the main point is that the valuation, "So and so should be done or is the best thing to do," is not just a repetition of this factual knowledge. It is a demand of the situation (i.e., of the interests and needs involved) in the light of the relevant facts. It is generated by our conative natures as illuminated by organized empirical knowledge, and *is* a valuation only because it is so generated *and* so illumined.

Thus we return to the question "How can Dewey rest the basic ends and norms of ethics on experience and science?" We saw that his program can be carried out if he can provide us with some such definitions as are suggested by the passages in *The Quest for Certainty,* provided of course that he can also show these definitions themselves to be somehow amenable to and called for by the facts of experience. But if he is holding that our most basic value judgments and norms (perhaps even our "definitions") are prescriptions or recommendations rooted in our interests and needs, as he is on the alternative interpretation proposed as his final view, then how are they corrigible in the light of experience? In general the answer would be that they are thus corrigible because our attitudes, which they incorporate, are or may be formed by what we believe about the world and especially about what we find in experience to be satisfying, all things considered. When our attitudes and the evaluations they engender are based on correct information on such matters they are justified or well-grounded; where they are not, experience and science may and should enforce a revision in our attitudes and so in our evaluations. This general answer applies to both of the two kinds of evaluations that Dewey sometimes distinguishes—judgments about what is good and judgments about what is right or obligatory—though in somewhat different ways. In both cases the evaluation must rest on empirical inquiry into the conditions and results of different courses of action.

But, it will be replied, this inquiry must be guided by some basic judgments about what is good and by some basic principles about whose good ought to be considered and promoted. This is true. The question is whether Dewey must regard such value judgments and moral principles as either arbitrary or a priori and not as hy-

WILLIAM K. FRANKENA

potheses amenable to correction in the light of experience. Consider such judgments as "Pleasure is the good" and "Growth is the end." Dewey holds that they are corrigible in the light of knowledge and reflection, and in this light he rejects the former and accepts the latter, both tentatively. The point is that, on the interpretation suggested above, even such "criteria" of goodness will be in principle subject to revision. They are (or should be) evaluational positions taken on the basis of reflective experience, and may turn out upon further experience and consideration not to be satisfactory after all (at least not unless we revise our conception of pleasure or growth). Even if we propose one of them as the "definition" of good, Dewey could plausibly argue that this definition, like all definitions, must itself be responsive to experience and hence open to correction.

More crucial, to my mind, is the question about the status of principles about whose good is to be considered. It is not difficult to see how my attitudes and so my value judgments and principles, even the basic ones, may be shaped by my beliefs and knowledge about the consequences for my own life and growth of what I do or of what goes on about me. But is it their bearing on my own life and growth that is to be my standard for judging them? A. C. Garnett interprets Dewey as thinking so, but it seems to me more plausible to read him as believing that the moral standard of judgment is to judge in terms of conduciveness to the general welfare, to the growth of everyone alike. Then all lesser judgments about what is right, and even judgments about what is good on the whole, must for Dewey be testable by looking to see what promotes "the well-being of all concerned." But what about this principle itself? It is true, as Dewey points out, that any conception of what well-being, individual or general, consists in must be regarded as subject to revision in the light of experience, but what about the principle that we *are to* promote the general well-being, and to find our own well-being in so doing, on which Dewey so much insists? This seems to be presupposed in the verification of all other moral judgments and evaluations. How is *it* to be "tested" by experience? It must, on our present interpretation of Dewey, be "justified" to my conative nature by a full knowledge of the facts. Yes, but which facts count as justifying a basic moral principle—

facts about its bearing on my life and growth or facts about its bearing on the general life and growth? If we say the latter, we are in a circle, if the former we have a kind of egoism after all.

At this point Dewey would probably remind us of the artificiality of separating the facts bearing on my life and growth from those bearing on the general well-being, for this is one of his favorite themes, even if it does not show why an individual should be any more interested in society than he already and inevitably is. Dewey has, however, another way of avoiding the dilemma. The question is about the status of the utilitarian principle "I ought to promote the well-being of all concerned." For Dewey this either asserts that I will choose or approve of promoting the general well-being after reflection on the relevant consequences of my choice (on the naturalistic interpretation) or it expresses a favorable attitude toward it based on such reflection (on our preferred interpretation). In either case it will be empirically grounded, though in different ways. No circle is involved, nor is any egoism, since no limit is placed on what Mill calls the "considerations capable of determining the intellect to give or withhold its assent." We might ask here if there must not be some limit on the considerations that are relevant if the doctrine assented to is properly to be called *moral*, but we must admit that, if Dewey's account of the nature of a valuation (whether naturalistic or not) is acceptable, then he can show how even the most basic of our value judgments and ethical principles may be placed on a scientific footing.

It seems clear, however, that Dewey is assuming here and elsewhere in his thinking, not only "a systematic over-optimism about human *willingness* to follow the lead of intelligence," as Hook points out, but also, to use Dewey's own words, that intelligence (i.e., applied scientific knowledge) will lead human individuals to take as their supreme interest "the enrichment of the lives of all," since it will bring them to see that "the final happiness of an individual resides in the supremacy of [such] interests." [1] In a sense his whole program for ethics and politics depends on these assumptions, as Niebuhr and other critics of liberal secular thought are constantly remarking. M. G. White and Charles Frankel have shown that something can be said in defense of "modern" or

[1] John Dewey and J. H. Tufts, *Ethics,* rev. ed. (1932), p. 335.

Deweyan man, and it does not seem to me just to label Dewey's beliefs as complacent and superficial, if "touching," as Niebuhr does, but surely they cannot today be simply taken for granted. There are important psychological questions here that bear on the whole enterprise of ethical empiricism (except for such theories as were dealt with in Chapter IV), and, while Niebuhrish answers to them may not be correct, they must be taken more seriously by moral philosophers than they have been.

At the same time, I do not believe that Dewey can be refuted, as many seem to think, simply by arguing that science has already been adequately tried as a guide to life and pointing to what we have had: Hitler, the atom bomb, a mass media culture, the organization man, and all that. Much of what we have had has involved a considerable application of science, but the fact that it has been wanting or worse does not prove that human conduct needs some guide other than human nature and science. A Deweyan may well reply that our troubles are due to a defect, not an excess, of science and enlightenment—that we have not yet really tried to live our whole lives, all of us, in the light of science, and that our science in any case still has much to learn. He might also maintain, with much plausibility, that nothing else has stood mankind to better avail. Perhaps science cannot save us, but this cannot be shown by such an easy appeal to recent history as is often made by otherwise serious writers.

Much more might be said about Dewey's ethics, politics, and social philosophy, since they represent a whole way of life that is conceived as an alternative to all forms of supernaturalism, authoritarianism, and totalitarianism, as well as to any other isms that decline to base all belief and action on scientifically enlightened intelligence. One further point is needed to supplement what has been said about Dewey's "reconstruction in moral conceptions." My account thus far has stressed his belief that ethical conclusions may somehow be based on those of science. This is, however, not the only way in which Dewey and his followers have sought to derive an ethics from science. He and others, not all of them his followers, have often tried to show that an ethics is involved in the very method and spirit of science, independently of any conclusions to which science may come. Devotion to truth, impartiality, freedom of inquiry, tolerance, respect, sense of dignity, integrity, and awareness of fallibility, they say, are virtues that are inherent in scientific inquiry and that must be present in a society of scientists. Without them science would languish and die. Extended, they may become the virtues of human society as a whole in all of its activities. Such a society, in fact, is what is meant by democracy, and a society in which science is full and free must be a democratic one. Science is not only a tool of democracy, it is also, or at least may be, the source of its moral principles. Thus some writers link science and democracy in a way in which others seek to link religion and democracy.

To say, however, that ethical principles have or may have their source in science in this way is not to say that they can be justified by appeal to the findings of science, as the ethical empiricist holds they can. It may still be that they can be so justified. But what this last line of thinking suggests is that the justification of moral principles is to be found, not in the results of science, but in the very rationale of the scientific enterprise itself. Something like this is what I take C. I. Lewis to be thinking.[2]

Other pragmatists have developed the pragmatic theory of ethics in a variety of ways. G. H. Mead wrote only fragments on ethics; his main contributions have been in social psychology, especially his notion of "roles" and his social theory of mind and conscience. C. W. Morris has been important for working out a behavioristic theory of signs, including ethical terms, and for making empirical studies of preferential behavior and valuation. Although he regards himself as a pragmatist throughout, he was first a straight naturalist in ethics like Perry, then a noncognitivist of sorts, and now seems to be moving back to naturalism. On this point Abraham Kaplan definitely takes (or once took) an emotivist position, arguing that moral judgments are not assertions but rather perform certain "pragmatical functions" such as expressing the speaker's emotions, committing him to certain courses of action, and urging others to share his attitudes, though insisting that they do not do so capriciously. It would seem, then, that we must regard pragmatism as susceptible of taking either a naturalistic or a noncognitivist form. Perhaps this is why some pragmatists—Ray Lepley for example—

[2] See also J. W. Smith, *Theme for Reason* (1957).

385

have been seeking for a rapprochement between these two points of view.

Dewey's closest important follower, however, is Sidney Hook, who has been unusual among recent philosophers for the way in which he has addressed himself to such problems as civil liberties, academic freedom, judicial review, etc., though in this too he has been following Dewey's example. His basic theory is an interesting kind of contextualism or situationalism, which he thinks he finds in Dewey. It is summarized in the following sentence: "A moral ideal is a prescription to act in a certain situation or class of situations in determinate ways that will organize the human needs and wants involved so as to fulfil a set of other values which are postulated as binding in relation to the problem at hand." [3]

These other values, however, may be tested by an appeal to experience together with still other values postulated as binding in relation to the problem then in hand, and so on. This view (which Hook sometimes expresses in a naturalistic form, i.e., as involving certain definitions, but which can also be given a noncognitivist interpretation) offers a way of reconciling the Dewey thesis that every value and ethical judgment is corrigible in the light of experience and science with the dictum that the establishment of any such judgment presupposes another one as a premise. It does not seem to me to be quite Dewey's view, however, and it implies that our reasoning about moral ideals and other values is involved in a circle, narrow or wide, of such ideals and values. One wonders, then, how one reasons with others who share none of these ideals and values. Or are there no such people? If not, why not?

The sentence quoted from Hook also serves to introduce his justification of the democratic ideal of social equality, which we may take as an example both of his method and of his conclusions. He asks the question "Why should we treat individuals of unequal talents and endowments as persons who are equally entitled to relevant consideration and care?" We should do so because doing so fulfills a set of other values postulated as ultimate for the problem in hand: it evokes a maximum of creative, voluntary effort

[3] Y. H. Krikorian, ed., *Naturalism and the Human Spirit* (1944), p. 57. For another statement of contextualism see Abraham Kaplan, *The New World of Philosophy* (1961), pp. 19, 35-40.

and intelligent loyalty from all members of the community; it enlarges the scope of our experience by giving us insight into the lives of others; it promotes peaceful living and socially harmless forms of competition, and minimizes duplicity, fear, and toadying; it maximizes the fulfillment of each individual through art and science; it makes for less cruelty of man toward man than any other way of life; and it makes possible the widest forms of mutual consultation and free intellectual communication and inquiry. In spite of my questions about Hook's views on method I must say that this kind of justification of democracy is good enough for me, assuming that the factual claims made for it can be substantiated by empirical investigation. One may, of course, point out that the values postulated here are not accepted by all, but this disagreement, even *if* it is irreducible through the increase and free spread of empirical knowledge, cannot be used as a basis for resort to metaphysical or theological beliefs or even intuitions, for about these there is just as much difference of opinion, and it is at least as irreducible by free rational methods.

Apart from Dewey the most important and also the most independent of those who have called themselves pragmatists is C. I. Lewis. With him pragmatic ethics and value theory take a different turn, or rather two different turns. Lewis holds that all knowledge is either a priori and analytic or a posteriori and empirical.[4] Intuitionism, transcendentalism, and all forms of nonnaturalism he rejects, as any pragmatist would. Valuations and ethical judgments must therefore be either empirical assertions, analytic truths, or noncognitive utterances. But in *An Analysis of Knowledge and Valuation* (1946) Lewis condemns the view that they are noncognitive utterances as "moral skepticism" and "one of the strangest aberrations ever to visit the mind of man" (p. 366). They must then, for him, be either analytic or empirical. But which? Here Lewis distinguishes sharply between the good and the right (or at least between the nonmorally good and the morally right), and gives very different accounts of the two kinds of judgments, taking judgments about the good first.

---

[4] Here and hereafter "analytic" means "true by definition" and "synthetic" means "not true by definition"; "a priori" means "known independently of experience" and "a posteriori" means "dependent on experience."

Lewis recognizes several kinds of goodness or value: intrinsic, extrinsic, final, contributory, and social value, and just plain utility. Except for utility all of the other species of value can be defined, he thinks, in terms of intrinsic value. But judgments of utility are clearly empirical, and judgments of the other kinds of value will also be empirical if those of intrinsic value are. Most philosophers argue at this point that judgments of intrinsic value are in the nature of the case incapable of empirical verification, resorting either to intuitionism or to some kind of noncognitivism, and Dewey is so convinced of this that he feels he must attack the whole notion of intrinsic value in all its forms if he is to make out his program of ethical empiricism. Lewis, however, thinks he can show that evaluations are a form of empirical knowledge even if he accepts the notion of intrinsic value, as he thinks one must.

What then is intrinsic value? It must, Lewis holds, be something that involves an imperative for action and gives direction to rational conduct. Hence he adopts an affective theory of value. Intrinsic goodness is an immediately felt empirical or natural quality or family of qualities or rather a "dimension-like mode" that pervades all experience. One must have experienced such qualities to know what intrinsic goodness is; it cannot be explained in other terms, though it may be described. Pleasure, enjoyment, satisfaction, happiness—these are all species of it. It cannot be defined in terms of pleasure, however, because this predicate is too narrow. In fact, says Lewis, the best term for it is just the familiar term "good" if this is limited to directly found goodness. This theory reminds one of Moore, of course, but it seems clear that Lewis means to identify intrinsic goodness with something like hedonic tone, and that he is from Moore's point of view a naturalist about good.

Such statements about the nature of intrinsic goodness, Lewis maintains, are not themselves valuations, since they are analytic of the nature of value itself. There are also "expressive statements" like "This is good" said of an experience one is enjoying at the moment. These, he contends, are not mere expressions of feeling, as emotivists hold; they are direct apprehensions of felt hedonic quality and are true or false. But they cannot be mistaken, and not being predictive, they are not properly forms of knowledge, even though they are empirical. In fact, they are not really evaluations. These are of two kinds: judgments of intrinsic value like "It will be good to hear that concert" and others like "Knowledge is intrinsically good." Both of these kinds of judgment, however, can be verified empirically by observing whether hearing the concert, acquiring knowledge, etc. are enjoyable for their own sakes. All sorts of judgments of intrinsic value, Lewis concludes, are forms of empirical knowledge not fundamentally different in what determines their validity from other forms of empirical knowledge.

Lewis's first new turn (new in the history of pragmatism, not in that of value theory), then, is his making central the notion of intrinsic value, which Deweyans reject. Nevertheless he accepts, so far as evaluations of what is good are concerned, the general Deweyan program; in fact, he shows more clearly how it may be carried out, even if one admits judgments of intrinsic value. I am tempted to think that in this area Lewis has said what Dewey should have said, and has given us the most plausible and best worked out of all the empiricist theories of value. Now comes Lewis's second new turn. He separates the right and the good more clearly than Dewey does. Though he agrees that determining what is right involves a knowledge of what is good, he believes that it involves something more also. Even if we know all about the intrinsic, extrinsic, and even the social values of our alternatives in action, he contends, we still cannot tell which one we are to take, because we still do not know whose good we are required to promote, or how we should distribute the available good. We need here an ethical principle that cannot be derived from a knowledge of good and evil by itself. In fact, we cannot use such a knowledge as a guide unless we have a principle telling us how. Even the utilitarian principle that we ought to do what will produce the greatest balance of intrinsic good over evil in the world as a whole cannot be arrived at merely on the basis of a knowledge of what will produce such a balance. Nor will it do as the ethical principle we are looking for, since it begs the question against the egoist who offers a rival ethical principle. What we need here is a categorical imperative that is formal in nature, as Kant pointed out. But this cannot consist in a prediction about what is intrinsically good; in fact, it cannot be an empirical assertion at all. "Valuation is always a matter of empirical knowledge. But what is right and what is just, can never be determined by empirical facts alone" (*An Analysis of Knowledge and Valuation*, p. 554). For ethics proper, then, Lewis herewith gives up the Dewey program, ethical naturalism, and ethical empiricism.

It will be recalled that this is the point at which we found difficulties of one kind or another in Dewey, Parker, and even Perry. The problem is that of grounding an imperative asserting that we have obligations to others. This, says Lewis, is perhaps *the* distinctive question of ethics, and it cannot be answered by the theory of value or by empirical inquiry. Where then are we to look for our basic ethical principles? Must we go beyond the bounds of a naturalistic position altogether, as so many think? Lewis thinks not. A mere knowledge of good and evil entails no imperative, he says, but human beings cannot help being affected by it, for they are necessarily concerned about the future. They are inevitably concerned about future good or ill to themselves but do not automatically act in accordance with their knowledge of it. This is a datum of human nature. Out of it comes an imperative to be rational, consistent, and objective, which we cannot wholly repudiate without repudiating all concern whatsoever, and which, while it cannot be proved, requires no reason because it is presupposed in all reasoning. It is a priori in the sense that to deny it involves one in a "pragmatic," though not a logical, contradiction. One cannot deny, though one may not always obey, the "inbuilt teleology" or "basic bent" of conscious life to seek the good and avoid the bad. Here one is reminded of Aquinas's basic natural law, of the "natural norms" of S. C. Pepper and J. D. Wild, or of P. B. Rice's "congenital a priori" (which was indeed suggested by what Lewis says). But Lewis goes on, for he has not yet established an ethical norm. In *Our Social Inheritance* (1957), he tries to do this by extending the above imperative of rationality beyond the confines of mere prudence to the realm of social morality.

> The gist of the matter may be briefly put. Given the basic capacity to subordinate immediate feeling to the dictates of the cognitive recognition of objective actualities, and given the intelligence to appreciate the gratifications and griefs of others as realities fully comparable to our own, the imperative to respect the interests of

others as we would call upon others to respect our own, is a dictate of rationality. Recognition of this imperative requires only that capacity to generalize which is essential to human thinking altogether and is required for any learning to govern our behavior by reference . . . to objective facts. More clearly and obviously: a way of acting, to be right in a given case, must . . . in the same premises of action, be right in every instance and for anybody [pp. 92f.].

This too is involved in being consistent.

In this principle of justice Lewis discovers two subprinciples: that of respecting all conscious life for what it is, and that of taking no decision of a kind that one would call upon others to avoid. These principles are analytic of the notion of justice, and so a priori, but the imperative of justice, an application of the imperative of rationality or consistency, is also a priori, though in another sense—that is, it is "pragmatically a priori." [5] From these principles, taken together with a knowledge of good and evil, we may derive our needed guidance in the conduct of life.

There are questions one may ask about this attempt to solve our problems, of course. Is the domain of ethics only that of justice, or does it also include benevolence? How is a conflict between prudence and justice, both of which are equally requirements of rationality, to be adjudicated? Does the imperative of rationality, generated by the individual's concern for his own future, in fact bind one to concern oneself equally for others? Has Lewis solved his problem? In any case, why should we be any more rational than we inevitably or in fact are? One wonders too about Lewis's saying that the basis of his imperatives is a "datum of human nature." Is the statement that something is such a datum empirically verifiable or is it somehow analytic? But these are only questions, and they may well have answers. One may also ask whether anyone has done better than Lewis has, all things considered.

Thus "pragmatic ethics" turns out to be a number of things. Its typical proponents are ethical empiricists, but of these some are naturalists in Moore's sense and some are noncognitivists of a sort;

---

[5] To say "P is pragmatically a priori" means that the opposite of P is "self-contravening" but not in a strictly logical sense. Lewis argues that "Be consistent" is a priori in this sense because one *cannot* adopt the opposite maxim, since to do so would require one to be consistently inconsistent.

Dewey himself is somewhat ambiguous on the issue, while Hook's position on it seems to be indeterminate; and one important pragmatist, Lewis, is not even an ethical empiricist, except about "good."

Pragmatism has also expressed itself in the philosophy of law, where it has been associated with the rise of a "new jurisprudence" variously referred to as pragmatic jurisprudence, sociological jurisprudence, or legal realism, and involving such names as Holmes, Brandeis, Cardozo, Pound, Frank, and Llewellyn. This movement is related to the ethical theories I have been reviewing, and accounts of it may be found in such books as E. N. Garlan's *Legal Realism and Justice* (1941), L. L. Fuller's *The Law in Quest of Itself* (1940), and Roscoe Pound's *An Introduction to the Philosophy of Law*, rev. ed. (1954).

❈❙ 5 ❙❈

NONCOGNITIVE THEORIES

General introduction. Critical Realists: George Santayana; R. W. Sellars; A. K. Rogers. Postulational theories. Logical positivists: Rudolf Carnap; Hans Reichenbach; Herbert Feigl. C. L. Stevenson's emotive theory.

While ethical empiricism is a natural product of an age in which the natural sciences are achieving such spectacular successes and psychology and the social sciences are so confidently setting out to do likewise, the fact that this is an age of science has not meant that its offspring has been without critics. Actually, ethical empiricism has been much attacked, first by the intuitionists and the metaphysical moralists, then by the logical positivists and emotivists, and most recently by the new Oxford moralists and their followers as well as by the existentialists and the resurgent forces of religion. Even scientists and philosophers of science themselves have often aligned themselves against it, especially when dealing with political theory or the methodology of the social sciences. It has, nevertheless, remained strong, and even naturalism is showing signs of regrouping its forces for a new campaign.

About 1930, just as Perry and Dewey were at the height of their campaign to harness science to the ethical chariot, and just as Urban was proclaiming the victory of objectivism in value theory, a movement arose that seemed determined to say them all nay. This was not a revival of antinaturalisms or antihumanisms of various kinds, though we have had a revival of them also; it was a point of view that found particular favor among the very empirically and scientifically minded philosophers to whom Dewey and Perry, if not Urban, might well have looked for allies. In fact, some of their cruelest foes were fellow members of the larger family of empiricists and naturalists to which they themselves belonged. The noncognitivist movement was not entirely new, but it did enjoy a new vogue after 1930, especially since it became the typical ethical theory to

393

go with the analytical philosophy that was then coming to the fore (together with its antithesis, existentialism).

Intuitionism and naturalism are agreed in holding that ethical terms stand for properties and that ethical judgments are assertions ascribing these properties to actions and objects, or, in other words, that normative ethics constitutes a body of knowledge, be it natural or nonnatural. Contrary to intuitionism and naturalism, noncognitive theories hold that ethical terms do not stand for properties, that ethical judgments are not property-ascribing assertions, and that normative ethics is not a body of knowledge. In some forms noncognitivism holds that value judgments are simply or primarily expressions of emotion or attitude, but the movement as a whole must not be identified with the "emotive theory," since many of its exponents reject this theory, holding that value judgments are imperatives, prescriptions, recommendations, postulates, performatory utterances, or even that they are *sui generis,* having a nature different from any other kind of utterance but still not cognitive or descriptive.

There is no necessary connection between such a view and empiricism, positivism, or analytical philosophy. Empiricists, analytical philosophers, and even positivists may be ethical naturalists. Analytical philosophers may even be intuitionists, as Moore was. On the other hand, existentialists may and usually do subscribe to a noncognitive position, and theologians may and often appear to maintain that ethical principles are not cognitive assertions but divine imperatives. Even a divine command is not as such true, though it may be true that God has uttered it, and that it is based on infinite knowledge.

Indeed, the vogue of noncognitive theories among analytical and empirical philosophers has something paradoxical about it. Such theories could be expected to become popular among the anti-rationalists and anti-intellectuals whom we have had with us since the nineteenth century. Yet, and this is one of the most interesting facts about the last three decades, noncognitivism has been most prominent precisely where the influences of analytic clarity, logic, mathematics, and science have been strongest—among the empiricists and logical positivists, and even among scientists themselves. For example, a central point in the "scientific philosophy"

394

advocated long ago by Russell, and more recently by Reichenbach, is that normative ethics is not and cannot be a science.

How then has the recent vogue of noncognitive theories come about? In spite of what was just said, it may be in part a result of the irrationalism that has been fed by so many streams in our century, including the other development that is known as "analysis," namely, depth psychology. Partly too, as has often been remarked, it is a result of Moore's arguments. For these seemed to many to prove conclusively the untenability of naturalism and metaphysical ethics; and since they also found intuitionism untenable they were forced to look for a noncognitivist analysis of ethical language. They were encouraged in this both by the "discovery" in the Twenties and Thirties of the fact that language has other meanings and uses besides those of describing, informing, reporting, etc., and by the relativistic conclusions suggested by the findings of anthropologists and psychologists. No doubt, the then still growing conviction that science must be neutral and must have nothing to do with values and ethical judgments also came into play, as it does with Arnold Brecht, though it is hard to be sure which is cart and which horse here—the theory that science is *wertfrei* or the theory that value judgments are not cognitive. In any case, one of the factors that certainly played a part was the Humean conviction that moral and value judgments must be "practical" in the sense that their acceptance tends directly to influence our conduct, together with the belief that they could not do so if they were susceptible of a purely cognitive analysis, as intuitionists and naturalists think they are. And, of course, the history of our period itself must have had an effect.

The Critical Realists have been noted since 1920 for an epistemological manifesto but unduly neglected as moral philosophers. Some of them, J. B. Pratt and Durant Drake, for example, are straightforward naturalists in ethics, but some of the others appear to be noncognitivists of a unique kind. The most famous of them all is George Santayana. His discussion of "Hypostatic Ethics" in *The Winds of Doctrine,* published in 1912, shows that he was already holding: first, that "good" is an indefinable quality or essence, but one that is conditional and relative, accruing to or being read into things when we take an interest in them, and, second, that when we say a thing is good we are really using this predicate, not to describe it (if we did, we would simply be making a false statement), but to express our interest in it. In some places Santayana sounds more like a naturalist, and he is usually classified as one, but in a chapter on "Moral Truth" in *The Realm of Truth* (1938), as in 1912, he is clearly a noncognitivist. "The nerve of moral judgment is preference: and preference . . . cannot be either false or true." But he recognizes that our desires and preferences may be enlightened and sincere or ignorant and insincere, and that our moral judgments may or may not express what we genuinely desire when faced with the facts, and so may have a kind of "moral truth" or "moral falsity." "Moral truth . . . signifies only complete, enlightened, ultimate sincerity." In other words, while "ultimate" moral judgments are not strictly true or false, even they can in a sense be corrected or sustained by experience, since experience can revise or support the attitudes that underlie them. They are not necessarily arbitrary, but may be rooted in attitudes taken in the light of full knowledge. Like Dewey, as I have interpreted him, Santayana would add that moral judgments not only can but should be enlightened and sincere in this sense.

The views of R. W. Sellars, the next most important of the Critical Realists, represent an attempt to match the Critical Realist analysis of perception with a parallel analysis of valuation.[1] Briefly this means that he holds: (1) that valuation involves an empirically generated but irreducible predicate, (2) that we judge objects in terms of this predicate when we find them bearing on our interests, (3) that when we so judge them our intention is not to describe them, but to appraise or grade them or to take a certain stand with respect to them, and (4) that this judgment, though not strictly true or false, may be "justified" or "unjustified" by evidence about the relations of objects to human satisfaction and happiness. Accordingly Sellars was as insistent on the difference between cognition and valuation as any later noncognitivist could be, though he held both to be amenable to correction or support by empirical facts.

[1] For references and discussion see my "Sellars' Theory of Valuation," *Philosophy and Phenomenological Research*, XV (1954).

The fullest system of moral philosophy to be worked out by a Critical Realist, or by any of our noncognitivists, is, however, that of A. K. Rogers, who wrote *Theory of Ethics* (1922), *Morals in Review* (1927), and *Ethics and Moral Tolerance* (1934). Rogers' style is poor, but he was an able and perceptive moral philosopher for all that, and can be read with considerable profit. I shall indicate briefly his theory of "natural" or nonmoral goodness; that of moral goodness is similar though it differs in detail.

In opposition to the rationalists, Rogers associates himself with the "ethics of sentiment" of Shaftesbury, Hutcheson, Hume, and Smith; like them he regards sentiment as the basis of ethical judgments, though he finds an important place for reason. He uses Moore's open question argument to show that goodness cannot be identified with pleasantness or any other such natural property. But, rejecting Moore's own intuitionist conclusion, he argues that judgments like "X is good" express approval. They do not, however, simply express an immediate liking for X, as emotivists usually think; they express a "reflective" or second-order approval or liking. That is, they express an approval of the fact that X is liked in a first-order way. Rogers is not unambiguous about this, but he seems to mean that "X is good" does not *assert* that I approve of X's being liked when I reflect, but *expresses* my reflective approval of its being liked. At the same time, Rogers insists that "X is good" professes to find a quality of goodness in X; in it we project the abstract essence of the pleasure felt on contemplating X into X, just as we attribute bitterness to coffee when it is too strong. Goodness, he says, is a new and imported quality, a "tertiary" quality, not a constitutive one. As an abstract character it may be the inhabitant of a special realm of ultimate being, but what is existentially behind its involvement in a valuation is the presence of feeling, and we can discover by psychological analysis that this feeling is the real crux of the matter.

This Critical Realist analysis of ethical and value judgments, variously stated by Santayana, Sellars, and Rogers, has both difficulties and virtues, but it has not had the attention it deserves. It serves at least to show that emotive and noncognitive theories were already present in America before 1930 and were not all imported from abroad along with positivism. The postulational theory of ethics is also not wholly a foreign import, although in some of its versions it was at least partly a product of reflection on both the strong and the weak points of intuitionism as argued by Moore and others. In fact, it is more than suggested by what Santayana said in 1912 when he was attacking Moore and Russell. For postulational ethics as for intuitionism, moral reasoning rests on certain basic or ultimate premises, one or more in number. These cannot be deduced from any other premises, for there are by hypothesis no more basic ethical principles or ends to appeal to, and, of course, no ethical proposition can be deduced from premises that are not ethical. But neither are they self-evident as intuitionism claims. So, it is argued, they must represent postulates or basic commitments by which we have consciously or unconsciously chosen to live—our "rock-bottom axioms," as D. C. Williams has called them.

Postulational theories of this sort were offered in the Thirties by Barnett Savery, Leo Abraham, Morris and Felix Cohen, Ledger Wood, and G. H. Sabine, but the best-known statements are those of C. M. Perry and D. C. Williams in articles published in 1933 (see my bibliography), although Williams recanted in 1937 when he adopted a closely related form of naturalism. Some of these authors stress the arbitrary character of these ethical postulates, e.g., Perry in "The Arbitrary as Basis for Rational Morality." Williams, however, suggests that there may be some kind of rationale even for choosing postulates, though he ends on an existentialist note with the thought that just here may be "the dreadful and desperate last freedom at the growing point of the universe." It seems clear, as has often been pointed out of late, that what leads people to the postulational theory is (1) a belief that ethical reasoning is linear and presupposes certain ultimate principles or values, combined with (2) a belief that nothing can be rationally justified unless it can be deductively or inductively established. Dewey, Hook, and Stevenson accept (2) and therefore attack (1). But others have recently begun to question (2), and to argue that there are other modes of rationality besides the inductive and deductive ones, and that, whether (1) is true or not, our most basic ethical judgments are susceptible of the appropriate kind of rational justification, and need not be thought of as "arbitrary" or even as "postulates."

The best-known among the so-called analytical philosophers are the logical positivists, but analytical philosophers are not all logical positivists. Moore, Russell, and Broad, for instance, were not, yet in effect they inaugurated "the age of analysis." It is, however, typical of analytical philosophers to avoid metaphysical speculation on the one hand, and empirical inquiry on the other. Their reasons for doing so vary but need not concern us here. More to the point is the fact that they tend to avoid doing normative ethics (though Moore and Ross did not); that is, they tend *qua* philosophers not to make normative judgments or value judgments, though of course they do make them as much as anyone else when not speaking *ex* armchair. Philosophy for most of them is neither speculation, empirical science, nor normative guidance; it is the attempt to achieve conceptual and methodological clarity in an increasingly wide number of areas. In ethics, then, they are usually meta-ethical rather than normative or practical in their interest, and are concerned with the analysis of ethical terms and judgments, with the logic of ethical reasoning, and with certain related topics.

Nothing about the programs of the analysts or positivists requires them to be noncognitivists. Since they tend to be empiricists in their theories of knowledge (though they need not be), they could consistently be naturalists in ethics. In fact, however, they have also tended to think, for various reasons, that naturalistic theories of ethical judgments are untenable. Even though noncognitive theories, independent of foreign influences, existed here before the advent of the age of analysis, the noncognitivism of our analytical philosophers is not a fruit of our native stock, but an import from abroad. Especially is this true in the case of the logical positivists, for logical positivism was translated bodily from the Continent in the Thirties. Itself influenced greatly by Russell and Wittgenstein, it represents the major impact of the Continent on professional philosophy in America. Since its chief proponents here came from abroad, it is not clear that this country made any contribution to the movement besides that of being its second host, but even so some account of the ethical theories associated with it must be given.

In a well-known passage in *Philosophy and Logical Syntax* (1935), Rudolf Carnap says that insofar as ethics includes psychological or sociological investigations it is an empirical science, but he argues that the case of normative ethics is very different. For example, the statement "Killing is evil" does not imply any proposition about future experiences, hence is not verifiable, and hence, by the verifiability criterion of meaning that is central to logical positivism, is cognitively meaningless. Normative and value judgments are thus neither true nor false, they are "expressive" and are best interpreted as commands put in a misleading grammatical form. Normative ethics therefore is not an empirical science, but consists of disguised commands. Clearly Carnap is here simply assuming that empirical verifiability is the criterion of cognitive meaning and that a naturalistic rendering of ethical judgments is not possible. These two premises are characteristic of logical positivism in ethics, though they are not always so simply assumed.

A fuller but still brief and inadequate statement of a positivist position is given by Arthur Pap in a 1946 article, "The Verifiability of Moral Judgments," and again in *Elements of Analytic Philosophy* (1949). For our purposes the best statements are those of Hans Reichenbach and Herbert Feigl. In *The Rise of Scientific Philosophy* (1951), Reichenbach remarks that the conception of ethical insight as a form of knowledge was first held by the Greeks and was not present among the Hebrews, who thought of ethical rules as imperatives. Then he contends that, if ethics were a form of knowledge, its judgments would have to be either analytic or synthetic. But if they were analytic they would be empty, and, if synthetic, would inform us about mere matters of fact. In neither case would ethics be what moralists want it to be, for it would not be normative, it would not supply directives. In a sense Reichenbach is here forgetting about the naturalists on the one hand and Lewis on the other, but also in a sense he is indicating an argument against them, namely, that ethical judgments can be seen on analysis to be directives, not statements that may be true or false. Ethical axioms, then, are basic directives, not basic truths. They are not self-evident, analytic, or logically provable by induction or deduction. Are they simply an individual's basic postulates, as D. C. Williams suggested? Reichenbach thinks not, arguing that moral directives are accompanied by a feeling of obligation and thought of as applying both to ourselves and others; they express both the will of the speaker and that of his group. Having said this, however, he himself ventures the directive that we should be more autonomous, each setting up his own moral imperatives and demanding that everyone follow them. This he calls the "democratic principle."

Is there any way in which one can justify one's imperatives against those of others? Reichenbach does not believe there is in the case of basic directives. We must give up the quest for certainty here; the choice of a goal is not a logical act, but a spontaneous affirmation of desire. He agrees with Dewey that we should illuminate our choices wherever possible with knowledge of a scientific kind, for only so can we find out what we really want. Reichenbach insists, however, that basic choices cannot be scientifically validated and he says that he wishes the pragmatists would recognize this.

The problem of justifying ethical principles is more fully explored by Feigl. For him too an ethical imperative is an expression of emotion, volition, or wish, and is most accurately put in the form "Would that everyone behaved. . . ." Feigl makes a useful distinction between "validation" and "vindication": Validation applies to all ethical judgments except the most basic ones and consists in deriving the judgment in question from a more basic one plus relevant factual premises. Vindication applies to basic ethical judgments and the question is what it may consist in, if it amounts to anything more than motivation for adopting the goals or principles at issue. For Feigl, vindication cannot rest on an appeal to intuition or self-evidence. Nor can it be simply a deduction or induction from factual premises, since factual statements alone cannot possibly entail normative conclusions. Saying that the principle in question is true by the very definition of "right," "good," or "ought" will not do either, he says, since no such definition incorporates what we all mean, and anyway the acceptance of a definition is tantamount to the acceptance of the principle involved, and so we still have the problem of vindicating it. Vindication, he concludes, can only take the form of "pragmatic justification," that is, an ethical principle can be justified only in the sense that it may be found to be acceptable by us in view of our purposes as illuminated by empirical knowledge concerning means-ends relations or by logical truths. It follows that vindication is as relative as our purposes are. (Here, like Reichenbach, Feigl is skeptical of the belief in a common human nature, though he is willing to allow for a cautious optimism on the possibility of a convergence toward common standards.) It does not follow, he insists, that our choice of principles is arbitrary, for our choices are determined by the culture and subculture in which we live and by our (more or less) intelligent reflection upon the facts as they impress "us-as-we-are."

The discussions of the nature and justification of ethical judgments by Carnap, Pap, Reichenbach, and Feigl are programmatic pieces written by philosophers whose main interests lay outside ethics, but they present a penetrating challenge to moral philosophers. Logical positivism as known to the Thirties and to its enemies is dead or dying, but it has served, in ethics as elsewhere, as a training school for and as a spur to the formation of more adequate theories.

The most important name connected with noncognitivist theories is that of C. L. Stevenson. In following a plan of taking each general movement and tracing its development from 1930 to 1960 I have already dealt with some writers who read Stevenson and reacted critically, for example, Pepper, Dewey, Hook, Brandt, Wild, Northrop, and Blanshard, and others who read and were affected by him, such as Feigl, Kaplan, Pap, and Parker. The breadth of his influence must be remembered if we are to see his contribution in perspective. Stevenson published his views in articles in 1937 and 1938. Even so, he was not the first to publish an "emotive theory" of the recent vintage. Earlier in the Thirties this was done in Britain by A. J. Ayer, Carnap, Russell, and W. H. F. Barnes. He was, however, working out his emotive theory independently of them at the same time, under the influence, not of any earlier native noncognitivists, but of C. K. Ogden, I. A. Richards, and Wittgenstein, as well as that of Dewey and Perry. In any case his *Ethics and Language* (1944) is, except perhaps the works of A. K. Rogers, the first book-length statement of a noncognitivist position in English, possibly since the eighteenth century. Many philosophers regard it as the most important book in ethics by an American in this century, comparing it with those of Moore and Ross in Britain. Almost certainly it has been the one most widely read and discussed in recent years, both here and abroad. In England and in this country alike it played a large part in the drift away from intuitionism and naturalism. The theory propounded in it is itself more adequate than the more extreme views of Ayer and the logical positivists, but, like them, it has served to spur many readers to attempt to find still more adequate theories and to help in preparing them to do so.

The emotive theory, in Stevenson's form, is not easy to state accurately in brief compass. It certainly cannot be formulated, as it often is by opponents, by saying "Values are simply attitudes" or "A value is merely an expression of emotion." It is not a theory about the nature of "values" (i.e., things that are or are called good), but only about the nature of value judgments. Nor can it be adequately expressed by saying "Value judgments are *merely* expressions of attitudes or emotion." It would be more adequate to say that for Stevenson such sentences as "A is good" and "B is right," in their *typically ethical* uses, are *primarily* emotive in meaning, or *primarily* expressions of attitude, but this is still not the whole story. Even the account that follows is over-simplified.

Stevenson is trying to answer two related sets of meta-ethical questions: (1) questions about the analysis, function, meaning, or nature of ethical terms, judgments, and disagreements, and (2) questions about the methodology of supporting ethical judgments and settling ethical disagreements. His conclusions, he says, are based on and must be tested by observations of ethical discussion in everyday life, but they are not meant to be mere transcriptions of ordinary ways of thinking. Rather, they represent a theory about what is going on in everyday ethical discussions that will enable us to engage in them more intelligently.

Stevenson does not deny that ethical words and sentences may have a cognitive or descriptive meaning. In fact, while he denies that they can have a nonnatural one, he insists that they often do have a natural descriptive meaning. When I say that my grandfather was a good man I mean, in part, that he was honest and kind. But Stevenson also insists that there is something about ethical judgments that is not provided for if they are thought of as cognitive or descriptive, either naturalistically or nonnaturalistically, namely, the fact that they have emotive meaning and serve to embody and evoke favorable or unfavorable attitudes toward the actions or objects referred to. Indeed, he maintains, this fact is their primary feature. Ethical sentences are basically tools for expressing and propagating the speaker's attitudes (emotions and interests), not his beliefs. What generates them is ultimately a favorable or unfavorable attitude toward an object or action, not just a piece of cognition, real or fancied. It is because we take a favorable attitude toward, say, honesty and kindness that these characteristics get built into the descriptive meaning of "a good man," and it is because we take a favorable attitude toward them that I can cite certain of my grandfather's actions as evidence that he was a good man. The actions cited and even honesty and kindness would simply be irrelevant to my claim if we were not for them or against them.

It follows that ethical agreements and disagreements are primarily agreements and disagreements in attitude toward an object, not in belief about it. An ethical disagreement is resolved if and only if the parties involved end up taking the same attitude toward the object or action in question. I can "prove" my claim that my grandfather was a good man by proving that he was honest and kind if and only if my opponent B is also in favor of honesty and kindness, and is merely mistaken about the facts of my grandfather's life. In this case a basic agreement underlies our initial disagreement; our opening disagreement in attitude toward my grandfather is rooted in a disagreement in belief about his actions, and when this is resolved it disappears too, since we share a more basic attitude. More generally, an ethical disagreement can be settled by rational methods and inquiry only if it is rooted in a disagreement in belief. This is often the case, as in my disagreement with B about my father's father, but it may not always be the case. Suppose that when I have shown B that my ancestor was honest and kind, it becomes clear that B thinks of kindness and honesty as vices. Then we are agreed about the facts but it turns out that our opening disagreement in attitude toward my grandfather is rooted in a more basic difference in attitude toward honesty and kindness.

Now perhaps even this difference rests on some difference in our beliefs about the effects of honesty and kindness. Stevenson believes, however, that we may sooner or later arrive at an irreducible disagreement in attitude. He does not say that this is so, but he seems inclined to think it is. If it is true that ethical disagreements are not always based on differences in belief, then, he insists, the use of reasons comes to an end at some point. Unless and until we come to such a point, however, we may use reason and evidence in trying to bring about agreement. In fact, this is the place for science in ethical discussion. But we must be prepared to find that the reasons that are relevant to ethical judgments, in the sense of bringing about agreement, have a peculiar variety and complexity, for they will consist of any and all beliefs or facts that will produce agreement in attitude, not merely of those that will establish the descriptive part (if any) of the judgment in question. Moreover, since an ethical judgment is basically an expression of an attitude, it cannot be logically related to the reasons that may be relevant to it; the final relation of reason to conclusion here is purely psychological. Even if the evidence adduced does logically establish the descriptive part of the ethical judgment, it can bring about assent to the judgment only if the required attitude is present. This does not mean that the connection between reason and conclusion is accidental, however, for the attitude involved may be a basic one in human nature.

To "justify" an ethical judgment to someone, then, is to *move* him to take a certain attitude toward a certain object or kind of action. It may be possible to do this by giving reasons, but it may not be. Even definitions of ethical terms, if offered, must be "justified" by moving the reader to take a favorable or unfavorable attitude toward whatever has the defining properties in question.

It follows, says Stevenson, that normative ethics is not a science. If the first part of the above theory is true, the naturalistic claim that ethical judgments are primarily empirical assertions is mistaken; and, if the second part of it is true, especially if attitudes are not rooted in beliefs, then even Dewey's claim that ethical questions may be settled by science cannot be sustained. Or rather, the naturalistic claim must be thought of as a "persuasive definition," and Dewey's as a normative judgment to the effect that we ought to let our attitudes form themselves only on the basis of empirical knowledge. Then these claims are themselves essentially expressions of attitude and not neutral meta-ethical statements.

Stevenson does not reject any such normative proposals; he merely stops short of committing himself to them, reminding us that they must be recognized for what they are.

Virtually every aspect of and item in Stevenson's form of the emotive theory was attacked, not only by nonnaturalists, but by fellow empiricists and fellow noncognitivists. The notion of emotive meaning, the distinction between beliefs and attitudes, and, of course, the various substantive theses—not one escaped criticism as Stevenson's opponents and even sympathizers went about seeking to avoid his conclusions. Some reactions consisted of simple shocked rejection, counterassertion, and name calling, others of careful constructive exploration. Those of the more constructive kind were directed especially at Stevenson's conclusion that, while factual reasons may be given for an ethical judgment, their relevance and relation to the judgment is essentially psychological and not logical, so that one can exclude certain reasons as bad, irrelevant, or invalid only by taking a normative position about the reasons that may be used, which is itself an expression of attitude. Both those who agree that disagreements in attitude may not all be rooted in belief and those who do not have often balked at his views about the place of reason in ethics.

I myself sympathize with such reactions. The general noncognitivism of Stevenson's position does not especially disturb me, but I have questions about his particular kind of theory. He seems to me to distinguish too little between moral judgments and other kinds of value judgments. Hence he talks as if a moral disagreement between A and B about C is settled if they both end up taking a favorable attitude toward C, whatever the grounds of their doing so may be. Hence too he talks as if there can be no nonmotive distinction between reasons that are morally justifying and reasons that are simply motivating, and as if giving a moral justification of "X is right" is merely providing motives for doing X. Of course, all kinds of reasons and nonreasons can be relevant in the sense of motivating, but are they all relevant and valid if what we are looking for is a *moral* justification? Here I am inclined toward the Aiken-Dewey-Hook view that nonrational influences and appeals are misplaced in a discussion of what is morally justified or right, but I would go further, as the British philosopher S. E. Toulmin does, and claim that not all kinds of reasons are in place either. Here Stevenson would cry "persuasive definition," of course, but at this point his own position involves a contrary inclusive persuasive definition, as is shown by the way he asks, in one of his articles, "But how could such an ethics be of interest to anybody?" This question may not be easy to answer, but it is not simply rhetorical, and one need not supply Stevenson's answer, even if one is not a cognitivist. Perhaps every answer involves some proposal about the meaning of "moral" or "ethical" in this context, and, if so, the pot may be at least as black as the kettle it is addressing.

Nevertheless, Stevenson and the emotive theory have had a considerable following, including, besides the people already mentioned, W. R. Dennes (*Some Dilemmas of Naturalism*, 1950). Now, many opponents of this movement, and even some of its sympathizers, feel that it represents or entails moral skepticism. If this means that emotivists do not have any moral principles or subscribe to any normative propositions, it is simply false. They may not propound such principles in their philosophizing, but in their daily lives they certainly often do. If the claim is that they are logically inconsistent in doing so, it is also mistaken. There is no inconsistency in believing, on the one hand, that ethical judgments are emotive expressions, commands, or postulates, and in holding, on the other, that killing is wrong, that knowledge is good, or that democracy is the ideal form of society. If skepticism means not accepting any normative judgments, noncognitivists need not be and generally are not skeptics. It may still be said, however, that if the emotive theory were to prevail, the upshot would be a general moral skepticism and loosening of standards. This is a question of empirical fact on which the evidence is by no means clear; the critics simply assume that it would be in their favor, and never do anything to show that it is.

"Skepticism" may, however, have a somewhat different sense. Instead of meaning a suspense of judgment on all normative issues, it may mean simply the view that normative issues cannot all be settled by rational methods. But an emotivist need not be a skeptic even in this sense, for, even if he holds that ethical disagreements are disagreements in attitude, he may still hold that such disagreements are rooted in disagreements in belief, that human nature is fundamentally the same in all men, and hence that ethical disputes can all be settled, in principle at least, by rational methods. Only those who doubt such further claims, as Stevenson does, are skeptics in the second sense. Other noncognitivists, like Dewey as I have interpreted him, are not. In any case, even if Stevenson and others are skeptics in the second sense, it does not follow that they are or should be skeptics in the first sense. Also, it may be pointed out, little is gained by saying that ethics must be based on metaphysics or theology, if it is added that these depend on faith and not on reason and empirical evidence. For such a position is also skeptical in the second sense, though not in the first.

6

THE LATEST INVASION FROM BRITAIN

Oxford analytical philosophy and ethics. H. D. Aiken.
A. I. Melden. John Rawls.

The next group of analytical philosophers to be considered represents the impact of the latest invasion from Britain. As a result of the work of Moore and Wittgenstein there has been a "revolution in philosophy" in England, and, as revolutionary movements almost always do, it has reached across national boundaries and spread out into the world. Much influenced by Stevenson's writings, it first showed itself in ethics after 1949, in articles and books by S. N. Hampshire, P. F. Strawson, H. L. A. Hart, S. E. Toulmin, Margaret Macdonald, J. O. Urmson, R. M. Hare, P. H. Nowell-Smith, Kurt Baier, and Bernard Mayo. Related views have been expressed in America by H. D. Aiken, Paul Edwards, A. I. Melden, John Rawls, S. M. Brown, Kai Nielsen, M. G. Singer, J. W. Smith, F. E. Sparshott, and others. Few books have yet appeared here that show the influence of this movement, but there have been many articles pro and con, and the works of the British authors mentioned are the favorite diet in the graduate ethics seminars of today.

This is not the place to give an account of the moral philosophy of this movement as a whole, since relatively little has yet been contributed to it by Americans; nevertheless, because of its still growing importance in our schools and journals, it is necessary to sketch in at least a few of its main features. In general this "Oxford philosophy" rejects the Russell-positivist view that ordinary language must be replaced by some more ideal language that is logically and semantically more satisfactory. We only need to know how to use it correctly, as in fact we generally do. It also rejects the earlier conception of analysis as translation, which Moore shared with Russell and the positivists; that is, it gives up the notion that the paradigm of analysis is the finding of a second sentence that can replace the original one and yet be an improvement on it. There are other ways, it claims, of clarifying our language. Being anti-Platonist it prefers to ask, however, not for the "meaning" of an expression, but for its "use." In short, it conceives of philosophy as an elucidation of the rules according to which we ordinarily use various kinds of expressions, especially those related to its traditional problems. It is not the construction of speculative or quasi-scientific theories, nor the reconstruction of our everyday discourse.

The proponents of this movement begin by finding that language has many uses in everyday life besides those of describing, reporting, informing, etc., more than were recognized by the positivists or by Stevenson. They find next that ethical expressions are generally used in certain of these other ways. Thus they reject all forms of naturalism and even intuitionism, on grounds similar to those of Moore and Stevenson respectively. But, unlike the emotivists and imperativists, they deny that ethical sentences can be reduced to or translated into exclamations, expressions of attitude, commands, etc. We do express our attitudes in them, and are misusing them when we do not, but we are primarily using them to commend, demand, prescribe, give advice, tell people what to do, and the like, and doing this is not adequately described as evoking or inciting certain attitudes in others. Nor is it accomplished by employing some kind of emotive meaning as a tool. In fact, whatever may be true of other value expressions, our moral utterances, to be correctly used, must meet certain requirements: we must be willing to universalize the judgments expressed, and we must be ready to give factual reasons in support of them. It is such implications of moral judgments that earlier noncognitivists missed, and that their cognitivist opponents were seeking to retain, though in a mistaken manner.

Thus, on the one hand, this Oxford philosophy rejects the whole program of our American ethical empiricists of reconstructing ethics into a science, but, on the other, it insists with Dewey (but unaware of this fact) that moral judgment is inherently reasonable, and must be supported by factual reasons, not implemented by non-rational sources of persuasion, if it is appropriately to be called moral at all. In accord with this insistence, the Oxford philosophers and their followers argue that it is not incorrect to speak of true or false ethical judgments, to call them beliefs or statements, to say that certain reasons are relevant to them and others not, or to claim that they are rationally justifiable even though they cannot be deductively or inductively inferred from factual premises alone. In this way they remove much of the disturbing paradox of earlier more extreme theories, and reduce the gap between noncognitive theories and the theories of the ethical empiricists.

Hence stems the great concern of recent analytical philosophers with "the logic of moral reasoning." They believe that there is moral reasoning and that it has a logic, even though they also hold that ethical judgments are not primarily pieces of cognition. They deny that such judgments, or even the most basic ones, are "arbitrary," "irrational," "illogical," or without justification. About the logic of our reasoning in connection with them, however, they disagree, sometimes in very fundamental ways. Some believe that moral reasoning has its own peculiar logic, a third logic to be added to the deductive and inductive logics of our textbooks. Others deny this. Many of them represent our moral reasoning as taking the form of a "rule-utilitarianism," but a few describe it as deontological and others as "act-utilitarian."

As one example of this current of thought, we may take H. D. Aiken, whose recent book, *Reason and Conduct* (1962), contains many of his articles. In some of his articles, Aiken has stoutly defended the value for education, action, and the spiritual life of the kind of analytical moral philosophy it embodies. In others, he adumbrates in a variety of ways a moral philosophy that indeed exemplifies it, but that also shows considerable independence and promise. Throughout he is an acute and resolute critic of the emotive theory and other more extreme forms of noncognitivism. At first he did so from a naturalistic point of view similar to those of Perry and Parker, but after 1949 from an Oxfordish point of view. All along he contends that ethical judgments are not simply expressions and tools of private attitudes or volitions, casual or deeply rooted, and that to say so is unnecessarily to discredit rational procedures and invite irresponsibility just where it is most dangerous. In about 1949, however, Aiken gave up naturalism on the ground that it cannot provide for the normative character of ethical judgments, that is, their "power to influence the will." Ordinary moral language, he now insists, does not need the kind of reconstruction required to realize the programs of Dewey, Perry, or Pep-

411

per. It is no sacred cow, but "when correctly employed it is a sufficiently precise and flexible tool for the ordinary conduct of human affairs."

[It] is not a crude, pre-scientific form of speech which must be reconstituted so as to render it more amenable to the requirements of a "moral science." Such a science is not even a possibility, and any such reconstruction, were it to prevail, would in effect mean the supercession of the institution of morality altogether. . . . Morality could not become a science without a radical reconstitution of the very uses of such terms as "good" and "ought"; but such a reconstitution would no longer enable us to say (or do) "the ethical thing" [*Reason and Conduct,* pp. 20, 22].

That is, we could no longer make normative judgments of a moral kind but only descriptive ones.

The emotive and imperative theories remedy this defect of naturalism, Aiken recognizes, but they do not provide for the objectivity, universality, impersonality, or authority that ordinary moral judgments claim to have, and they miss the fact that there is a logic of moral reasoning by which such judgments achieve a kind of interpersonal justification. In "A Pluralistic Analysis of the Ethical Ought,' " he says:

What we want is an account which (a) does not reduce the ethical judgment to a mere description of desire under certain circumstances (Perry), and (b) does justice to the normative impersonality of the moral judgment and the generality of the rules by means of which a particular moral judgment is justified. My suggestion is this: the ethical "ought" voices or expresses, but does not simply state, what would, upon reflection, be regarded as binding upon any normal person within a given social system, and enjoins the addressee, as such a person, to act accordingly. Thus when I state that X is morally desirable, I am, in effect, voicing the approval which upon reflection would be bestowed upon X by any normal person in the society to which I belong, and demanding, in the name of that society, that so and so, as a fellow-member do likewise and, if appropriate, act accordingly [p. 500].

Of course, one may ask about the moral adequacy of the rules of one's society, but then, Aiken argues, one is recognizing "another quasi-moral or 'ideal' sense of ought," and even then

. . . I challenge the moral code . . . not in my own name or in my own behalf, but, so to say, in the name of an ideal humanity of which I claim actual society to be implicitly a part. I am voicing a claim which, *because I put it in ethical terms,* transcends my own approval of it [p. 502].

In any event my judgment can be rationally justified, granted the point of view from which I speak.

Here we seem to have an example of the noncognitivist form of ideal or at least demi-ideal observer theory to which favorable attention was called earlier. Working it out somewhat in other articles, Aiken maintains that moral reasoning has its own criteria according to which we may perfectly well call its reasons "good," "relevant," or "valid" and its conclusions "justified," "rational," or even "true," all in an interpersonal sense. He does not accept the usual utilitarian conception of these criteria even for "ideal" morality, however, for he believes that, at the highest level of moral discourse, there are other principles to be considered besides that of welfare or least suffering, namely, those of justice, equality, and respect for persons. These criteria, for him, define the sphere of moral reasoning. Conclusions arrived at on the basis of empirical facts in the light of this set of principles are moral, and, if illumined by adequate knowledge, they are rationally justified in the only sense that is morally relevant.

Valuable and penetrating studies of particular topics have recently been made by A. I. Melden and John Rawls from the general point of view here being described. Working on the nature of rights and duties, and of our reasoning about them, Melden contends that certain "moral relations" are built into many of the terms or concepts that are used in justifying ascriptions of rights and duties, and that have usually been regarded as "descriptive" or "factual" rather than normative, for example, those of "father" and "son." We may and do justify saying that X has a certain right and Y a certain duty by pointing out that X is Y's father. We can do this, not by virtue of any implied premise or rule like "One ought to give special consideration to one's father," nor by virtue of any special logic that permits us to go from "X is Y's father" to "X has a right to such and such treatment by Y" without the use of such a premise or rule, but simply because it is part of the meaning of

X's being a father of Y that X has a right to special consideration from Y. In this and other such cases (e.g., promising) there is a "moral structure of relations" between the parties involved, and the right act is the act that preserves the moral relations obtaining between all of them, that is, that preserves "the moral community of which one is a member." This does not mean, however, Melden insists, that the moral institutions and relations of one's community cannot be reappraised. For morality has a point, namely, to facilitate the diverse forms of happiness possible for those who participate, and the moral structure of a community may be judged in the light of this point.

In an acute and original article on justice, Rawls rejects the utilitarian view of justice as a kind of efficiency or utility for the concept of justice as fairness. Beginning with the notion that questions of justice arise when mutually self-interested agents in similar circumstances are trying to deal with each other in moral terms, he suggests that the principles of justice are those principles that such agents can reasonably accept as governing their behavior toward one another or, in Kant's terms, can will to be universally acted on by all of them alike. He identifies two such principles: (a) that each person has an equal right to the most extensive liberty compatible with a like liberty for all, and (b) that inequalities are arbitrary unless it is reasonable to expect that they will work out to everyone's advantage, provided also that the positions and offices involved are open to all.

It seems to me fair to say that Aiken, Melden, and Rawls are not merely borrowing from Toulmin and the British, but are improving on what they borrow, possibly because of the different and richer background provided by previous moral philosophy in this country. At any rate the members of this latest school of moral philosophers are saying very interesting and illuminating things. It is not too much to claim that there has been no movement in the field since the war that has made comparable contributions, if we count the British writers in our estimate, and I am not forgetting the existentialists or the theologians yet to be discussed. I am not convinced, however, that in their findings its proponents are simply elucidating the ways in which we actually use words like "good," "ought," "moral," "rational," "justified," "valid," etc., as some of them seem to think. Indeed, I rather doubt that any fullfledged meta-ethical theory can be merely elucidatory of the rules of ordinary ethical discourse and reasoning. At the very least, is must be an implicit endorsement of the prevailing rules, and then it is in a sense a normative position, and moreover a conservative one. This would not mean that it is mistaken, but it does mean that reasons must be given for not revising the rules, as well as for revising them (as Perry on the one hand and Stevenson on the other are recommending that we do). After all, as Aiken himself says in *Noonday,* II (1959); "The part of intelligence is to conserve and reform the old patterns when we can and to fashion new ones, gradually, as we must, creating but also recreating our spiritual destinies [including, perhaps, morality], as we go along" (*Reason and Conduct,* pp. 372-73).

7

ROADS TO REUNION

P. B. Rice. M. G. White.

We have had a good deal of talk about a "crisis," "deadlock," "impasse," or "stalemate" that is supposed to be present in ethical and value theory. This talk is symptomatic of the nervousness of our time, and so seems natural, and yet it is curious that philosophers themselves should use it. For philosophers have always been divided into disagreeing camps, and it is doubtful that they would really want it otherwise, since, as far as we now know, the only way to achieve a monolithic intellectual culture is to have an inclusive state or church that "establishes" it by proclaiming it to be authoritative, on whatever ground. Be this as it may, we must conclude our review of ethical theories that are empirical, naturalistic, or "analytical" by noting that there have lately been some which have sought a "way out" of our strife of systems by proposing "roads to reunion" along one route or another.

As a matter of fact, we have already noticed certain approximations of friend to foe among the empiricists. Other such rapprochements between cognitivist and noncognitivist empiricists have been indicated or proposed by C. A. Schuster, Ray Lepley, Alexander Sesonske, and J. W. Smith. In 1955, Sidney Hook heralded Paul Edwards' *The Logic of Moral Discourse* by proclaiming it as "a fusion . . . of the emotive and objective naturalistic points of view." Actually Edwards' position does not differ from Stevenson's in any substantive way, as far as I can see, though he seems to think it does. But, following S. N. Hampshire, he does make the position verbally less paradoxical and bring it closer to ordinary usage by finding senses in which terms like "true," "prove," "rational," "relevant," and "implies" can be applied to ethical judgments. Thus he approximates the Oxford point of view without actually leaving the emotivist camp.

The most important recent synthesis is that offered us by P. B.

Rice in *On the Knowledge of Good and Evil* (1955). He thinks of himself as reasserting naturalism in a revised form in which it can meet the attacks of Moore, Stevenson, Aiken, and the Oxford ordinary language philosophers. Actually he is proposing a synthesis, for he holds that in an ethical judgment one is both asserting truly or falsely that an object or action has a certain naturalistic "identifying" (or defining) property, and recommending, prescribing, or committing oneself to that object or action. That is, an ethical judgment has both a descriptive meaning and a noncognitive "matrix meaning." Thus, he argues that "X is good" means "X is satisfying or conducive to satisfaction; MM!" and that "Y is morally obligatory" means "Y promotes the greatest general good; MM!" Why does Rice call this position naturalism rather than noncognitivism? Possibly because he thinks the descriptive meaning is more basic than the emotive one, but his position on this is not clear, and he sometimes talks as if the latter were primary, as Stevenson holds. His main clear difference from Stevenson, Edwards, Hampshire, Hare, and others lies rather in the fact that he holds, as any naturalist does, that there is a single "identifying" property for each ethical term that constitutes the descriptive part of its meaning. This means that he is faced with the problem of justifying his basic definitions in a very crucial form, and in wrestling with it he has very interesting things to say, which carry the problem somewhat beyond the points at which Feigl and Lewis leave it.

In his stimulating book, *Toward Reunion in Philosophy* (1956), M. G. White represents himself as "beyond" all of our recent isms in a land where the lion may lie down with the lamb (whether beside or inside him is not clear). On one count or another he calls a plague on all houses except his own new one—intuitionism, naturalism, positivism, the emotive theory, pragmatism, and Oxford philosophy. All their main theses, White argues, are really normative or "quasi-ethical" proposals, hence he is also against the distinction between meta-ethics and normative ethics, at least in its usual form. It follows that to adjudicate such theses we must use methods similar to those in ethics.

Now ethics, White insists, has no special logic. In fact, he propounds a one-hopper theory of justification for ethical judgments and all others. That is, he regards all of one's thinking as (ideally)

WILLIAM K. FRANKENA

forming a single system. Into its hopper go sensory data, moral feelings, and everything else. Out of it come one's logical rules, one's ethical principles, and one's factual and scientific beliefs. But these do not form three separate bodies that are impervious to one another. To shift metaphors, anything may in principle trump anything else—sensory experiences, moral feelings, rules of inference, factual beliefs, or scientific hypotheses. For instance, if my moral feelings balk at the conclusion of a piece of moral argument, I may question its ethical premise, its factual premise, or even the rules of inference involved. On the other hand, if I am not ready to revise any of these, my moral feelings may have to give in. Nothing is in principle unquestionable in the system of my thought; though I may accord privileged positions to some items, these may be of any sort. Our ethical principles are "the principles which together with our other beliefs systematically organize our elementary moral convictions," but the other beliefs and the elementary moral convictions are not in themselves incorrigible and may on occasion be revised.

This is the old coherence theory of justification, still thought of as all-inclusive, but de-absolutized. It desegregates ethical and factual judgments, without reducing one to the other, and for both it disowns the linear theory of justification by deduction from unquestionable principles or by induction from incorrigible data. Thus it gives the lie at once to all forms of intuitionism, naturalism, postulationism, and any other isms that depend on one or another of the familiar dichotomies of recent philosophy. According to it, to justify any judgment, moral or otherwise, is to think out with care one's system for organizing sensory experience and moral feeling, and to place the judgment within it.

It is hard to believe that moral feelings and judgments may ever legitimately move us to revise our factual beliefs, as White implies they may. Moral reasoning seems to accord a definite primacy to the facts, as Maurice Mandelbaum has shown. On this point R. B. Brandt's view, otherwise similar to White's, strikes me as the more plausible. Nevertheless, it is an interesting road to reunion that White has sketched for us, involving as it does, not just a synthesizing of two or more prevailing theories, but a transcending of them all.

418

All of these proposals are irenic in purpose, if not in tone, and foretell an idyllic issue out of crisis and debate. Out of the eaters, they aver, shall come forth meat, and out of the strong, sweetness. But none of these roads to reunion has yet been so well laid out and paved that such a happy ending is now visible. Wars and rumors of war will therefore presumably continue to prevail in our philosophical life, and the philosophical lamb will continue to shun the philosophical lion.

∽§ 8 §∾

RELIGIOUS ETHICS AND
EXISTENTIALISM

General account of recent Judeo-Christian ethics. Paul Til-
lich; Reinhold Niebuhr; H. Richard Niebuhr. Relations of
ethics to religion. Views of human nature. Social applica-
tions. Existentialism.

Not all of the recent opposition to ethical naturalism and empiricism has come from proponents of theories such as those described
in the last three sections. Those theories were worked out within
the framework of a view of knowledge and reality that is just as
naturalistic or secular as the framework of Perry or Dewey. But we
have also had a lively movement, amounting to a revival, among
those who reject all naturalistic or secular views of man and the
world in favor of a religious one, and its spokesmen have preached
a veritable counterreformation to the reformations proposed by
Perry, Pepper, Dewey, Sharp, etc., on the one hand, and by Stevenson, Reichenbach, Aiken, etc., on the other, as well as to the more
ecumenical programs of Rice and White.

This "anti-naturalism *in extremis,*" as Dewey calls it, comes primarily not from philosophers, but from theologians on one side
and political theorists, literati, and even scientists on the other, and
thinks of itself as baptized by fire in the events and heart searchings
of our period. Fed by the "upsurge of religiousness" that these have
engendered, it has expressed itself politically both in the Christian
radicalism of Niebuhr and others in the Thirties and in "the new
conservatism" of many writers of the Fifties. It agrees with the intuitionists and noncognitivists that ethics is autonomous with respect to science, but, like Perry and Dewey, it holds that ethics is not
wholly autonomous; unlike them, however, it seeks to associate
ethics with metaphysics or theology instead of with psychology or
the social sciences. In all its forms it denies the adequacy of any
ethical theory that is not conceived, at least in part, in supernatural-

istic terms taken more or less directly from the Judeo-Christian tradition.

I cannot try here to cover recent religious ethical theories in any adequate way. I shall, therefore, confine myself to the minimum of description and comment that seems necessary to round out the picture, hoping to be less superficial than philosophers usually are when they review the ethical theories of theologians. I should like to encourage more dialogue on the problems of ethical theory between philosophers and theologians, and so will say what seems to me most helpful all around, sticking mainly to what the latter write about issues of the sort that we have been dealing with, and neglecting somewhat their contributions to the development of religious ethics as such.

The outstanding figure by all odds, for our purposes, is Reinhold Niebuhr. He has been centrally concerned with the application of Christian ethics to the political and social problems of our day and has been widely influential in the circles of those who think and write or try to do something about these problems, much more influential than any of our philosophers, with the possible exception of Dewey. No moral philosopher can ignore Niebuhr's disturbing neo-orthodox challenge to and criticism of our modern liberal and secular ethics and social philosophy, even if it is filled with baffling paradoxes and has little of the clarity or rigor called for by contemporary philosophical standards. Also prominent are H. Richard Niebuhr and Paul Tillich, both stimulating teachers and authors of widely read books and articles. These theologians are to a considerable extent taking the intellectual and cultural places once occupied by James, Royce, Dewey, Santayana, and Whitehead. It is not only unclean spirits who will move into a house that is empty, swept, and garnished, as the parable has it, though it remains to be seen if the last state of this generation will be worse than the first.

Other writers exemplifying this revival of Judeo-Christian ethics are Paul Ramsey, G. F. Thomas, J. A. Hutchison, J. H. Hallowell, Eric Voegelin, Abraham Heschel, and Will Herberg, not to mention Jacques Maritain and Dietrich von Hildebrand. With some of them, as with the more important trio just mentioned, there enters another influence from the Continent that has not figured so far in our story of American ethics, namely that of the religious existentialism and dialectical theology of thinkers like Kierkegaard, Barth, Jaspers, Brunner, Marcel, and Buber—an influence that has been particularly strong in Protestant and Jewish circles.

In general terms, the claim of this group of thinkers is that ethics and morality crucially involve a religious or supernatural dimension or reference. But this claim is ambiguous, and is seldom, if ever, clearly stated by those who make it. Even if we talk roughly, we may distinguish the following theses: (1) that the only adequate or tenable set of basic normative principles is or includes the Judeo-Christian ethic; (2) that certain religious or supernatural propositions are necessary as minor premises in the development of a normative ethics, given a set of basic ethical principles to serve as major premises; (3) that the major premises of ethics themselves rest on certain religious or supernatural experiences or beliefs; and (4) that the capacity or motivation for being moral depends on the presence of such experiences or beliefs. Theses (2), (3), and (4), it should be noted, may be advanced as holding for any morality whatsoever in its entirety, or only for some part of morality, or only for the kind of morality described in thesis (1). Most Judeo-Christian thinkers would assert all four theses in some form or other, but they generally do not distinguish them sufficiently clearly, or define their scope with enough care. Perhaps the most careful of them are A. C. Garnett and Eliseo Vivas, who argue only for a form of thesis (4). Here we shall center on discussions relating to (3) and (4).

First, however, we must say something about morality as our religious writers conceive of it. Among philosophers the debates in normative ethics have been between (a) the ethical egoists and self-realizationists, (b) the utilitarians or universalistic teleologists (and, among these, between the "extreme" or act-utilitarians and the "restricted" or rule-utilitarians), and (c) the deontologists. In them some writers, for example Garnett and Stace, have identified Christian ethics with utilitarianism. But among religious thinkers the debates have taken a somewhat different form, even though there are interesting parallels. Almost all of them agree that there are certain "supernatural" principles, values, or virtues—roughly indicated by the terms "faith," "hope," and "love"—which are properly regarded as forming at least a part of morality, but which are not within the competence of the kind of natural knowledge afforded by the empirical sciences. Most Roman Catholics, however, and some Jews and Protestants, hold that there is another part of morality, another set of principles, values, or virtues, that is effectively independent of the first, namely, the area of "natural law," "human virtue," or the "principles of justice." For them morality forms a kind of duality; the two parts may be harmonious (as Thomists hold), and the second may be improved by association with the first, but they are distinct, and there may even be a "tension" between them (as Protestants sometimes say). But most Protestants and Jews, and some Catholics, deny that there is any valid morality or true virtue that is in this way independent of the law of faith, hope, and love. They tend to a more monolithic or simplistic view of morality that regards the whole duty of man as a direct function of religious faith and love. Paul Ramsey and Will Herberg illustrate this tendency in their books. Most extreme in this respect is the position of certain recent writers who may be called religious contextualists or situationalists, some of them influenced by H. Richard Niebuhr and some by existentialism. This is virtually a form of antinomianism that minimizes the role of reason and principle and makes the moral life a direct expression of faith, love, or communion with God in each situation as it comes up, guided by a knowledge of the facts involved but not by any moral rules or principles. In *True Morality and Its Counterfeits* (1955), von Hildebrand criticizes a Catholic version of this antinomian view that has appeared in Europe. In general there has been much discussion among religious writers of the relations between faith and the law of love, between the law of love and the principles of justice and other moral rules, and about the existence of a natural law and the extent to which it can be formulated in definite principles.

A moderate position on these matters is maintained by G. F. Thomas in *Christian Ethics and Moral Philosophy* (1955)—and perhaps, in recent writings, by Ramsey. According to Thomas there are genuine principles and values, especially justice, that can be grasped, though not with complete clarity, by moral philosophy, and that are needed to complete the Christian ethic of love. But they do not suffice to constitute the whole of morality and must be supplemented by the Christian ethic; and when this is done they do not remain unchanged, but are "transformed" in character and more clearly apprehended, besides being provided with a more adequate motivation.

Most interesting and stimulating, but also most ambivalent, is the position of Reinhold Niebuhr. Much of the time he writes as if there are two parts of morality, the law of love and the principles of justice (e.g., equality), and as if the latter are known by reason independently of revelation and grace (possibly he takes them as self-evident or as a priori in Lewis's sense), not simply deduced from the former together with empirical or theological premises about how love may best be implemented in the world. Then he seems to think of justice as a more practicable ideal than love. Sometimes, however, he suggests that the principles of justice are simply a function or application of the law of love, as when he says that equality is a "symbol" or "political version" of the law of love or that the law of love is the "source" of the norms of justice. On the whole the former seems to be his more dominant view, for example, when he speaks of the "dialectical" relation between love and justice. Even in holding it, however, he insists that love and justice require one another, that love is the fulfillment of justice, and that it is the final norm by which the structures of justice are to be judged.

This ambivalence of Niebuhr's position extends to the question of the existence of a natural law, but, in line with his dominant view, Niebuhr generally recognizes the existence of such a law, known by reason and involving the ideals of equality and justice. He insists, however, that no formulation of this law can be final, as Roman Catholics think; an absolute norm is involved, but any historical formulation of it has only a relative validity, even though it may be closer to the ideal than any previous one. It is always possibly corrupt because reason is never wholly free from the influence of our natural egoism and lust, and it is also subject to revision in the light of further experience and insight.

Aside from whether a religious normative ethics is dualistic or monolithic, other questions arise. What is the meta-ethics involved? What is the meaning of "good," "right," and "ought"? What is the nature of ethical judgments? What is the status of the law of love or the principles of justice? How, if at all, can these judgments, laws, and principles be vindicated? On such questions the writings of the theologians and their followers are particularly unclear to a philosopher who has been reading the works reviewed in previous sections. Almost without exception, possibly because they are uninterested or untrained in philosophy, it is very difficult to see just what the theologians are maintaining. In claiming that ethics depends on religion they seem to be making a meta-ethical claim, but what they mean is rarely, if ever, made clear, and it is hard to see how it can be, as long as such meta-ethical questions as philosophers have been discussing are not carefully considered and fully answered by them.

About the "natural" part of morality, if he believes it has such a part, a theologian might hold any of the meta-ethical theories reviewed in earlier sections. I have already suggested that Thomists are ethical naturalists in Moore's sense about this part of their ethics, if not about its "supernatural" part. And, logically, one can subscribe to the Christian law of love as a normative principle, no matter what meta-ethics one holds. Garnett, a naturalist, argues that it can be established on an empirical basis. An intuitionist might hold it to be self-evident. Those who regard it as a divine command, on the other hand, may be regarded as noncognitivists; if one takes them literally, their position differs from Carnap's only because they claim that a supernatural being is the source of the command. For those who prefer not to stress the command conception of Christian standards another noncognitivist line is open; they may maintain that Judeo-Christian moral judgments are not assertions about but expressions of a love or gratitude that we cannot but feel if we have certain religious beliefs or experiences, for instance, the belief that God has redeemed us or the mystical experience of him as love. On this view one who has such beliefs or experiences might say, as Luther did, that one cannot do otherwise than adopt a certain norm or goal for one's life, e.g., the law of love. Such a view would differ from Stevenson's only in holding that moral judgments are linked with a specific attitude and that this attitude is rooted in religious beliefs or experiences. For it, ethics (or at least part of it) depends on religion, but only psychologically, not logically; religious beliefs can be given as reasons for ethical principles, but the principles will follow from them, not logically, but only psychologically (or, if one prefers, "existentially").

Most of our religious writers would, of course, insist that, whatever is true of "natural law" and "justice," the law of love is not a norm that can be known "naturally," whether by intuition, demonstration, empirical science, rational ontology, or natural religion. Faith, revelation, divine grace, or a supernatural light, they contend, are necessary for its recognition. But just what meta-ethics is involved they do not make clear. What they say seems to rule out intuitionism, Cartesian rationalism, and Deweyan empiricism, at least for this part of ethics, but not ethical naturalism or noncognitivism.

This said, let us look at the relevant views of a few of the writers in question. In *Love, Power, and Justice* (1954), Paul Tillich takes up the "ontological analyses" or "foundations" and the "ethical applications" or "functions" of love, power, and justice, claiming that the answer to each of the questions of ethics "directly or indirectly depends on a doctrine of being." What he has to say is, as usual, very interesting, but his conception of the logic of the relation of ethics and ontology remains most obscure; he does not explain just how ethics depends on ontology, and once says that ethics verifies ontology, as if the relation were reciprocal. Perhaps his most interesting point is that ethics is neither autonomous as "pragmatists" think nor heteronomous as "theologians" think who regard moral commandments "as expressions of a divine will which is sovereign without criticism," but theonomous and therefore ontological. By "theonomous" he means "that the law given by God is man's essential nature, put against him as law. . . . It is natural law. . . . Every valid commandment is an expression of man's essential relation to himself, to others, and to the universe." This is much too cryptic to be very helpful, however. It suggests that one can prove a moral principle by showing that it is a requirement of man's nature, but does not explain why it can be proved in this way. Does Tillich think, for example, that "I ought to love" *means* "Loving is necessary for the fulfilment of my essential nature?" Then he seems to be a naturalist like Garnett and Wild, and must defend his definition. Also, since he is putting all of ethics, even the law of love, under natural law, he is not really resting

426

any of its basic principles specifically on religion; even though he uses the word "theonomous," he does not explain just how a reference to God comes in. The crucial question seems to be, not what God, but what human nature requires.

In *An Interpretation of Christian Ethics* (1935) Reinhold Niebuhr says that religious ideas are the ultimate sources of moral standards, and that Christian faith is the foundation and roof of an adequate morality. By this he seems to mean, at least in part, that religious premises are the logical basis of moral norms, for he also says that the ethics of Jesus proceeds "logically" from the presuppositions of prophetic religion. He then offers what appear to be arguments in which the law of love is deduced from such religious presuppositions. In one place he argues that we are to love and forgive because God does, in another that we ought to do so because all life is essentially a "unity," and yet elsewhere that we ought to love because God commands us to. Nowhere, however, does he try to explain just how one can move from the religious premise to the ethical conclusion in these apparent arguments. Until he does, one can always claim that in each case there is a suppressed ethical premise to the effect that we ought to imitate God, that we ought to obey him, or that we ought to love what we are one with, and that this more basic ethical premise has not been derived from religious presuppositions. Neibuhr may be thinking that his inferences are justified by defining "the right" as what God does or commands or as what unifies, but then he should say which definition he means to adopt and why we should join him in adopting it.

In *The Nature and Destiny of Man* (1941) Niebuhr suggests another line of thought, also suggested by Tillich, namely, that the law of love is a law for man because loving is a necessary condition of his self-realization. If this is his basic doctrine, then his view is like those of Garnett and Wild—perhaps even like that of Dewey! Then his ethics is that of self-realization, even if he hastens to add the paradox that gaining one's life entails first losing it, as Dewey also does. The principle of self-realization itself, however, does not seem to rest on any religious presupposition, though the belief that we can gain our lives only by losing them in love may depend on one. Then it cannot be claimed that the basis of ethics is specifically religious, but at most that its further development requires religious

427

premises, and, while this may be true, it is not obvious and must be shown.

A similar view is expressed by H. R. Niebuhr in an essay in Ruth Anshen's *Moral Principles in Action* (1952). The logical basis of his position consists of two "relational" definitions: "good" means that which fulfills the potentialities of an existent thing, and "right" means that relation between beings in which their potentialities for each other are realized. He thinks of this as an ontological analysis of value and obligation, but in Moore's sense it seems to be a form of ethical naturalism, like those of Wild and Tillich. In any event, nothing specifically religious is referred to in these basic definitions, and so the most their author could claim (and he does claim at least this) is that theological premises about what is needed to fulfill our potentialities are required for the development of an adequate ethics. This may be so, but it is not obvious, and, even if it is so, the validity of the basic definitions themselves would seem to be independent of religion.

If Tillich and the Niebuhrs seem thus to approach ethical naturalism, without quite admitting it, other theologians seem to be non-cognitivists without quite saying so. They seem to regard our basic moral and value judgments as arbitrary commitments that cannot be justified at all, but can only be espoused, freely and perhaps anxiously. Thus J. A. Hutchison, in one of the very few attempts made by religious spokesmen to make clear "the nature of moral reasoning" (*The Two Cities*, 1957), writes that "we must boldly assert that all basic moral rules are essentially postulates of faith," not deducible from anything more basic, not self-evident, and not arrived at by inductive reasoning. This must also be Herberg's position, for he insists that no Ought follows from any Is, and seems to deny that any Ought is self-evident to reason. Such a view does not assert that moral principles are logically dependent on religious truths about God or the world, for it says that they are logically autonomous premises taken on faith or, perhaps better, that they are themselves ultimate commitments. Yet Hutchison wants to maintain that religious faith is "the creative source of ethical values." He manages to do this by arguing in effect that any ultimate value commitment is *ipso facto* an act of religious faith. But to argue this is to define religion as the making of basic commitments,

428

thus rendering the thesis that morality depends on religion true simply by definition. Then anyone who accepts the definition of religion involved—which is essentially that of Dewey in *A Common Faith* (1935)!—can accept that thesis even if he is a naturalist or a positivist. For all the thesis says is that a basic value commitment is a basic commitment. Hutchison may be right, but his victory is a hollow one. Similar comments apply to similarly misleading moves made all too often by other theologians, including both Niebuhrs—and even by Garnett.

Perhaps what such writers are really holding is that basic ethical principles and goals are psychologically or existentially dependent on specifically theistic beliefs and experiences in the sense indicated earlier. In fact, this, it seems to me, is what those who contend that morality depends on religion ought to hold. But to take this position is to subscribe to a kind of noncognitivism also—to an ethical postulationism within a theological framework. And to defend it one must show, not only that religious beliefs and experiences are sufficient to generate basic ethical convictions, but that such convictions cannot be generated without them.

We may point out that even if ethical norms depend logically or existentially on religious beliefs, it does not follow that ethical norms can be justified rationally. Everything depends on what is said about the religious beliefs on which ethics is held to rest. If they can be rationally justified, then ethical ideals and principles can also be justified rationally or at least existentially. But, if the religious beliefs appealed to as the basis of ethics are themselves matters of faith that cannot be reasoned about, then our ethical norms turn out to be unjustifiable at least at the second remove. One may, then, ask what is to be gained by the quest for a religious ground for morality, if morality is thereby made to inherit all of the uncertainty of religion. Little seems to be achieved if the theological premises involved are propositions about which there is no general agreement and no publicly available method of providing a reasoned justification. It may be wiser to argue from the beginning that, save for special religious values, principles, or virtues like communion with God, piety, etc., ethics does not require any transmundane support, except possibly in the sense of motivation.

The thesis that morality depends on religion may be true, but a philosopher may perhaps be forgiven if he presses the theological critics of moral philosophy to formulate the thesis more clearly and to argue for its validity more circumspectly than they have in their recent writings. If they really mean to appeal to reason at all, they must at least say just what part of morality depends on religion, in just what sense it depends on religion (logically, psychologically, etc.), and just what it is that morality is being said to depend on.

All of these comments apply to a more specific thesis that has been characteristic of religious thinkers in the last few decades, namely, that Western ideals and democratic principles require a religious foundation and cannot be justified on a secular, naturalistic, or humanistic basis; that apart from their religious roots "freedom, brotherhood, justice, and personal dignity", to use Will Herberg's words, are like "cut flowers" (a much-used phrase which comes, I believe, from Reinhold Niebuhr) that soon must wither and die; and that therefore our culture must return from its secular ways to its traditional religious faith or perish from the earth. Virtually all the writers referred to in this chapter insist on this point, as Herberg does, and J. H. Hallowell makes it central to his *Moral Foundations of Democracy* (1954). Yet, like the more general thesis I have been discussing, it is never clearly stated or carefully argued for. Until this is done Perry and Stace, Dewey and Hook, and all the philosophers who believe in "freedom, brotherhood, justice, and personal dignity" may well continue to maintain that they do not need a religious foundation—as even Garnett does when he concludes "that the basic moral principles of the Hebrew-Christian tradition can be supported by the methods of naturalistic ethical inquiry."

A large part of what the theologians have had to say against the philosophers on this and other points relates to what I have called thesis (4) and belongs to moral psychology rather than meta-ethics. It is in this connection especially that Reinhold Niebuhr *et al.* have made an impact on recent moral and political thinking, for example, on Arthur Schlesinger Jr., George Kennan, Hans Morgenthau, K. W. Thompson, and many others. Niebuhr in particular has been famous for hammering in a somewhat pessimistic or at least "realistic" estimate of human nature, its abilities, and its tendencies. He does not agree with the extreme Protestants who hold that man's nature has been wholly corrupted and depraved, but he does insist that modern culture, including both Christian and political liberals, and especially thinkers like Dewey and Perry (and also the Marxists), has "a confidence in human virtue which human nature cannot support." In fact, according to Niebuhr, all such views as we have previously discussed are in one way or another unrealistic in assessing man's capacities and inclinations. In particular, they suffer from an inadequate recognition of man's demonic tendencies and original sinfulness. Such "scientistic" programs as Dewey's and the typical social programs of the modern reformer are alike misled by optimistic assumptions. Utter pessimism is not called for, and certainly Niebuhr is not advocating an aloof despair, but he does think that a too idealistic approach is both doomed to fail and positively dangerous. He is not therefore against "impossible ideals" like love and perfect justice—he insists on their validity and relevance—but he also urges that a great deal of accommodation and compromise is required in practice if any victory at all is to be gained and its fruits preserved. He especially emphasizes that human finiteness and sin are revealed with particular force in collective relationships, and is sharpest in contending that, although we must have and take part in group action, we must guard against or allow for the egoism of groups, which is even more inveterate than that of individuals.

With this view of human nature in mind, Niebuhr argues that reason is in constant danger of corruption and that the rational resources of the individual for moral living are very limited. No kind of rationalism, naturalistic or nonnaturalistic, according to him, can provide an adequate "dynamic" for the moral life, nor can our natural social affections do so. Only the dynamic provided by the Christian faith in God and his love can come anywhere near being sufficient, and even these religious resources have their limitations, Niebuhr says, which religious idealists are apt to neglect. "The Christian doctrine of love is thus the most adequate metaphysical and psychological framework for the approximation of the ideal of love in human life." It may be interesting to note that Garnett comes to the same conclusion even though he holds to a much more optimistic conception of man's nature.

In a book called *Children of Light and Children of Darkness*

(1944) Niebuhr criticizes the traditional defense of democracy as depending on a too optimistic view of man and thereby inviting chaos and confusion. He also points out that a too consistent pessimism about man's capacity for justice invariably leads to absolutism in political theory and practice. He then offers "a more compelling justification and . . . a more realistic vindication [of democracy] than is given it by the liberal culture with which it has been associated in modern history." He argues that man's capacity for justice is enough to make democracy possible, and that man's inclination to injustice is so great that democracy is necessary. No one can be trusted with absolute power. Man's inclination to injustice is also so strong, he goes on to say, that we cannot expect to achieve a just society in history; the hope of both the liberals and the Marxists that such a society will emerge is the height of illusion, even though perfect love and equality remain the ideal. It is doomed to disappointment by the facts of human nature. "Social conflict [is] an inevitability in human history, probably to its very end."

One may challenge Niebuhr's view of the facts, as M. G. White and Charles Frankel have. Niebuhr never does much to give a solid empirical or scientific demonstration of these "facts." He can and does appeal to the findings of depth psychology, but we may note that not all depth psychologists agree with him, in particular Erich Fromm, whose Man for Himself (1947) is a widely read statement of a kind of humanism. Niebuhr especially likes to claim that the facts of recent history prove his view, but he never shows very carefully just how they do so. A good deal of empirical evidence can be marshaled in favor of his general position, but it is not at all clear that it proves anything like his doctrine that man sins inevitably but not necessarily. Such dour dicta go beyond the pale of empirical evidence, and for them Niebuhr seems to depend on scripture, prophetic insight, and dialectical metaphysics— grounds that he can hardly expect others to find compelling. Whatever one thinks of these grounds, however, it remains true that Niebuhr, and others like him, are calling attention to matters that philosophers have been neglecting, and to possibilities that the modernist culture for which they tend to speak has too blithely pushed under the threshold.

A philosophical moralist cannot help thinking, after such a review of recent religious ethics as I have just made, that theological moralists could learn a good deal from the work of contemporary moral philosophers. What is less clear from what has been said is that he himself can learn something from the work of contemporary moral theologians, but it is, in my opinion, equally true. Much of our most profound ethical thinking and much of our best effort to apply such thinking to the solution of present problems is to be found in the writings of theologians. So also are some of our most serious analyses of moral experience and moral psychology. Moreover, the theological discussions of love and justice, of the role of principles, and of the existence and nature of natural law are instructive for ethical theory, as are the debates between what I have called the dualistic and the monolithic conceptions of morality. In particular, philosophers who seek to elucidate the nature of morality must think carefully of the Judeo-Christian claim that love is the essence of morality. Lewis's view that justice is the whole of morality is not obviously correct, and it may be that its supplement lies rather in the Christian than in the utilitarian direction. Judeo-Christian conceptions have become a part of our ordinary moral consciousness—so much so that for most people, perhaps, morality just means Christian ethics or the law of love—and it would seem to follow that any philosophical attempt to elucidate or to reform our moral ways of thinking must take them seriously.

In this connection, we must note again the great interest of Reinhold Niebuhr and other spokesmen of religion in social and international problems. The voice of religious liberalism is muted these days, but much of Rauschenbusch's social gospel and this-worldly concern is still present among contemporary theologians. There is much debate about "ethics and public policy," and the theologians and their followers, rather than the moral philosophers, are taking the lead in it. This is nicely illustrated, not only by Niebuhr's own writings, but by such books as *Ethics in a Business Society* (1954) by Marquis Childs and Douglass Cater, *Ethics and United States Foreign Policy* (1957) by E. W. Lefever, and two books by K. W. Thompson, *Christian Ethics and the Dilemmas of Foreign Policy* (1959) and *Political Realism and the Crisis of World Politics* (1960). There is a very interesting review of these debates by John

Courtney Murray in *America* (March 1960). Most of the participants think of ethics rather monolithically in terms of the law of love, and they wonder how public policy can be guided by such an ideal. It is a good question whether *public* policy should be guided by a specifically *religious* norm at all, but other issues are also involved. The most popular view is what Father Murray calls "ambiguism," which regards every situation and every action as morally ambiguous. It thinks of itself as "realistic" and is rough with idealists, sentimentalists, and utopians, but its moral theory remains obscure; it includes a Niebuhrish estimate of human nature, and sometimes goes so far as to suggest that ethical ideals and principles are not even applicable to political decisions. Here Niebuhr seems to be undone by his own ambiguities.

This is as good a place as any to say something about the impact of existentialism (besides analytical philosophy the other newish philosophical movement of our period) on ethical theory. In its religious form existentialism has had a considerable impact on theology, and in its Sartrian form on literary writers, but in neither form has it had much influence on moral philosophers, though they often read existentialist writings. Its chief native sympathizers are Wild, William Barrett, William Earle, and Geoffrey Clive; Marjorie Grene is more critical. Wild in *The Challenge of Existentialism* (1955) was partly sympathetic, but nevertheless criticized existentialism in the light of the Aristotelian-Thomistic position noticed in Chapter 3. In *Human Freedom and the Social Order* (1959), however, he criticizes the tradition of natural law and self-realization and seems to go all the way over to an existentialist form of Christian ethics.

Though existentialism is in a broad sense ethical in character, it has expressed itself rather little in the field of ethics specifically. It seems to involve a noncognitive theory of the nature of moral judgments and a rejection of all proposals for making ethics scientific. It characteristically denies that man and his works, especially his choices, are susceptible of scientific treatment, and also that ethical and value judgments are either self-evident or capable of rational justification. For it ethics is fundamentally a matter of "decisions," which are arbitrary in the sense that, even if reasons can be offered, they cannot establish or justify one alternative to the exclusion of the others. Indeed, the reasons are only relevant if they represent prior decisions. To accept an ethical judgment is to commit oneself to a course of action or a way of life, and it involves an act of choice in which one is at least partly on one's own, anxious but free. Even particular judgments have this character of decision; they are not, except in artificial situations, mere conclusions from general principles plus the facts. In fact, existentialists tend to discard general principles as otiose or dishonest; but, insofar as they admit them, they insist that basic ones are simply ultimate postulates. Clearly this way of thinking has affinities with those of Stevenson, Reichenbach, Feigl, and the postulationists, as well as with those of Herberg and Hutchison. At least some of the same influences and considerations that produced existentialism have been at work on our philosophers, even when its own direct influence on them is negligible. Thus White thinks, with approval, that we are moving from the age of meanings through the age of words to the age of decisions; and Aiken, though he insists that morality has its own interpersonally valid patterns of deliberation and justification, and hence is rational in a way that emotivists and existentialists fail to see, nevertheless agrees with the latter that the pattern of moral reasoning is not that of inductive or deductive logic, that the individual moral agent is autonomous, and that when one comes to the question "Why be moral?" one can answer it only by an appeal to his own commitments freely made. "Decision," he says in *Reason and Conduct,* "is king. . . . The existentialists, for all their strange ways of saying things, have really understood a fundamental fact of the moral life." (p. 86).

I must also mention here an influence of a very different sort from the other side of the globe, namely, that of Buddhism. This is not very considerable as yet, and is spearheaded by visitors from abroad: Aldous Huxley, Gerald Heard, Alan Watts, and D. T. Suzuki. A number of Americans, however, have become interested in Oriental philosophy, especially Zen Buddhism, and some of them, like Northrop, are beginning to take it into consideration in thinking about ethics, feeling that the East has an important contribution to make, and hoping that Kipling is wrong about the time of its meeting with the West.

NORMATIVE ETHICS AND
SOCIAL PHILOSOPHY

Issues in normative ethics. Social and political philosophy.
Philosophy of law. Anthropological and psychological studies.
Free will; responsibility; punishment.

Thus far I have concentrated mainly on the more theoretical or
meta-ethical views of our moral philosophers and value theorists of
the last three decades. In this respect my emphasis has reflected the
general one noted at the outset. In many cases, however, when
authors did make normative commitments, these have at least been
indicated, so that normative ethics has by no means been neglected,
even though such commitments have been to very general goals
or principles rather than to solutions of particular practical problems; for example, to a hedonistic or nonhedonistic view of
what is good or to a utilitarian or nonutilitarian view of what is
right.

Perhaps the chief normative issue in recent discussions, as always,
has been the one between the teleologists, who hold that what is
right is ultimately to be determined simply by seeing what promotes
the most good, and the deontologists, who deny this and insist that
other considerations such as justice must come in as well. Among
the teleologists there has also been a debate between ethical egoists
and ethical universalists on the question whose good it is that ought
to be promoted. There is today a tendency to adopt a certain compromise between the deontological position and that of the universalistic teleologists better known as utilitarians. This mediating
position has been called rule-utilitarianism and is contrasted with
act-utilitarianism, which holds that in each and every case we are to
answer the question "What is right?" by looking to see which of
the alternative acts open to us will probably produce the most good.
As against this, rule-utilitarianism contends that in most cases we

are to determine what is right in a particular situation by appealing to the prevailing moral rules rather than to consequences. But it does not leave the rules unchallenged, as the deontologist tends to do. Nor does it judge them in terms of their consequences for the individual, as an ethical egoist would. It argues that, if we ask whether actions conforming to a certain rule are right, as we may, then we may or should answer our question by looking to see if acting according to that rule has better consequences for the general good than acting according to alternative rules would have. As S. E. Toulmin has put the view, we are to proceed in morality "by applying to individual judgments the test of principle, and to principles the test of general fecundity." In this country it has been most nearly advocated by John Rawls and M. G. Singer. More on the act-utilitarianism side are C. A. Baylis and Lucius Garvin. Toulmin states his position as if it were a purely meta-ethical account of the prevailing method of moral reasoning, but it may be questioned whether it can be maintained in this form, and even whether it is not a normative theory in disguise. In any event, it may also be advanced as a proposal as to how moral choices should be justified, and then it definitely is a normative position. I myself doubt, as Aiken, Lewis, and Melden do, that we can be satisfied with a purely utilitarian justification in morality, even at the level of rules or principles. Even at this level it seems appropriate to bring up questions of just distribution and of respect for the individual that do not appear to be resolvable merely on utilitarian grounds.

The similarity between this debate among philosophers and the discussion of the relation between love and justice that goes on among theologians has not been sufficiently recognized by either group.

We have seen that even when they have been ready to propound normative principles or to advocate goals, American philosophers have been relatively unpreoccupied in their official capacities with the practical and cultural problems of the day, a fact that has often disturbed their readers, as well as some of their own number. For instance, a recent visitor complained at lunch that moral philosophers are not trying to help solve the problems of gerontology, even though all of them are growing older. However, our philosophers have not been entirely remiss. Dewey and his followers, especially, cannot be accused of staying aloof from current social problems, even though, as some of his supporters have admitted, Dewey's own answers to them leave something to be desired. Perry also wrote much, well, and cogently, during and after the war, to provide a rational but spirited rationale for "our side" and to outline principles for the "one world" he hoped was in the making. In a different way Northrop has also sought to bring about a meeting of East and West. Stace too tried to provide an ideology for our side in *The Destiny of Western Man* (1942). On another level A. E. Murphy's *The Uses of Reason* (1943) likewise took part in the ideological wars of the Forties, and, for quality and substance, deserves more attention than it has received. And, all the time, Hook has been contending in the lists on living issues of politics, education, and civil rights.

In general, it remains true, however, that the central concern of most of our moral philosophers has not been with the more practical or immediate problems of culture and society. They have usually contented themselves with offering general principles for the solution of such problems, and a very influential school of thinkers has disowned even the responsibility of doing this. Among those who have tried to provide such principles are some who have ventured into the field of political or social philosophy, which is closely related to ethics, since it is usually conceived as involving an application of value judgments and ethical principles. For the most part it was the older philosophers who interested themselves in this field, especially Dewey, Perry, and W. E. Hocking. One of them, G. H. Sabine, more disillusioned and Humean, wrote a distinguished *History of Political Theory* (1937), one of the best books of our entire period. A few younger men like Hook and Murphy at least kept their hand in. Most of them, however, were led by the analytic conception of philosophy, or even, perhaps, by events themselves, to neglect the area of social thought in favor of other things. For, to be fair to them, we must admit that the very developments that made this area so crucial were also not very encouraging to anyone who might wish to seek a reasoned and principled solution of its problems. Partly perhaps because of the temper of the times, the bulk of the more influential writing in the field recently has come from theologians, political scientists, and nonacademic thinkers, many of them influenced by the theologians, though philosophers are currently revving up an interest in political and social theory again, both analytic and normative. This revival of political interest among philosophers should not be a surprise; ethics in general has taken a social rather than an individual direction in the last decades, and this naturally brings moral philosophers closer to political thinkers. Perhaps, also, the pendulum has reached its highest point on the side of analysis and is about to swing back.

A large number of articles and books on social thought, most of them not by professional philosophers, might be mentioned here, besides those already referred to in one way or another. With much inaccuracy, the drift of the discussion can be described as follows. Already at the beginning of the Thirties the older political individualism and liberalism was coming under attack. Dewey, Hocking, and others sought to formulate a new individualism or a new liberalism. Many went off to the left, some all the way to Marxism, later labeled "the God that failed" and "the illusion of an epoch"; some moved to socialism, and others looked for a "New Deal" from a "welfare state." For most of these people the ideal was a revised democratic society inspired by a liberal religion or by philosophical naturalism. For yet others, including Niebuhr, a neo-orthodox Christianity served as a basis for a democratic theory and program of social action, sometimes in combination with a modified Marxism. They attacked alike religious and secular liberalism, Christian idealism, and totalitarianism, as well as all forms of social injustice. Events conspired with such "realistic" thinkers, or so they thought, in "proving" false the modern concept of man and the idea of progress, even in its Marxist form. Even since then liberalism has been stoutly reasserted—by Commager, Frankel, Hook, Murphy, Nagel, Perry, Schlesinger, White, and Adrienne Koch. But more and more writers have proclaimed the end of the modern era and "the demise of liberalism as the dominant political and social philosophy," and are asking, as Hallowell does, if democracy can survive the change; and more and more of them feel that the answer is either a new liberalism regrafted upon a revitalized religion or a new conservatism linked with a traditional religion. On both views politics is religious. There is also some romantic irrationalism

439

remaining from the nineteenth century, largely reclothed in existentialist styles. The result, according to Judith N. Shklar in *After Utopia* (1957), is a "decline of political faith" and of political philosophy in the manner of confident reason, a kind of romantic or Christian social despair and fatalism. Not ready to give up the rational methods of the ideology under attack, but "being neither able nor willing to build an original theory of politics," she herself prefers to resort to a "reasoned skepticism." So completely demolished does "the case for modern man" appear in many eyes.

Since much of political and social theory rests, on the one hand, on value judgments and ethical principles, and, on the other, on psychological views about the nature of man, the discussion just summarized has centered on meta-ethical and psychological questions just as those in ethics have. The parallel on meta-ethical issues between the debates in ethics and those in politics is brought out nicely in an article by Adrienne Koch on "The Status of Values and Democratic Political Theory" (*Ethics,* 1958). She distinguishes the same points of view we have been reviewing: ethical empiricism (her own position), noncognitive theories, and transempirical ones. The parallel also comes out in *What Is Justice?* (1957) by Hans Kelsen and in *Political Theory* (1959) by Arnold Brecht. The pros and cons of the natural law theory, for example, involve just such meta-ethical issues as have concerned the philosophers. If I may say so, however, these issues are generally not handled as clearly or adequately by political theorists as by philosophers. On the whole, although political science is moving in the direction of an empirical "behavioral" science, the prevailing point of view among political theorists, as among theologians, seems to be a transempirical one. Hence also their debates about the nature of man tend to parallel the polemics of the theologians against Dewey and the naturalists in the field of moral psychology. This does not mean, however, that political theorists are mostly conservatives; many of them are, but many of them, like Niebuhr and other theologians, are still liberals of a sort on social questions.

These parallels between ethical and political thinking absolve us from having to give a fuller account of the latter. Good critical reviews of recent social thought may, however, be found in M. G. White's *Social Thought in America* (1947, 1957) and Charles

Frankel's *The Case for Modern Man* (1955), both already referred to. These authors defend "modern man" against his critics, not with any startling new insights, but clearly, reasonably, and without panic, as does Miss Koch in her more recent book.

Much of what has been said of social thought generally applies to the philosophy of law, which is especially close to ethics and has been mentioned above in one or two connections. This has been an active field in America recently, and important work has been done in it. The basic issues and points of view here too parallel, to a very considerable extent, those described before. This has been shown by George Nakhnikian in an article in the *Natural Law Forum* (1957), and comes out in the books of F. C. S. Northrop, Hans Kelsen, and Lon Fuller. As was just remarked, the various attitudes toward the theory of natural law and natural rights reflect meta-ethical points of view corresponding to those of moral philosophers. One can, in fact, classify the prevailing philosophies of law under such headings as we have used, though, in doing so, one may have to do some violence to those used by legal thinkers. Legal pragmatism and legal realism go well with pragmatism in ethics, as has been observed. Analytical jurisprudence and legal positivism, however, seem sometimes to be naturalistic and sometimes noncognitivist. The natural law theory itself, as we have seen, may take an intuitionist or a naturalistic form, and perhaps others. Such correspondences arise either because law and jurisprudence depend on value and ethical judgments, as some think, or because law and morality, though independent, are in important respects similar, as others think. In fact, the relation between law and morality is itself a problem to both legal and moral philosophers. For this reason many moral philosophers are today very much interested in law and legal philosophy, partly under the influence of H. L. A. Hart, an Oxford philosopher who is also a lawyer. The interest is, no doubt, reciprocated by legal thinkers, but one feels that they could profit from an even closer study of moral philosophy, especially meta-ethics.

The emergence of "realism" both in legal philosophy and in social thought and practice generally deserves attention that I cannot give it here. It is associated with theology on the one hand and pragmatism on the other. Partly it represents an insistence on the

441

facts, however unpleasant or unideal they may be, as a basis for thought and action—the facts about man, about judges, or about the situations calling for action. But this insistence may be combined with an appeal to a moral ideal, as it is in Niebuhr and Dewey alike, and the so-called realists often seem, in their reaction to "idealism," "moralism," and "utopianism," to disown any such appeal to moral ideals or principles. They frequently seem to want to live, at least at the level of public policy, by facts alone—or, perhaps more accurately, by self-interest enlightened by a knowledge of the facts and accompanied by an assumption of self-interest on the part of others, both individuals and groups. This is a kind of amoralism that moral philosophers may well ponder.

Besides peoples' meta-ethical theories and normative views, I have had occasion to touch on their relevant psychological doctrines, explicit or implicit. Philosophers and theologians in this country have been relatively fully aware of developments in psychology, though they often feel that the psychologists are not as helpful as they might be. Some philosophers, as we have seen, have even sought to assimilate ethics, at least in part, to psychology, sometimes working out their own psychology in the process, as Perry and Pepper do. C. W. Morris's researches in the psychology and anthropology of valuation have already been mentioned. Some philosophers have tried on occasion to estimate the bearing of current psychological findings and theories on morality and moral philosophy, for example, Brandt and Edel. Perhaps the main question is that of the implications of work in psychoanalysis both for ordinary morality and for ethical theory. A number of philosophers have made efforts to estimate these: S. C. Pepper, Eliseo Vivas, Abraham Kaplan, John Hospers, and L. S. Feuer. Some psychologists have likewise done this, of course, in particular Harry Hollingworth, Edmund Bergler, Gordon Allport, and, in a book already cited, Erich Fromm. There is also the question of the working ethics assumed by psychiatrists, but this, I believe, has not been much discussed in print. At least it has not been scrutinized by moral philosophers.

There has been much more discussion of the bearings of cultural anthropology on ethics, especially since many writers have thought that ethical relativism is established by anthropological evidence (and some that it is disproved by such evidence). Anthropologists and social psychologists like Clyde Kluckhohn, Bronislaw Malinowski, Ralph Linton, S. E. Asch, Ruth Benedict, and Margaret Mead have said interesting things in this connection. Several philosophers have also studied their writings and those of other anthropologists to see what light they shed, if any, on questions either of meta-ethics or of normative ethics. Especially crucial is the question of whether anthropological evidence supports the view that ultimate disagreement on ethical issues is possible even when people have the same factual beliefs, and that ethical disagreement is therefore irresolvable by rational methods. Most anthropologists seem to tend toward an affirmative answer, though some are inclined to a negative one. Philosophers are some on one side, some on the other. Abraham Edel in *Ethical Judgment* (1955), for example, argues strongly for the view that science can in principle resolve ethical disagreements, while Mandelbaum and Brandt hold that there are or may be ethical differences that are irresolvable.

In order to obtain empirical background for the discussion of this and other problems about morality, but not feeling that this is satisfactorily provided by anthropologists themselves, two moral philosophers have actually done fieldwork—Brandt among the Hopi and John Ladd among the Navaho. What they report is very interesting. Ladd claims, for example, that the ethics of the Navaho is a kind of ethical egoism or prudentialism, a claim which, if true, tempts one to say that what the Navaho have cannot properly be called a morality. Sensing this, Ladd seeks to prepare his way by defining at some length the distinction between ethical or moral judgments and rules and nonethical or nonmoral ones, a distinction that has been much debated in recent ethical theory. Ladd's discussion should be of interest to the anthropologists, who often seem to confuse the moral and the nonmoral. In any event, the work of Brandt and Ladd should do much to raise the treatment of the relations of anthropology and ethics to a new level. Indeed, what this new level is like may already be seen in *Anthropology and Ethics* (1959) by May and Abraham Edel, a book that reviews many of the topics of moral philosophy in the light of anthropological find-

443

ings and that should also help clarify for anthropologists just how and where their findings bear on the questions of philosophical ethics.

The problem of freewill and determinism has recently been receiving increasing attention, and many American philosophers have written on this topic, though their work still stands somewhat in the shadow of that of the British. An excellent collection of current views on this subject is contained in *Determinism and Freedom in the Age of Modern Science* (1958), edited by Hook; apart from this, the most important discussions have been those of R. E. Hobart (D. S. Miller), C. L. Stevenson, John Hospers, and the California Associates who wrote *Knowledge and Society* (1938). The main question is whether determinism is compatible with the kind of ascription of freedom, obligation, responsibility, and blame that is involved in morality. In general, unlike most Continental philosophers, most American philosophers (as distinct from theologians) are determinists, but they deny that determinism is incompatible with the requirements of morality. This is the position of Hobart, Stevenson, and the California Associates, and Blanshard opens the Hook volume with a statement of one form of it. With it there usually goes a utilitarian or at least teleological conception of morality. Hobart also argues forcefully that free will, responsibility, etc. *require* determinism and are "inconceivable without it," a contention in which he has been followed by many others (but which has been attacked by F. B. Ebersole and Maurice Mandelbaum). John Hospers and Paul Edwards, however, maintain in the Hook volume, not only that determinism is true, but that moral responsibility is inconceivable *with* it, and that therefore we cannot be held morally responsible for our actions; for them, this kind of moral judgment must be given up, and perhaps others. At the other extreme are a few existentialists who reject all forms of determinism and hold that we can be and are in fact responsible, not only for our actions and our characters, but for our native endowments themselves. Displaying yet another kind of hardihood, Ebersole maintains that determinism and indeterminism are alike compatible with (and so irrelevant to) morality, and Richard Taylor that they are both inconsistent with it, the two men agreeing that what is

444

needed is some third conception of "action," "agency," or "person," which they try briefly, but none too satisfactorily, to provide.

Thus our philosophers reason high of will and fate, and if they are not "in wand'ring mazes lost," like the devils in Milton's hell, then at least they have "found no end" on which they can agree. Ebersole argues, rightly I think, that this is partly because they fail to distinguish several different questions. And, in one of the latest contributions to the debate, Mandelbaum correctly identifies the main question as a normative one, namely, whether it is morally right or justified to praise and blame, punish and reward, if determinism is true or held to be true. Then the answer depends, at least in part, on one's general normative ethics and not the other way around. In his own answer Mandelbaum tries an interesting new line with which to thread the maze (with Gestalt psychology and a nondualistic metaphysics acting as Ariadne): that our choices are determined, not by the past as past, but by the present, including present "unlearned" insight into the nature of the situation.

In any case, whatever one may think of this subject, one may ask about the grounds on which people may be praised, blamed, excused, and held responsible for their actions, dispositions, etc. This question is getting a good deal of attention today from both legal and moral philosophers, largely as a result of the work of J. L. Austin and H. L. A. Hart of Oxford. It is still too soon, however, to see what new developments are likely to emerge from this discussion.

⋙ 10 ⋘

CONCLUDING REMARKS

Any number of threads remain that ought to be woven into the story of ethical theory in America in recent decades, especially threads from the skeins of normative ethics, moral psychology, and social philosophy. I must content myself, however, with some comments on the story as a whole and with a few remarks on its further development.

I have reviewed the development in this country after 1930 of several sorts of ethical theory: intuitionism, naturalism, pragmatism, noncognitivism, and supernaturalism. Actually these groupings are not mutually exclusive; pragmatists may be either naturalists or noncognitivists, naturalists may be religious moralists, and religious moralists may be intuitionists, naturalists, or noncognitivists. This suggests that I might have used only three headings: intuitionism, naturalism, and noncognitivism. Perhaps so, but it must be admitted that some writers—e.g., Hall, Dewey, Lewis, Aiken, and Niebuhr—would then be hard to place, while others— e.g., Rice and White—who explicitly propose views that seek to synthesize or transcend those named, could not be placed at all.

On the basis of my review, it seems that intuitionism is in decline, that naturalism and pragmatism are strong but on the defensive, and that noncognitive and religious theories are in the ascendancy (the former among philosophers, the latter among nonphilosophers). However, though it is not easy to envisage a revival of intuitionism, none of these types of theory can be said to have been finally refuted. Naturalism has often been regarded as disposed of, but notices of its death have been premature, and, even in Britain, where it has never been strong, philosophers are beginning to think of reopening the shallow grave in which Moore buried it.[1] The claims of the theologians have certainly not been

[1] See Mary Warnock's *Ethics since 1900* (1960); for reassertions of naturalism in this country, see C. W. Morris's *Varieties of Human Value* (1956) and Paul Ziff's *Semantic Analysis* (1960).

446

established, and the proposed roads to reunion have not been adequately laid out. And so the debates must and will continue.

Yet it seems clear that they can hardly go on in the same ways. Perhaps the main issue of 1930-60 has been between the cognitivists and the noncognitivists. But noncognitivism has been becoming more cognitivist, and cognitivists have been making concessions to noncognitivism. In fact, it is becoming increasingly difficult to state the issue involved in any clear and general way. In part, this is because of the problems involved in distinguishing between ethical and nonethical judgments, between cognitive and noncognitive utterances or aspects of utterances, etc. The older facile ways of making such distinctions seem no longer to do the job. Even if one talks in terms of the familiar distinctions between what asserts and what expresses or between what can be called true or false and what cannot (as I often have here), one is not out of the woods. For virtually every assertive theory one can conceive a corresponding expressive theory and vice versa (e.g., the cognitive and noncognitive forms of the ideal spectator theory mentioned in Chapter 3), and, if this is so, one may at least wonder whether the correspondence between them is not more important than the difference, or even whether there really is a difference or not.

One might go on in this vein, but comments of other kinds must also be made. It cannot be claimed that many American philosophers of the first importance have played a part in our story; Dewey and Santayana alone are candidates for that rank, and they belonged to a previous generation; the only names of comparable importance are those of theologians and nonacademic writers like Niebuhr and Lippmann, or of authors who are only doubtfully regarded as American, for example, Maritain and Tillich. The period from 1930 to 1960 simply has not been an age of greatness for philosophers who had not already reached their prime. Nevertheless, it has seen a good deal of moral philosophy and value theory produced in this country, much of which compares very favorably in all respects with that produced on the Continent after Scheler, Hartmann, and Bergson, and in quality even with that produced in Britain, which it surpasses in richness and variety. Many very able people are working in ethics—more than ever before—often with a great deal of clarity and rigor and with a con-

447

siderable mastery of the subject and of related disciplines and sciences, some of them doing better work than philosophers of greater general importance. Some of this work is in book form, but it is characteristic that much of it has appeared only in articles or chapters. The best recent review of the principal questions of morals in the light of these recent discussions is Brandt's *Ethical Theory*. But, after Dewey and Niebuhr, the most important contributions are clearly those of Perry, Lewis, and Stevenson.

As always there have been heavy influences from abroad, partly because so many scholars from elsewhere have come here to live in the United States, or at least to teach here for a term or two. These influences have come mainly from Britain, and have been described where relevant. Yet one may without chauvinism claim that much of our ethical theory has been relatively independent and that even when it is borrowed it usually goes through a sea-change, as Aiken calls it, in coming across. This comes out clearly if one makes a comparative list of books by British writers in the Thirties, when intuitionism was dominant in Britain, and in the Fifties, after the "revolution in philosophy" took over the field of ethics there, with those written by Americans during the same periods. In both cases, though it is clear that the Americans have read the British (but not vice versa, except for Stevenson), the books by the former show surprisingly little resemblance to those by the latter; the views and arguments of Moore and others are often referred to and discussed, but the general approaches and points of view are different. If one looks at articles in our philosophical journals, especially recent issues, the story is somewhat different, for here the Oxford influence is very strong. This may mean that the picture is about to change, but at least so far our full-dress ethical theories have not simply copied transatlantic styles. We may perhaps hope, then, that, even if the picture changes, our rising moral philosophers will take only the best ideas in styling that come from abroad and combine them with what is good in those already here. It must be admitted, however, that our young men appear to be unduly impressed by Austin, Hare, Hart, *et al.*, and fail to put a proper value on Perry, Pepper, and Parker, or even on Dewey and Lewis, let alone on Rogers or Sharp.

It is in the development of naturalistic and pragmatic forms of ethical empiricism that American philosophers have been most distinctive. Even if it should prove that these were all mistakes, as intuitionists, existentialists, positivists, and the Oxford philosophers believe, it will still have been worthwhile to have such theories fully worked out in the most up-to-date fashion. However, they have never been thoroughly discussed in their most adequate forms by those who claim to have dispatched them. And, if it should turn out that they were on the right track, or that the British or Continentally inspired theories must be supplemented by something they have incorporated, as may well be the case, then their elaboration by their authors will have been a contribution indeed. In any event, we must not forget the important contributions of Stevenson, Aiken, and Melden to the development of noncognitive theories—especially Stevenson, whose articles and book played a considerable role in bringing about the British revolution in moral philosophy of the Forties, either by action or by reaction. Nor should we forget the contributions of the Niebuhrs and others in this country to the development of Judeo-Christian ethics, which is still the dominant ingredient, at least in theory, in the morality of most of the West— a point that philosophers are too apt to forget.

Besides being largely humanistic, naturalistic, or secular (except for the theologians), the moral philosophy and value theory of our period has been primarily meta-ethical rather than normative in character. It has tended, especially more recently, to avoid normative questions about what is right or good, as well as questions of psychology, and to confine itself to questions about the meaning or function of ethical and value judgments and the possibility and manner of their justification, plus certain other questions to be detailed below. This is by no means the whole story, but it represents perhaps the major tendency among philosophers proper. This meta-ethical preoccupation of recent moral philosophy has disturbed some readers. In at least partial reply it may be said that the concern of philosophers with questions about the nature and justification of moral and other value judgments is itself a response to a major need of our time. This is often called an age of crisis, of "the shaking of the foundations," to use Tillich's phrase, and surely one of the central ingredients in this cultural crisis is a feeling of insecurity about the foundations of our beliefs about what is good or what is right. If this is so, it is entirely appropriate for some of us—our philosophers—to ask what such beliefs signify and what bases they may have, even before they propound such beliefs for us to consider and perhaps adopt. Actually, theologians and others have also been concerned with the same meta-ethical questions —as have European philosophers—and, while what they say is often more exciting, it is also much less careful and clear, possibly because they could not maintain the same degree of detachment.

We must not forget, however, that some of our philosophers have offered us general goals or principles of action. Yet even these philosophers have been somewhat abstract and detached, and so, whether analytical or normative, they have been charged with irresponsibility and irrelevance, with ivory-towering and fiddling while the world burns. In fact, American and British philosophers have often been unfavorably compared with their Continental brethren in this respect, and there is probably some justice in the comparison (more in the case of the British than of the Americans). Nevertheless, there is much to be said for having some thinkers who are not impatient, panicky, short-sighted, lost in the concrete, the present, or the situational, even if maintaining such a class involves a risk of waste. If they should give us only the goals or general principles by which to guide our actions, they would have conferred a great boon, especially if accompanied by "the rational cogency of ordered and tested thought." Even if they were to contribute nothing but conceptual clarity and methodological rigor to our thinking about actions, policies, and institutions, they would have made a gift of inestimable value, though only indirectly, in the guidance of individuals and groups. For, as Aiken says in *Reason and Conduct,* "the task of clarifying such golden words as 'liberty,' 'justice,' 'democracy,' 'person,' and 'love' is . . . essential to the well-being of any people whose way of life is expressed in terms of them. For if they are unclear or confused or inconsistent, then the way of life is also" (p. 30). Even analysis has its sweet uses.

However, while I am ready to defend the prevailing concern of philosophers with meta-ethical and apparently impractical questions, I am not one of those who hold that the whole function of philosophy is analysis. In fact, like White, I am inclined to think that even analysis must take a normative form, and not merely elucidate actual linguistic uses, but whether this is so or not, it seems to me entirely appropriate and desirable that philosophy should be a guide to life, as the motto of a famous honorary society has it, sometimes going even beyond the formulation and defense of basic goals and principles to more specific problems.

The complaint that moral philosophy has been becoming not only meta-ethical but linguistic exaggerates the linguistic character even of the concerns of analytical philosophers, and it minimizes the fact that much of what is said by other philosophers, for example, existentialists and phenomenologists, can also be put in a similarly linguistic way. In any event, I, like many others, should prize highly answers to such "linguistic" questions as "What is or should be the meaning or function of sentences like 'I ought to do A'?" and "How are they to be justified?" With the critics, I doubt that the answers to them can be found without looking at anything nonverbal, but I also doubt that any so-called linguistic philosopher thinks they can. Even those who seek "merely" to describe or elucidate the rules for the ordinary use of "right," "good," "moral," etc. must talk about things other than these words, namely, people, feelings, motives, and situations. And there is no inconsistency in their doing so. A linguistic formulation of meta-ethical questions runs a danger of being thin and unreal, but it need not be so and often is not so in fact; and it also makes possible a clarity and rigor that is missing in the writings of many of its detractors.

Nevertheless, it seems to me that the questions of moral philosophy cannot be resolved without the help of knowledge from fields like anthropology, psychology, and sociology, together with such nonlinguistic phenomenology of moral experience as is provided by Mandelbaum, von Hildebrand, Continental writers, and theologians. Especially is this true if its questions are to include normative as well as meta-ethical ones.

Both in this chapter and earlier the desirability of greater clarity and rigor of thought and expression has been mentioned, not only on the part of theologians but also on that of philosophers. In respect of such clarity and rigor, with some exceptions, we compare unfavorably with British philosophers, though we do no worse, and often better, than Continental philosophers. There is still too

451

much loose and opaque use of language in ethics and value theory. Part of this is due to the influence of the social sciences and psychology, where jargon and bad writing are notoriously prevalent. Part of it, I believe, is an unfortunate legacy of the general theory of value. In fact, I am of the opinion that very little except harm has come from the broad use of terms like "value," "values," "valuation," and "value judgment" that is rampant in philosophy, theology, criticism, and the social sciences. Perry himself pled that "value" should be our "careful word," but I for one am almost prepared to cry "Let us swear by all that we value never to use the word again!" When people use "values" to mean not only things that are good, but all sorts of principles, virtues, and beliefs; when they make statements like "There is value" or "There are values"; when they describe the emotive theory as holding that there are no values or that values are attitudes or emotions—and they do all of these things—then matters have come to a sorry pass, and one cannot but wish that we could return to the older and more ordinary words, "good," "right," "ought," etc. Clarity and rigor are not less but more desirable in an age of crisis when all coherence seems gone. How else, except by a lucky accident or a divine dispensation, can we find the way out of our intellectual and spiritual troubles than by marshaling our information and our thoughts as carefully as possible? This probably cannot be done without some reconstruction of our concepts and our language, even in the area with which we are concerned here, but it does not require the gobbledygook that one finds on so many hands. The least a philosopher can learn to do is to think clearly and to write well. If he does, and also knows what he is talking about, he may be able to do a great deal.

What he should try to do, I have suggested, is both analytical and normative. There are a number of areas into which moral philosophers, thoroughly trained in recent methods and theories, should venture more than they now do, though, of course, not without obtaining the knowledge necessary to speak with some authority and point. In each case there is room for them to analyze and clarify terms and concepts, to evaluate reasoning, and to uncover assumptions, thus helping to sharpen the tools of those who work in the area, and also to pass such normative judgments about ends, means, or principles as they may then feel qualified to make. One such area is the philosophy of law. This has the advantage that the joint study of law and morals may be rewarding to both. Another is the philosophy of education in general and of moral education in particular. R. M. Hare has said in *The Language of Morals* (1952), "The question 'How shall I bring up my children?' . . . is one to . . . which, since ancient times, few philosophers have given much attention" (p. 74). A third field is that of psychoanalysis, the ethics of its practice and its implications for morality and moral theory. Aiken and Vivas have rightly pointed out that it has not yet played a sufficiently important role in American moral philosophy, though it has begun to have an impact on practical moral thinking. Still other areas are those of foreign policy and international or intercultural relations, civil rights, social justice, ethics in business and government, professional ethics, perhaps even gerontology. On a broader scale, moral philosophers might well take a look at and try to deal with the tendencies and problems of our present-day culture—besides the problem of foundations, with which they are already concerned—for example, the problem of religious pluralism, the effects of mass communication, automation, and increasing leisure, the phenomenon of other-direction, what Joseph Wood Krutch has recently called "the new immorality," the question of what traits of character or personality are being produced or should be produced, etc. In all these matters philosophers should take a hand, as critics and commentators, and, if possible, as guides. Else they will be left wholly to the Niebuhrs, Voegelins, Heilbroners, Riesmans, and social scientists—most of them able minds whom we cannot well do without, but nevertheless not such as any philosopher can be wholly content with.

Yet, though the hearts of moral philosophers may and should go out to such concerns, the heart of their subject must remain in meta-ethics where the center of our current crisis lies. I shall end, then, with a brief attempt to state systematically, though still rather generally, the main questions of this part of ethics as I now see them.

(1) What is the meaning, nature, function, analysis, or elucidation of ethical and value terms, sentences, or judgments?

453

(2) What are the principles of ethical reasoning? How, if at all, are moral and other value judgments to be justified or reasoned about?

(3) What is the relation of questions (1) and (2)? Does an answer to one presuppose or entail an answer to the other? How are the reasons for an ethical judgment related to its meaning?

(4) What is the analysis or meaning of terms like "moral" and "ethical" when these are applied not to actions, but to judgments, sentiments, institutions, etc? What is the definition of "morality" not as opposed to immorality but as distinguished from what is not morality, e.g., from what is aesthetic, legal, scientific, or religious?

(5) What is the relation between answers to (4) and answers to (1) and (2)?

(6) What is the justification of morality itself? Why be moral or have a morality? Should morality be retained in its present form, reconstructed, or replaced by something else? Do such questions make sense?

(7) What is action, choice, conscience, deliberation, intention, freedom, responsibility, etc.?

(8) What is the methodology to be used in answering questions (1) to (7)? Is it linguistic, phenomenological, psychological, or normative? How is one meta-ethical theory to be established as against another? What is meta-ethics anyway? Is it really distinct from normative ethics? From psychology?

In general, (1) and (2) have been the standard questions of ethical theory in our period, and I have centered on them in this study, emphasizing somewhat the differing views about the relation of ethics to science. But recently questions (4) to (8) have been coming more and more to the fore, not only in England but in America, and with them a group of problems involving the notions of moral authority, moral autonomy, and moral responsibility. This change has added greatly to the excitement of moral philosophy, even in its analytical or "linguistic" versions, for it opens new vistas and reopens old ones for a new look. It should also do much to answer the current detractors of ethical theory, since the newer questions obviously raise large and important issues such as befit an age of cultural crisis and revolution. In dealing with such questions, everything that has been mentioned is grist for the mill—moral experience, our ordinary moral discourse, law, psychoanalysis, the social sciences, political "realism," and religious ethics, as well as the whole history of morality and moral theory. If we can set ourselves to think on these things with critical care and relevant knowledge, we may at least hope that, while much of what we have had in moral philosophy has been excellent, what is to come will be even better.

BIBLIOGRAPHY

Abraham, Leo, "The Logic of Ethical Intuitionism," *Ethics*, XLIV (1933).

Adams, E. M., *Ethical Naturalism and the Modern World-View* (1960).

Aiken, H. D., "Emotive Meaning and Ethical Terms," *Journal of Philosophy*, XLI (1944).

————, Review of C. L. Stevenson's *Ethics and Language*, in *Journal of Philosophy*, XLII (1945).

————, "A Pluralistic Analysis of the Ethical 'Ought,'" *Journal of Philosophy*, XLVIII (1951).

————, *Reason and Conduct* (1962).

Allport, Gordon, *Personality* (1937).

————, *Becoming* (1955).

Asch, S. E., *Social Psychology* (1952).

Barrett, William, *Irrational Man* (1958).

Baylis, C. A., "Confirmation of Value Judgments," *Philosophical Review*, LXI (1952).

————, "Intrinsic Goodness," *Philosophy and Phenomenological Research*, XIII (1952).

————, "Utilitarianism and Moral Obligation," *Philosophical Review*, LXI (1952).

Benedict, Ruth, *Patterns of Culture* (1934).

Bergler, Edmund, *The Battle of the Conscience* (1948).

Blake, R. M., "Why Not Hedonism?" *Ethics*, XXXVII (1926).

Blanshard, Brand, "The New Subjectivism in Ethics," *Philosophy and Phenomenological Research*, IX (1949).

————, *The Impasse in Ethics and a Way Out* (1954).

————, *Reason and Goodness* (1961).

Bourke, V. J., *Ethics* (1955).

Brandt, R. B., "The Emotive Theory of Ethics," *Philosophical Review*, LIX (1950).

————, "The Status of Empirical Assertion Theories in Ethics," *Mind*, LXI (1952).

456

———, *Hopi Ethics* (1954).

———, "The Definition of an 'Ideal Observer' Theory in Ethics," *Philosophy and Phenomenological Research,* XV (1955).

———, *Ethical Theory* (1959).

Brecht, Arnold, *Political Theory* (1959).

Brown, S. M., "Duty and the Production of Good," *Philosophical Review,* LXI (1952).

———, "Inalienable Rights," *Philosophical Review,* LXIV (1955).

California Associates, "The Freedom of the Will," *Knowledge and Society* (1938).

Carnap, Rudolf, *Philosophy and Logical Syntax* (1935).

Childs, Marquis, and Douglass Cater, *Ethics in a Business Society* (1954).

Clarke, Mary E., *A Study in the Logic of Value* (1929).

Clive, Geoffrey, *The Romantic Enlightenment* (1960).

Cohen, Morris, *Reason and Nature* (1931).

Cohen, Felix, *Ethical Systems and Legal Ideals* (1933).

Conklin, E. G., *Man: Real and Ideal* (1943).

Dennes, W. R., *Some Dilemmas of Naturalism* (1960).

Dewey, John, and J. H. Tufts, *Ethics,* rev. ed. (1932).

Dewey, John, *Experience and Nature* (1929).

———, *Individualism Old and New* (1929).

———, *The Quest for Certainty* (1929).

———, *A Common Faith* (1934).

———, *Liberalism and Social Action* (1935).

———, *Theory of Valuation* (1939).

———, "Some Questions About Value," *Journal of Philosophy,* XLI (1944).

———, "Ethical Subject Matter and Language," *Journal of Philosophy,* XLII (1945).

———, *The Problems of Men* (1946).

Duncker, Karl, "Ethical Relativity," *Mind,* XLVIII (1939).

Earle, William, *Objectivity* (1955).

Ebersole, F. B., "Free Choice and the Demands of Morals," *Mind,* LXI (1952).

Edwards, Paul, *The Logic of Moral Discourse* (1955).

Edel, Abraham, *Ethical Judgment* (1955).

457

————, and May Edel, *Anthropology and Ethics* (1959).

Feigl, Herbert, "Validation and Vindication," in *Readings in Ethical Theory*, ed. W. S. Sellars and John Hospers (1952).

Feuer, L. S., *Psychoanalysis and Ethics* (1955).

Firth, Roderick, "Ethical Absolutism and the Ideal Observer," *Philosophy and Phenomenological Research*, XII (1952).

————, "Reply to Professor Brandt," *Philosophy and Phenomenological Research*, XV (1955).

Frankel, Charles, *The Case for Modern Man* (1955).

Frankena, W. K., "The Naturalistic Fallacy," *Mind*, XLVIII (1939).

————, "Moral Philosophy at Mid-Century," *Philosophical Review*, LX (1951).

————, "Sellars' Theory of Valuation," *Philosophy and Phenomenological Research*, XV (1954).

————, "Obligation and Motivation in Recent Moral Philosophy," in *Essays in Moral Philosophy*, ed. A. I. Melden (1958).

Fromm, Erich, *Man for Himself* (1947).

Fuller, L. L., *The Law in Quest of Itself* (1940).

Garnett, A. C., *The Moral Nature of Man* (1952).

————, *Can Ideals and Norms Be Justified?* (1955).

————, *Religion and the Moral Life* (1955).

Garvin, Lucius, *A Modern Introduction to Ethics* (1953).

Grene, Marjorie, *Dreadful Freedom* (1948).

Hall, E. W., *What Is Value?* (1952).

————, "Practical Reason(s) and the Deadlock in Ethics," *Mind*, LXVI (1955).

————, *Modern Science and Human Values* (1957).

————, *Our Knowledge of Fact and Value* (1961).

Hallowell, J. H., *The Moral Foundations of Democracy* (1954).

Herberg, Will, *Judaism and Modern Man* (1951).

Hildebrand, Dietrich von, *Christian Ethics* (1952).

————, *True Morality and Its Counterfeits* (1955).

Hill, T. E., *Contemporary Ethical Theories* (1950).

Hobart, R. E. (D. S. Miller), "Free Will as Involving Determinism," *Mind*, XLVIII (1934).

Hollingworth, Harry, *Psychology and Ethics* (1949).

Holmes, S. J., *Life and Morals* (1948).

Hook, Sidney, *Reason, Social Myths, and Democracy* (1940).

————, "Naturalism and Democracy," in *Naturalism and the Human Spirit*, ed. Y. H. Krikorian (1944).

————, "The Desirable and Emotive in Dewey's Ethics," in *John Dewey: Philosopher of Science and Freedom*, ed. Sidney Hook (1950).

————, ed., *Determinism and Freedom in the Age of Modern Science* (1958).

————, *Political Power and Personal Freedom* (1959).

Hospers, John, "Free Will in Psychoanalysis," in *Readings in Ethical Theory*, ed. W. S. Sellars and John Hospers (1952).

————, "What Means This Freedom?" in *Determinism and Freedom*, ed. Sidney Hook (1958).

Hutchison, J. A., ed., *Christian Faith and Social Action* (1953).

————, *The Two Cities* (1957).

Johnson, O. A., *Rightness and Goodness* (1959).

Kaplan, Abraham, "Are Moral Judgments Assertions?" *Philosophical Review*, LI (1952).

————, *The New World of Philosophy* (1961).

Kelsen, Hans, *What Is Justice?* (1957).

Kluckhohn, Clyde, "Universal Categories of Culture," in *Anthropology Today*, ed. A. L. Kroeber (1953).

————, "Ethical Relativity," *Journal of Philosophy*, LII (1955).

Koch, Adrienne, "The Status of Values and Democratic Political Theory," *Ethics*, LVIII (1958).

Köhler, Wolfgang, *The Place of Value in a World of Facts* (1938).

Ladd, John, *The Structure of a Moral Code* (1957).

Ledden, J. E., "On the Logical Status of Value," *Philosophical Review*, XLIX (1950).

Lefever, E. W., *Ethics and United States Foreign Policy* (1957).

Lepley, Ray, *The Verifiability of Value* (1944).

————, ed., *Value: A Cooperative Inquiry* (1949).

————, ed., *The Language of Value* (1957).

Lewis, C. I., *An Analysis of Knowledge and Valuation* (1946).

————, *The Ground and Nature of the Right* (1955).

————, *Our Social Inheritance* (1956).

Linton, Ralph, "The Problem of Universal Values," in *Method and Perspective in Anthropology*, ed. R. F. Spencer (1954).

Lippmann, Walter, *The Good Society* (1937).

———, *The Public Philosophy* (1955).

Mandelbaum, Maurice, *The Phenomenology of Moral Experience* (1955).

———, "Determinism and Moral Responsibility," *Ethics*, LXX (1960).

Maritain, Jacques, *The Rights of Man and Natural Law* (1943).

———, *The Person and the Common Good* (1947).

Mead, G. H., *Mind, Self, and Society* (1934).

Melden, A. I., "On the Method of Ethics," *Journal of Philosophy*, XLV (1948).

———, "Two Comments on Utilitarianism," *Philosophical Review*, L (1951).

———, ed., *Essays in Moral Philosophy* (1958).

———, *Rights and Right Conduct* (1959).

Morris, C. W., *Pragmatism and the Crisis of Democracy* (1934).

———, *Paths of Life* (1942).

———, *Signs, Language, and Behavior* (1946).

———, "Axiology as the Science of Preferential Behavior," in *Value: A Cooperative Inquiry*, ed. Ray Lepley (1949).

———, *Varieties of Human Value* (1956).

Murphy, A. E., *The Uses of Reason* (1943).

———, "Coming to Grips with 'The Nature and Destiny of Man,'" in H. N. Wieman, *et al.*, *Religious Liberals Reply* (1947).

Murray, J. C., "Morality and Foreign Policy," *America*, CII (1960).

———, *We Hold These Truths* (1960).

Nakhnikian, George, "Contemporary Ethical Theories and Jurisprudence," *Natural Law Forum*, II (1957).

Niebuhr, H. Richard, "The Center of Value," in *Moral Principles of Action*, ed. Ruth Anshen (1952).

Niebuhr, Reinhold, *Moral Man and Immoral Society* (1932).

———, *An Interpretation of Christian Ethics* (1935).

———, *The Nature and Destiny of Man* (1941).

———, *Children of Light and Children of Darkness* (1944).

———, *Faith and History* (1949).

Nielsen, Kai, "The Functions of Moral Discourse," *Philosophical Quarterly*, VII (1957).

———, "Justification and Moral Reasoning," *Methodos* (1957).

Northrop, F. C. S., *The Meeting of East and West* (1946).

———, *The Complexities of Legal and Ethical Experience* (1959).

Pap, Arthur, "The Verifiability of Moral Judgments," *Ethics*, LVI (1946).

———, *Elements of Analytical Philosophy* (1949).

Parker, D. H., *Human Values* (1931).

———, "The Metaphysics of Value," *Ethics*, XLIV (1934).

———, "Reflections on the Crisis in Theory of Value," *Ethics*, LVI (1946).

———, *Philosophy of Value* (1957).

Pepper, S. C., *A Digest of Purposive Values* (1947).

———, *The Sources of Value* (1958).

Perry, C. M., "The Arbitrary as Basis for Rational Morality," *Ethics*, XLIII (1933).

Perry, R. B., *General Theory of Value* (1926).

———, "A Theory of Value Defended," *Journal of Philosophy*, XXVIII (1931).

———, "Value as an Objective Predicate," *Journal of Philosophy*, XXVIII (1931).

———, "Value as Simply Value," *Journal of Philosophy*, XXVIII (1931).

———, "Value and Its Moving Appeal," *Philosophical Review*, XLI (1932).

———, *Shall Not Perish from the Earth* (1940).

———, *Our Side Is Right* (1942).

———, *One World in the Making* (1945).

———, *Realms of Value* (1954).

Pratt, J. B., *Naturalism* (1939).

———, *Reason in the Art of Living* (1949).

Ramsey, Paul, *Basic Christian Ethics* (1953).

———, ed., *Faith and Ethics* (1957).

———, *War and the Christian Conscience* (1961).

———, *Nine Modern Moralists* (1962).

Rawls, John, "Two Concepts of Rules," *Philosophical Review*, LXIV (1955).

——, "Justice as Fairness," *Philosophical Review*, LXVII (1958).

Reichenbach, Hans, *The Rise of Scientific Philosophy* (1951).

Rice, P. B., *On the Knowledge of Good and Evil* (1955).

Rogers, A. K., *Ethics and Moral Tolerance* (1934).

Ryan, J. A., and F. J. Boland, *Catholic Principles of Politics* (1940).

Sabine, G. H., *History of Political Theory* (1937).

——, *Social Studies and Objectivity* (1941).

Santayana, George, *The Realm of Truth* (1938).

Savery, Barnett, "The Unique Quality Goodness—a Myth," *Ethics*, XLVII (1937).

Savery, William, "A Defense of Hedonism," *Ethics*, XLV (1934).

Schuster, C. A., "Rapprochement in Value Theory," *Journal of Philosophy*, L (1953).

Selsam, Howard, *Socialism and Ethics* (1943).

Sesonske, Alexander, *Value and Obligation* (1957).

Sharp, F. C., *Ethics* (1928).

——, "Voluntarism and Objectivity in Ethics," *Philosophical Review*, L (1941).

——, *Good Will and Ill Will* (1950).

Shklar, Judith N., *After Utopia* (1957).

Singer, M. G., "Moral Rules and Principles," in *Essays in Moral Philosophy*, ed. A. I. Melden (1958).

——, *Generalization in Ethics* (1961).

Smith, J. W., "Should General Theory of Value Be Abandoned?" *Ethics*, LVII (1947).

——, *Theme for Reason* (1957).

Sparshott, F. E., *An Enquiry into Goodness* (1958).

Stace, W. T., *The Concept of Morals* (1937).

——, *The Destiny of Western Man* (1942).

——, *Religion in the Modern World* (1953).

Stevenson, C. L., "The Emotive Meaning of Ethical Terms," *Mind*, XLVI (1937).

——, "Ethical Judgments and Avoidability," *Mind*, XLVII (1938).

——, "Persuasive Definitions," *Mind*, XLVII (1938).

BIBLIOGRAPHY

————, *Ethics and Language* (1944).

————, "Brandt's Questions about Emotive Ethics," *Philosophical Review*, LIX (1950).

————, "The Emotive Conception of Ethics and Its Cognitive Implications," *Philosophical Review,* LIX (1950).

Swabey, W. C., "Non-Normative Utilitarianism," *Journal of Philosophy,* XL (1943).

Taylor, Richard, "Determinism and the Theory of Agency," in *Determinism and Freedom,* ed. Sidney Hook (1958).

Tillich, Paul, *The Religious Situation* (1932).

————, *The Protestant Era* (1948, 1957).

————, *The Courage to Be* (1952).

————, *Love, Power, and Justice* (1954).

Thomas, G. F., *Christian Ethics and Moral Philosophy* (1955).

Thompson, K. W., *Christian Ethics and the Dilemmas of Foreign Policy* (1959).

————, *Political Realism and the Crisis of World Politics* (1960).

Urban, W. M., *The Intelligible World* (1929).

————, *The Fundamentals of Ethics* (1930).

————, "Value Propositions and Verifiability," *Journal of Philosophy,* XXXIV (1937).

Vivas, Eliseo, *The Moral Life and the Ethical Life* (1950).

White, M. G., *Social Thought in America* (1947, 1957).

————, *Toward Reunion in Philosophy* (1956).

Wild, J. D., *Plato's Modern Enemies and the Theory of Natural Law* (1953).

————, *The Challenge of Existentialism* (1955).

————, *Human Freedom and the Social Order* (1959).

Williams, D. C., "Ethics as Pure Postulate," *Philosophical Review,* XLII (1933).

————, "The Meaning of Good," *Philosophical Review,* XLVI (1937).

Williams, Gardner, *Humanistic Ethics* (1951).

Wood, Ledger, "Cognition and Moral Value," *Journal of Philosophy,* XXXIV (1937).

Ziff, Paul, *Semantic Analysis* (1960).

PHILOSOPHY OF SCIENCE

◦§§◦

HERBERT FEIGL

PROFESSOR OF PHILOSOPHY AND DIRECTOR,
MINNESOTA CENTER FOR PHILOSOPHY OF SCIENCE
UNIVERSITY OF MINNESOTA

PREFACE

In this essay I have attempted to relate some of the more important issues, contributions, and developments in the philosophy of science in America during the last three or four decades. A general objective of the Ford Humanities Project—that participating scholars direct their essays to the educated layman rather than to specialists in their own respective fields—clearly necessitated a good deal of selection and simplification on the one hand and omission of highly technical aspects on the other. Since American philosophy of science in recent times is a product of many minds (scientists and philosophers, philosopher-scientists, and scientist-philosophers) I decided to deal with my subject matter *topically,* rather than historically. This procedure suggested itself also for the reason that—despite much diversity in orientation and basic commitments—there is perhaps a larger measure of agreement in this field than in any other area of philosophy. To be sure, different metaphysical and epistemological viewpoints do express themselves in the various contributions to the philosophy of science. This will become quite evident in my report about the many controversial issues. Nevertheless, there are in the philosophy of science no "towering figures" or "schools of thought" in quite the sense in which they are so prominent in other branches of philosophical endeavor.

A. N. Whitehead and Albert Einstein are, of course, "towering figures," but the work of neither can strictly be claimed to be American. Whitehead completed his work in philosophy of science before he came to this country, and thereafter devoted most of his work to metaphysics; Einstein, perhaps the greatest scientist-philosopher of our time, also made his most significant contributions while in Europe. Some of his later writings, however, fall within the scope of my survey and will be discussed as American contributions to scholarship. The logical empiricists (or scientific empiricists) formed perhaps the most influential and productive group at work in the United States during the past three or four decades. Their divergencies, however, are as important as their basic agreements and are sufficient reason for considering them as individuals rather than as members of a leading "school of thought."

In keeping with the objectives and the scope of "The Princeton Studies," this study deals primarily with work done in the United States and refers to contributions from abroad only to the extent that they significantly influenced American thought. But, of course, my report does cover the work done on American soil by scholars who migrated to this country in the last thirty years.

I have limited my exposition to the philosophy of the *empirical* sciences, with special attention to the logic and methodology of the natural sciences and psychology, and I have dealt only very briefly and superficially with the philosophy of the social sciences. Some such limitation of scope was inevitable both in view of the space allowed, and my own predilections in weighing the significance of the extant contributions to the field.

The brief bibliography appended to my essay will help interested readers to pursue more intensive and extensive studies in this field. Several of the books listed also contain ample references to other books, and to articles in the periodical literature.

Philosophy of science came to be recognized in America as a field of research and study only some thirty years ago. There were important contributions by just a few men in the second half of the nineteenth century and during the first thirty years of our century. The names of J. B. Stallo, C. S. Peirce, William James, and John Dewey are the first to come to mind. Morris R. Cohen's work, though not exactly trailblazing or greatly original, was certainly influential in stimulating the growth of the young discipline. P. W. Bridgman's book *The Logic of Modern Physics* (1927), which puts emphasis on the operational outlook (in many respects similar to Peirce's pragmatist view of meaning), affected the thinking not only of philosophers of physics but also of the methodologists of psychology and the social sciences. A little later, a group of prominent teachers and writers, such as A. C. Benjamin, F. S. C. Northrop, W. H. Werkmeister, Henry Margenau, Ernest Nagel, C. W. Churchman, Nelson Goodman, Max Black, W. V. Quine, and Patrick Suppes, contributed much toward the establishment of this field of scholarship in the institutions of higher learning. The immigration in the 1930's of the logical empiricists Rudolf Carnap, Hans Reichenbach, Philipp Frank, Richard von Mises, C. G. Hempel, Henryk Mehlberg, Gustav Bergmann, and Herbert Feigl added a great impetus. Since then a younger generation of numerous philosophers of science has grown up to contribute highly valuable studies, many of them fairly specialized and highly technical. Prominent in this younger group are Adolf Grünbaum, N. R. Hanson, P. K. Feyerabend, Arthur Pap, Michael Scriven, Israel Scheffler, Morton Beckner, May Brodbeck, Hilary Putnam, Wesley Salmon, and Grover Maxwell. There are several dozens of others who have produced valuable work in the logic of the natural and the social sciences. Special mention should be made also of the many prominent scientists who by way of methodological studies, or at least by occasional philosophical "asides," have made significant contributions: Hermann Weyl, Alfred Landé, Norbert Wiener, Nicolas Rashevsky, Wolfgang Köhler, C. C. Pratt, E. C. Tolman, C. L. Hull, B. F. Skinner, S. S. Stevens, K. W. Spence, P. F. Lazarsfeld, P. E. Meehl, W. W. Rozeboom, Victor Lenzen, H. A. Simon, John Kemeny, Sigmund Koch, K. S. Lashley, F. A. Hayek, and G. A. Lundberg. There are many others, too numerous to mention here.

Because of the tremendous scope, the varying degrees of technicality, and the great diversity of the extant work in recent American philosophy of science, I decided that a "distillation" of its more generally important and interesting aspects would be the task called for in this essay.

WHAT IS PHILOSOPHY OF SCIENCE?

The vast and impressive structure of modern science, as well as its ever increasing impact on human affairs, has given rise to a variety of reflections and speculations. There are those who deplore the "cleavage in our culture," and seek for a better understanding between the sciences and the humanities. There are serious misgivings about the future of civilization in the age of automation, of nuclear energy, and of the biological, psychological, and social manipulation of man. And more relevant to the object of this essay, there is an increasing concern with the nature of scientific method and with the meaning and validity of the fundamental principles of science.

"Philosophy of science" as currently understood designates a variety of critical reflections upon the basic concepts, assumptions, and methods of the formal and the factual sciences. It may concentrate on highly intricate aspects of concept formation, theory construction, proof techniques, etc., or it may deal with such general issues as the (alleged) limitations of science, the relations of science to the arts, ethics, religion, metaphysics, or theology. It involves logical and epistemological analyses of such problems as the existence of theoretically postulated entities, or of the validity of probable inference. It may involve reflections upon problems traditionally classified as "metaphysical," such as the nature of space and time, of matter and energy, of causality, of organic life and the relation of the mental to the physical. But the present trend favors a restriction of the discipline of philosophy of science to the logical analysis and clarification of the knowledge-claims of the sciences. It therefore differs quite sharply from the "Naturphilosophie" of the nineteenth century. Speculative anticipations of scientific syntheses and unifications can hardly be regarded any longer as a proper task for philosophy. It is true there have been occasions in the past when thinkers who may be more properly designated philosophers rather than scientists have introduced trailblazing ideas that were later developed and confirmed by scientific procedures. The atomic hypothesis of Leucippus and Democritus, the Ionian anticipations of evolutionary theory, the perceptive remarks of Nietzsche on the psychology of the unconscious—these and possibly just a few other instances are pertinent illustrations. But it seems that in recent times the imagination of the scientists has outrun that of the philosophers and the poets. No philosopher even vaguely anticipated the theory of relativity, or the quantum theory. Nor have the theories of genetics or of biochemistry been foreshadowed by philosophical speculations. It does seem that nowadays and in the future fruitful theorizing can be expected only from competent scientists. They must have an expert grasp of the observational and experimental facts, they must be thoroughly conversant with the extant theories, and they have to be able to utilize advanced mathematical techniques. The great scientific syntheses of the modern age have often been prepared by the development of borderland sciences, such as the "hyphenated" disciplines of physical chemistry, biophysics, biochemistry, psychophysics, psychophysiology, and social psychology, and such auxiliary disciplines as cybernetics and information theory. To be sure, many philosophically minded scientists have initiated, or contributed to, these developments. The German chemist Wilhelm Ostwald was instrumental in establishing physical chemistry as a scientific discipline in its own right, and he was one of the first to use the term "Naturphilosophie" in the modern sense of philosophy of science.

All this does not mean that professional philosophers of science are disinterested in synthesis or synopsis. Quite to the contrary, a good deal of their work concerns precisely the logic of unifying syntheses. They share the scientific theorist's fascination with the synoptic power of the hypotheticodeductive method. One may interpret this fascination psychologically in various ways. There is the "economic" aspect: Theories are attempts to cover a maximum of facts by means of a minimum of basic concepts and assumptions. The predictive efficacy of scientific theories in a way demonstrates how much one can get for how little. Another aspect may be that of a sublimated power drive. Instead of dominating other persons, the scientific theorist masters and marshals a great number of facts. I refrain from such "deeper" psychoanalytic interpretations according to which the quest for scientific understanding may be traced to infantile sexual curiosity. No matter how we explain the fascination, it exists, and it accounts for at least one aspect of the high regard for this monumental contribution of the human intellect, the theories of modern science. Hence it is understandable that philosophers have attempted to achieve a "science of science" that would make the almost miraculous achievements of scientific theories somehow comprehensible. This is perhaps the purest and most commendable motivation for philosophical analyses of science. But, of course, other motivations have also yielded worthwhile results. There are logicians who use the sciences as a domain in which to exercise their formal (and often formidable) intellectual powers. And there are others, perhaps more artistically inclined philosophers, who prefer to rhapsodize quite informally about the scientific enterprise. Still others are preoccupied with epistemological or metaphysical puzzles, and prefer to tackle them within the arena of "metascientific" reflections.

In what follows I shall deal with American contributions to the philosophy of the empirical sciences regardless of the motivation or provenance of those contributions.

There is a fair measure of agreement today on how to conceive of *philosophy* of science as contrasted with the history, the psychology, or the sociology of science. All these disciplines are *about* science, but they are "about" it in different ways. The history of science traces the development of scientific problems, ideas and solutions, preferably within the entire sociocultural context. The psychology of scientific discovery tries to account for the creative, problem-solving activities of the scientists in terms of the requisite mental processes. The sociologist of science tries to account for the development and reception of scientific theories and points of view. Investigations of styles and fashions in scientific theorizing, reflecting the "Zeitgeist" of a given period of cultural, social, economic, or political conditions clearly belong in this area of the sociology of knowledge.

In the widely accepted terminology of Hans Reichenbach, studies of this sort pertain to the *context of discovery,* whereas the analyses pursued by philosophers of science pertain to the *context of justification.* It is one thing to ask how we arrive at our scientific knowledge-claims, or what sociocultural factors contribute to their acceptance or rejection; and it is another thing to ask what sorts of evidence, and what general objective rules and standards govern the testing, the confirmation or disconfirmation, and the acceptance or rejection of knowledge-claims in science. The question "How do we know?" is thus typically ambiguous; it may amount to asking "How did we come to know?" or it may mean asking "What reasons can we give by way of objective support for our claims to know?" As a prerequisite for answering the second, i.e., the philosophical, kind of questions, we need to be clear about the *meaning* of scientific assertions. This involves a scrutiny of the logical structure of scientific concepts, and it involves critical reflections upon the lines of demarcation of the scientific from nonscientific and unscientific endeavors. These two questions, then, "What do we mean?" (i.e., by the words and symbols we use) and "How do we know?" (i.e., to be true, or confirmed as likely to be true what we claim as scientific truths), guide the inquiries of modern philosophy of science. Analyses of the empirical bases and of the logical structure of the factual sciences are the primary concerns. On many signal occasions great scientists have been their own philosophers in that they have produced new theories or methods aided by incisive critical scrutinies of the total relevant conceptual frame. But with the increasing specialization in all fields, two or three generations of philosophers of science have arisen. Competent understanding of at least some scientific disciplines, combined with logical acumen and philosophical insight, is a distinction achieved only by a rather small group of philosophers of science. But the efforts of these specialists have yielded results that are eminently enlightening.

The approaches and procedures used by individual philosophers of science differ widely. They range from rather informal studies to formidably formal reconstructions. Personally, I think there is a place for all of these. To be sure, there are dangers at the extreme ends. The British preoccupation with the analysis of ordinary language and the attendant inclination to reduce philosophical to philological problems has not been very influential in American philosophy of science. A modicum of Oxford-type analysis, however, has yielded some very interesting results—as in some of the work of Max Black, N. R. Hanson, and Michael Scriven. On the

473

other side, the "precisionists," i.e., the constructors of formal systems, have contributed a great deal, and there can be no doubt that some work of this kind has been outstandingly fruitful. In the spirit of Euclid's method as it has been tremendously improved and refined in modern mathematics, entire disciplines in the empirical sciences have been cast in the form of deductive systems. The danger here is that formalization and axiomatization becomes an end in itself. The ideals of mathematical compressions and "elegance" have their place, but not necessarily in the logic of the empirical sciences. What is most needed here are systems of maximally independent testability. Such systems enable us to see which postulates may need revising or supplanting if and when contrary evidence should emerge.

᪥ 2 ᪥

THE AIMS OF SCIENCE AND THE
CRITERIA OF SCIENTIFIC METHOD

This chapter is to report essentially on the definitions and the delimitation of the scientific enterprise. Fortunately there is a large measure of agreement on how to answer the question "What is science?" It is true there have been occasional doubts about the possibility of an adequate definition. Impressed with the tremendous changes in the content, techniques, and general outlook of science, some thinkers have discouraged all attempts at a general characterization. But even if the common denominator for the various stages of the historical development of science may be tenuous it is not nil. Moreover, it is not too difficult to arrive at a definition of the *modern* scientific quest, accurate at least for the period since the Renaissance. Limiting myself again to the factual-empirical sciences, I think it is fairly well agreed that their aims are adequate description and explanation of the facts of the world. Prediction per se is not one of the aims of the pure sciences. It is of course of the utmost importance in the testing of explanatory laws, hypotheses, and theories; and it is indispensable in all the applied sciences, such as the technologies, medicine, etc. whose practical aims are control, production, therapy, or guidance. Nothing is more vital in science than reliable knowledge of what happens under what conditions, or what is correlated with what to which degree. But this is precisely the sort of knowledge that the laws of science formulate. Logically speaking, predictions are statements about specific future states of affairs, just as retrodictions are statements about specific past states of affairs. Hence they are descriptions, and if scientifically respectable, they are descriptions inferred according to rationally acceptable rules from reliably established other descriptions, together with well-confirmed laws or theoretical assumptions.

Although a more detailed discussion of the logic of scientific explanation will be presented later, a brief preliminary characteriza-

475

tion is required at this point. There is still a small minority of thinkers, especially among the experimental scientists, who maintain that there is no such thing as explanation in the empirical sciences. These ultrapositivists cling to the views of Kirchhoff, Mach, and Stallo according to which the task of science consists in an "economical description" of the empirical facts. This view, however, obliterates the useful distinction made already on the level of everyday life and common sense (and in common language) between *giving an account of* and *accounting for* the facts. It is clearly one thing to *describe,* e.g., the phenomenon of the rainbow, the sequence of the seasons in the temperate zone, the growth of an organism, etc., and it is another thing to *explain* how these phenomena come about. We do the latter by (respective) reference to the laws and theories of optics, of the celestial motion of the earth (and the radiation impinging on its surface under the conditions of the inclination of the earth's axis to the orbital plane), the biological regularities of cell division, etc. In all scientifically justifiable explanations we *derive* the facts or regularities that are to be explained (the "explananda") from laws or theoretical assumptions in conjunction with descriptions of individual states of affairs or with other laws and assumptions. The premises required for such derivations are called the "explanantia." In the context of any given explanation there are then always unexplained explanantia. This does not preclude the possibility of explaining these same explanantia on a "higher level." Since this process invariably comes to a natural stop at some level, this (at a given stage of scientific investigation) highest level of explanation can only be accepted on the basis of its explanatory power. The objection that we therefore never obtain a genuine explanation is mistaken, because the objector cannot even specify what such a "genuine explanation" would amount to. If he insists on *self-evidence* of the explanatory premises, then he must be reminded that we have many excellent explanatory theories in modern science whose postulates are far from self-evident. If he insists that the ultimate premises of scientific explanation must be true on purely logical grounds, then we have to point out that purely logical truths do not contain any information regarding matters of fact. Scientific explanation as we know it and as we appreciate it is thus *relative* in a twofold way:

476

It is relative to the premises that on the given level of scientific investigation are themselves unexplained; and it is relative to the strength of the empirical evidence that supports those premises. If new and contrary evidence emerges in further research, those premises will at least be modified, or even abandoned in order to be replaced by entirely different assumptions. In our day and age it scarcely needs emphasizing that scientific truth-claims are unexceptionally open to revision, i.e., that all laws and theories can be held only "until further notice." By this I do not mean to endorse the popular notion that the progress of science is chaotic and anarchic. Quite to the contrary, a closer analysis of the history of scientific theories reveals that quite frequently the new theories contain the older ones as special cases, still approximately correct within a limited range of the pertinent variables. On the other hand there can be no question that there have been incisive and pervasive changes in theoretical outlook. The "revolutions" of science, such as the replacement of the Aristotelian physics by that of Galileo and Newton, the replacement of Newtonian physics by that of Einstein and the quantum theorists, the Darwinian revolution in biology, the Freudian innovations in psychology, are only some of the more spectacular examples.

With these clarifications understood it can be asserted that the aims of the pure factual sciences are indeed description and explanation. Turning now to the criteria or standards of scientific method, I shall present and examine the views prevalent in recent and current philosophy of science regarding the distinctions of *scientific* from *nonscientific* and from *unscientific* procedures.

There is a large measure of agreement concerning the line of demarcation between scientific and nonscientific endeavors. There is little trouble in distinguishing science from literature, from the arts, and from religion. Here even the aims are different. Science attempts to provide reliable knowledge. Literature and the arts may utilize knowledge, they may convey knowledge, but they do not systematically test knowledge-claims. The question has often been asked whether *history* is a science. I think the answer is quite clear: inasmuch as history aims at a reliable reconstruction of past events by a scrupulous scrutiny of present evidence, it is a scientific enterprise. After all, geology in reconstructing the formation of the various features of the surface of the earth is a historical discipline. So is paleontology in its attempt to reconstruct the evolution of organic life in our planet. The history of civilization concerns human affairs, and the interpretations or causal explanations it has to offer involve psychological, sociopsychological, economic, ecological, etc. premises. History as presented in the books of great writers, however, also involves an artistic component, in that it enables the readers to project themselves imaginatively into cultures and personalities other than their own. Similarly, a great novelist may be able to convey psychological insights by vividly depicting various characters in various life situations. These insights may well go beyond what one could find in textbooks of psychology or sociology. But it is important to recognize that the criteria by which we appraise a scientific knowledge-claim are only of secondary significance in the evaluation of a work of art; and that the aesthetic criteria that we apply to works of art are only of secondary importance for the acceptance or rejection of scientific theories. As Boltzmann said, and as Einstein quoted him: "Let elegance be a matter for tailors and cobblers." It might be argued against this that Einstein, of all people, should have realized that in the construction of his theories he was guided by considerations of mathematical symmetry and harmony. Still, even the formally most beautiful theory may be hopelessly inadequate in regard to the facts of observation. It is these facts of observation, the results of measurements, experiments, or statistical designs, that are decisive in the confirmation or disconfirmation of scientific theories.

The line of demarcation between science and religion requires special consideration because of the truth-claims that are explicitly made especially in those religions that are connected with a theology. The same sort of question arises in regard to the boundary between science and metaphysics. Unfortunately the word "metaphysics" is used in at least six different senses.[1] What I have in mind here is the sort of knowledge-claims that are transcendent in that they are in principle irrefutable (and as some would add, unconfirmable) by any kind of empirical evidence. This is presuma-

[1] One may distinguish the following types of "method": (1) intuitive, (2) deductive, (3) inductive-synthetic, (4) dialectical, (5) categorial-analytic, (6) transcendent.

bly what many philosophically unsophisticated people have in mind when they say that theological and metaphysical assertions can be neither proved nor disproved, and hence that they are a matter of faith. At this point we encounter a good deal of disagreement among the philosophers of science. The logical positivists and the logical empiricists have for a long time maintained that assertions that are absolutely beyond the possibility of test are devoid of factual meaning and that whatever significance they have consists in their evocative expressions and appeals, i.e., in their pictorial, emotional, and motivational potencies, but that they could not have any cognitive (factual, empirical) reference. This implies that questions concerning the truth of such assertions cannot even arise. Other, less radical thinkers merely say that immunity to test removes metaphysical and theological truth-claims from the domain of the empirical sciences, but not from the domain of the cognitively meaningful. In short, the issue is between adopting a criterion of (factual) meaningfulness versus a criterion of demarcation. The pragmatist-operationist tendencies in this country favor the former. If there is no difference that *makes* a difference in observable consequences between the affirmation and the denial of a given statement, then this statement is not a genuine proposition at all, but a sentence, i.e., a sequence of words that may express or arouse mental images and emotions, influence attitudes, or stimulate action. In such cases we are precluded from asking how reliable the statement is in the light of evidence—and this for the simple reason that we have (often unwittingly) made the statement immune to any kind of test, and thus "proof against disproof." As the positivists have emphasized, it is not only pointless but strictly meaningless to ask questions that we have so conceived as to make them in principle unanswerable. Problems of this sort are guaranteed 100 per cent insoluble! All this is relevant not only for the critique of traditional theology and the speculative metaphysical systems propounded by the philosophers throughout the ages. It is also most pertinent for the type of metaphysical admixtures that we find again and again in the history of scientific ideas. Doctrines concerning absolute space and time, absolute substance, the ether theories, certain conceptions of causal necessity, of vital forces and entelechies, of the human soul or mind, of group minds, etc. have some-

479

times been so conceived as to make them in principle immune to even the most indirect or incomplete tests. It is this sort of intellectual self-stultification to which the radical empiricists object, and which they attempt to remove by closer attention to the functions of language and the types of significance. There is no question that in ordinary discourse the cognitive and the emotive (pictorial, emotional, and motivative) types of significance are usually combined or fused. The positivistic critique admits the fusion, but warns against the confusion of one type of significance with the other. What the positivists object to is the mistaking of emotive appeals for factual meanings. Sentences in religious discourse, for example, may serve the purposes of exhortation, fortification, edification, or consolation, but they do not communicate *information.* Similarly, many a metaphysician mistakes the wish for experience with the quest for reliable knowledge. Intuitive and mystical "insights" may consist in powerful emotional experiences, they may even produce radical reorientations in one's attitude toward the values and ideals of human life, but they are by themselves not a basis for the validation of knowledge-claims. To the radical empiricist (positivist, operationist), religion may indeed be a way of life, an attitude of devotion to certain moral ideals, but neither religion nor theology can be considered as a branch of knowledge parallel (or superior) to scientific knowledge. The factual sciences as we understand them nowadays make genuine knowledge-claims precisely because they are so conceived as to make them susceptible to severely scrupulous tests.

Rudolf Carnap, Hans Reichenbach, and other logical empiricists have been much concerned with a precise formulation of a criterion of scientific (empirical, factual) meaningfulness. I shall try first to give an informal account of these attempts, then to interpret their larger significance, and finally to evaluate them in the light of recent criticisms. The simplest logical forms of statements are the singular, the universal, and the existential (particular). A singular statement may assert in subject-predicate form that a specific thing has a certain property, or that two or more specific things stand in a specified relation to each other. On the quantitative or metrical level of concept formation the statement may ascribe a numerical value of a certain magnitude to a space-time point or small space-

480

time region. If the state of affairs thus described is open to direct observation (or measurement) such a singular statement may be verified if true, or refuted if false with relative finality or practical certainty. Universal statements that formulate laws are definitively refutable, but—because of the unlimited range of reference— never definitively verifiable; and existential statements are verifiable by confirming instances, but are never conclusively refutable. For example, a fundamental law of physics, such as the law of the conservation of energy or the law of gravitation, may be said to be refutable if instances to the contrary should be observed; but they are never *completely* verifiable. Most positivists have therefore chosen confirmability-or-disconfirmability for a criterion of factual meaningfulness. If, as in the last stage of the ether theory, it is in principle impossible by tests of any kind to determine the velocity of a body relative to the ether, then the conception of a stationary ether—a sort of "incarnation" of absolute space—is not only fruitless, but scientifically meaningless. The phrase "in principle" needs a little elucidation. It was generally agreed that merely practical or technical difficulties of testing have no bearing on meaningfulness. Questions or statements about the physical characteristic of the far side of the moon were perfectly meaningful long before they could be more directly tested by the means of recent astronautics. Or, for another example, the "private" thoughts or sentiments of a silent thinker are difficult to ascertain, but it is conceivable that detailed neurophysiological evidence, together with psychophysiological correlation laws, may yet make them "publicly" ascertainable once scientific techniques have developed to such a higher state of perfection. It is only when the very assumptions of a given theory *logically* preclude even the most incomplete and indirect testing that the empiricists rule out as meaningless the question at issue (as well as any answer to it). An ancient puzzle may illustrate this. If two persons, when subjected to the most incisive color vision tests, discriminate colors equally well, if all the assertions they make about colors-as-experienced coincide, some philosophers still raise the question as to whether the private color qualities experienced by those two persons could not be fundamentally different. One of them might "privately" experience, e.g., green when the other experiences red, and vice versa. This riddle can be so conceived as to be absolutely insoluble; the underlying assumption is, of course, that no one can possibly ever inspect the contents of someone else's consciousness. But in actual psychological practice we do decide questions regarding immediate experience on the basis of behavioral tests. Such tests of course may well utilize verbal utterances as a part of the subject's behavior. This makes the questions answerable. But philosophers who are not satisfied with this way of answering questions of this kind obviously cut themselves off altogether from *giving reasons* for whatever beliefs they may hold on such matters. Another example will illuminate what is the logic of the situation. It is obvious that statements about the past, be it in natural history or any other branch of history, are justified by appeal to currently available evidence. But this justification is possible only if rules of inference are utilized. If these rules of inference consist merely of the rules of deductive logic, then some law(s) must be assumed in the premise(s). If we had the suspicion that these laws do not hold, or if we supposed that what we call the "laws" are subject to drastic change, we would leave no basis for our inferences, even if the currently available evidence be stated very accurately. For example, if we assumed that written or printed documents, or fossil bones, or other remnants of the past could undergo entirely unpredictable changes, then we could never confirm or disconfirm any retrodictive assertions. Or if we assumed that the world with all its traces, documents, remnants, and memories sprang into existence, say, one second ago, then all inferences of past events would be illusory, even though the evidence is in every respect "as if" there had been a long historical development. Common sense and scientific practice ignore such "perverse" assumptions. The inductive, analogical, and hypotheticodeductive types of reasoning we employ quite universally involve assumptions of a basic uniformity at *some* level of analysis. It is one thing to doubt some specific laws, and to be ready to revise them when good reasons for such revisions can be given. But it is another thing to call into doubt *all* laws indifferently. This extreme form of skepticism would reduce us to complete ignorance and silence. Normal and legitimate doubt can be resolved only if, at least in the given context, we retain other assumptions. Hence it is useful to distinguish ordinary, legitimate doubt from the all-encompassing philosophical or metaphysical doubt.

Applying these considerations to the problem of our knowledge concerning the experienced contents of other people's minds, we find that doubts in this domain, if they can be removed at all, are removed by empirical evidence regarding behavior, or possibly neural processes. This presupposes that we utilize correlation laws that enable us to infer the mental contents from behavioral responses to given stimulus situations, or from the occurrence of certain brain processes.

The examples from psychological and historical knowledge illustrate something that is important for all scientific knowledge: that verifications or refutations are almost always *indirect,* as well as incomplete. They also show that the sort of tests we apply must utilize evidence that can be ascertained *intersubjectively.* This is at least part of what is meant by the much vaunted "objectivity of science." It amounts to the demand that knowledge-claims, if they are to be *scientific,* must be in principle open to tests by any observer, sufficiently equipped with the requisite instruments and with the intelligence to perform the tests and to interpret their results. The significance of this requirement becomes clearer if we ask what it excludes. It obviously excludes the sort of dogmatism that answers the question "How do you know?" by simply asserting "I just know." This answer is clearly taboo among responsible scientists, as it should be taboo also among rational thinkers in any intellectual domain. The implications for intuition or mystical insight are obvious. The *occurrence* of intuitive or mystical experiences is not to be denied. It can itself be intersubjectively certified. But no matter how much agreement there may be in the intuitive experience of a great number of individuals, this by itself does not validate the knowledge-claims concerning anything over and above those experiences. If the defender of intuitive knowledge then goes on to say that the immediate intuitive experience or mystical insight provides *evidence* for the inference of something beyond, e.g., the existence of an absolute, a God, or the like, then the scientific attitude demands that we scrutinize this claim. The mentioned experiences may well be evidence for something beyond themselves, but this may turn out to be something perfectly natural, such as the infantile situation of man, or unconscious remnants thereof.

The requirement of intersubjective testability also rules out as scientifically meaningless (if we adopt the meaning criterion), or as beyond the scope of science (if we are satisfied with a criterion of demarcation) any speculations about disembodied minds. If part of our mental life were to continue beyond our bodily death, it might well be possible to verify this *subjectively*. But if we assume that there can be no physical manifestation of such a surviving mind, then intersubjective tests are in principle impossible.

The implications of these considerations for the philosophy of psychology and of the social sciences will be sketched at a later point. Suffice it to say here that one of the major aims in American behaviorism was to transform psychology into a science with the same degree of objectivity as physics or biology.

Intersubjective testability, we may conclude, is the criterion by which we can distinguish scientific from *non*scientific endeavors. Entirely different considerations are relevant for distinguishing scientific from *un*scientific procedures. The question of *reliability,* or of *degree of confirmation,* is decisive. We condemn the doctrines of astrology, alchemy, phrenology, quack medicine, etc. as superstitious because the available evidence speaks very strongly against them. These enterprises are nowadays considered as pseudo-sciences. They have the same aims as the respectable sciences, i.e., description, explanation, and prediction. But the manner in which they pursue their aims, the way in which they validate their knowledge-claims, is highly suspect. They either choose to disregard patent disconfirmations or hedge their theories against refutation by ad hoc hypotheses. In the first case they violate one of the most essential principles of scientific method, namely, the policy of the open mind, the readiness to revise or abandon refuted knowledge-claims. In the second case, in making their assumptions safe against refutation, they invoke hypotheses that are not defensible on the basis of independent evidence—that is to say, though *auxiliary* hypotheses (which do rest on independent evidence) are entirely legitimate, ad hoc hypotheses serve the only purpose of salvaging favored beliefs or theories.

The more detailed logical and methodological analysis of the criteria of reliability, or of confirmation and disconfirmation, are still a matter of controversy in current philosophy of science. Three major points of view may be noted in this connection. They differ in the way in which they interpret the notion of *evidential support*. The first is the theory of probability of Hans Reichenbach (based on the much more restricted theory of Richard von Mises), according to which all ascriptions of probability (e.g., to predictions, laws, hypotheses, or theories) are reducible to statements about relative frequencies. More precisely, according to Reichenbach's account, it is *limits of relative frequencies,* i.e., what we usually and loosely call frequencies in the long run, that must be introduced here. The "weight" of an individual prediction, e.g., the likelihood of an earthquake tomorrow in the San Francisco area, is determined by the relative frequency with which earthquakes have occurred in that area in the past. The likelihood of a law or law-like theoretical postulate would accordingly have to be determined by the success frequency of its confirmations. Right here is a difficulty for this outlook. Without considerable emendations and qualifications it seems inapplicable to law-like statements, because laws are considered definitively refuted by a single bona fide contrary instance. Reichenbach's view is most plausible for statistical generalizations, as, e.g., in the case of demographic extrapolations, or in the statistical regularities concerning the disintegration of radioactive substances. Reichenbach does accommodate the variations of the probability of such generalizations as they are forced upon us in the light of new additional evidence. This he achieves by attention to the reference class in which we determine the relative frequency of a given sort of event. If, for example, we say that in periods of famine the likelihood of the birth of male children is increased, we simply choose as our reference class all the births that have occurred in such periods in the past and compare the relative frequency of boys born in such periods with the relative frequency in periods free of famine.

Rudolf Carnap's analysis proceeds differently. Stimulated by some suggestions contained in Ludwig Wittgenstein's *Tractatus logico-philosophicus,* and pursuing objectives somewhat similar to those of J. M. Keynes and Harold Jeffreys, he has developed a systematic account of inductive logic. According to Carnap's view the inductive probability or the *degree of confirmation* of a proposition is defined as a logical relation between that proposition and its supporting evidence. Just as deductive logic rests on the notion of necessary implication, so inductive logic is based upon the notion of partial or probable implication. The concept of degree of confirmation is understood in the sense of such a partial implication. The propositions that formulate the evidence bestow a certain degree of confirmation upon another proposition (prediction, hypothesis, etc.). Carnap has succeeded in making such an analysis plausible for propositions in a relatively simply constructed language, and has made some promising starts in extending the same principles to the quantitative language of the physical sciences. In some respects his analysis is parallel to Reichenbach's. For example, what in Reichenbach's view is the choice of a reference class corresponds to Carnap's choice of a certain body of evidence. And statistical frequencies are an essential part of this evidence. Moreover, the special definition of degree of confirmation that Carnap proposes is based on measure functions that yield the highest probability for those predictions that correspond to whatever uniformities are suggested by the regularities, be they statistical or deterministic, in the instances that make up the evidence. In Reichenbach's analysis this all-important feature is contained in the rule of induction, the so-called straight rule, according to which the "posits" made should conform to the frequencies thus far observed in the total evidence, and modified in the light of whatever deviations from those frequencies are exhibited by further accumulating evidence. This is the way in which both Carnap and Reichenbach incorporate in their respective accounts the *self-corrective* character of scientific method.

The deeper philosophical issue concerning the *justification* of either Carnap's choice of a definition of degree of confirmation or of Reichenbach's rule of induction pertains perhaps more properly to the general theory of knowledge than to the philosophy of science. I shall therefore deal with it only briefly. Ever since Hume's incisive discussions of causality and induction, it has been patently clear that inductive inference cannot in any way be reduced to deductive inference. If, for example, in scientific theories we deduce natural laws (empirical regularities, experimentally testable functional relations, be they statistical or deterministic) from theoretical premises, then it is those premises that transcend their always limited evidential support. Even if not *arrived* at by inductive generalization, they are inductive in their validity. Moreover, Hume made it equally clear that we cannot justify the acceptance of inductive validations by reference to the previous successes of these procedures. Only on pain of vicious circularity, or of an impossible and equally "vicious" infinite regress, could this be done. Hume's own skeptical solution simply rests its case by reference to the psychological regularities according to which beliefs and expectations are formed. This reduces inductive inference to what Santayana called "animal faith," and does not provide a rational justification of any sort. The psychological account itself depends on inductive generalizations concerning the formation of expectations. On the animal level this is treated in the theory of learning or of the acquisition of habits through conditioning, trial and error, reinforcements, etc. On the level of advanced science as pursued by human beings, there is still the feature that we put our trust in theories that have thus far been highly confirmed. To the question with what *right* we do this, various answers have been given. Some philosophers maintain that the whole problem is spurious in that we demand a demonstration that would show that what we generally consider as *good reasons* are really good reasons. But according to these philosophers the question itself is mistaken because it asks in effect why it is reasonable to be reasonable. They repudiate the question as a pseudo-problem because it invokes *philosophical* doubt of the kind that could never be responsibly removed by any sort of appeal to either logic or experience. Such appeals can be seen to be question begging. Hence, philosophers of science like N. R. Hanson (in agreement with the spirit of Wittgenstein's later outlook) will allow only critical questions regarding the goodness of any specifically advanced reasons (for the acceptance of inductive conclusions), but they see no sense in any attempts in an overall justification of inductive inference. Reichenbach, however, insisted that an empiricist philosophy must finally give some sort of justification for what after all is the very life nerve of all scientific knowledge. Lacking such a justification we are stranded either with a hopeless extreme skepticism, or an empty conventionalism, or a

487

useless psychologism, or else with an indefensible rationalism (a priorism). What Reichenbach tried to show is that if any method of generalization can be successful, then the inductive method will ultimately also be successful. He agreed that we have no a priori guarantee for an order of nature. But *if* there is an order of nature, the inductive method is the only one of which it can be demonstrated (deductively!) that it *can* be successful in disclosing it. It cannot be shown that it *will* be successful (let alone that it is necessarily successful). The order of nature may be so complex, or so deeply hidden, that any and all attempts at deciphering it may fail. But, "nothing ventured, nothing gained." Or, to add another familiar saying—"if at first you don't succeed, try, try again." According to the most plausible interpretation available, this is also what Einstein intended to convey by his famous pronouncement, exhibited at the Princeton Institute: "Der Herrgott ist raffiniert, aber boshaft ist er nicht" (The Lord is subtle, but not malicious). In plainer and duller words, it is the optimistic attitude of the scientists that the regularities of our world may well be quite intricate, but that they are not too complicated for discovery by ingenious minds.

The third point of view in regard to induction and probability is only just beginning to gain acceptance in America. It was elaborated in the early Thirties by the Viennese Karl R. Popper (now at the University of London, and currently perhaps England's most prominent philosopher of science). Taking Hume's critique of induction seriously, Popper repudiates "inductivism" altogether. Not only does he maintain that science *arrives* at its knowledge-claims by the hypotheticodeductive method; he also rejects radically the idea that there can be inductive validation by verification. According to Popper the procedure of the sciences consists in the free invention of hypotheses and theories and in the severe testing of their logical consequences. Theories can be refuted, but they cannot be verified. However, Popper does speak of the "corroboration" of a theory if incisive attempts to refute it have failed. The "degree of corroboration" is not a probability in any usual sense, and differs fundamentally from Carnap's degree of confirmation. Popper does have a place for the probability of events. In his analysis such probabilities are to be assigned in the light of thus-far-unrefuted (but severely tested) statistical hypotheses. The question that "inductivists" must ask of Popper is, of course, with what justification scientists can be so confident that a well-corroborated theory will hold also in domains of space and time (or in ranges of the pertinent variables) in which they have not yet been tested. Moreover, and analogously, one must ask what justifies us in expecting that a refuted theory will not suddenly sometime begin to "stand up" again—i.e., while refuted up to a certain moment, might it not be confirmed ever after?

Other issues connected with confirmation and reliability are too technical for exposition here. One much discussed question concerns the conception of *simplicity*, which is of great importance in this context. Many scholars agree with Reichenbach that one must sharply distinguish at least two kinds of simplicity: the purely formal and the factual. Modern logic and mathematics provide many ways in which the factual content of a scientific theory may be represented. There are differences in the degree of formal simplicity in such different representations. In some cases it may be merely the choice of a coordinate system, or of the type of coordinate system (Cartesian or polar); in others it may be the choice of a metric, or other more incisive conventions upon which the logico-mathematical simplicity of the systematization depends. But differences in this type of simplicity do not affect the factual content. In this regard the various systematizations are factually equivalent; as in the simple case of coordinate transformations, there is the possibility of a strict *translation* of one representation into another. The transformations are, as we might say, "fact-invariant." The choice of the simpler system is guided by considerations of convenience only. *Factual* or *inductive* simplicity is something very different. The principle of parsimony as commonly understood is a norm of scientific theorizing. It is as such part and parcel of the inductive and hypotheticodeductive procedures, and merely reminds us not to introduce more factual hypotheses if few will achieve the same explanatory power. In his first *regula philosophandi,* Newton had precisely this in mind when he urged not introducing more causes than are necessary for the explanation of natural phenomena. Theories that differ in the degree of factual simplicity thus are not logically equivalent; they make different assertions. A precise definition of the concepts of formal and of factual simplicity is still being sought by several logicians of science, and no unanimously accepted solution has been attained thus far. But it is fairly clear that factual simplicity is closely related to the inductive probability or to the degree of corroboration of theories. Work on the clarification of "evidential support," "confirmation," "corroboration," "reliability," and the related concepts of probability and simplicity is being carried on in many quarters.

There is, in this connection, also some controversy regarding the possibility of "crucial experiments" by means of which we are to decide upon the acceptance or rejection of rival theories. One point of view (which originated early in this century, with the French philosopher and historian of physics Pierre Duhem) has come to the fore more recently again, especially through the work of the American logician W. V. Quine. This school of thought maintains that crucial experiments are impossible because the test of any theory is essentially "global"; i.e., tests always concern a whole set of hypotheses and laws, and the refutation of any experimentally testable consequences of this set reflects unfavorably upon the *whole* set or system, and does not enable us to tell which part of the system is defective. While this is formally unassailable, another school of thought opposes this view by pointing out that experimental tests can in practice be so arranged as to yield at least tentative confirmations or disconfirmations of *parts* of theories. In some cases it seems quite possible to secure independently the validity of whatever auxiliary assumptions may be needed for the testing of a given hypothesis or theory. Thus, for example, the laws of optics relevant for telescopes (or microscopes) can be tested independently of whatever astrophysical (or biological) hypotheses may be at issue. Even in the much discussed controversy regarding the relation of geometry and physics, it has been shown by Adolf Grünbaum that the acceptability of a certain geometry (be it Euclidean or non-Euclidean) is experimentally decidable, and relatively independently of physical assumptions, once a certain definition of congruence has been adopted by convention.

In addition to intersubjective testability and reliability, there are other criteria of scientific method. These criteria are the definiteness (and/or precision) of scientific concepts; the coherence of scientific systems of description or explanation; and the scope (or comprehensiveness) of scientific theories. In these three regards science differs only in degree, although often enormously, from the knowledge constituted by the common-sense outlook upon the world.

The meaning of scientific concepts is of course much more definitely specified or specifiable than the meaning of terms in the common language of ordinary usage. The classificatory concepts of the descriptive natural sciences, such as mineralogy, crystallography, botany, zoology, anatomy, pathology, etc., are much more sharply delimited than whatever concepts are available for similar purposes to untutored common sense. The discrepancy is even greater in the case of the quantitative concepts whose definition is given by rules of measurement. Nevertheless, empirical concepts without exception lack the precision so characteristic of purely mathematical concepts. It is generally agreed that this is no reason at all for regret or despair. The concepts used in the description of factual states of affairs need to be only as precise as the purpose on hand requires. Geometrical measurements of distances on the surface of the earth, for example, can be made much more exact than necessary for our practical affairs. But in the testing of scientific theories it is often indispensable to go to the very limit of the measuring accuracy afforded by the best instruments.

It has long been recognized that the sciences also differ in degree from the unaided knowledge of everyday life in regard to *coherence* or systematic character. On the level of common sense we have only loose collections of miscellaneous items of information. But all the way from the taxonomies of the descriptive sciences up to the postulate systems of explanatory theories we find coherent and interlocking sets of concepts and assumptions with ever increasing degrees of coherence. "Coherence" as here understood presupposes logical consistency, but is much more than that. It involves the fruitfulness (or should I say "fertility"?) of systems of premises from which an indefinite, usually unlimited, number of conclusions can be derived. Geometry as first axiomatized by Euclid (and later much more fully and rigorously by Hilbert, Veblen, and others) is the paradigm. Newton proceeded in a similar manner in mechanics and astronomy. And ever since then we have had a most impressive series of systematic theories in the various natural sciences, and to some extent also in the social sciences.

Closely connected with the systematic and "fertile" character of theories is their *scope*. The task of scientific explanation consists in subsuming a maximum of observable facts under a minimum of "uppermost" concepts and assumptions. The remarkable success of modern physical theories bears vivid testimony to this effect. The biological and the social sciences have often, perhaps sometimes prematurely, attempted to emulate this pattern; but even here some syntheses or unifications have been achieved.

~§ 3 §~

THE PURELY FORMAL SCIENCES AND
THE FACTUAL SCIENCES

Though it is not the task of this essay to discuss the work done in the philosophy of logic and of pure mathematics, a few remarks seem required at least on current views regarding the relations of logic and pure mathematics to the empirical sciences. Many American thinkers have adopted either the logicist or the formalist view of pure mathematics. According to the former, i.e., the view that stems essentially from Frege, Russell, and Whitehead, mathematical truths are ultimately reducible to logical truths. In the light of recent criticisms, the situation is probably not as simple as all that. The mathematics of the infinite (including Cantor's set theory) requires postulates that may well be irreducible to the principles of even the modern symbolic logic. Nevertheless, this does not abolish the sharp distinction between *pure* and *applied* mathematics. Arithmetic, number theory, algebra, group theory, etc. do not by themselves furnish, or add to, knowledge of the real (empirical, factual) world. These disciplines may more properly be regarded, as it were, as "storehouses of forms," i.e., forms that may be applicable to the facts of reality. The truths of pure mathematics are "a priori" in the sense of being valid independently of the facts of experience. Observation and experimentation have no jurisdiction over the acceptance or rejection of purely mathematical propositions. According to the formalist view, mathematical proof consists in the derivation of theorems from postulates and definitions, and is thus fundamentally different from "proof" in the other, empirical use of the word. (In the empirical sense, "proof" amounts to showing by observation that something is the case in the world of facts.) The ancient doctrine that the postulates or axioms of mathematical systems must be self-evident has long been abandoned. Only criteria of consistency, and to some extent of nonredundancy, and of such completeness and "fertility" as can be achieved, count in pure mathematics. The formalists regard mathematical proofs as

493

manipulations of signs according to preassigned rules. Since these signs may be entirely uninterpreted, machines can be "programmed" to produce proofs. Bertrand Russell's famous quip applies here: "Mathematics is the science in which we never know what we are talking about. . . ." Kurt Gödel's proof of the essential incompleteness of most mathematical systems demonstrated the ever present possibility of raising questions that within postulate systems of certain types are absolutely undecidable. This was a severe blow to those formalists who hoped that a general theory of proofs could show that every problem stated in terms of the concepts of the system must be solvable.

The logicists, represented in the United States most prominently by Rudolf Carnap and Alonzo Church, admit that for the purposes of proof theory the formalistic conception of mathematical systems (or "pure calculi") as "games" played with uninterpreted symbols is useful. But they insist that at least some mathematical concepts, such as those of elementary arithmetic, can be given an interpretation in terms of basic *logical* concepts. The very fact that the notions of "at least one" and "at most one" are easily defined on the basis of the existential operator, identity, negation, and conjunction (all of these are elementary concepts of modern logic) shows that the natural numbers in their common use (as in counting) can be defined on the basis of logic alone.

The case of geometry is different. For the assessment of the deductive demonstration of theorems the formalistic view is again entirely adequate. But if geometry is to be a science of *physical* space, the basic concepts or "primitives" in the geometrical postulates need to be interpreted. Without such an interpretation, geometry would remain a purely abstract system, self-contained and devoid of empirical reference. The concepts of "point," "straight line," "plane," "intersection," etc. would be like mere "X's," "Y's," "Z's," and "R's" linked together in a network of postulates; but definition (if we can call it that at all) is ultimately circular here, and hence of no help for the description of reality. As C. I. Lewis once so nicely said "A circle is the less vicious, the larger it is!" He obviously had in mind the "fertility" of postulate systems with richly interconnected primitives. Geometrical postulate systems as pure calculi are thus in no way distinguished from other calculi. They attain *geometrical* significance in the usual sense only if interpretations by means of reference to *empirical* concepts of space are added. In essence this is generally agreed, only the terminologies differ. The connecting links by which such interpretations are achieved are variously called "coordinative definitions" (Reichenbach), "correspondence rules" (Carnap, Margenau), "epistemic correlations" (F. S. C. Northrop), "definitions of congruence" (Adolf Grünbaum). Once such an interpretation is provided, the question as to which geometry—Euclidean or any one of the many types of non-Euclidean—"fits" the world of physical reality becomes empirically decidable.

More generally, the applicability of certain logical or mathematical forms to the world of experience is partly a matter of convention, partly a matter of empirical test. Considerations of formal simplicity prevail in the former respect, considerations of inductive simplicity prevail in the latter. In any case, there is no need for metaphysical speculations about the "mathematical order" of the universe. Mathematics provides the symbolically most concise formulation of whatever the order of nature might be. Our world happens to yield to our attempts of finding functional relations among its quantitatively measurable magnitudes. *That* there is such an order of nature that can be formulated mathematically is ultimately just as much a "brute fact" as is the very existence of nature. There is no need for and no point in falling into mystical bewilderment over the order of nature. Metaphysical or theological attempts to explain it invariably make use of verbal sedatives. All scientific explanations rest on premises that may themselves remain unexplained. But this does not detract in the least from the possibilities of offering genuine explanations of countless facts and regularities—except of course those "deepest" regularities that we formulate in the "highest" theoretical postulates. There are a few intimations in Einstein's later work (somewhat similar to those in Eddington's) that the "highest" premises might be purely mathematical in that the relations of the basic constants of nature to each other could be reduced to purely arithmetical patterns. Considering Einstein's otherwise great concern with empirical confirmation this is somewhat surprising. Even if the dimensionless constants exhibit such patterns, the meaning of the constants can be explained only by their role in the laws in which they occur; but these laws fall ultimately and undeniably under the jurisdiction of experimental test.

❧ 4 ❧

PRINCIPLES OF CONCEPT FORMATION
AND MEASUREMENT

Analyses of the nature of scientific concepts have been pursued by many philosophers of science, most notably P. W. Bridgman, Rudolf Carnap, C. G. Hempel, Ernest Nagel, and S. S. Stevens. Until rather recently it has been quite generally agreed that the concepts of the empirical sciences may be classified according to the level of description or explanation to which they pertain, and that it is useful to distinguish the level of observation from the level of empirical laws and both of these from the level of theories. In keeping with the general empiricist tradition most contributions in this area distinguish at least *observation language* from *theoretical language*. For example, the lines as seen in a spectrum may be described in the language of direct observation; but the explanation of spectra in terms of energy levels in atoms, quantum jumps, etc. is given in the language of a theory (the quantum theory in this case). Similarly, descriptions of phenotypical traits in botany or zoology is a matter of observation. The explanation of the scattering of these traits through successive generations is achieved by the theory of genes. Since the testing of any theory, according to the empiricist view, invariably and ineluctably requires recourse to observations, the very facts of observation should be stated in a language that must not be contaminated by any theory, certainly not by the theory at issue.

All of the philosophers of science mentioned above either take it for granted or else make it quite explicit that the observation language is intersubjective. They do not insist, and most of them do not even believe, that there must be a ground-level language suited for the description of immediate (purely private, subjective) experience. Instead of pursuing what they consider chimerical, namely, a language of sense data, they are satisfied with a purified language of common sense by means of which we can give an account of the observed properties and relations of perceptible ob-

497

jects. The results of scientific measurements, for example, are describable in terms of what we see when we read the indications of measuring instruments. Pointer readings are publicly observable. And of course on the more primitive level of the classificatory disciplines, we may simply group a large number of objects according to their observable properties. Hence the observation language employs proper names for objects and predicates for their properties. This is the *qualitative* level of concept formation. The meaning of such qualitative concepts can be specified by explicit definition. Such definitions have often been considered entirely arbitrary. But the actual scientific procedures clearly indicate that this is not so. True, the choice of a verbal label or symbol is, logically speaking, a mere convention. But the manner in which predicates are selected, and how they are joined together in explicit definitions, far from being arbitrary, is guided by important considerations of fruitfulness. This becomes clear from the analysis Hempel has given of the distinction of "nominal" and "real" definitions, and of the corresponding distinction between "artificial" and "natural" classifications. While it may be impossible to draw a sharp line of demarcation between them, there is an eminently practical distinction here. The taxonomies of the descriptive natural sciences attempt to define kinds, species, etc. in such a manner that the defining characteristics are associated with a maximal number of other characteristics. Thus, for example, the definition of "vertebrate" in terms of the possession of a spinal column is scientifically useful because a number of other characteristics, such as the presence of certain types of circulatory and of nervous systems, is as a matter of *empirical* regularity inferrable from the defining characteristic. In contradistinction to a purely artificial classification, natural classifications are based on empirically ascertained clusters of properties. In many cases, the clusterings are in the nature of statistical correlations rather than of fully deterministic connections. Nevertheless their value resides in the fact that in them we have the beginnings of the formulations of laws, and hence the possibility of at least low-level explanations.

Natural classification attempts to "carve nature at its points," as the classical precept indicates. This is, however, not always as simple as the Platonic doctrine assumed. In many fields we encounter practically continuous gradations. The type of concept that lends itself best for description here is that of *relations*. Equalities are represented by symmetrical and transitive relations. Directed inequalities (such as "more than," "greater than," "warmer than," "harder than," etc.) are represented by asymmetrical transitive relations. Under certain conditions rank orders can be formulated. These may be one-dimensional, as, e.g., in the case of temporal succession, or intensities of heat, etc. Or they may be two-, three-, or multidimensional. The order of color qualities requires a three-dimensional arrangement according to hue, brightness, and saturation. The colors in the well-known color octahedron are ordered simply in terms of their degrees of similarity or dissimilarity. Or, to take an entirely different example, once Kretschmer's simple tripartite classification of human body types proved inadequate, it was supplanted by the Sheldon-Stevens system, in which each body type is represented in a topological space by a point or small region. Even in one-dimensional rank orders we have of course a topological order in that only the *rank* determines the place of a given item on the scale. If numbers are used at all, as in the old scale of hardnesses set up by Mohs, they play only the role that might just as well be fulfilled by the letters of the alphabet.

The assignment of numbers in a *metrical* scale is based on measurement, and this is based on definitions of equality of intervals, of a zero point and of a unit. These definitions presuppose a topological (or rank) order, but go beyond it, in that the numbers used now enable us to answer questions on a fullfledged *quantitative* level. The simple example of the thermometric concept of temperature will illustrate the point. Once we have empirical criteria to determine whether two bodies are equally warm, or which of the two is warmer, we introduce the convention by which the indications of a mercury thermometer give us the concept of equal differences (or equal intervals of temperature). The convention simply stipulates that these are proportional to the intervals in lengths of the mercury column in the thermometer. The traditional zero points of the centigrade or the Fahrenheit scales are similarly a matter of arbitrary stipulations; and so are the respective conventions regarding the units. All this seems seductively simple until we take a close look at the development of thermodynamics. First, there are excellent experimental and theoretical reasons for the adoption of an "absolute zero" point of the scale. The units remain arbitrary, but the definition of the equality of intervals is no longer tied to the thermal expansion of any thermometric substance. In fact, the rates of expansion for different substances are not strictly proportional to one another. Only a naïve and dogmatic procedure would fasten upon one substance as the standard. (In that case we might have had contending parties in physics—"mercurialists," "alcoholists," etc.) The actual history of thermodynamics shows that the temperature concept was redefined in the light of the energy and entropy laws. This sort of development took place with practically all concepts of science. Only a very naïve form of operationism could insist on purely *procedural* definitions of scientific concepts. As I read Bridgman, he was not given to such simple-minded ideas. There were some psychologists who thought they were operationists in Bridgman's sense when they declared "Intelligence is what intelligence tests test." But how could one then responsibly even ask about the "validity" of tests, or speak about improving them, if all there was to a concept was nothing but a certain standardized procedure for ascertaining its applicability. Operationism in this crude form is reminiscent of, and indeed akin to, the early phase of logical positivism according to which the meaning of a statement is its method of verification. As a counterbalance to deep metaphysical speculations these radically empiricist views have been salutary. There is indeed no reason to be mystified by scientific concepts. But the analysis of their meaning cannot be given in such simple terms. To be sure, as a general guiding maxim, the pragmatist-operationist slogan "Concept is what concept does" can be useful. But great care and considerable finesse are required for determining precisely what concepts do in the scientific enterprise.

Bridgman distinguished between "physical" and "mental operations," insisting that both types are equally essential to the meaning of scientific concepts. In a perhaps more illuminating, though more cumbrous terminology, this amounts to the distinction between experimental-mensurational-observational and logicomathematical procedures. In some cases this may be illustrated very simply. The concept of the mean velocity of a moving body may be defined as the space traversed divided by the time it took to traverse it. Arithmetical division is a very elementary mathematical operation. The measurement of the distance traversed, and the time elapsed, say, by yardsticks and stopwatches, respectively, again is something that seems prima facie quite unproblematic. But if account is taken of the intricacies that enter into the notions of space and time in modern physics, this simple analysis, though still adequate for the purposes of practical life, will have to be greatly amended. There are problems concerning the definition of "rigid bodies," needed for the measurement of length, and concerning the definition of "temporal congruence," needed for the measurement of time. The modern relativistic conceptions of space and time clearly show that length and duration can be more precisely understood only within the framework of the theory of relativity. Further incisive modifications in the concept of measurement were introduced in quantum mechanics. These are especially relevant in the domain of microphysics. All this indicates clearly that Bridgman's "mental" operations, properly understood, involve the logical relations among the concepts of scientific theory. This is not to deny that carpenters and architects can afford to ignore these refinements, as far as their practical purposes are concerned. But experimental physicists can no longer disregard the revolutionary effect of the new theories on their concepts. No sharp line can be drawn between experimental and theoretical physics today.

The operationist analysis was especially plausible for some time as applied to *dispositional concepts.* These concepts, no matter whether on the qualitative, semiquantitative or fully quantitative level of science, invited a radical empiricist explication especially because of the positivist aversion to "occult qualities." What does it mean to say that a given material is elastic, or magnetic, or that it has a certain degree of thermal or electric conductivity? It is obviously no help to say that these are inherent properties whose existence explains certain types of behavior. For it is precisely the regularities of the behavior on the basis of which we ascribe those dispositional properties to various substances. From the positivistic and operationistic point of view, dispositional predicates are merely shorthand for those regularities. In one of his most influential essays ("Testability and Meaning," *Philosophy of Science,* 1936-37), Carnap attempted an exact logical analysis of dispositional concepts in terms of test-condition → test-result conditionals. This famous doctrine of "reduction sentences" was later discredited by Carnap himself, but it is perhaps the most precise formulation of a basic tenet of operationism. Carnap attributes little importance to this sort of analysis nowadays because he has come to realize the all-important role of theoretical concepts. This does not involve a return to a metaphysical doctrine of occult qualities, but amounts to the realization that even the disposition concepts are essentially theoretical. That is to say that their meaning is specified by postulates, and that this meaning can be enriched by further postulates. A dispositional predicate introduced at first only operationally becomes a place holder—i.e., at least a promissory note—for fuller theoretical specification. Thus, for example, the concept of magnetization, to begin with, may indeed be merely shorthand for the various experimental conditionals, but it is soon replaced by micro-concepts (referring to the spin of electrons) that connect it with the theories of electrodynamics and quantum mechanics.

THE LOGICAL STRUCTURE OF
SCIENTIFIC EXPLANATION

The prevalent view of scientific explanation as expounded especially by Carnap, Hempel and Oppenheim, Nagel, *et al.* conceives
of scientific theories as postulate systems interpreted by rules of correspondence. The postulates are conceived as a network of sentences or formulas that connect the concepts of a theory with one
another, and these concepts are linked with the help of correspondence rules to concepts of the observation language. If the facts to
be explained (the "explananda") are matters of direct observation,
then their explanation consists in the derivation of observation sentences from theoretical premises. The derivation may be strictly deductive, as it undoubtedly is in classical mechanics, classical thermodynamics, electrodynamics, and the relativity theory; here the
theoretical postulates are deterministic in form. But the derivation
may be probabilistic if it proceeds from postulates that are statistical in form, as they are in statistical mechanics, quantum theory,
genetics, and in several postulate systems of psychological theories
of learning and motivation.

This modern view of the nature of scientific explanation has almost completely replaced the older and traditional views according to which an explanation is adequate only if it reduces the unfamiliar to the familiar. This requirement is understandable in the
light of the long history of two prominent thought patterns: the
mechanistic and the animistic. The wish for explanation is strongest
when we are confronted with unusual, unexpected, strange, or
weird phenomena. And, again psychologically speaking, an explanation seems most satisfying if it enables us to understand such
phenomena as due either to a mechanism or to intentions, desires,
or volitions. This is the way we understand and explain in everyday life. Nothing is more familiar to us than, on the one hand, the
"pushiness and pulliness of things" (Whitehead's phrase), and the
efficacy of our will, on the other. The animistic pattern of explana-

tion has come to be increasingly discredited since the Renaissance, and survives only in the views of a small minority of biologists, psychologists, and philosophers. Its decline was originally due to the spectacular success of mechanistic explanations, but its more recent rejection is based on considerations of testability or fruitfulness. The mechanistic type of explanation, at least in its classical (Newtonian) form has also been abandoned in modern physics. It has been supplanted by explanation in terms of theories whose postulates are largely very strange indeed, and certainly lack the "self-evidence" on which the classical tradition had insisted for a long time. Far from explaining the unfamiliar in the light of the familiar, or reducing the new to the old, the trend has fairly generally been reversed. This of course does not mean that modern science explains the known by the unknown. The premises of modern theories can be, and have been, stated quite clearly and precisely, but they do not appeal to us intuitively. It is familiarity that breeds intuition, and we have not been long enough familiar with the modern theories to regard their postulates as immediately self-evident. The only criteria scientists use nowadays in explanations accepted as adequate are: (1) consistency; (2) absence of ad hoc assumptions; (3) intersubjective testability, and (4) explanatory power, i.e., the capacity to subsume a maximum of observable facts under a minimum of basic concepts and principles.

Explanation may be desired for *individual facts* (e.g.: Question: What caused this devastation? Answer: An earthquake) or it may be desired for *regularities* (e.g.: Question: How do earthquakes come about? Answer: Through underground shifts in the structure of the earth's outer layer). Quite generally scientific explanation may be construed as having a level structure, such that individual facts are subsumed under empirical regularities (as formulated in empirical laws) and such that these regularities may in turn be explained by deriving them from higher order regularities assumed in theoretical postulates, and existential hypotheses. In the historical development of the sciences we can discern often even two or three distinct levels of theory, similarly related to each other in a hierarchical structure. Thus, for example, the empirical regularities formulated in the empirical laws concerning the conduction of heat were explained in terms of the principles of classical thermodynamics. These latter ones in turn were explained by the kinetic theory of heat and the principles of statistical mechanics. And, finally, the interaction of the molecules assumed in the kinetic theory of heat has been more recently explained by the principles of quantum mechanics. This is where the present theory stands.

All this makes for a rather plausible account, until we look a little more closely into the logical relations involved in this level structure. The first thing we notice is that the higher levels almost always involve some severe corrections or modifications on the lower levels. More bluntly speaking, the original formulation of the lower level laws or theoretical postulates is outright false, if viewed from the vantage point of the higher levels. Thus, for example, Newtonian mechanics is logically incompatible with the Einsteinian theory. Similarly classical thermodynamics is incompatible with statistical mechanics; and the assumptions of the latter clash with the principles of quantum mechanics. Many more examples for the same point could be given. Some thinkers like Rudolf Carnap, W. S. Sellars, and P. K. Feyerabend have recently concluded that the whole story of the hierarchical level structure should be abandoned. Their new and different account deals with the historical succession of laws and theories in terms of radical *replacements* rather than in terms of a standing hierarchy of levels. They view what is traditionally called a higher level as a *new theory,* involving a new set of concepts. In short, the erstwhile "higher levels" simply *supplant* the "lower" ones. There is much that speaks in favor of such an analysis. Indeed, the older claim of the deductive derivability of the lower level laws from the higher level theoretical postulates can be made good only if the lower level laws are formulated in terms of the theoretical concepts of the higher levels. This involves the "corrections from above," and thus often very radically affects the meaning of the "empirical laws." Carnap and Nagel, to be sure, operate with the notion of correspondence rules (tantamount to the "epistemic correlations" of Northrop and Margenau). But these correspondence rules (also styled "bridge laws"), far from being explicit definitions introduced by convention, formulate empirical relationships, and are hence in principle open to revision in the light of experimental evidence. In fact, if we accept the new way of looking at them, most correspondence rules would be outright false. They are not mere semantic rules by means of which an erstwhile uninterpreted calculus is given empirical reference. If, for example, we say that the mean kinetic energy of the molecules in a gas "corresponds" to the temperature of the gas as determined by macro-measurements, then this is a statement whose truth depends on empirical confirmation. In many, though by no means all, cases the "correspondence" may be understood to consist in an identity of the events, states, or conditions referred to by macro- and micro-descriptions. Thus it is a certain state of the gas, namely, its intensity of heat, that is designated by two (or more) alternative descriptions. If the "corrections from above" are not applied to the concept of macro-temperature, then the alternative descriptions may be congruent only approximately, or in limited parts of the range of the relevant variables.

These considerations are especially important for the analysis of the type of scientific explanation that constitutes a *"reduction"* of one scientific discipline to another. I am referring here especially to the work of Ernest Nagel, Hilary Putnam, Paul Oppenheim, John Kemeny, and others. Thus when we consider statistical mechanics as reducing (part of) classical thermodynamics to the mechanics of molecular motion, or when we say that chemistry is "in principle" reducible to quantum mechanics, this implies such a qualified identity of the referents of the concepts of the reducing discipline with the referents of the reduced discipline. What, for example, is referred to as the "chemical bond" by the older chemistry turns out to be identical with what in the more recent stages of modern physics is designated by certain quantum mechanical forces and "resonances" for which there is independent evidence in areas outside classical chemistry.

The logic of reduction as it emerges today from the work of numerous philosophers of science (i.e., P. W. Bridgman, Rudolf Carnap, Ernest Nagel, Arthur Pap, P. E. Meehl, P. K. Feyerabend), and as I attempt to view it synoptically, may be made clearer and more explicit by a few more detailed illustrations from the comparative methodology of physics and psychology. The current theory of ferromagnetism in physics explains the phenomena in this domain by assumptions concerning the spin of electrons, together with certain postulates of quantum theory and electrodynamics.

A highly derivative, i.e., very complexly defined, concept of this theory then corresponds, for example, to the experimental concept of magnetic pole strength. This latter concept is usually understood as operationally definable. That is, following Bridgman's well-known analysis, we merely have to ask ourselves by what sort of experimental and, wherever possible, mensurational, procedures the experimental physicist, without any "high level theory" about "deep level structures of reality" in fact does determine the pole strength of a bar magnet. A little reflection on these test-operation → test-result procedures shows in this case, as in countless others, that the experimentalist is ascertaining the quantitative degree of a *dispositional property*. The logical explication of dispositions reveals that dispositional predicates or functors are to be understood as ascriptions of properties on the basis of the evidence of the empirical regularities of sets of one or several test-conditions → test-results.

Dispositional properties are, however, not just shorthand expressions for test-operation → test-result conditionals. They cannot be construed even in terms of a total set of many such conditionals. Positivists and operationists did maintain this view. Nowadays a more realistic interpretation seems much more adequate. By a dispositional property we mean a state or condition that when more fully known would explain, i.e., enables us to *derive,* that total set of conditionals. To be sure, before a science attains such perfection, there is little else one can say except that each member of the set of operational conditionals serves as an *indicator* (usually probabilistic, i.e., neither necessary nor sufficient) for the dispositional property. Once we have formed a more definite conception of the disposition, it will enable us to see how its presence, in the light of relevant nomological assumptions entails the empirical regularities that, epistemologically speaking, were the original grounds for the ascription of the disposition. From a methodological point of view dispositional properties may be regarded as temporary place holders for (relatively) micro-states that are inserted in their place once a theory concerning those micro-states achieves a sufficient degree of confirmation. In the terminology familiar to psychologists, "intervening variables" are later replaced by "hypothetical constructs." Once we have a sufficient number of evidential "fixes" on the hypothetical constructs, they become the theoretical concepts of the *reducing* theory.

Even experimental concepts derive part of their meaning from the set of laws in which they occur. Hence the concepts of the experimental sciences—no matter whether in physics, chemistry, biology, or psychology—are nodal points in nomological nets. It is therefore a matter of terminological preference whether we say that even the language of the experimental sciences is essentially a language of theoretical terms, or whether we reserve the label "theory" only for the "higher level," more comprehensive and more unifying explanatory syntheses. One could say (with Goethe) that it is important to remember that what we ordinarily call a fact involves almost invariably a theoretical interpretation.

As long as all this is kept in mind, it does not matter too much whether we say that an experimental discipline has been reduced to a theory, or whether we say that one theory of narrower scope has been reduced to another theory of wider scope. The point to be remembered is that successful reductions allow us to make *identifications,* not of the concepts, but of their *referents.* In the example of ferromagnetism, the condition or state ascribed to the iron bar on the usual observational evidence is one and the same as the state that is more precisely and (from the point of view of explanation and prediction) much more fruitfully characterized in terms of the micro-account involving the spin of electrons.

The case of psychological concepts seems to me in many ways quite parallel. Let me illustrate this in terms of the concept of memory trace. If we wish to avoid "action at a distance in time," we cannot let our scientific account rest with a narrative about a succession of stimuli, exteroceptive or interoceptive, that have impinged on the organism; just as in the case of the magnetization of an iron bar we do not restrict ourselves to a narrative about the things done to the iron bar (such as inserting it repeatedly into an electric coil). We assume that both in the organism and in the iron bar some as yet unspecified modification of structure has occurred, and it is this modified state to which the modified behavior is due. It is of course perfectly legitimate to tabulate the results of various schedules of reinforcement, just as it would be legitimate to tabulate the cumulative results of the treatment of the iron bar. It is also perfectly legitimate and useful to study quite empirically the maximal habit strength that can be attained in a given species by repeated reinforcements, just as it is to study the maximal pole strength that can be attained in a given kind of metal by repeated treatment in the electric coil. Other empirical regularities can be found on this same level of investigation—e.g., that the magnetization is completely destroyed by heating the iron bar to a temperature of about 600°C, or that intensive electroshock eliminates (in this case temporarily) all memories of recent events. I hardly need to remark that I use the analogies of memory and magnetism only from a *methodological* point of view; I am suggesting no similarity whatsoever in the processes or the structures involved. The analogy I am stressing concerns merely the replacement of the respective macro-concepts by corresponding micro-concepts, once the latter can be specified.

There is still a good deal of dispute about neurophysiological theories of memory. For a while it looked as though short-term memory might be explained in terms of reverberating neural circuits, whereas long-term memory was interpreted as due to relatively permanent lowerings of synaptic resistances. Problems of localization versus mass action also are not completely resolved as yet. It has become increasingly clear that memory and habit are much more complex concepts than had been assumed in earlier phases of psychology. The interaction and "cooperation" of many relevant variables must be taken into account. Wilder Penfield's striking experiments showed that quite specific recollections can be elicited by electric stimulation of a very small area in the temporal lobes of the cortex. But other aspects of memory seem to be much more diffusely and vicariously localized. Scientifically, it will of course be most exciting to watch the further experimental developments, and to see what sort of neurophysiological theory will turn out to be the most adequate for the multifaceted facts and regularities of memory. But it is perhaps not premature to say that, whatever the most satisfactory neurophysiological theory might be, it will have to achieve a reduction, and that it will thus be possible to *identify* the referents of the various "macro"- or "molar"-psychological concepts of memory with the referents of the corresponding micro-concepts of neurophysiology.

Analyses of the kind I have sketched only in outline may suggest a fruitful way in which to discuss the problems of the unity and the alleged limitations of science. Especially in the work of Carnap has the idea of the unity of science become more fully clarified. Carnap distinguishes two theses of the unity of science. The first is the assertion of the unity of the language of science, which says that the confirmation of all scientific knowledge-claims must ultimately be in terms of evidence that can be described in an intersubjective observation language. The second, more exciting thesis may be formulated as the convergence of the sciences toward a unitary schema of explanation. Carnap has stressed that this second thesis cannot be justified on purely logical grounds. Here the philosopher can at best hazard some extrapolations from the trends of explanatory unifications thus far achieved. It is logically quite conceivable that the laws of a given domain, such as that of biology or psychology, may remain autonomous in the sense of being irreducible to the laws of physics. But the progress in reduction of chemistry to physics, the successes of physicochemical explanations (as in biophysics and biochemistry) of multifarious phenomena of organic life have encouraged many thinkers to believe in the thesis of unitary science, according to which all phenomena of nature could in principle be explained by the postulates of physics. This is, however, not only a problematic thesis; it is also a very vague one. With all the changes, expansions, and revisions continually occurring in physical theory, one must ask *which* physical postulates are to be the basis of reduction. It is fairly plausible that present-day physics will not be equal to this ambitious job. And if we merely say that "some sort" of physical postulates will achieve the reduction, this is too indefinite. Nevertheless, a qualified and cautious reductionism (as advocated by Carnap, Nagel, and myself) does exclude not only the various doctrines of vitalism, but tentatively also the doctrine of emergent evolution. The vast majority of present-day biologists acknowledge readily that talk of vital forces, entelechies, *élan vital,* etc. is entirely fruitless (if indeed not factually meaningless). Such talk is at best a more or less poetic phraseology by means of which one may describe the undeniably marvelous teleological features of organic life. But it contributes nothing to the explanation of these features because no independent confirmatory access to those vital forces is provided. If such access is excluded by the very conception of the vital forces, then the logical empiricists repudiate hypotheses of this kind as devoid of factual meaning. Even if independent confirmability is not logically excluded, vitalistic hypotheses remain questionable as promissory notes whose explanatory or predictive "cash value" is not anywhere in sight.

The case of emergent evolution versus reductionism is different from that of vitalism. The facts of emergent novelty in the course of evolution are patent and undeniable. But the question of their explanation may be left open. In incisive analyses, especially those by Ernest Nagel and Gustav Bergmann, it is made quite plausible that the properties of organic wholes may well be derivable from the basic laws pertaining to their parts together with a few composition laws. Even in atomic physics there are composition laws such as Wolfgang Pauli's exclusion principle. According to Henry Margenau this is a principle of organization that could never have been gleaned from the behavior of isolated free electrons. The problem of emergence then consists in the question how far up we have to go in the study of complex structures and processes in order to catch hold of the relevant composition laws. Putting it in another way, properties are emergent in the logical (as distinct from the historical) sense if they are underivable from a given set of theoretical premises. This makes the concept relative, and hence much less mysterious. In this sense, the electromagnetic properties of matter are "emergent" with the respect to the laws of classical mechanics.

Many philosophers of science, notably F. S. C. Northrop, have hailed the rise of *cybernetics* (the work of Norbert Wiener, Warren McCulloch, Walter Pitts, and others) as the most promising breakthrough in the explanation of the behavior of teleological systems. The "wisdom of the body" (W. B. Cannon's phrase), i.e., the remarkable self-regulating, mutually attuning activities in organisms, may be explained in terms of homeostatic devices, negative feedback, and other mechanisms of the "cooperation" of the parts that make up an organic whole. Ernest Nagel has shown most lucidly in which way we may fruitfully conceive of parts and wholes, and that the old saying "The whole is more than the sum of its parts" is hopelessly vague and fruitless. And this not so much because the concept of an "organic whole" is not very precisely understood, but rather because it is left entirely unclear just what is meant by the "sum of the parts." More importantly, Nagel (in his incisive chapter "Mechanistic Explanations and Organismic Biology" in his book *The Structure of Science*) has presented a most suggestive analysis of the concept of teleology. Perhaps less exuberant than Northrop, but equally in consonance with the basic ideas of cybernetics, he has shown that it is not a contradiction in terms to speak of "teleological mechanisms," i.e., that by due attention to the structure of organisms we can give *causal* explanations of their self-regulated and goal directed behavior.

It remains to be seen whether the challenging problems posed by the Gestalt psychologists (especially Max Wertheimer and Wolfgang Köhler) will be resolved by further developments in the field of cybernetics. The scientific progress here, and in information theory as applied to biological and neurophysiological problems is extremely rapid. The logical analysis of these new disciplines is also well under way, but it is difficult to summarize their results in a nontechnical manner, or to assess their philosophical significance. In general there can be little doubt that the discussions of machines that simulate organisms and of organisms that can in some respect be viewed as intrinsically "programmed" machines are immensely promising. Very likely new contributions to the methodology of reduction and explanation will result from these exciting developments.

৵§ 6 §৵

CAUSALITY, DETERMINISM, AND
INDETERMINISM

Discussions in recent American philosophy of science have subjected the concept of causality to searching analyses. The predominant view of the causal relation among empiricist philosophers of science has remained close to Hume's classical analysis in terms of regularity and predictability, but four important emendations have been added. These concern (1) the logical and mathematical form of scientific laws on the quantitative (metrical) level of concept formation; (2) the special features of causality in classical (deterministic) science; (3) the difference between "accidental" and "essential" regularities; and (4) the severe modifications involved in the acceptance of basic statistical laws (indeterminism) in quantum mechanics.

Most philosophers of science grant that the concepts of cause and effect have a legitimate place in the accounts we give of many phenomena on the macro-level of ordinary observation. To be sure, there are some ambiguities in this respect in common language. Sometimes we mean by "cause" merely the differential or additional factor or event that, against a background of "standing conditions," may be said to bring about or "trigger off" a given effect. The well-known "ceteris paribus" clause, i.e., the phrase "all other things being equal," indicates just this conception. Thus we say that it was the occurrence of a tornado that caused the devastation; or that the taking of aspirin relieved the headache. But in order to justify assertions of this kind, it is necessary to take account of all the rest of the relevant conditions. In doing that, we refer to the total set of factors or conditions, which when so taken together (i.e., in conjunction) provide us with a sufficient condition for the causal explanation of the effect. For a scientifically satisfactory causal explanation, it is required to make explicit all the relevant regularities of conditions and consequences. In this connection it is important to distinguish between necessary and sufficient conditions.

In many situations, a group of conditions when conjoined are sufficient, but possibly no single one of the conditions is necessary, in the sense that it might not be replaced by a different, equally "potent" condition.

Once the quantitative level of concept formation has been attained, causal relations are formulated in terms of functional dependencies between measurable variables. Thus, for example, Ohm's law in the experimental physics of electricity formulates the causal dependency of the intensity of an electric current upon the electromotive force of that current. The mathematical form of such laws may be as simple as "$E = I \cdot R$" as in this case, or as complex as in the differential equations of Maxwell's field theory, or of Einstein's theory of gravitation.

Two questions have been much under discussion in this connection. First, since it is in principle always possible to formulate mathematical functions that "fit" a given course of changes in the magnitudes we are interested in, is it still possible to distinguish "chaos" from causal order? The only answer that seems to stand up is that the criterion of causal order is successful predictability, i.e., the possibility of extrapolations that on independent observation turn out to be correct, at least to a high degree of approximation. The second question arises in view of the elementary mathematical truth that to every function an inverse function can be formulated, thus interchanging independent and dependent variables. While from a purely mathematical point of view there can be no fundamental distinction between the two kinds of variables, common sense and scientific practice seem to indicate that in many of the laws of the empirical sciences it makes very good sense to say, for example, that the period of oscillation of a pendulum depends on its length, that the intensity of light depends on the distance from the source, and not vice versa. This can be explicated by the pragmatic notion of accessibility for experimental manipulation or intervention.

There are still the much more interesting questions regarding the temporal asymmetry or symmetry of natural laws. The general consensus of researchers in this area (Henryk Mehlberg, Hans Reichenbach, Adolf Grünbaum) is that the basic laws of nature as formulated in classical physics as well as in quantum physics are temporally symmetrical, and that the obvious irreversibility of most natural processes hinges on their "initial and boundary conditions." Beyond this agreement there is much controversy, too technical and involved for presentation here.

Besides the temporal symmetry of laws, other important, logically contingent features of classical physics are the continuity of the functions by which the quantitative dependencies are expressed; the repudiation of "action at a distance" and its replacement by field theories; and the deterministic formulation of the laws. In its crude form, this is the principle "same causes, same effects," which in the understanding of classical physics involves the relational (nonabsolute) character of space and time. While it is true that strictly lawful relationships can be conceived also in case the space or time coordinates enter explicitly into the functional equations, the denial of this is a basic—though again logically contingent—feature of the ideology of classical physics.

Most empiricists have refused to allow for "causal necessity" except in the entirely ametaphysical Humean sense of "assumed exceptionless regularity." These empiricists, countenancing only the notion of *logical* necessity, locate this necessity in the relation of implication between the premises and the conclusion of an explanatory deductive inference. Nevertheless it is possible, at least in principle (though never with finality in practice) to distinguish between accidentally and essentially universal statements. The basic laws of nature, at any given stage of scientific progress, may be called nomological universals. But it is possible to conceive of a universe of deterministic structure in which some regularities depend not only on the basic nomologicals, but also on the contingent constellation of facts, i.e., on the initial conditions. If we accept for the sake of illustration a strict determinism (à la Laplace), then, the momentary total condition of the universe at a given time together with the basic laws of the universe might enable us to derive the universal statement that the element helium, anywhere and at any time, is in the gaseous form; and this simply because the initial conditions are such that in the total history of the universe, both past and future, the temperature nowhere ever falls below, say, $-200°C$. Nonetheless, the contrary-to-fact conditional "Helium would liquefy if the temperature were to be lowered to $-272°C$" might conceivably be derivable from the basic nomologicals. To put the point differently, the basic laws (nomologicals) characterize an infinite class of universes, differing among each other only in initial conditions. If a limitless regularity could be shown to depend on a peculiar type of initial conditions, then it is in this sense merely accidental, important and reliable though it would be for the purpose of predictions.

Perhaps the most incisive re-examinations of the concept of causality originated from the probabilistic character of some of the basic laws of quantum physics. To forestall misunderstandings, let me distinguish "external" from "internal" probability. The degree of evidential support of any law, be it deterministic or statistical, is external. In this sense any and all scientifically accepted empirical statements can be said to be "probabilified" (confirmed, corroborated) by relevant evidence to some degree. It is the *internal* probability that concerns us in the shift from the deterministic to the indeterministic outlook. By way of speculative reasoning C. S. Peirce before the end of last century developed his doctrine of "tychism," i.e., the view that there is a significant element of "absolute chance" in the processes of nature. This is antithetic to the classical determinism that dominated the thinking of most scientists and philosophers at least since the seventeenth century. The laws of Newtonian mechanics, of Maxwell's electrodynamics, and of Einstein's theory of relativity were all formulated in a deterministic manner. Whether they are expressed in terms of differential equations or in terms of variation principles (as in Hamilton's principle of least action), they allow for completely strict and precise predictions once they are applied to precisely ascertained initial and boundary conditions. In a world so conceived there can only be "relative" (but not "absolute") chance: "relative" in the twofold sense that events may appear fortuitous in that they result causally from conditions too complex or too delicate for precise ascertainment by measurement, and in that "coincidences" may be considered as a matter of "chance" if they result from the crossing of causal lines (or "chains") that are physically independent of one another. This is the only concept of chance that is compatible with classical determinism. We find it beautifully exemplified in classical statistical mechanics as conceived by Maxwell, Gibbs, and Boltzmann. The probability distributions of the positions and moments of individual molecules are represented in assumptions about the contingent features of the initial conditions. The great revolution of thought marked especially by Max Born's statistical interpretation of wave mechanics (in 1926), following upon the formulation of Heisenberg's principle of indeterminacy, involved a repudiation of determinism for atomic and subatomic processes. There is still some controversy about whether this should best be understood as the denial of the simultaneous precise measurability of all relevant initial conditions, or whether this very limitation should be viewed as due to the ineluctably statistical interaction of particles and fields, and of particles with one another. These interactions are essential in any measurement of the state of a micro-system. Some philosophers of science (e.g., Hans Reichenbach) maintained that the facts and theories of microphysics force upon us a radical revision even of logical principles—namely, the replacement of the traditional two-valued logic by a three-valued logic that allows for "indeterminate" as a third truth value beside the customary "true" and "false." Henry Margenau and Ernest Nagel have attempted to show that the deterministic view of physical laws can be upheld if the concept of "state" of micro-systems is reinterpreted. Thus the psi-function in Schrödinger's wave mechanics conforms to a differential equation of the classical type. But serious objections have been made against this redefinition. The "psi" of the Schrödinger equation does not by itself represent a physical state in ordinary space-time. According to Born's interpretation (still accepted by the majority of today's physicists) certain mathematical expressions involving "psi" represent the *probability* of the occurrence of certain micro-events in given regions of space-time. This probability manifests itself in relative frequencies in the long run of such micro-events. For the individual event we have thus far (in 1963) nothing better than probable predictions. To be sure, this matters little if we are concerned with large masses, or with large populations of events. Here, just as in the case of classical statistical mechanics, we have practical certainties and extremely high precision for our predictions. However, as has been pointed out by A. H. Compton, Ivan London, and others, there are situations in which the micro-indeterminacies, through amplification mechanisms, may well manifest themselves in macro-events. For example, in the Compton effect in which an electron is propelled by a photon in an individually unpredictable direction, the electron may impinge on any one in an array of Geiger counters; and these may be hooked up by way of amplifying devices with a variety of end results, such as the ringing of a bell, the lighting up of a bulb, or the detonation of a bomb. While it is true that even according to the deterministic ideology extremely small differences in initial conditions may result in tremendous differences in final effects, this very ideology declares that the final effects are precisely predictable only if we can ascertain the relevant initial conditions with full precision. Just this is, however, "in principle" ruled out by the well-confirmed postulates of quantum mechanics. Naturally, the first reaction of many deterministically oriented thinkers (scientists and philosophers) was that the indeterminacy principle expresses merely a "technical" or "practical" difficulty, but not one of "principle." It may be granted that the alleged "impossibility in principle" is not a logical impossibility. But many philosophers who have made careful studies of the logic of quantum mechanics (Reichenbach, Hanson, Feyerabend) pointed out that a restoration of determinism in microphysics is logically incompatible with the extremely well-confirmed principles of quantum mechanics. The "impossibility in principle" of which I have spoken, while therefore neither purely logical nor merely technical, is a "natural impossibility"—in the same sense in which a perpetual motion machine is impossible in view of the law of the conservation of energy.

Einstein, who contributed so much to the early development of the quantum theory, agreed that quantum mechanics was extremely fruitful and explanatorily powerful. But to the end of his days he could not reconcile himself with the indeterministic ideology held by the vast majority of contemporary physicists. In a brilliant discussion with Bohr he maintained staunchly that quantum mechanics does not achieve a "complete description" of nature. But a close analysis of the requirement of "completeness," as Einstein conceived it, reveals that he considered a theory complete only if it allowed for strictly deterministic predictions. It is understandable why Einstein thought in this way. His triumphant achievements in the special and the general theory of relativity, their otherwise revolutionary character to the contrary notwithstanding, were based on the geometrical method and thus in a general manner were patterned after the classical paradigms of Euclid's, Newton's, and Maxwell's work. Despite many attempts in the direction of a recovery of determinism on a deeper level of reality, Einstein's unitary field theories are generally regarded as tragic failures of a brilliant mind. Theoretical physicists who still pursue somewhat similar programs are confronted with the difficult task of either refuting essential postulates of quantum mechanics or providing a deterministic substructure logically compatible with quantum mechanics, and accessible to at least indirect but independent experimental tests. In view of the rapid and exciting developments in quantum field theory and in the theory of atomic nuclei it is probably premature to assess the chances of success of further quests for a deterministic theory.

Purely logically speaking, it is of course conceivable that the universe is "infinitely deep," so that the question as to whether it is "at rock bottom" deterministic or indeterministic loses its empirical significance altogether. As long as we have no criterion for "rock bottom" we do not even know what we are talking about when we ask (or answer) the question. The only fruitful way to discuss it is in terms of a given stage or level of scientific analysis. And there is considerable agreement that as of 1963—i.e., in terms of the "elementary particles" known today, and without any clear indication of further substructures—the basic laws of micro-interactions are statistical, and that hence the principles of indeterminacy are thus far unassailable.

A few remarks on the controversy regarding free will, determinism, and indeterminism are in order at this point. Various philosophers and philosophizing scientists have welcomed the indeterminism of modern physics as at last providing for the "leeway" necessary for genuinely free choice and action. In their, to be sure, widely differing ways, A. H. Compton, Hans Reichenbach, and Henry Margenau maintain that the determinism of classical physics excludes freedom. If we analyze the behavior of human organisms from a physical, and ultimately microphysical, point of view and if we assume strict lawful connections between antecedent conditions and their ensuing consequences, we cannot account for the introspectively evident freedom of choice. Without such freedom of choice there can be no meaning to moral responsibility either. Hence any breach in the causality of human behavior is gladly accepted as a basis for free choice. But a little reflection (as pointed out long ago by Hume and Mill, and brought up to date by Grünbaum, Nagel, and others) reveals that freedom of choice cannot be based on "absolute chance" or indeterminism. Far from being incompatible with determinism, such freedom as we have and cherish presupposes at least a certain measure of causal order in the processes involving choice and action. We are the "choosers of our choices" and "doers of our deeds" only to the extent that our personality expresses itself in our choices and actions. And we are unfree to the extent that our choices or actions are imposed upon us by factors external to the core of our personalities. In other words, the contrary opposite of freedom is not determinism, but coercion, compulsion, or constraint. The problem of free will, engendered by conceptual confusions, thus requires no solution through the findings of empirical science. It can be "dissolved" by a logical clarification of ideas. This is not to deny that there are many as yet unsolved problems concerning the causal explanation of human behavior. Only further progress in biology, physiology, psychology, and psychophysiology will afford answers to questions of this type. Such progress is indispensable also for the solution of the problems pertaining to the relations of mind and body. Attempts to show by logical analysis that the mind-body problem is a spurious one have not succeeded as they did so convincingly in the case of the free will–determinism problem.

COMPARATIVE METHODOLOGY OF THE NATURAL AND THE SOCIAL SCIENCES

Concern with the logic and methodology of the social sciences has become increasingly emphatic and has expanded enormously in the recent decades. Among professional philosophers of science, Morris R. Cohen can perhaps be credited more than any one else with initiating closer analyses in this area some thirty years ago. Quite recently, Cohen's erstwhile student Ernest Nagel has (in several chapters of his book *The Structure of Science,* 1961) presented a most judicious, penetrating, and comprehensive discussion of the problems in the comparative methodology of the social and the natural sciences. But there are also the very many psychologists, sociologists, anthropologists, economists, and historians who, in numerous books and countless articles, have voiced their views on this vital topic. The general outlook is roughly this: Among the empirical sciences we may distinguish the natural and the social sciences, with psychology somehow "straddling the fence" between the two domains. Striking differences in approach appear even on first glance. It has been maintained that the natural sciences aim at *nomothetic* knowledge, i.e., that they are concerned with the discovery of laws, and that they differ from the social sciences in that the latter are *idiographic,* i.e., concerned with individual facts regarding persons, events, or cultural situations. Indeed, if we compare, for example, theoretical physics with history, the difference is striking. But does the distinction nomothetic versus idiographic really characterize a fundamental difference in method? A little reflection suffices to show that there are nomothetic *and* idiographic components in both the natural and the social sciences. Physical geography is a natural science, but clearly idiographic; so are the geological history of the earth's surface, paleontology, and descriptive astronomy. Moreover, on the other side, even if the search for reliable laws in the social sciences cannot be regarded as so spectacularly successful as it has been in the physical sciences, the search is

going on, and the results in psychology, social psychology, economics, and sociology are certainly respectable. It is unfair to point to
the failures of historical generalization. The political, cultural, and
social history of mankind may find its explanations on a deeper
layer of the processes in question. Psychological, social-
psychological, and economic laws and theories have contributed a
great deal in this direction. But the "historicist" search for over-all
extrapolatable patterns or periodicities (à la Spengler, Toynbee—
or even à la Marx) seems fruitless, if not indeed entirely ground-
less. In this respect meteorology (a natural science!) appears to be
more hopeful in that there are at least the obvious regularities of
the seasons and other cycles of the weather. But real progress in
meteorology became possible only with the introduction of the explanatory principles of the physics of the atmosphere. Once the
role of such factors as air pressure, air velocities, temperature, hu-
midity, radiation, etc. were introduced, explanation and prediction
were greatly enhanced. If historical processes are analyzed in terms
of the underlying psychological, ecological, economic, etc. factors,
the outlook for explanation, and possibly even for prediction, becomes much more hopeful.

It has also been maintained (e.g., by the psychologist G. W. Allport, somewhat in the spirit of the German philosophers Dilthey,
Windelband, and Rickert) that the idiographic procedures of the
social disciplines are coupled with the method of *understanding*
("Verstehen," empathy); and that they differ from the natural
sciences, which seek explanations. There can be little doubt that
the techniques of clinical psychologists, psychiatrists, historians,
and anthropologists involve a good deal of the sort of imaginative
projection that is called empathy ("Einfühlung"). But as it has
been clearly pointed out, e.g., by Carnap, Hempel, Abel, and Nagel,
the technique of empathy is at best a source or a way of arriving
at explanatory hypotheses. It is not a method of validation for
such hypotheses. The clinical psychologist or psychiatrist, as it
were, uses his own person as a sort of diagnostic instrument, in that
his intuitions ("hunches") may turn out to be more or less reliable
indicators of the conditions ascribed to his patient. Just how reliable they are, how much their reliability may be improved by rich
and manifold experience in the field, is a matter that can be es-

tablished only by objective (intersubjective) tests, usually by clever statistical designs. It remains true that such empathy is of strictly no use in the natural sciences (especially in physics, chemistry, astronomy, but also in general biology). But this, I repeat, establishes only a difference in the techniques of the production of hypotheses, and does not demonstrate a fundamental difference in the *method* of justification of knowledge-claims.

Closely associated with the alleged differences discussed thus far is the alleged difference between *causal* and *teleological* explanations. Dramatic illustrations of this difference may be found in Plato's *Phaedo*. We are told that it is one thing to explain a given event in terms of its causal antecedents and the relevant causal laws, and that it is quite another thing to provide explanations in terms of motives, reasons, purposes, or intentions. The controversies on this point are far from settled. But, as I have hinted already in my general discussions of the structure of scientific explanations, it is questionable whether teleological explanations are genuine explanations at all. That there is goal directed behavior is of course undeniable. But can we explain such behavior, except in a very "low-level" superficial manner by utilizing such phrases as "he did it in order to" or "for the sake of"? Must we not ask how the idea of the goal or purpose of action is incorporated in the causal antecedents of the behavior in question? Cybernetics, which originated from a study of servomechanisms, has been extended to the explanation of the self-regulated behavior of organisms. It is in this sense the most hopeful step in the direction of causal explanation of teleological processes.

Before going on to one more (and last) point of the fundamental differences that have been asserted to exist between the natural and the social sciences, a very condensed report regarding the philosophy of psychology must here be inserted. Under the influence of the Darwinian revolution in biology and its own characteristic causal explanations of the evolution of organisms adapted to their environment, American psychology turned first to functionalism, later to behaviorism and its theories of learning and motivation. Some of the philosophical controversies that are still unsettled concern the general problem of the scientific status of psychology, and this is closely related to some issues of the traditional mind-body problem. Others pertain to the logic and methodology of concept formation and theory construction in psychology. American behaviorism, beginning with the work of J. B. Watson and culminating in the theories of C. L. Hull (continued notably by Neal Miller and K. W. Spence), E. C. Tolman, and B. F. Skinner (who, however, in somewhat positivistic fashion declares that he proposes no theories) attempted to transform psychology into a respectable branch of natural science. The logical behaviorists among the philosophers (especially Carnap and Hempel—in their earlier work) aided and abetted this movement in supporting it with philosophical and methodological arguments. As I have pointed out in the discussion of the criterion of intersubjective testability, the logical empiricists were behaviorists because they could not connect any factual meaning with *purely* mental terms. In its early phase logical behaviorism construed mental terms as logical constructions based on concepts designating the behavior of organisms. This was made fairly plausible even for the concepts of introspective psychology, in that introspection was viewed as a response to previous responses; and in that the very acquisition of subjective or mental terms in one's language could be explained by a learning process that occurs in a social environment. Thus even terms designating moods or emotions are from the very start linked to what other persons can observe of the behavioral situation.

Some behaviorists were inclined to deny the existence of mental phenomena altogether—and were thus close to a materialistic outlook. But the majority of behaviorists were only methodologically oriented, and refused to commit themselves on what they regarded as the metaphysical question of the status of mental entities and their relation to behavior or neural processes. The behavior of animals and human beings, under various conditions of previous positive or negative reinforcement, strength of drives, stimulus patterns, etc., could be examined in a completely objective manner. Psychology in this sense became part of general biology. Some psychologists and a good many philosophers raised a storm of objections. It was said that psychology, having lost its soul (with the abandonment of theological and metaphysical speculations), later had lost its consciousness and finally its mind. For several decades the behaviorist views were triumphantly victorious. But mentalistic psychology still retained some strongholds in the schools of Gestalt psychology and phenomenological psychology. Some philosophers, greatly concerned with science (though perhaps not typically philosophers of science) like C. J. Ducasse could not be discouraged in their arguments for an essentially Cartesian, i.e., dualistic and interactionistic, view of mind and body. Others, like Reichenbach and myself, have proposed identity theories of the mental and the physical. Impressed with the advances of neurophysiological explanations one could be tempted to adopt an epiphenomenalistic view of the mind, i.e., the doctrine that complete explanations and predictions of even the highest forms of human behavior can in principle be given on a physiological (or more specifically, neurophysiological) basis. The data of direct experience, i.e., the "raw feels" (E. C. Tolman's term) of sensations, images, thoughts, emotions, moods, sentiments, desires, volitions, etc. are merely regular concomitants of neural processes, but in themselves causally inefficacious. Since this sort of view obviously clashes with the experientially all too convincing role that our mental life plays in the determination of our behavior, only some sort of monistic view seems adequate. Behaviorism as well as its philosophically opposite counterpart, phenomenalism, were largely motivated to repress the difficulties of the mind-body problem. But no amount of logical ingenuity in either direction could avoid reductive fallacies. Double aspect and double language solutions that shun reductionism have been proposed ever since Spinoza; they were revived and modernized by twentieth century critical realists: in Germany in the early work of Moritz Schlick, in America by C. A. Strong, Durant Drake, R. W. Sellars, and George Santayana, and in England by Bertrand Russell (see his *Human Knowledge*). The American psychologist and historian of psychology E. G. Boring adumbrated a somewhat similar theory in his book on *The Physical Dimensions of Consciousness* (1933). Stimulated and encouraged by these developments, as well by the (however rather cautious) suggestions contained in Wolfgang Köhler's philosophical contributions, I have attempted (most fully in *Concepts, Theories, and the Mind-Body Problem, Minnesota Studies in the Philosophy of Science,* vol. II, 1958) to establish a semantical monism or identity theory. According to this view the very same events are designated on the one hand directly by the phenomenal terms of introspection and on the other indirectly by certain concepts of neurophysiology. The identity as here understood is ascertainable on empirical, i.e., not on purely logical, grounds. For this reason I prefer not to call mine a double language view any longer. While this empirical identity view of mind and matter avoids the various pitfalls mentioned previously, it is not without difficulties of its own. I have listed these candidly in the monograph referred to above. As I see it, a great deal of further work, both in logical analysis as well as in empirical psychophysiology, will be necessary before we can be satisfied with any solution of the great problem, the "world knot" as Schopenhauer called it.

Less speculative and hence more promising are the many studies of theory construction in psychology. With several rival approaches in practically every field of psychology, here is a splendid opportunity for methodologists to contribute clarifying ideas. The hypotheses concerning unconscious mental processes in psychoanalytic theory and other "depth psychologies" are still a matter of controversy. Some philosophers of science, such as Ernest Nagel, are extremely skeptical regarding the explanatory power, or even the logical legitimacy, of the Freudian and other related theories. Others, impressed by the growing empirical confirmation and the refinements of those theories, find it worthwhile to retrace their logical structures and to assess their factual validity.

In sorting out the various schools and systems of current psychology, the late Egon Brunswik (a psychologist highly interested also in methodology) has contributed valuable suggestions toward the alternative ways in which experimentation and theorizing may "focus" on their subject matter. Such a view allows for a more tolerant attitude among theoreticians of different schools of thought. It allows for the possibilities of mutual supplementation where a more superficial examination had concluded that there are genuine incompatibilities. There can be no question about the central and strategic position of psychology for the settlement of the problems of the unity or the diversity of method in the natural and the social sciences.

Finally, I shall discuss briefly the assertion that the natural sciences are value-free or value-neutral, whereas the social sciences are invariably evaluative. This notion is prima facie plausible for two reasons: First, many historians, sociologists, and economists do make evaluations—moral or nonmoral, as the case may be. Second, investigation into the relations of the conditions to the consequences of social action serve as a basis for planning, guidance, or control. Perhaps more than any one else, John Dewey opposed the dualism of fact and value, already very clearly seen by Hume and emphasized, developed, and subjected to more penetrating analyses by the logical empiricists. This issue is discussed elsewhere in this volume in William Frankena's essay on "Ethical Theory"; that is indeed where it properly belongs, but it is also relevant here. The issue of science and evaluation has been discussed briefly by Carnap and Reichenbach, as well as by other philosophers of science of logical empiricist convictions. As they (and I with them) see it, it is one thing to *study evaluations* and valuative attitudes in the manner in which psychologists, anthropologists, sociologists, and historians pursue this task, but it is another thing to *make evaluations.* The logical empiricists staunchly maintain that, while the first task is a legitimate and important part of the social sciences, the second is part of the life process itself, and not a scientific activity at all. For even if we had complete knowledge concerning what conditions produce what consequences (or what means ensure with what probabilities and what utilities certain ends), it is an extrascientific question what consequences we *ought* to desire, or what ends we *should* aim at. It is admitted that knowledge regarding the probabilities and utilities in question is indispensable for rational action. But the evaluation of the utilities and of the purposes of action must at some point become a matter of commitment rather than of knowledge. Many of our fundamental commitments are so much taken for granted as a matter of course that we are interested only in the—admittedly vital and indispensable—information regarding means-ends relations. Thus we emphatically prefer the perpetuation of human life on our planet to its extermination, or we prefer health to sickness, fairness to injustice, and so on. But these are commitments, matters of attitude, which in and by themselves are not susceptible to scientific justification. Of course, as commitments and attitudes they can be studied by social scientists. Their historical development and possibly their causal explanation may be disclosed by scientific study.

But to questions of ethics—e.g., why we ought to perpetuate human life rather than destroy it—there are no answers that science can validate. Any attempt in this direction is bound to beg the question at issue.

There have been occasional voices saying that the whole scientific enterprise rests on evaluations. It has even been maintained that the scientific method involves ethical decisions. I believe that those views that would, as it were, turn the tables are generated by certain confusions. It should be clear that both a saint and a scoundrel can utilize the best scientific information for their very different purposes. And while of course commitment to the aims of science in a sense underlies all scientific activities, it is in itself not part of the knowledge-claims of science. It is equally clear that even though value judgments play a role in the selection of problems and of techniques with which to attack them, such value judgments do not as such become part of the corpus of science. They are essentially like the considerations of utility and probability that enter into rational planning for practical action. In this sense they pertain to the pursuit of the scientific enterprise but not to its cognitive content.

The conclusion that seems to me to emerge from the foregoing discussions in this: While there is much diversity in techniques among the various sciences, the fundamental method of testing and validating hypotheses is throughout essentially the same. If the program of unitary science should prove feasible, there would not be even a basic difference in subject matter. But practically speaking, and for the time being, divisions of labor are undeniable and indispensable. It is conceivable that psychology will ultimately be reducible to neurophysiology, and the latter to physics. Similarly it is conceivable that sociology may in some respects and some way be reducible to psychology. According to "methodological individualism" (opposing methodological collectivism) this should be a fruitful avenue of theory construction. This is not to deny that in the sociopsychological explanations of historical events or processes, a proper balance must be struck between the "mass factors" and the roles of "key individuals." Overemphasis of either side in this issue is apt to lead to factually inadequate explanations. There is a place for the "heroes" in history, just as there is a place for more global and statistical conceptions of mass action. (Cf. Sidney Hook's *The Hero in History;* Edgar Zilsel's "Physics and the Problem of Historico-Sociological Laws" in *Readings in the Philosophy of Science,* ed. Feigl and Brodbeck; and May Brodbeck's "Methodological Individualisms: Definition and Reduction," *Philosophy of Science,* XXV [1958], 1-22.) Even if we could ever attain reductions of psychology and the social sciences to a unitary scheme—say of the physicalistic sort—of explanation, this would always be a matter of "in principle only." In practice neither psychologists nor social scientists will become "unemployed" by such reductions. It is just conceivable that "theory-engendered unemployment" may come to pass in chemistry. Once chemistry is fully reduced to atomic and quantum theory, perhaps the time will come when chemists will no longer have to experiment in order to find out the properties of to-be-synthesized compounds. Given sufficiently powerful computers perhaps these properties will be derivable by calculation. But the tremendously more complex subject matter of the bio-psycho-social sciences renders this sort of extrapolation too fanciful, if not entirely utopian.

THE SCOPE AND THE LIMITATIONS
OF SCIENCE

The foregoing chapters have repeatedly touched upon the scope and the limitations of scientific inquiry and explanation. It remains to discuss various views about the *reach* of science—both regarding its own subject matter and regarding its delimitations from nonscientific (or extrascientific) endeavors. The first issue centers upon the factual reference of scientific theories. Essentially this is a problem in epistemology. The majority of scientists are *realists,* usually in a quite unsophisticated way. They take it for granted that the sciences have disclosed the existence of a variety of entities beyond the range of direct observability. Thus, atoms and subatomic particles, the various fields (gravitational, electromagnetic, etc.) in physics, but also the deeply unconscious parts of the human mind, are assumed to exist independent of observation, measurement, experiment, or inferences based on these procedures. Most scientists not only admit but insist that the scientific *knowledge* of reality can be attained only by observation and inference. But they, together with an increasing number of philosophers of science, unhesitatingly ascribe *reality* to what is "referred to" by many highly inferential concepts of the sciences. More "tough minded" philosophers of science (logical positivists, instrumentalists, operationists), however, either repudiate such a realism as unjustified or find the notion of "independent reality" quite obscure, if not outright meaningless.

Essentially this is the controversy of "realism versus positivism," as it stems from the contrasting positions of Boltzmann, Planck, *et al.* on the one side, and Mach, Ostwald, *et al.* on the other, at the turn of the century. Influenced by Russell's early work, Carnap developed a phenomenalist epistemology in a logically highly refined manner. Taking for his guiding maxim Russell's famous saying "Wherever possible, logical constructions are to be substituted for inferred entities," Carnap (in his *Der logische Aufbau der Welt,*

1928) attempted to show that all concepts of the natural and the social sciences can (in principle) be "constituted," i.e., constructed by various logical types of definitions, out of very elementary concepts that refer only to certain qualities or relations of immediate experience. This sort of epistemology is *positivistic* in that it claims that all factual statements of the sciences can be translated back into (complicated) sets of statements couched in a phenomenal language. While this point of view was soon abandoned by Carnap himself, and is left with hardly any adherents (except, in their different ways, perhaps Nelson Goodman and Gustav Bergmann), it has been supplanted by an equally antirealistic instrumentalism. According to the instrumentalistic outlook scientific theories and theoretical concepts are "nothing but" computational devices. For example, the "unobservables" of modern physics (e.g., fields, electrons, the spin of electrons, etc.) are mere auxiliary constructions (earlier positivists called them at best "fictitious entities"), designed to enable physicists to make inferences from one set of observables to another. This same ideology prevails in only slightly changed form in the "Copenhagen interpretation" of quantum mechanics (originally proposed by Bohr and Heisenberg and now accepted by many American philosophers of science). Here we are told, for example, that the observable frequencies and intensities of radiations as ascertainable spectroscopically, together with the macroscopic entities of classical physics, are the starting and the end points of interpolated auxiliary micro-concepts. Such a restrictive attitude is typical of the positivist's and operationist's temper, with its phobia of the invisible and the intangible.

But this rather narrow minded positivism appears open to serious doubts on general epistemological grounds. Any adequate account of empirical knowledge-claims must differentiate between the *factual reference* and the *supporting evidence* of the statements making such knowledge-claims. In historical statements it should be obvious without much discussion that the reference is to events of the past, while the evidence may consist of currently available (or future) observational data. Similarly, according to well-confirmed assumptions, the observed spectra of distant stars are *indicators* of astrophysical and astrochemical conditions. In the same way, the evidence presented in the Brownian motion of colloid particles supports the theoretical assertions about the number, masses, and motions of molecules in the surrounding liquid or gas. Cloud or bubble chamber tracks constitute important evidence for statements about the properties and motions of micro-particles too small for direct observation. Moreover, "observability" itself is a rather vague and slippery concept. Bacteria (and viruses) become observable in optical (and electronic) microscopes. Even an ordinary magnifying glass makes things visible that are not discernible by unaided inspection. Finally, from the point of view of logic and semantics it is useful (I think in fact indispensable) to define the meaning of a factual statement by its truth-conditions. But these conditions, which when actually obtaining render the statement true, are identical with the evidence only in the case of statements about immediate, fully particular observations. In all other cases—and the sciences consist of almost nothing but these other cases—the factual content of scientific statements invariably transcends the observational evidence. This transcendence is not to be confused nor to be burdened with the objections against metaphysical transcendence. The scientific theories themselves, if properly spelled out, tell us in a confirmable way how the indicating evidence is related to the indicated states of affairs. If the metaphor be permitted, we "triangulate in logical space," i.e., we obtain "fixes" on the "unobservables" from multifarious domains of the observable evidence. Objections against the assumption of hypothetical entities are justified only if the assumptions are clearly "ad hoc," i.e., if they are based on only one item or kind of evidence.

The "critically realistic" position I have just sketched and defended is in keeping with Carnap's own more recent views—although he still dislikes the label "realism" because to him it has the objectionable connotations of transcendent metaphysics. But many of the younger philosophers of science (e.g., Grünbaum, Feyerabend, Rozeboom, and others) have no misgivings in adopting the sort of realistic philosophy that Moritz Schlick (in his earlier phase), Hans Reichenbach, and I have been advocating. The somewhat Kantian position of Henry Margenau (in his *The Nature of Physical Reality*) is certainly not phenomenalistic or instrumentalistic either, though his realism is more guarded and qualified.

Against all this it may be asked whether the "neutral" views of

Philipp Frank and especially those of Ernest Nagel (recently more fully expounded in Chapter 6 of his *The Structure of Science*) do not put an end to the controversy. The point of view of these two thinkers is close to positivism and pragmatism. In effect they raise the poignant question "What is the difference that makes a difference whether we accept an instrumentalistic or a realistic interpretation of scientific theories?" It must be granted that if this question refers to the differences in observable phenomena, then there is no difference. There may well be a difference in the attitude between positivistically and realistically oriented scientists. But this is relevant at most only psychologically or heuristically, in that the realist will be inclined to pursue theory construction in a bolder (and possibly more fruitful) manner than the positivist. This, however, does not touch the central issue. In my own view the "neutralist" test question is misguided. It would properly apply if we were to choose between two rival *scientific* theories. But the issue here is one of the *interpretation* of scientific theories. This is a metascientific query. It is not a "metaphysical" question in the sense in which "metaphysical" speculations are repudiated as either fruitless or even as meaningless by most empiricists. Metascientific queries can be answered by such logical and semantical examinations of the structure of scientific theories as I have suggested above. In this context the realistic distinction between evidence and reference seems to me highly clarifying, and in any case indispensable. Just as in the general theory of knowledge we must render justice to the obvious way in which the "knowing subjects" (i.e., human organisms) are embedded in the to-be-known world, and thus come to endorse a "causal theory of perception," so in the theory of scientific knowledge we must relate the readings of our instruments to what these readings indicate. Of course, this does not abrogate the empiricist conviction that the only meaningful and legitimate way in which we can support scientific knowledge about the world must be in terms of observational evidence. Slightly amending William James's famous saying, I would put it this way: Things are what they are knowable as; i.e., there is no better way to provide information about the world (ourselves included) than by the scientific method.

Lest the point of view here defended be misunderstood, the al-

533

leged and the real limitations of science must be distinguished. I can do this succinctly by reporting on the large common denominator that characterizes the views of many philosophers of science, most prominently perhaps those of the logical empiricists, scientific empiricists, and naturalists.

That terminal value judgments are not subject to scientific validation is true, but this fact cannot be considered a "limitation" of science. Science as we have come to understand it since the Renaissance is not designed to validate terminal value judgments. One might as well deplore the fact that a weaving loom cannot produce beautiful music. Ultimate concerns (to use Tillich's phrase) reflect ultimate commitments. These commitments can be *studied* scientifically (psychologically, sociologically, etc.) with regards to their origins and their historical developments, but no scientific studies can yield anything like a justification for them.

Is intuition or mystical insight an alternative to the scientific way of knowing? "Intuition" is a notoriously ambiguous term. We would first have to sort out its various meanings in order to come to grips with the question. Let us take just a few of these meanings. As I have pointed out before, intuition in the sense of the "hunch" may well be a way of arriving at hypotheses, but by itself it furnishes no basis for their justification. Some thinkers have wondered about extrasensory perception as an extrascientific way of knowing. Without going into the still controversial questions regarding the actuality of telepathy, clairvoyance, or precognition, it should be evident that the reliability of these "paranormal" ways of knowing still has to be tested and assessed on the basis of scientifically scrutinized (statistical) evidence. Once the occurrence and relative reliability of such "ways of knowing" is established (if it can be established), then it is time to ask whether and in what manner parapsychological phenomena can be explained. It is too early to speculate what sort of theories—either within the frame of present-day science or outside of it—will be adequate for this purpose. However this may be, it is clear that the power of extrasensory perception itself can be appraised only by the usual scientific (inductive, statistical) procedures.

Proponents of mystical intuition, be it religious or metaphysical, often claim that their insights attain an "Absolute Reality" that is in principle beyond the possibility of scientific investigation. This is usually accompanied by the admission that the language of the mystic is unavoidably metaphorical or allegorical, and that there is something completely ineffable about "ultimate reality." But equally characteristic of this outlook is the assertion that mystical insight consists in an identification or coalescence of the knowing subject with its object of knowledge. From the point of view of the vast majority of philosophers of science, these contentions reveal that the very word "knowledge" as used by the mystic for his trans-empirical insights means something utterly different from what this word means in common life and in science. Strict identification of the knowing subject with the to-be-known object is a logically in-coherent notion. The best sense one can make of it is that immediate experience provides "acquaintance" with the qualities of con-sciousness. But as soon as we represent even only the relations of these qualities among each other in propositional form, we make knowledge-claims in the ordinary sense. And if the mystic main-tains that he uses his extraordinary experiences as data that "indi-cate" a transempirical reality, then we are back again in the arena of scientific criticism. The question then is whether the intuitive ex-periences of the mystic are not susceptible to perfectly naturalistic (e.g., psychological) explanations that, if valid, would render any supernatural explanations superfluous. Although no one can af-ford to be dogmatic in these matters, it seems plausible that the powers of scientific explanation, combined with those of logical analysis, are sufficient to show that the mystical claims of transcend-ence are untenable. But it may well be granted that mystical ex-perience, just like religious experience more generally, can be ex-tremely influential in the formation of one's attitude toward life and human affairs in moral and social respects.

The thinking of most modern American philosophers of science in regard to all the alleged "limitations of science" is that of a cau-tious optimism. Tremendous difficulties have been overcome and are continually being overcome by the ingenuity of the experi-menters and the theorists.

Many a problem that appeared as an unsolvable "riddle of the universe" only some eighty years ago has been successfully ap-proached by the advance of scientific knowledge. The origin of the universe is responsibly discussed by modern astrophysics and cosmology. The question of the origin of life, in the light of recent biochemical research, is no longer so deep a mystery as it used to be. The relations of mind and body have been considerably illuminated by the progress of psychophysiology, and by epistemological reflections. The nature of force and matter is increasingly disclosed by the results of modern physics. The wish to know what reality is "absolutely" and "intrinsically" is misguided in that it strives for mystical "identification" rather than for relational knowledge—the only kind of knowledge that is responsible and intelligible. If there are any absolutely unsolvable problems, they seem to be of our own making. They arise out of confusions that can be dispelled by logical analysis.

—§—

SELECTED REFERENCES

The American literature in the field of philosophy of science during the last thirty years is quite voluminous. Many books and a great number of articles have been published and are being published at an increasing rate. The following references represent either introductory readings or "landmarks" in the field.

Systematic Expositions

Bergmann, Gustav, *Philosophy of Science*. Madison: University of Wisconsin Press, 1957.

Frank, Philipp, *Philosophy of Science: The Link between Science and Philosophy*. Englewood Cliffs, N. J.: Prentice-Hall, Inc., 1957.

Kemeny, John G., *A Philosopher Looks at Science*. Princeton: D. Van Nostrand Company, Inc., 1959.

Mehlberg, Henryk, *The Reach of Science*. Toronto: University of Toronto Press, 1958.

Nagel, Ernest, *The Structure of Science: Problems in the Logic of Scientific Explanation*. New York: Harcourt, Brace & World, Inc., 1961.

Pap, Arthur, *An Introduction to the Philosophy of Science*. New York: The Free Press of Glencoe, Inc., 1962.

Reichenbach, Hans, *Experience and Prediction*. Chicago: University of Chicago Press, 1938.

————, *The Rise of Scientific Philosophy*. Berkeley: University of California Press, 1951.

Anthologies and Collective Volumes

Baumrin, Bernard, ed., *Philosophy of Science,* vol. I. New York: John Wiley & Sons, Inc., 1963.

Colodny, Robert G., ed., *Frontiers of Science and Philosophy*. Pittsburgh: University of Pittsburgh Press, 1962.

Danto, Arthur, and Sidney Morgenbesser, eds., *Philosophy of Science*. New York: Meridian Books, Inc., 1960.

Feigl, Herbert, Grover Maxwell, and Michael Scriven, eds., *Concepts, Theories, and the Mind-Body Problem,* Minnesota Studies in the

537

Philosophy of Science, vol. II. Minneapolis: University of Minnesota Press, 1958.

————, and Grover Maxwell, eds., *Current Issues in the Philosophy of Science*. New York: Holt, Rinehart & Winston, Inc., 1961.

————, and Michael Scriven, eds., *The Foundations of Science and the Concepts of Psychology and Psychoanalysis,* Minnesota Studies in the Philosophy of Science, vol. I. Minneapolis: University of Minnesota Press, 1956.

————, and May Brodbeck, eds., *Readings in the Philosophy of Science.* New York: Appleton-Century-Crofts, 1953.

————, and Grover Maxwell, eds., *Scientific Explanation, Space and Time,* Minnesota Studies in the Philosophy of Science, vol. III. Minneapolis: University of Minnesota Press, 1962.

Frank, Philipp, ed., *The Validation of Scientific Theories.* Boston: Beacon Press, Inc., 1955.

Hook, Sidney, ed., *Determinism and Freedom.* New York: New York University Press, 1958.

————, ed., *Dimensions of Mind.* New York: New York University Press, 1960.

————, ed., *Psychoanalysis, Scientific Method, and Philosophy.* New York: New York University Press, 1959.

Kyburg, Henry E., Jr., and Ernest Nagel, eds., *Induction: Some Current Issues.* Middletown, Conn.: Wesleyan University Press, 1963.

Madden, Edward H., ed., *The Structure of Scientific Thought.* Boston: Houghton Mifflin Company, 1960.

Nagel, Ernest, Patrick Suppes, and Alfred Tarski, eds., *Logic, Methodology and Philosophy of Science.* Stanford: Stanford University Press, 1962.

Neurath, Otto, *et al.,* eds., *International Encyclopedia of Unified Science.* Chicago: University of Chicago Press, 1955.

Schilpp, P. A., ed., *Albert Einstein, Philosopher-Scientist,* 2nd ed. New York: Tudor Publishing Company, 1952.

Wartofsky, Marx W., ed., *Boston Studies in the Philosophy of Science.* New York: Humanities Press, Inc., 1963.

Wiener, Philip P., ed., *Readings in Philosophy of Science.* New York: Charles Scribner's Sons, 1953.

More Specialized Works

Beckner, Morton, *The Biological Way of Thought.* New York: Columbia University Press, 1959.

Bridgman, P. W., *The Logic of Modern Physics*. New York: The Macmillan Company, 1927.

Capek, Milic, *The Philosophical Impact of Contemporary Physics*. Princeton: D. Van Nostrand Company, Inc., 1961.

Carnap, Rudolf, *Logical Foundations of Probability*. Chicago: University of Chicago Press, 1950; 2nd ed., 1962.

Goodman, Nelson, *Fact, Fiction, and Forecast*. Cambridge: Harvard University Press, 1955.

Goudge, Thomas A., *The Ascent of Life: A Philosophical Study of Evolution*. Toronto: University of Toronto Press, 1961.

Grünbaum, Adolf, *Philosophical Problems of Space and Time*. New York: Alfred A. Knopf, Inc., 1963.

Hanson, Norwood Russell, *The Concept of the Positron: A Philosophical Analysis*. New York: Cambridge University Press, 1963.

————, *Patterns of Discovery*. New York: Cambridge University Press, 1958.

Lenzen, Victor, *Causality in Natural Science*. Springfield, Ill.: Charles C. Thomas, Publishers, 1959.

Margenau, Henry, *The Nature of Physical Reality*. New York: McGraw-Hill Book Co., Inc., 1950.

Northrop, F. S. C., *The Logic of the Sciences and the Humanities*. New York: The Macmillan Company, 1947.

Quine, W. V., *Word and Object*. New York: John Wiley & Sons, Inc., 1960.

Reichenbach, Hans, *Modern Philosophy of Science*. New York: Humanities Press, 1959.

————, *Philosophic Foundations of Quantum Mechanics*. Berkeley: University of California Press, 1944.

————, *The Philosophy of Space and Time*. New York: Dover Publications, Inc., 1957.

————, *Theory of Probability*. Berkeley: University of California Press, 1949.

Scheffler, Israel, *The Anatomy of Inquiry*. New York: Alfred A. Knopf, Inc., 1963.

Skinner, B. F., *Science and Human Behavior*. New York: The Macmillan Company, 1953.

Watson, William H., *Understanding Physics Today*. New York: Cambridge University Press, 1963.

Wiener, Norbert, *The Human Use of Human Beings*. Boston: Houghton Mifflin Company, 1950.

INDEX

Frege, Gottlob, 82, 493
Freud, Sigmund, 180, 365, 442
Friedländer, Paul, 46
Fromm, Erich, 432, 442
Fuller, B.A.G., 26

GALILEO, 3, 49, 63, 134, 477
Gallie, W.B., 122
Garnett, A.C., 364-65, 370, 382, 422, 425, 429-31
Garnett, C.B., 92
Garvey, Sister Mary Patricia, 62, 276
Garvin, Lucius, 350, 437
Gassendi, Pierre, 98
Gay, Peter, 23
Geiger, G.R., 123
Gentile, Giovanni, 111
Gentry, G.V., 110
Geometry, 491, 494-95
Gestalt psychology, 309, 352, 445
Geulincx, A., 98
Gewirth, Alan, 74
Gibbs, W.J., 516
Gilbert, K.E., 27
Gilbert, N.W., 80
Gilson, Emile, 26, 61, 72
Glanvill, Joseph, 29, 96
Glanville, J.J., 15
Glathe, A.B., 90
God, 129, 155-56
Gödel, Kurt, 494
Goethe, J.W., 508
Goheen, J.D.M., 66
Goodenough, E.R., 58
Goodhart, H.L., 58
Goodman, Nelson, 208-09, 216 n.,

228, 241, 272, 284-85, 333, 468, 531
Grabmann, Martin, 61
Grajewski, M.J., 73
Grattan, C.H., 120
Gray, J.G., 92
Green, T.H., 106
Greenberg, Sidney, 79
Greene, T.M., 91
Greene, W.C., 15, 30
Gregory of Nyssa, 61, 62
Grene, David, 45
Grosseteste, Robert, 8
Grote, J., 105
Grünbaum, Adolf, 469, 490, 495, 514, 520, 532
Gutmann, J.J., 107

HACK, R.K., 31
Hackforth, Reginald, 17, 37
Hahn, Lewis E., 329
Hainds, J.R., 93
Haldane, E.S., 18, 25
Hall, C.M., 76
Hall, E.W., 223-25, 227, 229, 351-352, 355, 368, 446
Hallie, P.P., 105
Hallowell, J.H., 421, 430, 439
Hamann, J.G., 101
Hamburger, Max, 53, 54
Hamilton, William, 105
Hamilton, W.R., 516
Hammerschmidt, W.W., 110
Hampshire, S.N., 409, 416
Hanke, Lewis, 54
Hanson, N.R., 469, 473, 487, 518
Hantz, H.D., 49
Hardie, W.F.R., 47